Miscellaneous Essays Relating to Indian Subjects

(Volume II)

B. H. Hodgson

Alpha Editions

This edition published in 2020

ISBN: 9789354174247 (Hardback)

ISBN: 9789354178504 (Paperback)

Design and Setting By
Alpha Editions
www.alphaedis.com
email - alphaedis@gmail.com

CONTENTS OF VOL. II.

SECTION III.

[*Bengal Journal*, 1849, vol. xvii., part i., pp. 451–460.]

PAGE

ON THE ABORIGINES OF NORTH-EASTERN INDIA . . . 1

COMPARATIVE VOCABULARY OF THE TIBETAN, BÓDÓ, AND GÁRÓ
    TONGUES 7

SECTION IV.

[*Bengal Journal*, vol. xix., pp. 1–8.]

ABORIGINES OF THE NORTH-EASTERN FRONTIER . . . 11

SECTION V.

[*Bengal Journal*, vol. xviii., part ii., pp. 967–975.]

ABORIGINES OF THE EASTERN FRONTIER 19

SECTION VI.

[*Bengal Journal*, vol. xxii., pp. 1–25.]

THE INDO-CHINESE BORDERERS, AND THEIR CONNECTION WITH
    THE HIMÁLAYANS AND TIBETANS 27

COMPARATIVE VOCABULARY OF INDO-CHINESE BORDERERS IN
    ARAKAN 34

COMPARATIVE VOCABULARY OF INDO-CHINESE BORDERERS IN
    TENASSERIM 44

SECTION VII.

[Bengal Journal, vol. xxii., pp. 26–76.]

PAGE

THE MONGOLIAN AFFINITIES OF THE CAUCASIANS . . . 51
COMPARISON AND ANALYSIS OF CAUCASIAN AND MONGOLIAN
  WORDS 59

SECTION VIII.

[Bengal Journal, vol. xvii., pp. 222–23.]

PHYSICAL TYPE OF TIBETANS 95

SECTION IX.

[Bengal Journal, vols. xvii., xviii., xix.]

THE ABORIGINES OF CENTRAL INDIA 97
COMPARATIVE VOCABULARY OF THE ABORIGINAL LANGUAGES
  OF CENTRAL INDIA 99
ABORIGINES OF THE EASTERN GHATS 112
VOCABULARY OF SOME OF THE DIALECTS OF THE HILL AND
  WANDERING TRIBES IN THE NORTHERN SIRCARS . . 119
ABORIGINES OF THE NILGIRIS, WITH REMARKS ON THEIR
  AFFINITIES 125
SUPPLEMENT TO THE NILGIRIAN VOCABULARIES . . . 145
THE ABORIGINES OF SOUTHERN INDIA AND CEYLON . . 152

SECTION X.

[*" Selections from the Records of Bengal,"* No. IV.]

ROUTE OF NEPALESE MISSION TO PEKIN, WITH REMARKS ON
  THE WATER-SHED AND PLATEAU OF TIBET . . . 167

SECTION XI.

[*Bengal Journal*, vol. xvii.; "*Selections from the Records*," No. V.]

PAGE

ROUTE FROM KÁTHMÁNDÚ, THE CAPITAL OF NÉPÁL, TO DAR-
JEELING IN SIKIM 191

MEMORANDUM RELATIVE TO THE SEVEN COSIS OF NÉPÁL . 206

SECTION XII.

["*Selections from the Records*," No. XI.]

SOME ACCOUNTS OF THE SYSTEMS OF LAW AND POLICE AS
RECOGNISED IN THE STATE OF NÉPÁL 211

    PART I. ON THE LAW AND POLICE OF NÉPÁL . 211

    PART II. ON THE LAW AND LEGAL PRACTICE OF
        NÉPÁL AS REGARDS FAMILIAR INTER-
        COURSE BETWEEN A HINDU AND AN
        OUTCAST 236

SECTION XIII.

[*Bengal Journal*, vol. i.; *Trans. Agric. Society, India*, vol. v.]

THE NATIVE METHOD OF MAKING THE PAPER, DENOMINATED
HINDUSTAN, NÉPÁLESE 251

SECTION XIV.

[*Letters: Serampore*, 1847, *and Friend of India*, 1848.]

PRE-EMINENCE OF THE VERNACULARS; OR, THE ANGLICISTS
ANSWERED: BEING LETTERS ON THE EDUCATION OF THE
PEOPLE OF INDIA 255

SECTION III.

ON THE ABORIGINES OF NORTH-EASTERN INDIA.

———◆———

PURSUANT to my plan of furnishing to the readers of the Journal a glance at the Ethnic affinities of the Aborigines of India, from the snows to Cape Comorin, I have now the honour to submit a comparative vocabulary, uniform with its precursors, of the Dhimál, Bódó, and Gáró tongues, preceded by the written and spoken Tibetan, for a reason that will presently appear.

I regret that I could not on a recent occasion, nor can now, give the Chépáng vocables on this model. But it is many years since I have had access to that secluded people, and I cannot now calculate on having it again.

As I have already, in a separate work, given the Dhimál and Bódó languages upon a scale much ampler than the present one, and as I have, moreover, in that work demurred to the sufficiency of summary vocabularies, it may be asked why I repeat myself on the present occasion, and in the very manner I have myself objected to? My answer to this question is ready, and I hope will prove satisfactory. Three years have now elapsed since I published the work alluded to, and in that time I have had ample opportunity to observe the general indisposition to enter the field of Indian Ethnology, bent upon serious labour like the author of that work. Now, general co-operation is the one thing needful in this case: and since I feel certain that there is no want of mental vigour in this land, I am led to ascribe the slackness I have experienced in obtaining co-operators according to the suggested model, to the novelty of the subject, whence it happens that few persons can perceive the extensive bearings and high interest of that subject.

By the present series of summary vocabularies I hope to make these points apparent, when I confidently anticipate that many able men who could not be won to give their time and attention to the elucidation of the barbarous jargon of this or that insulated and petty tribe of aborigines, will yet be stimulated to efficient exertion upon being made aware that the question, in fact, relates to the fate and fortunes, the migrations and improvement or deterioration, of the largest family of human kind. No question of ethnology is insulated. It is quite the contrary, and that by its very nature. So that wherever we begin, even with the humblest tribe, we must soon find that we are dealing with the history, and with a material portion of the history, of some great mass of the human race. Thus, the latest investigators of the general subject of human affinities include in the great Mongolian family not merely the high Asian Nomades, or the Túrks, the Mongols and the Tangús, but also (with daily increasing, though not yet conclusive, evidence) the Tibetans, the Chinese, the Indo-Chinese, and the Tamúlians. The Tamúlians include the whole of the aborigines of India, whether civilised or uncivilised, from Cape Comorin to the snows; except the inhabitants of the great mountainous belt confining the plains of India towards Tibet, China, and Ava. These last are, in the North-West, derived from the Tibetan stock; and in the South-East, from the Indo-Chinese stock: the 92° of east longitude, or the Dhansri river of Assam, apparently forming the dividing line of the two races, which are each vastly numerous and strikingly diversified, yet essentially one, just as are the no less numerous and varied races of the single Tamúlian stock. Thus, we cannot take up the investigation of a narrow and barren topic like that of the Kúkí, the Ché-páng, or the Gónd tribe without presently finding ourselves engaged in unravelling some, it may be, dark and intricate, but truly important, chapter of the history of one of those large masses of human kind, the Indo-Chinese, the Tibetans, or the Tamúlians. Nor can one prosecute this investigation

far without perceiving that our subject has yet ampler relations, connecting itself by indissoluble yet varied links with
those tremendous warriors who planted their standards on the
walls of Pekin and Delhi, of Vienna and Moscow. Much of
their fate and fortunes belongs to history, but much more to
pre-historic times, when vast bodies of these so-called Mongols
poured themselves upon India, from the North and from the
East, both before and subsequent to the great immigration of
the Arian Hindús. Have you no curiosity to learn what may
be learnt anent these important and, for us British denizens of
India, domestic events ? Or do you doubt the validity of any
available media of proof ? If the latter, as is probable, be
the ground of your objection to such inquiries, I would say in
the first place, look steadfastly at any man of an aboriginal
race (an ubiquitarian Dhánger for instance), and say if a Mongol origin is not palpably inscribed on his face ? Or, again,
take a score of words of his language and compare them with
their equivalents in Hindí, U'rdú, or any other Prakrit, and
say if you are not sensible of being in a foreign realm of
speech ? And what can that realm be but the North and North-
East, the North-West being no way available to your purpose ?
In the second place, I would observe that every medium of
proof which has been employed to demonstrate the unity of
the Iranian family is available to demonstrate the unity of the
Turanian ; whilst, with regard to prima facia improbabilities,
much greater ones once encompassed the now admitted fact that
Hindús, Persians, Germans, English, Irish, Russians, are members of one family, viz., the Iranian, than can attend any similarly
perfect demonstration, that Tamúlians, Tibetans, Indo-Chinese,
Chinese, Tangús, Mongols, and Túrks are so many branches of
another single family, viz., the Turánian. Nor are these questions of interest only to the speculative philosopher. They are,
on the contrary, of vital importance to the statesman who may
be led into the most serious practical errors for want of such
lights as ethnology affords. I will give a striking and recent
instance. The Chief Secretary of the Government, who is
likewise one of the most able and accomplished men in India,
in speaking of the educational improvability of the Hindús,

has formally alleged the *impossibility* of making them worthy and vigorous men and citizens by reason of their race,* when it is really as certain as that 2 and 2 make 4, that the race of the Hindús is identical with Mr. Elliot's own! Glottology and anatomy combine to place this great truth (and in every educational view it is pre-eminently such for all those who are now seeking to make this splendid country capable of adequate British, and eventually in the fulness of time of self-government) upon an unshakable foundation. Would that the science of Law, national and international, stood upon an equally stable basis of numerous, largely and irrefragably inducted facts.

Having said so much, by way of encouragement, upon the extensive bearings and high importance of Indian ethnology, I will now add a few words by way of caution. Mr. Robinson, in a recent paper upon sundry of the border tribes of Assam,† has not scrupled confidently to assert the affinity of these tribes (the Bódó and Gáró amongst others) with the people of Tibet. This may or may not be so. But I apprehend that this alleged affinity demands larger and more careful investigation than Mr. Robinson has yet had leisure to apply to it, and that in thus deciding upon a most interesting and difficult point, he has adduced maxims which are not very tenable. In the first place, he has wholly neglected the physical and psychical evidence which are, each of them, as important as the glottological towards the just decision of a question of ethnic affinity. In the next place, whilst adducing a copious vocabulary which makes against, and a curt survey of the mechanism of language which (we will allow) makes for, his assertion, he proceeds to lay down the doctrine that the former medium of proof is worthy of very little, and the latter medium of proof (thus imperfectly used and applied) is worthy of very much reliance. In the third place, whilst insisting upon the indispensableness of a written and fixed standard of speech, he has neglected the excellent standard that was available for the Tibetan tongue, and has proceeded to rest upon two spoken standards, termed by him Bhotia and Chángló, but neither of

---

* Preface to the Moslem Historians of India. I cordially assent nevertheless to the justice of Mr. Elliot's strictures. But I find the cause of the actual evil elsewhere.
† Journal, No. 201, for March 1849.

which agrees with the written or spoken language of Lassa and Digarchi. In the fourth place, he speaks of Bhót, alias Tibet, and Bhútán, alias Lhó, as the same country ; and also gives his unknown Chángló a position within the known limits of Bhútán,* without the slightest reference to the latter well-known country; besides, speaking of the cis-Himálayans and sub-Himálayans (p. 203) as separate races !

These remarks are by no means captiously made. But some sifting of the evidence adduced is surely indispensable when a question of delicacy and difficulty is (I must think) prejudged upon such grounds.

Mr. Robinson is possibly not aware how much of the mechanism of the whole of the Turanian group of languages is common to every one language of that group, nor that the Tamúlian and Tibetan languages are held to be integral parts of that group. Yet such are apparently the facts,† whence it must surely result that a cursory and exclusive view of the organisation of one of these languages, such as Mr. Robinson gives and rests on, cannot be adequate to settle the Tibetan affinities of the Bódós and Gárós (interalia), since the points of lingual agreement cited may be neutral quantities, that is, characteristics common (say) to the Tamúlian and Tibetan tongues, or to the Chinese and Tibetan : and certainly some of them are so far from being diagnostically, that is, exclusively, Tibetan, that they belong to Hindí, Urdú, and even to English ! We have yet much to learn touching the essentials of the structure of the Indo-Chinese tongues, the Chinese and the Tibetan; and until a philosophical analysis shall have been made of these languages, it will be very hazardous to rest upon a cursory view of the supposed distinctive (structural) characters of Mr. Robinson's exclusive standard, or the Tibetan ; in regard to the structure of which tongue, moreover, he has scarcely more fully availed himself of De Körös' grammar than he has in his vocabulary of De Körös' dictionary. Under these circumstances I am disposed to place at least as much reliance upon Mr. Robinson's copious list of vocables‡ as I can

* Viz., 92¼° east longitude.—*Pemberton's Report.*
† Prichard, Vol. IV. p. 199 ff., and Bunsen's Report.
‡ This list seems to gainsay Mr. R.'s theory, for if the Bódós (for example) were

do upon his incomplete analysis of structure; and with regard to Mr. R.'s disparagement of the words of any unwritten and uncultivated tongue as evidence of ethnic affinity, I must say there seems to me a good deal of exaggeration.*

Whoever shall take an adequate number, not more than Mr. Robinson's, of well-selected words, and shall take them with such care as to be able to reach the roots of the words and to cast off those servile particles, whether prefixes or postfixes, among which deviation is ever most rife, may confidently rely upon his vocabulary for much sound information respecting ethnic affinities, supposing, of course, that he has a good standard and makes the proper use of it. Of course, I reject, with Mr. Robinson, as neutral quantities, all adopted, imitative and interjectional words. But when I find Mr. R. insisting upon " casual " resemblances as a class of words equally worthless with the three above enumerated, I desire to know what this chance means ; for one of the highest of living authorities on ethnology and glottology, and one, too, who insists almost too much upon the mechanism of language,† declares that " the chance is less than one in a million for the same combination of sounds signifying the same precise object." ‡ With these cautionary remarks, which are given in a spirit of perfect courtesy towards Mr. R., I now conclude, any further observations being unnecessary to explain my purpose in appending the written and spoken Tibetan—the former from De Cörös, the latter from a native of Lassa—to my present series of vocables.

of Tibetan origin, it is hardly credible that their ordinary vocables should not more plainly reveal the fact, seeing that they have never been out of actual contact with races of the same descent as that ascribed to them. The sub-Himálayan dialects differ from the trans-Himálayan standard : but identity is here shown in the roots as well as in the mode of agglutinating the servile particles ; not to mention that the snows form such a barrier in this case as exists not in regard to the Bódó intercourse with tribes of Tibetan origin.

The same general result follows from a careful examination of the vocabularies now forwarded. Apparently the Tibetan, like the Hindi, words, are adopted ones.

* Mr. Kemble has lately made most important use of the Saxon of the Heptarchy, of its words, and words only, in his " Saxons in England." A yet higher and strictly ethnological use has been made of the vocables of the old Iberian tongue by the younger Humboldt, who was yet reduced to glean these vocables from maps ! What would not Bunsen give for 100 plain words of the old Egyptian tongue, as spoken !

† See Bopp's remarks on the structural diagnostics of Sanscrit and Arabic.— Comp. Gram.   ‡ Bunsen's Report to the Brit. Assoc.

COMPARATIVE VOCABULARY OF THE TIBETAN, DHIMÁL, BÓDÓ, AND GÁRÓ TONGUES.

English.	Tibetan. Written.	Tibetan. Spoken.	Dhimál.	Bódó.	Gáró.
Air	rSúngma	Shákpá	Birima Bhirma	Bár H	Lampár
Ant	Grogma	Thómá	Nhá múï	Hásá brai	Góngá, Sámbúr
Arrow	mDáh	Da	Khér	Balá	Phéé
Bird	Byú	Chyá	Jíhá	Dou-chen	Tou-chap
Blood	Khráng	Thák	Hiki	Thöï	Chí
Boat	Grú	Koá, Syén	Náwár H	Nou H	Rúng
Bone	Rúspa	Rúkó	Hárá H	Bégéng	Kéréng
Buffalo	Mahi. s	Máhé	Diá	Moisho	Moishi
Cat	Byila	Simi	Mén khou	Mouji	Myou
Cow	Bá	Phá chúk	Piá	Mash-hú-jo	Máshú
Crow	Kháta	Ablak	Kawá	Dou-khá	Koura
Day	Nyinmo	Nyi mo	Nyi tima T	Shyán	Rasán, Sán
Dog	Khyi	Uyó	Khíá T	Choï má	Kai T
Ear	Sá	Amchó	Nhá tóng	Khoma	Máchór
Earth	rNá	Sá	Bhónoï	Há	Há
Egg	sGónga	Gong ná	Túï	Dou-doï (fowl's water.)	Tou-chí (fowl's blood)
Elephant	gLángchén	Lámboché	Nária	Moï gédét	Nápló
Eye	Mig	Mik	Mí T	Mogon	Makar
Father	Phá	Pálá	A'bá	Bipha	A'bá
Fire	Má	Mé	Mé T	Wat	Ver, Wal
Fish	Nyá	Gná	Haiyá	Ná T	Ná T
Flower	Métog	Méntok	Lhép	Bibar	Parr
Foot	rKáugpá	Kángó	Khókóï	Yáphá	Chaplap
Goat	Rá	Rá	F'échá	Búrmá [mon	Púrún
Hair	sKrá, sPú	Tá. Krá	Múï tú	Khanai, Kho-	Kaman, Houru
Hand	Lág pá	Lángó	Khúr	A'khai	Chákréng
Head	mGó	Gó	Púring	Khóró	Dakam
Hog	Phag	Phak	Páyá	Yóma	Vak
Horn	Rá	Rajo	Dáng	Góng	Korong
Horse	rTá	Tá	Onhyá	Kórai H	Ghora H
House	Khyim	Náng	Chá	Noö	Nagou
Iron	lChags	Chhyá	Chír	Chúrr	Shúrr
Leaf	Lómá	Hyómá	Lhává	Lai	Léchak
Light	Hod	Hwé. Eu	Sánéká	Chúráng Shráng	Klángkláng
Man	Mi	Mi	Wával, Diáng	Híwá Mánshi *	Míva
Monkey	sPrébú	Tyú	Nhóyá	Mókhara	Kouwé
Moon	zLáva	Dáwá	Táli	Nókhábir	Ráng rét
Mother	Ama	A'má	Amá	Bímá	Ama
Mountain	Rí	Rí	Rá T	Hájó	Há chúr
Mouth	Khá	Khá	Núï	Khouga	Hótóng
Moschito	Súnbú mChurings	Syé dongma	Jáhá	Thámphóï	Sotsá
Name	Ming	Ming	Ming T	Múng T	Múng T
Night	mTshanmo	Chénmó	Nhishing	Hór	Phar
Oil	hBrúmár	Num	Chúïtí	Thou	Tél H
Plantain	Caret	Grálá	Yúmphí	Thálit	Laktai
River	gTsáng po	Cháng pó	Chí	Dóï	Chí
Road	Lam	Lani	Dámá T	Lámá T	Lam T
Salt	Tshá	Chhá	Dúsó	Shyúng kárö, Sayúng kri	Syang
Skin	Pág spa	Pág-pa	Dhálé	Bígúr	Holop

* Diáng and Mánshi express mankind, met. F. Wával and Híwá, man only.

English.	Tibetan. Written.	Tibetan. Spoken.	Dhimál.	Bódó.	Gáró.
Sky	Nam kháh	Nam	Sórgi H	Nó khoráng	Sórg H
Snake	sBrúl	Deu	Púnhá	Jíbou	Dúpú
Star	sKarma	Karma	Phúró	Háthot khi	Laitan
Stone	rDó	Dó	U'nthúr	Onthai	Lóng
Sun	Nyimá	Nyí má	Bélá H	Shán	Sán, Rasán
Tiger	sTag	Tak	Khúná	Mochá	Matsá
Tooth	Só	Só	Sí tong	Hathai	Phá tóng
Tree	lJonshing	Shin dong	Shing T	Bong-pháng	Pan
Village	Yúl tsho	Thóng	Dérá H	Phárá H	Sóng
Water	Chhú	Chhú	Chí T	Dóï	Chí-ká T
Yam	Dóvá	Thómá	Ling	Thá	Han
I	Ná	Gnyá	Ká	A'ng	A'ng
Thou	Khyod	Khé	Ná	Náng	Náng
He, she it	Kho	Khú	Wá	Bí	U'
We	Nachag	Gnánjo	Kyel	Jong	Ning
Ye	Khyodchag	Khenjo	Nyel	Nang chúr	Nanók
They	Khochag	Khonjo	U'bal	Bí chúr	O'nók, Wonók
Mine	Nahi, Nayi	Gná yi	Káng	Angni	Angni
Thine	Khoyod kyi	Khé yi	Náng	Nangni	Nangni
His, &c.	Khoyi, Khóhi	Khó yi	Wáng	Bíni	U'ni
Ours	Nachaggi	Gnánjo yi	King	Jong ni	Ning ni
Yours	Khyod, Changgi	Khenjo yi	Níng	Nang chúrni	Nanókni.
Theirs	Khochaggi	Khonjo yi	U'bal ko	Bíchúrni	O'nókni
One	gChig	Chik	E'-long	Man-ché T	Gó-shá
Two	gNyis	Nyi	Nhé-long T	Man-né T	Gi-ning, A-ning
Three	gSúm	Súm	Súm-lang	Man-tham	Ga-thám, A-thám
Four	bZhi	Zhyi	Diá-long T	Man-bré	Bri
Five	Hna	Gná	Ná-long T	Man-bá	Bóngá
Six	Drúk	Thú	Tú-long T	Man-dó	Krók T
Seven	bDún	Dún	Nhí-long	Man-chini	Sining
Eight	brGyúd	Gyé	Yé-long	...	Chét
Nine	dGú	Gúh	Kúhá-long	...	Jú T
Ten	bChú Thámbá	Chúh	Té-long	... [sha-ché	Chí T
Twenty	Nyi shú	Nyi shú	E'long bísá	Chokai-bá Bi-	Rúng shá *
Thirty	Súmchú	Súmchú	Caret	Caret	Rúng shá chi
Forty	bZhibchú	Hip chú	Nhé bísa	Bishá né	Rúng ning
Fifty	Hnabchú	Gnap chú	Caret	Caret	Rúng ning chi
Hundred	brGyá-thambá	Gyá, Gyá thambá	Ná bísa	Bishá bá	Rúng bóngá
Of	Kyi, Gi, Hi, Yi	Gi	Kó	Ní	Ní
To	Lá, Tú, Dú, Rá, Sú	Lá	E'ng	No	Ná
From	Nas, Las	Né, Diné	Shó	Phrá	Prá
By, inst.	Kyis, Gin S. His, Yis	I'	Dóng, Ou	Jóng	Man
With, cum, Sáth, in Hindi and U'rdú	Lhanchig	Lá, Dá	Dópá, Dósá	Lago, Jong	Mon
Without, sine, Bina in Hindi	...	Thána	Mánthú	O'ngá, Géyá	Tóng chani ga-mang
In, On	Lá, Ná	Lá	Rhútá	Chon, Nou, Ou	Púm vái, Pir vai

* Bísá, Bishá vel Rúng is a score, and the system of enumeration is one score, one score and ten, two score, and so on to 5 score for 100.

Cho kai ba in the Bódó column is 5 groats or Gandas for 20.

English.	Tibetan.		Dhimál.	Bódó.	Gáró.
	Written.	Spoken.			
Now	Déngtsé, Dá Déng	Thándá	E'lang	Dánó	Tayan
Then	Dé tsé	Thi dwi	Kólá	Obélá H	Té éng
When?	Gang tsé Nam	Khádwi	Hélou	Mábélá	Bíbá
To-day	Déring	Thíring	Náni	Diné H	Tingní
To-morrow	Sáng, Thoré	Sáng	Júmni	Gábún	Ganáp
Yesterday	m Dáng	Dáng	Anji	Míá	Mí vai
Here	Hadina	Dicho	I'sho	Imbo	Yayan
There	Héna	Hácho	U'sho	Hobo	Wáng
Where?	Gangná	Khácho	Hésho	Mouha	Bié
Above	sTengna	Teng, Ghe yégi	Rhútá	Chhá	Pír vai
Below	Hogna	Wó, Syú, Magi	Létá	Sying	Chúrik vai
Between	Bar, du	Bhar	Májhata H	Géjér	Majár vai H
Without, Outside	Phyi, rohna	Chi	Báhiro H	Báhirou H	Báhír vai H
Within	Nang, na	Náng	Lipta	Singou, Sing	Púma vai
Far	Né, Nyé	Tháring	Dúré H	Gaján g	Piján g
Near	Ring	Tháui	Chéng só	Khátai	Katai
Little	Nyúng	Nigúva	A'toïsá	Tísí, Kitisi	Kiték si
Much	Máng, Tu-mo [ma	Má gúá	E'shúto	Gabáng	Takkri
How much?	Tsam, Tsó-	Khá chevé	Hé joko	Béché báng	Bipáng
As, rel.	Hadétsúg	Khánda	Jédóng	Jirin	Jégándá
So, corr.	Détsúg	Théndá	Kódóng	U'rin	U'gánda
Thus, poz.	Jitsúng	Dindá	U'dóng	U'rin	U'gándá
How?	Tsúg, Chit-sug	Kháché Khánda	Hé sá, Hé dong	Bré	Bigándá
Why?	...	Khá ïn	Haipáli	Mánó	A'táng
Yes	...	I'n	Jéng *	O'ngó *	Há
No	Má, Mi	Mén	Má, Manthú T	Ongá	Ahá
(Do) not	...	Má	Má T	Dá	Tá
Also, and	Yáng	Yáng	Caret	Bi, Bo	Bá
Or	...	Mo	Ná	Ná	Ná
This	Hadé	Di	I'thoï	Imbé	I'mara
That [Jón	Dé	Phi-di	U'thoï	O'bé	O'mara
Which, rel.	...	Thinda	Jédong	Jé, Jai H	Jón H
Which corr. Tón	...	Thé	Kódong	Bi, (that)	Wón H
Which? Kón	Gáng	Khangi	Hai, Héti	Má	A'to, Bíyó
What? Kya	Chi	Kháng	Hai	Má	A'tó
Who? Kón	Sú, Kha	Khángi, Sú	Héti	Chúr	Cháng
Any thing, Kúcch	Chizhig	Khá ïn	Hété, Haidong	Múngbó, Jish-láp	Harj múrj
Any body, Kóï	Súzhig Kháchig	Sú ín	Hété	Jishláp	Já-tá?
Eat!	Zo	Só	Chá;	Já	Sá
Drink:	hThúng	Thúng	A'm	Lúng	Lúng
Sleep	Nyan	Nyé	Jím	Múdúláng	Gúr
Wake	...	Caret	Lho	Jakháng	Sarai
Laugh	bGad	Gá	Léng	Mini	Mini
Weep	Nú, Shúm	Gnó	Khár [dóp	Gáp	Hép
Be silent	Khrog	Chúm	Chiká pahi, Má-	Srithá	Tápchilip tong
Speak	brJod, Smrós	Caret	Dóp	Rai	Brot, Borot
Come	Hóng sByon	Syo	Ló	Phoi	Phoi

* Jéng and O'ngó mean rather it is, hast in Persian, than simple assent.

English.	Tibetan. Written.	Spoken.	Dhimál.	Bódó.	Gáro.
Go	Sóng, Gró, Gyú	Gyó	Hadé	Tháng	Loi
Stand up	hChhár	Lóng	Jáp	Jakháng	Chap
Sit down	hDúg	Deh	Yong	Jó	Abak
Move, Walk	hGro	Gyó	Tí, Hadé	Thó, Tháng	Loï
Run	rGyúg	Gyúgé Chong	Dháp	Khát	Talok
Give	hBúh, Phúl,Thona	Phing	Pí	Hot	Há
Take	bLán, Júng, Hén	Léng, Yá	Rhú	Lá, Ná T ?	Lé, Lau
Strike	bDún, rDig	Dúng	Dánghai T	Sho	Tok
Kill	Shig, Sod, h Gúm	Sé	Sé T	Shothát	Tok tat
Bring	hKhyon, sKych	Bá syo	Chú má	Lá bo	Láphá
Take away	hKhúr, bKhyer	Bák, song	Chúng pú	Láng	Léláng
Lift up,raise	hDég, Slon, sNyob	Khúr	Lhopá	Bokháng	Paicho
Hear	Nyám, gSon	Nyén	Hin	Khaná chong	Natám
Understand	Soms, Go	Sám	Bújhté rhú	Bújílá H	Bújai H
Tell, relate	hShod, hChhod	Láp, Chwé	Dop	Rai	Borot
Good	Bazáng-po	Yappo	Elká	Gham	Péném
Bad	Náng-po	Dúkpo	Máélká	Hamma	Sarchá
Cold	Gráng-po	Thammo	Tirká	Gúshú	Chikrop
Hot	Tshá-po, Dropo	Chábo	Cháká	Gúdúng	Gútúng
Raw	...	Zvémbo	Sinkhá	Gatháng	Piting
Ripe	Sminbo	Chémbo	Minká	Gamang	Papman
Sweet	...	Gnármo	Tááka	Gadoï	Sahmá
Sour	...	Caret	Dukká	Gaphá, Gakhoï	Phakká
Bitter	...	Kháko	Kháká T.	Gakhá	Háni
Handsome	Dsésmo, sTúgpo	Jébo	Rémká	Majáng	Némá
Ugly	Midsesma, Mistúg-	Mén Jébo	Máremká	Chápma	Sarchá
Straight	Dránpo [po	Thángbo	Ghenká	Thúng, júng	Préng dén
Crooked	sGúrbo, Túdpo	Kákpo	Kyoká	Khúngkrá	Kákrőï
Black	Nágpo	Nákpo	Dááká	Gatcham	Pénék
White	dKárpo	Kárpo	Jééká	Gúphút	Bok láng
Red	sMúkpo	Márpo	I'ká	Gajá	Písak
Green	hJáng, khú	Jhángú	Nélpá	Samsram, Kháng shúr	Héng jeléng
Long	Ringpo	Rimbo	Rhinká T	Galou	Pillo
Short	Thúngpo	Thún dúng	Tótóká	Gúchúng	Bandók
Tall, } man	...	Thombo	Dhángáká	Gajou	Pillo
Short }	...	Mábó	Bángraká	Gahai	Bandók
Small	Chhúng, Phra	Chún chúng	Mhoïká	Múdúï	Pamar
Great	Chhénpo, sBombo	Bombo	Dhamká	Gédét	Gódá
Round	zLumpo	Riri	Gúrmaká	Dúllút ni, To-lotni	Góglot-ni
Square	Grúb, zhi (*angles* 4)	Thúzí *angles* 4)	Dia thúni ká (*angles* 4)	Kónámanbréni (kóná is H)	Koná bri ni (kóná is H)
Flat, } Level }	...	Caret	Sáriká	Somán ni H	Gakshan
Fat	rGyagspo	Thó thembo	Dhámká	Gúphúng	Kánéntwa
Thin	Srobbo, Ridpo	Mábó ?	Syéuká	Gaham	Jot kréng
Weariness	...	Gyák	Caret	Myéng dúng	Réwé kou
Thirst	sKóm	Khakúm	Chí ámli	Gáng dúng	Chíka láng nóïtwa
Hunger	lTógs	Tok	Mhítú	U'nkwi dúng	Máyú phïtwá

N.B.—T post-fixed indicates a Tibetan etymon for the word ; and H post-fixed, a Hindí or Urdú origin.

Thus it appears that there are, out of the above, 190 words derived from Hindí, or from Tibetan, in Dhimál, in Bódó, and in Gáró, as follows :—

	Hindí.	Tibetan.
Dhimál	8	19
Bódó	10	6
Gáró	8	7

Out of a total of 190 words of prime use and necessity. Ergo, these are adopted words?

SECTION IV.

ABORIGINES OF THE NORTH-EAST FRONTIER.

———◆———

DARJILING, *September 16th*, 1850.

To the Secretary of the Asiatic Society.

SIR,—I have the honour to enclose another series of Vocabularies obtained for me by the Rev. N. Brown of Sibságor, in furtherance of my plan of exhibiting to the Society a sample of the lingual affinities of all the Aborigines of India on an uniform plan. The present series comprises four dialects of the Nágá tongue,—the Chútia, the Ahóm, the Khámti, the Láos,—and the Siamese. My valuable correspondent Mr. Brown has favoured me with the following remarks on the present occasion :—

" The first four columns of the table complete the variations, priorly given, of the strangely corrupted Nágá language. This tongue affords an extraordinary exemplification of the manner in which an unwritten language may be broken up even upon a small extent of territory. On the other hand, in the great Tái family we have a not less striking instance of the preservation of a language in almost its original integrity and purity through many centuries, and in despite of a vast territorial diffusion; for, from Bankók to Sadiyá, along the Meinám, Salwén, Irawádi, and Kyendwen rivers, up to the sources of the Irawádi, through fourteen degrees of latitude, there is but one language, notwithstanding the diversity of governments under which the speakers of it live.

" The Mithan and Tablúng Nágás (see table) reside on the hills east and north of Sibságor. The Kháris descend upon the plains near Jórhát. They are much superior to the other

Nágás. The Jabokas and Banferas are the neighbours of the Mítháns, with nearly similar tongues. The Angámis occupy the southern end of the Nágá country. The Chútia is the language of one of the old tribes of Assam, now nearly extinct. The Ahóm also is nearly extinct as a spoken tongue. The present Ahóms of Assam, descendants of the conquerors, still form one of the largest portions of its population. But their language, as well as their religion, has been relinquished for those of the Hindus. Their ancient creed had little resemblance to Buddhism or to Bráhmanism. The Khámtis retain their tongue, but have lost their creed. They have accepted Buddhism from the Burmas, from whom they have likewise borrowed many new words.

" In answer to your queries I can but say, at present, that I highly appreciate the importance of a standard for the Indo-Chinese tongues ; but which language has the best claim to be constituted such I do not know. I should be inclined, however, to assume the Burmese, which is at least *half-brother to the Tibetan.* This would bring the Tibetan, the Lhópá or Bhútánese, the Burmese, the Singhpho, the Nágá, &c., into a kind of family union. The Siamese Shyán, or, as the people themselves call it, the Tái, cannot be brought into the same category. It has little or no affinity with the neighbouring dialects, and may represent another whole class of languages not yet ascertained. It is probably allied to the Chinese, and is in importance not inferior to the Burmese."

English.	Mithan Nágá.	Tablung Nágá.	Khari Nágá.	Angami Nágá.	Deoria chutia.	Ahom.	Khamti.	Laos.	Siamese.
Air	rangbin	wang yak	aning	tikhe	beni	lóm	lóm	lóm	lóm
Ant	tiksa	tik há	hungzah !	hache	chimechi	nyuchu	mót	mót, puak	mót
Arrow	sán	láhan	takala	thiwu	átá	lem	lim	lempún	lukson
Bird	ó	ondá	ozah	pará	duá	nuktú	nók	nók	nok
Blood	áji	ih	ai	unhi	chui	let	lüt	leut	leuat
Boat	khón	iseng	aróng	ru	nu	ru	hú	heu	reua
Bone	rha	wan	taret	uru	pichon	tau	nuk	dók	kaduk
Buffalo	loi	tek	apang	rali	iné	khrai	khwai	khwái	khwái
Cat	miáh	ami	mochi	nunno	midige	men	mian	meau	meau
Cow	mádu	mádu	mastí	mithu	mósu	hu	ngó	ngóa	wóa, ngóa
Crow	okhá	ausapa	waru	chejá	duká	ká	ká	ká	ká
Day	anyi	tini	asónga	tiso	sánjá	bán	wan	wan	wan
Dog	hi	kui	ai	tastí	shi	má	má	má	má
Ear	ná	ná	tenhaun	anye	yáku	pik	lú	lú	hú
Earth	háwán	katok	ali	kije	yá	din	langmin	din	phendin
Egg	otí	kek	ansú	podzú	dujá	khrai	khai	khai	khai
Elephant	lóak	lok niu	sati	tsu	meu	tyáug	tsáng	tsang	chang
Eye	mik	mik	tenik	amhi	mukuti	tá	tá	tá	tá
Father	apá	opáh	tabá	apó	tsipá	po	po	po	po
Fire	van	áh	matsú	mi	nye	fai	fai	fai	fai
Fish	ngiá	nyále	anghá	kho	tsingá	plá	pá	pá	plá
Flower	maipóa	chupeng	taben	popu	ibá	blok	mok	dok	dokmai
Foot	tchyá	yah lan	tachang	uphi	yápásu	tin	tin	te	tin
Goat	rón	yun	nabóng	tarú	lipeduru	pengá	pe	pe	pe
Hair	khó	min, su	kwá	atsú thá	kin	phrum	phóm	phóm	phóm
Hand	chak	yak	takhet	abi	ótun	khá	mü	mü	mü
Head	kháng	sang	telim	atsú	gubong	rú	hó	hó	hóa
Hog	vak	ak	auk	thavo	chu	mu	mú	mú	má
Horn	róng	wong	tili	pokhye	nu	khau	khau	khau	khau
Horse	nan	kowai	kungri	chekwir	góri	ren	má	má	má
House	ham	nok	aki	ki	nyá	hón	hün	heun	reuan
Iron	jián	yan	ayin	je	sang	lik	lék	lek	lek
Leaf	pán chak	phum yak	tuwá	ponye	chiá	bón	mau	bai	bai
Light	rangai	bining	snaugo	ngukwi	dákári	leng	leng	leng, tseng	sawang
Man	nu	sauniak	aui	theme	mósi	kun	kun	khon	khón

English	Mithan Nágá	Tablung Nágá	Khari Nágá	Angami Nágá	Deoria chutia	Ahom	Khamti	Laos	Siamese
Monkey	mainuk	simai	kishá	takwi	iku	laling	ling	wok, ling	ling
Moon	letnu	le	leta	kharr	yáh	den	lün	deun	tawan
Mother	ánnu	onu	tü	azo	tsimá	me	me	me	me
Mountain	...	...	apih	ehaju	asü	doi	noi	loi	pukhau
Mouth	tun	chusim	tabaun	amü	dumju	sup	sóp	pák	pák
Musquito	...	...	mrilá	viru	dán	phreng	yung	yung	yung
Name	man	min	achu	nzá	mn	chu	tsu	tsü	chü
Night	rang nak	vang niak	áyáh	tizi	siri	dam	khün	khün	khün
Oil	mangá	mangá	tutsü	kakizu	tu	man ngá	nam, man	nam, man	nam, man
Plantain	...	...	mangó	tekwasi	tüzu	kui	kóe	kue	klue
River	shuá	yang nü	atsü	kharr	ji maji	klie	khye nam	nam me	mé nam
Road	lam	lam	ndi	cháh	tságu	táng	táng	tang	tháng
Salt	hun	hum	machi	matso	süz	kla	kü	kue, kem	kleüa
Skin	khóan	soh	tagap	bikhr	chikun	plek	nang	nang	nang
Sky	...	...	aning	thi	pichoni	fá	fá	fáfön	fá
Snake	pu	cháhá	ahü	thinhye	dubu	ngó	ngü	ngu	ngú
Star	lethi	yóng	peti	thenü	jiti	dau	náu	láu	dáu
Stone	lóng	wang hi	alóng	kache	yatiri	frá	hin	hin	hin
Sun	rang hán	sahnu	suhih	nakhi	sáoh	bán	wan	kang wan	tawan
Tiger	chianú	phá	akhü	taklu	mesá	sü	sü	seu	süa
Tooth	vá	peh	taphá	ulu	háti	khiu	khiu	khiau	fan, khiau
Tree	pan	tying	sundóng	si	popon	tun	tun	tón	tón
Village	ting	riang	ayim	aramo	átigu	bán	mán	ban	ban
Water	ti	...	atsü	zü	ji	nam	nam	nam	nam
Yam	...	...	...	...	...	...	...	...	man dóm
I	ku	tau	ni	á	án	kau	kau	hóuman	khá
Thou	nang	nang	nang	no	no, áni	mó	mau	óng, ku	tua, mũng
He, she, it	nih	taupá	pau	me	bareni	heu	man	tóa	khon, man
Wo	...	...	akan	áwe	járurau	rau	hu	man, tan	rau
Ye	...	...	nikhala	notoleli	jákugroni	khau	mau sú	hau	su
They	...	...	tungkhala	tothete	bário	khreu	man khau	...	khau ar ai
Thine	kukuhe	tesei	ní	...	ányo	au	kau	...	...
Mine	...	...	nang	...	niyo	mó	mau	...	...
His	...	...	...	...	biyo	heu	man	...	...
One	áttá	chá	akhet	po	dügshá	ling	nüng	nüng	nüng

English	Mitham Nágá.	Tablung Nágá.	Khari Nágá.	Angami Nágá.	Deoria chutia.	Ahom.	Khamti.	Laos.	Siamese.
Two	ányi	ih	anne	kane	dukuni	sang	song	song	song
Three	ázan	lem	asam	sü	dugdá	sam	sám	sám	sám
Four	áli	pili	phali	deh	duguchi	sí	sí	sí	sí
Five	ázá	ngá	phangá	pangu	dugumua	há	há	há	há
Six	árok	vok	tarók	sóru	duguchu	ruk	hók	hók	hók
Seven	ánath	nith	tani	thene	duguchi?	chit	tset	tset	chet
Eight	áchet	thath	sachet	thetha	duguche	pet	pet	pet	pét
Nine	aku	thu	tekü	thaku	dugnchuba	kau	kau	kau	kau
Ten	ban	pan	tarah	kürr	dugnchuba dugshe	sip	sip	sip	sip
Twenty	chá		makhi	makü		sau	sau	sáu nüng	yó sip
Thirty			samrá	sürr		sam sip	sám sip	sám sip	sám sip
Forty	panyí		lfrah	lhide		sí sip	sí sip	sí sip	sí sip
Fifty			tanam	rijangu		há sip	há sip	há sip	há sip
Hundred	pugá		rukrá	kre		pak	pák	hoi	roi
Of			(wanting)			(wanting)	(wanting)		thí
To			ná				hang, ti		ke
From			bine				luk		té
With		sah	ashe						duei
In	khá		gü	kinu	chikimi	chum	kannü	nai	nai
On			tarnüge	akihawo	pichoni	khau	nau	neu	bón
Now	atha	cháha	hikü	lilitiha	derereni	nu	tsang, ngai	teng	reu, than chai
Then?			jikü	tadzune	deremai	tinai			müa
To-day	anyí	tinyi	thani	teje	dumoni	turnnai		wanni	müa dai
To-morrow	nai ni	ngai ni	asang	thedu	dhinieni	phreu nai	maphók	phuk	wan ní
Yesterday	manyi	manyi	hashi	koshe	disuini	banai	mangá		phrungní
Here			nikó	haki	dupuroni	sang manai	phe, thai	ní	wa, wän
There?	pau pu	tau wai	wadengüojü	lithe	loliore	poi	hanpun		ní
Above	ding	kawang	kuchi	kiraporú	hobóng	u, tinai	thaü	tinai	thi nau
Below	hópang	opang	tamachingu	bale	boróng	tet	kalu	pin	thi nai
Between			tamóksing	chakise	picho	hó		lum	bón
Without			tiong	kite	kumo	nu			tí
Within			takigü	kinu	bajüni, chikimi	lep, klang	tinaü		wang, thi nok
Far	atai	kátike	tisingo, uragu	chawé	asain	lí, khunju, jau, sai	kai	kaf	thinai, kli

English.	Mithan Nágá.	Tablung Nágá.	Khari Nágá.	Angami Nágá.	Deoria chutia.	Ahom.	Khamti.	Laos.	Siamese.
Near	hole	ótike	anhagu	chaguno	butugain	klai	kaü	kai	klai
Little	olipia	echinghá	ichadango	katuno	poiani	chut	lek, kye	nak, lái	leknoi
Much	taihu	eselai	kwalangau	kyapür	poiní	rá	nam	kilam	lai, bundá
How much?	...	...	kuia	kiehuru	armeha	plai	...	...	ki lem
Thus	...	...	itangó	tsawe	lakireni	...	nang nai	...	yangnan, chen
How?	...	...	kotisaü	nokidihika	dakang	...	...	...	thaü, phrá het
Why?	...	...	chibatsaawi	kaji	dannno	wá	...	...	phrá aurai
Yes	vai	aiya	hau	e	loi	khewo	tsaü	tsai, nem	khá
No	mantai	mang cha	nongó	mowe	hóya	bukhewo	ma tsaü	bo tsai	michi
Not	...	...	tá	...	dá	bu, ma	le, tak	bo, mai, yá	mi, yá
And	...	...	...	...	...	...	...	le	le, kap, tak
This	hi ha	thoi nan	pio	hawe	taihoni	iu	an nai	ni	ní
That	hi ha	thoi theo	poicho chu	liwe	bare	heu	an nan	nan	nan
Which?	tem	tof nan	kubni	kiuru	boroshini	panku	an naü	...	khondai
What?	oveh	owai	chabaü	kaje	damdarini	re	sang	sang	arai
Who?	...	...	sui	soru	basani	phreu	phaü	khai, phai	khrai, süng
Any thing	...	...	kuiai	kajipuru	damasirini	pheu	kan phong	asang	arai
Any body	sá há	háchu	koi mürli	chakra paru	shámádu	...	...	...	...
Eat	singhá	yang ying shi	tsaung	chiliche	hurini	kin	kin	kin	kin
Drink	jipdau	chunshi	atsióng	dzü kretowe	jinine	kieu	kin nam	kin nam	deum
Sleep	nile	nichi	ipigili	zü	yung arini	non	non, nap	non, lap	lap
Wake	saple	saptike	sishaugó	sirto	harmamani	teng	tün	tün	tün
Laugh	...	...	manitli	nu	hatukari	khru	khó	hán, khóa	hóaro
Weep	...	...	chipli	krá	ugarini	hai	hai	hai	rong hai
Be silent	káh	táh	tukurú	chasibale	turucha	supmu	yú tsip tsip	dak dak yú	ning yú
Speak	ráhai	ongkoi	aihushang	pusiche	icharini	bok	wá	pak	phut
Come	tóng	angsi	hinnerang	akiphirche	nangkwá	má	mé	má	má
Go	ajóng	yong chi	wá	totache	ákená	ká	ká	ká	pai
Stand up	ngó dau	um chi	huæligili	thale	tákarini	ti	sau	pai, men	yün
Sit down	tóng, khá	angsi	manio	bache	dudurini	nang	nang	song	nang
Walk	rikle	phal chi	róng chwa	tothe	kerurini	ká	pai	nang	dün
Run	láhai	yakhu	semekwa	mhathele	jonoini	paikhan	len	men	wing pi
Give	paule	yakei	khiugó	süwawo	larini	heu	haü	len pai	hai
Take	maithun	set chi	hirangó	khriliwe	lario	au	au	hü	au, nap
Strike	...	...	yakohau	vashuwe	borini	dá, po	po	au, tí, bup	tí, boe

English.	Mithan Nágá.	Tablung Nágá.	Khari Nágá.	Angami Nágá.	Deoria chutia.	Ahom.	Khamti.	Laos.	Siamese.
Kill	langlau	toi chi	yaksitógó	dukhiawe	botechiro	potai	au tai	khá	khá, au tai
Bring	láhai	yakei	heneratli	seyawo	larini	ánmá	au ná	aumá	au má
Take away	pai pau	noh si	heneraugó	satele	laromni	sung	sóng	sóng, thü	thü
Lift up	lauko	noh si	chungótsó	tupele	lagaromni	yok, tang	yó, yóng	yá	yók
Hear	atluk	chai ha	jaugó	silowe	kanatori	nyin	hú, thom	...	dai yin
Understand	avan	tau singpu	metechau	siwe	takaruni	hú	wa	rü, hü	rú
Tell	...	...	...	...	...	bok	ni	wá	bok wá
Good	maile	mailuke	aró	viwe	churini	di	maní	di	dí
Bad	manmai	yemei	maró	sowe	chani	khyá	...	hái, bodí	chua, mai dí
Cold	ráng kham	wang sam	aiyang	sí	chepepe	khye, náu	yen	náu, yen	yen, nán
Hot	kham	shem	tetsá	khakwu	kaini	ran, lut	hon, mai, lút	hon	ron
Raw (green)	...	...	tachim	memo	pijo	lip	nip	dip	dip
Ripe	jum	yim	tenhing	me	munom	rung, suk	sík	sík	súk
Sweet	ti	urang	miang	che	jiri	oi	wán	wán	wán
Sour	shi	si	tehsan	khye	aitotoi	sum	sóm	sóm	sóm, preo
Bitter	khá	khá	khá	chási	kai	khum	khóm	khóm	khóm
Handsome	...	...	kubaitaró	visu	ichubare	khyeng	ngám	ngáin	ngám
Ugly	...	...	maró	shopur	úchini	khye plá	háng hai	hai	rái
Straight	kom	kom	mathunjau	theklia	pune	í	nan	...	trong, sü
Crooked	nak	niak	tikihang	krewi	kekurai	ke, ngok	ngok	kom, kót	ngo
Black	thoh	heng	nak	kati	sakokoi	dam	nam	dam, nin	dam
White	...	...	mesing	kacha	puri	phók	kháu, phúk	kháu, pheuk	kháu
Red	ló	lau	tamitram	mrí	saru	deng	neng	deng, kam	deng
Green	mau	soh	shim paluk	kapaje	pijoni	kyí	khyeu	kheau	kheau
Long	chóak	tau	tilhaun	josú	lui	lej au	yáu	yáu	yáu
Short	...	...	tútsizau	jú	sutugai	lot	lot	san, hun	san
Tall (high)	ahipin [nau sui	...	oregn	karkhre	suini	sung	sung	sung	süng
Short (low)	achung	...	orejute	khar uo	patigaini	tam	tam	tam	tam bóa
Small	...	yong nong	minghaji	kanachapo	suru suroni	noi	lek, on	lek, noi	lek noi
Great	...	...	tahpetiau	jopúr	am chá dini	lóng	lung, yaü	luang, yai	luang, yai
Round	...	nittan	meketang	khruhi	tumóru	klom, pán	món	kóm	klóm
Fat	chóng	...	tabiti	pomoja	mejirini	pí	pí	pí, tui	sai, man
Thin (lean)	...	...	achi	soponoru	dugumjini	heng	yom	...	mai man

SECTION V.

ON THE

ABORIGINES OF THE EASTERN FRONTIER.

In continuation of my papers already submitted to the Society having in view to exhibit summarily the affinities of all the aborigines of India, I now submit vocabularies, uniform with their precursors, of the written and spoken Burman, the Singpho, the Nágá in three dialects, the Abor and the Miri tongues.

For this series I am indebted to the Rev. N. Brown, of Sibságor, who, in forwarding it to me, favoured me with the following remarks :—

" These specimens appear fully to establish the fact that the *Burman, Singpho, Nágá,* and *Abor* languages are very close relatives, and ought not to be separated into different families, as they sometimes have been. The Burman and Singpho, it is true, have been regarded as nearly related; but I am not aware of its ever having been supposed that the Nágá or Abor were closely related to the Burman, or that there was any very intimate connection between the two. The Nágá tribes are very numerous, and every village appears to have its own dialect.

" I have not inserted the Khámti or Shyán, because I am not convinced that there is any very close radical connection between either and the Burmese. This affinity seems always to have been taken for granted as a matter of course, but without any just ground. It is true there are a considerable number of Burman words in the Khámti, but they bear the marks of recent introduction, and are not to be found in the old Ahóm, the parent Shyán, nor in the Siamese, with which the Ahóm was nearly, if not exactly, identical. I have inserted the Burmese as *written*, together with the spoken *form*. The Mags of Arakán, it is said, pronounce it *as it is written*, and not like the Burmese. It appears to resemble the Tibetan considerably. The first column of Abor Miri I have collected from a vocabulary published a year or two ago by Captain E. F. Smith (of the Bengal Native Infantry), commanding at Sadiya; the last column I got from a Miri residing at this place.

"In Burman I have used *th* to express the sound of *th* in *think*. Also a stroke under the initial letter of a syllable to denote the falling tone, and a dot under the final vowel to denote the short, abrupt tone. The Singpho and Namsang Nágá are taken from a vocabulary published several years ago by the Rev. M. Bronson, and may be depended on as correct. The other two Nágá dialects are given by two men from villages near Nowgong—the only Nágás I can find in the station just now; and as they do not understand Asamese very well, I may have introduced some errors from them. At all events, the words are evidently encumbered with affixes and prefixes that do not properly belong here. I have not, however, ventured to remove any of them, as you will be better able to do this. I am inclined to think that the radical forms in all these languages are monosyllabic, as the Burmese unquestionably is. The verbs, &c., would probably show a much greater resemblance if we had all the terms for each idea, as there will generally be many verbs nearly synonymous; consequently the lists do not always exhibit the corresponding forms, thus creating an apparent difference when there is none in reality."

As it is not my purpose to anticipate the results of the present inquiry, I will add nothing on this occasion to the above obliging and sensible remarks of Mr. Brown.

English.	Burman, Written.	Burman, Spoken.	Bronson's Singpho.	Bronson's Namsang Nágá.	Norgong Nágá.	Tengsa Nágá.	Capt. Smith's Abor-Miri.	Sibságor Miri.
Air	lé	lé	mbung	póng	mabung	mapung	asar	esār
Ant	parwakchhit	payuetseik	gagin	teipchák	machá	matháu	nirang	meráng
Arrow	mrá	myá	peliá	látchau	lasang	lasan	epuk	epug
Bird	nghak	nghet	wu	vó	üzz	usó	petang	pátang
Blood	swé	thwé	sai	hé	azü	ái	yilpi ui	íye
Boat	lhé	lhó	li	khuonkhó	surung	lung	ellóng	óilungá
Bone	aró	ayó	nráng	áráh	terap	telet	áiong	áiong
Buffalo	kwye	kyue	ngá	ló	chang	tyang	menjek	menjeg
Cat	krong	kyaung	ningyau	miang	tanú	neyau	mendari	menkuri
Cow	nwá	nuá	kanaú	mán	nasi	mási	gárúshameh	góru
Crow	kyí	kyí	kokhá	wakhá	waru	walo	piák	piág
Day	né	né	ningthói	rangyi	…	túnglú	longeh	longko
Dog	khwé	khwé	gui	hí	azz	arh	ekí	iki
Ear	ná	ná	ná	ná	tenaung	telánnu	norong	yerung
Earth	mré	myé	nggá	há	áli	áli	ámong	ámong
Egg	u	u	údi	ati	antsú	utú	áfplu	apú
Elephant	chhang	s'hen	magui	puok	shitf	sutf	sita	site
Eye	myakchi	myetsi	mi	mit	tenok	tenyik	ámik	amik
Father	phaó	phá-é	wá	vá	urpá	apu	yiai	bábá
Fire	mi	mi	wan	van	mi	unasi	eme	unme
Fish	ngá	ngá	nga	ngá	angu	angu	eugo	orgo
Flower	pan	pán	siban	chóngpó	naru	nolong	ápun	ápun
Foot	khré	khyé	lagóng	dá	tatsüng	tacliing	die	die
Goat	chhit	s'heik	bainain	kien	nabung	nabung	shuben	ságroli
Hair	chhanbang	s'haben	karí	kachó	kó	kn	dumit	dumed
Hand	lak	let	lettí	dak	teklaf	teklát	áfiák	elág
Head	khong	ghaung	bóng	khó	takolák	teko	tuku, mittuk	mittub
Hog	wak	wet	wá	vak	ák	ák	yóek	eyeg
Horn	khyo	ghyó	rung	róng	tazzü	tái	áreng	áreng
Horse	mraug	myen	guurang	mók	kórr	kuri	góre	gure
House	im	eing	ntá	hum	kí	kí	ekum	ekun
Iron	sau	thán	mpri	jan	yin	yen	ragurah	yogír

English.	Burman, Written.	Burman, Spoken.	Bronson's Singpho.	Bronson's Namsang Nágá.	Nowgong Nágá.	Tengsa Nágá.	Capt. Smith's Abor-Miri.	Sibságor Miri.
Leaf	rwak	yuet	láp	nyáp	ám	ám	anné	ekamane
Light	lang	len	ningthói	rangvó	tsángurh	sangagho	piudng	púáda
Man	lú	lú	singpho	minyán	nyesung	mésung	amie	dámme
Monkey	myok	myauk	woé	véh	sñtsü	suchí	sibeh	shibe
Moon	la	lá	sitá	dá	yitá	lutá	palé	polo
Mother	ami	ami	ná	incyóng	uchá	ápñ	nanu	náná
Mountain	tong	taung	bun	háhó	min áram	maaan	ádí	ádi
Mouth	nhup	nhók	ninggrup	tun	tepang	tabdug	napang	napñing
Mosquito	khyang	khyen	tsigrong	mang dóng	merila	anjang	songgóu	tauig
Name	amín	amí	nfong	min	tenung	teñying	ámin	ámin
Night	nyin, nya	nyin, nyá	siná	rangpan	annu	ásangdi	kamogah	kannno
Oil	achhi	s°hí	nam án	tánthí	tótsü	mángá	tuláng	tuláng
Plantain	nghakpyo	ughetpyo	lungu	kieke	tsülátsü	mongo	kópagü	kopage
River	mrach	myit	khé	jóau	saaun	túlá	asie	abunge
Road	lam	láin	láin	lam	lemang	unglan	lambeü	lámte
Salt	chhá	s°há	jun	sum	natsü	machi	álu	állo
Skin	sáró	tháyé	phi	ákhuon	takap	takap	dumóer	asüg
Sky	mógh	mó	mu	rángtung	mabat	phunching	teong	domür
Snake	mrwé	myué	lapú	pá	pürr	phalü	...	tábbe
Star	kre	kye	sigan	mérik	pitinu	lutingting	tákár	tákár
Stone	kyok	kyauk	nlung	lóng	lungzik	longmaanggo	iliing	iliing
Sun	né	né	jín	sán	ánnü	tingtü	dunié	doanye
Tiger	kyá	kyá	sirong	sá	kayi	khü	simiü	sümyo
Tooth	swá	dáwá	wá	pá	tabu	taphu	ipáng	áie
Tree	apang	apen	plum	bang	santung	sangtung	esing	ising
Village	rwá	yuá	mereng	há	yüm	yam	dulong	doliing
Water	ró	yó	ntsin	jó	tsü	tü	ásai	áche
Yam	myok	myauk	nai	hákhuon	shi	chu	ngunü	álie
I	ngá	ngá	ngai	ngá	nyí	ngai	ngo	ngo
Thou	naung, mang	nen, men	náng, ní	nangmá	ná	nang	nóna	no
He	sú	thú	khí	até	pá	pá	bü	bu
She	ditto	ditto	...	...	pá	pá	no	...

It	ngátó	ngadó	í	nímá	annok	akhala	ngolu	ngosin
We	nangtó	nendó	nitheng	nómá	nákara	nakhala	nolu	nolüsin
Ye	sátó	sátó	khiní	sening	yau	tebepá	búlu	üllü búlu
They	ngái	ngái	ngómá	ngá	ka	ngaichi	ngoke	ngokke
Mine	mangi	meni	nāná	má	ná	mechi	uókke	nokke
Thine	sái	thái	khiná	ató	pá	páchi	búkke	búkke
His					ásan	akhali		ngolükke
Ours	ngátói	ngadói			nú	nakhalá		nolükke
Yours	nuangtói	mendói			pári	pdli	bulüke	búlükke
Theirs	sátói	thátdói	aimá	vánthó	katang	khatu	ako	átero
One	tach	tit, ta	nkhong	vánoyí	anna	fánnat	aniko	ngoye
Two	nhach	nhit	masúm	vánram	ásan	ásám	aomko	auma
Three	sung	thong	meli	beli	pazr	phále	apiko	ápie
Four	ká	lé	mangá	bangá	puangu	phungu	pilingoko	üngo
Five	ngá	ngá	krú	frók	tarok	thelok	akeko	ákünge
Six	kiŋok	khyauk	sinit	ingit	tanot	thanyet	kunitko	künnide
Seven	khwan nhach	khunnhit	matsat	isat	te	thesep	puuitko	pinge
Eight	rhach	shyit	taekhá	ikhu	taku	thaku	konangko	konánge
Nine	kó	kó	sí	ichi	tarr	thelu	üingko	üyinge
Ten	ebhe	s'he	khín	ruakngi	matsii	machi	irlingko	üying ányiko
Twenty	nhachchhe	nhits'he	turnsí	ruakram	liri	machi lithelu	üing aomko	üying aumko
Thirty	sungehhe	thóngzhe	mlisí	ruakbeli		mesung annat	üing apie	üying apiko
Forty	léchhe	lézhe		ruakbangá		mésung annat té thelu		
Fifty	ngáchhe	nŋázhe	mangási		thanam	mésung phun-gu		üingo üyingko
Hundred	tarí	tayá	latsá	cháthe	rokrii			üyingüyingko
Of	i (affix)	i	na (affix)	wanting		gu		
To	á	á	fe	nang	tang	nai	met	lope
From	ka	ga					telópu	lokke
By	phrang	phyen			wá	nú	odánkáng	appünge
With	nhang	nhen			yasii	siiga	umnus	logolo
Without								
In	nhaik	nhaik	kátái	hum nyu	lóng	atap	áráng	áráflo
On	pomhá	bomhá	lethá	ákhónang	talak	tathak	teó só	talülo
Now	yakhu	yakhu	yá	dókko	tang	thong	supáb	su
Then	thó akhá	thó akhá			tas au	kabáng		kojo

English.	Burman, Written.	Burman, Spoken.	Bronson's Singpho.	Bronson's Namsang Nágá.	Nowgong Nágá.	Tengsa Nágá.	Capt. Smith's Abor-Miri.	Sibságor Miri.
When?	bhesokhá	bhethokhá	yango	matu suanta	kódang	kápá	...	údilo
To-day	yané	yané	daini	tajá	tannu	thanglu	silo	silo
To-morrow	nakphan	netphán	mphóní	ninap	asóng	ásang	idmpo	yampo
Yesterday	yanaanné	yanaanné	maní	majá	yashi	óst	milo	melobo
Here	simhá	támhá	náde	anang	yóng	iga	sho	so
There	hómhá	hómhá	tode	dinang	aunchi	ótiga	...	úlo
Where?	bhemhá	bhemhá	gadógui	makóa	kóng	ótiga	...	okolon
Above	apo mhá	apo mhá	ning tsang	ákhónang	taiak	tathak	ungkolo	talito
Below	okmhá	aukmhá	katái	akhannang	tasung	tachung	taleng	rúnktibe
Between	adrámhá	akyámhá	...	...	kimá	ulam	rumking	áráso
Without	prángmhá	pyenmhá	...	vákáhang	tamá	má	radang	rongongolo
Within	atwang	atwen	...	...	talóng	atap	lulo	áráso
Far	wé	wé	tsán	háló	talang	lángiá	áráso	modo
Near	ní	ní	ní	therkó	tatsaka	annangiá	...	áninse
Little	chhitkhaló	seikkhaló	katsí	achá	ishika	tesu	auinda	ájoda
Much	myá	myá	lo	éjá	ayúka	tebe	...	ábako
How much?	bhelok	bhelauk	gadómá	chento	kayúka	katekat	eritko	údiiko
As	kesó	gethó	...	...	...	...	...	...
So	ló, só	ló, thó	...	...	...	...	depú, au	sempidang
Thus	thosó	thothó	ndaisat	árarang	ányakáng	atti	pua	úmpe
How?	bhesó	bhethó	fári	rétó	kótau	katikiang	káppida	kapú
Why?	bhepruló	bhepruló	raia	ilanga	kashia	kadó	okkiduna	kappú
Yes	hótkhe	hókhe	galai	má	au	ho	iú	iú
No	mahut	mahók	ng, phung	nak	nau, nonga	nongo	mámá	má
No, not	ma (pru) nhang	ma (pyu) nhen	...	...	(tók) n' (sui)	(tha) m' (thi)	ioka	yoka
And, also	lin kong	ligaung	ndai	...	...	...	aiu	...
Or	sómahut	thómahók	orawá	...	...	...	...	...
This	í, sin	í, thí	...	óra	yáo	igáaé	sí, issi	shidebulu
That	thó, hó	thó, hó	...	frapá	aunchika	óchika	itina	ullibullu
Which?	abhe	abhe	gadónuá	mapd	yákung	kachi	ing kóno	okolone
What?	abhe	abhe, bluá	phakaimá	chená	kachisúr	chaba	ingkua, ong kokko	okko

Who?	bheaŭ	bheaŭ	gadaimŭ	haŭŭ	sirau	sinŭ	sekŭ	seko
Anything	bhemhya	bhaŭmhya	…	…	…	…	anjoko	okko
Anybody	bheaŭnhya	bheaŭŭmhya	…	…	…	…	…	sekodi
Eat	chŭ	sŭ	shŭŭ	chŭo	chijŭng	tyu	dol anka	dolangka
Drink	sok	thauk	luu	jŭko	chajamti	tünun	taipü	tüpü
Sleep	ip	eik	yŭpu	jŭpo	annanü	annü	iddo	yüm
Wake	nŭ	nŭ	dŭunu	chingo	ula	phayŭ	emü aipü	dŭrdoku
Laugh	re	ye	manŭu	ngfo	mannü	mannü	nilodopü	yírda
Weep	ngŭ	ngŭ	klrŭpu	sapo	ŭchaprr	chappale	kappü	kapda
Be silent	titchhit nŭ	teiksheik nŭ	temdingau	…	manakazong	ayok sulang	ŭsopü	ŭsopa
Speak	pro, chhŭ	pyo, s'hŭ	sŭu	thŭo	shang	suang	lüpü	saluto
Come	lŭ, rok	lŭ, yauk	sŭu	kŭro	arung	ahalü	giküpü	kŭpü
Go	swŭ, kwya	thwŭ, kyuŭ	wŭn	kŭo	tsu, wang	chennang	gupügikangka	sŭ
Stand up	tha, mat	thŭ, mŭt	tsapu rotu	chapo	nŭtak	septak	dangküpü	dŭrup
Sit down	thaing	thaing	dŭngu	tŭngo	manŭkarü	mannang	dŭpü	dutoka
Move, walk	le, kwya	le, kyuŭ	thotu, dannu	chŭo, khuanu	asŭmataur	asambat	iokoda	gümaudak
Run	prŭ	pyŭ	gagŭtu	chuano	ssŭmawaung	ŭ dsambat	dukpü	dupdandak
Give	pŭkhya	pŭ khyŭ	yŭu	kŭo	kwŭng	khalang	bŭpü	sopŭ
Take	yŭ	yŭ	lŭu	kapo	niagirr	chiokko ŭnno	lŭpü	lŭto
Strike	raik, put	yaik, pŭk	dŭpu	vŭto	tatsungr tatapŭap	taphetokŭ	pŭpü	…
Kill	sat	thŭt	satu	rikvŭto	dsoko	dseko	…	düto
Bring	yükhe	yŭghe	lŭu	vanro	ŭnyaung	siyang	pŭpu	dingketo
Take away	yŭŭwŭ	yŭthŭwŭ	lŭu wŭu	kapkŭto	penruang	khalnang	bombipu	bomkuka
Lift up	mhrang, mhrok	mhyen, mhyauk	phŭnu	tuons	achŭngatŭng	chebachenang	bomkang	bomkang
Hear	krŭ	kyŭ	nŭngu	tŭto	ŭŭshu	aiyŭang	lŭssŭpü	jowon
Understand	lin, si	le, thi	chŭiu	jjŭto	matürrmŭ	ŭngŭng	tadkapü	tŭttoka
Tell	chhŭ, krŭ	s'hŭ kyŭ	sŭu	ngŭo	shiang	nyangnang	ken	kintoka
Good	kong	kaung	gajŭ	asan	tateŭng	suang	lüpü	lubida
Bad	chhŭ	s'hŭ	ngaiŭ	achl	matsŭng	chŭngkolo	aidu	aida
						machŭng	aimang	aima
Cold	khyam, e	khyŭn, e	katsį	akį	kŭŭsütŭ	ŭchikale	ansinge	ansinge
								sikkire

English.	Burman, Written.	Burman, Spoken.	Bronson's Singpho.	Bronson's Namsang Nágá.	Nowgong Nágá.	Tengsa Nágá.	Capt. Smith's Abor-Miri.	Sibsagor Miri.
Hot	pá	pá	káthet	akhúm	tatsok	lamme	gudórong	gunáme
Raw;	chim	seing	ketsing	úhing	nútók	túi	...	leda
Ripe	mhin, rang	mhe, yen	nin	óchúm	túman	túman	mindó	minda
Sweet	khyó	khyó	dúi	átú	túnang	túnang	tídó	tídák
Sour	khyin	khyin	khrí	ásí	túsan	senla	kune	kudák
Bitter	khá	khá	khá	akhá	paklá	paklá	kónam	kodák
Handsome	lha	lhá	jásói	asamá	kángatsóong	chongthang	kampodó	kángkáne
Ugly	arup chhó	ayókahó	sannáng	pangtsí	matsóng	machóng	...	aimang
Straight	phrong	phy aung	preng	úting	tumutum	matungkolo	pundu	guyokdák
Crooked	kok	kauk	mágo	akuang	tikrak	kóikolo	muwat, gadó	gudák
Black	nak	net	cháng	anyak	tanak	nyakla	yákár	yákádák
White	phrú	phyú	phróng	apó	tamasóong	nasang	asidó	kámpodák
Red	ní	ní	khyeng	achak	maram	malamla	yalung	liúdák
Green	chim	seing	ketsing	ahing	tacham	tacham	...	gedák
Long	rhín	shó	gálú	ál	talang	lángkolo	baddoló	aúrdák
Short	tó	tó	kutún	atóon	tatsú	únanglá	adedi	úndúdák
Tall	mrang	myen	tsode	achnong	talángka	lánglá	...	aúrdák
Short	nim	neing	kutún	amienpa	tatsú	únanglá	adedi	úndúdák
Small	nge	nge	katsí	úring	tilala	tesu	angidó	úmedák
Great	krí	kyí	gubá	adóng	talulu	tapó	bóte	úttadák
Round	lun	lóng	dindin	útúm	tarang	litiúkpu	...	úttumdák
Square	lóthong	lóílhaung	...	...	tangakúku	taugík	...	...
Flat	pyá	pyá	ram	tode	matam	madamka	neing sudó	omandák
Fat	wá, tup	wá, tók	phím	atat	tabók	tabók	udó	juiname
Thin	lhyá	slyá	lasí	achá	apoprr	apo	...	gídák
Weariness	mo, pangźan	mo, penźún	bahá	bóan	únyokó	ngúchaho	...	amírse molámak
Thirst	ré ngat	ye ngat	pháng gerá	khamlán	tukula seratúr	chebalá chuale	tuling	túling
Hunger	chhá ngat	súngát	koslu	ramrio	yatúr	chulale	kinong	konóng

SECTION VI.

ON THE INDO-CHINESE BORDERERS

AND THEIR CONNECTION WITH

THE HIMÁLAYANS AND TIBETANS.

To the Secretary of the Asiatic Society.

SIR,—In further prosecution of my purpose of recording in the pages of our Journal a complete set of comparative vocabularies on an uniform plan, I have now the honour to transmit to you two fresh series, one for Arrakan, and the other for the Tenasserim provinces. The first comprises six tongues, viz., the Burmese, the Khyeng, the Kámi, the Kúmi, the Mrú, and the Sák; the second five, viz., the Burmese, the Talien, the Túng-lhú, the Shán, and the Siamese.

It is needless, I presume, to apologise for thus recording provincial dialects of well-known languages such as the Burmese and Siamese, because such deviations of a known kind afford inestimable means of testing those which are unknown, and of thus approximating to a just appreciation of the interminable varieties of speech that characterise the enormously-extended family of the Mongolidæ.

I am indebted for these vocabularies to Captain Phayre, whose name is a warrant for their authenticity, and who has kindly added to their value by the subjoined explanatory note upon the Arrakan tribes. On those of the Tenasserim provinces the only elucidatory addition is the important one that the Túng-lhú are "Hillmen," that is, dislocated aborigines driven to the wilds, or, in other words, broken and dispersed tribes, like the Khyeng, and Kámi, and Kúmi, and Mrú, and Sák of Arrakan, whose vocables constitute the greatest part of the first half of the vocabularies herewith forwarded.

In the course of recording in our Journal these numerous vocabularies, I have purposely avoided any remarks on the affinities they suggest or demonstrate, intending to take up that subject when they should be completed; but the high interest * excited by my Himálayan series, in connection with the bold and skilful researches which are now demonstrating the unparalleled diffusion over the earth of that branch of the human family to which the Himálayans belong, has induced me on the present occasion to deviate partially from that rule, and to at once compare Captain Phayre's Arrakanese vocables with my own Himálayan † and Tibetan ones. Having been so fortunate as lately to procure an ample Sifánese series, comprising the tongues of the several peoples bordering on China and Tibet between Konkonúr and Yúnán, and having, moreover, made some progress in a careful analysis of a normal and of an abnormal sample of the Himálayan tongues, with a view to determining the amounts of the Turánian and Arian elements, I shall ere long find occasion to recur to the general affinities of the Indian Mongolidæ. In the meanwhile, the subjoined comparison of several Arrakanese tongues with those of Tibet and of the Eastern Himálaya will be read with surprise and pleasure by many who, accustomed to regard the Himálayans as Hindus, and the Indo-Chinese, like the Chinese, as distinct from the people of Asie Centrale, and from the Tibetans, will be astonished to find one type of language prevailing from the Káli to the Koladán, and from Ladakh to Malacca, so as to bring the Himálayans, Indo-Chinese, and Tibetans into the same family.

That such, however, even in the rigid ethnological sense, is the fact will hardly be denied by him who carefully examines the subjoined table, or the documents from which it is taken, because not only are the roots of the nouns and verbs similar

---

* Latham's History of Man and Ethnology of British Colonies.

† My own Himálayan series will be found in the Journal, No. 185, for December 1847. The Arrakanese series is annexed hereto.

to identity, but the servile particles are so likewise, and that as well in themselves as in the uses made of them, and in the mutations * to which they are liable. It should be added that the resemblances cited are drawn not from "ransacked diction-aries," but from vocabularies of less than 300 words for each tongue.

To those who, not content with this abstract, shall refer to the original documents, I may offer two remarks suggested by their study to myself. 1st. The extraordinary extent to which the presently contemplated affinities hold good has been made out by the helps afforded by the series of cognate tongues, whereby the synonyma defective in one tongue are obtained from another, whilst the varying degrees and shades of devia-tion are a clue to the root or basis.† 2d. The other remark suggested by the comparison of the vocabularies is, that it is the nouns and verbs, and *not* the pronouns and numerals, which constitute the enduring part of these languages; and that con-sequently, whatever may be the case in regard to the Arian group of tongues, we must not always expect to find the best evidence of family connection in regard to the Turanian languages among the pronouns and numerals. Indeed the confused character of these parts of speech seems to be a conspicuous feature of the Mongolian tongues.

Comparison of Tibetan and Himálayan tongues on one hand, and of the Indo-Chinese on the other.

Blood.—Thak in Bhotia, Thyak in Lhópa, Vi in Lepcha.‡
        Thwé in Burmese, Thé in Sák, Ka-thí in Khyeng, A-ti in Kámi, Wi in Mrú.
Boat.—Thú in Sérpa.
        Thé in Burmese.

---

* In order to appreciate this remark and to trace the elements of the vocables, see analytic observations of the following paper on Caucasian and Mongolian Words, appended to the list of those words.

† Take the radical word for dog, as a sample. We have khyi, khíá, khí, ki, khwé, kwé, kwi, kú, kí-chá, kú-chú, khó, kyó, cho-i. For the appended particles and their mutations I must refer to the original documents, and to the future con-firmations to be supplied by my Sifánesc series of words.

‡ The first line gives the Northern series, the second the Southern.

Cat.—Si-mi in Bhotia, Si-mi in Sokpa.
     Min in Khyeng, Min in Kámi.

Crow.—O'-la in Lhópa, A'-wá in Limbu.
     O'-á in Kúmi, Wá á in Kámi and in Mrú.

Day.—Nyi-ma in Bhotia, Nhí in Newári, Nyim in Lhópa.
     Né in Burmese, Ni in Mrú.

Dog.—Khyi in Bhotia, Khi in Lhópa, Kú-chú in Kiránti,
     Ki-cha in Newári, Khia in Dhimali.
     Khwé in Burmese, Ta-kwi in Mrú, Kú in Sák.

Ear.—Ná in Bhotia, Na-vo in Lhópa.
     Ná in Burmese, Ka-ná in Sák.

Eye.—Mig in Bhotia, A-mik in Lepcha, Mó in Múrmi and
     Gúrúng.
     Myé-tsi in Burmese, A-mi in Kámi and Sák, Min in
     Mrú.

Father.—Phá in Bhotia, Amba in Limbú.
     Phá é in Burmese, Ampa in Kúmi.

Fire.—Mé or Mi in Bhotia, and' in all Himálayan tongues.
     Mí, Má, Má i, in Burmese, Kámi, and Mrú.

Fish.—Nyá in Bhotia, Ngyá in Lhópa, Ngó in Lepcha, Nyau in
     Súnwár.
     Ngá in Burmese, Ngú in Khyeng, Nghó in Kámi.

Foot.—Káng in Bhotia, Káng in Lhópa, Khwe-li in Súnwár.
     Khyé in Burmese, Ká-kó in Khyeng, Khou in Kúmi.

Goat.—Rá in Bhotia.
     Ta-rá in Mrú.

Hair.—A-chóm in Lepcha, Chúm in Magar.
     A-shám in Kámi, Shám in Mrú and Kúmi.

Head.—Gó in Bhotia.
     Ghóng in Burmese.

Hog.—Phak in Bhotia and Lhópa and Kiránti, Wak in Magar.
     Ta-pak in Mrú and Vak in Sák.

Horn.—Ar-kyok in Sérpa, A-róng in Lepcha.
     A kyi in Khyeng, A-rúng in Sák.

Horse.—Tá in Bhotia and Lhópa, Sa la in Newári.
     Tá-phú (phú, male suffix) in Kámi, Sapú in Sák (púidem).

House.—Khyim in Bhotia and Lepcha.   Yúm in Magar.
     Kyim in Sák, Kim in Mrú, Um in Kúmi.

Man.—Mi in Bhotia and most Himálayan tongues, Maro in
    Lepcha, Múrú in Súnwár.
        Ka-mi in Kámi, Mrú in Mrú dialect.
        (Ka-mi in Newári means craftsman.)
Moon.—Lá-va in Bhotia, Lhópa, Lepcha, &c., &c.
        Lá in Burmese and Khyeng, Pú-lá in Mrú.
Mountain.—Gún in Newári.
        Ta-kún in Kámi.
Name.—Ming in Bhotia and Lhópa and Limbú and Múrmi,
    Náng in Newári.
        A-mí in Burmese, A-mín in Kámi, Na-mí in Khyeng.
Night.—Sa-náp in Lepcha.
        Nyá in Burmese.
Oil.—Si-di in Magar.
        Shi in Burmese and Kámi and Mrú, Si-dak in Sák.
Road.—Lam in Bhotia, and all the Himálayan tongues.
        Lam in Burmese, Khyeng, Kámi, and Sák.
Salt.—Tshá in Bhotia and Lhópa, Chhá in Himálayan tongues
    (most) Súng in Bódó.*
        Shá in Burmese, Tsi in Khyeng, Súng in Sák.
Skin.—Pá-kó in Lhópa, Dhi in Gúrúng, Di in Múrmi.
        Pé in Kúmi, Pi in Mrú.
Sky.—Mú in Múrmi, Mún in Gúrúng.
        Mú in Mrú, Mó in Burmese.
Snake.—Búl in Magar, Bú-sa in Súnwár.
        Phúl in Khyeng, Pú-vi in Kúmi.
Stone.—Lóng in Lepcha, Lúng in Limbú, Lhúng in Magar.
        Lún in Khyeng, Ka-lún in Kámi, Ta-lún in Sák.

In the verbs, again, we have

Eat.—Sá in Lhópa, Zó, Só, in Bhotia, Ché in Limbú, Chó in
    Kiránti.
        Sá in Burmese, Tsá in Kámi, Tsá in Kúmi.
Drink.—Thúng in Bhotia, Thóng in Lhópa, Thúng in Limbú
    and Múrmi, &c.
        Thouk in Burmese.

---

* My Bódó and Dhimál vocabularies will be found in the Journal, as well as the
Himálayan series. I take this occasion to intimate my now conviction that the
Bódó, Dhimál, and Kócch tribes belong to the Tibetan and Himálayan stock rather
than to the Tamilian; that is, with reference to India, to the more recent race of
Tartar immigrants, not to the more ancient and more altered.

Sleep.—I'p in Súnwár, I'p in Limbú, Im in Kiránti.
　　I'p in Khyeng, I' in Kámi, I' in Kúmi.
Laugh.—Yé in Limbú, Nyé in Múrmi, Nhyú in Newári.
　　Yé in Burmese, A-nwi in Khyeng, Am-nhwi in Kúmi.
Weep.—Nú, ngó, in Bhotia, ngú in Lhópa and Sérpa, Khwó in
　　Newári.
　　Ngó in Burmese, and Khá in Kámi.
Say, tell.—Shód in Bhotia.
　　Shó in Burmese.
Come.—Wá in Newári.
　　Vá in Kámi.
Go.—Lau in Súnwár.
　　Lá in Kámi and in Kúmi.
Sit down.—Det in Sérpa, Ngú-ná in Magar.
　　Tat in Kúmi, Ngún-gé in Khyeng.
Move, Walk.—Dyú in Lhópa.
　　Kyú in Burmese.
Run.—Chóng in Sérpa, Lóyá in Kiránti.
　　Chó-né in Khyeng, Lei in Kúmi.
Give.—Bin in Bhotia and Lhópa, Pí in Limbú, Pai in Kiránti,
　　Pen in Gúrúng.
　　Pé in Burmese, Pé gé in Khyeng, Pei in Kúmi.
　　(Ná pú in Kami == Náng in Bhotia, asks for self.)
Take.—Yá in Bhotia, Lyo in Lepcha, Lé in Limbú.
　　Yú in Burmese, Lá in Kámi, Ló in Kúmi.
Kill.—Thód in Gúrúng, That in Bódó.
　　That in Burmese.
Hear, attend.—Nyen in Bhotia and Lhópa and Lepcha, Nyo in
　　Newári.
　　Né in Khyeng, Ka-ná-i in Kámi.

Remark, the materials for the above striking comparative
view are derived from my own original vocabularies for the
Northern tongues, as published in the Journal, No. 185, for
December 1847, and from Captain Phayre's for the Southern
tongues, hereto appended.

It is seldom that vocabularies so trustworthy can be had,
and had in series, for comparison; and yet it is abundantly

demonstrable that everything in regard to the discovery of the larger ethnic affinities of dispersed races depends upon such a presentation of these materials, the distinction of roots and of servile particles, as well as the range of synonymous variation, in each of these classes of words, being thus only testable, and these points being all important as diagnostics, even more so than grammatical peculiarities which, at least in our sense, are apt to be excessively vague, or else palpably borrowed, among the Mongolidæ. Syntactic poverty and crudity and etymological refinement and abundance seem to be the characteristics of this vast group of tongues, and hence the importance of its vocables and the necessity of obtaining them in a state accurate enough for analysis, and copious enough to embrace the average range of synonyms.

A common stock of primitive roots and of serviles, similarly employed, indicates unmistakably a common lineage and origin among the several races to which such stock belongs; preference for this or that synonym among the radicals, as well as various degrees and modes in the employment of serviles, whether prefixed, infixed, or postfixed, indicates as unmistakably the several branches from the same family stem with the relative ages and distances of their segregation. By the above comparison of vocabularies I purpose to illustrate the common lineage of tribes now and for ages most widely dispersed, and of which the intimate relationship is ordinarily overlooked; by a subsequent and more detailed examination somewhat differently conducted, I will endeavour to illustrate the true character of the minor distinctions of race, showing that these distinctions are by no means inconsistent with the common lineage and family relationship now exhibited.

COMPARATIVE VOCABULARY OF INDO-CHINESE BORDERERS IN ARAKAN.

English.	Burmese or Myamma.	Khyeng or Shou.	Kami.	Kúmi.	Mrú or Toung Mrú or Myú.	Sák.
Air	ló	kli	ga-li	a-lí	ra-li	mwi-ya-hé
Ant	payuetseik	lhing-zi-mi	ba-lin	pa-lin	loung-tsa-ring-já	phín-si-gyá
Arrow	myá	thwá	li	li-tá-i	sá, or qwá-i	to-lí-ma-lá
Bird	nghet	hau	ka-vá or ta-vá	ta-wú	ta-wá	wá-sí
Blood	thwó	ka-thi	a-thí	a-thí	wi	thé
Boat	thé	loung	m'loung	p'loung	loung	hau
Bone	ayo	ka-yok	a-hú	a-hú	a-hot	a-mrá
Buffalo	kyuai	nau	ma-ná	pán-no	ná	kro
Cat	kyoung	min	mim-bo-i	min-cho	ta-myin	heing
Cow	nuá	sharh	kha-bo-i	si-rá	tsi-yá	tha-mók
Crow	kyi	áng-au	wa-á	ó-á	wa-á	wúk-ká
Day	nó	ko-nup	ma-ni	ka-ni twun	ni	yat-ta
Dog	khwó	ú-i	ti-i	ú-i	ta-kwi	kú
Ear	ná	ka-nhau	a-ga-ná	ka-no	pa-rán	a-ka-ná
Earth	myó	det	ka-lái-hong	ka-loung	kroung	ká
Egg	u	to-i	du	dú-i	dú-i	wa-tí
Elephant	s'hen	mwi	ka-sái	ka-sá-i	nga-s'háit	u-kú
Eye	myetsi	mí-ú-i	a-mi	mó	min	a-mí
Father	phá-ó	pau	pá-ei	am-po	pá	a-bá
Fire	mi	mi	má-i	mhá-i	má-i	bá-in
Fish	ngá	ngau	mo-i	ngho	dám	pan-ná
Flower	khyó	pa-pá	a-pá	ka-shyoung	pá-ou	a-pán
Foot	páu	ka-ko	a-kho	khou	khouk	a-tar
Goat	s'heik	ma	tso-bó	mi-ó	ta-rau-a	ki-bí
Hair	s'haben	lu-sáin	a-s'hám	s'hám	s'hám	kí-mí
Hand	let	káth	a-ká	ka	rát	ta-kú
Head	ghoung	lá	a-lá	a-lá	lá	a-khú
Hog	wet	weuk	o	a-ou	ta-pák	vák

Horn	glyo	a-kyi	at-ta-ki	ta-ki	a-náng	a-ráng
Horse	myin	shó	ta-phú	koung-ngú	ko-ra-ngá	sapú
House	*eing*	im	im	úm	kin	kyin
Iron	*yuet*	thi	s'hein	ta-mhú	loung-há	*thein*
Leaf	len	shó	la-háng	ngám	a-rám	pwin-ták
Light	lú	...	a-ván-da-gá	...	wa-tá-i	...
Man	myouk	klóng	ka-mi	ku-mi	mrá	lú
Monkey	lá	young	ka-lái	ka-lu	ta-yút	ka-wuk
Moon	a-mi	khlau	lú	hlo	pú-lá	*that-tá*
Mother	toung	ní	na-ú-i	am-nú	a-ú	a-ná
Mountain	nhup	toung	ta-kún	mo-i	s'hung, or túng	ta-ko
Mouth	khyin	hak-kau	a-ma-ká	li-boung	naur	dáng-sí
Musquito	a-mi	young-yán	kán-sa-ká	chán-ráng	ta-tsáng	pí-chí
Name	nyá	na-mi	a-min	a-min	E-mi	tú
Night	s'hi	a-yán	ma-khún	wa-dúm	wár	ha-ná-hó
Oil	nghet pyo	to	s'hi	sa-rou	s'hi	sí-dák
Plantain	myit	nhám-pau	ka-tí	kú-ti	deng-kú-i	tsa-ú
River	lám	ha-loung	ka-vá	ka-wá	au	pi-si
Road	s'há	lám	láng	lám	ta-má	láng
Salt	tha-yó	tsi	ma-lo-i	pi-lo-i	wi-s'há	sáng
Skin	mo	wún	a-phú	pó	pí	mi-lak
Sky	myué	han-mhi	khau, or khú	ka-ni	mú	koung-gounglak
Snake	kyai	phol	ma-khú-i	pú-wi	ta-ro-a	ka-pú
Star	kyouk	dá-shé	a-s'hi	ka-si	ki-rek	*tha-geing-thi*
Stone	nó	lún	ka-lún	lún-s'houng	ta-whá	ta-lón
Sun	kyá	ko-nhi	ka-ni	ka-ni	ta-nin	sa-mí
Tiger	*thwá*	kyi	ta-ká-i	ta-ká-i	ta-pri	*ka-thá*
Tooth	apen	ka-hau	a-fhá	ho	yún	*a-tha-wá*
Tree	yué	thin	a-kún	din-koung	tsing-dúng	páng-ráng
Village	yé	nám	váng ...	a-ráng	kwá	thing
Water	myouk	tá-í	tú-í	tú-í	tú-í	o
Yam	ngá	ba-há	khá	ho	mau	káng-kú
I	men or nen	kyi	ká-i	ká-i	...	...
Thou	*thú*	náng	nán	nang	...	...
He		ni	ha-ná-i	hú	...	...

English.	Burmese or Myamma.	Khyeng or Shou.	Kami.	Kúmi.	Mrú or Toung Mrú or Myú.	Silk.
She	...	...	...	...	...	...
It	ngá-do	kin-ní	ka-chi	ká-í-no	...	...
We	mendo	náng-ní	nán-chi	náng-chi-no	...	...
Ye	thúdo	ni-di, or ni-li	hún-na, or ha-ni-	...	...	...
Mine	ngái	ki-ko	ká-í-un [chi	...	...	...
Thine	meni	náng-ko	nán-un	...	...	...
His	thái	ni-ko	ha-ná-í-un	...	...	...
Ours	ngádoi	ki-ni-ko	ká-chi-un	...	...	...
Yours	mendoi	náng-ni-ko	nán-chi-un	...	...	...
Theirs	thá doi	ní-dí-ko	ha-ni-chi-un	...	...	...
One	tít	nhít	há	há	loung	sá-war
Two	nhit	pan-nhí	ui	nhá	pró	nein
Three	thon	thúm	ka-tín	túm	shín	thín
Four	ló	lhí	ma-lí	pa-lá	ta-lí	prí
Five	ngá	nghau	páng-ngá	pán	ta-ngá	ngá
Six	khyouk	sauk	ta-ú	ta-rá	ta-rú	khyouk
Seven	khun-nhit	s'hó	sa-rí	sa-rí	ra-nhít	tha-ni
Eight	shyit	sát	ka-yá	ta-yá	rí-yít	a-tseit
Nine	ko	ko	ta-ko	ta-kau	ta-kú	ta-fú
Ten	s'hai	há	ha-suh	hau	há	si-sú
Twenty	nhit s'hai	kúr	ká-suh	a-pum-ró	ní-ra-mí	hún
Thirty	thon s'hai	tún gíp	ká-í-thún	m'phá-í-ró	tsím-gaum	thon-si
Forty	lóz hai	lhí-gíp	ká-í-ma-ll	wó-pa-lá-ri	...	prí-sí
Fifty	ngúz hai	nghau-gíp	ká-í-páng-ngá	wí-pá-rí	...	ngá-sí
A hundred	tayá	klá-át	ta-rá	chúm-wá-ri	...	ta-yá
Of	i	...	ún	...	...	...
To	á	á	á	...	...	...
From	gú	lá	má-í	...	...	...
By	phyen	...	mí	...	...	...
With	nhen	yung	há-í	...	...	...

English				
Without	uheik	dúka	yá	wá-i-mé
In				
On	bomhá	hté-nang	a-koung-bo	
Now	yakhu	tú-a	a-vá-i	
Then	tho akhá	ní-kho-á	ho-ná-i-gán	má-na-ká
When	bhetho khá	í-kho-á	há-ni-kán	wá-i-ni
To-day	yané	tun-ap	wei-ní	qui-dám
To-morrow	netphan	nhát-ta	cha-khon	
Yesterday	yamunné	yam-tú	ya-dúm	
Here	thimhá	ní-ám	lí ó, or yá	hí-báng
There	homhá	tsá-ó	há-bhé	
Where	bhemha	i-ní-ám	mé-ní-bó	mé-mo
Above	aponahá	ada-ma-ka	a-koung-bó	i-klín
Below	ouk mhá	dó-kan	ting-bó	i-klot
Between	akyá mhá	A-lhá-ka-ku	thinbó or u-thin-ó	si-lá
Without, outside	pyen mhá	kláng-á-me	a-khám-bó	a-ngám
Within	atwen	dú-gá-mé	a-thám-bó	thím
Far	wó	tsá-a-a-lhau a-me	khán-lá	pi-lá-pá-i
Near	ní	a-shyo-zo-yan	nei	ki-sá
Little	seikkhalé	a-lák-chá-i	pé, or ong-jó	a-htan
Much	myá	a-pá-lák	ha-yé-to	no-i
How much?	bhéßouk	hyau-úm	hí-ná-í	
As	gétho		ka	
So	lo, tho			
Thus	the-né	ß-bau	ná-ha-bé	
How	bhé tho	í-na-to-ám	ta-í-sá-né	
Why	bhé pyulo	a-hi	ta-ko-ká	
Yes	hokhó	hí-a	na-n-ká	
No	mahok	né-ó	né or nau	nán
(Do) not	ma (pya) nhen			na-o
And, also	ligoung			
Or	thomahok	ní	hi	
This	í, thí	oní	ma-há	
That	tho, hó	í-ní-a-ka	na-ná-i	
Which?	abhé			

English.	Burmese or Myamma.	Khyeng or Shou.	Kami.	Kúmi.	Mrú or Toung Mrú or Myú.	Sák.
What?	bhá	fní-hám	a-pá-í-mé			
Who?	bhéshá	ú-li-am	ta-ú-í			
Anything	bhámhya		a-pá-í-mé			
Anybody	bhéthámhya		tsá			
Eat	sá	ó	nei	tsá		
Drink	thouk	ú-ó	i	nei		
Sleep	eik	ip	thá	i		
Wake	no	kakák	ma-nwí	an-thá		
Laugh	yé	a-nwí	khá	ám-nhwi		
Weep	ngo	a-káp	on-vo	a-wú		
Be silent	teiksheikné	mhé	ta-pé			
Speak	pyo, s'ho	hé-we	va	tho-i		
Come	lá, youk	lo	la	you		
Go	thwá	tsit	ka-do	lá		
Stand up	thá, mát	tún-e	ka-ná	áng-thou		
Sit down	tháing	ngúnge		tat		
Move, walk	lé, kyuá		a-whí			
Run	pyé	cho-né	na-pú	lei		
Give	pé	pe-ge	lá	pei		
Take	yú	si	ma-lé	lo		
Strike	yáik, pok	mo-lé	dú-rhum-ma-lé	pu khou-orathum		
Kill	dát	tú-e	ma-há-í	pu-khou		
Bring	yá ghé		lá-há-í	lo		
Take away	yuthwá	youk-ké	ta-khún	lo-dé		
Lift up, raise	mhyouk	ka-yauk	thá-í	ka-tán		
Hear	kyá	né	ka-ná-í	thá-í		
Understand	lé, thi					
Tell, relate	s'ho kyá	be	hú-í	thó		
Good	koung	po-ya	s'hau	hau-í		
Bad	s'ho	ka-young	dé, or, di	hau-í-o		
Cold	é			si-wá-í		

English				
	: :			
	: :			
Hot	pá	kho-leik	bí	bi
Raw	seing	tein	ká-s'hí	káng-hei
Ripe	mhé	mhín	mín	mhún
Sweet	khyo	tá-í	tá	tá-í
Sour	khyin	to	tho	a-lto
Bitter	khá	khau	khá	a-kho
Handsome	lhá	pau-i	a-non	ho-i
Ugly	ayups'ho	a-si-í	a khé-sung	ho-i-o
Straight	phyoung	khán	to	tau
Crooked	kouk	ko-lák	ta-ko	a-kwé
Black	net	kán	ma-nún	ka-nún
White	phyú	búk	a-lún	kan-lúm
Red	ní	sen	é	kan-lein
Green	seing	nau	ma-ein-sin	kan-hein
Long	shé	sou	sá	a souk
Short	to	twé	dó-i	do
Tall } Man	myin	lhán	ka-sá	::
Short } Man	neing	..	dó-i	
Small	ngé	ná-ó	spí	a-thún
Great	kyí	len	leng	lén
Round	lun	pá-lá	pá-lún	ta-ki
Square	lédhoung	kyí-lhí	a-tí-kimli	kam-po
Flat	pyá	pé	phá-dá	len
Fat	wá, tok	tho-í	lén	thún
Thin	shyá	pán	ta-pá	a-kom
Weariness	mo, pen-bán	ka-no	má-sá	
Thirst	yé ngát	tá í-lan-a-dú-í	tá-í ma-kháng	ti-an-hei
Hunger	sá ngát	bu-lan-a-dú-í	búk ma-khang	bé-on lúm

NOTE TO ACCOMPANY VOCABULARIES OF LANGUAGES SPOKEN BY TRIBES IN ARAKAN.

1.—BURMESE.

This is the language of the Arakanese people, who for the most part live in the lowlands and on the sea-coast of the country called Arakan. Provincial words occur in this language, differing from those of Burmah proper, and the pronunciation in Arakan varies considerably from that current in the valley of the " Irrawaddy ; " yet the written languages of both countries are for the most part alike. Thus the word for a day written is ရက် pronounced Rák by the Arakanese, but by the Burmese is softened to Yet: the word for water is called by the Arakanese Rí, by the Burmese Yé. It is written with the same letters by both people. The Arakanese and Burmese are of the same race, and have the common national name of *Myam-má*, which is however a comparatively modern appellation for the several tribes, into which the race was originally divided. The term Mug is applied by the people of India to the Arakanese. It is exclusively a foreign epithet, unknown to the Arakanese themselves. It probably takes its origin from the tradition of a tribe of Bráhmans, termed *Mágas*, said to have emigrated Eastward from Bengal.

2.—KHYENG.

This name is given by the Burmese and Arakanese to a numerous race of people who live in the high range of mountains called *Yo-má* (that is " great ridge," or " back-bone "), which separates Arakan from the valley of the Irrawaddy. These people call themselves *Shyou* or *Shyú*. The word Khyeng (pronounced Khyáng or Kyáng by the Arakanese) is probably a corruption of *Kláng*,[*] their word for man; and

* Perhaps so ; but Kyáng or Khiáng is a well-known ethnic designation to the Northward, where, by the way, with Chinese and Tibetans, many of the ethnic designations of the Indo-Chinese religion are familiar terms of their own, as Mon, Lho, Lao, Sák, Kyáng, Myau. Nearer at hand we have, as terms allied to Khyeng, Rakheng (whence our Arakan for "the Mugs"); Khyi for the "Cossiahs," Kho or Kyo and Ká for Kambojian tribes, and Ká Khyen for "the

their own present distinctive name for their tribe is no doubt recently adopted. An Arakanese in writing down for me words from the mouth of a man of this race, wrote Khyáng for what appeared to me to have the sound of *Kláng*. The Khyeng country extends along the Yo-má range (which runs nearly N.N.W. and S.S.E.) from about the nineteenth to the twenty-first degree of north latitude. The people inhabit both the Burmese and British side of the range. The ascertained number of this race under British rule in Arakan is 13,708 souls. An equal number probably reside within the Burmese territory. There are also a large number of Khyeng tribes, which, though living within the nominal British frontier, yet, from the rugged inaccessible nature of their country, are really independent, and which have never yet submitted to any foreign Government, whether Arakanese, Burmese, or British. Their language is unwritten. There appears to be some difference of dialect between the Northern and Southern tribes of Khyeng. The words here given were taken from a man belonging to the Northern tribes. The Khyengs believe themselves to be of the same lineage as the Burmese and Arakanese, the stragglers from armies or moving hordes left in the mountains.*

3.—KAMI' OR KU'MI'.

This race of people, of which there are two divisions called by themselves Kamí vel Kimi and Kúmí, and by Arakanese respectively Awa Kúmí and Aphya Kúmí, inhabits the hills bordering the river which is named by the Arakanese *Kulá-dán* (that is, limit or border of the *Kula* or Western foreigner),

---

Karens," whilst the Kambojian Kyo or Gyo reappears in the Kho of the Koladyne river, and in the "Moitay" of Manipúr we have the combined appellations of the Siamese Tai and the Kochin Chinese "Moy." In other words, the Manipurian tribe, called Cossiahs by the Bengális, belong to the Moi section of the great tribe called Tai by themselves and Shán or Syán by the Burmese, the sectional name being also foreign, and equivalent to the native. Khyi or Khyáng of Chinese and Khyeng of Burmese.

* This native tradition and opinion accord with what follows relative to the Khyau and Mrúng in corroborating the doctrine which assigns the whole of the border mountaineers towards Ava, or inhabitants of the Yo-má range from Assam to Arakan, to the Rakheng division of the Myam-ma.

and by the Kamís *Ye-man,* by the Kúmís *Yan pán.* It is the chief river of Arakan. It is probable that the Kamís and Kúmís have not been settled in their present seat for more than five or six generations. They gradually expelled therefrom a tribe called Mrú or Myú. The Kamí clans are now themselves being disturbed in their possessions by more powerful tribes, and are being gradually driven Westward and Southward. They state that they once dwelt on the hills now possessed by the Khyengs, and portions of the tribe have been driven out by the latter within the memory of man. The language of the Kamí portion of this interesting race has lately been reduced to writing by the Rev. Mr. Stilson of the American Baptist Mission. The Kamí words entered in this vocabulary have been chiefly furnished by an intelligent Kamí young man educated by that gentleman, and are more to be depended upon than the other portions. For it is exceedingly difficult to acquire from savages, through the medium of a language foreign to them, any words but those which they use to designate some object or quality. The number of Kamís within the British territory amounts to 4129 souls. They are divided into several clans, each having a distinctive name. The dialects of these clans differ more or less from each other. Many clans are independent.

4.—Mru' or Toung Mru'.

This is a hill tribe now much reduced from its ancient state. They once dwelt on the river Kuládán and its feeders, but have been gradually driven out by the Kamí tribe. They have therefore emigrated to the West, and occupy hills on the border between Arakan and Chittagong. The Rádzaweng, or history of the Arakanese kings, refers to this tribe as already in the country when the Myam-ma race entered it. It states also that one of this tribe was chosen king of Arakan about the fourteenth century of the Christian era. The traditions recorded in the same work also imply that the Mrú and Myamma races are of the same lineage, though this connection is denied by the Arakanese of the present day, who regard the

Mrú tribe as " wild men " living in a degraded state, and consider that it would be disgraceful to associate with them. The
number of the Mrú tribe in Arakan amounts to about 2800
souls. Their language is unwritten. They call themselves
Mrú. Toung Mrú * is a name given to some of their clans by
the Arakanese. *Mrú* is also used by the Arakanese as a
generic term for all the hill tribes of their country. The word
Khyeng is occasionally used in the same sense.

5.—SA'K.

This is a very small tribe mentioned by Buchanan in his
paper On the Religion and Literature of the Burmese, "Asiatic
Researches," vol. vi. p. 229. He calls them " Thœk " (that
being the Burmese pronunciation of the word), and states that
they are " the people inhabiting the eastern " branch of the
Nauf river, and are called by the Bengális *Chatn* and
" Chatnmas." *Chatn* is no doubt meant for *Sák*, which is the
name these people now give themselves. Their language is
unwritten.

There are other tribes in Arakan who have languages or
dialects peculiar to themselves. They consist of but a few
families, and some no doubt are the descendants of captives
brought into the country several generations back by the
Arakanese in their warlike expeditions against the adjoining
countries. Of these, the language of the tribe called *Dáing-
nák* appears to be a rude corrupt dialect of Bengálí. The
tribe called *Mrúng* state that their ancestors were brought as
captives from the Tripúra hills. There is also a curious tribe
called *Khyau* † in the *Kuládán* country, consisting of not

---

* Toung means wild, uncultured, as " hill-men " with us, and Pahari or Par-
batia with Hindus. Mrú alias Myú = Myau of Chinese, which again = Kyáng.

† Kyo aforesaid ? The tradition would ally them with the Kúki and Khyí,
whence Kyo, Khyen, Khyi, and Kúki may be conjectured to be radically one and
the same term, and to be an opprobrious epithet bestowed by the now dominant
races of Indo-China upon the prior races whom they have driven to the wilds, for
Khyi, Kyi, Kí, Kú has the wide-spread sense of *dog*. Not one of these tribes is
known abroad by its own name. Kami may be readily resolved into "men of the
Ka tribe," the Ka being a proper name or merely an emphatic particle. Ka,
mutable to Kí and Kú, is a prefix as widely prevalent in the Himálaya and Tibet

more than from fifty to sixty families. I have not yet been able to obtain satisfactory vocabularies of the languages of these last-named three tribes, but they will be procured on the first opportunity. I regret that there are so few words of the *Mrú* and *Sák* languages given, but as some time might probably elapse before more could be procured, I considered it best to forward them in their present state.

MEMO.

Scheme of vowels, &c., &c., a to be sounded as a in America.

á	.	.	.	.	.	a in father.
i	.	.	.	.	.	i in in.
í	.	.	.	.	.	i in police.
u	.	.	.	.	.	u in push.
ú	.	.	.	.	.	oo in foot.
e	.	.	.	.	.	e in yet.
é	.	.	.	.	.	e in there.
ai	.	.	.	.	.	ai in air.
ei	.	.	.	.	.	i in mind.
ou	.	.	.	.	.	ou in ounce.
au	.	.	.	.	.	au in audience.
o	.	.	.	.	.	o in note.
th	.	.	.	.	.	th in thin.
th	.	.	.	.	.	the aspirate of t.

I have endeavoured to express the sounds of the *Khyeng* and *Kamí* languages as near as I can, but there are a few which I could not exactly convey through any combination of European letters.

N.B.—In the next or Tenasserim series of words the system of spelling followed is the common English. I have not deemed it prudent to alter it. These words were taken down by Dr. Morton, not Captain Phayre, as above inadvertently stated. Valuable as they are, they lack the extreme accuracy of Captain Phayre's series, and hence I have not extended my comparisons over them.

as the word mí for man. The Kamís themselves understand the word in the latter sense—a very significant circumstance quoad affinities. Ka prefix is interchangeable with Ta (Ka-va or Ta-va, a bird in Kamí, and so in most of these tongues), and Ta varies its vowel like Ka ; and thus, in Gyarúng, Tir-mi, a man, answers to Kimi, a man. Ex his disce alia.

COMPARATIVE VOCABULARY OF INDO-CHINESE BORDERERS IN TENASSERIM.

English.	Burmese or Myamma.	Talien or Môn.	Toung-lhoo.	Shán.	Siamese.
Air	lé	kya	ta-lee	lónna	lon
Ant	parwet	khamol	h-tung	mot	mot
Arrow	hmya	lau	pla	pén	tsán
Bird	hnget	khaten	á-wa	lnót	lnót
Blood	thwáy	htsein	thway	leet	leét
Boat	hlé	hio	phray	hó	ró
Bone	ayo	htsot	htsot	sot	katot
Buffalo	kúwai	paren	pay-nay	kwihn	khwa
Cat	kyoung	pakway	nyen	myoung	may
Cow	nwan	karau	phou	wó	ngwau
Crow	kyée-gan	khatat	zank-ay	ka	ka
Day	na	ta-ngway	mo-yay	kawon	wan
Dog	khwá	kalé	htwe	ma	ma
Ear	nau	khato	nau	loo	hoo
Earth	myá-ghee	te	ham-tan	sen	tein
Egg	ó-o	khmatsan	de	khílt	khu
Elephant	tsheng	tsing	hsan	tsan	htsann
Eye	myet-sé	mot	may	mat-ta	ta
Father	a-hpa	má	phá	pau	hpau
Fire	mée	ka-mol	may	ipiln	thwa
Fish	ngá	ka	lita	pa	parz
Flower	pán	koung	ken	mau	towkrna
Foot	khyá-hloók	htsihn	khan	ten	ténn
Goat	hlsiet	khapa	bay	pá	hpá
Hair	htsa ben	swet	ta-lu	khon hó	hpóln
Hand	let	tway	su	mee	mó
Head	o-lhkoung	katau	katu	ho	kamon
Hog	wet	kalet	htau	moo	moo

English.	Burmese or Myamma.	Talien or Môn.	Toung-thoo.	Shán.	Siamese.
Horn	gyo	kareng	nung	khoung	khóung
Horse	myón	chway	thay	ma	ma
House	*seng	hnyee	sam	hien	rau
Iron	thán	kasway	say-thee	leit	leet
Leaf	aynet	kana-htsoo	lay	moung-mán	pihn-ma
Light	alóng	rá	liita lay	alen	psa-won
Man	loo-youk-ya	karoo	lan	konpoo-trihn	hpoohtso
Monkey	myouk	ka-nwee	khyag	lein	lenn
Moon	la	kha too	lu	len	hpya htoet
Mother	ama	ya	men	amyá	má
Mountain	toung	kha-lon-khyan	koung	pa-touk	khan-ta
Mouth	pazat	khamoupan	proung	htsot	pat
Moschito	khyen	khamcet	takhra	you	you
Name	amee	yámoo	meen	tsoo	htso
Night	ngyu-ngyeen	khatan	mó-ha	ka khán	than-khen
Oil	hteée	kalihn	ná-man	na-man	na-mau
Plantain	hnet-pyau	hpyat	gná	kwá	kalway
River	myeet	pee	nhrong	nán-howk	may-na
Road	kín	khapann	klay-taitha	tán	hon-tán
Salt	htsé	pó	tá	kó	ké ló
Skin	axá	nan	phro	nann	a-kat
Sky	mó	parwai	mó	hpa	
Snake	mywa	tha-roon	h'm	ngoo	ngoo
Star	kyay	noung	h'sa	loung	touk
Stone	kyouk	kamau	lung	mabein	hee
Sun	ná	ta-ngway	mu	kawon	kawon
Tiger	kyá	kala	ka	htso	tsó
Tooth	thwáu	nget	ta-gná	khyó	thóhn
Tree	apen	ka-noung	thing-mu	ton	tón
Village	yooa	koh	dung	mann	pann

* Jeng?

Water	ya	dhiik	h'tee	mán	nan
Yam	myouk-khoung	ka-wa	nwá	ho-mau	mau
I	ngá	awrai	khwá	koung	kha
Thou	nen	bai	na	moung	ren
He	tho	nyá	wá	khoung-nick	koung-nee
She, It	…	…	…	…	…
We	nga tó	pwá	nó	koung-niht	kha-aen
Ye	nen to	beén tau	ná-the	htsooh-niht	aen
They	thoo to	nyee tau	wá-the	mau-niht	loung-nee
Mine	nga ha	kharoo-awáy	…	khoung-kau	khon-kha
Thine	nen ha	kharoo-hpá	…	khoung-moung	khoung-aeng
His	thoo ha	kharoo-nyúng	…	khoung-pen	khoun-troung
Ours	nga-to ha	kharoo-away taw	…	khoung-houng	khonkhá tsoung
Yours	nen-to ha	kharoo hpaytau	…	khoung moung-pen	khrong tsoung-aen
Theirs	thoo to-ha	kharoomyeen-tau	…	khoung houng-pen	khonkha-tsooung-aen
One	teet	niway	ta	nein	nein
Two	hneet	pa	ne	htsoung	tsoung
Three	thóu	pe	thung	htsan	tsan
Four	lá	pón	leet	htse	tsee
Five	ngá	pa-tson	ngat	ha	hnga
Six	khyouk	karoung	ther	hoht	hoht
Seven	khwó-lneet	khapau	nwot	tseet	tseet
Eight	sheet	kha san	that	tet	tet
Nine	kó	kha-seé	koot	kowt	kowt
Ten	ta-htsay	tsau	tah-si	tseit	htseet
Twenty	hneet-htsay	pa-sau	he	htsoung	ya-tseet
Thirty	thon-htsay	pe-tson	thung	htsan-htsiet	tsan-tseet
Forty	sá-htsay	pon-tson	leet	hse htsiet	tsee-tseet
Fifty	nga-htsay	patsoo-tson	ngat	ha htsiet	ha-tseet
A hundred	ta-ra	kaloon	ta loyeu	bpat	yuay nén
Or	…	mken	a	…	…
To	go	pway	en	kohn	tway
From	ga	noo	a	…	…
By	…	nakeu	tóme	han	kha
With	hnen	ku	…	…	…

English.	Burmese or Myanma.	Talien or Môn.	Toung-thoo.	Shán.	Siamese.
Without	bá	hpa	...	nai	...
In	a-htámha	atway	pu	kanoung	khan-ná
On	apau	atoo	long	ka-nouk	khan-mon
Now	yákoo	la mod	ngá-khayen	nayóhnihn	pá-too-nee
Then	hto akha	akha	moung ma	chyain-hnigh	hpá la
When?	bay-thaukha	a-khalarau	teu ma	chyain-lu	hpalahighn
To-day	thu khana	tang waynau	han-né	ma-hniht	wan-nee
To-morrow	net hpangha	lee ya	mú-reu	má-hpot	hpoonei
Yesterday	ma-na-ga	let-ka-na	má-ha	ma-wa	ma-wa-nee
Here	thee mha	kha-na-nau	yo	kaniht	hta nee
There	ho-mha	kha-na-ko	ea-lí'sú	ka-po	hai-nan
Where?	bay-mha	alorau	eu-hmay	kalau	kalau
Above	a-htet-mha	atotá	en ké	pamon	tee-nan
Below	onk-mha	kha ta ta	enla	palon	khan la
Between	alay-mha	adho	akha	akhun	khalan
Without, outside	apyenmha	ma-ngá	ta-lí'tanu	ka-nouk	khan-nouk
Within	a-hlaymha	kha-tway	en-pu	ka noung	khan-noung
Far	awá-mha	noo-ma-way	hyá	an-kéhn	ka-ríhn
Near	anee-mha	tsonk	lan	an-san	ká
Little	ta-htset kalai	soot	pá	aet	net-ta-ró
Much	apon	hlau	a	taima	hton
How much?	bay-louk	ma-tsee	kheing hmay	hta-noung	htau riht
As	kai-tho	nway tseik-nau	nay-yó	neik-youk	nee
So	thu-kai-tho	nyoung-tseik-kau	nay-yo	tso-neik-yonk	ram-nee
Thus	thee atihn	top-peun	nay-yo	tso-na-youk	men-ran-nee
How?	bay-nay	tsou-la	leu-may	tso-hoo	ran-rihn
Why?	ban-pyoolo	moo-parau	h'twa may	pen-htsau	hta mihn
Yes	hot-kai	tot-kwai	mwá	htsonk-hóe	tsen
No	mahot-bóo	ha-tsen	ta-mwá tew	ma-tsouk	mai-htsa
(Do) not	ma-lot-boo	hó-ka-lon	...	ma-het-a	nai-htau
And, also	yuay	young	la	...	...

Or	tho-mahot	hó-to-tseik-ko	yo	tso-neik-ma-tsouk	mai-pen-yau
This	thee-ha	enan	...	tso-niāit	nóe lai
That	ho-ha	tai-kau	ta-hlon	an-loung-lai	nan-lai
Which?	bay-thin	ee-la-rau	lisa-may-nay	ka-tsan-lay	nhn-louk
What	ba-lai	moo-gau-rau	lo-may nay	hpoung	ayo-loung
Who?	bay-tho	nyay-gau-rau	pá-may nay	pen-htsaytsó-tsó	nihn-loung
Anything	tá-sontakhoo	mway-theik-payai	...	pen-htsaytsó-tsó	hpayla
Anybody	tá-tsontáyouk	kha-ra-tau-mwai-mwai	...	kyen	hpayla-righm
Eat	tsa-thee	tsee	am	kyen	kénn
Drink	thouk-thee	thou	nwa	nonn	kenn
Sleep	aick-thee	tet	ping	tón	nona
Wake	nó-thee	ngoo	ting	kho	tóin
Laugh	yay-thee	garihn	nga	hihk	ho-rau
Weep	ngó-thee	rán	ngen	yoo-hlseet-hlseet	raung-hihn
Be silent	tót-tet naithee	non-ka-nouk-ka-nouk	lingiug	sat	nenróo
Speak	pyauhtso-thee	han-kai	ung-dau	nha	hoo-tsa
Come	la-thee	ka-lon-ra	lóne	kwa	ma
Go	thwáu-thee	aara	lway	tsot-roo	pḥk
Stand up	mat-tai-nay-thee	monlet kha-tau	ung-h'hung	nan-yoo	roa
Sit down	htihn-thee	kha-gyo	ung-lau	lay-yoó	nan
Move, walk	lay-thee	kyay	lay	len-kwa	hta-ro
Run	pyai-thwau-thee	gareetaa	law	pan	wen pihn
Give	pai-thee	ka	pha	an	hihn
Take	yon-thee	keet	khone	pau-tihn	ouk
Strike	yeik-thee	tat	tway	out-tihn	pau tihn
Kill	that-thee	tsa	ma-thay	oung-ma	out-tihn
Bring	yoa-khal-thee	keet-nen	htoo-tone	oung-kwa	oung-nan
Take away	you-thwau-thee	keet-na	htoo-lway	hóh-khen	oung-kot
Lift up, raise	mhyouk-thee	ka-toung	hya or young	htan loo	houm-khan
Hear	na-htoun-thee	kalan	heung	hoo-likh	htawlon
Understand	náiay-thee	tiht-ma-ra	tha-na	lat	hoo-let
Tell, relate	pyau-thee	han-ma-rai	thou-than	lee yau	lat
Good	koung-thee	khá	heu	ma-lee	lee-youk
Bad	ma-koung	hakhá	kay	kat	ma-lee
Cold	chyann-thee	bá	khwá		kann

English.	Burmese or Myanma.	Talien or Môn.	Toung-thoo.	Shán.	Siamese.
Hot	poo-thee	kata	kheu	méik	met
Raw	tsen-thee	tsen-tsangeet	ta-theet	chyo	chyo
Ripe	mhai-thee	tóo	hma	a-htsot	wen
Sweet	chyáthee	tat	nen	tron	wann
Sour	khyen-thee	hpya	h'eya	ltsol	htso
Bitter	cháthee	ka-tau	khu	khon	khon
Handsome	hla thee	gau	tá-rá	han-leen	han lan
Ugly	ayot-htso-thee	hén	...	han-tichk	lou hiik
Straight	hpoung-thee	touk	tsone	tsoo	htsó
Crooked	konk thee	ta-nouk	ngá-ken	kot	kot
Black	mai thee	katsau	phreu	lan	lan
White	hpyoothee	hpa-tihn	bwá	khoung	khoung
Red	nee-thee	hpa-keet	tá-nya	len	tal
Green	tsein-thee	hnen-ta-nyeet	ling	chyo	khayo
Long	shac thee	kalein	l'to	young	young
Short	to-thee	kalée	deng	tot	tsánn
Tall } man	myen-thee	tha-lon	l'to	tson	thóhn
Short	poothee	kwa	pá	pauk	tee
Small	ngay thee	dhot	pá	leikh	let
Great	kyoc thee	tha-not	tan	youhk	kalóhn
Round	lón-thee	kha-toung	tung-lung	món	htsee
Square	lai-htouk nai thee	pon-ka-lan	seet-seng	pyay	htsee-len
Flat	pya-thee	kha-tai-thee	sau-pyay	pyee	hpen
Fat	wau-thee	ka-ra	pay	pyee	awen
Thin	pen-thee	tha rai	hyeng	raung	hpóhn
Weariness	anyoung	ka-won	tá-wa	kon	nai
Thirst	yai-nat-khyer	htan-tikh	h'ta-en-h'tee	rat-nan	rat-nan
Hunger	ngat-mot kihyen	ka-lo hpyo	ha-khó	ok-pyat	aotrat

N.B.—English system of spelling used in the above, which I have not ventured to alter.

SECTION VII.

ON THE

MONGOLIAN AFFINITIES OF THE CAUCASIANS.

ALL residents in the East who take an interest in the more general topics of Ethnology must have been exceedingly struck by Dr. Latham's recent imposing exhibition of the vast ethnic domain of the Mongolidæ. From Easter Island to Archangel, from Tasmania and Madagascar to Kamtchatka and the mouths of the Lena, all is Mongolian! Caucasus itself, the Arian Ararat, is Mongolian! India, the time-honoured Aryavartta, is Mongolian! Granting that this remarkable sketch[*] is in good part anticipatory with reference to demonstrative proofs, it is yet, I believe, one which the progress of research has already done, and is now doing much, and will do yet more, to substantiate as a whole; though I think the learned author might have facilitated the acceptance of his splendid paradoxes, if, leaving the Oseti[†] and the Bráhmans in unquestioned possession of their Arian honours, he had contented himself with maintaining that the mass of Caucasian and Indian population is *nevertheless* of Turanian, not Arian, blood and breed; and if, instead of laying so much stress upon a special Turanian type (the Seriform), he had been more sensible that the technical diagnostics, which have been set upon the several subdivisions of the Mongolidæ, are hindrances, not helps, to a ready perception of the common characteristics of the whole race.

---

[*] Natural History of Man : London, 1850.

[†] It will be seen in the sequel that in the course of those investigations which gave the " Comparative Analysis " its present amplitude, I satisfied myself that the Oseti are Mongolian.

I do not propose on the present occasion to advert to what has been lately done in India demonstrative of the facts, that the great mass of the Indian population, whether now using the Tamulian or the Prakritic tongues, whether now following or not following the Hindu creed and customs, is essentially non-Arian as to origin and race, but that this mass has been acted upon and altered to an amazing extent by an Arian element, numerically small, yet of wonderful energy and of high antiquity. These are indubitable facts, the validity of which I am prepared with a large body of evidence to establish; and they are facts which, so far from being inconsistent with each other, as Latham virtually assumes, are such that their joint operation during ages and up to this hour is alone capable of explaining those physical and lingual characteristics of the Indian population, which Dr. Latham's theory leaves not merely wholly unexplained, but wholly inexplicable. I must however postpone their discussion till I come to treat of the Newár and Khas tribes of Népál. In the meanwhile, and with reference to Dr. Latham's crowning heresy that the most Caucasian of Caucasians (the Irôn or Oseti) are "more Chinese than Indo-European," I have a remarkable statement to submit in confirmation of his general, though not his special, position; my agreement with him being still general, not special.

His general position quoad Caucasus is, that the Caucasian races are Mongolidan; and, availing himself with unusual alertness of the results of local Indian research, he has, at pp. 123-128, given copious extracts from Brown's Indo-Chinese Vocabularies, as printed in our Journal; and he has then compared these vocables with others proper to the Caucasian races. My recent paper upon the close affinity of the Indo-Chinese tongues with those of the Himálaya and of Tibet, will show how infinitely the so-called "Chinese" element of this comparison may be extended and confirmed; and my Sifanese series, now nearly ready, will yet further augment this element of the comparison, which in these its fuller dimensions certainly displays an extraordinary identity in many of the commonest and most needful words of the languages of Caucasus on the one hand, and of Tibet, Sifan,

the Himálaya, Indo-China, and China on the other. There is
no escaping, as I conceive, from the conclusion that the
Caucasian region, as a whole, is decidedly Mongolian, what I
have now to add in the shape of grammatical or structural
correspondences affording so striking a confirmation of that
heterodox belief, whilst Bopp's somewhat strained exposition
of the Arian characteristics of the Irôn (as of the Malayo-
Polynesian) provokes a doubt even as to them, despite the
"Edinburgh Review." * It is the fashion of the age to stickle,
somewhat overmuch perhaps, for structural or grammatical
correspondences, as the only or best evidence of ethnic affinity.
I am by no means insensible of the value of such evidence;
and, though I may conceive it to be less important in reference
to the extremely inartificial class of languages now in question
than in reference to the Indo-European class, I proceed to
submit with great pleasure a telling sample of structural
identity between the Gyárúng tongue, which is spoken on the
extreme east or Chinese frontier of Tibet, equidistant from
Khokhonúr and Yúnán, and the Circassian language, which is
spoken in the west of Caucasus.

The Gyárúng sample is the fruit of my own research into
a group of tongues heretofore unknown, even by name : the
Caucasian sample is derived from Rosen apud Latham, pp.
120–122.

Rosen, who was the first to penetrate the mysteries of Caucasian Glossology, states, 1st, that the Circassian pronouns have
two forms, a complete and separable one, and an incomplete
and inseparable one. 2d, That in their incomplete or contracted
and concreted form, the pronouns blend themselves alike with
the nouns and with the verbs. 3d, That these pronouns, like

---

* No. 192, article Bopp's Comp. Grammar—a work that cannot be too highly
rated, though its style of demonstration is not equally applicable beyond the
Indo-Germanic pale. Its spirit may pass that pale, but not its letter, as when
the Georgian sami is identified with the Sanscrit tri, Greek τρια, and Latin tres.
My doubt respects the Oseti, not the Malayo-Polynesians, for I am satisfied that
they are Mongolian, and would now add a striking and novel statement in support
of that opinion, but that I must by so doing go too far ahead of my yet unpro-
duced Sifan vocabularies. The true and endless Mongolian equivalents for the
Georgian numeral may be seen in the Appendix to this Essay.

the nouns, have no inflectional or other case signs; in other words, are immutable.* 4th, That the complete form of the pronouns is distinguished by the suffix Ra. Now, every one of these very arbitrary peculiarities belongs to the pronouns in the Gyárúng language not less than in that of Circassia, as the following examples will show; and I should add that by how much the development of this part of speech is anomalous throughout the Tartar or Mongolian tongues, by so much is the instanced coincidence with the Circassian more significant, the anomalous or irregular character of the pronouns of both not sufficing to conceal the coincidence, and therefore doubly illustrating it.

Circassian.—Ab, father. Wara, thou, the full pronoun. Wa, the contracted form, used in composition.

Hence Wáb or Wa-ab, thy father.

Gyárúng.—Pé, father. Nanré, thou, the full pronoun. Na, the contracted form, used in composition.

Hence Napé or Na-pé, thy father.

Verbal Use.

Circassian.—Wará, $\left\{ \begin{matrix} wa \\ ú \end{matrix} \right\}$ —kwisloit, thou ridest.

Gyárúng.—Nanré na—syo, thou knowest.

I have changed the Gyárúng verb, because I do not possess the equivalent in that tongue for to ride. It matters not, however, as the sample shows the grammatical form to be absolutely the same in both sentences, just as well as if ride were the verb used in both.

The other rules and examples (scanty, I admit) given by Latham from Rosen may be matched in each instance by

---

* I have now ascertained that the same principles prevail, with slight variations, in the Háyu, Kuswár, Kiránti, and Limbu languages of the Himálaya, in the U'raon, Ho, Sontál, and Gondi tongues of Tamulian India, and in the Tagala and Malayu languages of the Pelasgian group, though passing out of use in the last-named tongue as in several of the Himálayan tongues. See remarks in the Supplement. I may add that in the Háyu language (of which I have a detailed account nearly completed) the verbs are distinguished into the two classes of transitives and intransitives precisely as in Malay.

Gyárúng rule and sample, as will be seen in the sequel. But there is this difference in respect to the Ra suffix, that it is applied to the first and second pronouns in Circassian, though not to the third; and to the second only in Gyárúng.*

This, however, is in complete conformity with the other and typical Mongolian tongues; for in Mantchú, and in Mongol also, the Ra suffix is found, but attaching only to the *third* personal; and if we compare the Téré of those tongues † with the Chinese Tá and the Sokpo Thá, we shall perceive the perfect analogy of the suffix throughout these tongues, in spite of its varying applications.

But is there no clue to the irregularities, none to the real force and signification, of this pronominal suffix? Clearly there is; for in the Tibetan language, the word rang, meaning self, and attaching to all the personal pronouns alike, ‡ affords us that clue, though the people of Circassia and the Gyárúng, whose common and familiar use of this suffix is so perfectly analogous, seem equally unaware of the fact, and can neither explain the meaning nor the partial application of their suffix, any more than can the Mantchús and Mongols. This I infer from the silence of authors, and should add that the explanations are wholly my own, my Gyárúng interpreter being able only to express very unsophisticated surprise when asked to analyse a word.

But I have not yet done with the analogy of Circassian and Gyárúng pronouns, having still to notice that the third personal in Circassian, which drops the Ra suffix, is not really a personal but a demonstrative, equivalent to ille, iste. Now, the Gyárúng language has a third personal, which the Circassian lacks; but it has also a demonstrative, and that demonstrative is the very

* The first and second pronouns are so nearly alike in Gyárúng (nga, na), that the ré suffix has probably been reserved to the second, in order to difference it more plainly.

† Recherches sur les langues Tartares, pp. 173, 183. I cannot thus revert to the thoughts of my old antagonist (voce Buddhism) without a fresh tear dropped on the untimely grave of that truly amiable and learned man.

‡ Nga, I, ngarang, I myself, egomet; and so khérang, khórang. Rémusat has sadly confused the Tibetan pronouns, and, as I suspect, those of the other "langues Tartares," though his work be a marvel for the time and circumstances of its publication. Rémusat ut supra, p. 365.

same as the Circassian one; that is, ú or w; and this pronoun has, in both tongues alike, a separate, full, and a concrete contracted form. Moreover, in the Gyárúng tongue the forms and uses of this demonstrative afford a perfect elucidation both of its strange metamorphosis (w to t) and of its anomalous suffix (i) in Circassian; for "watú" is the complete separate form in Gyárúng; whilst "wa," the contracted form, alone used in composition, constantly takes í, which is really a genitive sign and recognised as such in Tibetan, but is a mere "particule morte" in Gyárúng as in Circassian. Take the following samples from Gyárúng: Watú, he, iste, ille: Wapé, his father: Womo,* his mother: Waimyek, wa-i-myek, his eye (myek, eye): Shaimek, shai-i-mek, leaf of tree (shi, tree, mek, leaf); and then turn to the Circassian samples in Latham, ú-i, he; t-ab, his father;† í-kwisloit, he rides, and you will perceive that (ú being the same with w) the nominal t and the verbal í of Circassian are the secondary or suffix portions of the full Gyárúng pronoun exalted into primaries in order to difference the third person from the second, the second already having the wa or ú (wab, thy father; ú-kwisloit, thou ridest) form. And that such substitution of the secondary for the primary part of a word is no arbitrary assumption of mine, but a regular principle of the Caucasian and of the Mongolian tongues, may be seen by the numerous examples of it occurring in the subjoined list of vocables. The above elucidations of Circassian pronouns for which I am entirely answerable, are so thoroughly in the spirit of Bopp's system that I trust they may find favour

* The change of wa into wo, in wapé and womo, is an instance of that vocalic harmony which these languages so much affect, and which has been erroneously supposed to be peculiar to Turki. We have abundant alliteration both vocalic and consonantal out of, or beyond the Turki branch of, the Mongolian tongues.

Shaimek, from shi and mek, has other peculiarities precisely similar to what occur in the Altaic tongues, teste Remusat.

† In the supplement to this paper will be found an exact and beautiful pendant for this Circassian sample, derived from the Tamulian tongues, the Sontal language having ú and í for the third personal, and these commutable in composition into the conjunct form of tá, precisely as in the Circassian tongue. From the Gondi tongue is there given another example of the commutation of ú to t, so that my exposition from the Gyárúng instance is placed beyond doubt, whilst some fresh and beautiful links are added to the chain of affinities, as to which see prior note.

in his eyes, though I have ventured to demur to his Arianising
of the Tartars by too strained applications of that system.

I know not if Rosen at all explains the peculiarities of the
pronouns in Circassian, but Latham does not; and it will
therefore be felt as a truly interesting circumstance that the
explanation just given, like that of the Ra suffix, have been
fetched from Lhása and Litháng! The cultivated tongue of
Tibet proper continues, it will be seen, to afford the clue to
the labyrinth; and that it does so, is surely a strong presumptive proof, as well of its superior antiquity as of its
superior completeness. So judging, I cannot moreover doubt
that the Circassian preterite sign is the same with the Tibetan
preterite sign (chen-tshar), though this be beside the mark of
pronominal expositions—and to these I must confine myself,
or I shall not know where to stop, so constantly do these
Tartarian illustrations of the Caucasian tongue flow in upon
me. I am unaware whether the Circassian language is distinguished, like the Gyárúng, by a very ample employment of
those prefixes which, as more or less employed, characterise so
many of the Mongolian tongues, and which are dropped in
composition, like the Ra suffix. Thus, tarti, a cap, in
Gyárúng, is compounded of ti the root, and tar * the prefix;
but if we join a noun or pronoun to this word the prefix
disappears, and " his cap," for example, is wárti, compounded of
the wá above mentioned and the radical ti. In like manner
taimek, a leaf, when compounded with shí, a tree, drops the tá
prefix and becomes shaimek, as tápé, father, becomes ngapé,
my father.† Rosen, should this paper fall under his eye, or

---

* Ta, the common form, becomes tar, differentially as tími, fire ; tirmi, man,
root mi, used in both senses. In tirmi, tarti, warti, we have the ra particle,
which remains in its conjunct form as a medial, whilst the usual prefix ta disappears. The rá, too, would disappear in a compound of roots if not needed to
differentials and mark the special sense of such roots, or one of them, or if the
root commenced with other than a labial consonant, its prefix being servile.

† It has been queried whether the polysynthetic words of the American
tongues quoad their principle of construction, as to which there is so much
doubt, be not compiled from *radical* particles only. Judging by the method of
forming ordinary compounds in Gyárúng and its allies, I should say, Yes, certainly
they are to a great extent, though not exclusively, for the cumulative principle
ill brooks control, revelling in reiterations and transpositions of root alike, and of

Latham perhaps, whose quick eye will not fail to catch it, will be able to tell whether the same peculiarity distinguishes the Circassian tongue. For myself I doubt not it will so prove, because the rule for nouns is but another phase of the rule for pronouns.

In the meantime, the striking grammatical analogies* I have pointed out stand in no need of further elucidation, and these analogies, together with the explanation from the Tibetan of the widely-used but heretofore unexplained Ra suffix, constitute in themselves, and as sustaining all those numerous identities of the primitive vocables which have been adverted to, something very like a demonstration of the Mongolidan affinities of the Caucasians, though I would be understood to speak with a due sense of the disqualifications inseparable from my secluded position and want of access to books. I subjoin Latham's sample of the construction of the Circassian language, with its equivalent in Gyárúng.

"I give to my father the horse."

Circassian.—Sara	s-ab	acé	istap
I	my father	horse	give

Gyárúng.—Ngaré†	nga-pé	boroh	dovong
I	my father	horse	give

"In the house are two doors" is, in like manner, "house two doors" in the Circassian and Gyárúng tongues.

---

its servile adjuncts, though clearly, as to simple compounds, constantly observing the rules of contraction and of substitution noted in the text. In the Gyárúng sentence, Tizécazé papún, he summoned them to feast, the word for to feast shows the root repeated twice, and each time with a separate servile, though we have here only one verb, not two verbs; and in kalarlar, round, still no compound, we have the root repeated, but yet with a servile, though only one, being the prefix ka. In such cases that servile is usually omitted, as kaka, sky; pyepye, bird; chacha, hot.

* Those analogies might now be largely extended did health and time permit. Take the following instances :—Tam-bus, father; imbas, my father, in U'raon. Sampa, father; ampa, my father, in Kiránti, Ku-kos, child; ing-kos, my child, U'raon. Tam, sam, ku, serviles, replaced by the pronouns; compare Malayan sam-piyan, san-diri, kan-diri, ka-manus, k'anak, &c.

† Ra suffix subjoined for illustration though not in use with *this* person. See prior note.

The plural sign, kwé in Circassian, myé or kamyé * in Gyárúng, is in both languages alike "the beginning and end of declension."

The following list of Circassian and Gyárúng pronouns may facilitate the reader's apprehension.

	I	*Thou*	*He*
Circassian pronouns—	Sa-ra	Wa-ra	U-í
Gyàrúng pronouns—	Ngá	Nan-ré	Wa-tu

The same conjoined with a noun.

Circassian.†—	S-ab	W-ab	T-ab	} My, Thy, His, father.
Gyárúng.—	Nga-pé	Na-pé	Wa-pé	

COMPARISON AND ANALYSIS OF CAUCASIAN AND MONGOLIAN WORDS.

Man.—K'mari in Georgian
Maré in Suanic

{ K, prefix, servile, as in Indo-Chinese k'lun, a man, and Malayan k'anak, a child ; a sort of article and equivalent to the suffixed k.

Maro in Lepcha
Muru in Súnwár
M'ru in Mrú
Mano in Newári
Mansi in Bódó
Múa-máre nomen gentis

(Má, with the customary change of vowel (see on to mo-i and mi), is the root throughout, and it takes the common ra suffix, likewise with the usual vocalic diversity. But observe that in m'ru this servile absorbs the vowel of the root, as in m'se, Georgian for mé-se, voce fire.

Man.—Ló-g in Osetic

{ This is the first of numerous samples in which the name of the species is that of a tribe.

Ló-ng in Burmese

Means husband.

Len-ja in Magar
Lú in Burmese

{ Means male, especially human, lén, the root, having the sense of mankind, or both sexes.

Ló-k in Tai

{ K suffix, servile articular like the g in ló-g and ló-g.

Ló-g-nya in Khas

Nya, a synonym.

K'lú-n in K'lún

{ Compare k'amari and k'anak. Lú root. Nomen gentis necnon hominis.

Boy.—Lap-pu in Osetic

{ Pú suffix, a diminutive. Ló, lá, ló, the root, as in man.

Lok-pa in Tai

Pa, diminutive = pu. Ló, root.

---

* Ka is the prefix, appended as usual. I have already remarked that the Gyárún tongue is distinguished among its allies by its extensive employment of this class of particles. The Burmese tongue makes less use of them, and in its myá, much, many, we have the Gyárúng plural sign, myé, or ka-myé. The Suanic maré and Georgian k'mari for man, afford precise Caucasian equivalent quoad the servile ka, showing it to be dropped or retained according to circumstances or to dialects in Caucasus.

† Ab, father—pé, father, less the prefix.

Lúk-wan in Tai	Lú root with articular, k suffixed. Wan, doubtful. Compare wak, in Armenian, sá-wak, a child; sa in Burmese having the root only.
Young person of either sex { Bitshi in Georgian / Bi-shi in Lazic	Shi, euphonised sha = sa and cha and za, in the following words; or it may be bi, bo, bu, junior, and shi, human.
Bo-shi in Mingrelian	Means daughter.
Bo-zo in Lazic	Zo = za = sa and cha, the common diminutive, euphonised to vowel of root.
Bisha, Bishi in Bódó	Male and female respectively.
Bu-cha in Takpa	The diminutive cha is seen in the conjunct form in Osetic sa-ch voce earth.
Pu-sa in Maplu	Zo servile, as in Lazic bo-zo.
Po-ze in Pasuko	Z = S, alike in Caucasian and Mongolian series.
Man.—Moi in Osetic	I' servile. Mó, = má supra et mí infra, is the root.
Moi in Kong	Means sister.
Pú-moi in Ple	Means woman, pú being a feminine sign. Moi therefore is man.
Moi-tai	Nomina gentium. See note at end of supplement.
Mo-n	
Mo-cha in Newári	Means child, cha being a diminutive, = sa, supra.
Múi-bú in Takpa	Mú is the root. For change of vowel therein, see note, voce dog.
Mú-rú in Súnwár	Rú, the ra suffix, with its vowel harmonised to that of root.
Man.—Tsé-s in Georgian	Means boy, owing to the sa suffix. Tsé therefore is man.
Tsó in Chinese	
Man.—Zo-zi in Osetic	Zi, = si and shi, is the root. The latter appears in bit-shi, tsé, &c. It is a very widely-spread man root, signifying adults as well as juniors.
Ka-zi in Georgian	
V-zi in Horpa	
D-zi in Chinese	
Woman.—U's in Osetic	The root is ú, meaning man. The conjunct s is the feminising suffix. U'-er-ti, ú-shi, &c. have the same root. Rés is the ra suffix, with the sa particle repeated.
U's-res in Gyárúng	
Woman.—Swa-n in Osetic	
Swa-s-ni in Khas	
Brother or Sister { Dá in Georgian / Dá in Sóntal	
Dá in Kuswár	Means girl.
Da-s, Dá in U'raon	Mean boy and girl.
A-da in Bódó	
Dá-ni in Dhimáli	Means virgin.
D'si in Chinese	
Ego = Homo.—Mi in Suanic	Mean I, the pronoun. No fact is better established in Glossology than the frequent equivalency of the roots for man and I, and it is of much importance to note them here.
Mé in Georgian	
Mé in Mingrelian	
Má in Osetic	

Mi in Tibetan Mi in Lhopa Mi in Murmi Mi in Moitai Mhi in Gúrúng Bhar-mi in Magar Bar-ma, nomen gentis Tir-mi in Gyarúng Mi-va in Gáró Yap-mi in Limbu Mih-pa in Kuki	This and all the following mean man. It is remarkable how far the pronominal sense of mi prevails in Caucasus, and the nominal in the regions east of it. But they run into each other, and the root very generally is further employed to designate tribes from Caucasus to Indo-China, as mi-shi-mi, from the mi and shi roots, mú-r-mi, from the mu and mi roots, &c., &c.
Ka-mi in Kámi Kú-mi in Kúmi Pú-mi in Plé	Tribe names derived from name of species—a very extensively diffused principle. The etymology of Burma or the Burmese is thus recovered. See Supplement.
Mi-jang in Newár Mi-sa in Newár	Mi, the species; jang and sa sexual adjuncts. Jang = mas. Sa = fem.
Mi-ya in Newár Miyau-lau in Roinga	Means girl. Ya, differential servile with reference to the various senses of the mi root. *
Mim-ma in Burmese	Means woman. Root mi. Ma is a feminine and maternal sign.
Sa-mí in Burmese	Means girl. See note in sequel.
S'mé in Horpa Se-mé in Kolun	S'mé means girl, like sa-mi and sé-me. The sa particle in various phases, added to mi root.
Mé-jing in Lau	
I.—Sa in Circassian Sa-ya in Malay	Ya, a differential servile.
Sa in Tagalan	An article. See Crawford's work for proof how these so-called articles blend with the pronouns.
Sa in Malay	Means one. Smidt wittily remarks on the perpetual coincidence of the first personal pronoun, and the first numeral, which is also constantly equivalent to the indefinite article, where wanting.
Sú-m in Vayu	In composition only, as ha-sum, give to me.
I.—Má in Osetic Má in Mingrelian Má in Lazic Mi in Suanio Ma in Tinnic	
Mo-n in Sap	Compare moi, man, in Osetic and món the Indo-Chinese tribe name.
Mi in Mongol Mi in Mantchu	Deduced from the derivatives mi-ni and mi-ning-ge. So mi in the sense of man is deduced from mim-ma and sa-mi in Burmese.
I.—Jé-s in Armenian Ji in Newári vJa in Horpa	See remarks, voce dog, on the vocalic changes to which all roots nearly are subject.

---

* The basis of all these tongues from Caucasus to Oceanica is a small number of monosyllabic roots bearing necessarily many senses. Hence to distinguish between those several senses is the chief function of the servile adjuncts of the roots. In this language, for example, the root wa means come, tooth, rice, rain, throw, and he.

I.—A'-z, A-s in Osetic
  An-ka in Kiránti
  A-ku, A' in Malay
  A' in Manyak
  Ká in Dhimáli

A' is the root throughout, za, sa, ka, ku, being serviles, though some of them, as ka, frequently take the place of the root.

Thou.—She-n in Georgian
  Si in Mingrelian
  Si in Suanic
  T'shi in Mongol
  Se-n in Túrki
  Sa-n in Onigur
  Sa in Finnic
  Chhá in Newári
  Chú in Sokpa
  Sú in Tai

Sí, shí ; só, shé ; sá, shá, sú, are the several phases of the root, or cycle of customary variation, just as in the nouns. See remarks on "kha" voce dog.

The plural, Ye.

He.—Ná in Armenian
  Ná in Chinese
  Ná in Malay
  Ni in Khyeng
  No in Anam
  Ha-ná-i } in Kámi
  H'ná-i

Ha prefix and *Y* suffix, servile.

He.—U'-i in Circassian
  U'-i in Sóntál
  O'é in Magyar
  U' in Circassian
  U' in Gáró
  O' in Onigur and Túrki
  Wo in Newári and Gondi
  Wa in Gúrúng, in Dhimáli, and in Tunglhu

He.—I' in Circassian
  I' in Mantchu
  I' in Burmese
  I' in Dhekra
  I' in Malay and Tagala

Deduced from i-ti, i-tu, &c.

He.—Ta in Circassian
  Ta in Sóntál
  Ta in Gondi
  Té in Mongol
  Té in Mantchu
  Té-ún in Dhekra
  Tá in Esthonian
  Thá in Gyami
  Thi in Gúrúng
  Thé in Murmi

In composition as conjunct prefix or suffix or as disjunct, *e.g.*, t-ap, his father ; apa-t, his father ; handa-ta-r, he went. See Rosen, Phillips, and Driberg. With regard to the transposed pronoun, see note voce fire. The law of transposition is so important that I add the following samples to show that even where the actual practice has ceased, analogy supports its quondam use.

Suffix Possessive.	*Prefix Possessive.*
Baba-ku, Malay.	Ang-upa, Váyu.
Aba-im, Kuswar.	Im-bas, U'raon.
Apa-ing, Sóntál.	Nga-pe, Gyárúng.
= my father.	

  Thú in Burmese
  Tá-i in Dhekra

In i-thu, ithi. Means she.

He.—I'-s in Georgian
  I-ti-na in Mingrelian
  I-té in Dhekra

See Remarks in Supplement.

I-sé 〉 in Magar
I-se-ná 〉

Mean this, this very one, this one here.

I-ti in Malay
Sé-i-ti in Koch

Iste qui.

Sé-i in Dhekra
I'-ta in Khas

Means here.

Si-ni, si-tu, in Malay

Means here and there.*

Si-ya in Malay

Ille qui.

Sky.—Khá-k in Absné
Ká in Lazic
Ká-ka in Akush
Khá khau in Kámi

{ Khá is the aspirate, and ka-ka the reduplicate state of the root. K final is an articular servile, as in talak, bik, &c., &c.

Kbó-rang in Bódó
Nam-khá in Tibetan
Nam-khan in Magar

{ For nam compare nam-sin. It is frequently omitted. Khá is *the* place, metaphorically sky or heaven. Rang is an emphatic servile, for which see supplement to this paper.

Sky.—Ta-la-k in Tshettshentsh

{ La, root. Ta, the common prefix, and k, the articular suffix.

Ta-li in Georgian
A-li in Georgian

{ Doubtful, and can mean sky only metaphorically.

Ta-la-k in Ostiac

Means sun.

Ta-li-ang in Lepcha

{ Ta, as before. Ang, a form of the na suffix. Compare pett-ang.

Ta-li in Gyárúng

Means air.

Le in Burmese
A-li in Kumi

{ The nude root whereof the phases are lá, ló, li.

K'li in Khyeng
Ga-li in Kámi
La-k in Sák
Li in Rukheng

{ Valuable illustrations of the system of serviles, the root being palpable. Its general sense is air, sky, by metaphor. For k' prefix of kli, see k'mari.

Fire.—Mizh in Suanic = Mi-zhi
Msé in Georgian = Mé-só
Mzá in Absné = Ma-za

{ Zhí, só, zá, are three conjunct suffix forms of the sá particle which is seen in manyak in its separate unaltered form as a prefix. Here it is altered, 1st, by dropping its own harmonised vowel (see zhi, infra), 2d, by absorbing the vowel of the root. Div, den, for di-ni, day, and smé for sémé, girl, are parallel instances of change as of transposition are mi-sa and sa-mi,† voce man. See note below; and that on the ma particle, voce "day."

Zhi in Kuánchua
Zi in Dido
Za in Chunsag

{ These are introduced to show the servile particle of mizh, mza, and to show it superseding the root, as in fa for ma, here, and in ba for sa, voce cow, and in di for bi, voce skin.

---

* It is because the third personal is so perpetually identical with the demonstratives, of which the direct and exclusive principle is contrast, that the same elements come to express the contrasts of place and time and manner (here there; now then; as, so). He who would trace the remoter affinities of race, must treat languages in this thoughtful manner.

† Note. The mi-sa, sa-mi, sample of transposition of the sa particle, cited above to match the me-se, Georgian, sa-me, Manyak, sample here compared with it, is from my Tibeto-Himálayan vocabularies; thus in full, mi-sa, woman, in Newári, sa-mi, girl, in Burmese and Khyeng, and sme, in Horpa, root mi, me, mankind, and sa, a feminine and diminutive sign. In short, the sa particle, like all others, may be prefix or suffix, and separate or blended. Hence mse, Georgian = sa-me, Manyak. With regard to the suffixed zhi, zi, or za, clearly = sa, it would seem as if mi were the sun or great fire, of which mi-sa is the diminutive, just as sá is the earth, or terrestrial globe, and sa-ch (cha = sa) earth, soil. See "Earth" in sequel.

Má-fa in Circassian	Fa servile. We shall presently see it usurping the place of the root.
Mé in Tibetan Mé in Limbu Mé in Serpa Mé in Murmi Mé in Kolun Mhé in Magor Mi in Lepcha Mi in Kiránti Mi in Newári Mi in Gúrúng Mi in Sunwár Mi in Burmese Mi in Khyeng Mi in Moitai Mi-ung in Maplu Ma-i in Kámi Mha-i in Kumi	These abundant instances from the Mongolian series plainly prove the root in the Caucasian series, and they show that root precisely such in every phase (mi, mé, má) as it is seen in the Caucasian series. We thus securely proceed to the serviles or rather servile, and this the Manyak word, below, gives in the primitive state, unaltered by blending or by euphony. We are therefore certified as to its various altered forms (zhi, zá, só) in the Caucasian series. Observe also in the Mongolian series that all the tongues which use the mi root in the sense of man have mé instead of mi for fire.
Fá-i in Khamti Fá-i in Tai Fo in Kong	Turn to ma-fá, supra, and note again how the servile supersedes the root, as in zi for mi, fire. So also Tibetan ba for Circassian bsa, voce cow, and Anamese di for Dido bi, voce skin ; the last so decisively proved by the Murmi form of the word wherein root and servile both appear, di-bi. Thus the Circassian word ma-fa supplements and expounds the Tai and Khámti word fa-i; and this the Manyak word sameh supplements and expounds the Georgian word msé and its Suanic and Absné equivalents. The languages must have a deep and radical affinity which can thus be made mutually to illustrate each other.
Mé-n in Dhimáli Meh in Takpa Meh in Thochu	Return to the simple root again.
Sa-meh in Manyak Sa-mi in Sák	Here we have the sa particle above cited in its pure unaltered state. The Georgian msé shows it transposed and blended.
E'-mé in Abor Ti-mi in Gyárúng U-ma in He rpa Um-ma in Aka	Timi recurs to the mi form of the root, with the inseparable Gyárúng prefix (ta) harmonised in its vowel, ú servile, like é, in é-mé. These last words of the fire series afford excellent illustration of the wide scope of servile adjuncts.
Day.—Di-ni in Tshettshentsh	Di is the da prefix harmonised in its vowel to that of the root ni.
D-én, Dé-n in Ingush	Den shows the above prefix conjunct, and the ni root altered to né, become én per metastasin. Or, if we read dé-n, then the particle takes the harmonised vowel of the root which is absorbed, as in din for di-ni, below.
Ki-ni in Kasi Kamak	Has the ka prefix harmonised in its vowel to ni root.
Ki-na in Makash	Means to-day. Ki, as above. Na, a new phases of the root, as ma for mi, fire.

Di-ni in Magar Di-ni in Gúrúng Di-ni in Bódó	Tally exactly, root and servile, with the Tshettshentsh word, and similarly analysed of course.
D-in in Khas	Tallies with the den instance.
Ka-ni in Kumi	Means day and sun.
Ka-nhi in Khyeng Ko-ni in Koluu gNa in Hórpa	Means sun. The roots for sun and day run into each other to a great extent. Nhi, vel ni, vel ná, is the root.
Si-ni in Singpho	Si servile is the sa particle with harmonised vowel.
Nam-sin in Súnwár	Compare nam-kha, voce sky. Sin for si-ni is like din for dini, ni being the root.
Sak-ni in Lepcha	Sak, like nam, is a servile or particule mort;* not, however, so utterly dead that its radical sense of "sun" cannot be recovered.
Nhi in Newári	Shows the root again, free of all adjuncts, but varied by an aspirate, as khá for ká, voce sky; mhé for mé, voce fire.
Né in Burmese Ni in Mrú Ni-n in Koreng	
taNi-n in Mrú Ná in Súnwár	Means "sun." Day, sun, and sky run into each other perpetually.
Na-m in Limbu Na-m in Kiránti	Compare nam-kha, voce sky; mean sun or parent (ma) of day (na); or, "m" being servile, na = ni, will be sun vel day.
Ni-mo in Serpa	Means day and sun.
Ni-bha in Newári	Means sun.
Nhi-ga in Newári Ka-nhé in Newári Ba-ha-ni in Newári Ha-ni in Newári Tha-ni in Newári	Mean respectively to-morrow and yesterday, evening, then, and to-day, and are most valuable exponents of the function of the particles as well as of the flexibility of the roots nhi, nhé, ni, being as surely phases of one root as mhe, mé, ma, mi are, voce fire.
Má-né-k in Burmese	Means morning, from the roots ma, mother, and né, day, with the articular k suffix, as in kha-k, sky. The Chinese in like manner name the day the sun's son. Or the prefix ma may be a servile as in the next word.
Ma-ni in Kámi	The meaning here being simply day, from the root ní, ma must be a servile, no more affecting the sense of the root than the ka, da, and sa prefixes in Dini, Kani, and Sini.
Nyima in Tibetan	Here the ma particle becomes a suffix, and, as before, without touching the sense of the root.
Nyi-m in Lepcha	Ma suffix conjunct = ma in the preceding word. Seems conjunct in tsari chim, voce water.
Na-ni in Dhimáli	Means then. Na, servile.

---

* Observe therefore that what is said of the universal vitality of all the particles of these tongues, voce dog, is only true in the comprehensive view of the languages.

Nyi-ti-ma* in Dhimáli	Ti and ma, both servile differential. For ma suffix, see chi-m, voce water, si-ma, voce tree, &c. For ti suffix, see purti, voce bird, bi-t, voce cow, &c.
Snyi in Gyárúng	Sa prefix, conjunct.
Pish-nyi in Gyárúng Sos-nyi in Gyárúng	Mean respectively to-day and yesterday.

Night.—Ak-sá in Osetic	Ak servile as in akra, voce horn. Sa root = sha, Tibetan.
K'shé-r in Armenian	K prefix = ak, and the final r, the common ra particle, conjunct.
Séri in Mingrelian	Ri suffix, servile = r in ksher. See Supplement.
T'shá-n in Tibetan	Initial t' and final n serviles.
Chó-n, spoken Tibetan	Final n servile.
Kú-sén Sén-dik } in Lepcha	Kú prefix and dik suffix serviles. Sé root.
Sén-li in Takpa	Li servile, as in ché-li, Georgian, voce hand, and kué-li, Surawár, voce hand.
Chá-i in Chinese Cha-i in Buret	Tally exactly with the spoken Tibetan.

Summer.—Ach-ké in Mizjeji	Ach = cha, per metastasin. Ké servile.
Chá-ko in Tushi	Kó servile, like ké and ká. For vocalic changes, see "dog."
Cha-r-ka Chi-d-ka } in Tibetan	Mean spring. Medial r and d serviles, for which see the Supplement of this paper.
Chi-a in Chinese	Final a servile.
Chá-ko in Dhimáli Sá-ko in Dhimáli	Cha is hot and sá summer.† Yet the adjective and substantive are really but one word.
Chá-n-gu-la in Newári	"The hot months." Lá means month, and gu is a servile = ka, ko, supra.

Sun.—bShá in Mingrelian Shá in Tushi.	
Ta-chán in Tushi	Means day. Final n, servile as in the following words.
Sha-n in Bódó Sa-n in Gáró	N servile, as in the prior word and subsequent one.
Sá-ne in Dhimáli	Means sunshine.
Sá-cha-k in Lepcha	Sá-chá, sing, song, repetition of the root. K, articular servile.

Moon.—Twaiin Suanic = Tá-va-i	Compare tagalan Ta-vo and Bugis tau, meaning man, for proof of the wide prevalence of disjunct and conjunct styles. Final i, servile.

---

* Mani compare with nyima and nyitima afford further illustrations of the rule of transposition already illustrated from the msé and sameh instance, voce fire, as well as from the misa and sami sample, voce man. In fact, no law of these languages can be more certain than this of transposition, passing frequently into substitution (of servile for root), of which also we have seen various instances. The rationale is that every element is, in general, equally available in a primary or secondary sense, though there will of course be exceptions if the view be narrowed to one or two of the tongues, and more especially if these be regarded merely in statu quo.

† Compare Malay cha-bi and Endo sa, meaning pepper. Sense, sound, and system seem to tally with ours, the added or omitted servile and the change of root ! !

Twé in Georgian	
mTwá-ré in Georgian	Ré servile, the common ra suffix.
Twó in Newári	Epithet from colour, white.
Dá-va in Tibetan	
Dá-u in Lhópa	
Tá in Tai	
Tá-li in Dhimáli	Li servile, as in .cheli, sen-li, supra.

Earth.—T'shé-do in Dido — { Initial t', servile, and do suffix. For the suffix see remarks in Supplement.

T'shi in Georgian
T'shí-git in Osetic — { Initial t', the common ta particle ; git, doubtful.
T'shi-git in Dugoian
T'sé in Georgian.

Sá-ch in Osetic — { Ch suffix, a phase of the diminutive particle cha, sa.
Só-ch in Osetic — { Sa, the root, is *the* earth. Sach, earth, soil, a little of.

Mit-za in Georgian — Mi-t, double servile, modified like git.

Mi-sá in Andi
Mu-sá in Akush — { Mi and mu are indubitable serviles, sá being the root. They serve excellently to show how these particles attach to the roots. The mi prefix is very common in the Magar tongue, as mi-rong, misya-ros, &c.

Di-chá in Mingrelian — { Chá, the root, tallies exactly with Newári. Di is the common da prefix.

M'shá in Hórpa — { K' is the ka particle conjunct, as in k'mari, k'li, k'anak, &c. &c.

Ha-sá in Sóntál — Ha servile, or a synonymous root.
Séh in Gyárúng
Sá in Tibetan
Sá in Lhópa — { These numerous samples from the Mongolian tongues plainly demonstrate the root of the Caucasian words as before remarked in reference to the fire series.
Sáh in Takpa
Chá in Newári

Kat-ché in Karen — { Compare kat-shú, voce hand, and observe that the form is identical in the Caucasian and Mongolian sample (andi and plé). We have here the very same compound servile (ka-ta) similarly employed (prefix). Such perfect coincidence of all the elements of speech could result only from identity of origin and family unity.

Salt.—T'shé-a in Kubitsh — { The word is radically the same as that for earth, as proved by the Osetic and Wogul terms. The prefix also is the same, and hence a suffix is required to difference the senses. It is thus we learn the real function of the serviles. See note, voce ego = homo.

Za-ch in Osetic
Se-ch in Wogal — { See Earth.
D'zé in Akush,
Zi-o in Dido

Dé-só in Dhimáli — { Comparing this word with the Akush d'sé, we
Dé in Kolunj — see the equivalency of the conjunct and disjunct serviles.

T'si in Khyeng
T'sá in Takpa
T'sha in Tibetan
Shá in Burmese

Wi-shá in Mrú

> Wi = water? sha = salt. The salt procured from water. Else wi = bi, the common servile.

Chá-chá in Gyárúng
Chhá in Lhópa
Chhá in Serpa
Chi in Newári

> Root repeated as in ká-ká, voce sky.

Chhé in Manyak
Chhá in Horpa
Chhé in Gyárúng

> This aspirate ch is equivalent to the Tibetan and Kabitsh tsh.

Sú-ng in Sák
Syú-ng in Bódó

> Final nasal servile. Intercalate y, very common as ni, nyi, voce day. Khi, khyi, voce dog.

Dab-sú-n in Mantchu
Da-ba-sú in Mongol

> We cannot doubt that sú is here the root. Da-ba, therefore, are servile prefixes, though the existence of such has been denied to these tongues.

River.—O'r in Osetic
Hor in Avar
Or-(kyuré) in Akush

> O', ú, the root, r servile.
> The same aspirated.
> For Kyúré see on to "rain."

Wá-ran in Osetic

> Means rain. Wá root; ran servile. See Supplement.

sg-Wá in Georgian
O' in Sák
O'ng in Lepcha

> Means a lake; wá the root.
> O' is the nude root. O'ng the same, with the common nasal addition.

U'-(sú) in Sokpa

> U', another phase of the water root. For sú see on.

Wá in Newári

> Same as ú; means water.

Ha-wá
K'wá } in Kámi

> Prefixes h and k servile.

A'ú in Mrú
Wá-i in Dhimáli

> Unites the ó and ú roots.
> Means rain.

Hra in Hórpa

> Hra = ho-ra, ho-r, with the vowel of the root absorbed as in msé, voce fire, &c.

Hyúng in Serpa
O'ng-kyong
Wó-hóng in Limbu
Khyóng in Lau
Khwóng in Gúrúng
Khyong in Burmese

> Compound of yú and ong, synonymous roots.
> Compound of kyú (see rain) and óng, supra.
> Obvious compounds from the precedent elements. River, rain, water, so run into each other that no justice could be done to the real synonyms by technical separation.

Rain.—Kú-a, Kwá in Abassian

(Or) Kyú-ré in Akush

> For ré suffix see the Supplement. "Or" disposed of above. Kyu is ku with the intercalate y as in nyi for ni and khyi for khi.

Kú-i, Kwi, in Múrmi
Kyú in Gúrúng

Li-kú in Súnwár

> Li may be a root = sky, and then liku is sky water, or it may be the li servile.

Khu-(si) in Newári

> Compound of two synonyms Abassian kú and Kubitsh si! For si, apart, see on.

Lake.—D'zo in Armenian
T'so in Tibetan
Water.—Dú in Ingush
Dó-ú in Armenian
Dú-n, dó-n, in Osetic
Dú-í in Singpho
Dó-í in Bódó
Do-i in Gáró
Dá in Sóntál
Dá in Moasi
Dí in Magar
Tú-í in Khyeng
Tú-í in Kámi
Tú-í in Mrú
Chi in Mizjiji

Shi-n in Kubitsh
Shi-n in Kasikumak
Shé-n in Akush
pShi in Tsherkesik
dZék in Absné
T'cha-ri in Mingrelian

Chi-m in Tshari

Só in Altekesek

Chi in Gáró
Chi in Dhimáli

Ti-chi in Gyárúng

T'ché in Mopla
mChi-n in Jili

Cho-du-k in Mongol
I'-si-ng in Khyi

Wé-si in Ugorian

ntSin in Singpho

Chá-wa in Kiránti
Chá in Thochu
T'zú-n in Kubitsh
Shú-r in Armenian

T-sú-en in Samoiede

Chhú in Tibetan
Chhú in Lhópa
Chhú-a in Limbu
Chhú-wá in Kiránti
Shú-i in Gyami
Sú in Anam
Sú in Túrki

Voce "dog." We have summarised the changes to which the elements of words are liable when taken singly or when a single element constitutes a word : we may here take occasion of the great water root (or of available space, rather) to summarise the changes those elements are liable to in conjunction, or when more than one goes to the composition of a word. They are

1st. By reiteration, as ká-ká, voce sky, chá-chá, voce salt.

2d. By cumulation, as na-ma, si-ni, voce day, i-só-na, voce he.

3d. By contraction, as nt-sin, voce water; bb-só, voce tongue ; msé, voce fire.

4th. By permutation (euphonic of vowels and consonants), as kach-chur for katas kyur, voce sour.

5th. By transposition, as mim-ma and mi-sa, versus sa-mi, and s-mó, voce man.

6th. By substitution, as fa for ma, voce fire, di for bi, voce skin.

Final n servile. This is easily said by way of disposing of an inconvenient particle. But I appeal to the uniform tenor of the whole of my paper for my proofs.

M conjunct, ma suffix, as in Lepcha, nyim, voce day, and in Mrú sham, voce hair.
Often cited with the dú suffix as is dzó in Absne. See remarks on tshe-do, voce earth.

Has the inseparable ta prefix harmonised in its vowel.
The same prefix conjunct.
Initial m and final n serviles.
Means " spring." Observe that the dú suffix is frequently attached to Absnó zó and Altekesek só, though omitted here.
Compound of two synonymous roots.
N-t prefix, and n suffix, serviles, sí being the root.

Zú = sú = chú, the root.
R final, the common ra suffix, conjunct.
Cited to illustrate tzú just remarked on ; final en is metastatic ne, a servile.

Aspirate chh = ts and tsh by numerous examples, though the Tibetan alphabet has both letters.

U'-sú in Sokpa

{ U' and sú, are synonyms. U' is, in fact, the basis of a whole series of words for water.

Chú-rá in Kalmak
Chó-dú-k in Mongol

{ Mean rain. The ra suffix = dú, to which is added the articular k. Dú, however, may here be a root and synonym.

Cow.—bSá in Circassian

{ Turn to the Tibetan word, and mark how root and servile are commutable.

Sá in Newári
Sá-lo in Sokpa
Sha-r in Mongol
Sha-r in Khyeng

{ Lo, servile. La, li, ló, its phases; r, the common ra suffix.

Bá-shá in

{ Note how the surplus silent b of Circassian here becomes a regular prefix.

Bá in Tibetan

{ Takes up the servile b of the Circassian and makes root of it as already noted in various other instances.

Bi in Súnwár
Bi-t in Limbu
Bi-k in Lepcha

K-chú-g in Osetic
Má-shú in Bódó
Má-chú, spoken Tibetan

K and g serviles; chu, root.
Má, feminine sign.
Má, as before.

Dog.—Chó-í in Avar
Chó-í in Andi
Chó-í in Chansag
Chú-á in Akush

K-chú-d in Osetic

{ Initial k and final d, serviles. The latter is the conjunct form of the da, du, do, suffix remarked on in the Supplement.

Shu-n in Armenian
Chó-í in Bódó
Chú in Magar
Chí-ta in Moasi
Sé-ta in Sóntál

{ Ta, the common servile, which, like all others, may be prefixed or suffixed.

We may take occasion of the cycle of changes seen in this word to make a general remark: that homogeneousness and vitality belong to all the elements (roots and serviles) of words in these tongues is a very important truth, as well for the illustration of general philology as for the explanation of the extraordinary extent to which transposition and substitution among those radical and servile elements are carried. It is likewise true that these elements and the words resulting from them are less flexible and mutable than among the Arian tongues. But it is by no means generally or strictly true that "all the words are invariable." On the contrary, the words, whether consisting of monosyllable roots, or of such roots and their servile adjuncts, are constantly subjected to changes, which are clearly systematic, which belong alike to the radical and servile particles, and which may be summarised as follows:—

Khá in Circassian
Kó-a in Kubitsh
Gwai in Dido
Gwi in Dugoric
Khí-á in Dhimáli
Khí-á in Limbu
Khí in Lhópa
Khi in Gúrúng
Khwá in Thochu
Khwó in Burmese
Khyi in Tibetan
Geu, gyú, in Chinese
Na gyú in Gúrúng
Ká in Hórpa
Ká-í in Gáró
Kou in Gyami
Kú in Sák

1st, by aspiration, as khi for ki.
2d, by change of vowel, ko, ku, ke, ka for ki.
3d, by intercalation of y, khyi for khi.
4th, by metastasis, ain for nai, voce ear, &c.

Ta-kwi in Mrú
Kút-chik in Kurd
Khí-cha in Newári
Ko-chu in Kiranti
Kú-chúng in Súnwár

Kwi root = Ku-i.

} These are compounds of the two preceding words—a sort of term very common in all countries wherein many tongues prevail.

Dog.—Húé in Chunsay
Hwé in Tunglhu
U-i in Kumi
U-yo in spoken Tibetan

Tree.—K-Cha-d in Osetic
Ché in Mizjeji
dSé-g in Circassian
dSá in Lazic
Sé-k in Suanic
Shi in Gyárúng
Si-ng in Moasi
Shi-ng in Bódó
Shi-ng in Dhimáli
Shi-ng in Lhópa
Si-ng in Magar

The root varies from chá to ché, and sa to sé, to si, to shi. The suffixes have occurred too often to call for further remark in this place.

Si-n-du in Gúrúng

Here is a Mongolian sample of the dú suffix, so frequent in the Caucasian series. Ka-n-du, ka-do-t, &c., voce foot, are further samples.

Sá-ng in Anam
Si-ma in Newári
T-sing in Mrú

Sá, si, the root, ut supra. Of ma suffix we have had samples in nhi-ti-ma, voce day, chi-m, voce water, cha-m, voce hair, &c.

Forest.—Dish-chá in Mingrelian
Din-chá in Dhimáli

{ The Osetic chá = tree is clearly the basis of these two words for forest.

Bird.—Pú-r-ti in Andi

Compare ta-r-tí, a cap, ti-r-mi, a man, nyi-ti, day, of the Mongolian series, and the pú root will be easily apprehended.

Pét-tang in Avar

Tang, servile, is the ta particle with the common nasal addition. How common it is may be seen by consulting my Himálayan vocabulary. Pé is the root, borrowing the t from the servile suffix.

Pyé in Gyárúng

Pyé = pé. The frequent intercalation of y has been already noted in ni, nyi, khi, khyi, &c.

Pyá in Takpa.

Byú in Tibetan

{ Abstract the intercalate y, and the root reproduces that of the Andi pú-r-ti.

Bú in Limbu
Pho in Lepcha

= Andi pú.

Fish.—bZhéh in Circassian

{ Turn to the word for flesh, and you will see the differential function of the prefix b.

gZháh in Thochu

Initial g = b supra. These are merely the conjunct forms of the ba and ga prefixes. The conjunct and disjunct system of prefixed, as of infixed and postfixed serviles, prevail alike in the Caucasian and Mongolian tongues, as evidenced by this paper throughout; and the prevalence of both systems is another striking feature of that perfect analogy which pervades these tongues.

Di-shé in Magar

Di servile.

Flesh.—Zhéh in Abassian
   Jé-chu in Suanic
   Li-chá in Finnic   Li servile.   Chá root.
   Shá in Tibetan
   Shá in Takpa
   Ta-shá in Gyárúng   } The prefix ta is as common in Gyárúng as is
   A-sá in Burmese   } á in Lepcha and Burmese.

Egg.—Dú-khi in Akush   Du, Water ? Khi, fowl.
   To-kbá in Gáró   To, blood, and kha, fowl.
   Tou-chi in Gáró   Tou, fowl, and chi, blood.
   Tou-dóï in Bódó   Tou, fowl, and dóí, water.
                           ⎧ U', Burmese, meaning originally "water," is
   Tó-i in Khyeng   ⎪   the root of all the other words, for which
   Dú-i in Mrú   ⎪   see "Water." The metaphorical and now
   Dú in Kámi   ⎨   only current sense of the word is even more
   Tú-í in Dhimáli   ⎪   singular than that of the preceding terms,
   U' in Burmese   ⎪   amongst which the first is determined ana-
                           ⎪   logically. The literal sense of ú is lost in
                           ⎩   Burmese, like mi for man.

Ear.—Ná in Armenian.
   Ain in Tshari
   Ain in Avar   } Ain = ná-i, per metastasin.
   Ná in Burmese
   rNá in Tibetan   ⎧ Ná, the root, speaks for itself. Vo = bo =
   Ná in Singpho   ⎪   be = pe are phases of one and the same
   Ná-vo in Lhópa   ⎪   servile which = ko, ku. De Cöros calls
   Né-ko in Limbu   ⎨   these "articles," and, like all the serviles,
   Ná-ku in Karien   ⎪   they often perform the articular function of
   Ná-pé in Múrmi   ⎩   specification or emphasisation.
   Ná-bé in Gúrúng
   A-ga-ná in Kámi   ⎧ A rich fund of illustration of the serviles, the
   Ká-né in Sák   ⎪   ná root being unquestionable. My Himá-
   A-kha-ná in Tankul   ⎨   layan vocabulary affords numerous samples
   Ná-i-pong in Newári ⎪   of the pong and tong suffixes, which are but
   Nhá-tong in Dhimáli ⎩   pa and ta with the frequent nasal addition.

Hair.—T-shá-r in Kasikumak } Shá the root, t' prefix, and r suffix, as before
                               } in endless examples.
   Sá-b in Avar   } b final, the conjunct form of the ba, bo, suf-
   Sáb in Anzukh   } fix, so common in Tibetan.
   Sá-b in Tshari   }
   Shá-ben in Burmese
   Shá-m in Mrú   { M servile = b, and constantly commutable
   Chá-m in Magar   { with it.
   A-shó-m in Lepcha   { A prefix and m suffix, so common in Lepcha
   A-shá-m in Kámi   { that almost every adjective in particular is
   Lú-sá-m in Khyeng   { thus formed.
   Lú-sá-m in Khyeng   Lú = man. Hence lusam is human hair.

Head.—Tá-wi in Georgian } Wi servile = bi, vi, infra, compare wi-shá,
                            } voce salt.
   Tá-u in Khas.
   Thá-bo in Múrmi   Aspirate form of root, with bo suffix.
                         { Ng servile, the customary nasal appendage
   Tá-ng in Kiranti   { often superseded to other serviles.
                         { Gek servile. Compare git in Tshigit, voce
   Thá-gek in Limbu   { earth.
   Thau in Gyami   Aspirate root as in Murmi.

Ka-taú in Mou	Ka, the common prefix. Note that, in general, a servile may be known by the absence of accent, or of broad vowel where writing is used.
Káh. A-káh in Absnó	A servile, as in a-shom, a-sa, &c.
Za-ká in Altekesek	Za servile, the sa prefix in its usual Caucasian phase.
A-ká in Tangkul	
Ká-ng in Burmese	Ng servile.
Da ká-m in Gáró	Prefix da and suffix m, serviles.
K-ra in Gúrúng	Compare hra for hora, mse for me-se. So kra for ká-ra, the ra suffix absorbing the vowel of the root.
Kho-ro in Bódó	Ro servile with harmonised vowel.
Horn or } *Bone.—* } Ra-k-ka in Tsari	Ra root, ka servile adds k to it.
R-ka in Georgian	Servile ka absorbs the vowel of the root rá.
Rá-g-s in Lettic	G and s servile.
Rú-g in Slavie	G servile.
Ak-rá in Lazic	Ak servile as in ak-sa. It is the ka suffix changed per metastasin.
Rá, and Rú in Tibetan	Pure root, of which rá, rú, ró, ré, are the phases.
Rá-jo } Rú-ko } spoken ditto	Jo servile, and ka also, differential addenda.
Rá-k in Thochu A-ro in Rukheng	K final, conjunct form of ka suffix = prefixed k' in ak, which itself is merely metastatic ka.
Rou in Lhópa	
Ré-ra in Hórpa De-réng in Sóntál	Rá servile, or sing-song repetition of root. Dó servile, the da particle harmonised to vowel of root.
Am-rá in Sák	"Am" servile, metastatic ma.
A-ro-ng in Lepcha	A prefix, and ng suffix, serviles.
Rú in Gúrúng	Pure root.
Ró-s, Rá-ng in Magar	The roots for horn and bone are constantly the same, both in the Caucasian and Mongolian tongues. The senses are sometimes distinguished by an additional particle, as in Magar, which uses the prefix mi=human to demark bone. Just such is the form in lusan, voce hair.
Bone.—tLú-sa in Dido Lo-t in Shan	The root is lú, which is really only a varied pronunciation of Tibetan rú. But note how the servile t stands equally as prefix and suffix, just as does the servile r, voce stone.
Tsi-zyú in Suanic	Tsi = magar mi, just remarked on; zyú root, compare lusan, voce hair.
Gyó in Burmese Guro in Súnwár	Ró servile.
Mouth.—Mó-lé in Kubitsh	Mó the root, ló servile.
Mú-ra in Limbu	Mú the root; rú servile.
Mú-r in Khoibu	The same with ra conjunct.
Mbú-tu in Newári	Mbú, aspirate form of root, as mhó for mé, fire; nhi for ni, day, &c., &c.

Tooth.—dZéh in Circassian
    Zá-vi in Avar
    Sí-bi in Lesgian
    T-shi in Chinese
    Só in Lhópa
    Wá in Newári
    S-wá in Murmi
    S-wé in Thochu

D servile.
Z = s. Observe that in the Mongolian samples the conjunct form is used, swi, swá.
T' servile = d Circassian.

    Ti-swi in Gyárúng

Ti, the usual Gyárúng prefix harmonised to the root.

    Th-wá in Burmese
    Só in Tibetan
    Só in Serpa

Th servile.

    A-tha-wá in Sák

Repeats the Burmese prefix with an additional one.

    Sá-k in Gúrúng
    Sya-k in Magar

K servile, the *quasi* article so often noticed.

    Si-tong in Dhimáli

Tong is the ta suffix, with the nasal addition before noted.

    Syó in Hórpa

Intercalate y, as in khyi for khi, voce dog ; nha for na, voce ear.

Horse.—t'Shé in Circassian
    A-sé in Tuwash
    z-Ché-ni in Georgian
    Shé, só in Tibetan
    Shé in Khyeng
    Sá in Sák
    Sá-la in Newári

Sá, changing to só, is the root, the aspiration being neutral as to sense. Thus we have mhe or me, nhé or né, khi or ki, &c.

    Sá-dom in Sóntál

Dom, suffix, is the sexual sign.

Foot.—Pé-ché } in Georgian
    Pé-chi
    Pé-t-ché in Mantchu

Note the marvellous correspondence of this word with its Mantchu equivalent, roots and serviles tallying, as in katshu, voce hand.

    Po-g in Lesgian
    Pa-g in Chunsag
    Pa-g in Anzukh
    Pa-g in Khas
    Pá-li in Newári
    Bhá-lé in Gúrúng
    Bá-lé in Múrmi
    T'shé-ka in Andi
    Chhé in Horpa
    Ché-n in Anam
    Lip-ché in Manyak
    Lap-ché in Manyak = hand
    Chap-lap in Gáró
    Chhá in Gyami

The manner in which the words for hand and foot run into each other, *alike in the Mongolian and in the Circassian* series, is truly remarkable, so much so that it is difficult to distinguish the terms. The Georgian pé-ché, like the Mantchu pét-ché, in fact, blends the more special names for the lower and upper members, and so do the Manyak lipché and lapché, the latter word meaning hand, whilst chéli, hand, in Georgian, has the ché root of foot, with li servile.

    Ká-ch in Osetic
    Ko-ch in Tshetshentsh
    Ko-g in Ingush
    Ko-g, ko-ek, kwek in y, Mizjeji

Ká, kó, is the root in all these words and in the next one. Yet the two latter mean hand—a sufficient confirmation of what just said !

    Kó-da in Kabitsh

For dá suffix, see remarks on tshedá, voce earth, and compare ka-do and ka-do-t, infra.

    Kó-ng in Khyi
    Ka-ng in Tibetan

Final ng servile, as in many prior instances.

Ká-ng-lep in Lhópa   { Lep may be servile, or it may be the radical lip, lap, of lipché, lapché, &c.

Ká-n-du in Plé   Dú servile, also the annectant n.

Ká-do-t in Mon
Ká-do in Pasuko   { Mean leg, yet have indubitably the same root as the foregone, the do being servile, as in tshedo, voce earth.

Kó in Hórpa   { The nude root, vast numbers of such words occur in all the tongues alike.

A-kho in Kámi   A servile ; kho, the mere aspirate phase of ko.

Khó-khó-i in Dhimáli   { Root repeated, as in ká-ká, sky ; cho-cho, hot, &c.

Khyé in Burmese
Khau in Tunglhu
Khú-t in Khoibu
Khú-t in Khas
Khá-ng in Newári   Means leg.
Tá-i in Kubitsh
Tá-ra in Moasi   Ra, the common suffix.

A-tá-r in Sák   { Á, the servile, so frequent in Lepcha and Burmese ; r = ra.

Tá-mi in Gyárúng   Mi, servile, means human.
Ka-tá in Sóntál   Ta root. Ka, the common prefix.

Hand.—Ká-r in Tshari   { R servile, conjunct ra, as in the following words.

Kú-ch in Osetic   Ch servile ; compare só-ch, &c.

Kwé-r in Anzug
Ká-r in Sokpa
Gá-r in Mongol   { R final servile. Kú-er, observe here that kú, ká, gá, is the root throughout the whole series, and note the identity of the word in Súnwár and Anzak with reference to the alleged Greek etymon of kwér.

Ká in Kumi   The pure root.
A-ká in Kámi
Ta-kú in Sák   { Á and ta prefixes, serviles.

Kwé-li in Súnwár   { Li servile, as in ché-li, Georgian for hand. The word, therefore, is identically anzug, li being = r.

Kat-shú in Andi
Kat-shú in Plé   { Shú, the root. Kat, a double servile ; ka-ta, a marvellous accord !
Ché-li in Georgian
Ché in Mingrelian   { Such samples leave no doubt as to li being a servile.
Shi in Suanic
Shú in Gyami
Pat-shu in Pusako   Pat, double servile, pa-ta.
Chú-a-só in Plé   Compound of Andi shú and Mingrelian ché !!

Blood.—T'shá, shá in Absnó
Shá in Manyak
Sáh in Thochu
Séh in Hórpa
Syó in Gyami

Ta-shi in Gyárúng   { Compare the conjunct servile in the Absnó word, and observe that the so-called monosyllabic and polysyllabic character of languages has been made to rest on this frail foundation !

Thú in Osetic
Thwé in Burmese
Thé in Sák

{ Observe that the change of root from thú to thwé is exactly similar to that of kú to kwé, voce hand. This identity of plan prevailing throughout speaks trumpet-tongued for the truth of the affinity of races contended for.

Thé in Kasswi
Thó-i in Gáró
Ka-thi in Khyeng
A-thi in Kámi
Thá-k spoken Tibetan
I', é in Dido
Hí-n in Andi
I' in Khyi
Hí in Newári
Hí-t in Kong
Hí-ki in Dhimáli
Hí in Khoibu
Hí in Marúng
Hyú in Magar
Zí in Tshetshentsh
Zí in Ingush
Zí in Mezjiji
U'-sí in Súnwár
Chí in Gáró
A-zí in Champhang
A-zyé in Maram
Bí, pí in Avar
Ví in Lepcha
Wí in Mrú

Ka servile.
A' servile.
K, the articular suffix.

N servile.

T' servile.
Ki servile, the ka suffix harmonised.

U' servile as in ú-má, voce fire.

Skin.—fFé in Circassian
t'Ché-bi in Mingrelian
Ga-shi in Armenian
Pé in Kámi
Pí in Chinese
Fí in Gyami
Pí in Mrú
Ché-gú in Newári
Pá-ko in Lhópa
Pa-g in Tibetan

Gú servile, as in chan-gú, hot.

Skin.—Ká-ni in Georgian
Ka-n in Suanic
Kám-pa in Lhópa

Bi-k in Dido
Di-bi in Murmi
Di in Anam

Bi-gur in Bódó

{ Ka is the root passim. Ni and n, two phases of the same servile.
The "m" in kampa, a euphonic copula with reference to the labial of the root.
Pa, servile, the common ba, pa suffix of Tibetan.
Here is another sample of the substitution of servile for root, as fá for má, voce fire, &c.
Gu-ra, double servile. See remarks, voce ego = homo.

Tongue.—Bb sé in Circassian
rdZhé in Tibetan
Shé in Chinese

{ These repeated serviles bear direct reference to the very numerous senses of the sé root, and thus we learn the differential function of the serviles. See remarks, voce man.

Stone.—Dó-r in Osetic
rDó in Tibetan

{ Note again how the suffixed and prefixed serviles tally, the root (dó) being here indubitable. So Tsari chi-m and Jili m-chi, voce water.

Dóh in Lhópa
Dòh in Serpa
Dún-ga in Khas — Ga suffix, and annectant n, both servile.
Ló-di in Georgian
Lú-n in Khyeng — Root is ló, lú. The serviles have been too fre-
Lú-ng in Limbu — quently remarked on to need repetition.
Ta-lú-n in Sák — But note well how congruous they are, ab
Ló-ng in Lepcha — initio usque ad finem !
Ka-lú-n in Kámi

Great.—Di-di in Georgian — } Root repeated as in cho-cho, pyé-pyé, &c., &c.
Di-di in Mingrelian
Di in Tai.
Gé-dé-t in Bódó — Gé, the gá prefix euphonised ; t, conjunct ta.
Dá in Kuanchua
Dá-i in Anam — I final servile.
Dá in Plé
ta-Dhí in Newári — { Ta, the common prefix, and dhi, the aspirate form of the root, as mhé for mé, &c.

Three.—Sami in Georgian
Sami in Mingrelian
Jum in Lazic.
Sum, shum, sam, song, san, tham, tum, in all the Tibeto - Himálayan and Indo-Chinese tongues

Four.—pSí in Circassian — (Both root and servile are identical in all five
pShi in Abassian — words ; another marvellous instance of con-
bZhi in Tibetan — cord, capable, like the rest, of only one
Zhi in Lhópa — explanation.
Zhyi in Serpa — Intercalate y, as in the nouns.
Si, Si-kú in Gyami — Kú, a servile.
T'si in Siamese
T'sé in Shan — } T' servile, the common ta particle, conjunct.
Sí in Tai — The nude root.

Five.—Chú-ba in Circassian — { Chú, the root. Pat, a double servile, as in
Pat-chú in Talien — the Pasuko word for hand.

Eight.—Yat-sh in Tshetshentsh — } Final sh' servile. Another beautiful sample
Yat-sh in Limbu — of affinity.
g-Yet in Takpa — G servile = v, d, p, below.
Ka-yá in Kámi
Ba-yá in Tangus —) Yá, the root throughout the whole series, with
Ri-yá-t in Mrú — the common vocalic changes.
Re-yá in Kiranti
Yó in Súnwár
Or-yét in Gyárúng — Or servile, in Gyárúng.
Rwa in Georgian
Rú-a in Mingrelian — } Rá, rú, ré, is the root beyond doubt, though
Ré-ya in Kiranti — the Kiránti sample under both this and the
p-Ré in Murmi — preceding head shows how readily roots be-
Ryië in Hórpa — come serviles, and *vice versá*.
Rá-nit in Mrú

Nine.—bGú in Circassian
dGú in Tibetan

rGú-ré in Thochu

Gú-bi in Manyak
Gúh in Súnwár
Gú-n in Newári
Gó in Hórpa

Kan-gú in Gyárúng

{ Note again the wonderful accord of root and servile.
{ The ra particle here appears both as prefix and suffix.
Bi servile, as in Circassian.
The pure root.
N final, servile.
Nude root again.
{ Kan, double servile, ka-na = kam in kampa, voce skin.

Ten.—pShé-n in Circassian
Zhé-ba in Abassian
Swá-ba in Circassian = Sú-a
bChú in Tibetan
tSha-i in Burmese
hSú in Kámi
Chi in Gáró
ta-Chi in Gyárúng
Shi in Chinese
Sha-i in Tangus
ta-Shi in Tunghlhu
Sí-sú in Sák
t-Sa-u in Talien
p-Chi in Takpa
Chú in Serpa
Chá in Gúrúng
Chá in Lhópa
Sá-n-ho in Newári

} Sá, chá, is the root with the usual cycle of changes by aspiration and by alteration of the vowel; and to the root, moreover, are added the usual variety of servile appendages in some cases, whilst in others we have the nude root. All this is perfectly conformable to what has been seen in the nouns, and it follows, therefore, that the peculiarities commonly ascribed to the numbers do not really exist. The nature of the error, as derived from the examination of a few only of these tongues, may be appreciated by adverting to the remarks in the next paper on the differences presented to all *such* observations.

Chi-chi-bi in Manyak

{ Root repeated with ba suffix harmonised and *serial* as in Circassian. This feature of the numeral serviles is of frequent occurrence. See Essay on Bódó and Dhimáli for two good samples.

P.S.—The above paper has been considerably augmented in number of vocables, and in the analysis of them, since it was first presented to the Society, though not to the extent I had hoped and purposed if health had not failed me. If, however, the principles of the analysis (sufficiently revealed in their application and in the observations of this and the following paper) be sound, they may be easily carried as much further as is desired.

With regard to the soundness of those principles, I am fully prepared for censure of the presumption of attempting to analyse unknown tongues; prepared also to see many errors of detail detected, to afford apparent justification of such censure.

I can but solicit the particular attention of the candid to the perfect uniformity of the phenomena presented by the vocables, whether nouns, pronouns, or numerals, from the very beginning to the very end of my paper, and ask how this is to be explained, except upon those principles which a comparison of the numerous Himálayan tongues with each other and with that of Tibet led me first to detect, and which my opportunities of novel exploration beyond the Himálaya afforded me great advantages for testing the more extended application of? I have to regret that my investigations have been interrupted just when they were beginning to produce their ripest fruit, and to solicit the Society's favourable construction of what is now submitted as it is, rather than trust to an uncertain future for its improvement.

Supplement to the paper on the Mongolian Affinities of the Caucasians.

Since the above paper was hastily written I have obtained through the courteous aid of our Secretary the loan of the Mithridates and Asia Polyglotta. The ampler stock of Caucasian and Mongolian vocables thus placed within my reach (and illustrated too by occasional analytical notices) has needed only to be compared with my own large stores from the Himá-laya, Tibet, Sifán, Indo-China, and Tamúlian India, to satisfy me that the widest assumed scope of allophylian affinities might be placed on an unassailable basis. Again, a renewed reference to well-known works[*] has equally satisfied me that nothing short of a careful analytical demonstration would be accepted after the frequent insufficiently supported assertions and more or less superficial investigations that have been given to the world, even Dr. Latham's splendid panoramic view of the subject, though in fact well grounded on the opinions at least of numerous scholars,[†] and fortified, moreover, by the adduction of some special evidence[‡] either priorly overlooked or only recently accessible, having met with a cold, not to say a scoffing, reception.[§]

I therefore beg permission to withhold for the present the comparative list of Caucasian and Mongolian vocables which I had prepared to accompany the above paper on the resemblance of Circassian and Gyárúng pronouns, pledging myself

---

[*] Prichard, III. 13, *et seq.;* IV. 384 *et seq.* Report of the British Association for 1850, p. 174, *et seq.* Madras Journal for July 1837, and January, June, 1850.

[†] Klaproth, Dobrosky, Rask, Rolt, Norris, &c., &c.

[‡] Brown's Indo-Chinese Vocabularies, and Rosen's Caucasian Researches.

[§] "Edinburgh Review." Article, Bopp's Grammar.

that that list shall ere long be submitted to the Society, so amplified and analysed as to enable the scholar both to test and to extend the analogies sampled by the list.[*]

In the meanwhile, and with reference to the above paper, I subjoin some farther explanations which will not only serve to illustrate more fully its special topic (pronouns), but to show how continued attention to the general topic teems with fresh proofs of the soundness of the opinion that Caucasus is essentially Tartaric, and that the widest sense of the word Tartaric is the truest.

Klaproth, who was too well informed on the subject to insist on the Arian origin of the Caucasians generally, yet contended that the Osi were Indo-Germanic.

I shall soon be able, I think, to show that the elements and the mechanism of words in the Osetic tongue are purely Tartar, and that the very name of the race (O-si[†]), like that of the Georgians (Swan), proves their Tartaric progeniture, these names being significant, and significant in the special mode in use among the Tartar races. How Bopp could contend for the Arian origin of a race styling themselves Swan, and go to Sanscrit for Georgian etymologies, I am the more surprised, as swan in Sanscrit means dog, and we can hardly suppose that the Georgians or any other people would call *themselves* dogs, though their neighbours might so compliment them. Not to travel, however, beyond pronouns, I may mention that I have a long list of Mongolian equivalents for the Caucasian pronouns, and that, for instance, the má root in all its phases (má, mí, mó, mú), and in both its senses (nominal and pronominal), will be exactly matched by a long series of Tartaric equivalents. Nor are the so-called inflections or declensional signs less Tartaric than the roots; for instance, í or ní for the genitive; an, ang, náng, for the dative case; the í being Tibetan, Tákpa, Hórpa, &c.; the ní, Mongol, Mantchú, Túrki, Bódó; the an or ang, nan or nang, Dhimáli, Túrki, Ouigúr, &c. Here is a sample :—

---

[*] This has been done, I hope tolerably effectually, in the list as it now stands.

[†] See the note in the sequel on words with the ó and sí roots, o-as, o-su-ri, o-zu-r-ka, &c.

Pronoun I.

	Ouigúr.	*Osetic.*
N.	Ma, ma-n	Ma, ma-n
G.	Ma-ni-ng	Ma-ni
D.	Ma-nang ⎫ Máng-gé ⎭	Ma-nan

In Ouigúr the first na suffix is often dropped in the dative, and the second reiterated; and thus we have manggé for ma nang. Both changes are thoroughly consonant to the genius of these tongues, and are in perfect harmony with the alternative nominative form ma, or ma-n. The n final is here simply emphatic, and is the conjunct form of the na suffix. All these particles, in either their servile or radical character and function, may be used conjunctly and disjunctly, that is, with or without their vowel;* and all may be also augmented by various new elements or by reiteration, without affecting the sense in either case. Here are some samples of the disjunct and reiterated, or added ná, with one of these singular equivalents.

Pronouns I. Thou. He.

Tibetan	Na, nani	Khé, khéna	Khó, khóna
Esthonian	Ma, minna	Si, sinna	Tá, temma

We see here that the suffix má is equal to the suffix ná. So also is the suffix rá, which has been noticed as common, in form and function, to the Circassian and Gyárúng tongues, but which in fact has a wide and almost universal prevalence among these tongues, being attached like all the other serviles alike to pronouns, nouns, numerals, adverbs, and changing or dropping its vowel as well as taking the sur-suffix n, ng, without more alteration in its meaning than in the other cases of

---

* Here are some examples—k' ma-ri, man in Georgian, ka-mi, man in Kámi ; mú-rú, man in Súnwár, m-rú man in Mrú (root, mi, ma, mu); m-za, fire in Absné, mi-za, fire in Avar (root mi) ; s-mé, girl in Horpa, sá mé, girl in Thunglhu, sa-mi, girl in Burmese (root mé, mi). Note also the vocalic changes of roots and of the servile ra in ma-ri and mú-rú-and m-rú ; ka, servile of Georgian kmari, is dropped in Suanic maré, where again the servile ri becomes ré. In the Indo-Chinese tongues we have the ka prefix present and absent in this very word man, just as in the Caucasian, witness k' lun in kolun, being lun in Burmese. I may add l-ó-k in Tai and lé-g in Osetic, with the k vel g suffix (root, lú, ló, lé).

reiteration and elision and vocalic changes above illustrated in the pronominal roots and serviles, and in the nominal ones also, by the subjoined note.

In fact, such and much greater reiteration, cumulation, substitution and vocalic change, with concomitant contractions medial and final, affecting roots as well as serviles, are chief almost among the fundamental laws of these languages, and constitute the veil that has so long concealed their complete affinity. Who, for instance, would suppose namasini, or contractedly namsin, day, to be the same with ni, nyi, or nin? Show him, however, the intermediate forms nani, mani, and sini, and show him also this intercalate y and final n of the root, as well as this cumulation and these changes of the serviles, holding good in a great number of *other* instances, and you will carry him with you in this one and the rest, as I hope to do my readers by and by.

Here are some further pronominal illustrations of the ra suffix.

It attaches, as rá, to the first and second singular in Circassian, exclusively; to the second singular only in Gyárúng, as ré; to the third singular only in Mongol and Mantchú and Sokpo, as ré; to the third singular only in Gondi, as r; to the third plural only in Turki, as ré; to all three plurals, and to no singular in Rukheng, as ró; to the same in Burmese as dó (local difference and of pronunciation merely); to the first and third plural in Mongol as dá and dé respectively; to all three plurals in Takpa, and to them only, as rá; to all the persons singular and plural in Tibetan, as ráng, usually rendered by self; to the first and third plural in Ouigúr, as ár vel lár. The usual reading of olar, they, is o-lar, making lar a so-called plural sign. But if ol be "he," in Ouigúr and Turki, ol-ar must be "they." However, o is undoubtedly the root, as provable by numberless instances in the cognate tongues; and lá is an infix, and o-la-ra the true etymological analysis, as of the Turkish anlar and anlaré, the analysis is a-na-la-ra, á being here[*] the root (anggé, to him, a-ning, his), and na-la-ra, ser-

---

[*] The change of the root from ó to á in Turki and Ouigúr is continued in Mantchú, wherein it becomes í. Precisely in like manner we have mi, vel má vel mé, for five, and ni, vel na, vel né, for day, in Caucasus.

viles, whereof the first is the emphatic ná above illustrated; and ár, vel rá, vel lá-rá, the so-called plural sign or signs, though in my judgment it is to mistake the true genius and character of these tongues to give to any of their particles, except with extreme reserve, the attributes of strict grammar (declensional marks), or a precise independent signification such as self for ráng in Tibetan. Ráng is a compound of the rá and ang particles. The phases of the latter are á, an, ang, and the reflective or egoistic sense, such as it is (it is most like that of the Sanscrit swa), attaches, not to the compound ráng, but to the simple áng. In Bódó and Gáro and Hayu áng stands for the first personal pronoun; in Limbu and many other allied tongues it is the first possessive, in the form of á. In Tagala and Malayu á and áku represent the first personal, and ang is an articular prefix of the same drift. The first personal is an-ka in Kiranti and a-za in Osetic, prefix in all these instances, in others even of the same tongues it is a suffix;* but still, whether attached to pronouns, verbs, or nouns, and whether prefixed or postfixed or standing alone, as root or servile, it is apt to indicate a reflective character. This is the reason why it so constantly marks the possessive case, with or without a preposed particle; but if with one, usually the ná conjunct, which is only one phase, as ang-gé is another phase, of the repetition of itself; and this is also the reason why in so many of these tongues the áng suffix, when appended to verbs and their participles, designates the first person. Thus kazáng, I eat, kazángti, I who eat, I the eater, I eating, from the root zá, zó, in Gyárúng. Piré, give; pi-ráng or piráng-gé or piráng-né, give to me, in Limbú, from the root pi; davo, give, davóng, give to me, in Gyárúng, from the root va, vo. These forms are imperative. The indicative ones are similar, thus piré and dovo mean, you or he (quivis præter meipsum) gives; and piráng, dovong, I myself give, ang-né and ang-gé are equal, and are reiterations of the a, an, or ang particle.† Com-

---

* As ang is prefix or suffix, so is any other servile; for instance, the ká of anka, here cited; thus, k' mari, man in Georgian (mari in Suanic), and osurka, maid in Mingrelian (osuri in Lazic). See on to further note.

† In Sontal, Uraon, Ho, and Hayu, the ang becomes ing, and eng with the very same emphatic reiteration, viz., eng gna and ing ga.

pare ang-gé to me, in Turki and Ouigúr; and máng-gé to me in Ouigúr, with their equivalent má-nán in Osetic. Piré and Piráng show very pointedly that the reflective virtue resides not in the rá particle but in the áng particle. This case also exemplifies their conjunction. Má-náng is the disjunct form; máng, the conjunct; and máng-gé is the same, only more emphatic; máng, to me, máng-gé, to myself; and máng-né and máng-ré are both equivalents and emphasisers merely. So mini is mine; and mining-gé, my own, in Mongol and Mant-chú; the náng becoming níng euphonically to harmonise with the mi root. And, by the way, we may here, as in all the other derivatives, note the forthcomingness of the widely pre-valent mi root, though obsolete as a nominative in these two tongues, just as it is in the analogous sense of man (ego = homo plur. exem.) in Burmese, wherein, however, we similarly gather it from its derivatives, woman and child, mimma* and sa mi.

I have illustrated the pronominal and verbal uses of the rá particle, as well as explained its relation to rang. Here are some exemplifications of its nominal and other uses. I fear I shall weary the reader, but he must remember that what is true of this particle is true of all the particles; and that, whereas a confined view of the character and functions of this grand element of these tongues has led to very erroneous notions as to their general affinity, so a complete conception of the nature of the particles is the best guide to a just perception of that affinity. For instance, Rosen has dwelt on the unique character of the Circassian pronouns arising in good part out of the operation of the rá particle, and I, follow-ing him, have announced with reasonable surprise the fact that the same peculiarities are attached to the Gyárúng pronouns, whereas, in very truth, whatever he or I noticed in this respect as to the pronouns is equally true as to the nouns, adverbs, &c., and that not merely in the languages of the

---

* Compare Esthonian temma, supra, where suffix ma = emphatic na. All these tongues affect illiteration and consonantal as well as vocalic harmony to an extent quite perplexing, since each tongue has its fancies in this respect. Here má is a root.

Circassia and Gyárúng, but in every tongue from Caucasus to the Pacific. Here is the enumeration.

Ma-re, man, Suanic; ma-ri, man,* Georgian; ma-ro, man, Lepcha; mú-rú, man, Sunwár; m-rú, man, Mrú; ilé-ru, before, Turki; uz-ré, upon, Turki; herel-ri, man, Sontál.

Lan-ré, once, Tibetan; kyú-ré, river, Akúsh; thó-ré, to-morrow, Tibetan; wá-ran, rain, Osetic; mu-ran, river, Turki; mai-ran, arm, Mantchú; koöl-ron, child, Mongol; kho-rang, sky, Bódó; chák-reng, hand, Gáró; dí-rang, this, Serpa; dé-ring, to-day, Tibetan; ré-m-bú, man, Limbú; res-ga, where, Tibetan (samples of prefix); ús-rés, man, Gyárúng (sa added); rgu-re, nine, Manyak; ma-r, horse, spoken Chinese; ma-rhi, horse, Sokpa; gá-r, where, Tibetan; gá-rú, where, Tibetan; dé-r and dé-rú, there, Tibetan; ta-r-ti, cap, Gyárúng; ti-r-mi, man, Gyárúng; ok-ur, ox, Magyar; o-zu-r-ka, maid, Mingrelian (ka added, see note); o-sú-ri, maid, Lazic; u-er-ti, boy, Armenian; pu-r-ti, bird, Andi (ti, added, the rati suffix); do-r, stone, Osetic; teng-er, sea, Magyar; sha-r, ox, Mongol; khor, river, Avar; kú-er, hand, Anzúg; ka-r, hand, Tshari; ka-r, hand, Sokpo.

We thus see that the ra particle changes its vowel to the

---

* I here omit the ka prefix, with full warrant from usage :

See prior note on kmari and klún ; ka suffix in ozurka is the same thing and similarly omissible, witness osuri. Here ó is the root, = ú, meaning man, and it also takes the k prefix. Sú is the sa particle harmonised in its vowel to the root. It is a diminutive, so that o-sa, u-sa, or u-a-sa is child, and kusa is equally child. We have kusa and a-sa in Limbú, and u-a-sa in Aver, ú-s in Osetic, ú-as in Wogul, ú-er in Armenian ; sa in its capacity of diminutive means woman as well as child when added to any root for man, as ú or mi ; and hence Osetic ú-sá woman = mi-sa, Newári. Such and so concordant are *all* the elements. In Armenian uerti, child, erti vel rati being servile, it follows that the ú root for man may express juniors as well as adults, whilst the Gyárúng ús, man, and Osetic ús, woman, prove that the ú root expresses both sexes, meaning man-kind or the species man, and also that sa is not uniformly a diminutive but a synonym. This will be amply proved by and by, when the o-u-w and the sa, si, shi, roots for mankind are arrayed, and then it will be also seen that the name of the Osetic people is derived from two synonyms for man, and that, like tá-tá, or tshe-tshe-nsh, it is = Allemanni. The Caucasian puzzle as to us, ush, ushi, u-as, u-as-sa, u-er, o-su, o-zu, is solved by this explanation, and if we add the Murmi bú root for man (supra), we have the clue to the Caucasian bo-zo, bo-shi, bit-shi, bi-shi, for all which I have numerous Mongolian equivalents, thus po-zo in Pasuko, pu-sa in Karen, bu-cha in Tekpa, bi-sha and bi-shi in Bódó.

utmost (rá, ré, rí, ró, rú), takes the ang or other additional particle (ti, ka, sa), occupies the initial (res-ga), medial (pú-r-ti), or final (ka-r) position, or even both (r gú-re), with reference to the root, and lastly, blends itself with that root, dropping its vowel (gár), or stands apart, retaining its vowel (gá-rú); and all this without change or even modification of the meaning of the word as derived from the root further than a certain emphasising can be so termed, as kho-rang, *the* sky; ka-r, *the* hand.

Such elements of speech and all the serviles are essentially alike, can with little propriety be designated by our grammar terms or alleged to be conjugational or declensional marks, except with extreme caution. The essence of a grammatical rule or part of speech is generalisation; the essence of the function of these particles is the very opposite of specialisation; and thus it is that unlimited change of place and change of form belong to the latter, whilst nothing of the sort does or can belong to the former.

Of the habit of applying our grammatical terms to the elements of these tongues in central Asia without any apparent perception of their true character,* as noted in the south-eastern islands, I will give a sample from the Altaic group of languages.

The plurals of the Mantchú personal pronouns are thus stated and commented upon.

We.	*Ye.*	*They.*
Bé ⎱ Mousé ⎰	Souwé	Tését.

To this statement of the pronouns it is added that bé, sou wé, and tését constitute the ordinary series; that mousé is a sample of the dualistic form, and that it is regularly derived from mou, I, by the addition of the plural sign sé. Now it is quite true that the existence of a dual or rather of an inclusive

---

* To prove this it suffices to advert to Vater's derivation of the Caucasian kar and kwer, hand, from χειρ, and Klaproth's of Waran rainm for بَارَان and Máré from دْرِع. I shall give numerous Tartar equivalents for all three, and thus prove their roots to be respectively ka, wa, and ma, the ra, ré, and ran being serviles, or rather phases of one servile.

plural * is one of the characteristics of these tongues, and one
that prevails very generally from the Pacific to Caucasus. But
how it can be said that in the Mantchú tongue this inclusive
plural is formed regularly from the singular mou by means of
the plural sign sé, I cannot conceive, since a regular pluralising
particle would be uniformly applied and wear one shape,
whereas there is here in the three persons of the pronouns no
vestige of such attributes in the sé particle. The ordinary
" we " (bé) has no trace of this or other pluralising suffix ; the
ordinary " ye " (sou wé) has quite a different augment (wé) ;
and, lastly, the third person shows the sé particle indeed,
but with a foreign element or suffixed t (sét). Now surely a
grammatical rule must have some identity of character, what
it includes must be similar in form and application. But that
in the Mantchú pronouns the plurals cannot be said to be
regularly formed by the addition of sé, is self-apparent ; and if
we turn to any collated list of the pronouns of the Altaic
tongues generally, we shall immediately perceive the same
anomalies prevailing throughout this group of languages, and
affecting both the form and the application of all the particles ;
the áng suffix, for instance, being at once a genitive and a
dative sign in a single tongue (sanggé, of thee ; manggé, to
me, in Ouigúr), and also changing its form entirely in the same
case (meaning, of me ; sanggé, of thee) in that single tongue.
Look again beyond the Altaic group and you will see the
same anomalies. Everybody had noticed them in this or that
instance, and I have on this account myself demurred to the
use of the pronouns at all as a test of ethnic affinity. I am
now aware that I was misled by the authority of great names,
looking at these particles from a too grammatical point of
view. We first make the particles grammatical, and then we
declare them to be utterly anomalous ; the facts being, that
they are not strictly or uniformly grammatical, generally
speaking, nor perhaps anywhere so, except as the result of

This remarkable and arbitrary feature of a dual and two plurals I have already
detected in the Kuswar, Hayu, and Kiranti tongues of the Himálaya, and in the
Ho, Sontál, and Uraon tongues of Tamulian India. I need hardly add that the
same peculiarity belongs to the Tagalan and Alforian languages, as well as the
Altaic.

Arian influences (Tibetan, Newárese, cultivated Tamulian, and so in Caucasus); and that they obey their own law with perfect uniformity, and equally so when they attach to pronouns as to nouns and to verbs. That they are not strictly grammatical may be shown as well by their inconsistency with any intelligible conception of grammar,* as by the harmonious and simple elucidation they admit of according to their own norma loquendi or mechanism of speech.

Look, for instance, at the following explication of the Mantchú plurals above cited, or mouse, souwé, and tését. Mou-sé, we = I and thou; thus mou is the ma, mi, mo, root for I, obsolete as an ordinary nominative in this tongue, but found as such in most of the cognate series of tongues, and forthcoming even in Mantchú in all the oblique cases (mi-ni; mi-ninggé; mi-ndé); sé, again, is the sá, sé, sí, só root for thou, still extant as si in this tongue, as sé in Turki, as sá in Ouigúr, Finnic, and Esthonian, not to cite more instances from my ample store. Therefore mousé is beyond dispute a compound of two roots meaning I and thou. In like manner precisely is sou-wé, ye, a compound of the root above cited for thou, and of the o, ú, root for he; which latter, though obsolete in Mantchú, is extant in Turkí and in Ouigúr as o; in Magyar as óé or wé; in Circassian as úí or wí; in Garo as ú; in Dhimali, in Gyárúng, and in Thunglhu, as wá; in Newári, as wó, &c. &c. Sou-wé, ye, is therefore palpably a compound of the roots expressing thou and he; só changing to sou, as mó to mou, and óé to wé; the é moreover being a synonym of ó, and a phase of the í root, found alike in this very Mantchú tongue and in Circassian; so that the Magyar óé, Circassian úí, and Mantchú í, with other instances just cited, lead irresistibly to

---

* There should be, though there is not, a higher sort of grammar capable of reconciling Tartaric forms of speech with our own ; that is, of showing the equivalency of each to the other. In the meanwhile the use of our technical terms in discussing the Tartar tongues is natural, almost inevitable ; and at all events I beg earnestly to disclaim all purpose of censure whilst attempting to elucidate. There is much grammar in these tongues, but, as I think, borrowed, and shown to be so as well by reference to the much larger and unchanged portion of the languages as by the unharmonising character which the grammatical element wears when it exists.

wé = he in Mantchú. Therefore souwé, ye, is literally thou and he; as mousé, wé, is literally I and thou. In like manner the third plural or they, tését, is undoubtedly a compound of té = he, and sé = thou. The sé root has the tá particle added as a conjunct servile (sé-t), according to a rule of universal operation in these tongues. Té is extant in Mantchú in the sense of he. It has the rá particle suffixed and harmonised in its vowel to the vowel of the root (téré), also according to a universal rule governing these particles; and sé, in the sense of thou, is likewise extant, as sí in Mantchú, as sé in Turki, as sá in some one of its phases, in short (sá, sé, sí, só, sú) in twenty of these tongues. Therefore té-sé-t, or they, is literally he and thou; and the whole of the three plurals are constructed upon precisely the same principle thus :—

> Mou-sé = we = I and thou.
> Sou-wé = ye = thou and he.
> Té-sé-t = they = he and thou.

In like manner the Mongolian plurals, bi-dá, tá, and té-dé-t, might be analysed by means of the Tibetan demonstratives, dí and dé, with their analogues in allied tongues, and shown to be nothing more than reiterate pronouns of the singular number, and also that the dá, dé is no more a plural sign than the third phase of this particle or dou (dá, dé, dí, dó) is a dative sign, though widely as erroneously so regarded (just as De Cörös regards the equivalent ra* particle), witness t sé-do, to the earth; ko-dá, to the foot, &c., in the Caucasian group, according to Vater. In truth, the dá particle is in these latter instances a servile, not a radical, as is the sé before given; but apparently neither radical nor servile can be regarded in strictness as a declensional sign of case or of

---

* De Cörös, pursuant to his view of the rá particle, as a dative case sign, translates namgar in one instance and another, to heaven. Now, nam is the sun, and kha vel gá is place; and that the ra suffix only emphasises the sense of khá vel gá may be shown by a familiar pair of examples. Gár vel gáro and takla-khár are the names of two well-known places in Nari, gár meaning *the place* or fort, or headquarters of its district; and takla-khár, *the* place, or fort, or sadr, of Takla. Again, the thirteenth divisions of the spire of a chaitya are called chuksum-khár in Tibetan = trayodas bhuvan in Sanscrit, *i.e.*, *the* thirteenth mansion.

number. Nor in the great majority of these tongues from Caucasus to Oceanica do these or the other particles * ordinarily fulfil the necessary conditions of such a sign, with the scant and obvious exceptions before noted. The sá radical and the dá servile are both alike particles, and as such subject to the laws regulating particles, according to which all their alleged anomalies in either character can be explained, including not only every vocalic change incident to them in both capacities alike, but also that substitution whereby they interchange functions and the root becomes a servile, or the servile a root. Thus, for example, the sé particle is undoubtedly a root in the instances cited above, and it is as undoubtedly a servile in the Magar tongue, wherein í-sé means this, and ó-sé, that; í and ó being the near and remote demonstratives, with sé as a servile affix, answering exactly to the Georgian s in í-s, he. Compare Circassian í with Georgian í-s, and the servile and equivalent character of the sa suffix in these instances drawn from the Magyar and Georgian tongues will be at once apparent, and it will be also perceived how the alleged plural sense is here neither admissible nor possible, though the particle be assuredly the identical one to which in the Mantchú tongue the plural quality is attributed.

In explaining the Mantchú pronouns I have included almost all that need be said of the Circassian third personal singular, or ú, í, with its change to t' conjunct, as in t-ab, his father.

If we consider the ú, the í, and the t as all radicals, we may yet find numerous equivalents for each in that sense; and if, again, we regard the t' as a servile superseding the radical úí or wí, we may find abundant instances of such supersession alike among the Caucasian and the Mongolian tongues, as má, ma-fa, fá, fire; bí, dí-bi, dí, skin; sá, bá-sá, bá, cow; and many more for which I must refer to the forthcoming analysed list of vocables.

With regard to Mongolian equivalents for the radicals ú, í,

---

* The chá suffix in ma-ch, we, Osetic, is called a plural sign. What is it in sa-ch, earth? Probably what it is in a-ch, one, Circassian; viz., a servile with the usual differential function.

and ta, in the sense of he, the third personal, the subjoined
enumeration must suffice at present.

U´, Circassian = ú in Gáró; ú in Sontál; ó (óé) in Magyar;
ó in Ouigúr and Turki; wó in Newári; wá in Gyárúng, in
Dhimali,* and in Thunglhu. I´, Circassian = í in Mantchú;
í in Sontál; í in Burmese (this); é in Magyar (óé); é in
Kalmak; é in Lazig; í-s in Georgian; í-sé in Magar; í-tu in
Tagalan. Tá, Circassian = té in Mongol; té in Mantchú; tá
in Esthonian; tá in Chinese; thá in Gyámi; thí in Gúrúng;
thé in Murmi; thú in Burmese.

If, again, we take the Circassian ú, í, as one root and word,
we have parallels for it in the Magyar óé, similarly taken, and
in all the wá roots should we read wí (w for ú).

With regard to the Gyárúng wa, tú, which I have compared with the Circassian ú, í, changing in composition to tá,
it is very important to observe that if wa, tú, and ú, í, be considered as compounds of two synonymous roots, according to
the above detailed exposition of roots, then that such reiterated
pronouns are completely conformable to the genius of these
tongues, and as such harmonise perfectly with the preceding
exposition of the plurals. These tongues, in fact, revel in
cumulation, pronominal and nominal, varying as to the exact
applications of the emphasised or reiterated pronouns,† but

---

* The perfect agreement of the Circassian and Dhimali in regard to the singular of the third personal, ú being he, in both tongues, renders the proximate
agreement of the perplexing plural, ú-bert and ú-bal, very interesting. I have
tried the analysis in several ways, but have not succeeded to my own satisfaction;
but I submit the following.

U´-ba-rt = they = he and he; one he being the ú above elucidated, and the
other, a synonymous bá, bé, bi root, such as bí actually is in Bódó; rt, servile;
the ra and ta suffixes conjunct.

U´-ba-l = they = he and he, as before. The juxtaposition of the Bódó and
Dhimal tribes renders the adoption of the bí root from Bódó likely in this instance.
It is, however, a word and root widely diffused, and used as a noun and pronoun
also. Final l´, servile.———The Suanic al, he, and the Ouigúr and Turki ol,
he, and ol-ar, they, are very suggestive, as also the Turkish and Ouigúr bí, and
the Sokpo bú in abú, with all the numerous words for man having the bí root,
as bi-shi, juvenis, alike in Turki and in Bódó. Nominal and pronominal roots are
so apt to coincide that I have a long list of coincident roots for ego = homo : for
instance, the mi root, and ta root, and sa root, and ba root.

† See Mith. voce Turki, i. 467 *et seq.*, and Essay on Koch, Bódó, and Dhimal,
p. 120, and De Cörös' Grammar, p. 65, Crawfurd's Malayan Grammar, Phillips'
Sontal Grammar, and Brown's Asam Grammar.

preserving a general overruling similitude, of which the follow-ing instance from a Himálayan and a Caucasian tongue is too singular to be omitted. In Georgian the í root for the third personal singular, or he, becomes, by such accretion gradually augmenting, first í-s, and then í-ti-ná; and in Magar the same root with the same sense (ille iste) becomes í-sé and í-sé-ná, according as more or less of emphasis and dis-crimination is needed. Again, the Georgian ti in iti na is the Burmese thí in í-thi, a word compounded of two syno-nyms, both meaning this (ille), and conjointly equivalent precisely to iséná as well as itina in Magar and Georgian respectively. Thú, again, means he, the third personal, in Burmese, and this word, which is merely another phase of the thá particle (thá, thí, thú, thó—which last signifies that, and is Tibetan), brings us back to the Tagalan í-tú and the Gyárúng wa-tú, every particle, whether used in a primary or secondary sense, taking the aspirate indifferently (mé, mhé, fire; ni, nhi, day; ká, khá, sky; et cæt., ad libitum).

Now, if we look again at the Gyárúng wa tú through the medium of the Malayan and Tagalan í tú and the Circassian rí í and tá, all but the last equally involving a double pro-nominal root and single sense, we shall see in this identical composition and identical idiomatic use of the third personal pronoun, illustrated on all sides as they are by Altaic, Himá-layan, and Indo-Chinese equivalents, reproducing every form and phase of the roots, a marvellous proof of the affinity of all the tongues. But this is not all, for the Circassian ú and í, commutable to t, derives the highest and complete illustration from another and most interesting quarter, to wit, the unculti-vated Tamulian tongues of India, amongst which the Sontál exhibits both ú and í for the third personal pronoun, as well as their commutation into t,[*] whilst the Gondi has ú (w) similarly commutable. For the proof of these most remark-

---

[*] The transposableness of the particles in these tongues has been already stated and abundantly proved. With this hint, look at the following wonderful sample of analogous structure : t-ab, his father, in Circassian ; apa-t, his father, in Sontál. It is needless almost to add that the word for father is ab in the former tongue, apa in the latter. Not one of Bopp's celebrated Arian affinities surpasses the above in beauty and interest.

able coincidences I refer the student to the works of Phillips and Driberg, merely observing in conclusion that it is but a sample of those analogies derivable from the same interesting quarter which I have already made good progress in the development of, and which when fully exhibited will go far to confirm the conviction that the Tartaric family is one and indivisible from the Caucasus to the Pacific.

The prospect of a reunion of all the Tartars suggests the consideration of a fitting designation for the whole; and, whatever my leaning towards the term Scythian,* from veneration for the father of history who first introduced this mighty herd to our view, I prefer upon the whole the more familiar appellation Tartar; first, because it has a sense as ample as our present requirement, in which respect it has no advantage over Scythian; second, because it has an etymological significance thoroughly indigenous and in the highest degree appropriate, as well with reference to the structure of those tongues by the dissection of which we have come at a knowledge of the whole scope of Tartar affinities, as with regard to that characteristic idiom according to which the name of a tribe is the name of our species. Tá means man in a score of extant tongues; and tá designates numerous extant tribes stretching from the Altai to the Gulf of Siam, whilst the same or equivalent names prevail throughout the Mongolian countries and in Caucasus;† and, lastly, the reitera-

* Essay on Koch, Bódó, and Dhimal, preface, pages 8, 9, where the reader may see that seven years ago I had a strong presentiment of what I now hope to demonstrate.

† Tahá-ri, tahé-tahé-nah, &c., come from the tá and sá roots for man, and are seen in similar combination, being synonyms, in the Chinese and Georgian tsé meaning man, whereof tsé-s is a diminutive. The Chinese call the Tartars indifferently thá-thá and thá-tsé, and so do the Newárs of Népál, whilst ta-i, ta-i-mó, ta-i-lúng, ta-i-né, ta-i-yó, names of tribes from Asam to the Ocean, are all not only tá but tá-tá, since the second syllable is in all a synonym, and therefore as equivalent as tahé-tahé and tá-tá, which are reiterations. As instances, familiar to us in India, of a tribe-name signifying also man in the language of that tribe, I may mention a-nam, mru, k lun, ka mi, ku-mi, kong, lau, mó-n, mo-i, bar-ma. These are simple. Mi-shi-mi, mú-r-mi, &c., are compound. Occasionally, as in Burmese, the root may be obsolete in the human sense; but it will always be found in its derivatives or in the proximate tongues, leaving the principle of gentile nomenclature indisputable. In Mishimi we have the mi and

tion whereby *the* Tá, or Zenghis' clansmen came to be called tá-tá, vel thá-thá (men pre-eminently, quasi Allemanni) is a normal sample of one of the chief constructive principles of these tongues. Wherefore I would abide by that mediæval designation by which all the races beyond the confines of Europe have been known to Europe in modern times, and which from and after the middle ages superseded the classical term Scythian—a term of as wide import as the other and so far equally fitting, but now laid aside, and never so etymologically just as Tartar, the very r of which word, though carped at by half-informed critics, is in fact thoroughly in accordance with the jus et norma of Tartaric speech, everywhere from Oceanic to the Caucasian region.

shi roots for man, the former reiterated. In Múrmi we have the mi root reiterated in different phases (mú and mí). In Burma we have a third phase of the same root (má) with the bá root and synonym preceding it ; and lest this etymology should startle my readers, I will add that this very word barma means man in the Magar tongue, that is, in one of those Himálayan tongues whose close affinity to the Burmese language I have lately shown.

SECTION VIII.

PHYSICAL TYPE OF TIBETANS.

Pénjúr of Lhassa, 30 years old.

				ft	in	
Total height,	.	.	.	5	$9\frac{1}{2}$	
Length of head,	.	.	.	0	$9\frac{1}{2}$	Rectilinear measurements.
Girth of head,	.	.	.	1	$10\frac{1}{4}$	
Crown of head to hip,	.	.	.	2	5	
Hip to heel,	.	.	.	3	$4\frac{3}{4}$	
Breadth of chest only,	.	.	.	1	4	by curve.
Sh. point to sh. point,	.	.	.	1	5	
Arm and hand,	.	.	.	2	$6\frac{1}{8}$	
Girth of chest,	.	.	.	3	0	
Girth of arm,	.	.	.	0	11	Rectilinear measurements.
Girth of forearm,	.	.	.	0	$9\frac{3}{4}$	
Girth of thigh,	.	.	.	1	$6\frac{1}{2}$	
Girth of calf,	.	.	.	1	$1\frac{1}{2}$	
Length of foot,	.	.	.	0	10	
Breadth of foot,	.	.	.	0	3	
Length of head,	.	.	.	0	$7\frac{3}{4}$	
Breadth of head,	.	.	.	0	4	

A fine young man, but low in flesh from sickness, and the muscles flaccid. Colour a clear ruddy brownish or brunette rather deep hued, as dark as any of the Cis-Himálayans and as most high-caste Hindus. No red on cheeks, which are sunk and hollow. Hair moderately coarse, black, copious, straight, shining, worn long and loose, divided from the top of head. Moustache very small, black. No symptom of beard nor any hair on chest; sufficient on mons martis, where it is black, and on armpits also. No whiskers. Face moderately large, sub-ovoid, widest between angles of jaws, less between cheek-bones, which are prominent, but not very. Forehead rather low and narrowing somewhat upwards; narrowed also transversely, and much less wide than the back of head. Frontal sinus large, and brows heavy. Hair of eyebrows and lashes sufficient. Former not arched, but obliquely descendant towards the base of nose. Eyes of good size and shape, but the inner angle decidedly dipped or inclined downwards, though the outer not curved up. Iris a fine deep, clear, chestnut brown. Eyes wide apart, but well and distinctly separated by the basal ridge of nose; not well opened, cavity being filled with flesh. Nose sufficiently long and well raised even at base, straight, thick, and fleshy towards the end, with large wide nares nearly round. Zygomæ large and salient, but moderately so. Angles of the jaws prominent, more so than zygomæ, and face widest below the ears. Mouth moderate, well formed, with well-made closed lips hiding the fine, regular, and no way prominent teeth. Upper lip long. Chin rather small, round, well formed, not retiring. Vertical line of the face very good, not at all bulging at the mouth, nor retiring below, and not much above, but more so there towards the roots of the hair. Jaws large. Ears moderate, well made, and not starting from the head. Head well formed and round, but larger à parte post than à parte ante or in the frontal region, which is somewhat contracted crosswise, and somewhat narrowed pyramidally upwards. Body well made and well proportioned. Head well set on the neck, neither too short nor too thick. Chest wide, deep, well arched. Shoulders falling, fine. Trunk not in excess of proportionate length compared with the extremities, nor they compared with the trunk and whole stature. Arms rather long, within four inches of knees. Legs and arms deficient in muscular development from sickness. Hands and feet small and well formed, with instep hollow and heel moderate. Toes not spread, nor splay foot. Mongolian cast of features decided, but not extremely so, and expression intelligent and amiable.

DARJEELING, 30*th April* 1848.

SECTION IX.

THE ABORIGINES OF CENTRAL INDIA.

AT the close of last year I had the honour to submit to the
Society a summary view of the affinities of the sub-Himálayan
aborigines. I have now the honour to submit a similar view of
the affinities of the aborigines of Central India. The extra
copies of the former paper which were sent to me by the Society
I forwarded to Colonels Ouseley and Sleeman, to Major Naple-
ton, Mr. Elliot of Madras, and other gentlemen, with a request
that they would get the vocabulary filled up from the languages
of the several aborigines of their respective neighbourhoods.
The three former gentlemen have obligingly attended to my
wishes, and I am assured that Mr. Elliot also is busy with the
work. Of the seven languages which I now forward the comparative vocabulary of, the three first came from Chyebossa,
where Colonel Ouseley's assistant, Captain Haughton, prepared
them; the fourth and fifth direct from Colonel Ouseley himself
at Chota Nagpur; the sixth from Bhaugalpur, prepared by the
Rev. Mr. Hurder; and the seventh from Jabbalpur, where
Colonel Sleeman's principal assistant drew it up for me.
  The affinities of these tongues are very striking, so much so
that the five first may be safely denominated dialects of the
great Kól language; and through the U'ráon speech we trace
without difficulty the further connection of the language of the
Kóles with that of the "hill men" of the Rajmahal and Bhaugalpur ranges. Nor are there wanting obvious links between
the several tongues above enumerated—all which we may class
under the head Kól—and that of the Gónds of the Vindhia,
whose speech again has been lately shown by Mr. Elliot to have
much resemblance both in vocables and structure to the cultivated tongues of the Deccan. Thus we are already rapidly
approaching to the realisation of the hypothesis put forth in
my essay on the Koch, Bódó, and Dhimál, to wit, that all the

Tamulians of India have a common fountain and origin, like all the Arians; and that the innumerable diversities of spoken language characterising the former race are but the more or less superficial effects of their long and utter dispersion and segregation, owing to the savage tyranny of the latter race in days when the rights of conquest were synonymous with a license to destroy, spoil, and enslave. That the Arian population of India descended into it about 3000 years ago from the northwest as conquerors, and that they completely subdued all the open and cultivated parts of Hindostan, Bengal, and the most adjacent tracts of the Deccan,* but failed to extend their effective sway and colonisation further south, are quasi-historical deductions† confirmed daily more and more by the results of ethnological research. And we thus find an easy and natural explanation of the facts that in the Deccan, where the original tenants of the soil have been able to hold together in possession of it, the aboriginal languages exhibit a deal of integrity and refinement, whilst in the north, where the pristine population has been hunted into jungly and malarious recesses, the aboriginal tongues are broken into innumerable rude and shapeless fragments. Nevertheless those fragments may yet be brought together by large and careful induction; for modern ethnology has actually accomplished elsewhere yet more brilliant feats than this, throwing upon the great antehistoric movements of nations a light as splendid as useful. But if I hold forth, beforehand, the probable result of this investigation in the shape of a striking hypothesis in order to stimulate the painstaking accumulator of facts, and even intimate that our present materials already offer the most encouraging earnest of success, I trust that the whole tenor and substance of my essay on the Koch, Bódó, and Dhimál will suffice to assure all candid persons that I am no advocate for sweeping conclusions from insufficient premises, and that I desire to see the ethnology of India conducted upon the most extended scale, with careful weighing of every available item of evidence that is calculated to demonstrate the unity,‡ *or otherwise,* of the Tamulian race.

---

* Telingána, Gujerat, and Maharáshtra, or the Maratta country.

† Brachmanes nomen gentis diffusissimæ cujus maxima pars in montibus (Ariana Cabul) degit, reliqui circa Gangem. Cellarius, Geogr.

‡ This unity can, of course, only touch the grander classifications of language, and be analogous to that which aggregates, for example, Sanscrit, Greek, Teutonic, and Celtic.

COMPARATIVE VOCABULARY OF THE ABORIGINAL LANGUAGES OF CENTRAL INDIA.

English.	1. Sinhbhúm Kol.	2. Sóntál.	3. Bhúmíj.	4. U'ráon.	5. Mándala.	6. Rájmahali.	7. Góndi.
Air	hoïyo	hoyó	hoyó	tháká	hoyóh	táké, táphó	bárbá ítá
Ant	múí	múni	múó	póh	múnj	pók	patté
Arrow	sarh	sarh	sarh	chár	sár	chár	jíyatár
Bird	óó	chénó	chénó	órak	úró	pój	itté
Blood	myún	myún	myún	khéns	myún	kéní	nattúr
Boat	dúngá	dúngá	dúngá	dóngá	dóngá	návé, H.	dóngó
Bone	jáng	jáng	jáng	khóchal	jáng	kochal	hárá
Buffalo	kérá	kurú	kérá	mánkhá	bhítkil	mángó	háfíyá
Cat	bilaï, H.	bilaï, H.	bilaï, H.	bírkha	púsaí	bérgó	bílaí
Cow	gúndí	páeí	gaï, H.	údú	úrí	oí	dhóríyal
Crow	ká	gaï, H.	kóvá	khákhá	kóvá	kákó	káwá
Day	aúgi, mí	kahú	dín, H.	álláh	sing	dínó, H.	pattí
Dog	sétá	sing, mí	sétá	alla	sétá	allay	naí
Ear	látár	sétá	látár	khebda	látár	kheetway	kawí
Earth	óó	látár	óó	khókhól	wathó	kékal	dharti, S.
Egg	pítá	ót	pító	bí	billí	kírpan	méj
Elephant	háthí, H.	billi	háthi	háthí, H.	háthí, H.	atí, H.	yéje
Eye	mét	háthí, H.	mét	khán	mód	kánó	kank
Father	apáng	mét	bábá	bábó	apáng	ábá	wáwó
Fire	sengel	bábá	sengel	chík	singil	chichó	kis
Fish	háká	sengel	háí	injo	háká	mín	mín
Flower	bowh	hakú	baha	phúp	baha	púp	phúl, H.
Foot	kátá	bóhá	kata	dappó	kata	kév	kalk
Goat	méram	sáptíjánga	méram	óra	méram	cró	bókra, H.
Hair	úb	méram	úb	chítí	úp	talí	róbáng
Hand	thí	úb	thí	khókháh	tíhí	sésú	kaík
Head	bú	thí	búho	ktk	bóhú	kúpó	talla
Hog	súkri	búho	súkri	kiss	súkri	kis	paddí
Horn	dríng	súkri	derríng	nárág	daríng	márg	singh, H.
Horse	sadhaın	darring	sadhaın	ghoro, H.	sadaan	goro, H.	kóndaul?
House	óó	sadhaın	úrúú	erpá	úrúú	áwá	rón

English.	1. Sinhbhúm Kól.	2. Sóntál.	3. Bhúmíj.	4. Uráon.	5. Mundala.	6. Rájmaháli.	7. Góndi.
Iron	médh	mérhad	mérhd	panná	marhan	lóhá, H.	kachchi
Leaf	sákam	sakam	sikkam	átkhá	sikam	átgé	áki
Light	maskal	marsal	tetaytárra	billi	marsa?	ávoli	bérachí
Man	hó	horh	horro	alla	horl	málé	mánébábá maw-sal
Monkey	sarrha, gári	haná, gári	gari	bandra, H.	bandra, H.	mágé	bandara, H.
Moon	chándú, H.	chando, H.	chandú, H.	chando, H.	chandú, H.	bilpé	chanda, H.
Mother	éáng	i yo	nai, H.	ayyo	éngan	áyá	aval
Mountain	búrú	búrú	búrú	partá	bárú	tóké	dongar
Mouth	á	mocha	alang	iái	mocha	soro	údí
Moschito	siki	sikri	látí	bhúséndi	bhúséndi	minko'	misi
Name	nútúm	nútúm	núrná	nám, H.	natúm	námi, H.	batti paról
Night	níndhá*	níndhá	nídhá	nákhá	nidak	nákó	narkaát
Oil	súnúm	súnúm	súnúm	issúm	súnam	isgné	ning
Plantain	kodal	kaira	kodal	kérá, H.	kélá, H.	kalvi	kérá, H.
River	garra	garra	garra	khár	garra	caret	dóndá
Road	horra	hor	horren	dáhári	hórah	sarké, H.	sarrí
Salt	báláng	báláng	búláng	békh	bálang	békó	sabbar
Skin	úr	harta	úr	chapta	harta	chámé, S.	tól
Sky	sirma	sirma	rimmil	mírkhá	sirma	sarángé	bádár? H.
Snake	bing	bing	bing	nír	bing	nér	tarás
Star	ípil	ípil	ípil	binká	ipil	bindéké	suká
Stone	dirri	dirri	dirri	pakhná	diri	chaihó	tóngí
Sun	singi	sing marsal	singi	dharmi†	singi	bér	sádraj, H.
Tiger	garúmkúla	kúla	kúlá	lakhrá	kúlah	sad	púlli
Tooth	dáthá, H.	dátha	dátta	páll	dátá, H.	páll	palk
Tree	dárú, S.	dárú	dárú	man	dárú, S.	man	mará
Village	hattá	athú	hathújé	padda	hátá	kép	nár
Water	dáh	dáh	dáh	úm, chóíp	dhá	ám	yér
Yam	merúmtosang	dá sáng	sángá	álú, H.	árá, H.	caret	náska kángda
I	aing	ingé	ing	enan	ing	en	máná

* A misapplication, probably, of the Hindi word for sleep or sleepy.

† Sanscrit? and implies that the sun is worshipped.

	um	ungó	am	nien	am	nin	imna
Thou	ini	úní	ini	asán	inni	áth	caret
He, she, it	caret	caret	caret	en	allágó		caret
We	caret	caret	caret	ású	inkoghi	nam, om	úndó
Ye	caret	caret	caret	caret	ánkó	nina	caret
They	i yan	ingréá	inya	ónghi	jhátaná	ásabar, áwar	nává ángdo
Mine	úmmá	ami	úmmá	njenghi	amátaná	ongki	návútúránd
Thine	ini	únéá	aigé	ásghi	annerá tana	niongki	oná
His	alléá	alléá	ábásaban	émbi	ahúá tana	áhiki	mábaļ
Ours	appéá	appé	caret	ássghi	apiá tana	émki, námki	ná liilé
Yours	énkóá	únkúró	caret	caret	ankóá tana	nimki	oná ánd
Theirs				caret		ásá bériki	
One	mí	midh	moy	úntá	mtá	ort.+ oudong pándong, kivong, twr. mákis in dual	únddi
Two	barria	barria	barria	enótan	baria		raná
Three	apia	piá	apia	manótan	apia		máná
Four	úpúnia	ponia	úpúnia	nákhótan	úpmá		nálá
Five	moya	moné gótang	monaya	panjé gotan, H.	monia		saijhan
Six	túria	túrúi gótang	túrúyá	sé gotan, H.	túrisá	Same as Hindi and Urdu	sáróng
Seven	íyrá	fair gótang	sáth, H.	sat gotan, H.	sáth, H.		yénú, yétá
Eight	irlia	iral gótang	áth, H.	áté gotan, H.	áth, H.		anamúr
Nine	aréá	aró gótang	nou, H.	nó gotan, H.	nókó, H.		nó, H.
Ten	geléá	gél gótang	das, H.	das gotan, H.	dasgo, H.		pada
Twenty	hissi	caret	caret	bís, H.	bísa, H.		bísa, H.
Thirty	hissi geléá	hissi gél gótang	moy hissi dasti	dérh kori, H.	tís, H.		tís, H.
Forty	bárhissi	bár hissi	bár hissi	bísáénd	bár hiassidasgo		chális, H.
Fifty	moy hissigil	bár hissi gél	bar hissi dasti	dharihé kóri	bár hissidasgo		pachás, H.
A hundred	moy hissi	monay hissi	sou, H.	sé, H.	midaso		só, H.
Of	caret	caret	caret	ye	ki, H.	As in Urdu	orá, bará
To	tó	tó	caret	gai	kó, H.	By affix to the noun	baina
From	tó	tó	caret	tó	sé, H.		caret
By, instr.	tótó	táló	caret	caret	átam		túrsé, dúrsé
With, cum.	táli	táli	caret	sang, H.	gatt, minna	gúni	sang
Without, sine	banóá	banóá	caret	ni	sáiná	walo	bigúr

* Gótang is surplusage and Hindi.

† Ort. to human beings; others to diverse things.

English.	1. Sinhbhúm Kôl.	2. Sóntál.	3. Bhúmij.	4. U'ráon.	5. Múndala.	6. Rájmaháli.	7. Góndi.
In	ré	ré	caret	úlá	bhitar, H.	By affix to the noun	imitté
On	ré chitan	ré	caret	úlá	caret	"	inga
Now	ná	nítging	caret	úkú	náhá	únéké	ada
Then	en	ena, úní	caret	pisú	inam	úní	vang pur
When?	chúllá	tis	caret	éká héré	chúélo, chimto	I kono	naiú
To-day	ná	teheng	tising	inam	tihin	iné	ningnai
To-morrow	gúphá	gúphá	gúphá	nélá	gappá	lélé	nara khai
Yesterday	hólá	holánó	hóla	chólé	hólá	chéwr	ingabaré
Here	néthé	noéthi	néthai	isaan	nithi	ino	caret
There	entai	banati	éta thúí	háhá	únthi	úno	vagá
Where?	okotai	okáti	oko thúí	éksan	úthi	ikéno	parró
Above	sirma	sirma	sirma	méyah	chaitan	méehé	khálai mandar, H.
Below	súbá	phér	athé	kiyah	látúr	pissi	bćhte mandar, H.
Between	talaré	talaré	talaré	majin	talar	mújji, H.	bahiro mandar, H.
Without, outside	rachúré	rachúré	rachúré	búhari, H.	búhari, H.	dwúri	núpá mandar
Within	bhitur, H.	bhitar, H.	bhitar, H.	úlá	bhitar, H.	úlé	langkak mandar
Far	sanginiya	sangiuiya	súngiya	gécha	sangin	géchi	múntosa mandar
Near	nia	súrgí	járéyá	héúi	najk, H.	atgi	jarúsé mandar
Little	húring	húringi	húring	sani	húring	jóká	balé mandar
Much	úsú	oriúttar	burra	dhér, H.	dhér, H.	gúurí	banchur
How much?	chi miáng	tiná	chi miáng	yúng pagi	chinna	iná	inchur mandá
As	caret	carent	…	carent	nimnú	caret	aróbara
So					sú	caret	
Thus	inlikaté	húnkaté	nékagia	yéli	nikemeh	indéki	thán
How?	chi llka	chika llka	chi llka	yékassi	chilké	ikna	búlún
Why?	chikan minté	chér minté	chi llka	indarí	chikanlé	iudrik	búrad
Yes	hán, H.	hóá	hán, H.	hán	hán	ónón	ingé
No	bano	banga	bano	málá	bano	mállá	hillé
(Do) not	alam	alam	alapé	ampá	alá	caret	hillé bará
And, also	úndo	carent	…	our, H.	immi	inséki	údé
Or	nado	néá	ní	is	úni	malé	idaré
This	néá	hono	caret	edah	nia	íh	caret
That	énó			húdúh	únú	úh	caret

English							
Which, jón	carent omnino	…	…	ikrah	ókah	caret	caret
Which, tón	oko	hana	caret	…	…	caret	caret
Which? kón	carent	…	carent	carent	…	ik	caret
What?				indrári	chikína	caret	bará únd
Who?				ekóá	ókówó	ik	caret
Anything	oko bitté	oka dhon	okodhon	indara	jáhá, nági	indarbadi	bittlehjí, H.
Anybody	oko ho	okúrén horh	okoji	ékoárten	oko waihl	né gótó	vóndí úndi
Eat	júméman	júmmén	júniúbo	mokháh	jamómi	lápú, mókú minna	barátit
Drink	nuóman	nayman	nayman	úndi	noimi	oná	yérú undkar
Sleep	gitíman	gitikéman	gitijúm	khándara	dúróng	kúndré	súngji
Wake	birman	biritman	rúúrman	amha khaudara	adágya	ejra	jagémám
Laugh	landaiman	landman	landai	alíkah	caret	úlká	kavítoni
Weep	raiman	ragman	eyanman	chinkhdh	éyamtómi	olgá	arátó
Be silent	húpauman	hapókoman	hapiakanman	amha kach- nékrah	happá	aslúbehá	immakamnene- man
Speak	kajíman	rorhman	kajíman	kachnékrah	kajémi	auda	búrámankó
Come	hújúman	hijúman	hijúman	búrá	déla hájúm	búrá	búrúnigá
Go	sauóman	chalalman	sanóman	kálá	dásénáni	ekú, kálá	hannogáúná
Stand up	tingúnman	matingúnman	tingúakanman	illihá	tengúnni	choiyá	tedónigá
Sit down	dúbman	dúrúpman	dúrúbkanman	úkha	dúni	oká	uddáúigá
Move, walk	sanóman	dilangchalah- mau	dholóúúsanó- man	gúela	sénámi	sakrá?	táká
Run	níríman	dúrman	dúrman	bóngá	lírmi	bóngá	bittá
Give	immaiman	immaiman	únaainan	chhiá	dá	katá	si
Take	né	né	né	oárda	né	kinda	tará
Strike	goiman	dalmain	magirnan	khórah	dáll	lája	jim
Kill	margojokai	goidapolsmon	margogojiman	pítalchia	márgóji, H.	pitá	jaksívaústi
Bring	dá	dan	daigóúguúman	ondrá	ágómen	óndrá	tarúnigá
Take away	fóhman	dúdíman	idimengo	hóná	édimó	oiyá	oumaniga
Lift up, raise	rúkúbman	tdlrikúbman	úthaibaitman	chódá	rímómi	chivá	tóhá
Hear	jaimman	jyúmman	jyrúmuanmego	mijnka	jyoumómi	mené	caret
Understand	adaiman	únjúmkidda	etwanachigún	bhújarka	samójnai, H.	bújiá, H.	púttó
Tell, relate	kajíman	rorhman	kajíman	kíchana	kájí	tóngá	kantáná manjó
Good	búgí	búgí	búgí	bésri	bógí	crú	bósmanda, H.
Bad	etka	baríéna	júdajamna	maldau	réártana	búná	búró manda, H.
Cold	rabang	rabang	rabang	ekh	balhaltan	paniai	múragta
Hot	lóló	lóloa	gúmúr	bidáh		kúrni	kástai

English.	1. Sinhbhúm Kól.	2. Sóntál.	3. Bhúmij.	4. Uráon.	5. Mundala.	6. Rájmahali.	7. Góndi.
Raw	baral	baralgia	baral	khéna, arha	béral	kéné	kachchomanda, H.
Ripe	biriéna	biliéna	ihsinjanna	panja	bilia	panjéké	pútá
Sweet	sibíla	haramgia	sibíla	tini	sihil	émbé	mingatá
Sour	jójó	jójógia	jójó	tissa	jojou	tisé	chólk manda
Bitter	hárdá	hawéra	harrada	harkhá	harpand	karkeh	kadíta
Handsome	bági lika	úni bági	bágikúri	bésré, H.	bés, H.	crúgáré	assal, H.
Ugly	éstéčka lika	uni barigia	utea neloa	máli	kaibés	caret	búrótá manda, H.
Straight	múll	bágisajia	bági saj	újgó	sójhia, H.	jákró	tukrá
Crooked	kochamocha	ochúr	hessú bánka	béngko	kékándo	séró	téqhó
Black	héndé	héndé	hendé	mokharo	hendí	márgo	kariyal
White	pándi	úri pánda	hessá pínia	pándrú	pándí	jimpro	panguró
Red	*hessá árá	*úri árá	*bararanga, H.	khénsó	árrah	késó	ládl, H.
Green	gadésosang	hariyar, H.	gadé sosang	harria, H.	harriár, H.	kénkajro	haro, H.
Long	jilling	dri jilling	baroajlling	digha, S.	jiling	digaro	lamba, H.
Short	dángúya	hárikatógia	kándia	phádá	húding	jokka	chúndur
Tall } man	bátari salangi	úqi úsálai	baraisangaluma	micha	jiling	digaro	jhangchomanda
Short	hessá imitingia	bángorgaintia	bara bángarba	natúd, H.	húding	chápó	chúndúrmanda
Small	hádring	hádringia	huringia, káto	sanka	húring	caret	pataro, H.
Great	márang	márangia	lisso márang	kóhá	márang	bévó	mótó, H.
Round	dingtirúgia	gúkándia	golandia, gotagia	gólgól, H.	gótá?	golé, H.	gola, H.
Square	úpinkocha	pínkóna	úpán kón	chár kóna, H.	gótá	caret	ndlukhúnt
Flat	mitauligia	úri miraang	mórsóm	chaptí, H.	chaptia	bardbar, H.	naphúral mandáuur
Fat	kiriéné	úri móta	barai móta, H.	mota, H.	mota, H.	gandi tarvé	caret
Thin	bátaria	pátalia, H.	barai úsú	seriá	úsú	gandi walo	sirshattúr
Weariness	ésúbiagiéna	langiéna	laga jouálé	khárídkar	thakana, H.	caret	dikmandatúr, H.
Thirst	totáng tanna	totáng tanna	totang tanna	amín kala	titang	amkírvé	yétaksátúr
Hunger	réngé	réngé	réngé	kéíra	ringat	kiré	karúsátúr

N.B.—The postfix H. indicates a Hindi or Urdu etymon and the S. a Sanscrit origin.

* Hessú, udj, bara, bar, aj, mean "very," "extremely," and are mere expletives, I suspect.

ABORIGINES OF THE NILGIRIS AND OF EASTERN GHATS.

English.	Toda.	Kota.	Badaga.	Kurumba.	Irula.
Air	kátu (á = ou in bought)	gál̄ó	glai (l particular sound)	gáli	kátu
Ant	erb	irbó	irápu	irápu	irámbu
Arrow	ábu	ambe	ambu	ambu	ambu
Bird	bitti	pókó	hakibu	hakibu	páki
Blood	bách	netra	netru	netaru	litta
Boar	caret	gandu pandij	gand handij	gand handy	gandu pani
Bone	elf	yelave	yellu, illu	yellu	yellambu
Boy	moch (lit. son)	magó	máti	mati	kíge
Brother	ennon vót ó = German ó	anna, tamuma	kúda huttidava	...	annan, tambri
Elder brother	ennon etud	annan	anna	anna	anna
Younger brother	ennon kinud	királ	tamma	tamma	tambó
Cat	koti	pisó	koti	koti	páné
Child	pópen, enne	mágó	kúju	kusu	pálló
Male child	moch	gandu mage	gandu kuju	gandu kusu	ampálle
Female child	kuch	penue mage	hennu kuju	hennu kusu	pompálle
Cow	dánám	áve	dana, hasu	dana	mádu
Cock	caret	púse kóli	háva, hárja	hunja koli	javalu
Crow	kák	kákó	kákó	kákó	kákó
Day	nál	ndló	dina, jina	dina	nalu
Dog	noi	nai	nai	nai	nai
Ear	kervi	kivó	kivó	kivó	kádu
Earth	búmi	búmi	búmi	mannu, búmi	bumi
Egg	motte	motte	motte	motte	mottu
Elephant	án	...	ane	áne	áne
Eye	karm	kannu	kannu	kannu	kannu
Father	eyan	eyan	appa, tande	tande	ámme
Fire	nebb, dilth (th = English th)	dijó	kichchu	kichchu	tú, tee
Fish	mín	minó	minu	minu	minu
Flower	púf	párve	hávu	huv	pu

English.	Toda.	Kota.	Badaga.	Kurumba.	Irula.
Fowl	kádi	koli	krovi (Badaga)	koli	koli
Foot	kál	kálú	kálu	kálu	kálú
Goat	ádu	ádu	adu	ádu	ádu
He goat	caret	gandadu	hótu	gandádu	katai
She goat	caret	penádu	henadu	henádu	henádu
Hair	nír	míre	mande, kúdalu	kudalu	meiru
Hand	koi	kei	kei	kei	kei
Head	maḍḍ	mandó	mandó, táłé	mande	táłé
Hen	caret	pennekóli	hette krovi	kóli	heñukoli
Hog	pandij	panje	handij	handij	panni
Horn	kuar	kóbe	kodu, kombu	kombu	kombu
Horse	kadarao	kudare	kudure	kudure	kudure
House	todo house-ársh	pei	mane	mane	kúre
House of	{ badaga house and daśrypáłti Europeans, or Bungalow, Kúat	áłé	...	...	...
Husband	ál	ibbe	ganda	maneava	ganda
Iron	kabbun	yéllé	kabbuna	kabbuna	irrumbu
Leaf	ersh	belaku	yéllé	yélle	yélle
Light	velaku	ále, manijon	divige	dipa	valaku
Man	ál	pemmage	manija	manisha	manisha
Female	kuch	korté	hennu	hennu	ponnu
Monkey	turuni, kódan, pershk	tiggrulé	korangu	korangu	korangu
Moon	teggal	avve	tiggalu	chandra, tingla	ndlavu
Mother	avv	vettunne	avve, tai	ávve	ávve
Mountain	bana, dalta, mársh	vai	betta	beṭṭu	méłó
Mouth	boi	chukattu	bai	bai	vai
Musquito	chikattu	pér	chukattu	súgane	jolle
Name	pér	kattale	hesaru	hessaru, peru	hessuru
Night	kaggár	yenne	iru, kattale	iru	riṭṭu
Oil	emnei	yenne	yenne	yenne	éane
Plantain	pávóm	váhanne	bláóhannu	palehannu	páłepámbu

	arakk	akki	nellakki	nellakki	arai
Rice	arakk	akki	nellakki	nellakki	arai
Boiled rice	tugaru	kávo	kru, anna	kálu	jóru
River	ná	peye, révi	halla, holla	nirá	pálla
Road	ákdár	áldre	dári	dári	beiee, daḍá
Salt	uppu	uppu	uppu	uppu	uppu
Skin	tuvarsh	tuval	tólu	tolu	tolu
Sky	bán	vaname	banu	bana	vánu
Sister	enor vöt kuch	kedáse	akka tange	akka, amme	ákken, tánge
Snake	páb	pábe	hávu, pámbu	hávu	pámbu
Sow	pandi	penavajó	hemnohandij	henhandy	panni
Star	mín	mlné	mínu	mínu	vánu mínu
Stone	kall	kallu	kallu	kallu	kállu
Sun	bírsh	potte	hottu	hottu	pódu
Tiger	bürsh (ü = German ü)	puije	huli	huli	pulli
Tooth	pársh	palle	hallu	hallu	palhu
Tree	maen (ae = German ü)	marame	mora	mara	mara
Village	hatti, úr	patti	hatti	úru	úru
Toda village	mort	mande	mandu	mand	...
Water	nír	niré	uiru	níru	dani
Wheat	gádubi	godumbi	godumbi	godumbi	godumbi
Wife	kuigyó	pede	bendaru	bendaru	pondu
Yam	...	...	mulingó	...	...
I	ánu	áne	ná	ná	nanu
Thou	ní	niye	ní	ní	ni
He	adum, avan	avane	ava	avanu	ava
She	adum, adu	avale	avla	avalu	avla
It	adum, adu	ade	adu	adu	adu
We	am, em	yenge	yengla	yenga	navu
You	nív	ninge	ningla	ninga	nív
They	avar adum	avare	avaka	avaru	aduru
Mine	yennadú	yennade	yennadu	yennadu	namadu
Thine	ninnadu	ninnade	ninnadu	ninnadu	ninadu
His	avandu	avanade	avanadu	avanadu	avanadu
Ours	yennadu or nammadu	nangude	yengadu, nammadu	yengadu	nammudu
Yours	nitnmadu or ningadu	ningude	uingadu	ningadu	ninmudu

English.	Toda.	Kota.	Badaga.	Kurumba.	Irula.
Theirs	avardu	avarade	avaradu, avakaradu	avaradu	avarudu
One	vadd	vodde	vondu	like the numbers in Badaga	vondu
Two	ed	yeḍo	yeraḍu		irndu
Three	módu	mánḍe	máru		muru
Four	nánk	náke	nalku		náku
Five	útah	anjo	eidu		eindu
Six	ár	áre	áru		aru
Seven	el	yéye	yéḷḷu		elu
Eight	ett	yéṭṭe	yeṭṭu		yeṭṭu
Nine	anpath	vorupáḍe	vombattu		vonbadu
Ten	path	paṭṭe	hattu		pattu
Twenty	evoth	irváḍe	ibbatta	ibbatu	irvadu
Thirty	módbath	mávatte	muvattu	muvattu	mubbadu
Forty	narshbath	nalvatte	nalvattu	nalvatu	nábadu
Fifty	óboth	eivatte	eivattu	eivattu	ambadu
Hundred !	vaddnár	núr	nuru	nuru	náru
Of *	n. m.	n. n.	ya, na	ya, na	no
To	ge, g	ge	ga	ge, ke	ke
By or from	ind, ar	inde	inda	inda	irinda, inda
With, curr.	...	sengaḍa	kóḍa	sangaḍa	kúḍa
Without, sine.	allade	allade	allade	allade	ádalla
In	ult	vollage	vollage	vollage	úlle
On	méḷ, mok	méṣṭe	méle	méle	méle
Now	eni	innale	íga	igale	ípa
Then	áni	annale	ága	ágale	ápale
When	etvan	yennale	yégva	yega	yépa
To-day	édu	inde	indu	indu	indu
To-morrow	belkash	náḍke	náḍe	náḍe	náḍe
Yesterday	ennér	nér	ninne	ninne	nétu

* N.B.—Genitive case scarcely used, the nominative case is used instead of it.

Here	it, ing	iyáne	illi	illi	inge
There	at, ang	alle	alli	alli	ange
Where	et	yéya	yelli	yelli	yénge
Above	mēl	méte	méle, vodega	méle	mele, móke
Below	erg, neshg	kriyage	kria	kelage	kálake
Between	nárth, káshi	nadle	naduve	naduve	naduve
Without, outside	pormud	porenje	horasu	honage	valli
Within	ulf	diluli	volage	vollage	ulle
Far	podtchishi	dúrame	dura	dúra	dúra
Near	keehuri	vottle	vottura, sári	pakkaru	kitta
Little	yeddi, kimud	kunade	kuna, konji	vósi	konja
Much	upam	yeddame	tumba, appara	appara	tumba
How much	yet	yéje	yéja	yesaga	yettani
As	yingei	yeto	lyinge, yetate	yetate	yepadi
So	ingel	áto	hinge	háge	ipadi
Thus	ingei, angei	áte, angei	háge	háge	ipadi
How	hyage	yége	yétete, hyage	yetate	yepadi
Why?	áed	yendea	yéka	yéka	yenna
Yes	ha	ha	há	haudu	áma
No	á	illa	illei	illa	ille
Do not	achadi	veda	béda	bóda	vánda
Or	illade	illave	illave, illadhóle	innadhole	illavitta
That	avan	avane	avana	avana	ava
This	adu	adu	adu	adu	adu
Which?	yádu	yéde	yéadu	yavadu	yédu
What?	ēn	yéna	yéna	yénu	yenna
Who?	ár	áre	yáru	yaru	áru
Eat	thedth biné	tiggene	tinane		tinke
Drink	udth bini	unrikiene	kudidane		kúdike
Sleep	vorchth bin or vorginé	pat kene	voragine	like the Badaga verbs	rombuve
Wake	edaderth bini	mekikene	yleddane		yélke
Laugh	karth bini	karsibe	naggedane		jirike
Weep	atth bini	attabe	dátáné peculiar sound		óke
Be silent	bokkiru	bhévé	súmagiru, sappe niru		summa iru
Speak	eabth bini or arrersh bini	mausbe	nudi dane, mátádine		peshike

English.	Toda.	Kota.	Badaga.	Kurumba.	Irula.
Come	it vn	it va	ite ba	like the Badaga verbs	iti ba
Go	at fo	at hógu	áte hógu		bho
Stand up	mklo	nitullé	niddiru		niko
Sit down	neshkir	kisure	kuli, kútiru	nadedane	kukuve
I walk	nadedersh biui	nadegale	nadedane		nadake
Run	vádu	vóse	vadu		vódipoke
I give	tashken	kadube	tanane		tarke
Take away	ett fo	ett hogu	yettiund hogu		ededu konḍu poke
I strike	puis bini	puigabe	huidane	like the Badaga verbs	ádike
I kill	bóalt vers bini	taverigábo	koddane		kolluke
I raise	táchs bine, mokvers biné	yetti gabe	yettinetákine		yékkuke
I put down	háks biné, potsers biné	kriaga veigabe	hakine		irke
I hear	kelti biné, vonatth biné	vorutabe	kretine, voradiné		kélke
I understand	arth biné	arsibe	aridane		arike
Tell	bindudverth biné	peidibe	hlegine	volle	sollre
Good	vulti	volle	volle	volle	ndlla
Bad	vollade	ága	holla	ketta	polla
Cold	perthti, kuarthti	jalli	jalli, kóravu	jei	jalli
Hot	kiáti, kásviji	úri	uri, bissé	bissé	kája
Raw	paji	paje	húse	hasu	paje
Sweet	dijati	sé	sí	si	róse
Sour	pülthati	pulsa	hulli	hulli	pulli
Bitter	kithati	kaju	kthi	kthi	kósape
Handsome	nárthti	pasane, Sing ra	singara	singara	alagu
Ugly	álláli	máse	holla	hola	polla
Straight	caret	hasia, nettu	nettage	nettage	nette
Crooked	balug	kénke	gokke	gokke	kokki
Black	kárthti	kari	kari, kappu	koppu	kari
White	belpu	velape	belapu	bóle	vélle
Red	kebbu	kembu	kebbu.	kempu	jevve
Green	paje	paje	hase	hase	páje

		uddaune	udda	udda	uddya
Long	nirigiti	uddaune	udda	udda	uddya
Short	kurigiti	mone	mone	mone, kûle	kûle
Tall man	nirigi âl	uddaman	uddâva	uddalu	udda manisha
Short man	kuruḍa moch	mod âle	moneava	kûle alu	kûle manisha
Great	etud	daḍḍa	dadda	doḍḍa	doḍḍa
Round	caret	uuḍḍe	uruṭu	uruṭe	ruṭṭe
Square	caret	satto	jauka	jauka	javuka
Fat	bechiti	porâle	kobbu	gobbu	kolupu
Thin	kinud	vottale	kuna	melle	vaḍage
Thirst	nirchâsti	arthôje	arupu	arupu	vôke
Hunger	bîr eruhti	peṭṭi hoje	hasu	hasu	passi
Weariness	caret	salupu	salupu	salupu	salupu

The difference of the several dialects of the hill tribes consists not exactly in the idiom of the languages, but chiefly in their pronunciation. Therefore the same or nearly the same word in the mouth of a Toda with his pectoral pronunciation can scarcely be recognised as the same in the mouth of the Kotas with their dental pronunciation. The Badaga and Kurumba dialects are midway between the former two with regard to pronunciation, only the Badaga is a little more guttural than the Kurumba. There is a little difference in the dialects of the several Badaga tribes, those who came at a later period to the hills—for instance the Kangaru ("Lingaites"), who emigrated from Targuru—speaking a purer Canarese than the common Badagas.

The Todas also have some slight difference in their pronunciation according to the different districts they inhabit; for instance, some pronounce the s quite pure, others like the English th, and others like the z.* The names of the Toda tribes are not quite correct in the letter of Mr. Hodgson. They are the following five: Peikee, Kenna, Pekkan, Kuttan, Tôdi. The chief tribe is the Peikee, which pronounces the s like th.

---

* The th English is more especially Burmese; the rest is generally true of the northern tongues, which, even when they possess an ordinary sibilant series, prefer the use of the equivalent z series, or z, zy (Ellis' zh) and dz, whereof the first is a simple sound; the second a sliding sound, as in azure, pleasure, English, and = the French j in jeu; the third is the harsh modification of the sound. Several consonants besides z take the sliding sound represented by the blended y. This modification of the primitive sound of the precedent consonant may be seen in respect to the consonant p in the English pure and puling, which I write pyur and pyuling; and so of all consonants followed by y. Another almost universal trait of Tartaric phonology is the exceeding commonness of the French eu, as heard in jeu aforesaid. In the above paper I have not thought it prudent to meddle with Mr. Metz's orthography.

ABORIGINES OF THE EASTERN GHATS.

To the Secretary of the Bengal Asiatic Society.

SIR,—Pursuant to my purpose of submitting to the Society, upon a uniform plan and in successive series, samples of all the languages of the non-Arian races of India and of the adjacent countries, I have now the honour to transmit six more vocabularies, for which I am indebted to Mr. H. Newill, of the Madras Civil Service, at present employed in Vizagapatam. These six comprise the Kondh, Sávara, Gadaba, Yerukala, and Chentsu tongues. In forwarding them to me, Mr. Newill, a very good Telugu scholar, has noted by an annexed asterical mark such words of these tongues, and particularly of Yerukala, as coincide with Telugu. He has also remarked that many of the Chentsu vocables resemble the U'rdu.

Having, as you are aware, a purpose of submitting to the Society an analytical dissection of the whole of the vocabularies collected by me, I shall be sparing of remarks on the present occasion. But I may add to M. Newill's brief notes a few words, as follows:

The Chentsu tribe, whose language, as here exhibited, is almost entirely corrupt Hindi and U'rdu, with a few additions from Bengali, affords one more example to the many forthcoming of an uncultivated aboriginal race having abandoned their own tongue. Such relinquishment of the mother-tongue has been so general that throughout Hindustan Proper and the Western Himalaya, as well as throughout the whole of the vast Sub-Himalayan tract denominated the Tarai, not excluding the contiguous valley of Assam, there are but a few exceptions to this the general state of the case; whilst in the Central Himalaya the aboriginal tongues are daily giving way before the Khas language, which, though originally and still traceably Tartaric, has been yet more altered by Arian influences than even the cultivated Dravirian tongues. The very significant cause of this phenomenon it will be our business to explain by and by. In the meanwhile the fact is well deserving of this passing notice, with reference to the erroneous impression abroad as to the relative amounts of Arian and non-Arian elements in the population of India—an impression deepened and propagated by the further fact, still demonstrable among many of these altered aborigines, of the abandonment of their creed and customs, as well as tongue, for those of the Arians. We thence learn the value, in all ethnological researches, of physiological evidence, which, in regard to all these altered tribes, is sufficient to decide their non-Arian lineage, and to link them, past doubt, with the Himálayan and Indo-Chinese conterminous tribes on the east and north. It should be added, however, that, in a sheerly philological point of view, it becomes much more difficult to determine who are the borrowers and who the borrowed from, when both are non-Arians, than when one is Arian and the other non-Arian; and that, for instance, and in reference to the present vocabularies, we can decide at once that the Kondh numerals (save the two first) are borrowed from the Arian vernaculars, whereas it is by no means so certain that the Gadada and Yerukala numerals are borrowed from the Telugu and Karnata respectively, merely because they coincide; and so also of the pronouns where the same coincidence recurs. All such questions, however, are subordinate and secondary; and if we succeed in determining with precision—by physiological, lingual, and other helps—the entire Turánian element of our population, we shall then be able to advance another step and show the respective special affinities of the several cultivated and uncultivated Turánian tribes of India to each other and to certain of the tribes lying beyond India towards Burmah and Tibet, with at least an approximation to the relative antiquity of the successive immigrations into India.

A word in defence of these vocabularies, of which the utility has been impugned, and impugned by special comparison with brief grammatical outlines.

When I commenced this series of vocabularies I expressed as strongly as any one could do the opinion that their utility must be circumscribed; and that the ethnology of India would only then be done complete justice to when every branch of the subject should be carefully and simultaneously studied, upon the plan exemplified in my work on the Kóch, Bódó, and Dhimál. Much and toilsome labour has, however, since then, convinced me that inquiries confined wholly to India and its immediate vicinity would yield results far less satisfactory than such as should be greatly more extended even if they were less complete; whilst these continued labours have more and more satisfied me that limited grammatical comparisons are much more apt to give rise to error than limited glossarial ones. Perhaps the fascination of such extended inquiry may have somewhat biassed my judgment; but I am still decidedly of the opinion that the true relations of the most shifting and erratic, the most anciently and widely dispersed, branch of the human family cannot be reasonably investigated upon a contracted scale, while the subject is so vast that one must needs seek for some feasible means of grasping it in sufficient amplitude to comprehend its normal character (a thing rather of surface than of depth), at the same time that one neglects not more complete and searching investigation of certain actual or supposed characteristic samples. Such is the course I have been pursuing for some time past. I have examined, and am still examining, the complete grammatical structure of several of the Himálayan tongues; and I have at the same time submitted the whole of my vocabularies to the alembic of extended comparative analysis. I hope soon to be able to present the results to the Society. Those of the analysis have been fruitful beyond my hopes, owing to the extraordinary analogy pervading the Tartaric tongues in regard to the laws which govern the construction of all their vocables, save, of course, the monosyllabic ones, which, however, are very rare. Even a superficial examination of the vocabularies suffices to indicate this prevalence of common constructive principles; and to such persons as have neither time nor skill to trace and demonstrate those principles, the mere collocation of the terms as they stand, if done on a sufficiently ample scale, will afford such evidence of general relationship and family union between the whole of the Indian aborigines and the populations of Indo-China, Sífán, Tibet, and Himálaya, aye, and of China also, as philological superciliousness will seek in vain to ignore; and still more so will the results of the analysis, empirical though that analysis must, to some extent, be admitted to be. It may be conceded at once that these vocabularies must necessarily contain a good deal of error, which could only be completely avoided by a perfect knowledge of each recorded tongue on the part of its recorder. But as the languages are counted by hundreds, and as very few of them ever were or ever will be cultivated, either by those who speak them or by others, it is obvious that such precision can never be reached. On the other hand, it is certain that practical results of great value have been reached by a much less superfine process than that insisted on; and that if we suppose some thousands of facts, so simple in their nature as the mere vocables of a language are, collected with ordinary care, their failing to subserve effectually some of the highest ends of ethnological science, more particularly if taken in connection with other available evidence, must result rather from the incompetency of him to whom they are submitted than from their own intrinsic deficiency. Vocabularies illustrate one another, and furnish to the skilful no small means of correction of palpable errors, if sufficiently numerous. They also furnish means of sound induction from analogy, as I hope to prove by and by beyond the possibility of cavil.

In a word, vocabularies seem to me very much like the little instrument which Hamlet puts into the hands of Polonius; a mere bit of perforated wood, which yet in competent hands can be made to discourse sweet music. Nor can I avoid some emotions of surprise and pain (for to disparage vocabularies is to discourage their collection) when I see learned men citing with applause the inferences built upon a few doubtful words picked out of a classic writer, or perchance out of some old map, and which yet are supposed to furnish sufficient evidence of the affinity of a lost tribe, renowned in the history of past times, whilst these same learned and eminent men allow themselves to speak of vocabularies containing some hundreds of words, carefully selected and deliberately set down from the mouths of those to whom they are mother-tongues, as if these vocabularies could not furnish any legitimate basis for inference

respecting ethnological affinities.   But the objection adverted
to is sufficiently answered by the valuable purposes which my
series of vocabularies, long before completion, and with little or
no resort to analysis, has been made actually to subserve; and
therefore, I trust, it is no presumption in me to expect to be
able to educe yet more ample and important results from their
careful analysis* after completion.   Fresh ones continue to flow
in upon me still, and I have obtained not less than thirty,
almost all new, since my analysis was nearly completed.   This
is the reason why it has been withheld—this, and the daily

---

* I subjoin a sample or two of my method of dealing with the vocables, to
demonstrate, 1st, identity of roots; 2d, identity of adjuncts; 3d, identity of
constructive principles :—

Sá, Burmese, a son
A-sá, } Limbu { a child
Ku-sa, } Limbu { a son
Ku-sú, Karnatak, a child
Ku-sé, Mikir, ditto
Ku-ko-s', Oraon, ditto
Ta-ng-ko-s', ditto, ditto

Sa (vel chá) is the root.   It means a
non-adult.   Ka vel ga is the indefinite
article, and a, the definite, or its equivalent = my, so that ku-sa is any child,
and a-sa my child.   Ta is = ka, and
both take the nasal appendage, n, ng,
or m.   Oraon iterates the prefix and
elides the vowel of its root—ta-ka-sa =
ta-ga-pa below

Pá, passim, father
Ta-pó, Gyarung, ditto
Ka-pá, Kassia, ditto
Ta-ga-pá-n, Tamil, ditto'
Wa-pé, Gyarung, ditto
U-pá, Hayu, ditto
W-ab', Circassian, ditto
U-pá, Chintang, ditto
O-pá, Rangchhen, ditto
U-pá-p, Thulung, ditto
U-ka-pá, Kassia, ditto
Ap-ó, Chowrasi, ditto
A-pa, Waling, my father

The root speaks for itself.   Gyarung
has the ta and Kassia the ka prefix.
They are commutable—ta vel da and ka
vel ga—and the use of both is normal.
Tamil exhibits both, and also the nasal
suffix.   The ta vel ka, used as an indefinite article, is a contraction of the third
pronoun, another form of which is ú vel
ó vel w.   Hence u-pá, o-pá, wá-b vel
wá-p, ta-pá, and ka-pá = pater illius vel
istius, pater cujusvis, a father, whilst
á-pá = my father, as above.   Thulung
iterates the root, and Kassia the articular prefix, like Tamil u-ka-pá = ta-
ga-pá.ı

Yí-n } Chinese } Mankind, the
Yú-n } Chinese } species
E-yá-n, Toder, father
You-k, Burmese, man, the male
Yó, Bhramu, a man}
K-yó-ga, Tibetan, ditto
Yó, Savara, woman, mother
Yú-m, Tibetan, ditto
A-yú } Lepcha and Tamil { a wife
Ta-yú } Lepcha and Tamil { a woman
Ta-yí, Karnatak and Yerukala, a mother
Ta-ng-yó, Oraon, a mother
Ta-í } Khyi or Kassia } a mother; í =
Tha-i } Malabar } yi

Yá, yú, yí, the root, = man, the species,
or the male or female, or the emphatic
female, viz., mother.   Chinese, Burmese, and Tibetan have the suffixual
definitive m = n, as in Chinese and
Tamil supra; k suffix, the same as k
vel g prefix supra, such transposition
being normal and exemplified in ap-ó =
u-pá = wá-b, supra.   Observe that the
use of the prefixual a and ta, as respectively definite and indefinite articles, is
common to Tamil, Lepcha, and Limbu.
I might add Burmese, &c., &c.   Malabar
has ta prefix aspirated.

increasing skill in the use of that most potent of instruments, extended comparative analysis. But I cannot now expect, and

Er = Ré, Ouigur, man
Ar = Rá, Mikir, ditto
Ir = Rí, Bhaskir and Nogay, ditto
A-ir′ = A-rí, Armenian, ditto
E-ri-l, Hó, ditto
E-ré-l, Sontál, ditto
E-ró-s, Hungarian, virilis
Wi-ró, Scythic, man
U-ri, Kasikumak, man
G-rí, Kocch and Dhimál, Paterfamilias
G-rá, Bódó, head of Pagus
E-ri-n, Kasikumak, man
T-ri-n, Shan, ditto
Ta-n-d-ri, Telugu, father
Tá-g-ri, Lepcha, man, father

The rá, ró, rí root for mankind is palpable throughout, and the prefixes and suffixes, as well as the cumulation of the former, are normal, and therefore harmonise with the preceding samples ; thus, t-rí, g-rí, ta-g-rí, respond precisely to ta-pá, ka-pá, tá-gá-pá, aforegone, while n suffix of the Shan tri-n = the Tamil n in ta-ga-pá-n not less than the Telugu n in ta-n-d-rí. A vel e and u vel w prefixes recur just as in a-sá, a-pa, a-yú, e-yá-n, u-pá, and o-pá ; so also the nasal infix, whilst the suffixed labial and sibilant are as normal as the other adjuncts.

The above samples are selected out of thousands, whereby, collectively, perfect proof is afforded that Tartaric vocables are everywhere subject to identical laws of construction and built out of identical materials. In the absence of books of authority to cite, the demonstration must of necessity be *par la voie du fait,* and depend on the fitness and number of instances. I am prepared with thousands of instances whose applicability or fitness will, I think, be allowed to be irresistibly convincing. Though we have good grammars, dictionaries, and books on some few of the many tongues I cite, I am not aware that the composition of vocables has at all engaged the attention of their authors. It is the rock I build on.

Addenda.—Under the head "Sá," Burmese, a son, add—

Sá-u, Thai, a son
O-sú, U-sá, Lazic, a child
D-sí, vel D-zí, Kuanchua, a son
T-sé, T-sé-i, Kong, a child
D-chú-i, Mantchu, ditto
Chó-a, Kocch, ditto
Kó-a,* Hó, a child

* Sá = chá on one hand, and ká on the other. The soft sa passes into za or zya (French j), and the hard cha into ka, as in church = kirk. Thus Hó kó = Kocch chó as surely as the suffix á = the prefix a, whether used as a definitely *or* indefinitely definitive article. A′-yú, Lepcha, a wife, shows it as quasi-definite, whilst á-káp, a child, gives the a an indefinite sense rather ; and a-nak in Lepcha and Burmese, = the black, or a black one, is used either way.

The prefix da vel ta, by elision d′, t′, is as common a definitive as ka vel ga, with which it is constantly interchangeable ; or both are given, as in ta-pá, ka-pá, ta-ga-pá ; and a vel e prefix has often the indefinite-article sense, and thus also is used indifferently with ta and ka ; thus Burmese a-yén vel ka-yén, an aborigine ; and thus ta-vó vel ka-vó, a bird in Bugis. The most common of definitives, which are tantamount to articles usually indefinite, are t vel d, k vel g ; n, ng, vel m ; p, b, v, vel w ; r vel l, and the vowels i, e, a, u, o, which are all nearly commutable, as being in origin = ille, iste. And all are liable to transposition, and thus to become suffixes, as well as to be *repeated* both prefixually and suffixually, as in Chinese t-sé-i and Mantchu d-chú-i, where sa vel cha = little, is the crude, and t-sé-i vel d-chú-i precisely our English "a little one." That this is so, compare Chinese tá = great and sé = small with Newari tá and chí having the same senses. Newari takes the ka, ga suffix, like Mantchu ; thus, chí-ki, small ; and d-chá-ka, a thing, in those tongues respectively.

hardly desire, any more new materials; and I hope, therefore, soon to be able to submit my examination of the whole.

Under the head " Yu-n," mankind, after the word " You-k," add the word—

K-yó-ga, Tibetan, a man, the male

Tibetan k-yó-ga, from the yá, yú, yó crude, shows the ka vel ga definitive in both forms (soft and hard) and in both positions (prefix and suffix). The correspondent word for the female is ki-mi = ka-mi in Kassia, and not less = ka-mi and ku-mi in the tongues so named, after the name for our species, in them. The sexual distributive use of ka and u prefixes in Kassia is only of secondary value, like the prefixual or postfixual position of the definitives; thus ap-ó in Chourasi and o-pá in Rungchhen, = pater istius or ejus pater, viz., a father, any one's father, are from mere dialects of the same tongue, Kiránti. Thus also sá-u, Thai, filius ejus = u-sá, o-sú, Lazic. Compare yo and k-yo with mari and k-mari, lu-n and k-lu-n, &c., apud Mongol Affin. of Caucasians, Journal for January 1853; or above, pp. 51 ff.

Vocabulary of some of the Dialects of the Hill and Wandering Tribes in the Northern Sircars.

English.	Kondh.	Savara.	Gadaba.	Yerukala.	Chentsu.
Air	billu	ringe	gamváyi	gáli*	batás
Ant	...	bobo	gusalá	chíma*	peppido
Arrow	pinju	ám	sonni	yikke	kondu, kánd
Bird	propámannéru	onti	piti	kokku, sogide, kunju	chodai
Blood	rakko	miyamo	yignam	regam, vudaram	labu
Boat	tekkinga	vodá*	dóna	padava*	lá
Bone	pásu	ajágna	voudrángóyi	yamaka*	had
Buffalo	kóru	bognátel	vontsani	barre*	mohis
Cat	miyó	rámegná	girem	pína	billeyi
Cow	kháyi	tangli	bandi	alamádu, pútamádu	gáyi
Crow	káka	káká	guggá	selán, káka†	kovvá
Day	vujjyágu	tambá	simmyá	pammárá,‡ pangámáru	din
Dog	nahudi	kencho	guso	náyi	kukkúr
Ear	kirru	luv	nintiri	sóyi	kán
Earth	táná	labo	...	tarra	bháyi
Egg	vatánga	are	mittá	mutta	dimma
Elephant	hattánga	ra	kom	dina	hate
Eye	kannuka	amu	olló	supán	áyenkhi
Father	abbá	uwá	abbá	áva	bá
Fire	nádi	tógo	sungol	nerupu	agin
Fish	mininga	áyo	addán	mínu	matstsó
Flower	sáru	taraba	sari	puvvu*	phúl
Foot	vestámu	aji	adugésenáuu	medarán, kóru	khoju
Goat	vodangá	kíme	yimne	ádá	chheli
Hair	thámberakha	avu	jarli	vondu, mogurá	kéms
Hand	kúju	asi	titti	kayi, ki	hát
Head	tlávu	abóbunv, abumv	bo	vondu, talayi	mánd
Hog	pajji	kimbo	gibbi	pandri	suvvar, ghusiri

† In Telugu, káki

‡ Telugu, pagalu.

English.	Kondh.	Savara.	Galaba.	Yerukala.	Chentsu.
Horn	kosko	ajigna	nirri	kómmu*	sing
Horse	godá	kuḍata	kirtyám	kudara	ghóḍó
House	yiḍḍu	súgna	deyyón	váḍu	ghór
Iron	luharigá	lómá	vonchani	yerunbu	loho
Leaf	áka	olá	vollá	yale, yaláku	pát
Light	vujwḍlá	tambá	tarádutu	valuku	díp, vujjait
Man	lokká	mandra	lokko	munasaṃ	mánús
Monkey	kóju	karóyi	gusá	kóte*	mákaḍ
Moon	layiḍi	vongá	arke	tarra	mású
Mother	ayyá	yo	penamma	táyi	má
Mountain	soru	barṇ	kondá	gettu	parvat
Mouth	suḍḍá	amúká	tunnnó	váyi	má
Mosquito	vihángá	abubbo	kirigi	yeyyi	mussó
Name	paddá	vonneman	neninmede	andu	ná
Night		tógolo	tungol	ravu, náváru	ráyit
Oil	níju	miyyalo	sól	rganna, vauna	tél
Plantain	tádi	kinte	vusubullu	niráde	koḍel, sodail
River	jódi	náyi	roggilu	áru	loḍḍi, laḍi
Road	páhóri	tangóra	kingóru	yegi	báṭ
Salt	vuppanga	basi	bitti	sonava	nún
Skin	pándá	wusál	artá	tálu	chamaḍá
Snake	mudengi	agásá	kondá	ménu, túna	sarg, sáp
Star	soráso	ja	buḍubu	tsukka*	bhuḍaká
Stone	sukálá	tute	tsukka	kellu	paththar
Sun	viddi	arregna	birel	proddu, beruli*	belá
Tiger	belá	vuyu	singi	nálugáḍee	bág
Tooth	króḍi	kina	yekkili	pallam, pelivelu	dát
Tree	abúmu	ajágna	ginná	cheḍe, marom	gáṭa
Village	mránu	anóbagna	sunabbo	náḍu	
Water	náju	gorajáng, ḍa	yiugoma	tanni	páni
Yam	sridrá, gánḍikúna	gane, dá	ḍeyyá, dampu	aluvele	sarú, sakarkanda

I	anu	gua	naiai	nánu	hame, hami
Thou	yinu	aman	nó	ninú	tumyi, tá, yike
He	yanju	ani	tulokku	avanu	vú, vamhi
She	toliyadu	ani	tulo	avalu, paidi	mayyáta, vú
It	mónju	ani	tulo	adu	vahe, vú
We	...	móni	neyam	námu, namburu	hame
Ye	...	aman	pen	ningalu, avaru	te, tumyi
They		ani	mai	tilá, avállu	vamhi
Mine	nánde	gránate	noinyo	nungudedi, namburudu	hanoár
Thine	minde	amannate	nenne	ningadeo, ningadidi	thór
His	yevánetará	ani-nate	mayinó	avanudu, attanudidi	vahár
Ours	...	móni-nate	niyyinó	namburudu	hamar
Yours	...	aman-nate	...	ningalide, ninebududu	thór
Theirs		ani-nate	mayyinó	avanudu	vahár
One	ró:di	áboy	vokati*	vondu	yék
Two	jódeká	bágu	rendu*	rendu	duyi
Three	tinigottá	yági	mídu*	múme	tin
Four	sári	vonji	nálugu*	ndlu	chár
Five	pánchu	mollayi	ayidu*	anju	pánch
Six	só	kudru	áru*	áru*	chhé
Seven	sáta	gulji	yédu*	yégu, vógu	sát
Eight	áta	tamuji	yenimide*	yéttu, vattu	áth
Nine	nogattá	tinji	tommidi*	ombadu	ló, tótá
Ten	dosó	galiji	padi*	pattu, pottu	das
Twenty	kóde	bokodi	yiruvai*	yiravadu, yirapottu	bís, panchgandá
Thirty	tirisigottá	bokodigaliji	muppai*	muppadu	sátgandá dóyicha, pandrágandá
Forty	challisigottá	bágrukodi	nalabhai	nalubadu, nárarakapottu	poun, dasgandá
Fifty	panchásó	bágrukodigaliji	yábhai*	anjarakapottu	bárágandá doyicha
Hundred	sohó	molloyikodi	náru*	pattu padulu, pottarakapottu	panch vodi
Of	...	ti	móyi	rakka	vór
To	...	ti	nó	ku*	ku
From	...	sitholo	rón	nunche*	singa
By	...	sitholo	rón	valla*	soyi
With	...	ruhá	bonóm	tóte*	sang
Without		yejja	vuregusu	yilladóte	návunánai

English.	Kondh.	S'avara.	Gadaba.	Yerukala.	Chentsu.
In	séndó	lógna	r	kóre, kóku	t, gánt
On	iddáli	lanka	te	paini*	vuparóru, vuparót
Now	...	narni	á	yeppuḍu*	yekhán, yechini
Then	...	namóḍe	appuḍu	appuḍu*	tekhán, areghoḍi
When	yeseká	yenga	yiindoyi	yeppuḍu*	kekhán, kekkoneki
To-day	nenju	nangadini	yinchá	imán	ayije, éjko
To-morrow	rasi	biyo	beyyar	nesá	káyil
Yesterday	...	amanni	minḍe	nesu yennáyi	káyil, porusú
Here	...	tenne	tennó	yatukire, yinge	thaná, yechini
There	...	vodíte	tonnó	atukire, ange	unhaná, vuha
Where	...	téngá	ammanó	yiṭe, yenge	kuhaná, kahá
Above	nede	lanka	tommá	méne	vupár, vuparót
Below	madde	lanka	alóm	tallen	tolót, tól
Between	...	jáyitá	vomidi	neduve	mayidhit, móyid
Without, outside	...	lanka	valumúsá	bele	bahar
Within	aṭumané	vodíte	vomiḍi	vulle	bhitar
Far	...	alógna	sulóm	túra, kiṭṭe	dúr
Near	yíke	sangayi	tautel	kiṭṭa, kiṭṭáyi	lág
Little	púrá áte	tuya	khandiki	rátana	ráj, chone
Much	mesóni	tére	burre	mettá	bhóri
How much?	...	bari	aḍisugó	yiṭṭana	ketta, kettagulá
As	...	ḍite	...	...	lakha
So	...	...	voṭṭu	ate	vú, vumané
Thus	yísingi	kanínásan	vókke	yiṭe	jí, yemune
How?	...	yettáná	yeráuḍi	yaṭe	kemune
Why?	annáḍeki	yóngá	...	yemmatuku, phaláyá	kissále
Yes	vuje	jitásamgná	vón	ambó	schchhá, hoyyá
No	...	jáḍite, ó ó	víre	yillá	nahí
(Do) not	kunámá	yajja	ayide	mánu, yikkara	kámnai, kámnali
And, also	...	ṭiggo	tonnó	num	ke, ye, ye
Or	...	...	víre	taradote	nahí
This	...	ani	...	avanu	vahare, vu

	yeriri	ani	tónó, bhulúm	adu	vahe, ke
That	yestánju	vongá		yedu	vahe, ke / kahá
Which?	anná	vongádo		yanna, yemmatuku	kí, kochcher
What?	yestánju, yínu	bote	lári	ydru	ke, vuhe
Who?	annátki	yetagáni, jitagáni	mádisá	yenmadainá	kichu, jehaive
Anything	yestánáte	bote, bótegáni	loyisá	yeduayiná	kevu, jehaive
Eat	tírumu*	gába, jombá	sóm	vunu, kulla	khá, khayye
Drink	punamu	gába	yídu	kudi	pí, piyer
Sleep	dohamu	dimebá	eyyá	tuggudayi, varugu	súl, sutiyár
Wake	ningidaháwu	dimegó	módukusudukká	teigayirukku, dindugunduyiru	jágleró, jágalerahó
Laugh	kakkumu	mágnába	luddó	sirilá, chirike	hás
Weep		kam yite	borryó	agulá, agu	kánd, kandiyár
Be silent	kiuni jáminnú	kadaugáiná	vayisodukka	sumna, tsummateyiru	tisuperahó, tsupparo
Speak	katágehámu	birdána	sanmneva	vátéeula, véeetallá	kathháká, katthá
Come	ninju	jáyeba	phinge	ví, várá	asibo, asili
Go	nalákanju	maba	vóyindyaro	pó*	jíyivi, já
Stand up	nistámu	dedebá	tune ná	nikkebogu, nindrukonduyiru	thá dóño
Sit down	kukkumu*	góbá	vaisá	vulká, vukkárindiri	boa
Move, walk	kujinámu	yírba	vamsu	nadá	tsó
Run	gyáhamu	nadam	dugga	vódu	bég
Give	siyáainju	tilisibba	chedive	tá, vanko	ne diyo
Take	kúvay	yama	demá	váká, vánkemáto	niyyó, niyá
Strike	vetámu	teda	buvó	mottu	mái, maryó
Kill	veamáhudu	kilisibba	abboye	kolusu, kollu	marepheiá, morevaleyó
Bring	táma	pangayiba	yindre	yittikondu	áne, diyá
Take away	aháneamallinu	págná lá yírba	sógusiyyá	yittikondupó, váákondupómu	nikejá, niyá
Lift up, raise	densumu	lanka	lenó	yedudu	tól
Hear	venjámu	andángá	vóvo	keru, kétu	sún
Understand	anupunnenju	andángalayi	menyá avure	telentsu	málúm
Tell, relate	veaámu	appungá	tsúnó	sonnu	ko
Good	nekkánju áyo	ampase	jalem	nalla	achháye, bháiá
Bad	jilliminju	sedéle	ninmakávó	ketta, kettsu	khardó
Cold	rumúrumam	soyi vudedo	tsallari	musunu	síttalá
Hot	saddále	toggayi	gechem	vuduku*	jóru, tapta
Raw	mráutangi sen-dijaninju	amegna	broluká	pasuru	kanchó, káchuá
Ripe		agúruuate	mágegisá, bullo	mágisu, pandisu	mugilá pakhá

English	Kondh	Savara	Gudaba	Yerukala	Chentsu
Sweet	sendijáninju	mana	sabbuiká	teyyanikkiri*	miṭbá
Sour	trahane	aragna	susoká	pulladikkiri	amnutó
Bitter	pittáyine	asa	vusáin	ketatsu	titto
Handsome	...	ambasanate	limmókká	nalla	bhalláṭi, sundor
Ugly	sonjabasdho	ambaste	nimmokkvórá	nalladillá	kharáb
Straight	soddemanne	barídakó	lakoḍuttu	saduṇu	sorichhaiyye, sorikará-hache
Crooked	bankadájáne	kokkade	ḍairoyi	vankara*	bankó
Black	káújáná	je	yide	kaledó	kalló, kaliṭa
White	sukkáre	palu	tatár	valedá	vujula, savarniṭa
Red	gérú	soyipu	beraiḍuttu	yarraḍekirá	goriya, gorinṭa
Green	...	volámbidídakuvu	vólempatsta	yaláṭatsaggó	harihjal, sabuniya
Long	lambájámu	jelo	tiyyár	vasaram, aragam	vunchó, namóṭú
Short	koggári	ḍoyina	dille	kuraṭsa	khaṭa
Tall } man	...	lanka	tiyyár	vasaram	namó
Short } man	...	ḍoyina	poṭṭe	vasaram	khaṭóṭi
Small	...	sonna	mengen	ardullá	khopaṭi
Great	deranju	gogo	muḍó	chinnakerum, siruváyan	badaká
Round	...	gudi, solágundu onjimálalanka	biregunḍu	berudu / gunḍu*	chatan, goṭyaṭi
Square	taṭṭu	bagná, sagná-daku	duttu	tsadaram*	sadunúta, chakkaṭa
Flat	rósarola	samangadele	sadunugádulta	sadam*	chekunó, chakkakini
Fat	gellu ayininju	kovvuḍéle	bhirúgu	kovvitsu, nemamu	telubhariya, tellaraṭa
Thin	banda ayininju	palapalasan	palasanadulta	bakkadu	saruvoti, sakunaṭa
Weariness	lahite	...	burre	ayyóśu	haran, yusiki
Thirst	yeeengepekmanenju	araga	yide	daggа, dappikonu	pyaśiagí, pyas
Hunger	chatanganki pan-nenju	ḍolejan	kuddu	soda, peruntsu	bhúá, bhoku

NOTE.—The words marked thus * are also Telugu words. Many of the vocables of the Yerukala people correspond with the Tamil words representing the same objects; and many also of the Chentsu words resemble the Hindustani.

ABORIGINES OF THE NILGIRIS, WITH REMARKS ON THEIR AFFINITIES.

In the autumn of last year I forwarded to the Society a series of Nilgirian vocabularies. This paper was printed soon after in the Journal, but without the accompanying prefatory remarks, which seem to have been accidentally mislaid and omitted.

I now forward some corrections and additions to that paper, and shall take the opportunity to mention what, in substance, those prefatory remarks contained.

The Nilgirian vocabularies were prepared for me by the German missionaries at Kaity, particularly Mr. Metz, and were then examined and approved by the venerable Schmid, who is now residing at Utakamund, and who added some remarks, partly referring to his own valuable labours in Indian Ethnology, and partly consisting of corrections of my Ceylonese series of vocables. The latter are appended to the present paper.

When the Nilgirian vocabularies reached me, I immediately perceived that the verbs were not uniformly given in the imperative mood as required; and I therefore wrote again to Utakamund desiring that this anomaly might be rectified, and also supplying some further forms, the filling up of which might furnish me with some few essentials of the grammar of the tongues in question.

The subjoined paper exhibits the result, and from it and from some further remarks furnished by Mr. Metz and others I derive the following particulars relative to the people, and to the grammar and affinities of their speech.

The form and countenance of the Nilgirians, and especially of the Todas, have now been spoken of for years as though these people differed essentially in type from the neighbouring races, and had nothing of the Tartar in their appearance. The like has been said also of the Hó or Lerka of Singhbhum. I have always been inclined to doubt both these assertions, and I have lately had opportunity to confirm my doubt. My friend Sir J. Colvile, our Society's able President, having lately visited the Nilgiris, I requested his attention to the point, desiring him to procure me, if he could, some skulls * and photographic portraits.   Of the latter he obtained for me two, which are herewith transmitted, and which Sir James sent me with the following remarks:—"I am not much versed in these matters, and I confess I was at first insensible (like others) of the Tartaric traits you speak of, the Roman nose and long beard of the Todas more especially making me fancy there was something Semitic in their lineage.   But when I showed the passage in your letter to Dr. M'Cosh, he said you were right, and that, in spite of the high nose, there were strong Tartaric marks, particularly in the women.   The Badagas, who are considered to be of as old date in the hills as the Todas, have a very uniform cast of countenance, not easily distinguishable from the ordinary inhabitants of the plains below the hills."   These last are of course Dravidian or Tamulian, and the comparison drawn is therefore instructive, and doubly so when we advert to the indubitable evidence of language, which leaves no doubt as to the common origin of the highland and lowland, the uncultivated and the cultivated, races of Southern India, as we shall presently see.

Upon the origin and affinity of the highlanders Sir James observes, "People who know a good deal of the Todas say, that wherever they may have originally come from, they have less claim to be considered aborigines of these hills than the Kotas, not more than the Badagas, and are thought not to date higher than some four hundred years in their present abode." Mr. Metz, the resident missionary, who furnished the vocabularies, observes on this head, "The Kotas have so much intercourse with the Badagas that they are often not conscious whether they speak Badaga or their own language.   Their original home was Kollimale, a mountainous tract in Mysore. The Kotas understand the Todas perfectly when they speak in the Toda tongue, but answer them always in the Kota dialect, which the Todas perfectly understand."

* Neither Sir James nor any of the other parties I applied to could obtain for me any skulls.

"A Toda tradition states that the Todas, Kotas, and Kurumbas had lived a long time together on the hills before the Badagas came. I know places on the hills where formerly Kurumba villages existed, but where none are now found. It is well known that the Kurumbas were driven down from the healthful summit to the malarious slopes of the hills, and I have strong reasons for believing that the cromlechs and cairns of the hills were made by the ancestors of the Kurumbas, and not by those of the Todas, as is generally supposed by Europeans." In entire conformity with those views of the aspect and origin of the Nilgirians is the evidence of language, which palpably demonstrates the relationship of the highland races to the lowland races around them. The amply-experienced and well-informed Schmid has no doubt of that relationship, which indeed he who runs may read on the face of the vocabularies formerly and now submitted.* And it is well deserving of note that whilst that vocabular evidence bears equally upon the question of the affinity of the cultivated tribes around the Nilgiris, this latter affinity is now maintained as an unquestionable fact by the united voices of Ellis, Campbell, Westergaard, Schmid, Elliot—in short, of all the highest authorities.

We may thus perceive the value of the evidence in question with reference to the uncultivated tribes, as to whose affinity to each other and to the cultivated tribes Mr. Metz writes thus, "When I came up to the hills, the Badagas told me that the language I used, which was Canarese, was the Kurumba language." This reminds us of what we are told by another of that valuable class of ethnological pioneers, the missionaries, who reports that "Speaking Tamulian of the extreme south, he was understood by the Gonds beyond the Nerbudda." Nor can one fail to remark how this latter observation points to the great fact that Turánian affinities are not to be circumscribed by the Deccan, nor by the Deccan and Central India, nor, I may here add, by the whole continent of India, but spread beyond it into Indo-China, Himálaya, and the northern regions beyond Himálaya, irrespectively of any of those

* See the Tamulian proper, the Ceylonese and the Nilgirian proper.

specially marked barriers and lines of separation which Logan and Müller have attempted to establish—the former, on physical and lingual grounds; the latter, on lingual only. My own conviction is, that we find *everywhere* throughout the regions now tenanted by the progeny of Tur a large range of variation, physical and lingual, but one not inconsistent with essential unity of type, though the unity is liable, nay, almost certain to be overlooked, whether our point of view be anatomical, physiological, or philological, unless we carefully eschew confined observation such as misled Captain Harkness about the appearance of the Todas, and not less Captain Tickell about the appearance of the Hó. I have adverted to Harkness' mistake above. I will now add a few words as to my brother-in-law Tickell's. Last season Captain Ogilvie, Tickell's successor, in the charge of that very district wherein the latter studied the Hó physical and lingual characteristics, came to Darjiling. I questioned him regarding the alleged fairness and beauty of the Hó, and well knowing that, without samples before him, Captain Ogilvie must be unable to give a definite answer, produced, from among the many always here, four no doubt unusually fair, well-made, and well-featured U'ráon and Múnda men, but still all in the service of one gentleman, and I then interrogated him. Captain Ogilvie's answer was distinct, that the men before him were nearly or quite as fair and handsome as the Hó of Singhbhúm, and not either in feature or in form essentially distinguishable from the Hó, whose lingual characteristics, again, we now know, are so far from being peculiar that they are completely shared by the wide-spread tribe of Sontál, and almost as completely by the Múnda, Bhúmij, U'ráon, Male, and Gónd, not to speak of other and remoter tribes of Himálaya and Indo-China having the widely diffused pronomenalised verb type of the Turánian tongues.* Not that I would lay the same stress upon these nicer characteristics of language, as

---

* Viz., the Nága, Dhimáli, Háyu, Kuswár, Bótia, Kiránti, Límbu, Chepáng, Kusunda, and Bhrámu, of all which I hope soon to speak. All these tongues, of which the first is Indo-Chinese and the rest are Himálayan, belong to the pronominalised class.

seems at present to be so much the fashion in high quarters. But, on the contrary, I would choose, as a Turánian philologist, to rely rather upon extent than depth of observation, still remembering that by far the greatest number of Turánian tribes are not merely unlettered, but too many of them also, for ages past, broken and dispersed, barbarously ignorant and miserably segregated, like the Nilgirians.

The niceties of such men's languages can never be accurately reached by us, unless we would devote a whole life to the research; and, moreover, these niceties are certain to exhibit a great many anomalies, and to be now present, now absent, under circumstances which, whether the absence were originally caused by impatient rejection, by casual non-development, or by spontaneous or factitious decomposition, must detract greatly from the value and certainty of any inferences founded thereon; whilst in regard to the more civilised tribes, we often positively know and may always prudently suspect that *their* lingual refinements, when they differ from those of the ruder tribes, are so far from being special illustrations of the true *norma loquendi* of the Tartars that they are exotic and borrowed traits. From this digression (which has reference to Müller's remarks on the relative value of vocabular and grammatical evidence) I return to my subject by giving the following observation of Mr. Metz upon the affinity of the several Nilgirian tongues now before us, merely premising upon the interesting subject of the character and habits of these tribes what Sir James Colvile in his recent visit heard and observed. "They are idle, dirty, intemperate, and unchaste. Polyandry has always existed among them, and their women are now addicted to general prostitution with men of other races, so that they must soon die out; and, in fact, I think the population is scantier than it was when I was last here, though so few years back." Upon this I may remark that the traits observed in the Nilgiris are thoroughly Tartar, and as such are widely prevalent in the Himálaya and Tibet. Even the civilised tribe of the Newárs, who, by the way, have a recorded tradition uniting them with the Malabár Náirs—a name identical, they say, with Neyár or Newár (y and w being intercalary letters)—were once polyandrists, and are still regardless of female chastity, whilst the Tibetans were and are notoriously both.

Mr. Metz, on the subject of the dialectic differences of the Nilgirian tongues, observes :—

"The differences of the several languages of the hill tribes consist, not so much in idiom as in mere pronunciation. But that is so great that the same or nearly the same word in the mouth of a Toda, with his pectoral pronunciation, can scarcely be recognised as the same in the mouth of a Kota, with his dental pronunciation. The Badaga and Kurumba dialects are midway between the former two with regard to pronunciation, only the Badaga is a little more guttural than the Kurumba.

"There is some difference even in the speech of the several branches, or remotely located groups, of any one tribe. For instance, those of the Badaga tribe who, like the Kangaru or Lingaits, emigrated from Targuru and came to the hills at a later period than the others, speak a purer Canarese than the common Badagas. So also the Todas among themselves have differences of pronunciation according to the different districts they inhabit; for instance, some pronounce the s quite pure, others like z, and others again like the English th. And in like manner the Kurumbas round the slopes of the hills have so many little variations in their speech according to the situation of their villages (Motta) on the south, east, or west side of the hills, that it is difficult to say what the real Kurumba tongue is. In Malli, the chief Kurumba place on the south slope, the language is much mixed with Tamil."

I will now conclude with a few remarks on the grammatical traits exhibited by the subjoined papers.

PHONOLOGY.

As much as is forthcoming on this head has been expressed in the vocabular part of this paper and the remarks appended to it. It may be advisable, however, to repeat here that the presence of the English th, and its frequent substitution for s and z, and the equivalence of the two latter, are so far from béing exclusively Toda, as Schmid supposed, that they are common in Indo-China, Himálaya, and Tibet. Tibetan abounds in sibilants, having, besides the s, ch series, an equivalent z, zy, dz series. The former is possibly borrowed. At all events, z, zy, dz, and ts, tch are very much commoner in use than the Arian s, ch, series. The second z, represented by me by zy, and equal to the French j in jeu, is the same with the Tamil zh of Ellis and Elliot. It is a very prevalent sound, and equally prevalent is the French u, or eu in jeu aforesaid. Neither is ever heard from an Arian mouth; but the Himálayans most infected with Arian ways and habits are now gradually substituting Arian j for their own z, and Arian u for their own eu. D is also taking the place of their hard and aspirated z (dz and zh), and thus the Tibetan word zhí-ká-tsén and Newári Zhí-khá-chhén,* the name of the capital of Tsáng, has become Dígarché with those who use the popular and spreading Khas language, which language we hereby perceive also preferring sonants to surds (g for k), whereas the written Tibetan and Newári, like the Tamil and Toda, having a preference for surds.

But Tibetan is spoken with all the variety of hard and soft pronunciation noticed by Mr. Metz as characterising spoken Toda and indeed the whole of the Nilgiri dialects; and as there are few things more normally Turánian than the wide extent of legitimate, habitual commutability between the consonants and between the vowels also of the languages of the family, so I consider that to lay so much stress as is often

---

* The etymology of this word is curious and important with reference to the evident identity of the term Tibetan. And it is hardly too much to say that the family identity of the two tongues (Newári and Tibetan) might be rested on it.

It means in Newári "the four-housed," zhi or zyi being four, khá the generic sign for houses, and chhén being house. De Körös has said nothing about that most fundamental sign of the Turánian tongues, the generic or segregative signs; but I have good reason to assume that this is one of the several serious defects of his grammar, and that Tibetan ká is = Newári khá, as zhi = zhi, and tsén = chén, though khyim be now the commoner form of the word in written Tibetan. Zhi-khá-chhén or Zhí-ká-tsén Turanice = Dígarchén Arianice, is the name of the capital of Tsáng—why styled "the four-housed" I cannot learn. But three *such* elements, composing one word identical in form and in sense in two separate languages, involve the family oneness of these languages.

done on merely phonetic peculiarities is a great mistake on the part of Turánian ethnologists, and one apt to lead them much astray when in search of ethnic affinities. For example, the Myamma is questionless one language, notwithstanding that its phonetic peculiarities in Ava and in Arrakan are very marked; and a particular friend of mine, who is "genuinely Saxon, by the soul of Hengist," can by no means deal fairly by r, sh, or th, but calls hash has; shoes, soes or toes or thoes; brilliant, bwilliant; there, dere; thought, tought, &c.* A Londoner is not less Saxon, surely, because he is wont to " wow that weal, wine, and winegar are wery good wittals."

ARTICLE.

Mr. Metz says there is none whatever, but I feel pretty sure that the usual equivalents are recognised, viz., the numeral *one,* or the indefinite pronoun *some, any,* in lieu of the indefinite article; and the demonstratives in lieu of the definite, as also the segregatives van, val, and du, or an, al, and ad, for the three genders, or ál and pé for the major of gender, used as suffixes, and widely applicable to nouns (qualitives)—less widely and uniformly to verbs. We should always remember that the so-called segregatives or generic signs are essentially articles, definite or indefinite according to the context.

ADJECTIVES.

All qualitives which seem to embrace, as usual, the nominal (genitive), pronominal, participial, numeral, and adjectival, appear to be used both substantivally and adjectivally, and, when employed in the former way, to add to their crude, as a suffix, the appropriate generic sign, which, in the case of the participle, gives it a relative sense or an agentive, just as in English, *the* or *a striker,* or *the* or *a striking person* (*or thing*), and *the* or *a hard thing,* are equivalent respectively to *the person who strikes* and *the thing which is hard.* But the latter form of speech is quite Anti-Turánian.

---

* "Three fresh fishes in the dishes" is, in the mouth of the same friend, " Tree fes fises in the dises."

Qualitives are always prefixed when not used affirmatively or substantivally. If placed after the noun they become affirmative, including in their sense the substantive verb. *Man* (is) *mortal.* *That* (is) *mine.* *This the striker* = *this is the person who strikes.** *He* (is) *loving one* or *lover* = *one who loves.* *That one* (is) *the black* = *that is the black one.* Give me *the black* = *the black being* or *thing*—a difference which must be expressed, and with the sign of gender, too (an, al), in the former event. *This person two person* = *this one is the second person* (rend-al),† &c. Gender is fully marked in qualitives by the use of the suffixes van, val, du, or an, al, ad = hic, hæc, hoc. But these forms are very imperfectly reproduced in the verb, indeed can hardly be traced except in Badaga and Kurumba, where the following is unmistakable evidence of them.

English.	Badaga.	Kurumba.
He strikes	Hui-d-an	Hui-t-an
She strikes	Hui-d-al	Huiyu-t-al
It strikes	Hui-d-ad	Huiyu-t-ad

The major and minor of gender in beings, not things, seem to be denoted by ál and pé suffixes—words having still the independent signification of man and woman. In Toda, moreover, adum marks the common gender as a separate pronoun, and tan ‡ as a conjunct prefix. I am not sure as to the major and minor of gender, because the verb does not exhibit them in the peculiar manner of the cultivated Dravidian tongues or otherwise.

* In Newári it would be, ú-hma dáya-hma, which is in every particular of idiom Dravidian, hma being the van or ál suffix of the above tongues, and its affixing to the verbal form rendering that a relative participle.

† Here final ál is not the contracted sign of the feminine suffix aval, but is the name for man used as a suffix.

‡ The prefix ta, with or without the nasalisation tan, tang, and with or without the causulate equivalent ka vel ga, is widely prevalent to the north and south, as I have noticed in a recent paper; and so also the other equivalent a vel e, witness ta-pe, ka-pa, ta-ga-pa-n, a-pa-e-ri, g-ri, ta-g-ri, tan-d-ri, a-yi, ta-yi, tan-g-yo, for man and woman in Gyarung, Kassia, Kiránti, Bódó, Kócch, Tamil, Lepcha, Uraon, &c. Those who deny family connection between the Himálayan and Dravidian tongues are requested to pause over ta-g-ri (Lepcha), and tan-d-ri (Telugu), for man, and a-yi vel ta-ye, in both tongues, for woman—roots, ri and yi, vel i.

NOUN.

The papers furnish no sample of declension, but it may be safely inferred that it is simply postpositional with cases ad libitum, or none at all, according to the view taken of declension. Gender is marked either by separate words, such as *man, woman; cock, hen;* or by sexual prefixes like our *he-goat* and *she-goat;* or, lastly, the generic word bears also a male or female sense, when the feminine or masculine gender, as the case may be, is distinguished by the fitting sign prefixed. So Burmese sa means *child* and *boy*, and mí-sá, or *female child*, means *girl*.* I know not whether the suffixes van, val, and du, or ál and pé (pen, pem—the latter equal major of gender), are added to substantives as well as to qualitives, but I think not. Instances occur in Telegu, but not generally in the Dravidian tongues, nor in the northern.

The major and minor of gender (quasi, hic et hæc facilis; hoc, facile) are common in the Himálaya, Indo-China, and Tibet, but I have nowhere in the north found the fully-developed masculine, feminine, and neuter of the south.

In regard to number, the Nilgirian nouns are very defective, having no distinct and uniformly employed dual or plural inflexion or sign. But they seem to follow the cultivated Dravidian in so far as having no dual, but having the double, or exclusive and inclusive, plural at least in the separate pronouns and in the personal endings of the verb. Irula has not even the latter. In the Himálayan tongues it is often difficult to make out disjunct dual and plural forms of the substantive, even when the distinct and conjunct pronouns exhibit an exclusive and inclusive form both of the dual and of the plural of the first person, with correspondent verb forms as is the case in the Kiránti language. The source of the defective plural sign of nouns is to be sought in the fact that Turánian vocables generally, in their crude state, bear the largest and specific or generic meaning—a peculiarity well exemplified by the English word sheep. In the Nilgiri tongues neuter nouns

---

* The mí is often suffixed. Thus ta and ta-wa, a child, is tu-mi, a girl, in Háyu and Kiránti.

always lack, says Mr. Metz, a plural form. So also in Newári, which further agrees with the Dravidian tongues in annexing the generic signs to all qualitives, whereas the Himaláyan tongues, even those of the pronomenalised type, often omit the sign with pronouns and participles, though they annex it to other qualitives. Masculine nouns form it occasionally by changing final n into r in Toda (kullan, *a thief;* kullar, *thieves*), or by adding the plural sign kal vel gal in Badaga and Irula.

PRONOUNS.

Pronouns and pronominal forms are greatly developed in the Nilgirian languages,* as in all the Turánian tongues, reminding us, when viewed in connection with the paucity of true conjugational forms, of the fine remark that "rude people think much more of the actors than of the action." We have in the Nilgiris, 1st, personal and possessive forms; 2d, among the former forms excluding and including the person addressed (we—not you, and we—including you); 3d, among the latter, or possessives, two complete series, according as the pronouns are used conjunctively or disjunctively. I have given all these; and their forms, changes of form and uses, would alone suffice to prove the perfect identity of the Nilgirian tongues with those of the cultivated Dravidian class. The conjunct pronouns are prefixed to nouns, suffixed to verbs. But those which denote genders (proper to the third person only) are generally used suffixually with all qualitive nouns, which thus pass from the adjectival to the substantival category. This latter peculiarity is common to the Himálaya and Tibet, and is found even among the non-pronomenalised tongues, such as written Tibetan and Newári,† and likewise among the Indo-

---

* Kiránti, Váyu, &c., of Himálaya, show a wonderful agreement with what Müller calls the Múnda class of languages in Central India. In all these tongues alike not only the agents (singular, dual, and plural, and inclusive and exclusive of the two latter), but the objects, are welded into the verb, thus showing the maximum of pronomenalisation, whereas the action is nearly smothered by the actors, who, moreover, all reappear in the participial forms.

† *e.g.*, Sinya-hma, the wooden one (an idol), nominal (sin = wood, ya = genitive); u-hma, the that-pronominal; chha-hma, the one-numeral; dá-hma, the striker, participial; byáku-hma, the black-adjectival.

Chinese tongues, whose wong, pong is clearly the Dravidian van. The former also is found in the Himálaya, but, of course, among the pronomenalised languages only. But among them we have samples of the conjunct pronoun being used prefixually with nouns, and suffixually with verbs, as in the Dravidian tongues,* and others of the use of both suffixually, as in the West Altaic and Ugrofinnic groups of languages.* Separate

* Two forms :—

Háyu	am-pa um-pa wa } -pa u }	ang-upa ung-upa wathim- pa	My Thy His } father	To'-p-mum	struck me.
				To'-p-num	struck thee.
				To'-p-t-um or } To'-p-um }	struck him.
Kiránti Báhing	a-pa i-po † a-po	,, ,, ,,	My Thy His } father	Tip-t-óng Tip-t-ú Tip-t-á	I Thou } struck. He
Kiránti Bontáwa	ung-pa am-pa eu-pa	,, ,, ,,	My Thy His } father	Mo-v-úng Tá mó-v-ú Mó-v-eú	I Thou } struck. He
Kuswar	baba-im baba-ir baba-ik	,, ,, ,,	My Thy His } father	Thatha-im- ik-an Thatha-ir- ik-an Thatha-ik- an	I Thou } struck. He

REMARKS.—The Háyu conjunct pronoun (see first form) is falling out of use. Form second gives the full possessive before u-pa used for father, though it be literally a father, any father, his father, pater illius vel istius vel ejus vel cujusvis præter me et te. The verb is given in the objective or agento-objective form = the passive, the active voice no longer showing clearly the pronomenalisation. There is now used instead of this form, and perhaps ever was (it is a question of decomposition *versus* non-development), in the *active* voice the form seen in the sequel in khwa-chammi, I, thou, he, feed (self). Here it would be to'-p-ummi, or top-t-ummi (p = Bontáwa v, being the transitive sign, iterated or not, in the form of t), I, thou, he, struck. In Báhing also, which has a clear discrimination of time into present cum future and past, the former is ti-b-ú, ti-b-í, ti-b-á, I, thou, he, strike or will strike. In these samples we see again the transitive sign b = p = v, and this sign discriminated clearly from the temporal sign or t. The manner in which pá becomes pó in the Báhing noun (pá, my father ; pó = pa-u, anybody's father) is most suggestive, and should warn us against laying such undue stress on the position (prefix or postfix) of the conjunct pronouns. Frequently both are used, the former being in the full separate form and the

---

† The following is a better illustration :—

wá popo i popo } my, thy, his, uncle. á popo	tib-n = tib-wa } tib-i }I, thou, he, strikes. tib-a	

The change of áinto ó (a-pa, i-po) is confined to the words father and mother ; the words for uncle and aunt, which are mere iteratives (po-po, mo-mo), adhere to the latter form, which is very interesting as a sample of suffix pronouns coinciding with the verb form tib-u, pa-u-po ; vapulo, ego pater ejus, a crude pronoun (or noun), is substantival or adjectival according to its use ; thus, in Newári, ji is I or my, ji kai = my hand.

words, meaning two and all, can be added to pronouns and to
nouns, to form duals and plurals, and are often added to a true
inflective plural pronoun to mark that distinction; thus, nam
= *we;* namella = *we all,* plural; nam rendálu = *we two,* dual.
Sometimes the pronominal inflexion is repeated, as in emellam,
we (or *we all*); niv ellam, *ye;* avar ellam, *they,* of Toda.

VERB.

The verbal forms of the Nilgiri tongues clearly place them in
the same category with the cultivated Dravidian; that is, the
pronomenalised class. But, whether from non-development or
from decomposition, the pronomenalisation is very imperfect
on the whole. Nor is it easy to discern in the one or other
group of these southern tongues those generic and temporal
signs which are still so palpably traceable as a distinct element
of the northern tongue verbs. All of the pronomenalised class,
and some that can hardly be ranged in that class, in the
Himálaya, as in Altaic and Ugrofinnic, have the verbal root or
imperative followed by the transitive or intransitive (often
with many subdivisions) sign; and that, again, in the pronomenalised class, by the personal ending, which, too, is sometimes
agentive, sometimes objective (equivalent to active and passive
voice respectively), and sometimes both, in which case the
agentive form always follows the other and makes the ending.
But, even in the northern tongues, the transitive or intransitive

latter in the contracted, as in the Altaic tongues, and not less in Sontál and Hó,
and indeed in all. Thus, in Kuswar, my father is baba-im, or mahana baba-im
(maha, *ego,* ma-ha-na, the genitive). Kuswar beautifully demonstrates the
character of the infixed pronoun as a mark of the transitive verb, and it will be
seen that this language inverts the order of the agentive and objective, and
adds a common termination or an. The neuter verb, of course, omits the
transitive sign, and runs thus : walg-en-im, walg-en-ir, walg-en, I, thou, he, fell.
En is possibly the participial particle. But it is more probably the neuter sign
for the causal = transitive, whilst it resumes the transitive sign "ik," drops the
neuter sign "en," thus, walg-im-ik-an, I cause to fall. In topmun, tiptong, and
thathaimi kap, the tá vel dá root of Chinese, Newári, Sontál, &c., is palpably
traceable, despite its own modifications (to, ti, tha) and its numerous accessories,
all, as usual, suffixed with the single and most interesting exception of the second
person in Bontáwa, where ta-mo-vu shows ta prefixed, mo-v-ung, ta-mo-vu,
mo-v-en, mo being the root.

sign is constantly confounded with the temporal sign, whilst the personal endings likewise sometimes exhibit as much irregularity and defectiveness as they do in the Nilgirian verbs. Nevertheless, judging by analogy, and resting on the wonderful similarity of genius and character pervading all the languages of the sons of Túr, I should not hesitate to say that the cultivated Dravidian and the Nilgirian tongues are framed on the same model as that above described as belonging to the northern, and that the samples above cited from Badaga and Kurumba are palpable proofs of it, notwithstanding the silence of all Dravidian grammarians touching the generic or class sign (transitive, intransitive, &c.) of their verbs. For example :—

I have no doubt whatever about

Badaga	hui-d-an	} I struck (him)	
Kurumba	huiyu-t-an		
Kurumba	mad-id-en	I made (it)	
May be analysed precisely as are—			Active voice.
Turkic	sever-d-im	I loved (him)	
Hungarian	var-t-am	I waited for (him)	
Kiránti (Báhing)	tip-t-ong	I struck (him)	
Háyu	top-t-um	struck him	Active and
Háyu	*há-t-um	gave him	Passive voice.
Kuswar	tha-tha-im- ik-an	} I struck (him)	Active.

and numberless others of which I shall have, ere long, to speak in full. That is to say, I hold it for certain that all these verbal forms consist of, 1st, the root or crude ; 2d, the transitive and preterite sign ; 3d, the personal ending ; and that, moreover, the second of these elements may, in every case, be

---

* Hátum is active and passive in Háyu, and is regularly derived from the imperative transitive ha-t-o, give to him or give it, which is *common* to Khámti and Háyu ; and this leads me to add that the so-called monosyllabic tongues, like the simplest Himálayan ones, and the Tibetan and Burmese, exhibit in their imperatives the compound structure instanced in háto, *e.g.*, shat shod = kill, *i.e.*, kill him or it, in Lepcha and Burmese, where final t vel d is the well-known objective pronoun seen in all the above samples taken from the highest-structured class. Newári has sháta for the preterite second and third persons active and for all persons passive ; expressly because the "t" denotes the object or transitiveness of the action. So also Háyu has si-t- in the same sense, and si (sh) to in its imperative, which is modified by an enunciative sibilant, but shows the transitive "t" as before.

resolved into the third pronoun, current or obsolete, and used objectively. Kuswar baba-ik = *his father*, compared with tha-tha-ik = *strike* (*i.e.*, him, the object), settles the last point even more clearly than Samoiede lata-da = *his stick*, and Magyar Cicero-t = *Ciceronem.**

Having mentioned the wonderful analogy of these tongues, I will give a telling instance. In the Háyu language of the Central Himálaya and in the Mantchú we have khwachambi or khwachammi = *I feed*, that is to say, *feed myself;* for khwá, vel khóa is the root, chá the reflex sign, and mbi vel mmi the personal ending, and one, too, that in both tongues is invariable, though Háyu appears sometimes to drop the iteration in the second and third persons, khwachammi, khwá-chá-m, khwá-chá-m, *I, thou, he, feed* (self). Now, that root, reflex sign, and personal ending should thus concur to absolute identity, and that sense also should be as identical as form in two unconnected languages, is simply impossible. It follows, therefore, that we have people of the Mantchu race forthcoming now in the Central Himálaya close on the verge of the plains! And, again, what shall we say to such grammatical coincidences as—

Túrki	baba-im = my father,	sever-im = I love.
Kuswar	baba-im = my father,	saken-im = I can.

The answer is clear, that we have people of the Turkic stem also in the Central Himálaya, close to the verge of the plains of India. Nor need we doubt that such is the case in regard both to the Mantchúric and Turkic relations of the Himálayans, though the precise degree of such family connections can hardly become demonstrable until we have (what is now, alas! wholly wanting) a just definition of the Turánian family, and of its several sub-families, to test our Himálayan analogies by. The Mantchuric and Mongolic groups of tongues were long alleged to show no sign of pronomenalisation. It is now known that that was a mistake.

Other still maintained distinctions will, I anticipate, disappear before the light of fuller knowledge, when it will plainly appear that not mere and recent neighbours, such as

* Müller apud Bunsen, I. 319.

are alleged to be the Tibetans proper of our day (Bodpas), or they and the Ugrians, formed the Turánian element of Indian population, from the Himálaya to the Carnatic, but successive swarms from the one and same great northern hive—whether Turkic, Mongolic, Mantchuric, Ugric,* or these and others—who passed into Indo-China as well as India, and directly into the latter, as well as through the former into the latter, by all the hundred gates of the Himálaya and its southern off-shoots. Simple as the Mongolic and Mantchuric languages are wont to be called, they seem to me to possess entirely the essential Turánian characteristics; that is, in like manner as they have endless noun-relational marks without any distinct declension, so they have a rich variety of sorts of verb (but all reduceable into the two great classes of action, or that of things and that of beings, equal neuter and transitive), and this peculiar richness united with great poverty of voice, mood, and tense, whilst the participles partake fully of this character of the noun and of the verb; that is, they are poor on one side but luxuriant on the other, and throughout the whole Turánian area perform the very same function or that of continuatives, being employed to supply the place of conjunctions and conjunctive (relative) pronouns.

The Central Himálayan languages, but perhaps more especially those of the pronomenalised type, all present these characteristics with perfect general fidelity and with some instances of minute accord, besides those cited above, among which may be mentioned the hyper-luxuriant participial growth of Kiránti and of Mantchu, both of which have ten or rather eleven forms of the gerund, and these obtained by the very same grammatical expedient!

There is another very noticeable peculiarity common to the Himálayan and Nilgirian tongues, which is the emphatic distinction of the first person in conjugation, thus, piuthtstini, Toda, *I strike*, stands apart from puithtsti, *thou, he, she*, or *it strikes*, which are all the same. So Newári has daya in the present and dayu in the past for *I strike, I struck*, as opposed

---

* Are not Ugric, Uighur, or Igur, the same! and would not the identical name with the common characteristics (pronomenalised) of the tongues go far to identify the Ugrians with the E. Turks?

to the common terminations yu and la respectively for all striking present and past of every other kind save by the first person, da-yu, da-la, *any body or thing save me strikes or struck.* Hence these forms are used to constitute the passive, as in jita dála, of the sequel. Again, the hardening or doubling of the sign consonant of the intransitive verb in order to make it transitive, a principle supposed to be so peculiarly Dravidian, is quite familiar to the Háyu and Kiránti tongues. And again, the Báhing dialect of Kiránti is fully characterised by that indiscriminate use of the transitive and neuter signs for which the Tamil language is so remarkable. Another common characteristic of the Dravidian and Himálayan tongues is the double causal, *e.g.,* bokko = *get up;* pokko = *cause to get up;* pongpato = *cause to cause to get up*—in Báhing. Dun = *become;* thun = *to cause to become;* thumpingko = *cause to cause to become* —in Váyu.

Another common and radical feature of the Dravidian and Himálayan tongues is the amorphous character of their vocables, which become distinct parts of speech, as noun or verb, by the suffixing of appropriate particles. Thus kan, *the eye,* and *to see;* so neu, *goodness, to be good, good,* whence neu-gna, *I am good;* neu-ba, *the good one,* &c.—of Báhing. I, however, at present forbear to touch on more of these common characteristics of the Dravidian and Himálayan tongues, because they are so apt to run into the common property of all the Turánian tongues. But I may just add that Hoisington's Tamulian traits (in the " American Or. Journal ") are nearly all found characterizing the northern languages.

The general absence of a passive, the partial or total absence of tense distinctions, and the combination of the present and future when there *is* such partial distinction, as well as the denoting of tense by annexed adverbs (to-day, yesterday, and to-morrow) when there is *none,* are Turánian traits common to the (not to go further) Altaic, Himálayan, Indo-Chinese, and Tamulian tongues. Thus the Toda and Kota verbs are always or generally aoristic, and the three tenses are expressed by the above adverbs of time, used prefixually. Precisely such is the case with the Bontáwa dialect of Kiránti and with the Háyu,

whilst the Báhing dialect of Kiránti discriminates the past
tense from the other two by the use of an appropriate infix,
which is at once the transitive and temporal sign.   If such be
not visibly the case with the Badaga, Kurumba, and Irula
dialects, we may yet discern the cause, partly in the careless-
ness of barbarians, partly in that fusion of transitive and
preterite signs which cultivated Dravidian also exhibits, and
not less Ugrofinnic and Turkic.   But in the tin-d-é of Badaga
and Kurumba, and tid-d-é of Kota = *I ate*, as in the mad-id-é
of Kurumba = *I made*, not to cite more instances, I perceive
that identical preterite sign (t, vel, d) which marks it in Báhing
(tib-á, *he strikes;* tib-*d*-á, or tip-*t*-á, *he struck*), as in endless
other northern and north-western tongues.

I will add a few more words on these important points, for I
conceive that the passive of the cultivated Dravidian tongues
is clearly factitious, and suggested by contact with Arianism.
There are still extant long works in Canarese, says Mr. Metz,
in which hardly one instance of the use of the passive voice
occurs, and the fact that the *un*cultivated Dravidian tongues
have it not, is, I think, decisive as to its adopted character in
the cultivated.   Again, there can be no doubt that the negative
conjugation of the cultivated Dravidian tongues presents the
primitive form, and that form is aoristic; *e.g.*, mad-en, *I do,
did*, or *will, not make*.   In Himálaya and Tibet and Sifán the
passive is wanting.   Its absence is wholly or partially supplied
by the use of the instrumentive and objective cases of the
pronouns for the active and passive forms respectively.   Even
Khas still adheres to this primitive and indigenous form, over-
laid as that tongue is by Arian forms and vocables; and I have
myself not the least doubt that the anomalous né of the
preterite of Hindi and Urdu is nothing but the commutative
equivalent of the Khas instrumental sign lé.   A Khas of
Népál invariably says, *by me struck* for *I struck*, and *me struck*
for *I was struck;* and, moreover, there is still the strongest
presumptive proof, internal and external, that this, the present
preterite, was a primitive aorist, and the only tense in Khas.
Those who are fully conversant with the spoken Prákrits of
the plains can testify that the same traits still cleave to the

vernaculars of the so-called Arian class of tongues in the plains—traces, I conceive, of primitive Turánianism as palpable as are to be found in the secondary terms (bhat-*wat*, mar-*dal* (*vide* infra), kapra-*latta*, &c.) of the Prákrits, and which their grammarians can only explain by calling them tautological sing-song. That all such terms are really genuine samples of the double words so common throughout the Turánian area, and that the latter member of each term is Turánian, I trust by and by to have time to show. Meanwhile, and with reference to the Tartar substitute for the voices, here are a few examples :—

By me struck = *I struck*, active voice.

Tibetan, ngági dúng; Newári, jing dáye; Háyu, g'ha toh'mi; Khas, mailè kútyo; Urdu, main nè kúṭa.

Me struck = *I was struck*, passive voice.

Tibetan, ngála dúng; Newári, jita dála; Háyu, go toh'mi; Khas, manlai kútyo; Urdu, mujh ko kúṭa (subaudi, usnè).

The languages which employ conjunct suffix pronouns have a form precisely equivalent to the latter, *e.g.*, Soutál dál-éng, and Háyu toh'-múm = *struck me*. And observe that Sontál dál, *to strike*, reproduces not only the widespread dá vel tá root of the north, but also the l of Newári dála,* as to which see remarks on the transitive and preterite sign aforegone, and Urdu már-*dál*, with its comment.

With regard to the personal endings or pronominal suffixes of the Nilgirian verbs, their obscurity is sufficiently conformable to the cultivated Dravirian models, with due allowance for mistakes on the part of the rude speakers of the former tongues. Something may also be ascribed with probability to decomposition and disuetude. But upon the whole we cannot doubt that these tongues belong to the pronomenalised class, and that, for example, the ni and mi of Toda tinsbi-ni, *I eat;*

---

* Observe also that Jita dála reproduces the objective sign, ta vel da, above spoken of. Compare latada and Cicero *t.* As a transitive sign of verbs it is most widely diffused, and nearly as widely are ka vel ga, and pa, vel ba, vel va. Sa vel cha is a very widely diffused neuter sign which also can be traced indubitably to the third pronoun used to denote the object—in this case, the agent himself or itself. The French forms, Je lève and Je me lève, &c., very well serve to indicate the latter form, though not the former of Turánian verbs.

tinsbi-mi, *we eat ;* with the an, al, ad of nidre-madut-an, maḍut-al, maḍut-ad, *he, she, it sleeps,* of Kurumba, are instances of suffixed pronouns. And now, having already remarked sufficiently upon the other peculiarities of the Nilgiri pronouns under the head of " pronoun," I shall here bring these remarks, suggested by the Nilgirian vocabularies, to a close.

P.S.—Of the many resembling or identical words in the Himálayan and Dravidian tongues I say nothing at present. Those who meanwhile wish to see them, have only to consult the several vocabularies printed in the Journal.

But with reference to what I have stated above, that there exists an authentic tradition (reduced to writing some five hundred years back) identifying the people of the Malabar coast with those of Népál proper (or the Newár tribe), I may just point to such words as wá vel vá = *come,* and sumaka = *silent,* as perfectly the same in form and meaning both in the Newár language and in that of the Nilgirians.

SUPPLEMENT TO THE NILGIRIAN VOCABULARIES.

English.	Toda.	Badaga.	Kota.	Kurumba.	Irula.
Eat	tennu	tinnu	tinnu	tinnu	tinnave, tinduko (the latter to a superior)
Drink	únú	kudi	úne	kudi	kudidukove, kudidukoveko
Sleep	vorg	voragu	vorage (g = German g)	nidre madu (sleep make)*	kadandukove, kadandúko
Wake	vorigadi, **yecharichagirt**	yecharagiru (*awake be*)	yecharike iru (*awake be*)	yecharikeagiru (*awake be*)	néúevá girave
Laugh	kari	négó	kárje	nage	girkádu
Weep	aththi	laut (au = ou)	áge (g = German g)	alu	aluve
Speak	arvor	nudi (u = oo)	mániro	matádu, nudi	pôsu
Be silent	bokir	sumagiru, japaniru	pakiru	symaniru (*silent be*)	maniade iru (*speechless be*)
Come	itva? vá (it-va = *come here*)	ba, iti ba? (iti-ba = *come here*)	váge	ba	barave
Go	atfo? fo (at-fo = *go there*)	hógu, ate hógu? (ate hogu = *go there*)	athóge? hóge (at hóge = *go there*)	hógu	bhó
Stand up	mklo	lyettu	méke	reidu	yéndu kove
Sit down	neshkir (*be down*)	kuli	kúkiru (*be down*)	kutukó	ukandu kove
Move, walk	at nar? nar (at nar = *walk there*)	nade, ate nade? (ate nade = *walk there*)	nade	nade	nadandu kove
Run	vór	vódu	ate vódu	vódu	vódu
Give	ta, kor	ta, kodu	ta	kodu	tárave
Take	tegi, yettfo (*having taken go*)	tegi	vóde	tegi	bóúgu
Strike	burv	hui	puiye	hui	adi

* The brackets denote suggestions of my own. Former = guttural Scotch ch in loch, &c.
† Ch = kh. English ch represented by tsh.

K

English.	Toda.	Badaga.	Kola.	Kurumba.	Irula.
Kill	birshkir, koddu	kodd hóku	tavarsidade	kondu hóku	adidukove, kondu-kove
Raise, lift up	tách*	tắku	mékarse	táku	tákove
Put down	atvei (vei; at-vei = put there)	háku, idu, atebt (ate bi = put there)	vei	ate idu	bhodu
Hear	vorahir	kte, vorahiru (hearing be)	vóruttulle	kelu	kérukove
Understand	aridir	aridiru, aridutto	arsulle	ariduko	arindiru
Tell	eaht†	hlegu	parrde	helu	sollu
Strike	burv	hui	puiye	hui	adi
Strike not	burthtati	huiya béda	puiyade	huiya béda	adio-venda
To strike	burken	huiya	puikede	huiya	adia
Striking	burthtp	huiyuva	puika	huiyuva	adika
Stricken	burtht (used actively as well as passively, see remarks).	huida	possa	huida	adida
The striker, or He who strikes	Burthtpavan, or burtht-pál (= striking man)	huiynvavanu (van or vanu is masculine suffix, and ál or álu = man is equivalent. The two forms, therefore, are but one) huiyuva álu	puikálu puikálu	huiyuvava huiyuva álu	adikálu adika
Having stricken	burthtudd	huidu, huilundu	possutte	hui du gondu	adidu
I strike	burthtsbini, or burth-versbini	huidane	áne puikape	5) huiyutine	ná adi kallave
I struck	2) No preterite	huide	áne possupe	huide	ná adide
I will strike	No future	Present tense is used	Present tense is used	Present tense is used	ná adike

* Ch = kh. English ch represented by tah. Former = guttural Scotch ch in loch, &c.
† Esh-t is absolutely the same with Háyu ish-to, the t being the transitive sign? And moreover in Toda, as in Háyu, this is active and passive! See burth-t = stricken.

		ná voragine, vora-	*voragape, or inde	5) nidre madutine	ná kaḍandu kóge
I sleep	an vorchsbini	ná voragine, giunnane / ná voragidde	voragape, or voragape	nidre madutine	ná kaḍandu kónde
I slept	No preterite		3) voragape, or nór	nidre madide (*sleep made I*)	ná kadandu kóge
I will sleep	No future †	ná voragine	voragape, or nalke voragape†	Present tense.	
I eat	tetthbini, tinsbini	tinnane	tingape	tinnutine	ná tindu kóge
I ate	No preterite	tinde	tidde	tinde	ná tinde
I will eat	No future † nothbini, kadders-bini	4) tinnane	tingape	Present tense. kaudane, kaautine	ná tinge
I see	No preterite †	nódine	nósigape	kando	ná pátu kóge
I saw	The future is the same as the present tense in all these tongues	nodildo	nósipe		ná pátu kónde
I will see		voragine	voragape		
I sleep	vorchsbini	voragine	voragape	nidre madutine (*sleep made I*)	ná kada ke, na ka-dandu kóge
Thou sleepest	*vorchsti	*voragire	voragape	nidre maduti	ní kaḍandu kónde
He sleeps	vorchsti	voragina	voragapo	nidre madutane	avanu kadandu kónda
She sleeps	vorchsti	voragla	voriglo	nidre madutale	avla } kadandu kondala avala }
It sleeps	vorchsti	voragida	vorigo	nidre madutade	adu kadandu kónda
We two sleep	No dual in any of these languages				
We all sleep. Inclusive	amellam vorchsbini	angella voragineo	amella vorigame	navella nidre madu-teve	These have been casually omitted by Mr. Metz.
We all sleep. Exclusive	emellam vorchsbini	yengella voragineo	emella vorigame	yengella nidre madu-teve	
Ye all sleep	nivellam vorchsbini	ningella voragiari	*vorigire	nivella nidre madu-tiri	
They all sleep	avarellam vorchsbini	uvakaella voragiari	vorigoro	avarella nidre madu-tare	
I cause to kill	I have found no form for this	kodihákisine	tavarsiken	kondhakisutine	ná kollisó vittige
I cause to make	"	madisine	kesiken	madisutine	"

(About the Passive, see Remarks.)

* For omitted Pronouns, see elsewhere. † Adverbs of time used to mark tense. *I sleep yesterday = I slept. I sleep to-morrow = I will sleep.*

English.	Toda.	Badaga.	Kota.	Kuramba.	Irula.
I cause to love	I have found no, &c.	madisine	kesiken	madisutine	nâ pria pannisige
I love	"	"	"	"	nâ pria panni kandirige
I strike	*burthtsûini	huidane	*puikape	huiyutine	nâ adikallave, nâ adila vittige
Thou strikest	burthtsti	huidere	ni puikape	*huiyuti	ni adika
He strikes	burthtsti	huidana	avane puikapo	huiyutane	ava adika
She strikes	burthtsti	huidla	avale posso	huiyutale	avla adika
It strikes	burthtsti	huidada	adu posso	huiyutade	adu adika
We two strike. Dual	Dual is the same as plural ; adding only the numeral *two* after the pronoun instead of ella = *all*				
We all strike. Inclusive	am ellam burthts-bimi	angella huidaneo	âmella puiyame	angella huiyuteve	namella *adikeme* †
We all strike. Exclusive	em ellam burthts-bimi	yengella huidaneo	emella puiyame	yengella huiyuteve	The same
Ye all strike	nivellam burthtsti	ningella huidari	nîmella pórasire	nivella huiyutiri	nimella *adikiri*
They all strike	avarellam burthtsti noi	avarella huidara nai	avarella posso nai	avarella huiyutare nai	avarella *adikaru* nai
A dog	ded noi	yeradu nai	ded } yede } nai	yeradu nai	rendu nai
Two dogs. Dual	(1) No plural		(1) No plural. (See remarks.)	naigalu	No plural for neuters
Dogs. Plural		naigla	eiyune		
A father	eiyan	appa, tande		tande	amma, am-ma caused by euphony from ang-pa, my father
Two fathers, Dual	It is wanting	It is wanting	It is wanting	It is wanting	It is wanting
Fathers. Plural	It is wanting	It is wanting	It is wanting	It is wanting	It is wanting
A father. Indef.	No such distinction exists in any of these languages				
The father. Def.					

* For omitted Pronouns, see elsewhere.   † Dual is not a separate form, but rendu = 2, is added after pronoun instead of ella, as Nam rendal adikeme, &c.

	yen eiyan	yenna appa	yen eiyane	nana tande	yenud amma
My father	yen eiyan	yenna appa	yen eiyane	nana tande	yenud amma
Thy father	nin eiyan	ninna appa	nin eiyane	nina tande	ninnud / ninod } amma
His father	tan eiyan	avana / ava } appa	avan eiyane	avana tande	avanud amma
Her father	tan eiyan	avla appa	aval eiyane	avala tande	avalud amma
Its father	tan eiyan	aduna appa	adun eiyane	adara tande	aduna amma
Our father } Excl.	een eiyan	yenga appa	ema eiyane	yenga tande	yemmud amma, for both
Your father } Incl.	am eiyan	anga appa	anna eiyane	nama tande	
Their father	nim eiyan	ninga appa	nimud eiyane	nima tande	ninmud amma
I Ego	avar eiyan	avara appa	avara eiyane	avara tande	avarud amma
My	an, anu	nánu, na	ane	nanu, ná	ná, nánu
Mine	yen, yendu	yenna	yen	nana	yennudu, yennud
We	yendu, yennadu	yennadu	yennade	nanadu	yennádu
	em, am	yengla	yenge	yenga	navu
Our } Exclu.	yem, yemdu	yenga	yengo	yenda	yenmudu, or yem- mud, for both
	Inclu.	am, amdu	anga	emu	nama	
Ours } Exclu.	yemdu, yemmadu	yengadu	amu	yengalu	yemmadu, for both
	Inclu.	andu, ammadu	angadu, nammadu	emadu / amadu } nangude	nanadu	
Thou	ni	ni	ni, niye	ni	ni
Thy	nin, nindu	ninna	nin	nina	ninud, nina
Thine	nindu, ninnadu	ninnadu	ninnade	ninadu	ninnádu
Ye	niv	ning'a	ninge	ninga	niv
Your	nim, nimdu	ninga	nimudu	nima	ninmud
Yours	nimdu, ninmadu nin- gadu	ningadu	ninadu, ningude	ninadu, ningadu	ninmádu, ningadu
He, she, it	avan, aval, adu	ava, avla, adu	avane, avale, ade	avanu, avalu, adu	ava, avla, adu
His	avan	avana	avana	avana	avanud
Her } Con- junc. Common gender	aval	avala, avla	avale	avala	avalud
Its } tan	adun	aduna	aduna	adara	aduna
His } Dis- junc. Common gender	avandu	avanadu	avanade	avanadu	avanadu
Hers	avaldu	avladu	avalade	avaladu	avaladu
Its } adundu	adumdu	adunada	adunade	adaradu	adunadu
They	avar	avaka	avare	avaru	aduru
Their	avar, avaradu	avara, avakara	avare	avara	avarud
Theirs	avardu, avaradu	avaradu, avakaradu	avarade	avaradu	avaradu

Corrections by the Rev. B. Schmid, in the "Malabar" words of the Ceylonese Vocabularies.

ORIGINAL.	CORRECTION.
Akayam	Agiyam. Ak_gam : the y merely intercalary.
Irat-tham	Irattam. Rattam : the i servile = Sanscrit rak tam.
Pasú	Pású. Both syllables short: accent not = long vowel or syllable. It often falls on a short syllable.
Kákam. Kukkei	Kákam. Kukei. } Kakkei, which is the English mode of lengthening the a by making the accent coincide with it, could not be understood.
Naul	Náil. Naul would be pronounced Nowl on the continent of Europe, and would mislead.
Thenam, Malabar Dina, Singalese	These words, seemingly so different, are identical, the difference resulting merely from bad pronunciation and a bad spelling. Singalese (and Sanscrit) d is expressed in the Madras Presidency generally by th, and quite erroneously, and European foreigners might suppose this th = the English th, whereas in all the world only Todas and Danes have the English th. Even the Greek theta Θ is not quite the same. [I doubt the implied Arian etymology. Dina vel thína = day and to-day, is thoroughly Turánian.—B. H. H.]
Talappen	Tagappen. [Hard h = k vel g, throughout the Turánian area.—B. H. H.]
Thanthei. Thathei	Tandei. Tatei. } T = d, and aspiration neutral, are characteristically Turánian, and so also a hard nasal sound followed by t rather than by d.]
Poo Meen	Pú. } Mín. } [These are merely the Gilchristian and Jonesian representations of vowels.—B. H. H.]
Dawrasa Singalese Irattiri	Diása = Canarese Diasa and Latin Dies. [Query. W, like y, is an intercalary consonant, used normally to separate vowels.—B. H. H.] Irátir.
Natchetheram	Natchétiram = Sanscrit Nakshatra. The native word is ván mín = fishes of the sky, for stars. [In Newári the stars are called forest or jungle of the sky.—B. H. H.]
Keranam	Keránam } Better Krámann. The separation of the coalescing consonants being a mere trick of Támil. [Such separation is nevertheless normally Dravidian.—B. H. H.]
Alí-thu Niugal Averkal Avei	Adu. [Ah' is merely the abrupt accent separating the root a and the servile du ve thu.—B. H. H.] Niugal. [U for n is a misprint merely.—B. H. H.] Avargal. [Gal = kal, plural sign. But gal is better after a liquid.—B. H. H.] Avar. [Misprint merely.—B. H. H.]
Ennudeyathu. Enathu Ummadiathu. Unuathu Oné	Ennudéyadu. Enadu, } And so also read Avanudéyadu and erase Avarudéyadu, which is the Ummudéyadu, Unadu. } plural, Avarudéyadu, just cited. In the neuter, avatin.

Inthu — Eindu.
Pat-thu — Pattu.
Sympathu — Eimpattu.
Idat-thu — Idattu,
Netta — Nétu.
Inga. Angel — Ingé. Angé.
Engzei — Engé.
Kéiéi — Kúlé.
Met-tha — Metta.
Echukkuka — Edukkágru.
His. That — This. That.
Moschito — Moustachio.
Which. Kōn. H. — Which.
Which. Tōn. H. — Which.
Net-thirei — Tūngu.
Alukei — Alu.
Iru — Ulukkáru.
Kondurá
Eduttupōdu
Nadamadutha
Oduthal — Nada. Odu.

[I never use the diphthong ei so common in European writing of Drawidian tongues. With me ó makes ai, and á, au, and ó, ou. I never confound these two latter. The sliding French u I present in the form of eu, or in combination with a precedent consonant in the form of yú, thus English *puling* and *tune* I write pyúling and tyúin. The French j and u as seen in *jeu* d'esprit are among the commonest and most characteristic of Turánian sounds. I write them separately, z and eu, united zyú.—B. H. H.]

Long German dotted ú, or French ú.

These are slips of the pen in the English column. The latter is inferred from the Malabar terms.

The Hindi and Urdu relative and correlative are wholly unknown in Támil. Whatever is put down, therefore, must be incorrect.

Nittirei and Alukei (rather Alngei) are substantival forms = *the sleeping* and *the weeping.*

Iru means literally *be*, but is often used for *sit.* But ulukkáru is the proper word for *sit down.*

These are compounds from the verbs *come* and *go,* and mean *taking come* and *taking go.*

Thal suffix means *the doing;* maduthal in Canarese = *to do.* Nada and odu are quite enough for *walk* and *run.*

REMARKS.—I give the above as they reached me without entirely assenting to the value set on such precision by the venerable author of these corrections, or always even approving the corrections, for the more ample and careful becomes our survey of the Turánian tongues, the more deep is the conviction that the largest commutability of consonants and vowels is normal in this family of tongues, that local varieties of utterance are not to be reduced to a quasi-exotic standard, and that Akayam and Keramam, for instance, reflecting as they do the well-known preference of Támil for surds and its aversion to heaped consonants, may very reasonably be preferred to Akayam and Kramam. Mr. Schmid's conjecture that the English th is known only to the Tódas is incorrect, for the Burmese and Kúkis, as well as some Himálayan and Sifanese tongues, have the sound; and likewise the Todava proneness to blend the sounds of s, z, and the English th, and the latter also with d, like the Támulians of the Eastern Coast. My Ceylonese papers were prepared for me by a gentleman who used the ordinary English way of representing Oriental words. I myself always use the Continental, but the other does not mislead me. The Nilgirian vocabularies are framed on the latter model. The cerebral letters are indicated by an italic letter, thus, t, d, ḍ; ch is to be pronounced as in English *much*; ch with the mark > above, as in Gaelic *loch*; and in Toda th is always to be sounded the English way.—B. H. H.

ON THE ABORIGINES OF SOUTHERN INDIA
AND CEYLON.

To the Secretaries of the Asiatic Society.

GENTLEMEN,—In prosecution of the steps already taken by me, and recorded in our Journal, for obtaining ready and effective means of comparing the affinities of all the various aboriginal races tenanting the whole continent of India, I have now the honour to submit a comparative vocabulary of seven of the Southern tongues. Five of them belong to the cultivated class of these tongues, viz., Tamil, Malayalam, Telugu, Carnataka, Tulava; and two to the uncultivated class, viz., Curgi and Todava. The former are given both in the ancient and modern form, and care has been taken to procure the genuine vocables instead of those words of Sanscrit origin which are now so apt to be substituted for them, especially in intercourse with Europeans. I am indebted for these vocabularies to Mr. Walter Elliot of Madras, whose name is a sufficient warrant for their perfect accuracy.

In regard to these cultivated tongues of the south, Mr. Elliot observes that the aptitude of the people at present to substitute prákritic words for aboriginal ones is such a stumbling-block in the search for affinities as it requires pains and knowledge to avoid; and he instances (among others) the common use of the borrowed word rakta, for blood, in lieu of the native te rm néthar, by which latter alone we are enabled to trace the unquestionable ethnic relationship of the Gónds (even those north of the Vindhia) with the remote southerns speaking Telugu, Cannadi, and Tulava.

On the subject of the local limits and mutual influence at the present day of the cultivated languages of the south upon . each other, Mr. Elliot has the following remarks :—" All the Southern dialects become considerably intermixed as they approach each other's limits. Thus the three words for egg used indifferently by the people speaking Canarese (matté, tetti, gadda), are evidently obtained, the first from the Tamulian, matta; the last, from the Telugu, ga*dd*a. This intermixture, which is of ordinary occurrence in all cognate tongues, is here promoted specially by extensive colonisation of different races, as of the Telugus into Southern India under the Bijaynagar dynasty, where they still exist as distinct communities—and of the followers of Rámánuja A'chárj into Mysore, where they still are to be seen as a separate class speaking Tamil in their families, and Carnataka in public. The Reddies also, an enterprising race of agriculturists, have migrated from their original seats near Rajahmandry over the whole of Southern India, and even into the Maháráshtra country, where they are considered the most thriving ryots, and are met with as far north as Poona." *

Of the uncultivated tongues of Southern India, Mr. Elliot has been able to procure me on the present occasion only incomplete vocabularies of two, viz., the Curgi and Todava. But further assistance may be looked for from him in regard to this class of tongues, as to which he observes that "the dialects of the Kurumbers and Irulers and other mountain races of the south are well worth exploring." I have likewise myself made fresh application to Colonel Low, to our residents at Baroda and Sattara, and to other parties residing at Gúmsar, the Nilgiris, and Ceylon, with a view to completing the comparative vocabulary of all the Continental and Insular aboriginal languages; and to our authorities in Assam and in various parts of the chain of mountains dividing our provinces from those of Ava, in order to obtain the Indo-Chinese series of border languages—all upon one uniform plan.

These shall be hereafter forwarded as received, with such remarks as the study of the whole may suggest.

* * For the ordinary and proper locale of the several cultivated tongues of Southern India, see Ellis' Dissertation and Wilson's Mackenzie Manuscripts. Mr. Elliot speaks in illustration of the general and well-known facts of the case.

English	Tamil		Malayalam		Telugu		Carnataka		Tuluva.	Curgi.	Todava.
	Ancient.	Modern.	Ancient.	Modern.	Ancient.	Modern.	Ancient.	Modern.			
Air	kál	káttu	...	kátta	...	gáli	elaru	gháli	gháli	...	kott
Ant	uravi	erumbu	...	irumba	...	chima	...	irivi	pijin	...	erbb
Arrow	kanei	ambu	parva	amba	...	ammu	saralu	ambu	biru	pakki	pull
Bird	pul	paravei	...	pakki	...	pitta	...	hakki	pakki	chore	...
Blood	sennír	udiram	...	chora	...	netturu	kemniru	netturu	nettar	...	...
Boat	pakada	odam	...	vanji, or vallam	...	padava	páru	doni	oda	...	...
Bone	enpu	elumbu	...	ella	...	emika	elume	eluvu	elu	...	ir
Buffalo	kárán	erumei	...	eruma	...	enumu	...	emme	ermo	...	...
Cat	púsei	púnei	...	púchcha	...	pilli	...	bekku	puchche	...	...
Cow	á, pettam	pasu	...	payya	...	ávu	ávu	hasuvu, ákalu	petta	payyu	tanma
Crow	karumpil-lei	kakká	...	kákka	...	káki	...	kági	khákke	...	kak
Day	el	pagal	...	pagal	...	pagalu	pagalu	hagalu	pagil	pogal	pokhal
Dog	...	náyi	...	náya	...	kukka	...	náyi	náyi	náyi	náyi
Ear	sevi	kádu	...	káda	...	chevi	...	kivi, kimi	kebi	kemi	kavi
Earth	...	nilam	...	nilam	...	pudami	...	podavi	nela	...	nelan
Egg	sinel	muttei	...	mútta	...	guddu	...	tatti, or motte, or guddu	mutte, or tetti	...	mukshu
Elephant	kaliru	áne	...	ána	...	éniga	...	áne	áne	áne	án
Eye	náttam	kan	...	kanna	...	kannu	...	kannu	kann	kann	konn
Father	endei	tandei, ta-gappan, appan	...	achchan	...	tandri	...	appa, tande	anme	...	eyyan
Fire	azhal*	neruppu	...	tiyya	...	nippu	...	benki, kechchu	tu	...	...
Fish	puzhal	mín	...	mín	minu	chépa†	...	minu	mín	...	...

* Zh is employed, according to Mr. Ellis' plan, to represent the Tamil ழ which has the sound of the French j in jamb, Jacques, &c., but is often pronounced like a hard l by Europeans, Mohammedans, and other foreigners, and also by the Pariahs. Thus azhal would be alal.
† So written, but pronounced chápa.

s lower	alar	pâ	tingal§	puvva	—	puvvu	puvvu, or pâ a/di	huvvu, or	pu	—	puvvu
Foot	kazhal	adi		adi		adugu		hejje	hajji		orri*
Goat	vellei	âdu		vallâdu		mêka		kuri	êdu	kuri	âdr
Hair	kuzhal	mayir		talamudi		ventruka		kûdalu	kûdalu	orama	mir
Hand	tol	kai		kayya		cheyi	tol	kayi	kai		kayi
Head	senni	talei		tala		tala		tale	tare	mande	mudd
Hog	kêzhal	panri		panni			pandi	handi	panji	paudi	
Horn	kodu	kombu		komba		kommu		doda, or kombu / kombu	kombu		kurr
Horse	pâyimâ	kudirei		kudira		gurramu		kudure	kudare	kudre	kadar
House	illam	manei,uidu		vida, illam		illu		mane	illa		arra
Iron	karumbon	irumbu		irumba		inumu		kabbina	karba		err
Leaf	adei	elei		ela		âku		ele	ire		pelch
Light	oli	velichcham		velichcham		veluturu		belaku	bhoksha	elakand	âl
Man	makana	âl, see night		âl		koti		âiu	âl	mânus†	kodan‡
Monkey	kaduvan	kurangu		koranga				koduga, or manga	mango		
Moon	pirei	tingal	tingal		nela, or zâbilli			ac tingalu	tingalu		
Mother	inrâl	tâyi or âyi		amma		talli		tâyi, or avva	appe	avva	pann
Mountain	varei	malei		mala		konda	male	gudda	gudde		pâyi
Month		vâyi		vâya		noru		bâyi	bayi	bayi	
Mosquito		kosuvu				doma		solle			
Name	al	pêr		pêra		pêru	pesaru	hesaru	pudar		pêr
Night	nêyam	irâ		râv		rêyi		iralu	iral	iral	
Oil		ennei		enna		nûne		enne	enne		enn
Plantain		vâzhei		vâzha		arati		bâle	bâle		
River	varupunal	âru		puzha		êru	pole	hole	tude	pole	pâ
Road	neri	vazhi		vazhi		dâri, dova	pâde	hâli	sâdi	batte	morg
Salt	adal	uppu		uppa		uppa		uppu	uppu		upp
Skin		tol		tola		tolu		tovalu	tolu		torn
Sky	vin	vânam		mânam		minnu	nugilu, or bân, or bânu				pone

* These words signify footstep rather than foot. The common word for foot in all the S. dialects is kal. † Sansc.
‡ Macacus radiatus. § The common word is chandra, Sansc.

English.	Tamil.		Malayalam.		Telugu.		Carnataka.		Tulava.	Curgi.	Todava.
	Ancient.	Modern.	Ancient.	Modern.	Ancient.	Modern.	Ancient.	Modern.			
Snake	kadsevi	pámbu	...	pamba	...	pámu	pávu	hávu	parapunu	pamb	pab
Star	vin-min	vánmin	...	minganna	...	chukka	uinu	chukki	dáráya	...	ponémin
Stone	kan	kal	...	kalla	...	ráyi	pallili	kallu	kalla	...	kall
Sun	...	pakalon	...	súrya (common)	...	poddu		hottu	polutu	...	...
Tiger	pul	puli	...	puli	...	puli	puli	huli	pili	nari	pirri
Tooth	eyiru	pal	...	palla	...	palla	pallu	hallu	káli	pall	...
Tree	...	sedj, mar-am	...	che*i, maram	...	chettu	...	gida, mara	mara	mara	mén
Village	pekkam	úr	...	tara, désam	...	úru	palli	halli, uru	úru	...	modd, or mort
Water	punal	tanni	...	vellam	...	nillu	...	niru	nir	nir	...
Yam	...	valli*	...		...	...	...		...		...
I	yán	nán	...	gnán	...	nénu	án	nánu	én ... i (pronounced as in it)	nán	one
Thou	...	ní	...	ní	...	nívu	nin	niuu	í	nin	ní
He	...	avan	...	avan	...	vádu	avam	avanu	áye	...	...
She	...	aval	...	aval	...	áme	aval	avalu	aval	...	...
It	akudu	adu	...	ada	...	adi	...	adu	av	...	...
We	yám	nám	...	guángal, or nám	...	mému	ám	návu	enklu	eng	...
Ye	nívir	nír	...	uingal	...	míru	nim	nívu	innkulu	ning	namma
They	...	avar	...	avara	...	váru	avar	avaru	ákulu	avaru	ádám
Mine	...	enadu	...	enre	...	náli	...	nannadu	ennow	...	...
Thine	ninadu	unadu	...	ninra	...	nidi	...	ninnadu	innow	...	...
His	...	avanadu	...	avanre	...	vádidi	...	avana	áyanow	...	...
Ours	emadu	namadu	...	nangade	...	mádi	...	nammadu	enkulanow	...	...
Yours	numadu	umadu	...	ningade	...	míli	...	nimmadu	inkulanow	...	...
Theirs	...	ávarudu	...	avarude	...	váridi	...	avaradu	ákulunow	...	...

* Dioscorea alata, perin valli Malayálam; D. oppositifolia, avating tiga, Telúgu; D. aculeata, seru valli, Támil; gannau, Carnátaka; D. pentaphylla, nuran kighang, Támil and Malayálam.

English								
One	…	onru	onna	vokati	ondu	onji	minn	…
Two	…	irandu	renda	rendu	eradu	eradu	nonk	…
Three	…	mûnru	mûnnar	mûdu	mûru	mûji	yajj	…
Four	nângu	nâlu	nâla	nâlugu	nâlku	nalu	orr	…
Five	aindu	anju	anja	âyidu	ayidu	ayinu	ett	…
Six	…	âru	âra	âru	âru	aji	onbod	…
Seven	ézh	ézhu	ézha	édu	élu	él	pott	…
Eight	…	ettu	etta	etimidi	entu	ename	ivvod	…
Nine	onbakudu	onbadu	ombada	tommidi	ombhattu	orambo	muppéd	…
Ten	orupakudu	pattu	patta	padi	hattu	pattu	nalvod	…
Twenty	irupakudu	irupadu	iruvada	iruvai	ippattu	irvo	erbbod	…
Thirty	mupakudu	muppadu	muppada	muppai	muvvattu	muppo	…	…
Forty	narpakudu	narpadu	nâlpada	nalubai	nâlvatta	nârpo	…	…
Fifty	aimbakudu	aimbadu	ambada	yâbai	ayivattu	ayiva	…	…
A hundred	nûru	nûru	nûra	nûru, or vanda	nûru	nûdu	onnûr	…
Of	il	nedaiya	ude	yokka	na, or da	no, or du	k	…
To	…	kku	kk, nn	ku, ki	ge, or kke	ku, or ge	n	…
From	ân	ninru	ninna	nunchi	inda, or dosainda	…	…	…
By	…	âl	âl, âle	valla	inda	ath	…	…
With	odu	…	konda, ode, kûda	to	kûda, or sangada	otugu	ol	kude
Without	allâmal	…	illâda, kûdada	tappa	hortu	horata	…	…
In	kan	il	il	lo	olage	olsi idu	…	…
On	…	mél	mél, méle	payini	méle	mittu	…	…
Now	ippozhadu	ippodu	ippol	ippudu	îga	itten	…	…
Then	appozhadu	appodu	appol	appudu	…	âpal	…	…
When?	eppozhadu	eppodu	eppol	eppudu	yâvâga	épag	…	…
To-day	ittai	inru	inna	nédu	ihottu	ini	…	…
To-morrow	pinrei	nâlei	nâle	répu	néle	elli	…	nâle
Yesterday	nerunal	néttu	innale	ninna	nenna	kode	…	nenne
Here	iran	ingu	ivide	ikkada	illi	inchi	itwan	ikkalu
There	avan	angu	avide	akkada	alli	anchi	atwan	anda
Where?	evan	engu	evide	ekkada	elli	oleke	…	ekke
Above	misei	mél	méle	payina	méle	mett	mockol	…

English.	Tamil Ancient.	Tamil Modern.	Malayalam Ancient.	Malayalam Modern.	Telugu Ancient.	Telugu Modern.	Carnataka Ancient.	Carnataka Modern.	Tulava.	Curgi.	Todava.
Below	kizhakku	kizh	...	tázhe	...	kinda	...	kelage	sett	...	...
Between	náppan	na/tu	...	nadukke	...	nadama	...	na/tuve	na/tu	...	...
Without, outside	...	veliyil	...	purame, or puratta	...	bayila	...	horage	peli	...	parmutak
Within	...	ullil	...	agatta	...	lopala	...	olage	oli	...	ullu
Far	séimei	tulei	...	agale	...	davvu	...	hattara, or sáre	khayi, or tol	...	kéguri
Near	anmei	kitta	...	adukke	...	dápu	...	tusa, or thode	onda	chennang	...
Little	...	siriya	...	kora	...	kásta	...		dinj-a	...	...
Much	mikka	mikunla	...	valara, or éra	...	nindá, or mikkili	...	bahala		...	uppom
How much?	ettunei	evalavu	...	etra	...	enta	...	eshtu	ett	...	...
As	ka/tuppa	pol	...	pole	...	vale	pol	háge	anchane	...	...
So	...	appadi	...	angine	...	atla		háge	do	annane	iggas
Thus	...	ippadi	...	ingine	...	itlá		hige	inchene	innane	...
How?	ennei	eppadi	...	engine	...	etlá		hánge	jayekk	...	...
Why?	...	én	...	endina	...	éla		yatakke, or yáke		...	...
Yes	...	ám	...	ade, uvva	...	avunu	...	havudu	aml	akku	...
No	...	illei	...	illa	...	ládu	...	illa	iddi	alla	...
(Do) not	...	vénda	...	véndá	...	vaddu	...	béda	botri	...	...
And, also	...	um	...	um, nam	...	nni, nnu	...	u (added to the end of the words coupled together)	no	...	...
Or	...	alladu	...	engil, adal-la, allan-gal	...	16ka	...	ádaru	andala	...	...
This	...	avanudaya	...	avande	...	váni	...	avanu	áyino	...	...
That	...	adu	...	ada	...	adi	...	adu, &	avu	adu	ad

English							
Which?	yáźu	ádu	eda	edi	yáŝvadu	erno	
What?	yár	enna	ouda	émi	énu	jána	
Who?	yŝáákilum	ár	ára	evaru	yáru	uvanda	
Anything		eźáákilum	yáduonnen-gil	edainá	yáŝvadá-dara	éránda	
Anybody	áráŝinum	árákilum	yádarutto-rum	evaraina	yáŝádaru	...	
Eat	...	tin	tinnuga, or unnuga	tinu	tinnu	tinupuna	unn
Drink	...	kudi	kuźikka	tágu	kudi, nidde hogu	narapuna, nidri-idu-puna	
Sleep	...	túngu	orakkam	tongundu	echchehat-tiru	echchehirigi-dupuna, telepuna	
Wake	...	vizhittuk-kol	onartuga	mólukonu	nagu	alupuna	
Laugh	naku	nakai	chiri, or chirikkuka	navvu	alu	manipan-tippuna	
Weep	...	azhu	karaga	édchu	summage	...	
Be silent	...	summá-viru	mindá, thiru, or uriyádá thiru	uriké-undu	iru		
Speak	...	pésu	paraya, or samsárik-ka	mátládu	mátádu	pater puna	takparo
Come	...	vá	varuga	vachchu	baru	barapuma	
Go	...	po	poga	povu	hogu	popuna	
Stand up	...	níl	nilka	niluchun-du	nintukollu	entuna	
Sit down	udká	udkáru	kuttnirika, nadakka, or elakka	kúrchundu	kútu kollu	kullona	
Move, walk	...	nada		naduchu	nadi	...	
Run	...	odu	odiga, or taruga	parigettu	odu	párma	tá
Give	...	kodu	kodukka, or taruga	ichchu	koźu	koźupuna	
Take	ettukkol	eduttuk-kol	edukka	pnchehu-konu	tokkolu	...	
Strike	...	adi	adi, talla	kottu	hode	...	
Kill	...	kol	kolla	chiampu	kollu	...	kol

English.	Tamil. Ancient.	Tamil. Modern.	Malayalam. Ancient.	Malayalam. Modern.	Telugu. Ancient.	Telugu. Modern.	Carnataka. Ancient.	Carnataka. Modern.	Tuluva.	Curgi.	Todava.
Bring	koná	konduvá	...	konduva	...	techchu	...	taru	kondattu	...	...
Take away	kodupo	kondupo	...	koudupo	...	tisukonipo	...	oyyu	popuna	...	...
Lift up, raise	márkol	edu	...	pondikka	...	ettu	...	ettu	dirijana	...	...
Hear	...	kel	...	kélkka	...	vinu	...	kélu	...	...	...
Understand	...	ari	...	tirichchiri-ka	...	teliyu	...	tili	teriyunnu-puna	...	...
Tell, relate	...	sol	...	para	...	cheppu	...	hélu	panuppuna	nallad	...
Good	...	nalla	...	nama, or nallada	...	manchi	...	olle, or cheluva	eddattano	kuttad	...
Bad	...	ketta	...	chitta	...	chedda	...	ketta	pedikatta-no	kultat	pillele
Cold	tanniya	kulirnda	...	tanutta	...	challoni	...	tampu	ch'hali	kultat	...
Hot	veyya	sutta	...	chúda	...	védi	...	bisi	sekhe	bekkel	...
Raw	pozháda	pachchei	...	pachcha	...	pachchi	...	hasi	paje	pachche	...
Ripe	kaninda	pazhutta	...	pazhutta	...	mágina	...	mágida	paranda	mantat	...
Sweet	iniya	tittitta	...	...	...	tiyyani	...	si	tipe	...	pilba
Sour	...	palitta	...	puli	...	pullani	...	huli	puli	...	kachchatt
Bitter	azhakiya	kasanda	...	kayippa	...	chédu	...	khayyi	khayipe	kaipal	narradodi
Handsome	azhakiya	azhakána	...	koutuka-máya	...	anda maina	...	cheluva	eddattano	...	...
Ugly	payirpána	aruvarup-pána	...	vasalala	...	...	...	andagédi	padiketta-no	...	odeda
Straight	ozhungána	nérána	...	nére, chov-ve	...	sarigga-unde	...	sariyáda	sarta	nére	...
Crooked	kodiya	koniya	...	valanga	...	vankara	...	sotta	mont	...	...
Black	kariya	karutta	...	karutta	...	nalla	...	kari	khappa	kartad	kapp
White	velliya	velutta	...	velutta	...	tella	...	bile	bollane	baltad	pelpam
Red	seyya	sivanda	...	choganna	...	erra	...	kempu	kempu	chondad	...
Green	...	pachchei	...	pochcha	...	akupach-cha	...	ele hasuru	pachche	...	...

Long	niliya	nínda	nínda	nidupa	udda gidda udda	udda kuddya	niraka, ne-ragatti kullol
Short	…	kuriya	kuranna	kurachu	gidda	…	…
Tall	…	uyarnda	…	podugu	sanna, chikka	kennu	…
Short	…	kuriya	…	…	doḍḍa	…	…
Small	vaźtdána	siriya	chiriya	paṭṭi chinna	…	…	…
Great	śórváźa	periya	valiya	pedda	gundu	mallow	…
Round	…	tiranḍa	urunda	gunḍu	chouka	uruṭu	…
Square	aḍara	saduram	chadaram	chadaram	chappate	chouka	…
Flat	valatta	taźaiyána	paranna	…	kabbida	thora	…
Fat		kozhuppá-na, or va-lappámá-na	kozhutta	kovvina	…	…	pekkam
Thin	melliya	melinda	melinsa	palachani	tellaneya	sabara	…
Weariness	ayaríppu	ileippu	valachal	alupu	danivu	bajil	…
Thirst	…	nirveźkei	tanni keri-chal	dappi	niradike	…	nikhosti
Hunger	posi		visappa	ákali	hasivu	paduvu	…

VOL. II.

P.S.—In representing the vernacular terms in Roman characters I have followed the received mode of spelling; *d, t*, in italics, represent the hard cerebral sounds of those letters which have only one representative with us, as opposed to their soft dental sounds; *r* among the Todas has a peculiarly harsh and prolonged sound which I have represented by reduplication. The correct sound of the Tamil *zh* is a deep cerebral enunciation of the French *j*, formed by touching the back of the palate with the tongue. Such a sound is very common in Tibetan and its derivatives, wherein nearly every *d* and *g* and *ch* becomes a harsh *zh*, as *digarchi* pronounced *zhiggatzhi*.

ABORIGINES OF CEYLON.

English.	Malabar (of Ceylon).	Singalese.
Air	Agāyam	Hulanga
Ant	Erumbu	Kúmbeyá
Arrow	Ambu, Kanri	Sare, or I'yá
Bird	Kuruvi, Pullu	Kurullá
Blood	Irattam, Rattam, Uthiram, Kuruthi	Lé
Boat	Thoni, Odam, Morak-kalam	Arua
Bone	Elumbu	A'tá
Buffalo	Erumei	Miharaká
Cat	Púnei	Balalá
Cow	Pāsŭ, Au	{ Eladena (gawa is the generic term)
Crow	Kágam, Kākei	Kaputá, Kakká
Day	Nál	D'wăsă, Dina
Dog	Nāy	Ballá
Ear	Kádu, Sevi	Kana
Earth	Púmi, Puvi, Prithivi, &c.	Polawa
Egg	Muttei, &c.	Bijja
Elephant	Yánei	Atá
Eye	Kan, Vilzi	Aha
Father	Jagappen, Thathei, Tandei	Piyá, Appá
Fire	Neruppu, Jí, Kanali, &c.	Gini
Fish	Min	Matsia
Flower	Pú	Mal
Foot	Kál, Thál, Ade	Paya
Goat	A'du, Velládu, &c.	Eluá
Hair	Mayir	Kes
Hand	Kai	Ata
Head	Thalei	Olua
Hog	Pandi	U'rá
Horn	Kombu, Kódu	Anga
Horse	Kutherei, Pari, Asuram	Aswaya
House	Vídu, Manei, Illam, Akam	Geya
Iron	Irumbu	Yakada
Leaf	Ilei	Kolé
Light	Velicham	Eliya
Man	Manushen, A'daven, &c.	Minihá
Monkey	Kurangku, Manthi	Wandara
Moon	Melavu	Sanda
Mother	Thai, Annei Annei	Amma
Mountain	Malei, Vetpu	Kanda
Mouth	Vái	Kata
Mosquito	Visei, Melvísei	Madurua
Name	Pér	Nama
Night	Iravu, Irătir	Rae
Oil	Ennei	Tel
Plantain	Válei	Kesel
River	Yáru, Kangei	Ganga
Road	Theru, Valzi	Párá
Salt	Uppu	Lunu
Skin	Thól, Tholi	Hama
Sky	Vánam	Ahasa
Snake	Pámbu	Sarpaya
Star	{ Natchetiram, Vanamín (fish of sky) Natchetheram, Velli, &c.	} Tarawa or Tárakáwa

English.	Malabar (of Ceylon).	Singalese.
Stone	Kallu	Gala
Sun	Veyil, Poluthu	Súrya
Tiger	Puli, Vengei	Wayággraya
Tooth	Pallu	Datha
Tree	Maram	Gaha
Village	Kurichi	Gama
Water	Thannír, Nír	Watura
Yam	Kilangu	Ala
I	Nán, Yán	Mama
Thou	Ní, Nír	Tó
He, She, It	Avan, Aval, Ah thu, or Adu	Ohu, aó, éka
We	Nám, Nángal	Api
Ye	Níngel	Topi
They	Avergel	Owun
Mine	Ennudeyathu, Enathu, E'n-adu	Magó
Thine	Ummudeyathu, Umathu, U'n-adu	Togé
His	Avanudeyathu, { Avan-ádu / Avarudeyathu } }	Ohugé
Ours	Engaludeyathu, Emathu, E'm-adu	Apé
Yours	Ungaludeyathu, Umathu, Um-adu	Topé
Theirs	Oné, Avergeludéyadu, Aver-adu	Owngó
One	Ondu, &c.	Ekay
Two	Irandu	Dekay
Three	Múndu	Tunai
Four	Nálu	Hatarai
Five	Eintu	Pahai
Six	A'ru	Hayai
Seven	Elu	Hatai
Eight	Ettu	Stai
Nine	Onpathu	Nawayai
Ten	Pat-thu, Páttu	Dahayai
Twenty	Irupathu	Wissai
Thirty	Muppathu	Tihai or Tis
Forty	Nátpathu	Hatalehai
Fifty	Eympathu	Panahai
A hundred	Núru	Seya-yai
Of	In, Udeya, Thu	Caret
To	Ku	Ta
From	A'l, Irunthu	Gen
By, instr.	Kondu, A'l	Wisin
With, cum.	Udan, Odu, Idattu	Samaga
Without, sine.	Vittu, Allathu, Indi	Natua
In	Il, Ul	Atulé
On	Mél, Péril	Pita
Now	Ippothu	Dan
Then	Appothu	Ewita
When?	Eppothu	Kawadá
To-day	Indu, Indeikku	Ada
To-morrow	Nálei	Heta
Yesterday	Néttu	Eeyé
Here	Ingá, Ingé	Mehé
There	A'ngéi, Angé	Ehé
Where?	Engei, Engé	Kohéda
Above	Méléi, Uyara	Ihala
Below	Kéléi, Kú'le	Pahala
Between	U'déi, Idiyil	Atare or Mada
Without, outside	Veliyé, Purambér	Pita or Bahara
Within	Ulléi	Atulé
Near	Kitte	Langa
Little	Siru, Konjam	Tika

English.	Malabar (of Ceylon).	Singalese.
Much	Metta	Bohoma
How much?	Evvalovu	Koccharada
As	Pól, Ena	Caret
So	Appadié, Avoannam	Mesé
Thus	Ippadi, Avoethamaka	Mesí
How?	Eppadi, Evoethamaka	Kohomada
Why?	En, Edukkäga	Ayi
Yes	A'm, Om	Ou
No	Alla, Illei	Nœ
Do not	Seyathéi	Apá
And also	Um, Thanum	Ta, da
Or	Allathu	Nohot
His	Avanudeya	Ohirgey
That	Ah thu, Athu	Eka
Which, jón ⎫ Which, tón ⎭	Carent	Kókoda
Which? kón	Ethu	
What? kyá	Enna, Entha	Mokada
Who?	Yár, Ever	Kowda
Anything	Ethum	Monawá numut
Anybody	Everayenum, Yarainum	Kowru hari
Eat	Thin, Sappedu	Kanawá
Drink	Kudi	Bonaw á
Sleep	Tungu	Nidá, gannawá
Wake	Villippu	Nagitenawá
Laugh	Sirippu	Hinahawenawá
Weep	Alugei = weeping	Andanawá
Be silent	⎧ Immayiru, Silent be ⎨ Summayiru, Be still, Do nothing ⎩ Pésúdiru, Do not speak	⎧ Katákaranda épá ⎨ (*i.e.*, Do no speak)
Speak *	Pésu	Katákarapan
Come	Vá	Waren
Go	Pó	Palayan
Stand up	Nil	Hitapan
Sit down	Iru, Ulukkáru	Indagan
Move, walk	Nadamáduthal, Nadei	Awidapan
Run	Oduthal	Duapan
Give	Thá Kodu, Tá Kodu	Diyan
Take	Edu, Kai	Ganin
Strike	Adi, Thattu	Gahapan
Kill	Kollu	Marapau
Bring	Konduvá	Genen
Take away	Edúttupódu, Kondu-pó	Ganin
Lift up, raise	Uyarthu, Thúkku	Ussápan
Hear	Kél	Ahapan
Understand	Vilangu	Terunganin
Tell, relate	Sollu	Kiyápan
Good	Nalla	Honda
Bad	Agáda, Pulsada, Ketta	Naraka
Cold	Kulirmei	Sítala
Hot	Súdu	U'sna
Raw	Pachei	Amu
Ripe	Pazhutta	Iduná
Sweet	Inippu	Mihiri
Sour	Pulippu	Ambul
Bitter	Kasappu	Titta
Handsome	Alahána, Alagu	Laksana
Ugly	Avalatchana	Kata

* These Singalese verbs are here put in the imperative mood.

English.	Malabar (of Ceylon).	Singalese.
Straight	Néré, Nér	Kelin
Crooked	Kónal	Aeda
Black	Karpu	Kalu
White	Venmei	Sudu
Red	Sivantha	Ratu
Green	Pachei	Nil
Long	Nedia, Ninda	Diga
Short	Kattei, Kurukal	Kota
Tall } man	Uyarnta	Usa
Short } man	Kullan	Miti
Small	Siria, Sinna	Punchi
Great	Peria	Mahat
Round	Vattippu	Wata or Guli
Square	Sathuramana	Hataras
Flat	Shattei	Patali
Fat	Kolutta, Thúlitha	Tara
Thin	Melintha, Mellia	Tuní
Weariness	Ileita, Kalait-tha	Wéhésa
Thirst	Tāgam	Pipása
Hunger	Pasi	Badagini

SECTION X.

ROUTE OF NEPALESE MISSION TO PEKIN,

WITH

REMARKS ON THE WATER-SHED AND PLATEAU OF TIBET.

THE two following papers (it may be as well to state, in order to show their trustworthiness) were presented to me by the Maha Rajah of Népál in 1843, when I took my leave of him, after having resided at his Court for ten years in the capacity of British Minister. His Highness was pleased to say he desired to give me something which, not being of monied value, I should be permitted to retain, and which he knew I should set especial store by, and all the more because I was aware that the communicating of any such information to the "Feringé" (European) was contrary to the fixed policy of his Government. And therewith His Highness gave me these two documents, as well as several others of equal interest. The papers now in question comprise official summaries of the routes of two of those embassies of tribute and dependence, which, since the war of 1792 with Tibet (aided by China), Népál has been bound by treaty to send to Pekin once every five years. It is customary for these embassies always to keep nearly or quite to the same track, they being conducted through Tibet and China at the expense of the Celestial Empire and under the guidance of officers appointed by it.

The time of departure from Káthmándú is determined by the opening of the passes over the Himálaya, which takes place usually during the first half of June by the melting of the snows; and that accordingly is the regular period for the setting out of the ambassador, who usually reaches Pekin about the middle of the following January. The ambassador's suite is rigidly fixed as to number, and as to every other detail; and, well or ill, tired or not, His Excellency is obliged by his pragmatical Chinese conductor (perhaps we should add in candour, by the character also of the country to be traversed) to push on towards his destination with only one halt of about a month and a half at Lhása, where, luckily for him, there is always some necessary business to transact, the Népálese having long had commercial establishments in that city. The ambassador, who is always a man of high rank (Hindú of course) and rather advanced in life, can take his own time, and cook and eat his own food, and use his own comfortable sedan chair or more comfortable litter (dándi, hammock) as far as Tingri. But there the inexorable Chinese Mehmandar (honorary conductor) meets him with the assigned set of ponies for himself and suite, and His Excellency must now mount, and unceasingly, as inflexibly, pursue his journey through a country lamentably deficient in food, fuel, and water, by pretty long stages and without a halt save that above named, on horseback, over a very rough country, for some one thousand seven hundred miles, and then only exchange his pony for the still worse conveyance of a Chinese carriage (more properly cart), which is to convey him with like persistency some seven hundred miles further, fatigue and bad weather notwithstanding, and the high-caste Hindú's cuisine (*horresco referens*) all the while entirely in the hands of filthy Bhótias and as filthy Chinese! Of course there is a grand lustration after each embassy's return home, which usually happens about two years from the time of its departure for Pekin; and many a sad and moving story (but all reserved for friends) the several members of these embassies then have to tell of poisonous compounds of so-called tea* and rancid lard or suet given them for drink in lieu of their accustomed pure lymph or milk; of heaps of sun-dried flesh incessantly substituted for the farinaceous and vegetable food of all decent Pagans; nay, of puppies served up to them for kids, and cats

---

* The so-called brick tea, which is composed of the sweepings of the tea manufactories, cemented by some coarse kind of gluten.

for hares, by stolid beastly cooks of Bhót (Tibet), under the orders of a seemingly *insouciant* and really pragmatical China-man, who answers all objections with " Orders of the emperor," " Food of the country," " You nicer than us, forsooth," " Fed or unfed, you start at such an hour." It is singular to observe the Celestial Empire treating Asiatics with like impertinence as Europeans, and it is satisfactory to think that the recent treaty of Népál with Tibet has put an end to these and other impertinences.

I proceed now to a few remarks on the form and substance of the papers. The form is such as might be expected from men, of a nation of soldiers and statesmen, scant of words and having an eye to business in the survey of a country. Blucher regarded London merely as a huge storehouse of valuables, fit, and haply destined, to make spoil for a conquering army. And a Népálese regards Tibet and China, not from a picturesque or scientific point of view, but with reference to the obstacles their natural features oppose to a daring invader having an eye to business in Blucher's line. The chief item, therefore, of both itineraries, and the only one of the shorter, is an enumeration of the mountain ridges or ranges intersecting the way (a most valuable piece of information, as we shall soon see); and to this the longer paper adds a similar enumeration of the intervening rivers, with the means of passing them, or the ferries and bridges; the forts occurring all along the route; and, lastly, the lakes and tanks where drinking-water can be had—a commodity most scarce in those regions, where half the lakes are brackish. The several items, together with the stages and the distances (computed by marching-time as well as by reference to the Népálese kós of 2½ miles each), comprise the whole information conveyed. But it will nevertheless be allowed that so authentic an enumeration of so many important particulars, relating to so vast an extent of country so little known, is of no small value; and though here packed into the smallest compass, that information might, in the hands of a skilful bookmaker, suffice to furnish forth a goodly volume. But bookmaking is in no repute with the gentry of Népál. It belongs solely to pandits, whilst on the class of official scribes is devolved the task of recording all useful information, which they are strictly required to embody in the fewest possible words and smallest space. I will only add on this head of the form of the papers—

1st. That the records of the two embassies having been made at the several times of those missions, and quite independently of each other, the statements of one may be used to correct and explain those of the other; and that, where discrepancies occur, the longer paper, which is complete in its details, is probably, on the whole, more correct than the one which is not complete in its details, though I confess a strong leaning to the Chountra statement, because of its sound discrimination of interesting facts.

2d. That the assigned distances, though not measured but computed, yet having a double basis of computation * by marching time under given assigned circumstances, and by kós according also to a given standard in use in Népál, ought, I should think, to be capable of very definite determination in competent hands.

3d. That both papers are literal translations, and that the additional information procured by myself, and embodied for convenience in the documents, is carefully distinguished by the use of brackets; the rest of such information being thrown into foot-notes.

The Chountra's embassy, as I learnt before I left Káthmándú, set out in 1817; that of the Káji in 1822, as appears on the face of the document. Chountra and Káji are titles of ministers of state in Népál. I proceed now to the substance of the documents; and here, in imitation of my friends, I shall be as curt as possible, and endeavour, in a few words, to bring together the most generally interesting items of information furnished by the two papers. The total distance from Káthmándú to Pekin, according to the Káji, is 1268½ kós; according to the Chountra, 1250 kós; and in that space occur, according to the former authority, 106 mountain-ranges, which are crossed; according to the latter, 104. The Káji's paper gives us the further information, that 150 lakes and tanks occur in the

---

* I have heard that the whole road is measured and marked by the Chinese; and if so, the Népálese could never be much out, the only thing required of them being the conversion of Chinese li into kós.

route; 652 rivers,* crossed by 607 bridges and 23 ferries; and lastly, 100 forts.

It would be very desirable, in dividing the whole space into the political and natural limits of the several countries traversed, to make the Chountra's and Káji's papers coincide. But I have attempted this in vain, owing to the different names cited in the two papers and the different methods of citation. In regard to political limits, they concur sufficiently, but not in regard to natural limits. I therefore give the former according to both papers; the latter according to the Chountra's only, it being quite clear on that head. I annex the langúrs or mountain-ranges to both statements.

	Political Limits according to		Mountain-ranges according to	
	Chountra.	Káji.	Chountra.	Káji.
	kós.	kós.	langúrs.	langúrs.
I. Népál (from Káthmándú to Khása) . .	29	34½	6	5
II. Tibet (from Khása to iron bridge of Tachindo) . . .	636	649½	63	71
III. China (Tachindo iron bridge to Pekin .	585	584½	35	30
Kós	1250	1268½	104	106

REMARKS.

I. From Káthmándú to Khása there is a difference of 5½ kós, obviously caused by the Káji's detour *viâ* Sankhu, instead of keeping the direct road as the Chountra did.

II. From Khása to the iron bridge of Tachindo, the difference is 13½ kós. It is pretty clearly caused, partly by a small detour as before, and partly by a slightly different use of terms. In the Chountra's paper the specification in the body of the

---

* Say rather rivers and river-crossings, for the same mountain-locked stream is here and there crossed twenty or thirty times in a very moderate distance. When I pointed out this at Káthmándú, I got the explanation, and was referred to the crossings of the Ráputi River between Hitounda and Bhimphédy on the road to Káthmándú from the plains of India for a sample.

document is "on this side of Tachindo;" in the remarks appended to it "beyond Tachindo;" whereas the Káji's paper specifies Tachindo itself.

III. From the iron bridge of Tachindo to Pekin the difference is only half a kós, which is not worth mentioning.

Natural limits from the Chountra's paper.

	Kós.	Mountain ridges.
1. Cis-Himálayan region (Káthmándú to Bhaírav langúr)	50	7
2. Trans-Himálayan region (Bhaírav langúr to four kós beyond Chinchi Shan, where the *great* mountains cease) .	635	65
3. Chinchi Shan to Pouchin (where *all* mountains cease)	212	30
4. Plains of China (Pouchin to Pekin) .	353	2
	1250	104

To these distributions I subjoin, though it be a repetition, the excellent concluding remarks of the Chountra's paper:—

"Thus there are 104 langúrs (or mountain-passes) between Káthmándú and Pekin, and of these 102 occur in the non-carriageable part of the way, or the first 897 kós; and the last 2 langúrs only, in the remaining 353 kós, or the carriageable part. The last-named part of the way may be said to be wholly through plains, for, of the two hills occurring, only one is at all noticeable, and both are traversed in carriages. From Káthmándú to the boundary bridge beyond Tachindo (China frontier) is 665 kós, and thence to Chinchi Shan is 20 kós. Throughout these 685 kós from Káthmándú, mountains covered (perpetually?) with snow occur. In the remaining 565 kós no snowy mountains occur."

In the way of provincial boundaries we have the following. From Gnaksa, the 37th stage of the Káji's paper, to Sangwa, the 51st stage of the same paper, is the province of U, which contains the metropolis of Tibet or Lhása. At Sangwa, or in full Kwombo-gyamda-Sangwa, commences the Tibetan province of Khám, which extends to Tachindo or Tazhi-deu, which is the common frontier of China and Tibet. It occurs at the 104th stage of the Káji's paper. The native name of Tibet is Pót vel Bód. The Sanskrit name is Bhót. This is Tibet Proper, or the country between the Himálaya and the Nyénchhen-thánglá, which latter name means (and the meaning is worth quoting for its significance) pass of (to and from) the plains of the Great Nyen or Ovis Ammon, or rather, Great Ammon pass of the plains. That portion of Tibet which lies north of the Nyénchhen-thánglá (as far as the Kwanleun) is denominated by the Tibetans the Western half, Horyeul; and the Eastern half, Sokyeul, after the Hór and Sók tribes respectively. The great lake Namtso demarks Northern Tibet in the same way that the great lake Yamdotso denotes Southern.

A word more about the Bhaírav langúr, which is equivalent to Mount Everest, as recently explained to the Society. The Chountra's paper makes it 50 kós from Káthmándú; the Káji's, 52½ kós. But to obtain the latter result you must not blindly follow the entry in the itinerary, but remember that his " huge snow mass "* covers a large space of the road, which must be understood as *commencing* soon after leaving the 14th stage or Thólung, and not after leaving the 15th stage or Tíngri Langkót.

The documents now submitted themselves suffice to prove the meaning of langúr, since they show it to be equivalent to the lá of Tibetan and the shán of Chinese; consequently also (as we know from other sources) to the Turkic tagh and the Mongolic úlá. It may therefore be rendered "mountain" as well as "mountain-pass," and this is the reason, perhaps, why the Népálese often do not discriminate between the name of the pass and of the peak of Bhaírava, but blend them both under the name of Bhaírav langúr, which is equivalent to the Gnálhám or Nyánam thánglá of the Tibetans. Colonel Waugh, therefore, may be assured that his Mount Everest is far from lacking native names, and I will add that I would venture in *any* case of a signal natural object occurring in Népál to

* This great mass is visible alike from the confines of Népál proper (the valley) and from those of Sikim, and all the more unmistakably because it has no competitor for notice in the whole intervening space. It is precisely half-way between Gosain-thán which overlooks Népál Proper and Kangchán which overlooks Sikim.

furnish the Colonel with its true native name (nay, several, for the country is very polyglottic), upon his furnishing me with the distance and bearings of that object, although neither I nor any European had gone near it.*   For the rest, I cannot withhold my congratulations upon this second splendid result of Colonel W.'s labours, though, alack! it would seem fatal to my pet theory of sub-Himálayan water-sheds—a term carefully to be discriminated from *the Himálayan* water-shed to which I now purpose briefly to advert.

Since I presented to the Society in 1849 my paper on the Physical Geography of the Himálaya, a good deal of new information has been published, mixed with the inevitable quantum of speculation, touching the true character of that chain, and the true position of its water-shed, with their inseparable concomitants, the general elevation and surface character of the plateau of Tibet.

After an attentive perusal of these interesting speculations, I must, however, confess that I retain my priorly expressed opinion, that the great points in question are inextricably involved with, and consequently can never be settled independently of, the larger question of the true physical features of the whole of the Bám-i-dúnya of Asiatics and the Asie Centrale of Humboldt.

It *may be* that the Himálaya is not a chain at all, but an exemplification of the truth of Elie de Beaumont's theory, that so-called mountain chains are only parallel dispositions of a series of geological nœuds, which, if laid side by side, constitute the semblance of a chain of longitude, and if laid one over the other constitute the semblance of a chain of latitude.

It *may be* that the Himálaya is not a latitudinal but a meridional chain, and that the geological back-bone of the

---

* It is obvious to remark that no European has ever approached Dhavalagiri, which yet lacks not a native name known to Europeans ; and, in fact, I myself have been twice as near to Dévadhúnga, vel Bháirav thán, vel Bháirav langúr, vel Gnálhám thánglá, as any European ever was to Dhavalagiri.   The Bhótias often call the Bháirav langúr Thánglá, or "pass of the plain," viz., of Tíngri, omitting the more specific designation,† Gnálhám, which also might alone designate the object, nay, which is *the* name of the snowy mass as opposed to the pass over it and the plain beyond it.

† Potius Nyánám.

whole continent of Asia does not run parallel to the greatest
development of that continent or east and west, but transversely to that development or north and south, and that the
Khin gan úla is an indication of the northern extremity of this
back-bone, the Gángrí or water-shed of the Indus and Bráhmapútra an indication of its southern extremity.

It *may be* that the question of the water-shed is not to be
regarded with reference to the adjacent countries only, but, as
Guyot and others affirm, with reference to the whole eastern
half of the continent of Asia; and that the northern part of
Tibet, inclusive of the Himálaya, is to be regarded as shedding
the waters of Eastern Asia from the Arctic to the Indian
Ocean. Such things, or some one of them, I repeat, *may be*,
and one of the theories just enumerated *may* involve the
true solution of questions for some time past investigated and
debated on the frontier of India, though without any sufficiently
distinct reference to those theories, prior though they all be
in date. But the mere statement of them suffices, I should
say, to show that they will not find their solution on that
frontier, but only when the whole Bám-i-dúnya (dome of the
world, a fine Orientalism) has become accessible to science.

In the meanwhile, without seeking to deny that many facts *
seem to indicate that the axial line of the Himálaya lies beyond
the ghát line,† it is obvious to remark that this assumed line is
still parallel to the ghát line, though beyond it, and consequently *cannot be reconciled* with an essentially meridional axis,
such as the Gángri range presents.   And, upon the whole, and
with reference to organic phenomena especially, the ghát line
still presents itself to me as the best deviser of the Indian and
Trans-Indian regions and climates, though I am not unaware

---

* These facts are—1st, That several of the Himálayan rivers (beside the Satlúj,
Indus, and Bráhmapútra, which cannot be so reckoned) have more or less of Trans-
Himálayan courses as the Ganges, Karnáli, Salikrámi, old Gunduk of Hamilton,
Arún, Tishta, and Mónas.   2d, That some of these, after flowing a good way east or
west over the plateau of Tibet, are at length deflected southwards, instead of pass-
ing north into the Erú, or other stream or lake of Tibet.

† Per contra, the numerous determinations of the height of the gháts at far-
distant points seem to warrant our assuming 17,000 feet for the mean elevation of
the ghát line; and it may well be questioned if any line of equal height and extent
exists north of that line. It is the closing of the *ghátts* that annually stops all access
to Tibet, not any obstacle beyond them.

that Bráhmanic geography has, from remote times, carried the Indian frontier up to Mansaróvar and Rávanhrád, to the Brahmapútra and Indus line in Tibet. And, again, though I do not, nor ever did, doubt that Tibet is a very mountainous country, yet I conceive that there are good reasons for admitting the propriety of Humboldt's general designation for it. He calls it a plateau or elevated plain, and all those I have conversed with, who have passed from various parts of the Himálayan countries into those of Tibet, have expressed themselves in terms implying a strong distinction, at least, between the physiognomy of the former and the latter regions. I would add, that nothing can be juster or finer than Turner's original contrast of the two.

No one acquainted, as I have long been, with the native descriptions of Tibet,* or with the general and special delineations of the country by Danville, based entirely upon native materials, or with such enumerations of mountain ranges occurring between the Népálese and Chinese frontiers, as the accompanying documents contain, could for a moment question that mountains abound in Tibet. On the other hand, there are several reasons of a general nature, besides the specific allegations of the fact by the people, to prove that widespread plains also abound there. It may be worth while to enumerate these reasons. They are as follows :—

1st. One language only prevails throughout all the provinces of Southern Tibet, that is to say, throughout Balti, Ladák, Nári, Utsáng, and Khám; or,† in other words, from the Bolór nearly to the Yúnling, whilst in the same extent of country in the Himálaya very many languages are found.

2d. The language of Tibet has express and familiar terms for plain and valley, which are respectively called tháng and lhúng in Tibetan, whereas the Himálayan tongues have no word at all for a plain, no distinct one for a valley.

3d. It is well known that there are very many lakes in Tibet, and several of them of great size—a fact which involves the existence of large level tracts also, as the contrary fact in

---

* Journal No. IV. for April 1832, Article I.
† Journal No. IV. for April 1832, Article I.

the Himálaya involves (what is notorious) the absence of wide-spread levels.

4th.—The numerous names of places in Tibet which are compounded with the word tháng, a plain, as Chyan tháng in Nári, Pékhéu tháng in Tsang, Nar tháng in U', and Pá tháng in Khám, would alone suffice to prove that the general surface of Tibet is very different from that of the Himálaya.

5th.—The numerous names of places similarly compounded with the word lhúng, a valley, as Téshu lhúng, Lhása lhúng, Phemba lhúng, &c.

6th.—Tibet is the permanent habitat of wild animals of the true ox, deer, and antelope types—all creatures of the plain and not of the mountain, and none therefore found in the Himálaya.

7th.—Tibet is annually the seasonal resort of vast numbers of the wading and swimming tribes of birds, which pass from the plains of India to those of Tibet every spring, and stay in the latter till the setting-in of winter, whilst the whole of these birds entirely avoid the Himálaya. "The storks know their appointed seasons in the heavens," and their skilfully-disposed phalanxes periodically afford one of the finest sights we have. Kangchán is swept over as if it were a molehill ! *

There are few of the Tibetan plains more noticeable than that which occurs immediately on passing the Himálaya by the Bhaírav langúr or Nyánamlá—few contrasts more palpable than that of the Cis- and Trans-Himálayan regions at this well-known and central point; and when I lately requested Major Ramsay, the Resident in Népál, to get for me a confirmation or refutation of my opinion, he answered—"Dr. Hooker must be in error when he says there are no extensive plains in Tibet, because Tíngri maidan (plain), for example, is fully sixty miles in length and fifteen to twenty in breadth. Til bikram Thápa assures me that, in the recent war, he marched along that plain for several days and passed a lake three days in circumference, and which he estimates to be as large as the valley of Népál."† When asked if Tíngri maidan was anything like the valley of Népál, he said—"No ! horsemen could not gallop about Népál.

* See my paper on the Migration of Birds in Bengal Asiatic Society's Researches.
† The valley of Népál is about sixteen miles in diameter, or fifty in circuit.

They would have to keep to the roads and pathways. But numerous regiments of cavalry could gallop at large over the plain of Tíngri."* In a like spirit the Tibetans themselves compare the vast province of Khám to a "field," and that of Utsáng to "four channels"†—both expressions plainly implying abundance of flat land; and the latter also indicating those ranges parallel to and North of the Himálaya, which all native authorities attest the existence of in Tibet, not only in Nári, but also in Utsáng and Khám. The most remarkable of these parallel chains, and that which divides settled from nomadic, and North from South Tibet, is the Nyénchhén-thánglá, of which I spoke in my paper on the Hórsók‡ and of which I am now enabled pretty confidently to assert that the Karakorum is merely the Western prolongation, but tending gradually towards the Kwánleún to the Westward. But these parallel ranges imply extensive level tracts between them, which is the meaning of the "four channels" of Utsáng, whilst the East and West directions of these ranges sustain Humboldt's conception of the direction of all the greater chains of Asie Centrale, or the Himálaya, Kwánleún, Thián, and Altaí, as also of that of the backbone of the whole Asiatic continent, which he supposes to be a continuation Westward of the second of these four chains.

Upon the whole, I conceive, there can be no doubt that Tibet Proper, that is, Tibet South of the Nyénchhén-thánglá range, is, as compared with the Himálaya, a level country.§ It may be very well defined by saying it comprises the basins of the Indus (cum Satlaj) and Bráhmapútra; or, if you please, of the Mapham, Pékhéu, and Yamdo Lakes.

In this limited sense of Tibet—which the native geographers divide into Western, Central, and Eastern Tibet, called by themselves Nári, Utsáng, and Khám, or, when they would be more

---

* Tingri is the name of the town. The district is called Pékhéu or Pékhéu tháng, and the lake Pékhéu tso. By referring to the Itineraries, it will be seen that the plain of Pékhéu extends sixty-eight miles in the line of the route, and is succeeded by a still larger plain reaching to Digarchi from Tasyachola (see Chountra's route).

† Journal at supra cit.

‡ Journal, No. II. of 1853. Essays II., 65.

§ See Cooper in Bengal Asiatic Society's Journal, No. 5, for May 1869, and Royal Asiatic Society's Report of the Soiree of March 1870, wherein is given the report of Montgomerie's Pandit, who states that the Mukhtinath pass, 13,100 feet, is reached from the North by a long smooth grassy slope varied by occasional cultivation.

precise, Balti, Máryul vel Ladák, Nári, Tsáng, U', and Khám—Gángrí is the watershed of Tibet.

The region called Tso tso in Tibetan, or that of the lakes Mapham and Lanag, equal to the Mansaróvar and Rávanhrád of Sanskrit geography, is situated around Gángrí, where the elevation of the plateau is 15,250 feet. From this region the fall of the plateau to the points where the rivers (Indus and Bráhmapútra, or Singkhú-báb and E'rú) quit the plateau is great, as we sufficiently know from the productions of Balti and of Khám at and around those points. In Lower Balti snow never falls; there are two crops of grain each year, and many excellent fruits, as we learn from native writers;* whilst my own information, received *vivâ voce* from natives of those parts, assures me that the country towards the gorge of the E'rú or Bráhmapútra is, like Balti, free of snow and yields two crops a year; that rice is produced, and silk and cotton; and that these last articles form the ordinary materials of the people's dress. These points cannot therefore exceed four to five thousand feet in elevation, which gives a fall of above ten thousand feet from the watershed, both ways.

I will conclude these hurried remarks, suggested by the ambassadorial routes from Káthmándú to Pekin now submitted to the Society, with a statement, which I think the Society will perceive the high interest of, with reference to those recent ethnological researches, the whole tendency of which is more and more completely to identify the Turanians of India and Indo-China with those of the Trans-Himálayan countries.

It is this—E'ru tsángpo is the name of *the* river of Tibet: E'rawádi, that of *the* river of Western Indo-China or Ava: E'rú vel A'rú, that of *a* river in the Támil and Telúgu languages. Now, when we remember that Tsángbo is a mere local appendage to the Tibetan word,† and Wádi vel Váti a mere Prakritic appendage to the Burmese word; and further, that the Turánians of Tibet, the Himálaya, and Indo-China are still constantly

* Journal for April 1832.

† Tsángpo, of or belonging to Tsáng, the province of which Digarchi is the capital, and by which place the river (Erú) flows. Even the prefixing of a Y (Yéru—Yáru) is equally Tibetan (in speech) and Dravidian! Turner's is the first and correctest writing of the word—Erúchámbu to wit, for Chámbu is the soft-spoken sound of Tsángpo. (For erú read èru passim).

wont to denominate their chief river by the general term for
river in their respective languages (teste Meinám, Líkhu, &c.),
we shall hardly be disposed to hesitate in admitting that the
Northmen, as they moved Southwards into the tropical swamps
of India and Indo-China, clung to and perpetuated, even amid
various changes of language,* that name of the river of their
Northern home (viz., the river, κατ' ἐξοχήν) with which was
associated in their minds the memory of their fatherland.

"By the waters of Babylon they sat down and wept."

P. S.—Before I went to England in 1853, I had been so fortunate as to gain access to some Gyárungs and Tákpas or
inhabitants of Sífán and of the South-Eastern confines of Tibet.
In my paper on the Hórsók I gave the substance of their
information about Sífán.   I will here add a few scattered particulars about the country lying above Asám, and the rather
because, from the date of my return to India up to this hour,
I have never again been able to get access to these people.   The
Tibetans and Sífánese are wholly unacquainted with the terms
Daphla, Abor, Bor, Aka, Miri, Mishmi, Khamti, by which we
denominate the tribes lying East of Bhútán.   They recognise
Cháng vel Sáng (Changlo of Robinson) as the name of a Bhútánese tribe or rather profession.   They say that above Palyeul
or Népál (Easternmost part—alone known to my informants)
is Tíngri: above Deunjong or Sikim is Trinsam (the Dingcham
of Hooker and Damsen of myself): above Lhó or Bhútán is
Nyéro: above Towáng or Takyeul is Chóna or Jháng chóna:
above Lhókhapta is Kwombo: above Tsárung is Chozogon.
These are said to be the respective Cis and Trans-Himálayan
districts occurring from the position of Kúti in Népál Eastwards
to beyond that of Saddia in Asám.   It is added that the river
E'rú vel Yárú (Bráhmapútra) passes, from Kwombo into Lhókhapta, beneath the great snowy mountain called Kwombochári,
and that a great *mela* or mart is held there every twelve years.
Lhókhapta, or Lhó of the cut lips, is so called to distinguish it

---

* The word for river in De Körös's Dictionary is certainly erroneous, derived from
a misapprehension of the attached descriptive epithet of the great river of Tibet.
The common word for river is chú = water.   But I am assured that a *great* river is
as frequently called E'ru, A'ru, or with the prefix Yéru, Yáru, as in India a great
river is called Ganga.

from Lhó Proper, because the people have the habit of making a permanent cleft in their lip.

Tsáng province is said to be bounded on the South by the Ghúngra ridge, on the West by Mount Ghúndalá, on the North and East by the Kámbalá range; the province of U to be bounded East by Sangwagyámda, West by the river Tamchok-hamba, South by the Kámbalá range, and North by the Nyén-chhen-thánglá. Beyond the last-named great snowy range is situated the immense lake of Nám tsó, which is said to bear the same relation to Northern Tibet that the Yámdo* tso (Palte or Yárbrokyú) lake does to Southern. The former is the Terkiri and Téngri núr† of our maps, as to which maps we have the following further identifications:—Ghámda = Gyámda. Batang = Pátháng. Rywadzé = Rewáché. Lári = Lhá ríngo. Kiáng, added to great rivers = Gyárung. River Takiu = Gyamo gnúl-chu, and river Yang-tse = Nyá chú. Pampou of Huc = Phemba: river and valley both so called. Galdeso river = Galden, and is the East boundary of Phemba and Lhása valleys, as the Tolong river is their Western boundary.

Abstract of Diary of Route from Káthmándú to Pekin, as taken during the Embassy of Chountra Páúskker Sáh, showing the number and position of the mountains passed.

Position of the mountain passes with the names of some of them.	No. of passes (called *langúrs*.)	Distance in kós.
From Káthmándú to Dévapúr	one	six
Dévapúr to Bhót Sípa	one	four
Bhót Sípa to Choútára	one	three
Choútára to Bísambhara	one	six
Bísambhara to Lísti	one	three
Lísti to Khása ‡	one	seven
Beyond Kúti, called Bhaírava langúr §	one	twenty-one

* I have elsewhere corrected the prevalent mistake about the shape of the Yámdo. It is very long and narrow.

† Núr is Turkic for lake as tsó is Tibetan. Tengri núr, or celestial lake of the former tongue, is an exact translation of Nám tsó of the latter. The general prevalence of Turkic words in the geography of Northern Tibet more especially sufficiently evinces the presence of that wide-spread tribe in Tibet.

‡ Boundary of Népál and Tibet.

§ Mount Everest of Waugh.

Position of the mountain passes, with the names of some of them.	No. of passes (called *lan-gúrs.*)	Distance in kós.
Beyond Shékar jéung, called Tásyachóla*	one	thirty-four
Within the Digarchá limits	one	thirty-seven
Beyond Digarchá limits	one	ten
On this side of Lake Khádupainti	one	thirty-nine
Beyond Kapilapainti	one	thirteen
Beyond Lhása circuit	one	sixty-six
Beyond Chhanjugyámda of Khám	one	twenty-nine
Beyond Acharjéung	one	eleven
At Chhésu Khám	one	seven
At Namgye-kúng	one	thirty-six
At Tángtasáng	one	six
At Láché	one	twelve
At a nameless spot	one	three
At a nameless spot	one	one
At a nameless spot	one	four
At a nameless spot	one	four
On this side of Lhóju	one	sixteen
At Sáyansámócha	one	eight
At a nameless spot	one	one
At a nameless spot	one	two
At a nameless spot	one	three
At a nameless spot	one	four
At a nameless spot	one	two
At a nameless spot	one	two
At a nameless spot	one	two
At a nameless spot	one	one
On this side of Chhámdo	one	fifteen
At Páng-do	one	twenty-two
At Hyáphélá	one	five
At Thúmélá	one	three
At a nameless spot	one	nine
At a nameless spot	one	nine
At a nameless spot	one	fourteen
At a nameless spot	one	three
At Néwá	one	seven
Beyond Lángurikhúdé	one	four
At a nameless spot	one	one
At a nameless spot	one	two
At Kólósáng	ono	twelve
At Phúla	one	ten
At Gólá	one	four
At Phúnzadé	one	nine

* Tásya chólá = Thólá of the Káji's paper?

Position of the mountain passes, with the names of some of them.	No. of passes (called *lan-gárs.*)	Distance in kós.
At a nameless spot	one	two
On this side of Pátháng	one	seven
At Tásó	one	nine
At Sámbáthúm	one	eleven
At a nameless spot	one	six
At a nameless spot	one	two
At a nameless spot	one	three
At Lámáyá	one	one
At a nameless spot	one	two
At a nameless spot	one	three
At a nameless spot	one	one
Beyond Litháng	one	ten
At a nameless spot	one	one
At a nameless spot	one	seven
At a nameless spot	one	two
At a nameless spot	one	two
At a nameless spot	one	seven
At a nameless spot	one	two
At Góló	one	nineteen
On this side of Táchindó * or Tazhideu or Tazedo	one	thirteen
At the military post of Khwálechín	one	twenty-eight
On this side of Chhinchisyán (Sháin or Syán = mountain in Chinese)	one	fifteen
At a nameless spot	one	four
Thus far the mountain-ridges passed are generally large. Henceforward they are small.		
At a nameless spot	one	three
On this side of Yáto	one	fourteen
On this side of Paitán	one	ten
Beyond Thinda phú and Kháto	one	thirty-five
On this side of Lochángsyán	one	two
On this side of Mingtou	one	seven
At a nameless spot	one	four
At a nameless spot	one	three
On this side of Chatoú	one	two
On this side of Ulingnái	one	ten
At a nameless spot	one	six
On this side of Chantoú	one	three
At a nameless spot	one	two

* The iron bridge beyond Táchindó is the boundary of Tibet and China. See Diary of a Journey from Káthmándú to Táchindó, printed in our Researches.

Position of the mountain passes with the names of some of them.	No. of passes (called *langúrs.*)	Distance in kós.
At a nameless spot	one	one
On this side of Gamsú	one	three
At a nameless spot	one	six
On this side of Kwángsyán	one	three
Beyond Kwángsyán	one	six
On this side of Saichhâng	one	four
At Saichhâng	one	two
Beyond Saichhâng	one	five
At a nameless spot	one	three
At a nameless spot	one	two
On this side of Níchhángtoú	one	seven
On this side of Tángákú	one	six
Beyond Mínsyán	one	three
Beyond Poáthínsyán	one	sixteen
Beyond Lúpasyán	one	nine
On this side of Phúngsyán	one	twelve
On this side of Poúchingsyán	one	nineteen
Not carriageable thus far. Henceforward carriages may be used.*		
At Chhálúng	one	caret
At Sínghásyán	one	caret
[Distance of both, as cited below	...	353]
	104	1205

Thus there are 104 langúrs or mountain ridges and passes between Káthmándú and Pekin, and of these 102 occur in the non-carriageable part of the way or in the first 897 kós, and the last two only in the remaining 353 kós or the carriageable part. This latter may be said to be entirely through plains, for of the two hills occurring, only one is at all noticeable, and both are traversed in carriages. From Káthmándú to the iron boundary-bridge beyond Táchindó (China frontier) is 665 kós; and thence to Chinchi Shán or Mount Chinchi is 20 kós. Throughout these limits, or 685 kós from Káthmándú, mountains covered with snow occur. In the remaining 565 no snowy mountains occur.

Horses are used for the first 894 [query 897], and carriages for the last 356 [query 353]. Total, 1250 kós.

---

* This remark, as well as the prior one in the body of the paper, belongs to the original. The bracketed entry of distance is mine, taken from the remarks below of the original.

Systematic Summary of the Route from Káthmándú to Pekin, as traversed by the Népálese Ambassador to China, Kájí Dalbhanjan Pándé, A.D. 1822–23, and set down by his Secretary at the close of each day's journey.

No. of stages.	Halting place.	Distance in kós.	Time in ghadis and pals.	Mountain ridges or ranges crossed.	Lakes and tanks.	Rivers or river-crossings.	Boat ferries.	Bridges.	Forts.
1	Gourighát	one	1—5	none	one	two	none	two	none
2	Sánkhú	three	9—0	none	none	two	none	none	none
3	Devápúr	four	15—0	one	none	three	none	three	none
4	Sipá	three and a half	11—0	one	none	two	none	none	none
5	Chóntárá	four	10—0	one	none	one	none	one	none
6	Pairyá	four	13—0	one	none	three	none	three	none
7	Thama gáon	five	17—0	none	none	two	none	none	none
8	Lísti	two and a half	13—0	one	none	two	none	four	none
9	Túguná	two and a half	10—0	none	none	five	none	one	none
10	Khásá*	five	19—0	none	none	none	none	four	none
11	Chósyáng	five	21—0	none	none	three	none	seven	none
12	Kúti	four	17—0	none	none	three	none	three	none
13	Tháchéling	five	15—0	none	none	three	none	three	none
14	Thó-lúng	four	12—0	none	none	three	none	none	none
15	Tígri langkót	ten	20—0	one (Bhaírav langúr	none	two	none	none	none
16	Tígri or Tíngrí	three	9—0	none or Tháng lá)†	none	one	none	one	one
17	Mímo	six	13—0	none	two	one	none	none	none
18	Shékar jéung	six	15—0	one (Khyumrila)	two	two	none	two	one
19	Lólah	three	8—0	one (Gyachila)	none	one	none	none	none
20	Chyáchópé or Gyáchópé	four and a half	11—0	one (Thólá)‡	none	one	none	two	none
21	Tháng bú	nine	17—0	one (Phángso§thoulá)	two	one	none	two	one
22	Lalit jéung	five	11—0	none	none	two	none	none	one
23	Chyá táng	four and a half	12—0	none	none	none	none	none	one

* Boundary of Népál and Tibet since 1792.

† Bhaírav langúr is the name in the Khás language. Thánglá, in full Nyánám thángla, in that of Tibet. These names of the mountain-ridges crossing the route are not in the original, but obtained by me from other sources and therefore bracketed. This famous pass, the heights above which and constituting with the pass one immense snow mass, which mass is equivalent to the Mount Everest of Waugh, commences (see Chountra paper) 3 kós beyond Tsibolung, or 55's of from Káthmándú, so by the Chountra's more direct route.

‡ Thólá = Chólá or Tísrya chólá or Chountra's paper.

§ This ridge and the three above it are all very small, and none of them of course snowed. The first or Khyumri is situated between the towns of Shékar and Sákyá.

No. of stages	Halting place.	Distance in kós.	Time in ghadis and pals.	Mountain ridges or ranges crossed.	Lakes and tanks.	Rivers or river crossings.	Boat ferries.	Bridges.	Forts.
24	Phencholing	five	12—30	none (snowy)	none	one	none	one	one
25	Tási gang	four	9—0	none (Chhunglá not	none	one	none	none	none
26	Girí	five	11—30	none (Khyonglá)	none	one	none	none	none
27	Káti gúmba	nine	16—0	none	none	one	none	one	none
28	Digarcha * or Zhikatsé	three	5—30	one (Jiklá)	none	none	none	none	one
29	Pená	eight and a half	17—0	none	none	none	none	none	one
30	Ták chwe	seven	14—0	none	none	one	none	none	one
31	Gyáng chi or Gyáng-tse	five and a half	11—0	none	one	one	none	none	one
32	Kú-nashi or Geb zés	seven	13—0	none	one	one	none	two	one
33	Thúng toï or Itálung	five and a half	11—0	none	none	four	none	three	none
34	Nicháng-u or dzara	five ‡ (Yamdó lake on right)	11—0	one (Chapla) †	none	two	none	one	one
35	Nágakhú jéung or Nan-gáche	six (Yáru	10—0	none	one	two	none	two	one
36	Pai khú jéung or Pédié	six (cross the	11—0	none	one	one	none	one	one
37	Gnáksá or Khampa par-si	six	12—30	one (Kambalá)	none	none	none	none	one
38	Chusum jéung [chu	nine	17—0	none	none	two	one	one	two
39	Gne táng	six	14—0	none	one	three	none	two	one
40	Lhása	six	14—0	none	none	three	one	none	one
41	Tsi-chlin	thirteen	11—30	one	none	one	none	two	one
42	Mito gúnga	five and a half	24—0	none	none	three	none	two	none
43	Ringché láng	five	10—0	none	one	three	none	four	one
44	Usú cháng or Usír gyáng	five	10—0	none	none	four	none	five	none
45	Toïta	nine	17—0	none	none	five	one	seven	none
46	Nú gári or Nú mári	nine	17—0	one (Gyámda thölá) §	two	one	none	five	none
47	Sú sung tá	six	11—0	none	none	six	none	two	none
48	Chyáng táng	six	11—30	none	none	two	none	five	none
49	Ling ta	five and a half	10—0	none	none	five	none	five	one
50	Syáng-tá	five	11—0	none	none	three	none	three	one
51	Sáng-wá||	eight	15—0	one (Thónda lá)	five	two	none	two	one
52	Wó-cha	five	11—0	none	five	none	one	five	none
53	Lá-thí	five	11—0	one (Bendalá)	none	two	none	five	none
54	Tá-túng-khá	six	16—0	one	none	four	none	one	one
55	Túva-thúng	seven	11—0	one (Chaklá)	two	two	none	none	none
56	Chyá-kúng	six and a half	13—0	none	none	two	none	three	none

No.	Place	Stages	Distance	Pass	none	four	none	six	none
57	Walá-tó	eight	17—0	none	none	three	none	four	none
58	Gáwó	five	12—0	one (Syár káng lá)	none	none	none	none	none
59	Láchi-chó	five	11—0	none (Nup káng lá)	two	two	none	four	none
60	Tó-tá	eleven	19—0	one	one	one	none	three	none
61	Pyáng-pá	seven	13—0	one	one	seven	none	one	none
62	Lá chá	five and a half	11—0	one (Sorak lá)	none	one	none	one	none
63	Páli láng	twelve	16—0	two (Nak lá)	none	three	none	three	one
64	Lácha páng-wo	thirteen	19—0	none	none	two	none	none	one
65	Tha-tho	seven	12—0	one (Gabu lá)	none	one	none	three	none
66	Lilibá-jéung	nine	17—0	one (Gámu lá)	none	none	none	three	one
67	Chyai chhou	nine	17—0	five	one	four	none	one	none
68	Máli	five	11—0	one (Yutakh lá)	five	two	none	two	none
69	Wá khó	four	9—0	five	one	three	none	two	none
70	Gnángta táy	sixteen	24—0	none ¶	four	one	none	eight	none
71	Lá kúng	five	9—0	one (Syánam cholá)	none	none	none	two	none
72	Lá katá	eight	13—0	none	none	one	none	one	none
73	Tháng dú or Cham-do	eight	12—0	two	one	none	none	none	none
74	Mú phú or Mung bhu	six	11—0	two	two	two	none	none	none
75	Pow tyang	nine	17—30	one	none	two	none	two	none
76	Pá kúng or Ba-gung	nine	11—0	none	none	one	none	two	none
77	Wáng khá	five	13—0	none	two	two	none	none	none
78	Gnáng ti or Gam	seven and a half	21—0	one	one	one	none	none	none
79	Táyá	eight	12—0	none	one	one	none	two	none
80	Ló cháng chúng	six	16—0	two	none	one	none	two	none
81	Ang sá or Asú	nine	11—0	one	none	none	none	none	none
82	Sépang kow or Nówa	six	17—0	three	none	two	none	none	none
83	Li sú or Risyú	ten	23—0	one	none	two	none	two	none
84	Mang khám or Cháng [kha	eleven	17—0	one	none	two	none	none	none
85	Kúsú	eight	18—0	two	none	two	none	none	none
86	Mángali	nine	6—0	one	none	two	none	two	none
87	Khanchi khá	three		one	none	one	none	none	none

* Zhí-khá-chhén of Néwári, capital of province of Tsáng = zhí-ká-tsé of Tibetan and Digarcha of Khas.

† The Sikim Raja's Vakíl suggests Khárníá or Nyunzying Khangzan, a great snowy range.

‡ The Tsumding monastery is situated here.

§ Gyamda thol and the seven next-named mountains are said to be vast masses of perpetual snow. True of Gyamda tholá and Syakangla and Nhup Kangla (kangla = snowy mountain or pass), but not of the three intervening lá. The pass of Gyamdatho is very fatal to travellers. Recent vivâ voce information.

|| Sángwá is on the border of the provinces of U and Khám. From Gnaksa to Sángwá is the jurisdiction of Lhása. The full name of Sángwá is Kwon-xegyamda-sángwa.

¶ None of the above with the simple addition lá, instead of Kangla, are snowy.

No. of stages.	Halting place.	Distance in kós.	Time in ghadis and pals.	Mountain ridges or ranges crossed.	Lakes and tanks.	Rivers or river-crossings.	Boat ferries.	Bridges.	Forts.
88	Túngná lúng	eight	15—0	none	none	two	one	none	none
89	Pá tháng	eight	16—0	one	none	three	none	one	none
90	Pá páng	three and a half	7—0	none	none	one	none	one	none
91	Tá só	nine	18—30	one	seven	two	none	one	none
92	Tsáng pá	seven and a half	14—30	one	one	three	none	three	none
93	Láma yá	twelve	23—30	four	none	nine	none	eight *⎰ none	none
94	Tháng-tháng	ten	17—30	two	two	four	none	four	none
95	Lí than	five	9—0	none	none	two	none	two	none
96	Khwongtakhá	seven	11—0	one	none	one	one	one	none
97	Kúmó-lí	twelve	21—0	three	none	three	none	one	none
98	Mákai túng	nine	17—0	two	none	three	one	six	none
99	Khó khou	four	8—0	none	none	four	none	eight	none
100	Wó lési	nine and a half	16—30	two	none	two	none	one	none
101	Tángwá li	seven	15—0	two	none	three	none	two	none
102	Anyáng yá	five	10—0	none	none	four	none	four	none
103	Chéchain-to	nine	20—0	one	none	two	none	five	none
104	Táchindó or Tázi-do †	four	7—30	none	none	three	none	four	none
105	Thou-tháng-suung	five and a half	10—0	none	none	two	none	two	none
106	Luting chúng	eight	15—30	none	none	three	none	four	none
107	Phí syáng	ten	19—0	none	none	seven	none	nine	none
108	Ní thyáng	seven	17—0	one	none	two	none	three	none
109	Chhyá chhá-syáng	eight	18—0	one	none	six	six	ten	none
110	Pai-phou	seven	17—0	none	none	three	none	four	none
111	Lúchʼyáng syáng	four and a half	7—0	one	none	five	one	nine	none
112	Yá-tou	ten	21—0	one	none	seven	none	eight	none
113	Pai-táuá	nine	22—0	none	one	twelve	one	six	none
114	Chi-tou	eight	18—0	one	none	thirty-nine† (crossings)	one	eleven	one
115	Syáng chang-shen	eight	17—30	none	none		one	sixteen	none
116	Chhin-púl	nine	23—0	none	none		three		one
117	Sídhu syá	five	10—0	none	one	fourteen	none	fourteen	none

118	Tayáng	ten	19—0	none	none	forty-seven	none	forty-seven	two
119	Lyóchang-syáng	five	9—0	one	none	nine	none	nine	one
120	Myáng ton	seven	15—0	none	two	six	none	six	one
121	Chatáúng syáng	twelve	17—0	two	two	fourteen	one	three	one
122	U-liáng-i	eight	16—0	one	none	two	none	two	none
123	Chyá táng	nine	17—0	two	none	four	none	four	one
124	Tású sú	eleven	23—0	two	one	six	none	seven	none
125	Kwá yá syáng	ten	21—0	one	one	three	one	two	two
126	Syáayú-yan-i	twelve	28—0	two	none	one	none	two	one
127	Khwáng pá-i	six	12—0	one	none	three	none	one	none
128	Nichi-tou	five	10—0	two	none	one	none	none	one
129	Tá gnái	nine	16—30	one	none	three	none	none	none
130	Myá syáng	nine	16—30	none	none	three	none	none	one
131	Páú tyáng	eight	12—0	none	none	four	none	one	one
132	Mátá wei	ten	18—0	one	none	three	none	one	none
133	Tályó-pá	nine	16—0	three	none	three	none	two	none
134	Lángsyáng	nine	15—0	one	none	six	none	seven	one
135	Phrasyáng	nine	16—0	one	none	seven	none	seven	none
136	Khwá nyou-phú	eleven	20—0	two	none	six	none	four	none
137	Pau ching syáng	ten	18—0	two	none	nine	none	thirteen	one
138	Phráng-syáng-phra	nine	17—0	none	two	four	none	three	one
139	Chhí syáng syan	six	10—0	none	one	three	none	three	one
140	U kúm syáng	twelve	21—0	none	four	four	none	three	two
141	Syángphróngsyáng	nine	15—0	none	four	one	none	one	two
142	Sing-há-phú	ten	19—0	none	two	two	none	four	one
143	Lét-náng-shan	six	13—0	none	two	four	none	three	one
144	Pai-lán-syan	eight	19—0	none	eleven	four	none	fourteen	three
145	Khwáng myú	twelve	25—0	none	two	fifteen	none	two	two
146	Pháng thou ten	ten	23—0	none	none	five	none	two	four
147	Lyangpyáng-syán	ten	23—0	none	one	two	none	two	two
148	Sá-tou	six	11—0	none	one	five	none	three	three
149	Pápáng-syí	seven	14—0	none	none	three	none	six	two
150	Myá-thung-syang	seven	13—0	one	none	seven	none	six	one

* Figure for eight perhaps a cypher. See Diary of a Cashmerian journeying on the route thus far in our Researches. Khdun extends from Sángwá or 91st stage to this point.

† Boundary of Tibet and Chiua Proper.

‡ These and the next two noted are crossings of one mountain-locked river, not separate rivers. The fourteen of stage 121 is another instance of the same kind.

No. of stages.	Halting place.	Distance in kós.	Time in ghadis and pals.	Mountain ridges or ranges crossed.	Lakes and tanks.	Rivers or river-crossings.	Boat ferries.	Bridges.	Forts.
151	Syáng-lyáng-syáng	nine	20–0	none	one	fourteen	none	twenty-two	one
152	Khó lyáng syáng	seven	13–0	none	none	seven	none	seven	one
153	Múng syáng	nine	20–0	none	three	two	one	one	one
154	Phai-chhen phú	six	13–0	none	one	four	none	four	one
155	Yó khwá-i [syáng	seven	13–0	none	none [two	six	none	six	one
156	Khwó-khon-chang-	ten	21–0	none	two [two	five	none	four	two
157	Wei-khai-phú	twelve	18–0	none	twenty-four	four	none	four	two
158	Chhi syáng	six	12–0	none	four	five	none	four	three
159	I'ka-i	six	12–0	none	two	six	none	five	one
160	Tá-tai-phú	seven	3–0	none	two	seven	none	six	two
161	Sa-tou	seven	13–0	none	none	three	none	three	one
162	Kliáng-táng-syáng	seven	13–0	none	none	six	none	six	one
163	Súng-tou-phú	twelve	12–0	none	one	seven	none	seven	two
164	Lói chhi-syáng	six	11–0	none	none	three	none	three	one
165	Pai-syáng-syáng	six	12–0	none	none	two	none	two	none
166	Twá-tou	six	11–0	none	one	four	none	four	one
167	Lou thyáng-syáng	four and a half	7–30	none	two	three	none	three	one
168	Dyang-dyaug-phú	six and a half	13–0	none	one	three	none	three	one
169	Shito-syáng	nine	18–0	none	none	three	none	three	one
170	Chhipú syáng	nine	20–0	none	two	two	none	two	one
171	Phá khó-syáng	seven	16–0	none	two	two	none	two	one
172	Pou tyán plú	one	11–0	none	one	three	none	three	one
173	Pai-khwó	eleven	20–0	none	six	eight	none	eight	none
174	Tá-tou	eight	16–0	none	seven	six	none	six	one
175	Lóng syán	eight and a half	18–0	none	none	five	none	five	two
176	Pai-chin (Pekin)	seven	16–0	none	none	five	none	six	three
176		1267 (1263¼)	2576	102 (106)	150	652	23	607	100

REMARKS.—The above paper, like that which accompanies it, is deserving of implicit reliance, from the circumstances under which it was prepared and transcribed for me. The kós, according to which the computation of distance is made throughout, is that of Népál, equal to 2⅓ miles; and the time in ghadis and pals is the same, according to which 60 pals make a ghadi and 2½ ghadis an hour. The embassy set out on 7th of Asár (June) and arrived at Pekin on 12th of Mágh (January), halting forty-seven days, which are included.

In the fifth column of the original, the names of the passes (laugúr in Khas and lá in Tibetan) are not given. I have, however, set down in brackets such as I was enabled to procure before I left Népál.

SECTION XI.

ROUTE FROM KÁTHMÁNDÚ, THE CAPITAL OF NÉPÁL, TO DARJEELING IN SIKIM,

INTERSPERSED WITH REMARKS ON THE PEOPLE AND COUNTRY.

First Stage to Choukót, East, 7¼ kós.

PROCEEDING *viâ* Mángal, which is within a quarter of a mile of the city, we came to Nangsál, at the like distance from Mángal. Both are petty suburban Néwár villages. Thence to Deopátan, distance three-quarters of a kós, a large pakka * village inhabited by Néwárs. Thence to Thémi, one and a quarter kós. Thémi is a considerable pakka town of Néwárs, and is famous for its pottery. Thence to Bhátgáon, distant one kós. Bhátgáon is a large handsome Néwár town situated near the Eastern end of the valley of Népál, and is said to contain 12,000 houses. Its palace, temples, and tanks are very striking structures. Thence to Sángá, two kós. This bridge-like place stands on a low ridge separating the great valley of Népál Proper † from the subordinate valley of Banépa. It is a small place, but the houses are all pakka, as usual with the Néwárs.

---

* Pakka here means built of burnt bricks. This word and its correlative kachcha are most convenient terms, for which I know no English equivalents.

† The valley of Népál is about sixteen miles in either diameter, of shape between oval and lozenge, cultivated throughout, and yields two crops per annum, a spring one of wheat and an autumn one of rice. It is very densely peopled with a population of probably 350,000 souls, distributed in three principal and many subordinate towns, all of burnt brick and tiled roof, in the tent style of architecture so prevalent in China. Equidistant from snows and plains, elevation 4500. Centrally placed with reference to the length (E. and W.) and breadth (N. and S.) of the kingdom. For its people see on to p. 196 infra.

Compare note at exordium of vol. on Buddhism, and separate paper therein on Sambu Puran, (Essays I., 115), notices of Valley and Tersi of Nepalya Kallyana in Benga's A. S. Journal.

Thence to Banépa, one kós. Banépa is a small pakka town inhabited by Néwárs, and situated in the vale of the same name. Thence to Khanarpú, one kós. It is a nice little Néwár village, situated near the point where the dales of Banépa and Panouti blend with each other. Thence to Choukót, a quarter kós, ascending a low ridge and quitting the level country thus far traversed, and all of which is highly cultivated, yielding autumn crops of rice and spring ones of wheat.

2nd Stage to Kálápáni, East, 6 kós.

Ascend the large ridge of Batásia and come to the mountain village of Phúlbári, which is somewhat less than one kós from Kálápáni. Thence along the ridge two and a quarter kós to Syámpáti, another small village of Parbattias. Thence to Saláncho, one kós. Saláncho is a third small hill village, and it overlooks the glen of Káshi Khand on the left. Thence to Kánpúr, a Parbattia village, close to which is the halting-place, at a tank called Kálápáni, distant from Mithya Kót one and a quarter kós.

3rd Stage to Jhángá-jhóli, South-East, 6½ kós.

This stage runs along the same ridge of Batásia. But it is here called Ténnál. Half a kós to the hill village of Bhoatia, and another half a kós to that of Gimti, both inhabited by Múrmis. Thence half a kós to Pokri, another similar village of Múrmis. Thence to Cháp Khár, about three-quarters of a kós, a fourth Múrmi village. Thence to Gárchá, another hamlet of Múrmis, distant from the last rather less than two kós: a quarter kós more brings one to the descent into the Biási or vale of Dúmja, on the banks of the Rósi and Sún Cósi. The Biási is low, hot, and malarious, but fertile in rice, triangular in shape, and about a mile in greatest width. The Bar, Pipal, Sémal, and Khair trees* grow here, and large Dhanéses (Buceros Homrai) are seen eating the fruit of the Pipal. The Sún Cósi at Dúmja flows freely over a wide bed of sand, and is about

---

* The occurrence of the Indian figs, cotton-tree, and acacia, so far within the mountains, shows that the Biásis, wherever situated, have a tropical climate. See on.

forty yards broad and one foot deep. This river, if the Milanchi be regarded as its remotest feeder, arises from the eastern side of Gosain-thán, the great snowy peak overlooking the valley of Népál, and is the first of the "seven Cósi" (sapt Cósi) of the Népálese. Others contend that the true Sún Cósi is that which arises at Kálingchok, east of Kúti.* There are several upper feeders of the Sún Cósi, which form a delta of perhaps thirty kós either way, between Malanchi, Kálingchok, and Dallálghát, where the feeders are all united. From Dúmja, which lies a little below Dallálghát, proceed along the right bank of the River Sún Cósi to Jhángá-jhóli, by the rugged glen of the river two kós, the road impeded by huge masses of rock lying half in the water.

4th Stage to Sítalpáti, East, 4 kós.

Leaving the river on the left, you ascend the ridge of Sidhak and travel along its side, far from the top, to the village of Dharma, inhabited by Múrmis. It is one and a half kós from Jhángá-jhóli. Thence half a kós to Jhámpar, a village of Múrmis. Thence descending again to the bed of the Sún Cósi, you proceed along the right bank for one kós to Chyanpúr-phédi, or the base of the Cháyanpúr range. Thence an ascent of one kós to the top of Cháyanpúr, where stands the Powa or small Dharamsála of Sítalpáti, the halting-place, and which is close to the village of Choupúr.

5th Stage to Liáng, East, 6 kós.

Two kós along the heights of Cháyanpúr bring you to the confluence of the Támba Cósi and Sún Cósi, where the united rivers, of nearly equal size before their junction, are passed at Séliaghát, a little below the Sangam or junction. The Támba Cósi, or second Cósi of the Népálese, has its course at the base of Phallák, a Himálayan peak situated some ten kós perhaps east of the Kúti Pass, which is on the great eastern highroad from Káthmándú to Lhása. From Séliaghát the road makes a rapid ascent of one kós to the high level or plateau of Gum-ounia, one kós along which conducts you to Bhalaiyo, which is

* See annexed Memorandum and Sketch Map.

only another name for the same plateau. From Bhalaiyo-dánra, one kós to Bétáini village, still along the plateau. Thence one kós along the same high level to the halting-place or Liáng-liáng, which is a large village well inhabited chiefly by Néwárs. Some Parbattias also dwell there, and there is plenty of cultivation and water on the flat top of this low ridge, which is neither mountain nor plain.* The rice, called "touli" by the Néwárs, grows well, and wheat and generally all the field and garden produce of the valley of Népál.

6th Stage to Narkatia, South-East, 4½ kós.

One and a half kós along the plateau of Liáng-liáng, you come to Bhirpáni, having the Dápacha and Manthali glens on the left, by which there is another road, used chiefly in the cold season. Thence at half a kós you descend slightly to Wádi Khóla, a small hill stream, and passing it make the great ascent of Hiliapáni and reach Lámágáon after one kós of climbing. Close to the village of Lámágáon is another called Sálú, inhabited by Parbattias.† Thence one kós to the Likhú Khóla, a slight descent. Thence a small ascent to Bhálú-dánra, or the Bear's Ridge, half a kós along, which brings it to the village of Nigália or Narkatia, the halting-place. The Likhú Khóla is the third Cósi of the Népálese. It is a large unford-able river, which is crossed by a bridge, but is smaller than the Sún Cósi or Támba Cósi. It comes nearly due south from the snows at Kháli Múngali, and forms one of the seven chief feeders of the great Cósi.

7th Stage to Bájbisoúnia, East, 3 kós.

Still along the Bear's Ridge a quarter kós to a small village of Láchia, and another half a kós to the village of Chúplú. Thence quit the ridge, and by a slight descent reach Phédi Khóla, at one and a quarter kós. Phédi Khóla is a small feeder of the Molang. Pass the stream, and ascending slightly

* See note at stage the ninth.
† For tribes of Népál, see Journal for December 1847.

for one kós, reach the halting-place, which is a village of good size, where plenty of provisions may be had.

8th Stage to Búngnám Kót, East, 4 kós.

Along the same low ridge to the village of Sailiáni, close to which you come successively to the villages of Chilounia and Pokhalia and Aisiálú, all within the compass of less than one kós. Beyond Aisiálú, one and a half kós, is a small pond, the water of which, though not rising from rock, never fails. Its name is Dhimilopáni, and on its left runs the ridge of Thária-dánra and Katonjia village; on its right, the Bhanda ridge and the village of Jaljalia. Beyond Dhimilopáni commence a descent of somewhat less than half a kós, leading to the Molang or Morang Khóla, before named. Cross the Khóla and ascend one kós to Búngnám Kót, a large village and residence of the rural authority, having the smaller village of Bari on its right.

9th Stage to Chúrkhú, East, 6 kós.

After one kós of descent reach the Lipia Khóla, which stream you cross at once and ascend the Lipia-dánra, or ridge, travelling along which you soon come to Okal-dhúnga, a village of Bráhmans and Khas. Thence to Jyá-miria, another village close by on the right. Thence going a kós you reach Charkhú-dánra, merely another name for the Lipia ridge. Descending slightly and advancing one kós you come to Rúmjátár, a celebrated and extensive pasture-tract, where the Gúrung tribe feed large flocks of sheep (Ovis Barúal).* Thence two and three-quarters of a kós of slight descent to Dhanswár, the head village of the rural arrondissement, where the Dwaria, or deputy of Rankésar Khatri, who holds the village in private property, resides. Had the village belonged to the first, it would have been called, as the Dwária's abode, not Dhanswár, but Kót.

* The more general character of Tára is described in the sequel. This one must be very unusually lofty and cool, else neither Gúrungs nor their sheep could dwell in it. It is probably only a cold weather place of resort, otherwise it must be 5000 to 6000 feet high, like the plateau of Liáng, spoken of at Stage 5. Both are exceptional features of the country, which nevertheless, with all its precipitousness, has more numerous, divers, and extensive level tracts than is commonly supposed

10th Stage to Háchika, East, 6 kós.

After half a kós of descent, we arrived at Thotnia Khóla, a hill torrent which joins the Dúd Cósi about three miles ahead. Proceeded down the rugged stony glen of the Thotnia to the junction, which is reached at Rasuá Ghát. Thence down the right bank of the Dúd Cósi for two kós to Katahar Biási, where the river, which had thus far run through a narrow glen, encumbered with boulders, has a wider space on either bank, capable of cultivation, and yielding fine crops of wet rice, but hot and malarious. This sort of tract is what is called in the Parbattia language a Biási. Katahar Biási belongs to Bráhmans, who dwell on the heights above. The road leads down the Biási, which is above half a kós wide for more than one kós, and then ascends the ridge of Kúvindia for one kós to the halting-place, or Háchika, which is a village inhabited by Kirántis, whose country of Kiránt is bounded on the west by the Dúd Cósi, and begins on this route, where the Dhanswár estate ends. The Arún is the eastern boundary of Kiránt. The Dúd Cósi is the fourth great feeder of the Mahá Cósi, which latter enters the plains as one river at Váráha Kshétra above Náthpúr in Purneah. We have already passed three of these great tributaries, or the Sún Cósi, the Támba Cósi, and the Likhú Cósi. The remaining ones are three, or the Arún Cósi, Barún Cósi, and Tamór Cósi.* Thus there are seven in all; and Eastern Népál, or the country between the great valley and Sikim, is called Sapt Cousika, or region of the seven Cósis, from being watered by these seven great tributaries of the Mahá Cósi. Kiránt and Limbúán are subdivisions of the Sapt Cousika, so called from the tribes respectively inhabiting them; the Kirántis dwelling from the Dúd Cósi to the Arún, and the Limbús from the Arún to the Tamór. The country between the great valley and the Dúd Cósi is not so especially designated after the tribes inhabiting it; but the Néwárs and Múrmis of Népál Proper are the chief races dwelling there. Of all these tribes, the Néwárs are by much the most advanced in civilisation. They have letters and literature, and are well skilled in the useful and fine arts.

* See Memorandum at the end of the Itinerary and annexed Sketch.

Their agriculture is unrivalled ; their towns, temples, and images of the gods are beautiful for materials and workmanship; and they are a steady, industrious people, equally skilled in handicrafts, commerce, and the culture of the earth. The rest of the highland tribes of people are fickle, lazy races, who have no letters or literature, no towns, no temples nor images of the gods, no commerce, no handicrafts. All dwell in small rude villages or hamlets. Some are fixed, others migratory, cultivators perpetually changing their abodes as soon as they have raised a crop or two amid the ashes of the burnt forest. And some, again, prefer the rearing of sheep to agriculture, with which latter they seldom meddle. Such are the Gúrungs, whose vast flocks of sheep constitute all their wealth. The Múrmis and Magars are fixed cultivators; the Kirántis and Limbús, for the most part, migratory ones; and the Lepchas of Sikim still more completely so. The more you go eastward, the more the several tribes resemble the Bhótias of Tibet, whose religion and manners prevail greatly among all the tribes east of the valley of Népál, though most of them have a rude priesthood and religion of their own, independent of the Lámás.

11th Stage to Sólmá, South-East, 3 kós.

Leaving Háchika, which is itself lofty, you ascend for two kós through heavy forest by a bad road, exceedingly steep, to the Kiránti village of Dórpá, which is situated just over the brow of the vast hill of Háchika, the opposite side of which, however, is far less steep. Going half a kós along the shoulder of the hill, you then descend for half a kós to the village of Sólmá, the halting-place.

12th Stage to Lámákhú, East, 2½ kós.

An easy descent of one kós leads to Lapché Khóla, a small stream, which crossed, you ascend the ridge of Lámakhú *viâ* Gwálúng, a Kiránti village situated near its base. Thence the acclivity of the hill is steep all the way to the halting-place, which is about half-way to the hill-top, and one and a half kós from Gwálúng. Lámakhú is a Kiránti village like Gwálúng, but smaller.

13th Stage to Khíka-mácchá, East, 4 kós.

Descend half a kós to the Sapsú Khóla, a petty stream, which, however, the Kirántis esteem sacred. Cross it, and commence ascending the great mountain Tyám Kyá. Climb for one kós by a bad road to the village of Kháwa, and another kós equally severe to Chákhéva-bhanjáng, or the ridge, and then make an easy descent of one and a half kós to Khikamácchá, the halting-place. It is a village of Kirántis, in which a mint for coining copper is established by the Durbar of Népál. The workmen are Bándas (Bandyas) of the valley of Népál, of whom there may be fifty or sixty. There is also a Taksári or mint master, and a squad of twenty-five soldiers under a jemadar.

14th Stage to Jinikhésáng, East, 5 kós.

After a kós of tolerably easy travelling, you come to Júkya Khóla, a petty stream, which passed you arrive in half a mile at Pakri, a village situated at the base of the Khokan ridge. Thence slightly descending for half a kós, reach Pikhúá Khóla. Cross it, and ascend the hill of Bhaktáni for one kós and reach Múrkiahúlák, a post-station of the Government close to the 66th* mile-stone of the great military road leading from Káthmándú nearly to the frontier. Thence a descent of one kós to the Khésáng Khóla, one of the innumerable small mountain streams. Cross the Khóla, and ascend the ridge of Thaklia for half a kós to Bánskim and Powagaon, two small conjunct villages of Kirántis. Thence along the ridge of Khésáng for one and a quarter kós to Jinikhesáng, a large Kiránti village, the head of which is Balbhadra Rai, and whence there is a very fine view of the snows.

15th Stage to Jarai Tár, South-East, 5½ kós.

Descending slightly for one and a half kós reach Yákú village, and then descending more abruptly for one kós, come to the Ghongaria Khóla, a small stream. Cross it, and proceed along the nearly level base of the Yákú ridge for two and a half kós

---

* The route gives 61. The difference of five kós is owing to the travellers making an occasional short cut, for they kept, generally, the great military highway.

to Jarai Tár, a large village inhabited by Kirántis, Khas, and Bráhmans, and situated at the opening of an extensive and cultivated flat running along the right bank of the Arún River, and raised some thirty or forty cubits above the level of its bed. Such an elevated flat is called in the Khas tongue a Tár, whereas a low flat, or one on the level of the river, is termed a Biási. Every great river has here and there Társ, or Biásis, or both.* Társ, from being raised, are usually too dry for rice, but some can be well irrigated from the adjacent mountain, and then they will produce rice as well as Biásis. If not constantly irrigable, wheat, barley, millets, pulse, and cotton are grown in them. The elevation of Társ is too inconsiderable to exempt them from malaria, though they are usually rather more wholesome than the lower and often swampy Biásis. Jarai Tár is an extensive one, being one and a half kós wide, and, as is said, several miles long, following the river. The soil is red but fertile, and the whole of it is under cultivation. The village is large for the mountains, and has some fifty to sixty houses, some of which are pakka, as a caravansery, here called Dharamsála or Powa, and one or two more. The site of the village is higher than the rest of the Tár. The Pinus longifolia abounds in Jarai Tár, and peacocks are very numerous. Also Jungle-fowl † and Káliches (*Gallophasis melanoleucos*).

---

* It is remarkable how universally this phenomenon of high and low levels of the land, indicating change in the relative heights of the land and water, prevails wherever obvious sedimentary deposits are found in definite locations. Herbert and Hutton, in their Reports of the Geology of the Western sub-Himálayas, perpetually speak of the phenomenon as occurring in the mountains, and, according to Herbert, also in the Dúns and even Bháver; and Darwin ("Naturalist's Journal") constantly records it in the course of his long survey of South America from Rio Janeiro to the north point of Chili.

The same thing is very observable in the great valley of Népál, whose whole surface is almost equally divided into high and low levels, though the operating cause must here have been modified in its action, as indeed is perpetually the case in different localities. The high and low levels of Tár and Biási I consider to represent the pristine and present beds of the rivers, whose constant erosion has during ages created this difference of level, often amounting to 150 or 200 feet. The low level of the valley of Népál I consider to have been suddenly scooped out, when the waters of the pristine lake (for such the valley was) escaped in one tremendous rush under the action of an earthquake, which rent the containing rock and let off the waters at once.

† From these indications, which are altogether exceptional as regards the mountains, it may be confidently stated that Jarai Tár is not more than 1500 feet above the sea.

16th Stage to Pákharibás, South-East, 2½ kós.

Proceeding half a kós you come to the ferry of the **Arún**, which is a large river rising in Bhót, passing the Himáchal above Hathia, and forming the main branch of the great Cósi. It is also the conterminal limit of Kiránt and Limbúán. It is passed at Liguaghát by boat, and is there very rapid and deep, and some thirty to forty yards wide. Thence down the left bank of the Arún for one kós to Mángmá, a village inhabited by Kiríntis and Limbús, being on the common frontier of both tribes. Thence quitting the Arún, you reach the Mángmá Khóla in a quarter kós, and crossing it proceed half a kós along the mountain-side (manjh) to Ghórli Kharak, which is the name of a small village, and also of a celebrated iron mine, the workers of which dwell above the line of road. A vast quantity of fine iron is procured. This mine, like all others in Népál, is the property of the Government. Iron and copper abound in Népál. Most of the iron is consumed in the magazines for the army, or otherwise within the country; but a deal of the copper is exported, and forms a good part of the pice currency of the plains on this side the Ganges. The Népálese are very military. Khas, Magar, Gúrung, and even Bráhmans, except those of the priest-hood, constantly wear side-arms of home manufacture; and the large army of the State is furnished with muskets, swords, and khúkris from native ore. Thus much iron is consumed, so that none is exported, at least none in the unwrought state, possibly because from defective smelting the ore becomes hardened by the accession of fumes of charcoal, and is thus rendered unfit for those uses to which soft iron is applied. From Ghórli Kharak, an ascent of a quarter kós to Pakharibús, the halting-place, which is a Gúrung village, large but scattered, according to the wont of that tribe.

17th Stage to Dhankúta, South-East, 2½ kós.

After a severe ascent of one and a half kós, a wide flat-topped mountain is gained, whence there is a fine view of the plains, and on the top of which is a small lake, very deep, and about half a kós in circumference. Its name is Hilial, and the water is clear and sweet. Thence a steep descent of one kós brings you to Dhankúta, distant from Káthmándú seventy-eight standard* kós by the great military road, as recorded on the milestone at Dhankúta. Dhankúta is the largest and most important place in Eastern Népál, and the head-quarters of the civil and military administrator of all the country east of the Dúd Cósi† to the Sikim frontier, excepting only what is under the inferior and subordinate officer stationed at Ilám, who has a separate district bounded towards Dhankúta by the Tamór River. Bijaypúr, Cháyanpúr, Mánjh-Kiránt, and a great part of the Limbúán, are subject to Dhankúta, where usually resides a Káji or minister of the first rank, who likewise commands the troops stationed there. After defraying the local expenses, he remits annually nine lakhs of revenue to Káthmándú. Towards the plains the jurisdiction of Dhankúta extends over the old Bijaypúr principality, and towards the hills, over the country of the Kiránts and Limbús. But both the latter tribes are poor at once and impatient of control, so that the Népál Government is content with a lax general submission and a light revenue, levied and paid through the Rais or native heads of those tribes. And this is the reason why only nine lakhs are remitted from Dhankúta to Káthmándú. The present Governor of Dhankúta is a colonel, and brother to the Premier Jang Bahadur Konwar. There is a cantonment, a powder manufactory, a parade-ground at Dhankúta, where the Sri Jang regiment, five hundred strong, is now stationed. The place owes its origin to the Górkháli dynasty, and is therefore recent; but it is growing fast into a town, the pakka houses being already numerous, and the tradesmen and craftsmen abundant, active, and skilful. Provisions are plentiful and cheap, and the workers in Kánsa (mixed metal) are celebrated for the excellence of their commodities, many of which find sale so far off as Káthmándú. The Kirántis and Limbús, who constitute the soldiery or militia of the former Bijaypúr state, pay to the Górkháli Government annually, in

---

* The Itinerary gives seventy-one and a half kós. The difference has been explained in a prior note. The standard kós of Népál is equal to two and one-third English miles.

† The central administration extends to the Dúd Cósi. See Essay on the Laws and Legal Administration of Népál in the Transactions of the Society, Vol. XVII., and Section XII. of this volume.

lieu of all other taxes and claims, seven and a half rupees per house or family. The houses or families are large, so that each can cultivate a great extent of ground. But how much (or little) soever they may raise, each family is free on payment of the annual fixed assessment, which the Rais above noticed collect and deliver. The Rais also administer police and justice among their own people in all ordinary cases. Capital crimes are referred to the Governor of Dhankúta, who must have the Durbar's sanction for every sentence of death or confiscation. Dhankúta overlooks Bijaypúr, the old capital of the Eastern Makwáni or Bijaypúr principality, which stands on the skirts of the Tarai of Morang, but within the hills; and no part of the lowlands (Madhés) is subject to the Governor of Dhankúta. The Madhés is administered by Súbahs, of whom there are seven for the whole.*

18th Stage to Bháinsiátár, South-East, 6 kós.

A sharp descent of one kós brings you to the banks of the Tamór, which is a large river, though less than the Arún. It is never fordable, and is crossed in boats. It is very deep, rapid, but not clear, and about thirty cubits wide between the hot-weather banks. This is the seventh and last of the great feeders of the Cósi, which it joins at Tirbéni, a holy place of pilgrimage, so called from its being the point of union of the three rivers, Tamór, Arún, and Sún Cósi.† The Tamór rises from the western aspect of Káng-chán-júnga. We crossed the Tamór in a boat, and then proceeded half a kós down its left bank. Thence quitting the river, you skirt the base of the Mádi hill for one kós to the Tankhudá-nadi, a small hill stream. Cross it to Mámagá Tár, and then travel through this fine extensive flat for two kós. The whole is cultivable, and the most part cultivated by Denwárs and Mánjhis,‡ and it is situated on the

---

* The seven zillahs of the Népálese lowlands, which extend from the Méchi to the Arrah, are Morang, Saptari, Mahotari, Rotahat, Bárá, Parsa, and Chitwan. These seven constitute the Eastern Tarai. The Western Tarai extends from the Arrah to the Ghagra. It has lately been restored to Népál, which lost it in the war of 1416.

† Of the seven Cósis, the Támba and Likhú are lost in the Sún Cósi, and the Barún in the Arún, the latter four above the route. Tirbéni is immediately above Váráha Kshétra before noticed, as the point where, or close to which, the united Cósis issue into the plains.

‡ See Essays (1874), Part II., p. 60.

banks of the Tamór, to which the winding of the road again brings you. Quitting the Tár you advance a quarter of a kós to the Rasua Khóla, which forded, you proceed along the base of the Télia ridge for one and a quarter kós to another Tirbéni and place of pilgrimage, where the Cherwa and Telia rivers join the Tamór at Cherwa Ghát. A great fair is annually held at Cherwa, to which traders go even from Káthmándú. Thence proceeding a quarter kós, you reach the halting-place or, Bhainsia Tár. The Tár may be half a kós wide and one kós long; it is very hot and malarious, and is inhabited by the Mánjhi tribe.

19th Stage to Lakshmipúr, E.N.E., 5 kós.

A quarter kós of slight ascent brings you to the Nawa Khóla, a moderate-sized stream, which is ascended for three kós by a very bad road that crosses the bouldery bed of the river many times. Thence quitting the Khóla, you commence the severe ascent of Lakshmi-chúria, which is climbed incessantly till you reach the halting-place near the hill top. Lakshmipúr is a large and flourishing village of Limbús, where men and goods abound, and the climate is fine and the water cold—a great relief after the burning Társ recently traversed.

20th Stage to Ibhang, East, 3 kós.

After a slight descent of one and a half kós, you come to Pokharia Khóla, a small stream, which is at once crossed. Thence a slight ascent of one kós up the ridge of Nángi, along the top of which another half kós brings you to the halting-place, which is a Khas village of large size.

21st Stage to Khándráng, East, 4 kós.

A slight ascent of a quarter kós to the village of Múléi, inhabited by Khas. Thence a great descent of one kós to Kokalia Biási, or the Magpie's Glen, which is watered by the Dóé-mai, a small stream. Cross it, and ascend the ridge of Timkyá a short way, and then skirting along its waist (mánjh) for one and a quarter kós come to the Léwá Khóla, another of the innumerable streamlets of the hills. Cross it, and proceed for one and a half

kós along the base of the ridge of Khándráng to the village of
the same name, which is the halting-place and a small village
of Bráhmans.

22d Stage to Ilám, East, 5 kós.

Descend the Khándráng ridge for half a kós, and come to a
small stream called the Ratia Khóla. Cross it, and then make
a severe ascent of one kós up to the ridge of Gólákharak, whence
Karphók, the great ridge dividing Népál from Sikim, is visible.
Thence an equally difficult descent of one kós to the Ilám
Khóla, a small stream. Thence, crossing the stream, make
the severe ascent of Tilkiáni ridge for one and a quarter kós.
Thence skirt along the side of the hill (mánjh) for one kós to
the halting-place of Ilám, which is a small fort designed to
guard the eastern frontier of Népál. The Chatelain is a captain,
and has a hundred soldiers under him, with eight artillerymen
and one cannon of small calibre. This officer is also the civil
authority of the arrondissement, and raises the extraordinary
revenues thereof to meet the local expenses, sending the balance,
if any, to Káthmándú. The land revenue is wholly assigned to
his troops in pay.

23d Stage to Godhak, East, 2 kós.

After a steep descent of one kós you come to the Jógmai or
Mai River, a small stream, which passed, you commence the
steep ascent of Gódhak, and continue ascending to the halting-
place, which is a small village of Bráhmans, half-way up the
hill.

24th Stage to Siddhi, N.E., 3 kós.

Detained much by rain to-day and yesterday, and therefore
made short marches. Leaving Gódhak, ascended by a very bad
road, loaded with dense vegetation, for one and a quarter kós to
Karphók-chouki, a frontier Górkháli post, where eight soldiers
always reside. Thence one kós along the ridge or Lekh to
Súddúng, which is but another name for the ridge. Thence
a slight descent of one kós to the Siddhi Khóla, a small stream,
on the banks of which we halted on account of the rain.

25th Stage to the English Chouki, N.E., 7½ kós.

Crossed the Siddhi stream, and proceeded one and a half kós of slight ascent and skirting the mountain bases to Thaplia. Thence half a kós of descent to the small streamlet of Séchideu. Thence a quarter kós over low hills to the Méchi River. The Méchi is the present boundary of Népál and Sikim. It is a small stream which rises in the Singalélah ridge, a spur of Karphók. Crossed it and ascended the hill of Nágri, by a very bad road and severe ascent of one and a quarter kós to the top. Thence a severe ascent of one kós to the smaller Rangbhang Khóla, a streamlet merely. Thence along the glen to the great Rangbhang, distant one kós. Thence a steep ascent of one kós to Nágri Kót, an old fort in ruins. Thence a painful descent of half a kós to the Balason River. It is a moderate-sized stream, larger than the Méchi. Thence half a kós of rather uneven travelling to the halting-place.

26th Stage to Darjeeling, North, 4 kós.

A severe ascent of one kós, and then an easy half kós along a ridge, brought us to the Company's high-road, along which we travelled for two and a half kós to Jellapahár and Herbert Hill at Darjeeling.

Total kós 109.

At 2⅓ miles per kós = 254 miles.

Note.—The Népálese standard kós is equal to 2⅓ English miles, and the travellers had this standard to refer to along a great part of their way, as being coincident generally with the measured military road several times adverted to on the route. Hence their distances from stage to stage may be perfectly relied on, though in the details of each stage the same accuracy cannot be expected.

MEMORANDUM RELATIVE TO THE SEVEN COSIS OF NÉPÁL.

The enumeration of the seven Cósis by the Itinerists is doubtless the accredited one, and what I have myself often heard at Káthmándú. Nevertheless, names are not always applied in strict correspondence with things in geography. Witness the neglected Jáhnavi, the true and transnivean source of the Ganges! Now, if we are to estimate the seven chief feeders of the Great Cósi according to the length of their courses, or their effect on the physiognomy of the country, the enumerations ought seemingly to be as follows :—

1*st.* The Milamchi	
2*d.* The Bhótia Cósi	
3*d.* The Támba Cósi	
4*th.* The Likhú Cósi	Local series beginning from the West
5*th.* The Dúd Cósi	
6*th.* The Arún	
7*th.* The Tamór	

This list omits the Bárun of the usual enumeration, and substitutes the Bhótia Cósi for the Sún Cósi, and not without Népálese authority for both changes; for it is generally allowed that the Bárún hardly belongs to the sub-Himálayas, and that Sún Cósi is rather the name of the general receptacle of the Cósis till joined by the Arún, than that of a separate Cósi. The following remarks on each river will make this apparent :—

1*st.* The Milamchi rises above the Bhótia village of that name, and at or near to the eastern base of Gosain-thán, the great snowy peak overlooking the valley of Népál. From the snows, the Milamchi has a south-eastern course of probably sixty miles to Dallálghát. It is joined from the west by the Sindhu, the Tánd, and the Chák; and from the north and north-east by the Indrávati, the Balamphi, and the Jhári. The three former are petty streams, but the three latter are considerable ones, one of them rising in the snowy region, and another having two subordinate affluents. The Indrávati comes from the Hemáchal at Panchpokri, and flows nearly due south into the

Milamchi below Hélmú. The Balamphi and Jhári have only sub-Himálayan sources, situated south-east of Panchpokri, but they have longer independent courses than the Indrávati before they unite, after which they presently join the Milamchi not far above the confluence of the Chák. The subordinate feeders of the Balamphi, above adverted to, are the Boksia and Lipsia. They have short parallel courses W.S.W. into their parent stream. Thus the Milamchi is a notable river, and it is the more so as forming very distinctly the western boundary of the basin of the great Cósi, of which the equally distinct eastern limit is the Tamór.

2*d*. The Bhótia Cósi has its sources at Deodhúnga, a vast Himálayan peak, situated some sixty or seventy miles east of Gosain-thán and a little north and east of the Kúti Pass, being probably the nameless peak which Colonel Waugh conjectures may rival Kángchánjúnga in height. The river flows from the base of Deodhúnga past the town of Kúti, and has a south-west direction from Kúti to Dallálghát, where it joins the Milamchi after a course about as long as the Milamchi's; the two rivers of nearly equal size forming a deltic basin. In about its mid-course, the Bhótia Cósi is joined by the Sún Cósi from Káling-chok. But Kálingchok is no part of the true Hemáchal, nor is the stream thence flowing equal to that coming from the snows at Deodhúnga. Consequently the name Bhótia Cósi should prevail over that of Sún Cósi as the designation of one of the separate seven Cósis, and the name Sún Cósi be reserved for the general receptacle, within the mountains as far east as Tirbéni. The Bhótia Cósi is joined at Listi by the Júm Khóla, whilst from the Mánga ridge another feeder is supplied to it, much lower down or below the confluence of the Sún Cósi from the east. But as the Milamchi, below the junction of the Balamphi and Jhári, is often called the Indrávati vel Indhani, so the Bhótia Cósi, below the junction of the Sún Cósi, is frequently styled by the latter name, which others again with more reason confine to the more general confluence below Dallálghát. *There* no doubt the name Sún Cósi begins to be well applied, it being universally the designation of the great receptacle of waters running west and east from Dúmja to

Tirbéni. At Dúmjá, which is only a few miles south of Dallál-ghát, the Sún Cósi receives a considerable affluent from the west. This affluent is called the Rósi. It rises on the external skirts of the great valley under the names Biyabar and Panouti, from the respective dales watered by the two streamlets.

3*d*. The Támba Cósi. It rises at Phallák in the snowy region, about two journeys east and a little north of Káling-chok, or the fount of the upper and pseudo Sún Cósi. The Támba Cósi's course from Phallák to Sélaghát, where it falls into the receptacle, is nearly south, and, as far as I know, it has only one considerable affluent, which is the Khimti. The Khimti rises in the Jiri ridge, and flowing nearly south, parallel to the Támba Cósi, joins the latter in its mid-course at Chisapáni.

4*th*. The Likhú. This river is less than the Támba Cósi, and seems to rise somewhat beneath the snows, though its place of origin at Khali Mungali is said to be a ridge connected there-with. Its course is still more directly south than that of the Támba Cósi, to which, however, its general direction is very parallel. I know but one of its feeders, the Kháni, which comes from the Cháplú ridge on the east of the main river.

5*th*. The Dúd Cósi. It is a large stream, larger even than the Támba Cósi, though inferior to the Arún or Támor. It rises amid the perpetual snows, but at what exact spot I do not know, and it has a southern course to the Sún Cósi at Rasua. Its feeders are numerous, but I know only those near Rasua, which are the Thotia and the Sisnia on the west and the Rao on the east.

6*th*. The Arún or Arún Cósi. It is the largest by much of the whole, and consequently the main source of the Mahá Cósi, having several feeders in Tibet, one from Darra on the north, another from Tíngri on the west, and the third from the east from a lake. The Arún is not only the greatest of the Cósis, but of all the sub-Himálayan rivers, if the Karnáli be not its equal. None other can compete with it. The Bárún, often reckoned a separate Cósi, is a mere feeder of the Arún, and joins it so high up that there is little propriety in admitting the Bárún as a member of the Sapt Cósi. The Bárún is lost in

the Arún in the Alpine region at Hatia, the great mart for the barter trade of the cis and transniveans by the very accessible pass of the Arún. Lower down the Arún receives many tributaries, from the west, the Salpa and Ikhua; from the east, the Sawai, the Hengwá, the Pilwa, the Ligua, and the Mámágá. Its course on this side the Himálaya is generally north and south; but in Tibet it spreads to the west and east also, covering and draining a deal of ground there.

7*th*. The Tamór Cósi. The Tamór, also, is a very fine river, inferior only to the Arún. It is alleged to have more than one Trans-Himálayan source. It passes the snows at Wallungchung, or rises there from the snows. Its course from Wallung to the general junction at Tirbéni is south-west, and it receives many affluents on the way, as the Wallung, the Chung, the Yángmá, the Mewa, the Kabaili, the Kháwa, the Nhabo, the Tankhua, the Teliá, the Nava, the Chérwa, the Kokaya.

SECTION XII.

SOME ACCOUNT

OF THE

SYSTEMS OF LAW AND POLICE AS RECOGNISED IN THE STATE OF NÉPÁL.

INTRODUCTION.

[WITH a view to obtain correct and authentic information on the subject of Népálese law, both in its theoretical principles and practical administration, Mr. Hodgson addressed a series of questions to several individuals who were judged most capable of replying to them in a full and satisfactory manner. Copies of these series of interrogatories, with their respective answers, have been communicated by him to the Royal Asiatic Society (together with a separate paper on crimes and punishments); and the following article has been drawn up from a careful comparison of the whole, excluding as much as possible the repetitions unavoidably occurring, in many instances, in the various answers to any particular question. A reference to the works of Kirkpatrick, Hamilton, and others will show how little has hitherto been contributed to the knowledge of Europeans respecting Oriental systems of jurisprudence, as far as regards the kingdom of Népál ; it is therefore particularly gratifying to be enabled to produce so complete a view of the subject as has been furnished by Mr. Hodgson, whose perseverance and energy in obtaining an acquaintance with these and other matters hitherto kept sacred from all strangers, are only equalled by the intelligent and liberal manner in which he communicates to the public the information he has acquired.—ED. JOUR. ROYAL ASIATIC SOC.]

PART I.

ON THE LAW AND POLICE OF NÉPÁL.

QUESTION I.—How many courts of law are there at Káthmándú ? What is the name of each ?

ANSWER.—There are four Nyáyasab'hás, the first and chief

of which is called *Kót Linga;* the second, *Inta Chapli;* the
third, *Taksár;* and the fourth, *Dhansár.* [Another answer
mentions four additional courts, viz., the *Kósi,** the *Bángya-
bit'hák,†* the *Daftar Khána,* and the *Chíbhándel.* In the *Kósi,*
the *Sirkár ‡* itself administers justice. The *Bángya-bit'hák* is
the general record-office of the fisc, and a separate *dit'ha §* presides over it. It is also a *Mahal-Adálat.‖* The *Kót Linga,
Inta Chapli, Taksár,* and *Dhansár* are the proper *Adálats,*
exercising both civil and criminal jurisdiction. In the *Daftar
Khána* the disputes of the soldiers relative to the lands assigned them for pay are investigated, and the *Chíbhándel* is a
tribunal for the settlement of all disputes relating to houses;
neither of these courts possesses criminal jurisdiction; and
whatever penal matters may arise out of the cases brought
before them are carried to the *Inta Chapli.* All these *Adálats*
are situated in the city of Káthmándú, and within eighty or
ninety paces of each other.]

QUESTION II.—What are the territorial limits of the jurisdiction of each court?¶

ANSWER.—There are no limits expressly assigned. Any
citizen of Káthmándú or Bhátgáon, or any subject dwelling
in the provinces, may carry his cause to any court, provincial
or superior, that he pleases. [Another answer says, that
whencesoever a civil suit comes, and whatever may be its
amount, it may be heard in any of the four courts of the capital
at the plaintiff's pleasure; but that grave penal cases must be
carried to the *Inta Chapli.*]

---

* Also called *Bháradár Sabhá,* or great council of state.
† Also called *Kumári Chók.*
‡ The Government, or its representative.
§ A superintending minister of justice, who does not try causes, but watches over
the conduct of the court.—B. HAMILTON.
‖ A court for questions relating to land revenue.—ED.
¶ See note at Ques. LXXVI. The Sadr courts' jurisdiction (ordinary) extends east
to the Dud Cosi, west to the Trisul. Beyond these limits there are a class of royal
judges called mountain bicháris to whom, in assigned lands (and all nearly are
assigned), there is an appeal from the decisions of the assignee. Every assignee, save
the sipahis and inferior officers, has a good deal of magisterial and judicial authority,
and the fines he inflicts, particularly for breach of the law of caste, are a part of his
usual income. But grave cases can always be appealed to the capital, and sentences involving death or confiscation must be so, however high the local authority
passing such sentences. See p. 200. Palpa and Doti are administered like Dhankúta.

QUESTION III.—Are the four *Adálats* of the capital of equal and co-ordinate authority, or how far is one subjected to another?

ANSWER.—The other courts of the capital are subject to the *Kót Linga*, in which the supreme judicial officer or *dit'ha* personally presides.

QUESTION IV.—Do the courts of the capital always sit, or have they terms and vacations?

ANSWER.—They always sit, with the exception of fifteen days in the twelve months, viz., ten days at the *Dasahrá*, and five days at the *Dewáli*,* during which the courts are closed.

QUESTION V.—Are the courts of the capital permanently fixed there; or do their judges, or any of them, make circuits, civil or criminal?

ANSWER.—They are fixed, nor does any judicial authority of the capital ever quit it. When necessary, the *dit'ha* sends special judges (*bichári*) into the provinces.

QUESTION VI.—In what cases does an appeal lie from the supreme or provincial courts to the *Bháradár Sabhá?*

ANSWER.—If any one is dissatisfied with the decision of the courts of the capital on his case, he may petition the Government, when the *bháradárs* (ministers) assembled in the *nhólcha* (palace) receive his appeal and finally decide. [Another respondent says: "If the matter be grave, and the party, one or other, be dissatisfied with the judgment of the courts of law, he applies first to the premier; and if he fails in obtaining satisfaction from him, he then proceeds to the palace gate, and calls out, 'Justice! justice!' which appeal, when it reaches the *rájá's* ears, is thus met: four *kájis*, four *sirdárs*, four eminent *panch-men*, one *dit'ha*, and one *bichári* are assembled together in the palace, and to them the matter is referred, their award being final."]

QUESTION VII.—Are the *bháradárs*, or ministers, assisted in judicial cases by the chief judicial authorities of the capital, when they hear appeals in the *Bháradár Sabhá?*

ANSWER.—They are: the *dit'ha*, the *bicháris*, and the *dharmádhikári*,† sit with the ministers in such cases.

---

* *Dasahrá* and *Dewáli*, public festivals.   † A high law officer; the chancellor.

QUESTION VIII.—What concern has the *dharmádhikári* with the courts of law in civil and penal cases; and of a hundred cases brought before the courts, what number will come in any way under the cognisance of the *dharmádhikári?*

ANSWER.—Eating with those with whom you ought not to eat; sexual commerce with those between whom it is forbidden; drinking water from the hands of those not entitled to offer it —in a word, doing anything from negligence, inadvertence, or licentiousness, by which loss of caste is incurred, renders the sinner liable to the censure of the *dharmádhikári.* He must pay the fine called *Gáo-dán* to the *dharmádhikári*, who will cause him to perform the *práyaschitta.** In such matters only has the *dharmádhikári* any concern.

QUESTION IX.—Is any pursuer-general or defender-general recognised in the system?

ANSWER.—No; none whatever.

QUESTION X.—If the prosecutor fail to appear at the trial of an offender confined at his instance, is the offender dismissed, or what course is taken?

ANSWER.—The offender is not dismissed, but remanded to confinement, and the trial is deferred.

QUESTION XI.—What, and how many, provincial courts are there?

ANSWER.—For the provinces west of the capital there are two courts constituted by the supreme judicial authority there; that is, the *dit'ha;* and the provinces east of the capital have also two courts similarly constituted.†

QUESTION XII.—Is the regular appeal from the provincial courts of justice to the ordinary courts of the capital, or to the *Bháradár Sabhá?*

---

* See Question XXX.

† Palpa and Doti (and Kiránt also, see page 200) are viceroyalties, and their viceroys appoint the judicial establishment; the other districts beyond the ordinary limits of the Sadr courts' jurisdiction (Dud Cosi and Trisul) are administered by mountain bicháris nominated by the Rajah. There is no dit'ha in the provinces, but an appeal lies from all the mountain bicháris to the dit'ha of the supreme metropolitan court. To the westward there are eight, and to the eastward four mountain bicháris, besides which every assignee of superior grade exercises a good deal of indefinite magisterial and judicial power in the lands assigned to him for pay by the State. From the precision of such assignees there is an appeal to the court of the adjacent mountain bicháris and thence to the dit'ha of the Kót Linga.

ANSWER.—To the supreme court of the capital, or *Kót Linga.*

QUESTION XIII.—Are not the powers of the provincial courts regulated with reference to the rank of the officer who happens to be nominated to the charge of the province ? In other words, what are the limits of a provincial court, of a *súba*, of a *sirdár*, and of a *káji ?*

ANSWER.—They are not; whatever may be the rank of the officer commanding in the province for the time being, the authority of the provincial court is always the same. [Another answer states, that generally all *grave* criminal cases are carried to the *Sadr Adálats ;* and the officer receiving charge of a province has a clause inserted in his commission prohibiting him from exercising judicial authority in certain offences. These are termed *Panch-khát,** viz., 1, *Brahmahatya*, or slaying a *Brahman ;* 2, *Gouhatya*, or killing a cow ; 3, *Stríhatya*, or killing a woman ; 4, *Bálahatya*, or killing children; and 5, *Patki*, and all unlawful intercourse of the sexes, such as incest, adultery, or whatever involves a loss of caste by the higher party. All penal cases, with the exception of these five, which must be reported for the direction of the *Sirkár*, and all civil cases whatsoever, are within the jurisdiction of the provincial authorities.]

QUESTION XIV.—When a *súba*, *sirdár*, or *káji*, is appointed to the government of a province, does the *dharmádhikári* of Káthmándú send a deputy *dharmádhikári* with him ? or the *dit'ha* or *bichári* of Káthmándú send a deputy *bichári* with him ? or does the provincial governor appoint his own judicial officers, or does he himself administer justice in his own province ?

ANSWER.—The provincial governor appoints his own judicial authority, called usually *foujdár*, who transacts other business for the governor besides the administration of justice. The *foujdár's* appointment must, however, be ratified by the *Darbár.*

QUESTION XV.—What are the names and functions of every officer, from the highest to the lowest, attached to each *Sadr* and provincial court ?

ANSWER.—At the capital, one *dit'ha* for all the four courts ; and for each of them two *bicháris*, one *jámadár*, twenty-five *sipáhis*, twenty-five *mahánias*, and five *chaprássis*. The *dit'ha*

---

* *Panch*, "five," and the Arabic ﺟﻨﺎﯾﺖ "a crime, a sin, fault."

gives orders to the *bichári*, the *bichári* to the *jámadár ;* and the *jámadár* to the *sipáhis* and *mahánias*, who serve processes, and see that all persons are forthcoming when required for the purpose of justice. [Another authority adds the following to the list of officers, after the *bichári*, viz., the *bahidár*, *arz-begí*, and two *naikiá*. The *dit'ha* (he says) decides ; the *bichári* conducts the interrogation of the parties, and ascertains the truth of their statements; the *bahidár* writes the *kail-máma*, which the *bichári's* interrogation has forced from the party in the wrong; the *arz-begí* is the superintendent of the jail, and sheriff or officer who presides over, and is answerable for, executions. The *naikiás*, with their *mahánias*, inflict the *korá* * when needed, and they are also subordinate to the *arz-begí*.]

QUESTION XVI. — How are the judges and other persons attached to the courts paid ? By fees or salary, or both ?

ANSWER.—By both ; they receive salaries from Government, and take fees also.

QUESTION XVII.—Are there separate courts for the cities of Pátan and Bhátgáon,† or do the inhabitants of those places resort to the courts of Káthmándú ?

ANSWER.—There are separate courts for Pátan and Bhátgáon, one for each city ; and each court has the following functionaries attached to it, viz :—one *dwária*, one *bichári*, four *pradháns*, and fifty *mahánias*. There is an appeal from these courts to the chief court at Káthmándú, and important causes are sent by them to that court in the first instance.

QUESTION XVIII.—How far, and in what cases, do the *Sadr* courts use *Pancháyets?*—in civil and criminal cases, or in the former only ?

ANSWER.—Both civil and criminal cases are referred to *Pancháyets*, in any or every instance, at the discretion of the court or the wish of the parties. [The answer of another respondent is as follows :—" With the exception of cases of life destroyed, all matters may be referred to a *Pancháyet*, at the desire of the parties ; but cases of assault and battery are not usually referred to *Pancháyets*."]

---

* A kind of whip.—ED.

† Both places are situated in the great valley, the former at the distance of eight, the latter at that of only two miles from Káthmándú.—*B. H. H.*

QUESTION XIX.—Are the persons composing the *Panchâyet* appointed by the parties to the suit, or by the Government? or does each party nominate its own members and the Government add a president or casting-vote, or how?

ANSWER.—The members of the *Panchâyet* are never appointed by the Government, but by the judge (*dit'ha*), at the solicitation of the parties; and no man can sit on a *Panchâyet* without the consent of both parties. [Another reply adds, that the judge takes from the parties an obligation to abide by the award of the *Panchâyet* when given, and that the court or Government never volunteers to appoint a *Panchâyet ;* but if the parties expressly solicit it by a petition, declaring that they can get no satisfaction from their own nominees, the Government will then appoint a *Panchâyet* to sit on the case. A third respondent says generally, in answer to the query, " The parties each name five members, and the Government adds five to their ten."]

QUESTION XX.—What means are adopted to hasten the decision of the *Panchâyet*, if it be very dilatory?

ANSWER.—In such cases the matter is taken out of the hands of the *Panchâyet*, and decided by the court which appointed it to sit. [The answer given by another of the respondents states that there never can be needless delay in the decision of causes by *Panchâyets*, as these tribunals assemble in the courts out of which they issue, and officers of the court are appointed to see that the members attend regularly and constantly.]

QUESTION XXI.—With what powers are the *Panchâyets* invested to enforce the attendance of parties and witnesses, and the production of papers, and to give validity to their decrees?

ANSWER.—The *Panchâyet* has no authority of its own to summon or compel the attendance of any person, to make an unwilling witness depose, or to secure the production of necessary papers; all such executive aid being afforded by the court appointing the *Panchâyet*; and, in like manner, the decision of the *Panchâyet* is referred to the court to be carried into effect. The *Panchâyet* cannot give orders, far less enforce them, but communicates its judgment to the court, by which it is put in execution.

QUESTION XXII.—Are all the *Panch* required to be unanimous, or is a simple majority sufficient ? and what course is adopted if there be one or two resolute dissentients ?

ANSWER.—The whole of the *Panch* must be unanimous.

QUESTION XXIII.—Are there any persons at Káthmándú who are regularly employed as members or presidents of *Panchayets,* or are persons indiscriminately selected for each occasion ?

Answer.—There are no permanent individual members of the *Panchayet ;* but in all cases wherein *Parbattias* are concerned, it is necessary to choose the *panch*-men out of the following distinguished tribes, viz. :—*Arjál Khandal* or *Khanal, Pandé, Parat'h, Bóhara,* and *Rana ;* one person being selected from each tribe. And among the *Néwárs* a similar regulation is observed, the tribes from which the individuals are chosen being the *Maiké, Bhanil, Achar,* and *Srisht.* In matters affecting persons who are neither *Parbattias* nor *Néwárs,* there is no restriction as to the selection of the *panch*-men by the respective parties.

QUESTION XXIV.—Are the *Panchayets* allowed travelling expenses or diet so long as they attend, or not ? If allowed, by whom are these expenses paid ? Does each party defray its own, or how *?*

ANSWER.—Persons who sit on *Panchayets* are never paid any sum, either as compensation for travelling expenses, loss of time, or on any other account whatsoever.

QUESTION XXV.—What is the nature of the *dit'ha's* authority in those three courts of the capital over which he does not personally preside ?

ANSWER.—The *bicháris,* or judges of these courts, cannot decide independently of the *dit'ha* of the *Kót Linga :* the *bicháris* of those courts are not independent. [Another answer is as follows :—" In those two courts in which the *dit'ha* personally presides, causes are decided by the joint wisdom of himself and colleagues (*bicháris*). In those in which he is not personally present, the *bicháris* decide small matters absolutely, but their investigations of grave ones are reported to the *dit'ha,* and they decide according to his directions."]

QUESTION XXVI.—What officers of the court are there to search for and apprehend criminals, to bring them and the evidences of their guilt before the courts, and to see sentence executed on them ?

ANSWER.—The officers enumerated in the answer to QUESTION XV., as being attached to the courts of the *dit'ha* and the *bicháris.*

QUESTION XXVII.—What officers are there to serve processes in civil suits, to see that the parties and witnesses in such suits are forthcoming, and to carry the decisions of the courts into effect ?

ANSWER.—Those last mentioned, as being employed in criminal cases.

QUESTION XXVIII.—If the plaintiff or defendant in a civil suit neglect to attend at any stage of the trial before decision, is the plaintiff non-suited, the defendant cast, the parties forcibly made to appear, the decision suspended or pronounced conditionally, or what course is adopted ?

ANSWER.—If the plaintiff be absent and the defendant present, it is the custom to take security from the defendant to appear when called upon at some future time, and to let him depart : no decision is come to in such cases. If the plaintiff be present, and the defendant absent, the latter is not therefore cast ; he is searched for, and until he is found, no decision can be pronounced.

QUESTION XXIX.—What security is provided in criminal cases, that offenders, when apprehended, shall be prosecuted to conviction; and how are prosecutors and witnesses made forthcoming at the time of trial ?

ANSWER.—*Mál zámini* and *hazn zámini* are taken from prosecutors and witnesses.

QUESTION XXX.—What are *práyaschitta, chandráyan,* and *aptali ?*

ANSWER.—*Práyaschitta :* the ceremonies necessary to be performed by an individual for recovering his lost caste. *Chandráyan :* expiatory ceremonies performed by the whole city or kingdom, in atonement for the commission of some heinous sin or uncleanness, the consequences of which have affected a considerable body of the citizens. *Aptali*—escheats : the lapse of property to the prince, for want of heirs to the last possessor.

QUESTION XXXI.—Is the *Kumári Chók* an offence of record and registry for all branches of the Government, or for judicial affairs only; and has it any judicial authority?

ANSWER.—It is an offence of record and registry for the fisc; and has no connection with the courts of law, nor does it contain their records. [Another respondent, in answer to QUESTION I., reckons it among the courts of law—*Adálats.*]

QUESTION XXXII.—Describe the forms of procedure in a civil cause, step by step.

ANSWER.—If a person comes into court and states that another person owes him a certain sum of money, which he refuses to pay, the *bichári* of the court immediately asks him for the particulars of the debt, which he accordingly furnishes. The *bichári* then commands the *jámadár* of the court to send one of his *sipáhis* to fetch the debtor; the creditor accompanies the *sipáhi* to point out the debtor, and pays him two *annas* per diem, until he has arrested the latter and brought him into court. When he is there produced, the *dit'ha* and *bicháris* interrogate the parties face to face. The debtor is asked if he acknowledges the debt alleged against him, and will immediately discharge it. The debtor may answer by acknowledging the debt, and stating his willingness to pay it as soon as he can collect the means, which he hopes to do in a few days. In this case, the *bichári* will desire the creditor to wait a few days. The creditor may reply that he cannot wait, having immediate need of the money; and if so one of the *chaprássis* of the court is attached to the debtor, with directions to see to the producing of the money in court, by any means. The debtor must then produce money or goods, or whatever property he has, and bring it into court. The *dit'há* and *bicháris* then, calling to their assistance three or four merchants, proceed to appraise the goods produced in satisfaction of the debt, and immediately discharge it; nor can the creditor object to their appraisement of the debtor's goods and chattels. In matters thus arranged, that is, where the defendants admit the cause of action to be valid, five per cent. of the property litigated is taken from the one party, and ten per cent. from the other, and no more.* If the defendant, when

---

* This fine or tax is called *das-ónd-bís-ónd.*

produced in court in the manner above described, denies, instead of confessing, the debt, then the plaintiff's proofs are called for ; and if he has only a simple note of hand unattested, or an attested acknowledgment, the witnesses to which are dead, then the *dit'ha* and *bicháris* interrogate the plaintiff thus, " This paper is of no use as evidence; how do you propose to establish your claim ? " The plaintiff may answer, " I lent the money to the father of the defendant; the note produced is in his hand-writing, and my claim is a just claim." Hereupon the plaintiff is required to pledge himself formally to prosecute his claim in the court in which he is, and in no other. The words enjoining the plaintiff thus to gage himself are "*Béri t'hápó ;* " and the mode is by the plaintiff's taking a rupee in his hand, which he closes, and strikes the ground, exclaiming at the same time, " My claim is just, and I gage myself to prove it so ! " The defendant is then commanded to take up the gage of the plaintiff, or to pledge himself in a similar manner to attend the court duly to the conclusion of the trial, which he does by formally denying the authenticity of the document produced against him, as well as the validity of the debt ; and upon this denial he likewise strikes the earth with his hand closed on a rupee. The rupee of the plaintiff and that of the defendant, which are called *béri*, are now deposited in court. The next step is for the court to take the fee called *karpan*, or five rupees, from each party. The amount of both *béri* and *karpan* is the perquisite of the various officers of the court, and does not go to the Government. The giving of *karpan* by the parties implies their desire to defer the dispute to the decision of the ordeal; and accordingly, as soon as the *karpan* is paid down, the *dit'ha* acquaints the Government that the parties in a certain cause wish to undergo the ordeal. The necessary order is thereupon issued from the *Darbár ;* but when it has reached the court, the *dit'ha* and *bicháris* first of all exhort the parties to come to an understanding and affect a settlement of their dispute by some other means ; if, however, they will not consent, the trial is directed to proceed. The ordeal is called *nyáya*, and the form of it is as follows :—The names of the respective parties are described on two pieces of paper, which are rolled up into

balls, and then have *pújá* * offered to them.   From each party a
fine or fee † of one rupee is taken; the balls are then affixed to
staffs of reed, and two *annas* ‡ more are taken from each party.
The reeds are then entrusted to two of the *havildárs* of the court
to take to the Queen's Tank ; and with the *havildárs*, a *bichári*
of the court, a *Brahman*, and the parties proceed thither, as also
two men of the *Chámákhalak* (or *Chamára*) caste. §   On arriving
at the tank, the *bichári* again exhorts the parties to avoid the
ordeal by adopting some other mode of settling the business,
the merits of which are only known to themselves.   If they
continue to insist on the ordeal, the two *havildárs*, each holding
one of the reeds, go, one to the east and the other to the west
side of the tank, entering the water about knee deep.   The
Brahman, the parties, and the *Chámákhalaks* all at this moment
enter the water a little way; and the *Brahman* performs *pújá* to
VARUNA in the name of the parties, and repeats a sacred text,
the meaning of which is, that mankind know not what passes in
the minds of each other, but that all inward thoughts and past
acts are known to the gods SU'RYA, CHANDRA, VARUNA, and
YAMA : ‖ and that they will do justice between the parties in this
cause.   When the *pújá* is over, the *Brahman* gives the *tilak* to the
two *Chámákhalaks*, and says to them, " Let the champion of
truth win, and let the false one's champion lose ! "   This being
said, the *Brahman* and the parties come out of the water, and the
Chámákhalaks separate, one going to each place where a reed is
erected.   They then enter the deep water, and at a signal given,
both immerse themselves in the water at the same instant.
Whichever of them first rises from the water, the reed nearest
to him is instantly destroyed, together with the scroll attached
to it.   The other reed is carried back to the court, where the ball
of paper is opened, and the name read.   If the scroll bear the
plaintiff's name he wins the cause ; if it be that of the defendant, the latter is victorious.   The fine called *jit'houri* is then
paid by the winner, and that called *harouri* by the loser; ¶
besides which, five rupees are demanded from the winner in

---

* *Pújá*, worship—adoration.—ED.   † Called *góla*.
‡ This fee is called *narkouli*.   § A very low tribe.
‖ SU'RYA, the sun ; CHANDRA, the moon ; VARUNA, the regent of the ocean ;
YAMA, the deity presiding over the infernal regions.—ED.
¶ Vide answer to Question LXIII.

return for a turban which he gets,* and the same sum, under the name of *sabhásuddha* (or purification of the court), from the loser. The above four demands on the parties, viz., *jit'houri*, *harouri*, *pagrí*, and *sabhásuddha*, are Government taxes ; and, exclusive of these, eight *annas* must be paid to the *mahánias* of the court, eight *annas* more to the *kotmál*, eight more to the *kumhalnáikias*, and, lastly, eight more to the *khardár* or registrar. In this manner multitudes of causes are decided by *nyáya* (ordeal), when the parties cannot be brought to agree upon the subject-matter of dispute, and have neither documentary nor verbal evidence to adduce.

QUESTION XXXIII.—Describe the forms of procedure in a criminal cause, step by step.

ANSWER.—If any one comes into court, and states that such an one has killed such another by poison, sword, dagger, or otherwise, the informant is instantly interrogated by the court thus :—How ? Who ? When ? Before whom ? The *Corpus delicti :* Where ? &c., &c. He answers by stating all these particulars according to his knowledge of the facts ; adducing the names of the witnesses, or saying, that though he has no other witnesses than himself to the fact of murder, he pledges himself to prove it, or abide the consequences of a failure in the proof. This last engagement, when tendered by the accuser, is immediately reduced to writing to bind him more effectually ; after which, one or more *sipáhis* of the court are sent with the informant to secure the murderer, and produce him and the testimony of the deed in court, which, when produced accordingly, is followed by an interrogation of the accused. If the accused confesses the murder, there is no necessity to call for evidence ; but if he deny it, evidence is then gone into ; and if the witnesses depose positively to their having seen the accused commit the murder, the latter is again asked what he has to say ; and if he still refuses to confess, he is whipped until he does ; the confession, when obtained, is reduced to writing and attested by the murderer, who is then put in irons and sent to jail. Cases of theft, robbery, incest, &c., are also thus dealt with in Népál, and the convicts sent to prison. When the

---

* Hence this fee or tax is called *pagrí* (turban).

number amounts to twenty or thirty, the *dit'ha* makes out a calendar of their crimes, to which he appends their confession, and a specification of the punishment usually inflicted in such cases. This list the *dit ha* carries to the *Bháradár Sabhá* (council of state), whence it is taken by the premier to the prince, after the *dit'ha's* allotment of punishment to each convict has been ratified, or some other punishment substituted. The list, so altered or confirmed in the council of state, and referred by the premier to the prince, is, as a matter of form, sanctioned by the latter, after which it is redelivered to the *dit'ha*, who makes it over to the *arz-begí*. The latter, taking the prisoners, the *mahá-náikias*, and some men of the *Pórya* caste * with him, proceeds to the banks of the *Bishen-mati*, where the sentence of the law is inflicted by the hands of the *Póryas*, and in the presence of the *arz-begí* and the *mahá-náikias*. Grave offences, involving the penalty of life or limb, are thus treated. With respect to mutual revilings and quarrels, false evidence, false accusation of moral delinquency, and such like minor crimes and offences, punishment is apportioned with reference to the caste of the offender or offenders.

QUESTION XXXIV.—Do the parties plead *vivâ voce*, or by written statements ?

ANSWER.—They state their own cases invariably *vivâ voce*.

QUESTION XXXV.—Do parties tell their own tales or employ *vakíls* ?

ANSWER.—They tell their own tale—*vakíls* are unknown. [Another respondent says, that instances of a pleader (*mukhsár*) being employed have occurred ; it is usually a near relation, and only when the principal was incapable. Professional or permanent pleaders are unknown.]

QUESTION XXXVI.—In penal cases, are witnesses compellable to attend to the summons of the accused, and to depose with all the usual sanctions ?

ANSWER.—Yes ; the court compels the attendance and deposition, in the usual way, of the witnesses for the accused.

QUESTION XXXVII.—Who defrays the expenses of witnesses in criminal cases ? Are such witnesses obliged to feed them-

---

* The vilest of the vile.

selves during their attendance on the court, and journey to and fro, or does the Government support them?

ANSWER.—The witnesses in penal cases support themselves; no allowance for food, travelling expenses, &c., is made them by any one.

QUESTION XXXVIII.—In criminal cases, if the prisoner volunteers a confession, does his confession supersede the necessity of trial?

ANSWER.—It does, entirely.

QUESTION XXXIX.—If the prisoner be fully convicted by evidence, must his confession nevertheless be had?

ANSWER.—It must.

QUESTION XL.—If he be sullenly silent, how is his confession obtained?

ANSWER.—He is scolded, beaten, and frightened.

QUESTION XLI.—May the prisoner demand to be confronted with his accuser, and cross-examine the witnesses against him?

ANSWER.—He has both privileges always granted to him.

QUESTION XLII.—In civil cases, are witnesses allowed their travelling expenses and subsistence, or not? and when, and how?

ANSWER.—Witnesses must in all cases bear their own expenses.

QUESTION XLIII.—Must the expenses of a witness in a civil case be tendered to him by the party as soon as he is desired to attend, or may they be tendered after the witness has presented himself in court?

ANSWER.—Witnesses must attend without any allowance being tendered, sooner or later.

QUESTION XLIV.—In civil cases, how are costs, exclusive of expenses for witnesses, distributed and realised? Does each party always bear his own, or are all the costs ever laid as a penalty on the losing party when he is to blame?

ANSWER.—All costs whatever are distributed between the parties, after the decision, according to fixed rules.

QUESTION XLV.—If a witness in a civil cause refuse to attend or to depone, what is the course adopted with respect to him? May the summoning party recover damages proportioned to the loss sustained by the witness' absence or silence? and may any punishment be inflicted on such contumacious witness?

ANSWER.—The court will always compel the attendance of a witness required, and will compel his deposition too; and if there be reason to suppose he is prevaricating or concealing some part of what he knows, he is imprisoned until he makes a full revelation.

QUESTION XLVI.—What is the punishment for perjury and subornation of perjury?

ANSWER.—In trifling cases, the perjurer and suborner are fined; in grave matters, they are corporally punished, and even capitally, according to the mischief done.

QUESTION XLVII.—How many sorts of evidence are admissible—oral testimony—writings—decisory oaths—oaths of purgation and imprecation—ordeals?

ANSWER.—In civil cases, the *Hari-vansa* is put on the head of the witness preparing to depose, and he is solemnly reminded of the sanctity of truth. [Another respondent says: "Evidence of external witnesses is the first and best sort; but if there are none, then an oath is tendered on the *Hari-vansa* to both parties, and they are required to make their statements over again under the sanction of this oath; by these statements, so taken, the court will sometimes decide, or one party in such a case may tender the other a decisory oath, and, if he will take it, the tenderer must submit."]

QUESTION XLVIII.—Is oral testimony taken on oath or without oath?—what are the forms?

ANSWER.—On oath; the form is given above. [By another respondent: "If the witness be a *Sivamárgi* or *Brahmanical* Hindú, he is sworn on the *Hari-vansa;* if a *Buddhist*, on the *Pancha-rakshá;* if a *Moslem*, on the *Korán*."]

QUESTION XLIX.—In civil causes, if testimony of men and writings is forthcoming, may either party call for ordeal, or is it only a *pis aller?* and if one party demands, is the other bound to assent?

ANSWER.—Ordeals are only a substitute, the best that can be had when oral and writing testimony are both wanting.

QUESTION L.—May the prisoner in a penal cause rebut evidence by the ordeal, and are the ordeals allowed to any persons under accusation of crime?

ANSWER.—If the prisoner be convicted by evidence, but still

refuses to confess, and asserts his innocence, his demand for the ordeal must be allowed.

QUESTION LI.—Do parties ever depose in their own causes, and under the same sanctions as external witnesses?

ANSWER.—In all causes, civil and criminal, the parties may depose like external witnesses, and under the same penalties for falsehood.

QUESTION LII.—How are writings signed or sealed. and attested or proved? are the attesting parties summoned, or, if dead, is their hand-writing proved, or how?

ANSWER.—In cases of bonds, &c., the witnesses to which are dead, and no other satisfactory evidence is forthcoming, ordeal is resorted to.

QUESTION LIII.—How are unattested or casual writings proved? Must the writer be produced, or will evidence of his hand-writing be admitted?

ANSWER.—If the writer be forthcoming, he must be produced; if not, evidence of his hand-writing is admitted, and any other sort of evidence whatever that can be had; but if the result of the whole is unsatisfactory to the court, it will direct an ordeal.

QUESTION LIV.—Are tradesmen allowed to adduce their entries in their books to prove debts to them? and must the shopman or enterer of the items be produced to prove the entries?

ANSWER.—The value of entries in merchants' books, and in general mercantile affairs, are referred by the court to a *Pancháyet* of merchants.

QUESTION LV.—How is the evidence of a man of rank taken?

ANSWER.—He must go into court and depose like any other person. [Another authority, however, states, on the contrary, that such a person is not required to go into court and depone; but an officer of the court is deputed to wait on him at his house, and to procure his evidence by interrogatories.]

QUESTION LVI.—How is the evidence of a woman of rank taken?

ANSWER.—The court deputes a female to hear the evidence of a lady of rank, and to report it to the court.

QUESTION LVII.—Is oral evidence taken down as uttered, by rapid writers, and enrolled on record?

ANSWER.—In general, oral evidence is not taken down or preserved, nor is it ever taken in whole. In trifling matters, no record whatever of the evidence is made; but in grave affairs, the substance of the more material depositions is preserved and recorded.

QUESTION LVIII.—Is written evidence, when adduced, recorded; and, if so, is it in full or in abstract?

ANSWER.—Important writings are copied, and the copies are recorded after the decision of the case.

QUESTION LIX.—Is the decree recorded, and a copy of it given to the winning party?

ANSWER.—The decree is written, the original is given to the winner of the cause, and a copy is deposited in the record-office of the court. [Another respondent states: "The decree is not written or recorded."]

QUESTION LX.—Do the decrees record the cause in full or in abstract?

ANSWER.—In full, with respect to whatever they *profess* to record, which, however (as stated above), is not every stage of the proceeding.

QUESTION LXI.—Are the records of the several courts of justice preserved in the *Kumári Chók*, and sent there immediately after the causes are decided?

ANSWER.—The *Kumári Chók* is the general and ultimate place of deposit, whither the records of each court of justice are sent after explanation, and account of receipts rendered to the Government at the close of each year. In the interim, the records stay in the courts where the affairs are decided.

QUESTION LXII.—Where the party in a civil cause enters a suit, does he pay any fee, or when he exhibits a document; and in short, upon what occasions is anything demanded of him?

ANSWER.—There is no fee paid on any of the occasions alluded to; what is taken is taken when the cause is decided.

QUESTION LXIII.—What are *jit'houri* and *harouri?*—in what proportion and on what principle are they taken?

ANSWER.—*Jit'houri* is what is paid to the Government by the winner of a cause, and *harouri* what is paid by the loser. They are proportioned to the amount litigated.

QUESTION LXIV.—What is *dhúngá-chúáyi?*

ANSWER.—A stone (*dhúngá*), the image of VISHNU, is placed before the loser when he has lost, and he is commanded to touch it; he places one rupee and one pice on the stone, and then salutes it with a bow, and retires, leaving the offering.

QUESTION LXV.—Besides *jit'houri, harouri,* and *dhúngá-chúáyi,* what other expenses fall on the litigant?

ANSWER.—Half as much as is taken as *harouri* is taken as *jit'houri;* both go to the *Sirkár,* and are proportioned in amount to the property litigated. *Dhúngá-chúáyi* is one rupee per cause taken from the loser; *sabhásuddha* is one or two rupees per cause, according to circumstances; *dhúngá-chúáyi* is the perquisite of the *bichári.*

QUESTION LXVI.—Can a civil action or damages be brought for assault, battery, defamation, &c.; or must the party complained against be of necessity prosecuted criminally?

ANSWER.—A civil action may be brought by the injured party in any of the four courts of the capital.

QUESTION LXVII.—If the defendant in any case as above be cast, is he ever made to pay the plaintiff's expenses in prosecuting him?

ANSWER.—In cases of that sort, no expenses fall on the plaintiff, for the *Sirkár* takes no fines or taxes from him; witnesses have no allowance, and *vakíls* are unknown.

QUESTION LXVIII.—What is the jail-delivery at the *Dasahrá?* Are not offenders tried and punished at the time of offence? and, with courts always sitting and competent to hear all causes, how comes it that multitudes of prisoners are collected for the *Dasahrá?*

ANSWER.—The jail-delivery is a mere removal of prisoners from the city into an adjacent village, in order that the city may be fully lustrated and purified at that season. The usage has no special reference to judicial matters; but so many offenders as ought about that time to be heard and dismissed, or executed, are so heard and dealt with.

QUESTION LXIX.—Is the jail delivered at the *Dasahrá* by the *dit'ha's* court, or by the council of *bháradárs?*

ANSWER.—When the *Dasahrá* approaches, the *dit'ha* takes to the *Bháradár Sabhá* the criminal calendar of those whose offences have been tried, and states the crime of each, the evidence, and the punishment he conceives applicable. The *bháradárs*, according to their judgment on the *dit'ha's* report, set down the punishment to be inflicted on each offender, and return the list to the *dit'ha*, who makes it over to the *arz-begí* or sheriff, and he sees execution done accordingly through the medium of the *mahá-náikias.*

QUESTION LXX.—What is the prisoner's daily allowance ?—and what is the system of prison discipline ?

ANSWER.—Each prisoner receives daily a seer of parched rice and a few condiments. [Another respondent states that prisoners of the common class get one and a half *annas* per diem ; persons above that class receive, according to their condition, from four *annas* to one rupee per diem.]

QUESTION LXXI.—What is the preventive establishment in cities ?

ANSWER.—There is no civil establishment of watchmen, but the military patrol the streets throughout the night at intervals.

QUESTION LXXII.—To whom are night-brawls, and riots, and disturbances reported ?

ANSWER.—The night-watch of the city belongs to the soldiery, who go their rounds at stated times. If they apprehend any persons in their rounds, they keep them till morning in the guard-room, and then deliver them to the *mahánias*, by whom they are produced in court, when their affairs are summarily heard, and they are released or committed to prison, as the case may be.

QUESTION LXXIII.—What are the village establishments of the preventive and detective kind ?

ANSWER.—In each village one *dwária*, four *pradháns*, four *náikias*, and from five to ten *mahánias.*

QUESTION LXXIV.—In the villages of Népál is there any establishment similar to the village economy of the plains ?—any *bará alotaya*, or *bará balotaya ?*

ANSWER.—No; there is neither *pattél*, nor *patwarí*, nor *mirdhá*, nor *garait*, nor blacksmith, nor carpenter, nor *chamár*, nor washerman, nor barber, nor potter, nor *kándu*, on the public establishment of any village of Népál.

QUESTION LXXV.—Is the managing *zemindár* of each village,

or are the principal landholders collectively, bound to Govern
ment, in cases of theft, to produce the thief, or restore the
stolen property?

ANSWER.—No; there is no such usage.

QUESTION LXXVI.—Is the village *málguzár* usually a farmer
of the revenues, or only a collector? the principal resident
ryot or a stranger? and how do these fiscal arrangements affect
those for police purposes?

ANSWER.—The *dwária* and *pradháns* above mentioned collect
the revenues, and the same persons superintend the police, keep
the peace and punish with small fines and whipping trifling
breaches of it. The *dwária* is chiefly an official person, and the
representative of Government or its assignee; the *pradháns* are
the most substantial landowners of the village, and chiefly
represent the community. They act together for purposes of
detection and apprehension—the four *pradháns* under the
dwária.*

QUESTION LXXVII.—How much of the law depends on
custom, and how much on the *Shástras?*

ANSWER.—Many of the decisions of the court are founded on
customary laws only; many also on written and sacred canons.
[By another respondent: "There is no code of laws, no written
body of public enactments. If a question turn upon a caste of
a *Brahman* or a *Rájpút*, then reference is made to the *guru*
(*ráj guru*), who consults the *Shástra*, and enjoins the ceremonies needful for the recovery of the caste or the punishment
of him who has lost it. If a question before the courts affect a
Parbattia, or *Néwár*, or *Bhótia*, it is referred to the customs
established in the time of JÁYA THITI MÁ'L RÁJÁ, for each
separate tribe; *dhúngá-chúáyi* being performed as directed by

---

* *Note from Mr. Hodgson's Remarks on the Great Military Road which Traverses the
Whole Kingdom of Népál.* — "This State, instead of collecting its revenues and paying
its establishments out of them, prefers the method of assigning its revenual claims
directly to its functionaries, and leaving them to collect the amount; while, as judicial follows revenual administrations in Népál, the Government feels little concern
about territorial divisions: in the whole country, westward from Káthmándú as
far as the Nárayáni River, and eastward as far as the Dúd Kósi River, there is no
specific arrondissement district, or *zillah*. These large tracts of country are assigned
principally to the *Compú*, or army stationed in the capital; and their judicial
administration is for the most part in the hands of deputies of the officers, super-
vised by certain migratory royal judges, called mountain *bichárís*."

those customs.   Since the *Górkháli* conquests of Népál Proper,
the ordeal by immersion in the Queen's Tank has become the
prevalent mode of settling knotty points." *

QUESTION LXXVIII.—In general, what sort of causes are
governed by the *Shástras,* and what by customary laws ?

ANSWER.—Infringements of the law of caste in any and every
way fall under the *Shástra ;* other matters are almost entirely
governed by customary law (*dés-áchár*).

QUESTION LXXIX.—Do the *Néwárs* and *Parbattias* follow the
same or different law *Shástras ?*

ANSWER.—The customs of the *Bauddha* portion of the *Néwárs*
are peculiar to themselves.

QUESTION LXXX.—With respect to inheritance, adoption, and
wills, do you follow the *Mitákshará,* the *Dáyabhága,* or any other
Shástra of the plains; or have you only a customary law in such
matters ?

ANSWER.—We constantly refer to those books in the decision
of such cases.

QUESTION LXXXI.—How do sons divide among the *Khas*
tribe ?—sons by wives and those by concubines; also unmarried
daughters ?   What is the widow's share, if there be sons and
daughters ?   What if there be none ?

ANSWER.—Among the *Khas,* sons by concubines get a third
of what constitutes the share of a son by a wife.   [Another
respondent says in addition : " If a *Khas* has a son born in wed-
lock, that son is his heir; if he has no such son, his brother
and his brother's male descendants are his heirs : his married
daughters and their progeny never.   If he has a virgin
daughter, she is entitled to a marriage portion, and no more."]

QUESTION LXXXII.—Can the *Khas* adopt an heir not of their
kindred, if they have near male relations ?

ANSWER.—No; they must choose for adoption the child of
some one of their nearest relatives.

QUESTION LXXXIII.—Are wills in force among the *Khas ?*
and how much of ancestral and of acquired property can a *Khas*
alienate by will from his sons or daughters ?

---

* Dr. Buchanan Hamilton observes that ordeals were seldom used until the
Górkhá family seized the Government, since which time they have become very
frequent.--*Account of Népál,* p. 103.

ANSWER.—If a *Khas* has a son, he cannot alienate a rupee from him by will, save only, and in moderation, to pious uses.

QUESTION LXXXIV.—Do the *Magars* and *Gúrungs*, and other *Parbattias* differ from the *Khas* in respect to inheritance, adoption, and wills ?

ANSWER.—In general, they agree closely.

QUESTION LXXXV.—How is it with respect to the *Néwárs, Sivamárgi*, and *Buddha-márgi* ?

ANSWER.—The former section agrees mostly with the *Parbattias* on all three heads ; the latter section have some rules of their own.

QUESTION LXXXVI.—How is it with regard to the *Múrmi* tribe, and the *Kiránti* ?

ANSWER.—Answered above : in regard to inheritance, all tribes agree.

QUESTION LXXXVII.—Are the customs of the several tribes above mentioned, in respect to inheritance, &c., reduced to writing, collected, and methodised ? If not, can they be ascertained with sufficient ease in cases of dispute before the courts ?

ANSWER.—The customary law on those heads is reduced to writing, and the book containing it is studied by the *bichárìs* and others whom it may concern. [Another respondent, on the other hand, says, with reference to the customary laws : "They are not reduced to writing ; nor are the *dit'has* or *bichárìs* regularly educated to the law. A *dit'ha* or *bichárì* has nothing to do with the courts till he receives from the Government the turban of investiture ; but that is never conferred, save on persons conversant with the customs of the country, and the usage of its various tribes ; and this general conversancy with such matters, aided by the opinions of elders in any particular cases of difficulty, is his sole stay on the judgment-seat, unless it is that the *ci-devant dit'ha* or *bichárì*, when removed by rotation or otherwise, cannot retire until he has imparted to his successor a knowledge of the state of the court, and the general routine of procedures." A third reply is as follows :—" When cases of dispute on these topics are brought into the court, the judge calls for the sentiments of a few of the most respectable elders of the tribe to which the litigants belong, and follows their statement of the custom of the tribe."

Question LXXXVIII.—Are the *bicháris* regularly educated to the law ?

Answer.—Those who understand *dharma* and *adharma*, who are well educated and practised in law affairs, are alone made *bicháris.* [By another authority: " Those who are well educated, of high character, and practically acquainted with the law, are alone made *bicháris.* It is not indispensable that they should have read the law *Shástra*, though, if they have, so much the better."]

Question LXXXIX.—The *dit'ha* is not often a professed lawyer; yet, is he not president of the supreme court ? How is this ?

Answer.—Whether the *dit'ha* has read the *Nyáya Shástra* or not, he must understand *nyáya* (justice-law), and be a man of high respectability.

Question XC.—Are there separate *bicháris* for the investigation of the civil causes of *Néwárs* and of *Parbattias?*

Answer.—There are not.

Question XCI.—In the *dit'ha's* court, if the *dit'ha* be the judge, the investigator, and decider, what is the function of the *bicháris?*

Answer.—The investigation is the joint work of the *dit'has* and the *bicháris.* [Another respondent says: " They both act together; the decree proceeds from the *dit'ha.*"]

Question XCII.—In courts where no *dit'ha* presides, do the *bicháris* act in his stead ?

Answer.—See the answer to Question XXV.

Question XCIII.—Among *Néwárs* and *Parbattias*, may not the creditor seize and detain the debtor in his own house, and beat and misuse him also ? and to what extent ?

Answer.—The creditor may attach duns to the debtor, to follow and dun him wherever he goes. The creditor may also stop the debtor wherever he finds him ; take him home, confine, beat, and abuse him ; so that he does him no serious injury in health or limbs. [Another answer states that the creditor may seize upon the debtor, confine him in his own house, place him under the spout that discharges the filthy wash of the house, and such like ; but he has no further power over him.]

Question XCIV.—Is sitting *dhárná* in use in Népál ?

ANSWER.—It is.

QUESTION XCV.—Give a contrasted catalogue of the principal crimes and their punishments ?

ANSWER.—Destruction of human life, with or without malice, and, in whatever way, must be atoned for by loss of life. Killing a cow is another capital crime. Incest is a third. Deflowering a female of the sacred tribe subjects a man of a lower caste to capital punishment, and the confiscation of all his property. Robbery is a capital crime. Burglary is punished by cutting off the burglar's hands. [The subjoined scale is furnished by another respondent :—

Killing in an affray.—The principal is hanged ; the accessories before the fact severely fined.

Killing by some accident.—Long imprisonment and fining, besides undergoing *práyaschitta.**

Theft and petty burglary.—For the first offence, one hand is cut off ; for the second, the other ; the third is capital.

Petty thefts.—Whipping, fining, and imprisonment for short periods.

Treason and petty treason.—Death and confiscation : women and *Brahmans* are never done to death, but degraded in every possible way, and then expelled the country.]

QUESTION XCVI.—If a *Néwár* wife commit adultery, does she forfeit her *strídhan* † to her husband, or not ? and how is it if she seek a divorce from him from mere caprice ? If, on the other hand, he divorces her from a similar motive, what follows as to the *strídhan?*

ANSWER.—If a *Néwár* husband divorce himself from his wife, she carries away her *strídhan* with her ; if a *Néwár* wife divorce herself, she may then also carry off with her her own property or portion. Adultery the *Néwárs* heed not.

QUESTION XCVII.—Among the *Parbattia* tribes, when the injured husband discovers or suspects the fact, must he inform the courts or the *Sirkár* before or afterwards ? and must he prove the adultery in court subsequently ? What, if he then fails in the proof ?

ANSWER.—When a *Parbattia* has satisfied himself of the adultery, and the identity of the male adulterer, he may kill

---

* Vide answer to Question XXX.　　　　　† *Strídhan,* dowry.

him before giving any information to the court or to the *Sirkár;* he must afterwards prove the adultery, and if he fails in the proof, he will be hanged.

QUESTION XCVIII.—Are such cases investigated in the courts of law, or in the *Bháradár Sabhá?*

ANSWER.—The investigation is conducted in the *dit'ha's* court; but when completed, the *dit'ha* refers it to the *Bháradár Sabhá* for instructions, or a final decree.

PART II.

ON THE LAW AND LEGAL PRACTICE OF NÉPÁL AS REGARDS FAMILIAR INTERCOURSE BETWEEN A HINDÚ AND AN OUTCAST.

THE Penal Law of Népál, a Hindú state, is necessarily founded on the *Shástras;* nor is there anything material in its marvellous crimes, and more marvellous proofs, for which abundance of justificatory texts may not be produced out of the Code of MENU and others equally well known on the plains.

The only exceptions to the truth of the above general remarks are, first, that, by the law of Népál, the *Parbattia* husband retains the natural privilege of avenging, with his own hand, the violation of his marriage bed ; and, secondly, that this law expressly confounds Mohammedans with the outcasts of its own community. But it may be remarked, in regard to the first point, that the husband's privilege is rather a licensed violation of the law than a part of the law; and that all nations have tolerated, and do still, some such privilege.

Nor can it be denied, in reference to the second point, that if the followers of Islám are not expressly ranged with ordinary outcasts by the Hindú law *Shástras*, it is merely because the antiquity of the books transcends the appearance of the

Moslems in India; since, by the whole spirit and tenor of those books, " all who are not Greeks are *barbarians* "—all strangers to Hindúism, *Mléchchhas.*

If, then, there be any material difference between the Hindúism of Nĕpál, considered as a public institution, and that of the Hindú states of the plains, the cause of it must be sought, not in any difference of the law, the sanctity and immutability of which are alike acknowledged here and there; but in the different spirit and integrity with which the sacred guides, common to both, are followed in the mountains and in the plains.

The Hindú princes of the plains, subject for ages to the dominion or dictation of Mohammedan and European powers, have, by a necessity more or less palpable and direct, ceased to take public judicial cognisance of acts, which they must continue to regard as crimes of the deepest dye, but the sacredly prescribed penalties of which they dare not judicially enforce; and thus have been long since dismissed to domestic tribunals and the forums of conscience, all the most essential but revolting dogmata of Hindú jurisprudence.

We must not, however, forget the blander influence of persuasion and mutual concession, operating through a long tract of time. The Moslems, though the conquerors, gradually laid aside their most offensive maxims: the Hindú princes, their allies and dependants, could not do otherwise than imitate this example; and hence, if there is much diversity between the Hindú laws and Hindú judgments, now and for ages past given in the public tribunals of the Hindú princes of the plains, there is no less between the law of the Korán and its first commentators, and the judgments of AKBAR and his successors.

But neither persuasion nor example, nor coercion, has had room to operate such a change in these mountains; the dominant classes of the inhabitants of which, originally refugees from Mohammedan bigotry, have in their seclusion nursed their hereditary hatred of Islámism, whilst they bade defiance to its power; and they have latterly come very naturally to regard themselves as the sole remaining depositaries of undefiled, national Hindúism. Hence their enthusiasm, which burns all the fiercer for a secret consciousness that their particular and, as it were, personal pretensions, as Hindús, are and must be but lowly rated at Benares.

The proud *Khas*, the soi-disant *Kshatriyas* of Népál, and the *Parbattia Brahmans*, with all their pharasaical assertions of ceremonial purity, take water from the hands of the Kachár Bhótias—men who, though they dare not kill the cow under their present Hindú rulers, greedily devour the carrion carcase left by disease—men, whose whole lives are as much opposed to practical, as their whole tenets are to speculative, Hindúism.

In very truth, the genius of Polytheism, everywhere accom- modating, is peculiarly so to its professors and their like in Népál. Here, religious opinions are utterly disregarded; and even practice is suffered among the privileged to deviate in a thousand ways from the prescribed standard. The *Néwárs*, or aborigines of the valley of Népál, are, for the most part, Buddhists; but they are deemed very good Hindús neverthe- less, pretty much in the same way as R'AM MOHUN RAYA passes for a good Hindú at Calcutta. A variety of practices, too, which would not be tolerated even in a Hindú below, are here notoriously and avowedly followed. They are omissions, not commissions, for the most part. But there are daily acts of the positive kind done in the hills which could not be done openly in the plains.*

Still these are matters which the Darbár would not brook the discussion of with us; and I am afraid that their known deviations, in many respects, would only make them more punctilious and obstinate in regard to those few which it is so much our interest and duty to get compromised, if we can, with reference to our followers. Unfortunately, these few topics are the salient points of Hindúism; are precisely those points which it is the pride and glory of this state to maintain from the throne and judgment-seat, as the chief features of the public law; *because*, nowhere else throughout India can they be maintained in the same public and authentic manner, or any otherwise than by the domestic tribunals of the people. The

* The gallant soldiers of these hills cannot endure the tedious ceremonial of Hindúism. When preparing to cook, they satisfy the law by washing their hands and face, instead of their whole bodies; by taking off their turbans, instead of their whole dress. Nor are they at all afraid of being degraded to *kúlis* if they should carry ten days' provisions, in time of war, on their backs. *Et sic de cæteris.*

distinction between Hindús on the one hand, and, on the other, outcasts of their own race, as well as all strangers indiscriminately, it is the special duty of the judges of the land to ponder upon day and night, to pursue it through all its practical consequences, as infinitely diversified by the ceremonial observances created to guard and perpetuate it; and to visit, with the utmost vengeance of the Penal Code, every act by which this cardinal distinction is knowingly and essentially violated.

Of all these acts, the most severely regarded is intercourse between the sexes of such parties; because of its leading directly to the confusion of all castes, of the greatness of the temptation, and of the strong inducement to concealment; and the concealment is deemed almost as bad as the crime itself; for the Hindú agent or subject will, of course, proceed, till detected, to communicate as usual with his or her relations, who again will communicate with theirs, until the foul contamination has reached the ends of the city and kingdom, and imposed upon all (besides the sin) the necessity of submitting themselves to a variety of tedious and expensive purificatory processes, pending the fulfilment of which all their pursuits of business or pleasure are necessarily suspended, and themselves rendered, for the time, outcasts. This, to be sure, is a great and real evil, deserving of severe repressive measures. But is not the evil self-created? True: but so we may not argue at Káthmándú. The law of caste is the corner-stone of Hindúism. Hence the innumerable ceremonial observances, penetrating into every act of life, which have been erected to perpetuate this law; and hence the dreadful inflictions with which the breach of it is visited. Of all breaches of it, intercourse between a Hindú and an outcast of different sexes is the most enormous; but it is not, by many, the only one deemed worthy of punishment by mutilation or death. The Codes of MENU and other Hindú sages are full of these strange enormities; but it is in Népál alone (for reasons already stated) that the sword of public justice is now wielded to realise them. It is in Népál alone, of all Hindú states, that two-thirds of the time of the judges is employed in the discussion of cases better fitted for the confessional, or the tribunal of public opinion, or some domestic court, such as the *Pancháyet* of brethren or fellow-craftsmen, than for a King's Court of justice. Not such, however, is the opinion of the Népálese, who, while they are forcing confessions from young men and young women, by dint of scolding and whipping, in order to visit them afterwards with ridiculous penances or savage punishments, instead of discharging such functions with a sigh or a smile, glorify themselves in that they are thus maintaining the holy will of BRÁHMA, enforcing from the judgment-seat those sacred institutes, which elsewhere the magistrate (shame upon him!) neglects through fear, or despises as an infidel.

When the banner of Hindúism dropped from the hands of the Mahrattas in 1817, they solemnly conjured the Népálese to take it up, and wave it proudly, till it could be again unfurled in the plains by the expulsion of the vile *Feringis*, and the subjection of the insolent followers of Islám. But surely the British Government, so justly famous for its liberality, cannot be fairly subjected to insinuations such as this? So it may seem; but let any one turn over the pages of MENU, observe the conspicuous station assigned to the public magistrate as a *censor morum* under the immensely extensive and complicate system of morals there laid down, and remember, that whilst it is the Hindú magistrate's first duty to enforce them, to the British magistrate they are and have been a dead letter: let him look to the variety of dreadful inflictions assigned to violations of the law of caste, and remember, that whilst their literal fulfilment is the Hindú magistrate's most sacred obligation, British magistrates shrink with horror and disgust at the very thought of them; and he will be better prepared to appreciate and make allowance for the sentiments of Hindú sovereigns and Hindú magistrates. The Hindú sovereigns *dare* not, and we *will* not, obey the sacred mandate. But in Népál, it is the pride and glory of the magistrate to obey it, literally, blindly, unbiassed by foreign example, unawed by foreign power.

An eminent old *bichári* or judge of the chief court of Káthmándú, to whom I am indebted for an excellent sketch of the judicial system of Népál, after answering all my questions on the subject, concluded with some voluntary observations of his own. from which I extract the following passage :—

"Below, let man and woman commit what sin they will, there is no punishment provided, no expiatory right enjoined.* Hence Hindúism is destroyed; the customs are Mohammedan; the distinctions of caste are obliterated. Here, on the contrary, all those distinctions are religiously preserved by the public courts of justice, which punish according to caste, and never destroy the life of a *Brahman.* If a female of the sacred order go astray, and her paramour be not a *Brahman,* he is capitally punished; but if he be a *Brahman* he is degraded from his rank, and banished. If a female of the soldier tribes be seduced, the husband, with his own hand, kills the seducer, and cuts off the nose of the female, and expels her from his house. Then the *Brahman* or soldier-husband must perform the purificatory rites enjoined, after which he is restored to his caste. *Below, the Shástras are things to talk of: here, they are acted up to.*"

I have, by the above remarks, endeavoured to convey an idea of the sort of feeling relative to them which prevails in Népál. It will serve, I hope, as a sort of apology for the Népálese; but will, I fear, also serve to demonstrate the small probability there exists of our inducing the Darbár to waive in our favour so cherished a point of religion, and, I may add, of policy; for they are well aware of the effect of this rigour, intending to facilitate the restricted intercourse between the Népálese and our followers, a restriction which they seek to maintain with Chinese pertinacity. Besides, the *Shástras* are holy things, and frail as holy; and no Hindú of tolerable shrewdness will submit a single text of them, if he can avoid it, to the calm, free glance of European intellect.

Having already given the most abundant materials † for judging of the general tenor of the judicial proceedings and of the laws of Népál, it will not be necessary (or possible), in this paper, to do more than briefly apply them, as regards that intercourse between a Hindú, and a non-Hindú, at present under discussion.

The customary law or license which permits the injured

* It is the exclusive duty of one of the highest functionaries of this Government (the *Dharmádhikári*) to prescribe the fitting penance and purificatory rites for each violation of the ceremonial law of purity.

† In allusion to other papers by Mr Hodgson.—ED.

husband in Népál to be his own avenger, is confined to the *Parbattias*, the principal divisions of whom are the *Brahmans*, the *Khas*, the *Magars*, and the *Gúrungs*. The *Néwárs*, *Múrmis*,* *Kachár-Bhotias*, *Kirántis*,† and other inhabitants of Népál, possess no such privilege. They must seek redress from the courts of justice, which, guiding themselves by the custom of these tribes prior to the conquest, award to the injured husband a small pecuniary compensation, which the injurer is compelled to pay.

Nothing further, therefore, need at present be said of them. In regard to the *Parbattias*, every injured husband has the option, if he please, of appealing to the courts, instead of using his own sword; but any one save a learned *Brahman* or a helpless boy, who should do so, would be covered with eternal disgrace. A *Brahman* who follows his holy calling cannot, consistently with usage, play the avenger; but a *Brahman* carrying arms must act like his brethren in arms. A boy, whose wife has been seduced, may employ the arm of his grown-up brother or cousin to avenge him. But if he have none such, he, as well as the learned *Brahman*, may appeal to the prince, who, through his courts of justice, comes forward to avenge the wrong (such is the sentiment here), and to wipe out the stain with blood; death, whether by law or extra-judicially, being the doom of all adulterers with the wives of *Parbattias*. *Brahmans*, indeed, by a law superior to all laws, may not be done to death by sentence of a court of justice. But no one will care to question the *Parbattia*, who, with his own hand, destroys an adulterer, *Brahman* though that adulterer be. If the law be required to judge a *Brahman* for this crime, the sentence is, to be degraded from his caste, and banished for ever, with every mark of infamy. If a *Parbattia* marry into a tribe such as the *Néwár*, which claims no privilege of licensed revenge, he may not, in regard to such wife, exercise the privilege.

But must not a *Parbattia*, before he proceed to avenge himself, prove the fact and the identity of the offender, in a court of justice? No! To appeal to a court would afford a warning to the delinquents to escape, and so foil him. He may pursue

---

* Kachár = cis-Nivean.
† See above, Vol. I., pp. 176 ff. 397 ff.

his revenge without a thought of the magistrate; he may watch his opportunity for years, till he can safely execute his design; and when he has, at last, found it, he may use it to the adulterer's destruction. But he may not spare the adulteress: he must cut off her nose, and drive her with ignominy from his house; her caste and station for ever gone. If the wife have notoriously sinned with many, the husband may not destroy any but the first seducer, and though the husband need prove nothing beforehand, he must be prepared with legal proof afterwards, in case the wife should deny the fact, and summon him before the courts (no other person can) for murder and mutilation.

And what is deemed legal proof in this case? The wife's confession made in the presence of two witnesses. But who is to warrant us that the confession is free? This, it must be confessed, is an awkward question; since, by the law of Népál, the husband's power over his wife is extreme. He may beat her; lock her up; starve her *ad libitum*, so long as he endanger not her life or limbs; and that he will do all this and more, when his whole soul is bent upon procuring the necessary acknowledgment of her frailty, is too probable. But still, her honour, her station, and her beauty are dear to a woman; and every *Parbattia* wife knows, that the terrible avowal once made, she becomes in an instant a noseless and infamous outcast. There is little real danger, therefore, that a true woman should be false to herself, by confessing, where there was no sin, *for fear of her husband;* and no danger at all, I apprehend, that, as has been imagined, she could be won to become the *tool* of some *petty malice* of her husband, or of the covert *political spleen* of the Darbár. There are, indeed, some married *Brahmans* among the soldiery of Népál; and the wife of a *Brahman* may not be mutilated. But in proportion as the station of a *Brahmaní* is higher than that of all others, so must its prerogatives be dearer to her; and all these she must lose if she confess. She must be driven from her home by her husband, and be degraded and banished the kingdom by the State. But there is certainly a contingent hazard to our followers, arising out of the circumstance of the adulteress, if she have sinned with many, being required to name her first lover; for since she must, in every court, suffer the full penalties of her crime, it may well be supposed that, under various circumstances, she might be led to name, as her first paramour, one of our *sipáhis*, instead of a country fellow. This, however, seems to me a vague and barely possible contingency.

PROCEDURE.

The proofs and procedure before the Népál tribunals will fall more naturally under consideration, when we proceed to the next case. Suffice it here to say, that if, when the husband would cut off his wife's nose, or afterwards, the wife should hurry to a court of justice, and deny her guilt, the husband must be brought up to answer. In ninety-nine cases out of a hundred, the husband's answer consists in simply producing the two witnesses to his wife's confession of guilt. She, of course, affirms that the confession was extorted by unwarrantable cruelty towards her; and if she can support such a plea (it is hard to do so, for the husband's legal power covers a multitude of sins), in a manner satisfactory to the court, and if the husband have no counter-evidence to this plea, nor any circumstantial or general evidence of the guilt which he affirms, he may be condemned to death. But, in the vast majority of cases, his two witnesses to the confession, with such circumstantial evidence as the case, if a true bill, can hardly want, will suffice for his justification.

INTERCOURSE BETWEEN A HINDÚ AND A NON-HINDÚ—THE LAW.

He who may give water to a pure Hindú to drink, is within the pale of Hindúism; he whose water may not be drunk by a pure Hindú, is an outcast, an unutterably vile creature, whose intimate contact with one within the pale is foul contamination, communicable to the pure by the slightest and most necessary intercourse held with them, and, through them, to all others. If trivial and involuntary, it may be expiated by the individual, if he alone be affected; or by all with whom he and they communicated before the discovery of the taint, if any such persons there be. The expiation is, by a world of purificatory rites, as tedious as expensive; and the tainted must segregate themselves from society till these rites are completed. But there are many sorts of contact between a Hindú and a non-Hindú, or outcast, the sin of which is inexpiable, and the penalty, death. Such is intercourse between the sexes. But, by a primary law, the lives and members of *Brahmans*, and the lives of women, are sacred. Subject to the modification of this primary law, the utmost vengeance of the Code is reserved for this enormous sin. Men so offending are done to death. Women have their noses amputated, are rendered outcasts, if they have castes to lose, and are banished the kingdom.

A male outcast, who has intercourse, under any circumstances, with a pure Hindú female, and whether the female be the seducer or the seduced, be maid, wife, or widow, chaste, or a wanton, is adjudged to die; and the female is rendered noseless and an outcast; unless of the sacred order, when her nose is spared. If an outcast female pass herself off for one of a pure caste, and have commerce with a Hindú, she shall have her nose cut off; and he, if he confess his sin so soon as he discovers it, shall be restored to caste by penance and purification; but if he have connection knowingly with such a female, he shall be emasculated, and made an outcast. If a *Sudra*, or one of lower degree, but still within the pale, have commerce with a *Brahmaní*, he shall suffer death, unless the *Brahmaní* be a prostitute, and then he shall go free.

If any such Hindú have commerce with a *Khasni*, she having been a chaste widow up to that time,* he shall die. If she were a maid, and willing, he shall be heavily fined; if a wanton, he shall go free.

Hindús, however low, whose water will pass from hand to hand, are in no danger of life or limb from such commerce with any others than *Brahman* and *Khas* females. The latter are the *Kshatriyas* of Népál and wear the thread.

The following are the outcasts of Népál:—

NÉWÁRS.		PARBATTIAS.	
Kúllú.	*Chámákhalak,*	*Kámi.*	*Kingri,* or *Gáin.*
Pórya.	or *Phungin.*	*Damái.*	*Dhobi.*
Kassai.	*Dúng,* or *Dúni.*	*Sárki.*	*Músálmáns.*
Kúsúlliah.	*Sangat.*	*Bhár,* or *Bhánr.*	

* Chaste widows are supposed to be dead to the world, and devoted to religious exercises. Most of them burn with their husbands' corpses.

The above enumeration of outcast *Néwárs* may serve to introduce the remark, that the distinctions of caste, and their penal consequences, do not owe their existence in Népál to the *Górkhá* dynasty. It is true that before that event the majority of the Népálese proper were Budd'hists, having a law of their own; but so they are still. And when we advert to the facts, that the Budd'hism of the most distinguished tribe of them (the *Néwárs*) admitted the dogma of caste; that the sovereigns of Káthmándú and Pátan, though belonging to this tribe, were, for three or four ages before the conquest, with many of their subjects, Brahmanical Hindús; that the *Néwárs* and others, since the conquest, have all, as far as they were allowed, by availing themselves of the privileges of Hindúism, confessed its obligations to be binding on them; and that lastly, all tribes have now for seventy years acknowledged the paramountship, *quoad hoc*, of the Hindú law of the conquerors;—when I say, we recollect all these things, it will appear clear, I think, that we are not at liberty to question the equitableness of the application of this law to our followers in Népál, inasmuch as it is *the unquestioned law of the land.**

THE PROCEDURE.

The round of operations by which a judgment is reached in a Népálese court of justice is precisely such as a man of sense, at the head of his family, would apply to the investigation of a domestic offence; and the contracted range of all rights and wrongs in Népál renders this sort of procedure as feasible as it is expeditious and effectual. The pleasing spectacle is, however, defaced by the occasional rigour arising out of the maxim, that confession is indispensable; and by the intervention, in the absence of ordinary proof, of ordeals and decisory oaths.

An open court, *virâ voce* examination in the presence of the judge, confrontation of the accuser, aid of counsel to the prisoner, and liberty to summon and have examined, under all usual sanctions, the witnesses for the defence—these are the ordinary

---

* The objection that may be raised to this law, in reference to our followers, on the ground of its inconsistency with the general principles of justice and humanity, is altogether another question, with which I presume not to meddle.

attributes of penal justice in Népál; and these would amply suffice for the prisoner's just protection, but for the vehemence with which confessions are sought, even when they are utterly superfluous, but for the fatal efficacy of those confessions and but for the intervention of ordeals. Ordeals, however, are more frequently asked for than commanded; and perhaps it is true that *volenti non fit injuria:* at all events, with reference to enforced confessions, it must not be supposed that the infamous ingenuity of Europe has any parallel in Népál, or that terrible engines are ever employed *in secret* to extort confessions. No ! the only torture known to these tribunals is that of stern inter-rogation and brow-beating, and, more rarely, the application of the *kórá :* * but all this is done in the face of day, under the judge's eye, and in an open tribunal; and though it may some-times compromise innocence, its by far more common effect is to reach guilt. Besides, with respect to ourselves, the mere presence of the Residency *Munshí*, pending the trial of one of our followers, would prevent its use, or at least abuse, in regard to him. Or, ere submitting our followers to the Népálese tribunals, we might bargain successfully with the Darbár for the waiving of this coercion, as well as for the non-intervention of the proof ordeal, *unless with the consent of the party.* And if these two points were conceded to us, I should, I confess, have no more hesitation in committing one of our followers to a Népálese tribunal at Káthmándú, than I should in making him over to our own courts. I have mentioned, that the prisoner is allowed the assistance of counsel; but the expression must be understood to refer to the aid of friends and relatives, for there are no professional pleaders in Népál.

There are no common spies and informers attached to the courts of justice, nor any public prosecutors in the name of the State. The casual informer is made prosecutor, and he acts under a fearful responsibility; for if he fails to prove the guilt he charges, if he have no eye-witnesses to the principal fact besides himself, and the accused resolutely persevere in denial, a man of respectability must clear his character by demanding the ordeal, in which, if he be cast, the judgment upon him may be to suffer all, or the greater part of that evil which the law

* A kind of whip.

assigns to the offence he charged. At all events, deep disgrace, and fines more or less heavy, are his certain portion; and if it seem that he was actuated by malice, he shall surely suffer the doom he would have inflicted on the accused, be it greater or be it less. Informers and prosecutors, who have evidently no personal interest in the matter—those who are the retainers of the Darbár, or of the Minister—are expected and required, under a Hindú Government, to bring under judicial cognisance such breaches of the law of caste, and of the ritual purity of Hindúism, as they may chance to discover, and they are, of course, more considered than other informers; but they are liable, like ordinary informers, to the predicament of seeing their credit in society ruined, unless they dare the perilous event of purification by ordeal, with its contingency of ignominy and fines. Ordeals, however, whether for proof of innocence or for the clearing of the accuser, are rare, extraordinary, and seldom or never admitted where there is sufficient testimony of witnesses to be had. But whatever quantity of testimony be adduced, the confession of the accused must still be had. That confession is singly sufficient: without it, no quantity and quality of evidence will justify a condemnation; a strange prejudice, producing all that harshness towards the accused, which (omitting the folly of ordeals, and that the people seem to love more than their rulers) is the only grave defect in the criminal judicatures of the country.

In Népál, when the arraignment of the prisoner is completed, he is asked for his answer; and if he confess, his confession is recorded, he is requested to sign it, and judgment is at once passed. If he deny the fact, the assessors of the judge call upon the prosecutor to come forward and establish his charge. A very animated scene then ensues, in which the parties are suffered to try their strength against each other—to produce their witnesses and counter-witnesses, their presumptions and counter-presumptions. The result of this conflict is usually to make the guilt of the accused very evident; and he commonly confesses when the trial is closed. But if the accused persist in refusing confession, the assessors of the judge then go formally into the evidence, and urge upon the accused all the criminative circumstances, and all the weight of testimony. If these be strong and decisive, and he still deny, he is brow-beaten, abused, whipped till he confess; or, if all will not do, he is remanded indefinitely to prison.*

If there be no eye-witness but the informer, or if the informer be not himself an eye-witness to the crime, and have no external witness to back his charge, he must, at all events, be furnished with strong presumptive proof (for woe betide him as he well knows, if he have neither!) wherewith to confirm his accusation. This proof is vehemently urged upon the prisoner by the court and by the accuser; and if the accused prevaricate or be sullen, he is scolded and whipped as before, till he confess. If he cannot be thus brought to confess, and there be but the accuser's assertion to the denial of the accused, the accuser, if he profess to have been an eye-witness, is now expected, for his own credit's sake, to make the appeal to the God of Truth, that is, to demand the ordeal. But if he be a man of eminent respectability, the court will probably, in such circumstances, instead of permitting the ordeal, administer to the accuser, being an eye-witness, a very solemn oath (witnesses and parties are not ordinarily sworn), under the sanction of which he will be required to depose afresh; and if his evidence be positive and circumstantial, and in harmony with the probabilities of the case, his single testimony will suffice for the conviction of the court, which will commit the prisoner indefinitely till he confess.

In matters of illicit intercourse between the sexes, where there are two parties under accusation, if the one confess and the other deny; and there is no positive testimony, and all the circumstantial evidence, however sternly urged upon the non-confessing party, fails to draw forth an acknowledgment, the court, as a last resort, may command that the issue be referred to ordeal of the parties; or that the contumacious party be remanded to prison for a time, whence he is again brought before the court, and urged, as before, to confess. And if this second attempt to obtain the *sine quâ non* of judgment be ineffectual, the gods must decide where men could not; ordeal must cut the Gordian knot.

---

* This, in capital cases, is exactly the mode of proceeding formerly observed in the Dutch courts, and probably in many others in Europe.— ED.

Upon the whole, though it be a strange spectacle, and a revolting, to see the judge urging the unhappy prisoner, with threats, abuse, and whipping, "to confess and be hanged;" yet it is clearly true, that whippings and hard words are light in the balance, compared with hanging.

A capital felon, therefore, will seldom indeed be thus driven to confess a crime he has not committed, when he is sustained and aided by all those favourable circumstances, in the constitution of the tribunal, and in the forms of procedure already enumerated. Nor should it be forgotten, that if much rigour is sometimes used to procure a confession, the confession itself is most usually superfluous to justice; and is sought rather to satisfy a scruple of conscience, than as a substitute for deficient evidence.

SECTION XIII.

ON THE NATIVE METHOD OF MAKING THE PAPER, DENOMINATED IN HINDUSTAN, NEPÁLESE.

For the manufacture of the Népálese paper, the following implements are necessary, but a very rude construction of them suffices for the end in view :—

1st. A stone mortar, of shallow and wide cavity, or a large block of stone, slightly but smoothly excavated.

2d. A mallet or pestle of hard wood, such as oak, and size proportioned to the mortar, and to the quantity of boiled rind of the paper plant which it is desired to pound into pulp.

3d. A basket of close wicker work, to put the ashes in, and through which water will pass, only drop by drop.

4th. An earthen vessel or receiver, to receive the juice of the ashes after they have been watered.

5th. A metallic open-mouthed pot, to boil the rind of the plant in. It may be of iron, or copper, or brass, indifferently; an earthen one would hardly bear the requisite degree of fire.

6th. A sieve, the reticulation of the bottom of which is wide and open, so as to let all the pulp pass through it, save only the lumpy parts of it.

7th. A frame, with stout wooden sides, so that it will float well in water, and with a bottom of cloth, only so porous, that the meshes of it will stay all the pulp, even when dilated and diffused in water; but will let the water pass off, when the frame is raised out of the cistern; the operator must also have the command of a cistern of clear water, plenty of fire-wood, ashes of oak (though I fancy other ashes might answer as well), a fire-place, however rude, and lastly, a sufficient quantity of slips of the inner bark of the paper tree, such as is peeled off the plant by the paper-makers, who commonly use the peelings when fresh from the plant; but that is not indispensable. With these " appliances and means to boot," suppose you take four seers of ashes of oak ; put them into the basket above mentioned, place the earthen receiver or vessel beneath the basket, and then gradually pour five seers of clear water upon the ashes, and let the water drip slowly through the ashes, and fall into the receiver. This juice of ashes must be strong, or a dark-like red colour, and in quantity about two lbs., and if the first filtering yield not such a produce, pass the juice through the ashes a second time. Next, pour this extract of ashes into the metal pot, already described, and boil the extract; and so soon as it begins to boil, throw into it as many slips or peelings of the inner bark of the paper plant as you can easily grasp; each slip being about a cubit long, and an inch wide (in fact, the quantity of the slips of bark should be to the quantity of juice of ashes, such that the former shall float freely in the latter, and that the juice shall not be absorbed and evaporated with less than half an hour's boiling). Boil the slips for about half an hour, at the expiration of which time the juice will be nearly absorbed, and the slips quite soft. Then take the softened slips and put them into the stone mortar, and beat them with the oaken mallet, till they are reduced to a homogeneous or uniform pulp, like so much dough. Take this pulp, put it into any wide-mouthed vessel, add a little pure water to it, and churn it with a wooden instrument, like a chocolate mill, for ten minutes, or until it lose all stringiness, and will spread itself out, when shaken about under water. Next, take as much of this prepared pulp as will cover your paper frame (with a thicker or thinner coat, according to the strength of the paper you need), toss it into such a sieve as I have described, and lay the sieve upon the paper frame, and let both sieve and frame float in the cistern : agitate them, and the pulp will spread itself over the sieve; the grosser and knotty parts of the pulp will remain in the sieve, but all the rest of it will ooze through into the frame. Then put away the sieve, and taking the frame in your left hand, as it floats on the water, and pulp smartly with your right hand, and the pulp will readily diffuse itself in an uniform manner over the bottom of the frame. When it is thus properly diffused, raise the frame out of the water, easing off the water in such a manner, that the uniformity of the pulp spread shall continue after the frame is clear of the water and the paper is made.

To dry it, the frame is set endwise, near a large fire; and so soon as it is dry, the sheet is peeled off the bottom of the frame and folded up. When (which seldom is the case) it is deemed needful to smooth and polish the surface of the paper, the dry sheets are laid on wooden boards and rubbed, with the convex entire side of the conch-shell; or in case of the sheets of paper being large, with the flat surface of a large rubber of hard and smooth grained wood; no sort of size is ever needed or applied, to prevent the ink from running. It would, probably, surprise the paper-makers of England, to hear that the Kachar Bhoteahs can make up this paper into fine smooth sheets of several yards square. This paper may be purchased at Káthmándú in almost any quantity, at the price of 17 annas sicca per dharni of three seers; and the bricks of dried pulp may be had* at the same place, for from 8 to 10 annas sicca per dharni. Though called Népálese, the paper is not in fact made in Népál proper. It is manufactured exclusively in Cis-Himálayan Bhote, and by the race of Bhoteahs, denominated, in their own tongue, Rangbo, in contradistinction to the Trans-Himálayan Bhoteahs, whose vernacular name is Sokhpo.† The Rangbo or Cis-Himálayan Bhoteahs are divided into several tribes (such as Múrmi, Lapcha, &c., &c.), who do not generally intermarry, and who speak dialects of the Bhote or Tibet language so diverse, that ignorant as they are, several of them cannot effectually communicate together. They are all somewhat ruder, darker, and smaller than the Sokhpos or Trans-Himálayan Bhoteahs, by whom they are all alike held in slight esteem, though most evidently essentially one and the same with themselves in race and in language, as well as in religion.

---

* The pulp is dried and made up into the shape of bricks or tiles, for the convenience of transport. In this form it is admirably adapted for transmission to England. See the *P.S.*

† The Néwár language has terms precisely equivalent to these. The Rangbo being called in Néwári, Paloo Sen; and the Sokhpo here spoken of is not really a different being from the Soghpoun nomade, the name ordinarily applied in Bhote to the Mongols. But this word has, at least, a different sense in the mouths of the Tibetans, towards this frontier, on both sides of the snows.

To return to our paper-making,—most of the Cis-Himálayan Bhoteahs, east of the Kali river, make the Népálese paper; but the greatest part of it is manufactured in the tract above Népál proper, and the best market for it is afforded by the Népálese people; hence probably it derived its name: a great quantity is annually made and exported southwards, to Népál and Hindustan, and northwards, to Sokya-Gumba, Digarchi, and other places in Tramontane Bhote. The manufactories are mere sheds, established in the midst of the immense forest of Cis-Himálayan Bhote, which affords to the paper-makers an inexhaustible supply, on the very spot, of the firewood and ashes, which they consume so largely; abundance of clear water (another requisite) is likewise procurable everywhere in the same region. I cannot learn by whom or when the valuable properties of the paper plant were discovered; but the Népálese say that any of their books now existent, which is made of Palmira leaves, may be safely pronounced, on that account, to be 500 years old: whence we may, perhaps, infer that the paper manufacture was founded about that time. I conjecture that the art of paper-making was got by the Cis-Himálayan Bhoteahs, via Lhassa, from China; a paper of the very same sort being manufactured at Lhassa; and most of the useful arts of these regions having flowed upon them, through Tibet, from China; and not from Hindústan.

Népál Residency, November 1831.

P.S.—Dr. Wallich having fully described the paper plant, it would be superfluous to say a word about it. The raw produce or pulp (beat up into bricks) has been sent to England, and declared by the ablest persons to be of unrivalled excellence, as a material for the manufacture of that sort of paper upon which proof engravings are taken off. The manufactured produce of Népál is, for office records, incomparably better than any Indian paper, being as strong and durable as leather almost, and quite smooth enough to write on. It has been adopted in one or two offices in the plains, and ought to be generally substituted for the flimsy friable material to which we commit all our records.

A. CAMPBELL.

SECTION XIV.

PRE-EMINENCE OF THE VERNACULARS; OR, THE ANGLICISTS ANSWERED:

BEING FOUR LETTERS ON THE EDUCATION OF THE PEOPLE OF INDIA.*

PREFACE.

THREE of the four following letters were first published several years back, and lest it should be supposed that the course of time has antiquated their reasonings, I beg leave to suggest that arguments so general are not so rapidly affected by time, and that in point of fact the Macaulayism of one cycle is but the Trevelyanism †

---

* "In Alsace and Lorraine the peasantry after two centuries of subjection to France do not know one word of French. In Wales, in Sleswic, and everywhere in Austria and Russia, we see all efforts to force the ruling language on a subject race resented, even when light, civilisation, and enjoyment of equal rights follow in the train of this denationalising schoolmaster."—*Times*, April 25, 1872.

"There are in almost every department vast hoards of truth which do not exist 'n an available form, and which, however necessary for us, form no part of our ordinary teaching. When our school-books have been rewritten, and when the proved results of research have been incorporated with them, the benefit will be in every way immense."—Article on Mr. Gladstone's Address to the King's College Students, *Times*, July 10, 1876.

"Hitherto the English people have begun at the wrong end, and have been educating downwards instead of upwards. What is of real importance is to teach the poor man to do the best for himself, to enlighten the ignorance, and to dissipate the prejudices which make his life so much harder than it need be. We have confidence in English good sense, and expect the *training-school* to do much good."—*Times*, May 25, 1874.

† These words are used with all honour and respect as the readiest means of speaking of well-known *acta et scripta* of well-known men, of whom the genius of the one and the benevolence of the other command my unfeigned homage. Mr. Macaulay's Minute is but a second edition of Mr. Trevelyan's Treatise.

of another, and that the recent practical measures of Lord Hardinge
are but the effectuation of the doctrines contended against in these
letters. I admit the sagacity and decision with which Lord Hardinge
has carried out the most accredited educational maxims of his predecessors ; I admit the possibility of these measures of our revered
Governor-General supplying the public service with a superior class
of native functionaries, though I confess the apprehension that this
new class of functionaries may prove competent in *our* special
acquirements only by losing all competency in *their own !* But I
contend that anything worthy the name of national education, as
being addressed to remedy the intellectual and moral wants of the
mass of the people, is not comprised in these measures which
address themselves only or chiefly to the wants of the public
service ; and I would add with submission that the principles and
reasonings upon which rest that avowed preference for English,
which dates its present ascendancy from the days of Lord Bentinck
and Mr. Macaulay, are very far inferior in philosophic compre-
hensiveness, as well as in benevolence and expediency, to the
principles and reasonings whence were deduced, according to the
wants of that age, the educational maxims of a Hastings (Warren)
and a Wellesley. I confess an unlimited preference for the latter,
not only because it is infinitely more practicable to make Europeans
familiar with the words and things of India, than to make Indians
familiar with the words and things of Europe, but also because the
former course tends perpetually to rebuke and subdue, the latter
course to excuse and foster, those peccant idiosyncrasies of the
haughty island race to whom God has committed this land, which
half neutralise the blessings derived from the no less characteristic
integrity and energy of that race. The vivifying spirit of our
sound knowledge, which it is so desirable to diffuse throughout
India, is no way inseparably connected with its lingual vehicle;
and, whilst every step we make in the grand project of idigenating
that knowledge in India by means of vernacularisation will prove
a bond of blessed union between ourselves and the mass of our
subjects, and a safe, a sure, and an universally operative agent of
the desiderated change in them, the contrary project of Anglicisation will help to widen the existing lamentable gulf that divides us
from the mass of the people, and put into the hands of the few
among themselves an exclusive and dangerous power, quite similar
in essential character to that power which for ages past the scribes
and priests of the East have wielded, to the deplorable detriment

of the spiritual and temporal welfare of their fellows, and therefore possibly destined only to perpetuate in a new phase the ancient curse of this land, or exclusive learning ! Sanskrit, Arabic, Persian, have proved the curse of this land, not so much by reason of the false doctrines they have inculcated as by reason of the administrative mystery they have created and upheld; and I hold it to surpass the wit of man to demonstrate that that terrible mystery will not be perpetuated by English; for, long ages must elapse before public institutions and public opinion become omnipotent in the interior of this land, and in the meanwhile, all those who possess the exclusive knowledge will find but too ample a field for the exercise of its *power* in prosecution of the selfish ends of ambition and avarice, and in despite of our best efforts at prevention. But, without saying more in repetition of the letters themselves upon the dangers incident to an English organ of knowledge, I may glance at the objection founded upon its difficulty of acquisition and consequent unsuitableness to the wants and necessities of the many. But this topic also having been amply treated in the letters, I notice it here only to call attention to the essential fact that in the practical proposition I have deduced from my general reasonings, there is *nothing whatever savouring of preference for one over another organ* of instruction. The learned languages of the East and of the West, English and the vernaculars of India, all meet with equal favour in the proposed Normal College; and, whilst it is assumed that the vast project of Europeanising the Indian mind calls for express specific measures subsidiary to education properly so called, it is endeavoured so to shape those measures as to reconcile the *adequate* cultivation of *difficult* knowledge by the few with an *incessant supply* of *improved means* of *easy knowledge* for the many. It seems to me that English, not less than Sanskrit or Arabic, is far too difficult for the many ; that such studies to produce the expected fruit must form the life-long labour of an appropriate body, the pioneers of a new literature ; and that if this corps be adequately equipped and provided for, and dedicated to the specific functions of translating and of teaching, in the manner expressed in my fourth letter, the interests of deep learning will be duly attended to without any risk of its running into monastic dreaminess or subtilty, and at the same time that the two great wants of ordinary education, or good teachers and good books, will be systematically provided for. Thus the advocate for English and the advocate for the learned orient tongues, and the advocate for the vernaculars, may all find equal motive and inducement to uphold the proposition of a Normal College; and those who consider the extent of the work to be done in the way of education with the inadequacy of all our means and appliances, will do well to reflect that every ripe scholar trained in this college will not be a mere well-taught individual, at liberty so soon as he is free of his educational course to forget or misapply those gifts which the public has bestowed upon him for better ends, but a teacher, and a permanent teacher or translator, and consequently one to whom thousands may, and hundreds must, be indebted for the elements of learning at least. Mark, then, the diffusable energy, the expansive force of the institution suggested, and support it with active exertion if you deem it worthy of support.

NÉPÁL, 1843.

Since the following letters were written vernacular and normal teaching have made much way in public estimation. But still, even in England, if we may credit frequent leaders in the " Times," and how much more in India! there has been a fearful waste of time and money with very inadequate results, owing to the want of fitting books and teachers. Such consequences of the want of system in providing these indispensable pre-requisites were long ago foreseen in India by Dr. Ballantyne, and if we may trust the language of the recent native petition to the Governor-General of India, to say nothing of further evidence of the same fact, there is an abiding sense among the people of India of the necessity of adopting those means for supplying adequately, and systematically, and enduringly, good books and good teachers, which the following letters point out. This, perhaps, may excuse the reproduction of the letters here.

LONDON, *Feb.* 1876.

" For as for that our tongue is called barbarouse, is but a fantasye ; for so is, as every learned man knoweth, every strange language to other : and if they would call it barren of wordes, there is no doubt but it is plenteouse enough to express our myndes in any things whereof one man hath used to speke with another."—SIR T. MORE.

LETTER I.

TO THE EDITOR OF THE "FRIEND OF INDIA."

SIR,—In the question now under discussion, whether it is better to convey European knowledge to the natives, indirectly, through the medium of their own languages and literature, or directly, through that of ours—I observe with some surprise that you seem to prefer the latter alternative.* You have, too, with the majority of the Anglomaniasts, whilst disclaiming all express purpose of annihilating the indigenous literature, advocated the justice as well as expediency of the so-called negative course of withdrawing all public patronage from it.* But, sir, have you considered the paramount influence of Government acts in the East, and the consequent imperative effect of even those which *profess* to be merely negative ? Have you considered the extent to which the spread of the British rule from province to province, and kingdom to kingdom, has had the effect of closing the native seminaries throughout India, either by the political extinction of their patrons, or by the absorption of their resources ? Have you considered the people's title to be consulted on a question of this sort ? or do you doubt that if their sentiments *were* deferred to they would claim from our Government that protection of their own litera- ture which is conceded to it by every native state ? Thank God, I am no lawyer ; but to my plain understanding, the British Legislature, when it decreed a small pittance for the " revival of native learning," had in view the making of some small atonement for that fiscal rapacity which had merged in the ocean of revenue so many streamlets of national education !

* So far as the worthy editors in question are concerned, this is a mistake which I joyfully retract.

Vested rights are the cry of the West. Let the Anglomaniasts inquire how many of these, appropriated to native instruction, have been violated directly by our indiscriminating resumptions, or indirectly by our levelling system of rule, and they will be better prepared to judge of the justice of Lord William Bentinck's sudden refusal of the Parliamentary dole! The Government's *discretion* in India is, like the Parliamentary omnipotence in England, sufficient for all things but the changing of wrong into right; and whether I advert to the absorption of native seminaries by the progress of our sway, to the enormous portion of the annual produce of industry which we sweep into the Exchequer, or to our obligation to consult the sentiments of the people (let them square with our own *or not*) upon a question of this sort, I must equally deny the title of the Governor-General in Council, to withhold public patronage from the indigenous literature of our subjects. This is my view of the question, as one of right; but as I have no wish to push the plea of *merum jus* on behalf of the people, to the extent of injuring them by compliance with their wishes, I shall proceed to assign some reasons for the opinion I entertain, that their essential welfare, not less than their rights, may be urged against the scheme implied by Lord William Bentinck's decretum. It may be granted at once, as a general proposition, that that sound knowledge, to diffuse which throughout India is our purpose, is to be found in the European languages, and not in those of the East. What we want is the best instrument for the free and equal diffusion of that knowledge. One party contends that English is the desideratum, the other party that the vernacular languages are. It is *assumed* by the former that the English language is a perfect and singly sufficient organ, whilst the native languages are equally objectionable from their plurality and their intrinsic feebleness. These assumptions appear to me somewhat hasty and unfounded. A large portion of the sound knowledge of Europe is *not* to be found in the English language, but must be sought in those of France and Germany—to go no further. Does not every educated Englishman daily resort to the languages of France and Germany for those useful and important ideas which are strangers to his own tongue; and must not, therefore, the assumption that English is coequal with sound knowledge be received with great reserve? Certainly it must; and without pushing the argument beyond due limits, it will be found to be worth something, when placed fairly in the scales against that plurality which is *so extravagantly* objected to the colloquial media of India, for Bengalee is the speech of at least thirty-seven millions of people, and Hindee is everywhere current from the northern frontiers of Bengal to the Indus and the Himalaya, not to mention the ubiquitarian Hindoostanee! This surely is a range of language enough to satisfy the most ardent of reasonable reformers *—is a range rather above than below the average of Europe. With like cautious circumspection let us now endeavour to ascertain the real extent of that intrinsic force, as an instrument for the communication of thought, which is ascribed to English by those who insist so much upon the feebleness of the native languages.

Truth and precision require, that, in making this estimate of English, we should exclude the consideration of the unmixed sciences, as well as of most of the applied ones which are strictly physical. Those sciences have a language of their own, which is admitted on all hands to be highly efficient, and which is disconnected with all ordinary colloquial media, as well as with the passions and prejudices—the ordinary habits and sentiments, of mankind. These circumstances, coupled with the fact that in reference to the sciences in question the native mind is almost a carte blanche, induce me to join those who propose, as the general rule, to convey our knowledge of them to the people of India *directly:* and that in all senses of directness, lingual as well as others.† But the case is far otherwise with the moral sciences: for, blended as these branches of knowledge are, from their very nature, with the daily pursuits and thoughts, and quickly responsive as they are to the strongest prejudices and passions, of mankind; appealing, too, as they do, for their ultimate evidence, to universal consciousness, or to almost universal experience, powerful intrinsical

---

* See note at the end of these papers.

† The exception of astronomy rests, and rests well, on the conversancy of the people with *this* branch of physical science and on their attachment to their own achievements in it. We should avail ourselves of that attachment *as far as possible.*

reasons may come in aid of the lingual considerations I am about to show, against the direct communication of our superior lights to the Indians. To those intrinsical reasons I propose to revert in the sequel,* and meanwhile proceed to observe, that, of the lingual considerations, the first I shall note amounts to a demur to the asserted perfectness of our language; and I would request the particular attention of those who lay such undue stress upon the imperfection of the vernacular tongues of India, to the following quotations from two of the most enlightened of English philosophers on the subject.

"The inadequacy of the words of our ordinary language for the communication, as well as for the discovery of truth, is a frequent complaint of which the justice will be felt by all who consider the state to which some of the most important arts would be reduced, if the coarse tools of the common labourer were the only instruments available in the most delicate operations of manual expertness. The watchmaker, the optician, and the surgeon are provided with instruments which are fitted by careful ingenuity to second their skill: the philosopher alone is doomed to use the rudest tools for the most refined purposes. He must reason in words of which the looseness and vagueness are almost as remote from the extreme exactness and precision required, not only in the conveyance, but in the search of truth, as the hammer and axe would be unfit for the finest exertions of skilful handiwork. He may be compared with an arithmetician compelled to employ numerals not only cumbrous but used so irregularly to denote different quantities, that they not only deceive others, but himself." Again, "In a mathematical definition, although the words in which it is expressed may vary, the meaning which it is intended to convey is always the same. The case is not the same with the definitions of the less strict sciences. In those of morals and politics it is most difficult to use terms which may not be understood differently by different persons. The terms virtue, morality, equity, charity, are in every day use: yet it is by no means agreed what are the particular acts which ought to be classed under these different heads.

---

* See Letter No. II. on the use that may, and should, be made of the Indian *literature* as a means of diffusing our sounder knowledge. The present letter is devoted to the consideration of *languages*.

The terms liberty, constitutional liberty, civil liberty, political liberty, political economy, are frequently understood in a different sense by different persons. The sense of the words wealth, capital, productive labour, value, labour, profits, demand, has been lately called in question, though I think without sufficient reason. As a remedy for these difficulties it has been proposed that a new and more perfect nomenclature should be introduced. But in such sciences as morals, politics, and political economy, it is impossible to suppose that a new nomenclature would be submitted to, or, if it were, that it would render the same service to these sciences as the nomenclatures of Linnæus, Lavoisier, and Cuvier, did to the sciences to which they were respectively applied."

These quotations are from works which were among the last and maturest labours of a Mackintosh and a Malthus; and though their tenor be not entirely correspondent, I apprehend that Malthus's not less than Mackintosh's sentiments demonstrate the inaccuracy and scarcity of our specific terms, or, in other words, the poverty of our language; whilst those of the former have other bearings upon this question, which will be recurred to in the sequel. Those who are disposed to object to mere authority, however high, are requested to advert to the prominent facts, that terminology occupies a *large portion of the latest* and *ablest* works on the theory of Government, on jurisprudence, on political economy, on mental and on moral philosophy—in a word, on every branch of knowledge beyond the limits of the exact sciences ; and that the new vocables and definitions of one philosopher *are continually rejected by another.* And such inquirers will find that they can only excuse our language (if determined so to do), at the expense of our ideas or knowledge. If, then, we begin by a fair estimate of the value of our own language as an instrument of thought; and forbear, in proceeding to compare it with the vernacular tongues of India, from undue depreciation of *them*, I conceive that as much exaggeration will be found to have prevailed relative to the poverty of the latter, as to their multiplicity. When we speak of the multitude of Indian languages we are sadly apt to forget the extent of its territory and population ; nor less so, the important distinction between the merely dialectial, and the essential, differences of language. When, again, we speak of the poverty of those languages, as though they neither were, nor could be easily made, competent vehicles of European knowledge, we assume with equal rashness the power of our own speech, and the powerlessness of those of India—alike inattentive to facts directly bearing upon the matter, and to those general considerations which, unless I am much mistaken, may be made to demonstrate the *necessary* capacity of the Indian spoken languages to bear any weight of knowledge coming home to the *business and bosoms of mankind* that we can lay on them. I call upon you, sir, and upon your fraternity (which is best able to do so), to explain distinctly and to unfold my general assertions, that Bengalee, the language of thirty-seven millions, has good dictionaries and grammars, as well as works which, quoad language, exhibit a respectable share of precision and compass; whilst its connection with Sanskrit, and the peculiar genius of the latter, afford extraordinary means of enrichment by new terms competent to express any imaginable modification of thought. I call upon you, sir, to explain and unfold in detail my further assertions, that throughout the Bengal Presidency wherever Bengalee is not spoken, Hindee is the basis of that almost single vernacular language which is common to all Hindoos and all rural Moslems; that Hindee possesses books which in point of language exhibit very consider-able actual and latent power; that the latter may be educed and extended to any requisite degree through the connection of Hindee with Sanskrit; and that, lastly, scarcely any part of the population of our vast presidency, which uses *not* Bengalee or Hindee, has other language than Hindoostanee—a language rich in grammars, dictionaries, and written works; and from its flexible genius capable of amalgamating with its existing wealth any and every variety of new terms and vocables which Sanskrit and Arabic can furnish from their inexhaustible fountains.

Let us now, for a moment, advert to those more general con-siderations above glanced at. That language is an express image of thought is an old and exploded error.* Words do *not* expressly embody ideas—the function of language being limited to putting and keeping two minds in the same train

* Stewart's Phil. Essays, pp. 201-211.

of thought. If the precision of mathematical expression seem to contradict this important truth, the semblance is nothing more than a real independence upon language, properly so called. It is, further, possibly the fact that philosophy, from its very nature, is incapable of that conciseness which belongs to the exact sciences; and, at all events, it cannot be denied that it is very far indeed from now possessing such conciseness in Europe, whether from comparative defect of knowledge on our part, or from more intrinsical peculiarities. Indeed, the signal failure of those great men who have again and again attempted to subject moral discussions to mathematical restraints would seem to prove that *both* the above conjectures are sound.

Hence, not less than because of the necessary connection of philosophy with our ordinary thoughts and feelings, the difficulty—perhaps impossibility—of creating such a language as our philosophers deplore the want of. Whether Mackintosh's anticipation that some future Bacon will raise our philosophical language to the level of our scientific * be better grounded than Malthus's idea of the vanity of such a hope, I shall not presume further to indicate. But I assert without fear of contradiction, that the *existing extreme inaccuracy* of all European languages, as instruments of thought, in reference to the principles of every department of that portion of human lore coming home to the business and bosoms of mankind at large, is *notorious and undenied;* and that it is precisely *in this view* that our own language, no way distinguished from the rest, has nevertheless been assumed to possess such wonderful efficiency! So far, however, is it from the truth that it *does* possess such efficiency that the fact is, it is solely by means of *ample definition, of much circumlocution*, that the English language at present represents the English knowledge on these subjects.

And, whoever will advert to the nature and extent of this circuitous communication of ideas in our tongue (whether its

* "A system of names may be *imagined*, indicating the objects of knowledge, and showing the relation of the parts to each other—an order and a language somewhat resembling those by which the objects of Botany and Chemistry have, in the 18th century, been denoted. But so great an undertaking must be reserved for a second Bacon and a future generation."—Mackintosh's Eth. Phi. pp. 5, 6.

cause be the nature of language and the dependence of philosophy upon it, or, the nature of philosophy, or, our imperfect knowledge of the latter), can have no further room to doubt that the same ideas may be conveyed to Indian minds, in their own languages, *without much further* circumlocution.

To put two minds in the same train of thought is all that it is *ever* given to language to accomplish : to effect this by the cumbrous expedient of definitions, amounting almost to dissertation upon the most ordinary and necessary vocables, is all that it has *yet* been given to *philosophic* * language to achieve *in Europe.* Such being the case, is it possible to advert to that universal consciousness, or almost universal experience, which form the basis and evidence of all the truths of philosophy,* in connection with the long-sustained and literary character of Indian civilisation, without reaching the conviction that the alleged incapacity of the Indian vernacular languages *cannot* relate to the *ordinary* topics and functions of language, but must respect that peculiar function and those special topics in reference to which the feebleness of our own language is confessed ; or, that the *cure* of this particular defect of the oriental vernaculars need excite the despair of those only who are hopeless about its cure in reference to their own ?

We must exaggerate the perfection of our own language as much as we do the imperfection of those of India—we must further shut our eyes to the essential nature and function of speech, to the connection of philosophy with life, and to the high date of Indian civilisation, before we can admit the assertion that the Indian languages neither are, nor can readily be made, competent to express our knowledge. Their present competency is great, in most ordinary views ; and if a very moderate degree of public patronage continue to be bestowed on the learned languages whence they are derived, the efficient lexicographical and grammatical labours of the past upon the vulgar tongues may be completed so as, without extraordinary pains, delay, or expense, to render the latter as much more

---

* It may be as well, once for all, to say that by this term I mean to express *all* knowledge beyond the limits of mathematics and strict physics. The latter I indicate by the word science.

effective as can be required, or can be expected by those who either understand the real state of the English language at present, or the nature of language in general.

Any number of new terms, as clear to the mind and as little startling to the ear, as the oldest words in the languages, may be introduced into Hindee and Bengalee from Sanskrit, owing to the peculiar genius of the latter,* with *much more* facility than we can introduce new terms into English: nor does the task of introducing such new terms into the Indian vernaculars imply or exact more than the most ordinary skill or labour on the part of the conductors of education, *so long* as they *disconnect not themselves wholly from Indian literature.* With such views of the nature of language in general, and of the existing comparative value of the languages of Europe and of India, I foresee that I may be set down for a lingual sceptic, or, may be, perchance, enlisted under the banners of that party which, without substituting English for the living tongues of India, would improve the latter by *directly grafting English terms upon them,* in preference to resorting to Sanskrit and Arabic. So far, however, from the truth is it, that my views of the general question are sceptical, that I am thoroughly convinced there *is* such a thing as idiosyncracy and genius in every cognate group of languages, and that this genius is of so *rigid and commanding a nature* that it is indispensably necessary humbly to bow to it, in all schemes for the improvement of any given tongue: for, if not, how happened it that those wonderful men who flourished in England between the Reformation and the Revolution, placed as they were close to the sources of our language, and endowed as they were with the highest faculties, yet failed utterly in becoming models of style? and how happened it that the wits of Queen Anne, much remoter as they were placed from the sources of our language, and incomparably inferior as were their mental powers, became so at once and for ever? The sole reason is that the former opposed, and the latter yielded to, the genius of our tongue, both in their terms and in their sentences.

* I borrow this idea, in his words, from Mackintosh, who applies it to German. Every scholar knows, and knows why, it is singularly applicable to the Indian Prakrits, through Sanskrit.

If, again, it be not necessary to consult idiomatic law, the usage of society, and vernacular euphony, whence arises a great part of that difficulty in respect to the introduction of a more copious and precise phraseology into English, which as we have seen, Malthus deemed it impossible to conquer ; and Mackintosh but faintly hoped some future Bacon might subdue ?   And how, yet again, are we to account for the steady and successful resistance which our language has made, for the last fifty years, against incorporation with either the peculiar nomenclature of science, or that of fashion ?   In that period, to go no further, a thousand modish ephemeral phrases have striven in vain to mix themselves with the great stream of our language; nor has the unusual popularity of the physical sciences, in the same era, enabled them, dignified and valuable as they are, to wed their phraseology to our common speech ?

Facts like the above will satisfy all those who are capable of appreciating them, that the people of India would never endure such an olla podrida as Anglo-Hindee or Anglo-Hindoosthanee ; and that if the vernacular languages of this country are to be preserved, their *improvement,* so far as it is requisite to convey European ideas, must be effected in the manner *exacted by the genius of these languages.*

The vague declamation, with which we are overwhelmed upon the subject of the feebleness and inefficiency of the native languages, is partly caused by the unfairness of that controversial spirit, which has laid hold of this question of the best vehicle for communicating our knowledge to India, and partly also by the difficulty of procuring and applying a measure of the value of languages.   Standard works, dictionaries and grammars, certainly furnish a relative measure; yet is it one which few persons *can,* and many fewer *will,* apply, even when there is *room to apply it.*   If, however, we look back to the state of our own language three centuries ago, nobody, I presume, will be found hardy enough to assert its superiority, as an organ for the communication of knowledge, to the Bengalee, Hindee, or Hindoostanee of the present day.   Now should we be able to adduce express evidence, that the most competent of judges deemed the English of 1530 entirely capable of performing that very function which the Indian vernaculars of 1835 are alleged to be incapable of performing, such an evidence, it might be hoped, would convince many who cannot, or will not, examine the question more deeply. It is thus then that Sir Thomas More expresses himself in 1530 :—" For as for that our tongue is called barbarouse, is but a fantasye, for so is, as every learned man knoweth, every strange language to other : And if they would call it barren of wordes, there is no doubt but it is plenteouse enough to express our myndes in any thinge wherefore one man hath used to speke with another." May we not, after this, say, for that the Indian vernaculars are called barbarouse and barren of wordes, it is but a fantasye ? No one, at least, can pretend to assert that the English language of 1530 had, or that the vernaculars of India at present, have not, dictionaries and grammars ; and he must be lost to all sense of impartiality who would maintain that the English chronicles and romances of the Middle Ages are superior in matter or style to such works as are now extant in Bengalee, Hindee and Hindoostanee. And as for capacity of rapid and facile *improvement*, who shall venture to deny it to the Indian vernaculars who considers with what a giant's pace his own tongue advanced to almost all the power it *yet possesses*, when the impulse to improvement had once been given ?

The English works of the age *immediately* following that of Sir T. More yet excite our wonder, and despair of rivalling their characteristic excellences. No one has confessed this more freely than that very writer, himself a master of our language (Mackintosh), whose complaints of its poverty and inefficiency, in *other respects*, were exhibited in the preceding part of this letter. Should not contrasted facts such as these warn us to forbear from dogmatic opinions upon the prospective or latent power of foreign languages ? Should they not teach us to examine the question modestly and carefully ? Let us awake the popular mind in India, and assuredly *the natives*, with our aid and example, will soon demonstrate that their languages possess capabilities equal to any demand. The history, not only of our own language, but of every vulgar tongue in Europe, justifies the presumption that, so soon as effort is directed towards their improvement, the Indian vernaculars will almost immediately and spontaneously put forth the ordinary strength of language ;

and as for what may be called its extraordinary strength, I think I have shown that our own tongue has *not yet* put it forth. Our inability to express without extreme periphrasis the recently-elaborated truths of all departments of the philosophy of life is confessed, as we have seen, by the greatest men of the age. In respect to the *remedy* of this peculiar defect of all known languages, so far as it is remediable, the Hindoos will enjoy, in the genius of the Sanskrit, and in their freedom from our conventional embarrassments, a liberty denied to us; and they will in the meanwhile probably be able to express, as we shall for them, all this class of ideas without more circumlocution than we are now compelled by our poverty of direct terms to use in English.

But it may be urged that Sir T. More's assertion in 1530, relative to the then power of our language, was confined to its capacity for colloquial purposes, and did not contemplate its permanent prospective use as an instrument of thought and medium for the communication of knowledge. No, indeed ! Let us then advert to the circumstances under which these remarkable words of More were uttered, and see how the case stands.

The proposition of that age in England was the general diffusion of sound knowledge. The existing stock of such knowledge possessed by the few, and which it was proposed to make the heritage of the many, was derived from without. The language of that without (Latin or Greek, or both, it matters not to the argument) was a highly-wrought instrument of thought, whilst the English vernacular was a comparatively rude one. Hence arose the question, whether the end to be accomplished (that is, the general diffusion of sound knowledge) might be more readily and happily attained by setting aside the homely Saxon, and diffusing the new ideas *directly* through their appropriate tongue (a ready-made and powerful instrument), *or*, by adherence to, and improvement of, the unfashioned vernacular. One party took the former side of the question; Sir T. More and his friends, the latter; and it was with express reference to *this state of things* that Sir T. More expressed himself in the words I have quoted. Now I apprehend, that the question at issue between the Oriental and Occidental parties in India at this moment, is precisely that which was proposed to the regenerators

of England in 1530. And whilst I do but glance at the speedy
and triumphant confirmation of More's views, I proceed to
insist that unless the Occidentalists can show, either that the
feebleness and plurality of the Indian vernaculars are greater
than those of the English vernaculars of three centuries back,
or that the power of our present English exceeds the force, as
an instrument of thought, of Greek and Latin, they will be
required to demonstrate one or other of these further points, viz.,
that our means of spreading English in India are superior to
those possessed by the regenerators of England for the diffusion of Greek and Latin, or, that the *more general* grounds upon
which More so wisely rested his main defence of the vernaculars, are unsound or inapplicable.

More did not deny that the English of his day was an inac-
curate organ for the communication of knowledge, as compared
with Greek and Latin. He only denied that it was anything
like *so much so* as was asserted. Such (mutatis mutandis) is
the argument of the Oriental party to the present debate. More
asserted that whatever present obstacles to the general diffusion
of knowledge might occur from the use of an *imperfect* instrument, much greater present obstacles must arise from the resort
to an *unknown* one. More further asserted that whatever
cost and trouble might be requisite for making English prospectively an *adequate* organ of thought, a hundred-fold greater
cost and trouble would be required to change the national organ.
With More the Orientalists make the like assertions, in reference to the Indian tongues and to the substitution of English.
The first of the assertions demonstrates itself, and is not denied
by the Occidentalists, however much they overlook its practical
importance. Pass we then on to the second—Is it easier to
improve the Indian vernaculars, or to substitute English for
them? Towards the decision of this question we possess advantages denied to More. To us the wonderfully rapid and facile
improvement of the vernaculars of Europe, so soon as effort was
directed that way, is matter of historic fact.

To us too the invincible tenacity of the habit of language is
not less matter of historic fact.* Those only who shall venture
to deny the merit of our *earliest* writers, after the revival of let-

* See "Times" of April 23, 1872, and of May 25, 1874. Note of 1876.

ters, can dispute the first position, or the *facility of improvement.* Those only who shall venture to deny that the immutability of language has served, by its clear and broad light, to guide us to the determination of many most important points relative to the affiliation and connection of the various families of the human race—points which not even the strong impress of distinctive physical conformation could help us to decide—can challenge the second position, or the *difficulty of change.* Let us attend for a moment to the nature of this evidence demonstrating the truth of the latter position. In the last age it was thought, that those striking differences of physiognomy, which contradistinguish and designate the varieties of our species, are *less* changeable than differences of language, how permanent soever the latter were *admitted to be.* The further and completer researches of the present age have proved the contrary. In the almost Georgian features of the modern descendants of the western Turks, we look in vain for the physical signs of their origin; whilst we find that origin still distinctly imprinted on their speech. Here is a familiar instance : others may be found in the works of those still living authors, who, from a survey of the whole old world, have deduced the general and uncontested inference, that of all the mutable characteristics of mankind *national language is the most obstinately adhesive !*

Sir T. More was reduced to argue the comparative feasibility of change and of improvement upon far less strong data than the course of events and knowledge has enabled us now to rest it on ; and looking at this point from the vantage ground of present experience, I maintain, that, quoad feasibility, an incalculable preponderance of reason belongs to the argument of the Orientalists, who hold that, whatever the difficulty of improving the popular languages, the change of them—in other words the conquest of the *most tenacious of habits* amongst that people which, of all upon the face of the Earth, *is most wedded to habit* —is a hundred times more difficult.

Lest I should swell my letter to inconvenient bounds I forbear to press a detailed comparison of those means of influencing the popular mind to the adoption of a new speech, which were possessed by the antivernacular party in England in 1530, and which are now at the disposal of the same party in India. Upon this point, I assume, as I am well entitled to do, that the former had preponderant advantages in their compatriotism with the objects of the proposed experiment, which the latter are wholly devoid of. If, then, the antivernacular party in England failed to answer the following cardinal objection to their scheme, and having failed, lost their cause, I may still hope that the ultimate defeat of the antivernacular party in India is certain; since the objection, great and vital in itself, applies with double force, here and now.

Both parties in England admitted that the end in view was the making of knowledge the portion of the *many:* but unless the instrument of its communication were generally acquired, the thing communicated must be perpetually restricted to the few. Now, Sir T. More contended, that the inspiring of a general love of knowledge, in itself most difficult, would be rendered hopeless, if the aditus of the temple were rendered so steep and thorny as the necessary acquisition of a difficult foreign language must make it; and that, therefore, in all human probability, the *practical consequence* of Greek or Latin becoming the sole organ for the communication of truth would be, the defeat of the end by the means; and that, *not* simply with the loss of the *benefit* sought, *but* with the *entailing in perpetuity* on *England* those *worst* of *evils resulting from monopolised* and misapplied *learning.* Such a consequence flowed directly and necessarily from the partial prevalence of a foreign medium—and no general prevalence could reasonably be anticipated. But even that anticipation could not be entertained unaccompanied by apprehensions lest such a slavish imitation of foreign models should extinguish freedom of thought, and all the generous impulses bound up with the speech of our fatherland. The success, therefore, as well as the failure of the antivernacular organ, was liable to induce mischiefs for which knowledge itself could poorly compensate; and as the vernacular organ was free from such damning liabilities, the latter was preferred upon this preponderant ground of preference! In reference to the question as it occurred in England in the beginning of the 16th century, no scheme so extravagant as the change of the national language was openly or, at all, willingly, broached by the antivernacular party: and it was only More's far-reaching sagacity which, by demonstrating this to be a pre-requisite to the success of the antivernacular plan (if, as was pretended, the *general spread* of knowledge were the object), brought the question to that issue, *there*.   It was reserved for our Indian regenerators to cope directly with such a difficulty—to make nothing of it—to shut their eyes to the consequences of failure: and that under circumstances multiplying infinitessimally the chances of failure, and peculiarly aggravative of its consequences!

Does any one mean to deny, that the researches of the last and present age have demonstrated the extraordinary tenacity of the habit of language?*   Does any one mean to deny the peculiar subserviency of the people of India to the dominion of habit?   And if not, then I would further ask, whether, few as we are in India, and limited as are the pecuniary means at our disposal to this end, our absolute incommunity of sentiment with the people does not strip of all the semblance of probability a successful attempt by us to vanquish the most rooted of human habits amongst a people entirely wedded to custom? To me it appears that nothing short of a miracle could avert failure from such an attempt; and that therefore it is peculiarly incumbent on those who have the permanent weal of India at heart, to inquire into the *consequences of failure*.   The proposal is to make English the sole organ of sound knowledge—the sole instrument of its communication: and it needs no words to prove that, if the organ be but very partially adopted, the knowledge must be restricted in the same degree.   Either, then, we must succeed in anglicising the speech of the Indians, or we must, by such an attempt, create a small exclusive body of proficients in our lore.   But knowledge is power: English knowledge is in India power of the most formidable character: and if that power *do but get associated with office*, is it possible to doubt its becoming, in the hands of those natives who possess it, an instrument for the oppression of their fellows more formidable even than the present priestly monopoly of learning? Now it so happens that all the advocates for making our language the medium of education, have likewise contended for making it the instrument of administration.   Such was Mr. Grant's doctrine in 1792: and such is the doctrine of the

* See "Times" above referred to.

present day. It is needless, therefore, to argue tendencies: the association of anglicised education to anglicised administration, is avowed, and declared to be a grand desideratum! This is, indeed, taking the bull by the horns; for the worst exacerbations of the antivernacular organ must doubtless flow from such association, how mischievous soever its effects might be, unaided by such direct connection with power. Were the question, indeed, a political, and not a philanthropical one; *did* we seek the *stabilitation of our dominion over India*, and in *this* view seek to measure the effects of an English compared with a *Persian* organ of administration, there might be some room for hesitation—perhaps for even the preference claimed for our language. Such, however, is *not* the question: our aim is the people's increase in happiness through increase in knowledge. We seek to regenerate India; and to lay the foundations of a social system which time and God's blessing on the labours of the founders shall mature, perhaps long after we are no longer forthcoming on the scene. Let, then, the foundations be broad and solid enough to support the vast superstructure. Let us *begin* in the right way, or fifty years hence we may have to retrace our steps, and commence anew! Sound knowledge generally diffused is the greatest of all blessings: but the soundness of knowledge has ever depended, and ever will, on its free, and equal, and large communication. Partially diffused it is not only no good, but a bitter and lasting curse—the special curse which hath blighted the fairest portion of Asia from time immemorial, and which for hundreds of years made even Christianity a poison to the people of Europe! Would you inchoate plans of education liable to produce such a result? Do you mean to deny the liability? or to contend that it is not a damning one? No one asserts that it is *impossible* to change the speech of this vast continent. It is only contended that the attempt is of all others the most difficult, and one for which your means are enormously disproportionate to the end. You are a drop, literally, in the ocean, and a drop, too, separated from the mass of waters by the strongest antipathy. So circumstanced, should you not consider that the many are unapt to seek knowledge for itself, though the few can always be won to pursue, *through it*, the path of profit and of power? and should you not reflect that to wrap up knowledge in a mysterious garb and to connect it directly with authority, is the sure way to cause it to be turned into an engine of oppression of the many by the few ?   True, Persian is such an instrument at present, and perhaps working more mischief than English could do: true, were English the language of administration, it would tend greatly to the strengthening of our power, in every sense but that large and ultimate one, which identifies the security of dominion with the happiness of the mass of its objects.   But the cardinal and overruling truth is, that dominion as well as knowledge should have *no secrets.*   Now, foreign organs of communication universally tend to create and maintain such secrets; whilst all the circumstances of our situation in India are pregnant with aptitude to educe that tendency; and as the evils flowing from the existence of those secrets are proved by the experience of all ages and countries to be the direst to which a nation can be exposed, this damning liability suffices for the rejection of such organs.   It sufficed in England—in all Europe —in the hour of its regeneration : far more should it suffice in India, where the *one thing* to *be eschewed* by those who have the happiness of its countless millions at stake, is the hazard of making knowledge an official monopoly in the hands of a small number of the people.   Any plan for regenerating India which involves such a hazard should be rejected at once on that single ground; and the preference of the vernacular over the English instrument of knowledge is sufficiently established by the exemption of the former, and the non-exemption of the latter, from this hazard.   Compare the character and effects of Greek and Roman civilisation (amongst those nations themselves I mean) with Chaldean, Egyptian, old Persian, and Indian civilisation; and tell me precisely why the one called forth all the sublime energies of our kind, whilst the other debased even whilst it refined the nations ?   Why, but because knowledge associated with power was made a monopoly with the latter, and expressly so by means of an inscrutable medium, whilst with the former it was the common heritage of all, because linked to common use by its vernacular organ.

We are told that but for the incessant motion and unrestrained range of the waters of the ocean, they would become a mass of corruption which would speedily poison the world. Have not the waters of knowledge, wherever restrained in their circulation, become corrupt themselves, and corruptive of all else? And are there any facts better established by the history of all ages and nations, than first, that it is almost better for a nation to have *no knowledge at all* than one which is denied a free and general circulation? And, secondly, that the strong tendency of knowledge is to centre in the few, who, as surely as they possess, abuse the monopoly?

Leisure and ease are the parents of knowledge, which reveals not its charms to the neophyte: hence the inability and the disinclination of the many—an inability and a disinclination so deeply founded in the nature of things, that he who overlooks them, or fails to make the obviation of them the basis of a national scheme of education, may, if there be any truth in history, any reliance on human nature, be pronounced a mischievous friend or traitorous enemy of the many, who, under the pretence of benefiting, would inflict the direst evils on them. It would seem that a certain degree of ease in the circumstances of a people, and a certain degree of popularity in their public institutions, must *conspire* with the facility and aptitude to common use of vernacular media of education, before knowledge can become a blessing, by becoming the heritage of the many, identified with their household wants and familiar experiences, and deriving from such identity the power of influencing and being influenced by them, in an easy and effectual manner. This, I say, would *seem* to be the case: but there can be no question that, under any conceivable circumstances of the people of India in relation to us, for the next fifty years, any attempt to make our difficult and strange language the organ of the communication of our effective knowledge is infinitely more likely to entail on the country the curse of a monopolised and perverted, than the blessing of a diffused and justly applied, learning. Where shall we find among the people of India the leisure and the ease for anything like a general and disinterested conquest of the vast and odious obstacle we thus place at the threshold of the temple of knowledge, obscuring all the beauty within? And what more certain than that such obstacle, if it exist, will only be vanquished by the few who are sustained in their efforts, *not* by the quiet impulse of a love of truth, but by the lust of profit and power combined? Let us do *nothing* rather than do this: and let us consider that the regeneration of India must be so essayed as to avoid the *possibility* of inflicting on the people evils so great, at once, and so incident to every feature of our situation as their teachers and rulers, as those which have never yet failed to flow from knowledge monopolised and associated with office!

The mystification of knowledge and of administration, separately evil, are dreadful when combined; and were we to anglicise our courts and our schools, we could scarcely fail, under all the circumstances of the case, to fix on India the curse of this double iniquity. There would soon be no want of English officials among the natives, who would rush to our schools like vultures to the battle-field: but the end of such a system would be worse than the beginning: nor can I find words to express my surprise, that those, who deplore the evils of a Persian organ of administration, should fail to perceive that an English one would perpetuate the greater part of the mischief flowing from the former: for, though the inexpertness of the governors in the use of that instrument work no doubt much evil, by far the largest share of the mischief proceeds from its use being *utterly unknown to the governed*—a condition of things which the substitution of English would leave where it was before, if it did not even aggravate it. Why did we immortalise our Edward for vernacularising the language* of the courts of law? because it is of the last importance to the happiness of nations, that the people—the many—should have the readiest possible means of rightly appreciating legal proceedings. And is it not, indeed, perfectly monstrous to impose on the many, who are stripped of all the appliances for its accomplishment, a task which the few alone can perform, by reason of their exclusive possession of those appliances? But what else than this is it to anglicise the administration in India, in order that our functionaries may be spared the labour of learning the speech of the people, who are thereby obliged to

---

* Remember too Whitelock's noble speech, when the question went further and involved the vernacularisation of the *whole* language of the law, and not merely the pleadings as in King Edward's time.

learn ours? *To us*, with our leisure, and formed capacity to learn, the acquisition of *their* speech is most easy; and the knowledge of one suffices to meet the need of thousands, nay, millions. *To them*, doomed to daily toil from their youth upwards, the acquisition of our language is next to impossible; nor can the knowledge of one be made subservient to the need of another.

This, the essential view of the case, is not less applicable to educational than to administrative organs: and yet, because of the obvious and comparatively trivial fact, that, so long as a native has not learnt our language, his knowledge must be bounded by the extent of our translations into his, it is coolly said, that for us to put our knowledge into the native garb is a "confined and ineffectual" manner of enlightening the countless myriads of our poverty-stricken subjects, in comparison of that of requiring them to master the prodigious difficulties of our speech, ere they shall be allowed to gather a particle of our knowledge! Folly methinks could scarcely go further than this; for I need not say that such a mastery of our language as should empower a native of India to use it *safely* as an instrument of thought, is a far different thing from such a knowledge of it as suffices to enable him to make his bread as a copyist. Bad English scholars will make little effectual use of the stores of English meditation: and whoever adverts, but for a moment, to the relative capacity and means of the natives and of ourselves to make a right use of the languages, each of the other, in the communication and search of truth, and yet insists that they should be required to adopt our instruments, and not we theirs, may be safely said to be either too shallow, or too lazy, to understand the subject. It is, however, no less an authority than Mr. Grant who propounds this notable maxim, instancing (to crown the absurdity) in religion! Now, since the *immutable* truths of religion are all bound up in *one small* volume, the labour of one competent translator may, it is obvious, suffice, with the aid of the press, to make those truths for ever accessible to all who can read their mother tongue; nor is it less obvious that such a translator may be reared in our ranks with a tithe of the labour which would be requisite to unseal the original volume to one single native. Compare this state of things with that flowing from the opposite plan of making English the *sine qua non* of knowledge; no single native can learn the truths of your religion till he has mastered your difficult language— mastered it, I say, and not merely learnt to parrot it! Nor can the knowledge of one suffice, in strictness and in truth, for more than himself—unless he take on himself the office of translator; and in such event the reiterative labour objected to the ver- nacular plan equally attaches to the antivernacular—only stripped of all its power and energy! No *instance* could be more unfortunate than the special one selected by Mr. Grant to illustrate his doctrine; and which, I humbly submit, is the very one that the skilful adversary would seize for its *reductio ad absurdum,* for the strongest illustration of its falseness.

Without taking undue advantage of the instance of religion, let us use it merely to throw light upon the *principle* contended for, viz., that as a good translation, once made, directly opens the knowledge contained in the work translated to millions of the people, whereas the teaching of our language can only tell *quoad* the individual taught, the objection that the knowledge conveyed by the first mode must be limited by the extent of our translations, is cast entirely into the shade by the necessary regard for those cardinal difficulties, springing out of the con- dition of the people, which absolutely *preclude them from availing themselves of the second mode.* WE, who have leisure and ease, and minds highly trained, and practical conversancy with divers tongues, can, therefore, readily master the languages of India; and provide, with no insuperable labour or cost a sufficiency of translation to convey the substance of our know- ledge to all its millions. *They,* who have neither leisure, nor ease, nor minds highly trained, nor practical conversancy with any language differing from their mother tongues, can scarcely, by possibility, master your speech. Yet you would put off the weight from your own shoulders and lay it upon theirs! would make *their* acquisition of *your* most difficult and utterly alien tongue the indispensable preliminary to the communication of your blessed gifts of truth and science: And, lest the still and quiet impulse of a love of knowledge should fail to animate the toil-doomed and custom-ridden multitude to so vast and irksome and apparently useless a preliminary labour, you would anglicise your administration of the country, in order to make *palpably intelligible* the connection of English with popular utility! And wherefore would you do all this? because, because I say—translations reveal no truths that are untranslated, and because (but this by way of appendix) "community of feeling through the medium of a common language" is an acknowledged tie of subject to sovereign, and one which your barbarian predecessors in dominion thought it proper to knit, for their own convenience and safety, without wasting a moment to consider the effects of such a constrained bond upon the happiness of their people!

So feeble an argument as the former is aptly backed by so iniquitous a one as the latter.

Compare the means and opportunities of learning possessed by the few and by the many; and then, unless you hold that knowledge and administration should be mystified for the sole benefit of the former, and in despite of the most terrible consequences to the latter, you will have no difficulty in perceiving that the few, who rule and who teach, have no duty comparable to that of laying open the secrets of both, as far as possible, to those whose ignorance and necessities are but too apt, under the most favourable circumstances, to make them bitter sufferers by such secrets! The aptitude of knowledge to become a fraudful mystery, as well as the miserable consequences to the weal of the many of its becoming such, are, I repeat, facts attested by all history; and facts of which the causes may be at once found in the difficulties inseparable from the acquisition of knowledge, and the overwhelming pressure of those difficulties on the leisureless and necessitous multitude. All history proclaims, too, that of all the circumstances which facilitate and confirm the growth and duration of this evil, an unvernacular medium is the most operative; as of all those which prevent or destroy the evil, a vernacular medium is so. Why? Because the former at once carries away knowledge (in itself an abstraction) beyond the pale of those household and imminent cares which necessarily engross almost the whole attention of the many; whilst the latter tends incessantly to approximate, to reconcile, and, as far as possible, to identify them. Glorious approximation; thrice glorious reconciliation, to which alone the too helpless and too little heeded many owe *their* exemption from the curse of knowledge, as well *their* partial admission to its blessing!

This is the commanding and overruling view of the question of the best instrument for the communication and search of truth, as it occurs to us at present in relation to the people of India. *Their* numbers, *their* necessities, *their* prejudices prescribe the sole use of the most facile and popular instrument, imposing the whole labour of facilitation upon us. Every circumstance of *our* situation, as joint teachers and rulers, prescribes the sole use of the safest instrument. But the welcome, and easy, and safe instrument is the vernacular. The unwelcome, and difficult, and unsafe, is the English. On each of the three counts, but especially on the last, the preference is due to the former, and would be still so, though its intrinsical feebleness as an organ of thought were considerably greater, in comparison of the English instrument, than it can be allowed to be.

I do not *deny* the reality of those objections to the vernacular plan which consist in the necessary reiteration of translation, and in the augmented difficulty of it, arising out of the inunity and inaccuracy of the living languages. On the contrary, I say of such objections, *valeant quantum valeant.* Let those difficulties be duly considered; but let them not be exaggerated; and above all, let them not be pushed forward so as to exclude from view the difficulties *and hazards* which are inseparable from the antivernacular plan of education.

The one class of difficulties principally falls on ourselves, as the teachers; the other class, principally on the people, as the learners. Now because our appliances are, in comparison of those of the people, as infinity almost to unity, I *therefore* lay the burden where it can best be borne. But it is because the vernacular is free from all liability to *do mischief*, whereas the antivernacular scheme threatens to make "the food of one the poison of many," that I abandon all hesitation in my preference of the former. Let us do no harm, at least, if we do but little good. Learning is not, in itself, a blessing: it is so only according to its use and application. *Generally diffused*, and identified with the *ordinary pursuits*, and *thoughts*, and *wants*, of society at *large,** it is beneficent power—power at once incapable of mis-application to the purposes of tyranny, and capable of aiding, in the highest degree, the accomplishment of every useful and generous aim and end. But *not* so identified, it becomes stale and unprofitable: *not* so diffused, it becomes noxious, and noxious in the highest degree—the certain engine of deception and oppression!

Adopt the vernacular organ, and you may at least hope for such general diffusion, and such household identification; be-cause the strong tendency of the instrument itself is to work them out, despite of all obstacles. Adopt the antivernacular organ, and you may not hope for either; because the strong tendency of the instrument selected is to counteract their development, by favouring that natural proneness of knowledge to contraction and perversion, which results but too easily from the necessities of the many and the temptations of the few! Consider, above all things, those necessities of the many: beware, above all things, of those temptations of the few: for the whole circumstances of the people of India, as well as all those of our relation to them, tend to give those temptations a fatal strength, and to direct it point blank against those necessities. The whole of the circumstances in question consti-tute *in themselves*, and *in despite of your protective prerogatives*, an invitation to the few to turn their gifts against the helpless multitude. Would you, indirectly but effectually, sanction and ratify that invitation, *anglicise* your courts and your schools: would you do all that human prudence can suggest to reverse this doom of Asiatic sovereignty, *vernacularise* your courts and your schools, and draw the mass of the people yet nearer to you by the largest possible association of themselves to the task of governing them. But ye have heard that the people, like their languages, are inefficient instruments: I deny it not; but verily I say unto you there is a holy aim and end in such courses *far beyond instrumental efficiency*, and which thus only shall you reach; and that end is to lift the people from the dust, and to breathe that generous fire into their torpid souls, the kindling of which must be the *beginning* of their regenera-tion! Why does Elphinstone observe that if Providence should

* See " Times " of April 25, 1872. Note of 1876.

ever bless the Affghans with a wise lawgiver, they might be far more easily regenerated than the people of India? Because the former possess, and the latter want, intellectual and moral stamina—those seeds of character which alone admit of culture.

It is this deplorable want which in India defies the best efforts of education and of administration, and ever will do so till both are principally directed to supply the deficiency, instead of (as at present) compassing inferior ends. The aim is high—its perfect realisation far distant—and probably not reserved for us. But let us do nothing to counteract it—to render its reali-sation yet more impossible: and if we take the direct road to this chief object, let us be encouraged to proceed by the double reflection upon our own abjectness in time gone by, and of our present noble and universal erectness of spirit.

Now, I object to the antivernacular organ of education, and of administration, not merely as aiding and confirming the tendency of knowledge itself to become monopolised and per-verted to the uses of oppression, but also because, firstly, it is apt to generate or confirm servile intellectual habits, especially when combined with the absence of political liberty; and be-cause, secondly, it is not less apt to divorce speculation from experience, theory from practice, abstraction from life.

Those who are accustomed to consider the despotic in-fluence of words over ideas—an influence which even that intellectual giant Locke declared his frequent inability to subdue when it was connected with a foreign language, save by rendering the passage *into his own tongue*—will be able to appreciate the nature of the first objection; or, if not, they have only to consider the effects upon national character of the servile adoption of the Greek and Roman learning by the Gauls, and Iberians, and Britons; and, in later times, by those nations who, having thrown down the Roman colossus, were content for ages to crouch beneath its literature.

Those whom Rome subdued, became twice subject by their slavish acceptance of her language: and those who subdued Rome were only saved from vassalage to her learning by the free genius of their political institutions.

If, again, you would appreciate the quality of the second objection, look at the character of learning in modern Europe, until it became vernacularised. It consisted entirely of thorny dialectics, or of flowery mysticism: and this, notwithstanding that its stock and root was the eminently useful and practical lore of Greece and of Rome! Can proof more strong be offered or required as to the debasing and disutilitising tendency of a foreign medium, however valuable *itself*, that is, as an organ of thought! I think not: and *therefore* would I not employ such a medium in India!

Had it been possible to emasculate the Teutonic national character, the Greek and Roman languages would have laid their chains on it: had it been possible among those energetic races of men to divorce learning from every species of utility, again the Greek and Roman languages would have accomplished the divorce. And yet those languages, in their natal soils, were the very heralds of liberty and of utility!

To the Greeks and Romans themselves, the breathing words lent double power to the burning thoughts; because those words were autochthonous, were the heritage of every single Greek and Roman, blended inseparably with his daily experiences, as well as with every movement of those more generous impulses, which made all Greek and Roman weal and woe a part of his own.

The very same noble and useful ideas when transplanted to foreign soils were stripped of their nobility and their usefulness, by that very same instrument of their communication, which at home had so well sustained and diffused the energy of both those splendid qualities.

And how was change so singular wrought? for the instrument, as an instrument, retained its identical character. Was it that the Teutons, the Franks and Saxons, had in *their own hearts* no chord responsive to the majesty of Greek and Roman ideas, to all compact of liberty and of practical usefulness?

No supposition could be less true! *What* was it, then? It was that the difficulty of acquiring the use of the instrument coinciding with the intrinsic difficulty of knowledge, compelled the many to abandon the pursuit of knowledge altogether, and thus enabled the few to turn it into an engine of deception: it was that the unfamiliar nature of the instrument coinciding with the intrinsic tendency of knowledge to abstraction, speedily shut out utility from the view of scholars, and left them, a segregated

and separate caste, with the sole alternative of becoming syllo-
gists or mystics.   If we may trust the concurrent experience of
the Middle Ages in Europe, and of all ages in Asia, it would
seem that a vernacular medium is the only expedient for preserving either the generous, or the simply useful, properties of
knowledge.   Would you, then, make English knowledge a
wholesome food—would you prevent its speedily becoming
innutritive or poisonous—to the people of India, give it a
vernacular organ; for by such an organ only can it acquire and
preserve those vital principles of accessibility, and of proneness
to identification with household experiences, upon which it must
wholly depend, whether that knowledge shall *ever* be a *blessing*,
and shall not *presently* be a *curse*, to this land.

August 1835.

LETTER II.

SIR,—Should the picture I have drawn of the difficulties and
hazards inseparable from the adoption of the English language as
the organ of education (and of administration) be allowed to be,
upon the whole, correct, it will follow that paramount considerations connected with the weal of the many enjoin and enforce
the *rejection of* that organ.   Should, on the other hand, the indication I have given of the advantages inseparable from the adoption
of the vernaculars as the media of education (and of administration) be allowed to be, on the whole, accurate, it will follow
that paramount considerations connected with the weal of the
many enjoin and enforce the *acceptance* of those media.

Before considerations weighty as those adverted to, the question of merely instrumental efficiency sinks into an insignificance
from which nothing could redeem it, but demonstrative proof of
such an utter and extreme degree of feebleness attaching to the
vernacular languages, in this view, as absolutely to compel a
resort, at whatever risk, to other instruments.   But that no semblance of such proofs has been, or can be adduced, I think I have
satisfactorily shown in my preceding letter; and by so doing, I
have, I trust, placed the preference due to a vernacular organ

upon unassailable grounds. It can scarcely be necessary for me to say, that my objections to an English organ of instruction are, in substance, not less applicable to a Sanskrit or an Arabic one. And, as I freely admit that the latter languages, notwithstanding their difficulty, lead to nothing deserving of general study, but to much, the even partial study of which, as heretofore, is on every higher account to be deplored, it may be asked with what possible aims I can seek to uphold the dead languages and literature of India, and to uphold them by public patronage?

I answer distinctly that those aims are, 1st. The improvement and literary application of the living languages, considered as the principal *organs* and *instruments* of general instruction in European lore. 2d. Means of facilitation and inducement, suited to the prejudices and ineptitude of the unlearned many, and of conciliation and check, adapted to the adverse interests and unbounded influence of the learned few, with reference to the introduction and establishment of our knowledge, considered as the sole *subject matter* of general instruction. The use of the learned languages of the country I contemplate merely as subsidiary to the first purposes; that of its literature sheerly as conducive to the last; and whilst I concede that these purposes are entirely preliminary, I expect, in the course of this letter, to be able to prove their indispensableness in that view.

If I have succeeded in demonstrating by my precedent letter the cardinal importance and necessity of vernacularising our knowledge, it would seem that *systematic means* to that end form an indispensable feature of our plans for the regeneration of India: And unless it be meant to be asserted, that the most rooted maxims and most cherished opinions of Indian society do not *necessarily* militate against the direct and unqualified acceptance of our staple truths, it would seem that *systematic means* of accommodation and compromise constitute *another* indispensable feature of those plans. I shall recur to these features of educational reform (heretofore so miserably obscured with dust and rubbish), in the sequel, in order to prove the obligation of Government to fix them in a collegiate establishment having for its object the cultivation, with exclusive reference to them, of the learned languages and literature of the country. Meanwhile, having I trust established the necessity of vernacularisation, and

its dependence upon the dead *languages,* I proceed to consider
the necessity of accommodation and conciliation, with *their* dependence upon the *literature.*

In approaching this topic, I feel a singular perplexity arising,
not out of the difficulty of the subject, but out of that hardihood
of assertion which has, of late, attempted to confuse and invali-
date the clearest, largest, best-grounded inductions from our
experience of the character and condition of the people of India.
Until recently, the extremity of their poverty had been as little
liable to question as the extremity of their prejudices.   But
now, it seems, the general acquisition of the English language is
as entirely compatible with their means, as the direct adoption
of English ideas with their inclinations.   Fie upon such stulti-
fying extravagances ! for, who not wholly blinded by his impetu-
ous pursuit of some favourite theory, can fail to perceive that
were the people indeed so easy in their circumstances, and so
liberal in their minds, as is here assumed, there could be little
or no occasion for our educational interference ?   Nay, were the
assumption in question anything but the *very reverse* of *truth,*
we towering Europeans should be ourselves demonstrably reduced
to take shelter under the most grovelling scepticism, entirely
without *motive* to amend others or ourselves, how much soever
they or we might need it.   Because if extreme moral and
physical evil and hindrance did not *practically* flow from such
notions as prevail in this land, the relative value of all conceivable human notions, must be reduced, universally, to such
stuff as reveries are made of !   How comes it that the advocates
of these extremely liberal opinions do not perceive, that their
tenets lead distinctly to the conclusion that all opinions whatever
are matters of indifference ? Take away from gross error its
practical malignity and impotence, and you take away, at the
same time, the practical importance of truth !   God forbid that I
should dwell upon the hostility, the alienation, the imbecility, of
the natives with a view to make them objects of execration or
contempt.   But for the physician to deny the disease at the very
moment of prescribing the remedy, is surely too monstrous a
procedure to be attended with advantages. Familiar as I am, and
long have been, with the deep seat, and the wide spreading
taint, of the disease, I could as soon dismiss the conscious-

ness of my own identity as the awfully solemn impression I entertain, that if this malady be at all remediable with the means at *our* disposal, it can be so only by a treatment as nicely as possible adapted to the constitution and habits of the particular patient, whilst it is, at the same time, consistent with the general rules of the healing art. I oppose myself unwillingly to the opinions of those who have recently so much distinguished themselves by philanthropical efforts on behalf of the people of India. But, the more I consider the drift and scope of these opinions, the more am I convinced that the great cause of native regeneration would be retarded, not advanced, by their adoption into general practice; and that in proportion to the unparalleled obstacles which exist to the mental emancipation of Indians by Britons, is the inexpediency of direct measures to that end. If we would indigenate a European plant to the plains of India, it is universally admitted that the first stock must be sent to the Hills in the hope of procuring seed; that there, to the advantage of climate the utmost care must be superadded, if we would realise that hope; and that, in the retransfer of the gradually-acclimated produce to the plains, we must redouble our previous pains in order to be ultimately successful in the experiment. And will those who make this admission, assert that the moral and intellectual regeneration of the people of India by the people of England is an experiment which may be safely and successfully essayed *without any sort* of *preparation?* Yet what but this is the assertion—the proposition of those, who, having in view the dissemination of our knowledge throughout India, contemptuously repudiate all connection with its literature, *or* with its living languages? Our institutions, civil and religious—political, social, and domestic, are not merely dissimilar from, but the very antipodes of, those of the Hindoos. And our knowledge—what is it but the fused extract of our institutions? And is not *their* knowledge the same of *theirs?* And is the prodigious gulf which now separates their minds from ours, to be, indeed, bridged over by measures involving an equal and utter neglect of the pride and power of the learned, of the necessities and imbecility of the unlearned, and of all the prepossessions, prejudices, and accustomed thoughts and feelings, of both? Surely not: nor, in a choice of difficulties, can the adoption of such measures be,

for an instant, admitted to be a closing with the *lesser* ones.
Once for all, I would distinctly state, that I conceive the question
to relate to the plan and outline of a system of general* education
for the people of India. It is high time that some such plan
should be devised, and having been devised, should be steadily
adhered to by the majority of private educational establishments,
as well as by the Government, quoad the extent of its patronage
of education. Nor can I fail to deplore that bias towards the
fashionable Anglomania which led Lord William Bentinck, when
his attention had been momentarily arrested by this question, to
proceed *per saltum* from the obvious absurdities of Orientalism
to the obvious excellences of Occidentalism, without perceiving
that, as usual, the real practical case—involving of necessity the
consideration of local fitness as well as of abstract perfection, and
of means as well as of ends—could have little affinity with such
a vulgar palpable extreme. How long are we to go on picking
up straggling students, and instructing them according to the unaided dictates of individual caprice ? The smaller the funds at
the disposal of Government to this end, the more carefully should
they be husbanded by uniform system steadily prosecuted. I
admit, at once and freely, the folly of squandering any portion
of those funds upon oriental literature considered as, *per se*, the
matter of instruction—or upon the learned languages considered
as, *in any way*, its *media*. But if the most insuperable obstacles
exist to the unqualified transmission of English ideas in the
English language, are we not necessarily thrown upon those
languages and that literature for the indirect means of removing
such obstacles, through vernacularisation and through the countenance and sanction of established notions ? And to what
source save the public exchequer can we look for the *adequate*
and *steady* supply of these appliances and helps of the only sort
of education in European lore which the people or can or will
accept ? If the obstacles to direct measures be real, of what use
can be the hardy denial of them ? And is not their reality attested by the concurrent testimony of history, of the laws and in-

---

* This is the point, a general system or what is needful to lay the foundation
of such : for particular cases, as of princes and men of rank, the question is different, or rather there is here no question of admissible *exceptions* to the general
plan, and it may be readily admitted that such persons should be taught in the
English language or rather taught that language as well as other things.

stitutions of the land, and of our daily and hourly experience of the people's conduct, towards us and towards one another ? *
And is it not most unworthy of us to oppose to such testimony as the above, which is *co-equal with the magnitude of what is testified to*, the favourable state of our schools at Calcutta and at one or two other little Goshens, bearing some such proportion to that magnitude as the contribution of a single river to the mass of the oceanic waters ?

Let me ask you, sir, as a Christian missionary, what you think of the general result of those efforts at *sowing the seed without dressing the ground*, which belong to the story of religious missions in the East *generally*, during the last two and a half centuries ? The miserable failure of these efforts, after so much apparent promise, I have always heard ascribed principally to their unprepared and exotic character, incapable of striking root into the household wants and habits of the instructed. As it is with religious, so is it with temporal, Truth : the difficulty is to work it into the warp and woof of the popular mind : and until it is so interwoven, it can neither have durability nor efficacy, let zealots affirm what they please. How often was not Europe amused, for a century, with the tale that the East was rapidly and generally evangelising ? Such as were those assurances, such are the present allegations about the ability and the eagerness of the people of India to drink our knowledge undiluted from the fountain head of English. They cannot, and they may not, so drink : they have neither the means, nor the will, nor the permission so to do. The English language is too costly for them ; sheer English truths are too alien to their distorted judgments, narrow experiences and immediate wants, as well as too repugnant to that dominant influence presiding over their minds, to find *unprepared* admission. Let it be granted that the first object is to disenchant the popular mind of India! Do you propose to break the spell which now binds it by the *facilities and attractions* of the English *language ?* Or, do you imagine that those magicians to whom the spell is power and wealth and honour unbounded, and whose vigilance has maintained its unabated influence for 3000

---

* Of the 100 Brahmans and Kshetriyas composing my escort, no ten will eat together ; no ten of the one or of the other tribe. Yet the natives have no prejudices ! ! !

years, have, merely to serve your ends, been suddenly stricken
with infatuation ?   To them belong the parents' minds ; to those
of the parents, the minds of the children.   Say that the children
were yours for six hours per diem ; would not the rest of their
time be necessarily passed at home amid home's habitual associations ; which, of what nature they are, may, I trust, be briefly
indicated without offence, by a glance at the seemingly forgotten
frame work of Indian society.

Two circumstances remarkably distinguish and designate the
social system of India : one, its inseparable connection with a
recondite literature : the other, the universal precurrency of its
divine sanctions through all the offices of life, so as to leave no
corner of the field of human action as neutral ground.

Can these premises be denied ?   And, if not denied, can it be
necessary to deduce from them a demonstration of the unbounded
power of the men of letters in such a society ? or of the consequent necessity for procuring, as far as possible, their neutrality
in respect to the inchoation of measures, the whole virtual tendency of which is to destroy that power ?   Touch what spring
of human action you please, you must touch, at the same time,
the established system.   Touch the spring with any just and
generous view of removing the pressure which that system
has laid on its native elasticity ; and you must, at the same
moment, challenge the hostility of that tremendous phalanx
of priestly sages which wields an inscrutable literature for the
express purpose of perpetuating the enthralment of the popular
mind.

However much the splendour of our political power may seem
to have abashed these dark men, the fact is that *their* empire
over the hearts and understandings of the people has been and
is almost entirely unaffected by it.   With the Saga of Pompeii
they say, ' The body to Cæsar, the mind to us.'—A profound
ambition, suited to the subtile genius of their whole devices,
and which I fear some of us commit the lordly absurdity of
misinterpreting into impotency or indifference !   Before we have
set foot almost upon *their* empire, it is somewhat premature
to question their resources for its defence against intrusion.
Their tactics are no vulgar ones ; nor will they commit themselves or sooner or further than is needful.   We now purpose to

spread our knowledge ; they know it, and they know the consequence. But so have we, for half a century, purposed the
spread of our religion! The purpose must become act, and
the act become, or seem likely to become, *generally* successful,
ere these subtile men will confront us openly; and perhaps not
then, if heaven inspire us with the prudence to conciliate, check,
and awe them by the freest possible resort to that sacred literature which they *dare not* deny the authority of, *however used ;*
and which assuredly is capable of being largely used for *the
diffusion of Truth !* * Time has set its solemn impress on
that literature : the last rays of the national integrity and glory
of this land are reflected from its pages : consummate art has
interwoven with its meaner materials all those golden threads
which nature liberally furnishes from the whole stock of the
domestic and social affections and duties. To the people it is
the very echo of their heart's sweetest music : to their pastors
—their dangerous and powerful pastors—it is the sole efficient
source of that unbounded authority which they possess. To
deny the existence of that authority is mere moon-struck idiocy.
To admit it is, I conceive, to admit the necessity of compromise
and conciliation, so far as may be.

Facillime jubetur exemplo. The text is in Seneca. Now for
the commentary. The Moslems, our immediate predecessors in
dominion, swayed the sceptre of India, with all the pomp and
resources of *domestic* rule, for 500 years. They had a national
system of opinions; and millions of immigrants flowed into the
adopted land to back the precepts of imperial pleasure in recommending that system to general adoption.

They colonised; they naturalised; they bade the administration adopt their speech; and, from first to last, nor prince nor
peasant among them forgot that their first duty to their new
country was to make it consentaneous in doctrine with themselves. What was the ultimate result ?

That India cleaved to its own institutions, and half imposed
them on the conquerors! Now, sir, let me ask you seriously,

---

* Reasoning may be refused attention. Wherefore I propose for consideration
the *fact* of Mr. Wilkinson's success. Can the fact be denied? Mr. Wilkinson
and myself are now about to extend the experiment by printing Ashu Ghosha's
argument from the Shastras against caste.

whether, with such an instance staring us in the face, it be not the very extremity of fraud or folly to allege that the people of this country have no material prejudices in favour of the language, the literature, or the customs, of their fathers ?

I am sorry, as I have said, to dissent from the prevalent dicta of well-disposed and active friends of India. But I believe a deep and abiding sense of the nature and extent of existing prejudices to be a cardinal maxim never to be lost sight of, by those who would safely and successfully rebaptize the Indian mind in the fount of European knowledge. And when I see and hear the *proceedings of our native schools* daily urged in proof that no such prejudices exist, and the Government lending itself, quoad the resources at its disposal, to a system of education implying their non-existence, *by reason of this supposed proof*, I am lost in astonishment. Granting the premises, the conclusion has no more just proportion to them, than a molehill to the Himalaya ! I admit that our knowledge is better fitted, by its superior practical utility, to make way in India, than that of the Moslems. I admit that our technical means of diffusion (the press), are vastly more efficient than any they could employ. But, sir, schools and scholastic lessons are neither the only, nor the most potent, media for the inculcation of new modes of thought and action among nations : And when I contrast the plenitude of those other and more operative means in the hands of the Moslems with their penury in our hands, I am compelled by superior evidence to own that where *they* failed, success cannot crown *our* efforts, unless consummate prudence in the use of all local appliances be added to the intrinsic efficacy of our knowledge and of the aid of the press. I point solemnly to the uniform language of the laws, the unchanging voice of history, and the general tenor of what we daily see and hear among the people, as concurring to prove beyond a question, that the prejudices and prepossessions of this land are the profoundest, most exclusive, and most pervading through all acts and motives, of any upon record ! And such being the case, I ask in God's name what probability is there that we, few as we are and miserably insulated as we are, should make any durable beneficial or general impression upon those prejudices and prepossessions, by means of such an abstraction as knowledge, without deliberate measures of general instruction combining the utmost modal facility with the furthest practicable use of existing sanctions of opinion ? Our knowledge itself militates necessarily, plainly, and directly, with the highest interests of the few, and with the warmest affections of the many. How, then, are we to procure acceptance for it without preliminary measures calculated to neutralise the hostility of the former, and to draw the sympathies of the latter ? Let our knowledge *have* come fairly into the field against the knowledge of the East; and who could doubt the result ? Not we; nor, assuredly, those who are so deeply interested in maintaining the present mental darkness of the land ! *The* difficulty is to bring our knowledge into action, in despite of popular penury and imbecility, backed by the utmost covert opposition of those dark men ! How is it to be done—generally and effectually done ? And, mind you, I speak not of the perfect realisation— be that the care of the Almighty—but of such inchoative measures as shall be not unworthy of His blessing from their prudence as well as benevolence, and, above all, from their being grounded in a due preference for the superior claims and extreme helplessness of the many ! To seek to spread our knowledge directly through an English organ is to fling away every species of facilitation, conciliation, and compromise. Is *this* the way for a few insulated strangers to make a durable or useful moral impression upon a country in which the whole mass of opinions has been welded by consummate fraud into one compact system bearing the highest of possible sanctions, which it derives from a sacred literature, the monopolisers of which wield at will the hearts and understandings of the people ? Those formidable pastors of the flock are the apostles of mental thraldom : *We* are the missionaries of mental liberty. Is it necessary to insist further on their hostility to us ? Surely not : How, then, shall we foil them ?—Let us give to our eminently generous and useful truths the facility and homely aptitude of vernacular media. So, and so only, may we hope gradually to draw over the multitude to our side.* And let us, in the meanwhile neutralise the hostility of the learned, and smooth the passage

---

* Ours is "the poor man's Raj." It is so really such that the truth has already passed into a proverb. The *few* hate and fear us, with and without cause. Let us, then, bind the *many* to ourselves by community of language : let us *vernacularise ourselves* and our *knowledge* for their and our common benefit !

of Truth into minds so biassed against it, by borrowing, as often, and as far as possible, the maxims and examples of that sacred literature which in our hands is the only charm to conciliate confidence, lull suspicion, and paralyse opposition. The many cannot, and the few dare not, resist its spell. To the former it recalls the long-past ages of their national greatness : to the latter, it is all things, the source of their power, the mystery of their iniquity ; enabling him who knows it to command their *willing and unwilling* homage ! I have spent many years in India, remote from the Presidencies and large towns and almost entirely amongst the natives, whom consequently it was ever an object with me to conciliate for my own comfort, and whom I trust I always felt anxious to win, in order the better to accomplish my public duties, as well as to influence the people to their own advantage and improvement. Yes ! I say I have *so* spent many, many years, during which I solemnly declare that the only unequivocal voluntary testimonies I have received of influence over either the hearts or heads of the people have been owing entirely to some little knowledge on my part of their literature ! With this instrument I have warmed hearts and controlled heads which were utterly impassive to kindness, to reason, and to bribery ; and deeply am I persuaded, by experience and reflection, that the use of this instrument is indispensable in paving the way for any general, effective, and safe measures of educational regeneration.

It is a splendid compliment we pay to the people to master their difficult literature. The memory of better days connected with it elevates their lowliness to something like a communicable distance from our loftiness. Their shy and shrinking affections, to which we have no direct access of any description, may be poured out to us through this indirect and modest channel which carries the whole waters of their hearts, reflecting from its tranquil bosom every rite and custom, and thought and feeling, of the land ! Hence its influence, with the many, in *our* hands : and, as for the few, with them to know it is to have been initiated into those mysteries, the participation of which is the *ne plus ultra* of authority ! they may tremble, but must obey, and, ample as is the ground occupied by this all-pervading literature, we may use its sanctions for general truths to a vast extent as righteously as efficaciously. Could anything surprise me in reference to the manner in which this all-important question has heretofore been treated, it would be the strange inconsistency of those whose extravagant applause of the people is combined with no less extravagant censure of their literature ; and the scarcely less strange inconsistency of those others who would borrow the sanction of that literature for our physical truths, but on no account for our moral ones.

The people, say the former, have no material prejudices or prepossessions : for, if they *had*, it might be necessary to consider them when a handful of insulated strangers purposed to lay an absolutely new bias on the popular mind! The literature of the people (they add) is sheer folly and iniquity : for if it were *not*, its pervading and mighty authority might seem to suggest it as a necessary means of laying that new bias on the people's mind! To a reflecting mind such propositions as the above evidently cannot consist together : whatever be the merits of the people, those merits cannot have been forgotten in that deliberate portraiture of themselves which they have embodied in their literature! The character of that literature is mixed : but it is more faithful to their virtues than to their vices ; else the limners had not been men. For the rest, those conductors of education who seek that literature not as an end but as a means—nor for itself but for its inducements—may safely borrow many of its precepts, examples, and illustrations to recommend to general attention the substance of a higher knowledge. Of this obvious truth the second class of objectors to which I have just alluded have not been unaware. But they have drawn a strange distinction between the licitness of such recommendation of our physical science, and its illicitness in reference to the other and more important branch of our knowledge,[*] founding that distinction upon what I conceive to be a false and narrow view of the subject. " Much as I approve of Mr. Wilkinson's suggestion to teach the natives astronomy by means of the Siddhantas, I am very far from thinking that any good use could be made of their moral system. This is a very different question from the former : for the truths of astronomy are derived from mathematical demonstration, whereas morality,

---

[*] " Calcutta Christian Observer," for August, 1843.

when disjointed from revelation, is *not* so indisputable: but is, even in *material points, open to objection:* witness the different systems that have been formed concerning the principle of moral approbation." This is, I confess, language such as I never expected to hear at the present day, and which is certainly opposed to the sentiments of the greatest and best men of Europe. With *them* the Divine geometrician is likewise the universal lawgiver and judge, whose moral attributes and ours alone cause it to *be* that there is, or hath been, such a thing as Religion in the world. That those attributes, on our part, are His work, is a proof that they are immutable and universal: that they are indispensable to His honour and our happiness, is a proof that they are indisputably vouched to all human apprehension. Were morality disputable there could be no religion: were there no religion there could be no Revelation. Have not the mass of mankind in all ages and countries by the *general tenor of their lives* demonstrated the practical indisputableness of morals? Conscience! does it speak one language at Benares and another at Canterbury? Or is that to which it testifies less satisfactorily evidenced, than that two and two make four? Certainly not!

" If we bear in mind that the question relates to the coincidence of all men in considering the same qualities as virtues, and not to the preference of one class of virtues by some, and of another class by others, the exceptions from the universal agreement of mankind in their system of practical morality will be reduced to absolute insignificance."*

" On convient le plus souvens de ces instincts de la conscience. La plus grande partie du genre humain leur rend temoinage. Les Orientaux, et les Grecs et les Romains conviennent en cela."†

As to the speculative disputes respecting the *principle* of moral approbation and disapprobation, they have no more to do with the fact that mankind naturally approve what is right, and disapprove what is wrong, or with the practical system of ethics resting on that fact, than have the laws of motion and their

---

* Mackintosh, Eth. Phi.

† Leibnitz, Œuvres Phil. To the same effect might be quoted Butler, Berkeley, and all the greatest lights of the Anglican Church.

practical consequences, and axioms with the question whether space be a plenum or a vacuum. Let the sense of right and wrong be a rational or sensitive principle, an original or a derivative one, it will still be the *very same* sense after these doubts are solved as it was before they were started ; and it is indeed surprising that an intelligent writer should cite such doubts to bear witness against that which they have no earthly relation to, viz., the immutability and universality of moral distinctions, and the consequent harmony of the moral precepts thence derived by the sages of all nations and of all times. But it is obvious that, beyond the limits of ethics, strictly so called, there is a very large and most important field which the most captious must concede to be neutral ground, quoad objections on *our* side to the use of Oriental sanctions of opinion.

The elemental laws of thought,—including a designation of the necessary boundaries of human inquiry, and the best rules of investigation within those limits—the law of population, the philosophy of wealth, the general principles of jurisprudence, of judicature and of reformative police ! How are we to inculcate the elements of our knowledge upon these topics, which are at once infinitely more essential to the welfare of the people of India than mathematical and physical science, and infinitely more liable to the adverse influence of prejudice and prepossession ?

Physical science is almost unknown in India, and hence there will be little for us to undo : it stands almost wholly aloof from the turmoil of the passions and interests of men, and hence there will be little difficulty in removing obstructions to fair and patient attention.

But the philosophy of life, however ill it is yet understood, has been an object of study in this land for 3000 years, in all which time the falsest interests, and the most turbulent passions, and the most fantastic opinions, have contributed the warp, as nature and experience have the woof, to its network.

To leave the woof as it is, and to supply a new warp from the schools of European wisdom—*hoc opus, hic labor est !* To attempt to remove both warp and woof were, I believe, to disorganise society, and to insure our own destruction in its disorganisation ! Here it is, certainly, that the countenance and support, real or seeming, of established maxims and examples, is most needed and most readily to be had—most needed, because of the prejudices and passions that are indissolubly bound up with the topics—most easily to be had, because of that universal consciousness, and almost universal experience, which necessarily supply the ultimate evidence of such topics.   High dated and literary as is the character of Indian civilisation, it *could not be* that their literature should have failed to gather ample materials for the just illustration, in some way or other, of most, if not of all, parts of the philosophy of life.   And, with respect to the *fact*, you, sir, need not be told that it has not failed to gather them.

In mathematical science, again, the premises must be absolutely known or unknown; and there is a long and rigorous process intervening between them and the conclusion.   It is otherwise in the philosophy of life, not to mention that examples furnish their own illustration, data carrying pretty obviously their consequences with them; and just data are deducible, to an astonishing extent, from *every* cultivated nation's existing stock of ideas, merely by superior arrangement and larger generalisation.   But, on the other hand, the whole host of prejudices compasses this latter class of ideas—prejudices of opinion, of affection, and of interest, so much so that, even in the most enlightened part of Europe, it is accepted as a maxim, that "it is impossible to make too much allowance for friction."

If the immediately preceding remarks be tolerably well grounded, I think it can scarcely be denied that the inducements and sanctions derivable from Oriental literature are at once infinitely more requisite and more procurable, in reference to the diffusion of our moral than of our physical sciences. Nor can I here avoid the expression of my surprise, that those who have been compelled to acknowledge the success of Mr. Wilkinson in removing, by means of the Indian astronomy, those formidable obstacles which stand round the threshold of the native mind, resisting the entrance of our knowledge, should refuse to attend to his repeated declarations, that his object is general, not particular, is moral, not scientific, is mediate, not ultimate!

Mr. Wilkinson's experience of the people of India is of that genuine sort which arises out of close intercourse with them, remote from our Presidencies and large towns.   *There* he learnt the necessity of preparation, conciliation, and compromise; and *there* he found the means of them all—the means of closing that gulf which separates European and Indian affection and intellect—in *the use of that literature which,* I shall venture to say, *cannot be dispensed with,* and least of all in relation to that very department of our knowledge from which there would seem to be a disposition to exclude its instrumentality upon grounds erroneous as far as they go, and which fail yet more by defect than by error.   Whatever may be the case at the Presidency, I trust I have now assigned some solid reasons for the conclusion that the general acceptance, as well as the safe and beneficial and durable operation, of our knowledge must depend upon the facilities of the living, and the inducements of the dead, languages of the country : and even with respect to the Presidency, it would seem that the apparent anxiety to Anglicise, which is there manifested by the people, is nothing more than a pestilent craving after the profit and power to be derived from the perverted use of our language.

The following is an extract from " The Englishman " of the 7th September :—" A report of the Hindoo Free School has been lying on our table several days.   We should have noticed it sooner could we have brought ourselves to view with calmness this *further* testimony to the disgusting and culpable indifference of the wealthy Hindoos to the solid interests and intellectual advancement of their poorer countrymen.   Will it be believed, out of Calcutta, that a school containing 250 scholars has not received pecuniary assistance from more than seven native gentlemen ?   Were we to tell the story that *all* the good service rendered to 80 millions in the way of education proceeds from Englishmen, and from poor students, whose *parents shamefully stint them,* and whose *intelligence is laughed at,* we should obtain no credit for our narrative."   The Editor's surprise may be real ; but beyond all question his story, were it told, *would* obtain universal credence everywhere without the limits of Calcutta, as far as the Himalaya and the Indus, both from the whole native community, and from all Europeans accurately conversant with the means and habits and sentiments of that community! To those means and habits and sentiments, sheer English knowledge in an English garb has some such relation of fitness, as have the English ball-room habiliments to the persons of the 80 millions in the pursuit of their ordinary avocations! Ah! would we, instead of circling round and round the pale of the Presidency, but elevate our contemplation to the physical and moral condition of those 80 millions, and to the possible means of influencing it beneficially, through our knowledge, with due advertence to our scanty numbers and miserable insulation, *then* should we perceive the indispensable necessity of a deliberate, systematic, and uniform plan of education, combining the utmost facilities with the utmost inducements to change. And *then* would the small funds at the disposal of Government to this end be devoted entirely to the steady and adequate supply of those facilities and inducements, leaving their application and use to the public. One of the most philosophic writers upon the progress of society in Europe has remarked,* that the vernacularisation of learning produced a greater effect in disabusing the general intellect of the prejudices of books, and of those of existing institutions and opinions, than all the rest of the glorious events and discoveries of that age which witnessed it, including among those events the invention of printing! Now, is it not the alpha and omega of our hopes, to produce such an effect upon the general intellect in India? Is not our knowledge itself but a means to that end? And shall we overlook vernacularisation in India, when neither availability, nor safety, nor adequacy, can belong to the instrument of our knowledge, save by and through it? If there be but a tolerable warranty for the truth of that pre-eminent liberalising influence ascribed to the vernacularisation of learning in Europe by the author I have adverted to—and he must be a bold man who will dispute the judgment of the finest intellect in Britain—vernacularisation should be our chief engine in India, apart from all advertence to its instrumental indispensableness towards the diffusion of *our* knowledge. But if we combine the consideration of its independent moral agency with that of its unequalled energy in spreading abroad any particular truths, what on earth should lead us to overlook its title to be made the corner-stone of the

* "Edinburgh Review," vol. xxvii. p. 203.

edifice of public instruction ? It is argued that there is no saying whence the moral spark may be elicited ; and that *therefore*
it is expedient to teach our language, in the hope that the seed
of our knowledge, thence procurable, may fall on some happy
spot where it may take root, and whence it may be generally
propagated. Now, I would observe, in the first place, that, as
the fructifying power belongs to our knowledge and not to our
speech, the chance of the seed falling upon a congenial soil must
be proportioned to the extent of the experimental ground employed to raise it. But the vernacular intrument may convey the
seed to hundreds of thousands of minds, whilst the English one
must limit it to a few hundreds at most. Need I make the application, according to the arithmetical rule of chances ? This,
however, is but half the answer to the argument I have stated ;
for, in the second place, it is beyond a question that sound knowledge may be accepted, taught, and studied, for ages, without
" awaking the strong man "—without stirring the deep waters of
a nation's intellect ; and that universal experience strongly indicates the *entire dependence*, in a national sense, of this vivifying
power of knowledge upon that complete fusion of its precepts
with a nation's familiar experiences and wants which neither
hath been, nor can be, without a vernacular medium !

If, then, it be our object to free the Indian mind from the
thraldom of prejudice, by means of knowledge, the chances of
success from the use of an antivernacular and of a vernacular
process are, according to the first of the above modes of computation, as very many to one in favour of the latter—and, according to the second mode of estimation, the unit disappears !
Again, it is argued, let us once reach and move, by English or
other media, the Indian intellect ; and the people will presently
direct that movement into the vernacular channels of communication. I do not deny the possibility : but, with respect to the probability, I ask, is there not the strongest prejudice in this country
against popular learning ? And is not much precious time and
opportunity like to be lost by reason of this prejudice, if we ourselves do not set the example of deriding it—if we *sanction* it by
the use of an antivernacular organ ? More than that : obvious
causes, always and everywhere, so much tend to make the cultivation of knowledge the special business of the few, and at

the same time to lay so many conscious and unconscious biasses on the minds of those few, disposing them to mystify, if not to abuse, it, that the history of letters since the dawn of civilisation on earth, hardly yields a few solitary exceptions to the general issue of the monopoly of knowledge in impotency or *in* knavery. And is it in *India*, and in respect to *our* knowledge, that we are to presume an easy, voluntary, and necessary transmission from the few to the many? Never was presumption made, so plainly opposed to reason and to history! * Nor is it, by any means, necessary to suppose an *artificial* and *deliberately fraudful* monopoly of our knowledge—though that is too probable, if it wear an English dress—since the natural monopoly, resulting from its difficulty, and from the incompetency of the means and wit of the many to cope with that difficulty, may abundantly suffice to strip our knowledge of all useful energy, and reduce it to the character of an idle curiosity in the possession of a small number of the people. The noble science of Greece and Rome, what else was it but an idle curiosity to all modern Europe for more than a thousand years? And why? Because of its costliness, and because of its disconnection from ordinary use and experience, partly by reason of its lingual, and partly by reason of its essential, incongruity with existing modes of thought and sentiment. And do we really imagine that there are more points of contact (so to speak) between English knowledge in an English dress, and the existing means and modes of thought and feeling in India, than there were between those means and modes in modern Europe from the fifth to the fifteenth century, and Greek and Roman knowledge in their respective lingual garbs? Do we really imagine that Anglicised Indians will presently and readily acquire either the *power* so justly to appreciate the philosophy of speech and thought as to do justice to English words and ideas in their transfusion to the Indian vernaculars; or the *will* so utterly to set their country's prejudice at defiance, as to bend their efforts to the peculiarly painful and compensating task of working out the literary application of those tongues to the substance of an alien knowledge?

---

* It cost *us* AGES to shake off the prejudice in favour of learned knowledge! Is this th. *reason* why Mr. T. affects to underrate the hazard of perpetuating this prejudice in India?

If we *do* cherish such fond imaginations, we are destined to be miserably disappointed : nor can there be a question that all those noble preliminary toils, by which alone European knowledge can be indigenated in India, must owe their entire design and plan, as well as the superior tendency of their execution, to ourselves.

To enlarge, strengthen, and purify the common Indian channels of thought—to pour into them the strong waters of our knowledge, duly tempered to the feeble stomachs of the people—to lead them on from truth to truth under the seeming guidance of their own venerated lore, till they have insensibly learnt to perceive its folly and iniquity—these are labours as much above the unassisted capacity of the people of India as contrary to their unguided inclinations !

The moral and intellectual fetters of thirty centuries are not to be sundered by unprepared and random efforts. To suppose so, is utterly to overlook the strength of those principles which hold society together, alike under the worst as under the best social systems. *Pas à pas on va bien loin.* If, in India, the whole mass of opinions bear the most authoritative of sanctions—if the affections of the many and the interests of the few combine to root that sanction in the very core of all hearts—we must *borrow* it, as often and as far as we can : so only shall we check the few, and attract the many, especially in the *first stages of our progress.* But to employ the indispensable sanction (the literature of the land) sufficiently freely, and yet so as not to counteract our ultimate object of discrediting and dispensing with it—does it not imply system, perseverance, cost, with such an habitual concurrence of native learning and European direction and control as we may look for in vain, if Government stand aloof ?

If, again, the moral energy of knowledge depend wholly or chiefly upon its intimate fusion with the household thoughts and words of a people, whilst there exists in India the strongest bias against thus lowering the dignity of learning, whence but from the patronage of Government to the systematic, persevering, and costly concurrence of native learning and European superintendency, in the improvement and literary application of the vulgar tongues, can we look for the adequate development of this moral energy ? It was because the Moslem scorned the aid of the established sanctions of opinion, in a land where their force was as pervading as imperative; and because he knew not whence springs the reformative vigour of knowledge, and therefore never poured his own into the popular channels of Indian thought, that the Moslem failed to make the least moral impression on India, despite his vast command over the influences of example, of time, and of domestic sway.

To us, those potent influences are wanting: and, few and insulated as we are, it *cannot* be that such an abstraction as knowledge should in our hands work out that impression unless we give to the agent its maximum of moral power by systematic vernacularisation, removing at the same time all obstacles to its incipient operation by systematic compromise with existing prejudices. With *these* ends and aims the continued public patronage of the learned languages and literature of India is not only legitimate but desirable—not only desirable but indispensable. Indispensable for what? for the moral and intellectual regeneration of India! How? by the communication of general truths! How, again? solely through the living languages of the country! How, once again? with all the recommendation of acknowledged precepts and examples that can be safely borrowed from the vast and various literature of the country!

Until these views be realised in a public college of translators and vernacularisers, it is impossible that the business of education should progress steadily and safely throughout the country, for want of the requisite means and appliances in the hands of the teachers.

But how, it will be asked, are we to realise the uses of the study of Oriental lore, and to prevent the abuse of that study to pristine purposes, on the part of those scholars who are to be educated in such a college? make the privilege of learning Arabic or Sanskrit at the public expense contingent upon the learning simultaneously of other things—English, for example, or anatomy and chemistry: and you ensure the mental superiority of these favoured scholars to the errors of their country, fitting them at the same time either to go forth as the accomplished apostles * of truth, or, more usually, to remain

---

* They should go forth, specifically, as *schoolmasters;* and the college spoken of should be appropriated to training schoolmasters only, and translators. See Letter No. IV.

about you, engaged in concert with yourselves in such lexi-cographical and grammarian labours as are required for the improvement of the vernaculars, or for transfusing our know-ledge into these channels, or for recommending it to general acceptance under the cover of admitted sanctions of opinion, preceptive or exemplary!

If the moral energy of knowledge can be shown to be com-patible with an *antivernacular* organ: if the learning of the English language can be shown to be compatible with the *means* of the people of India: if the very partial spread of our know-ledge can be shown to be consistent with their *welfare :* or lastly, if a voluntary and unaided disposition, on their own part, to popularise our knowledge by identifying it with the cultivation and literary use of the vulgar tongues can be shown to be probably deducible from *their own unaided views and habits in respect of letters*—I am content to give up my argument. But as for proofs of the contrary of any one of these propositions drawn from the alleged eagerness of the people to Anglicise, as manifested in our own schools, I must again repeat that were the particular premises granted they are no more adequate to support the general conclusion than I am to poise the Andes in the palm of my hand! And not merely so: for let the number of those scholars be quintupled, and the whole might still be presumed to belong to that pestilent class which seeks merely the means of turning the power of our knowledge *against* the universal helplessness! Where is the stress of education now laid in Europe? upon facilitation! Wherefore? because the procuring of the blessing, as well as the averting of the curse, of knowledge depends upon the *free access* and *effectual participation* of *the many;* which may not be without the utmost facilities of all kinds. So long as the acquisition of knowledge is difficult, so long must it centre in the few; and so long as it centres in the few, so long will it lapse into useless mysticism or subtility, if it be not turned into an engine of oppression.

It is *not* the quality of knowledge, how good soever, which makes it work beneficially : it is its identification with familiar general thoughts and feelings in the land where it is planted : and if Greek and Roman knowledge attained no such identi-

fication in modern Europe for a thousand years, and consequently stirred not the slumber of the strong man (according to
Milton's noble allegory); whence is derived the presumption
that European knowledge is so capable of allying itself to the
familiar thoughts and feelings of India, that we may dispense
with all facilities in the mode of propagating it? a proposition
more directly opposed to reason and to history was never, I
conceive, hazarded.

For knowledge to produce any moral effect, it must be
wedded to general sympathy: for knowledge to produce any
intellectual effect, it must be wedded to general practical
experience. And that a handful of strangers, shut out from
popular sympathies and from all the intimate things of local
experience, should cause these banns to be celebrated in India
by the sheer agency of European science, without deliberate,
systematic, public measures of education exclusively directed
to the one end of creating a popular disposition and means towards their celebration, appears to me a chimera!

But such popular means entirely, and such popular disposition
mainly, ever have depended, and ever will, upon the use of
vernacular media: and that part of popular disposition which
hath not hinged upon those media, where shall we look for its
subjection to the moral influence of learning, save in the use
of acknowledged sanctions of opinion.

To enable the people to think, have not the great minds of
Europe forced themselves to think with the people? To *induce*
them to think, have not those minds, in all ages, deferred to
prejudice? Christ Himself and His favourite disciples were "all
things to all men:" nor, if we exclude the agency of uncon-
trolled enthusiasm—an energy which we neither dare nor
purpose to employ—has one great and happy moral change
been effected in the world except by long and careful compromise and conciliation and preparation? Now, no case can
be imagined in which compromise and conciliation are more
requisite than in the present one: and because all *personal*
means of either are almost wholly denied to us, I point to those
ample means which the sacred literature of the land can afford
us. True, its employment is liable to objections: but what
then?

It is necessary—it is indispensable: it sways all interests—it hallows all opinions: and the Babel of thirty centuries, resting upon *its foundations,* will stand for ever, in despite of our knowledge, unless that knowledge be worked into the people's hearts and understandings with the precepts and examples of this omnipotent make-way! As to religious or moral scruples on *our* part, they are more than answered by the conduct and sentiments of the founder of our creed; and by the innocuous use of classic paganism by Europe for ages. There is, or recently was, somewhat more pith in the objection from expediency, that to protect the study of the learned languages and literature by public patronage tended to maintain their influence and that of the evils they support. I admit the force of this objection as it applied to the system of instruction in the public schools prior to Lord William Bentinck's reform. That system made Sanskr*i*t and Arabic the direct means, and Oriental lore the direct end, of instruction; and it sought further to recommend those languages by conveying into them the treasures of *our* knowledge! Such a plan of education, acting under the continuance of the jurisprudential sanction of those languages, and under the disadvantages of so difficult and alien an instrument for the general communication of European truths as the English language, might indeed have realised the apprehension adverted to.

But these measures, except the last, belong to obsolete follies: and, in respect to retrospective censure of the first of them, it should not be forgotten that so long as the ultimate reference in all legal questions was to Oriental lore, the public could scarcely be excused from the obligation of protecting the study of those difficult languages which formed its sole depositaries. The great question still remaining to be settled is, whether. assuming *our* knowledge to be the sole subject-matter of instruction, we can dispense with the facilities of vernacular media and with the inducements of established opinion? and, if not, whether the public patronage of the learned languages and literature in such a college as I have indicated the necessity of, be not indispensable to the adequate and steady supply of those facilities and inducements to all those who shall be directly engaged in the business of education? With that

business the college of translation and vernacularisation would
have no direct concern, the sole function of its masters and
students being the conjoint preparation for our teachers, public
and private, of those indirect means and appliances of education
without the fullest aid of which it is believed that the tree
of European knowledge can never take root in this land; and
the *adequate furnishing* of which appliances and helps implies
labours as much above individual means and leisure on *our* part,
as transcending the capacity, and repugnant to the fixed bias,
of the *native* mind.

The higher uses and influences of vernacularisation have heretofore failed entirely to attract attention. Knowledge itself,
even sound knowledge, owes its moral energy to this instrument. If the word of Junius * be an insufficient warrant for
this cardinal truth, let reference be had to any and all the great
writers of Europe who have expounded the causes of the progress of society : there is no difference of opinion amongst them
on this point. But, if vernacularisation be indispensable, it can
scarcely be denied that the highly skilful, steadily continuous,
and purely preliminary labours involved in the successful
effectuation of it in reference to the substance of our knowledge,
are pre-eminently *European* in the whole conception and
direction ; and at the same time, so remarkably the business of
no one, as to fall, quoad cost, to the care of the State. Hence
my impression of the necessity of public patronage of these
labours—involving, of course, such patronage of the study of
the learned languages and literature of the country : but their
study directed to ends how different, and by methods how
remote, from those lately in practice, I need not further explain.
I may remark, however, in reference to the applicability of the
objection just stated, to the protected pursuit of Orientalism that,
thus restricted and *directed*, it could not, by possibility, produce the
apprehended effects, were, as I propose, our eminently useful and
generous knowledge recommended to general attention by the
facility and aptitude to common use and experience of vernacularisation—including in that term the accommodation of

* These letters were first published under this signature.

thoughts as well as of words to the state of popular intellect and affection in this land.

September, 1835.

P. S. I have perused an article on the education of the people in the third No. of the Meerut Magazine. So far as I understand the writer's views, it would seem that he considers their education ought to consist in a very extended application of legal sanctions to the enforcement of moral duties. If this be the real scope of the essay—as I suppose—I would suggest to its author, 1st, that we are too few and too ignorant of the intimate framework of Indian society, to play the censor's part, magisterially or judicially, with much probability of success. 2d, That the glory of morality consists in its perfect voluntariness —a truth the neglect of which by Eastern lawgivers has led them to extend public coercion over the whole field of human action with no better general consequence than the *dwarfing and emasculation* of the national character! I fully admit, with this writer, the importance of the "concurrence and co-operation of the people themselves" in the business of education. Upon that rock I too build, laying the corner-stones of my edifice in facilitation, and conciliation, with reference to *their* penury and prepossessions. Pity so vigorous a writer will have nothing to do with the *first* half of the maxim, *Suaviter in modo: fortiter in re !*

It is scarcely practically convenient to give so unlimited a sense to the idea of education as does the writer in question. But I have not hesitated to say, incidentally in my first letter, that I consider the general association of the people to the business of administration, through Juries,* to be, educationally, at least as important as the general admission of them into the circle of European speculation, through vernacularisation. Sound doctrines are not everything : *neither are they nothing ;* and I think the author of the paper adverted to will admit, upon reflection, that his notion of creating a general spirit of industry by public means of coercion or punishment—in other words, by the

---

* Panchayets are, in a large view, essentially the same thing, viz., a qualification of the sheerly official administration of justice by certain popular elements.

instrumentality of the laws—is a sad mistake. *Mitius jubetur doctrina.* In respect of industry, in particular, it is universally allowed that the operation of the laws of all Europe has been —from the times adverted to by this writer up to our own day almost—singularly injurious ; so much so that the celebrated *'laissez nous faire'* has passed into a proverb.

LETTER III.

My reason for reverting to the subject of these letters, is to be found in the following extract from the "Friend of India :" "It is a truism, which we almost fear to hazard, that our only chance of effecting permanent and extensive good in India, must arise from the adoption of a system of vernacular education ; and yet, viewing the apathy which prevails on this subject, it would almost appear as though this fact was not yet received into the number of truths. It is now nearly twenty-five years since Parliament appropriated a large grant for educational purposes in India, and to this moment no single effort has been made to give the great body of the people the benefit of this grant. It has been invariably applied in succession to the encouragement of some foreign language or other, the Arabic, the Persian, the Sanskrit, the English ; never to that of the vernacular languages. It is a twelvemonth since the Education Board stated in their Report, that the creation of a national literature and of a national system of education, was the ultimate object to which all their labours were directed. What step has been taken to attain this ultimate object—what book has been translated into Bengalee or Hindustani — what indigenous school erected ? Of what system of education has even the foundation been laid ? Mr. Adam's report of his researches, which it was understood would form the basis of an educational structure, has now been before Government a twelvemonth. What single measure has grown out of his labours and researches ? The answer is lamentably simple ; none. The stillness of death reigns in the department of vernacular education." This is a lamentable statement: but as I have an unabating and full confidence in the *cause*, so I believe that further discussion must and will eventually open the eyes of the public.

With the hope of conducing to that end, I now reprint my two first letters, and add some further remarks suited to the changing and I think improving aspect of the subject, though there is, alas, but too much room for amendment still, and for continued revertence to first principles.

The letters are an answer to Mr. Trevelyan's Essay * on the means of communicating the civilisation of Europe to India. No other person has yet attempted formally to justify by argument the novel and exclusive measures of the Education Committee. Wherefore an answer to Mr. Trevelyan's Essay is an answer to all that has, thus far, been deliberately advanced in favour of Anglomania.

In the last Report of the Committee there are, indeed, a few stray sentences mentioning the vernaculars with respect: but those "epea pteroenta" are so foreign to the general scope of that Report, are so signally at variance with the whole previous sayings and doings of the Committee, and are so belied by the subsequent acts and *attempts* (buried in the archives of the Council Room!) of that body, that charity must seek to cover these egregious sentences with oblivion.

Such persons, however, as are content to be thankful for small mercies, may congratulate the vernacularists upon their having at least compelled the other party to *speak* respectfully of the languages of the people! Should Mr. Trevelyan feel inclined to favour me with a response, now that I avow my letters (challenging him directly to appear and answer), I would beg of him to address himself exclusively to the main topic of the letters, or the pre-eminent and overruling importance of vernacular media, universally, or in all times and places. I have assigned the largest and most pervading reasons deducible from history and from the nature of man, for that transcendent energy which I have ascribed to such media; and I have endeavoured to show that, were the objections made to the vernacular languages of India, in their present state, much stronger than

* Mr. Grant's essay on the same subject may be considered as the basis of Mr. Trevelyan's. I have studied them both.

they really are, the reasons above alluded to would still suffice to justify a present practical preference on the part of Government of the vernaculars to English—if our object be really to *renerve*, and to *give a right direction to*, the mental vigour of this land, safely, gradually, and with a reasonable prospect of producing expansive and durable effects. Let, then, Mr. T. address himself to the *express grounds* and *reasons* upon which the paramountship of the vernaculars is rested. If the corypheus of the Anglicists (whose active benevolence I honour and love) can show that these grounds are less comprehensive, or less firm than I assume, well and good; but, if he cannot show it, let him be assured that less comprehensive ones, though just as far as they go, must yet leave the *vital merits* of this great question untouched. And let him remember, too, that the real question is the regeneration of this land, or the means of breaking its intellectual torpor by a fresh and vigorous impulsion from sound knowledge, that is, from European knowledge.

As a practical measure for the immediate adoption of Government, I have no hesitation in saying that to found a college for the rearing of a competent body of translators and of schoolmasters—in other words, for the systematic supply of good vernacular books and good vernacular teachers (leaving the public to *employ* both, in case the Government fund be adequate to no more than the maintenance of such college), would be an infinitely better disposal of the Parliamentary grant than the present application of it to the training of a promiscuous crowd of English smatterers, whose average period of schooling cannot, by *possibility*, fit them to be the regenerators of their country, yet for whose further and efficient prosecution of studies so difficult and so alien to ordinary uses, there is no provision nor inducement whatever!!*

Mr. Trevelyan seems to have thought it enough for his argu-

---

* Note of 1846.—These have been partially afforded by Lord Hardinge. I trust the experiment may work well for the country beyond meeting the calls of the Government for native functionaries, and that these may be found sufficiently at home in the appropriate knowledge of their class in addition to their European lore. My proposed college, it will be seen in the sequel (Letter IV.), makes no distinction between mental culture in the English and vernacular languages. It proposes to combine the two and to give the combination the most definite at once and most effective form with reference to the general intellectual wants of the people of India.

ment (see Essay *passim*) to cite the *bare fact* that knowledge
has been generally communicated and spread through exotic
organs. I shall not attempt at present to bring any fresh proofs
that Mr. Trevelyan's historical *examples* may be easily turned
into solemn and fearful *warnings:* I shall not attempt further
to show that the general history of knowledge is, " propter hanc
causam exotici medii," a *disgraceful* and *lamentable story ;* that
(not to travel for illustrations out of the limits of Europe) it
was the practically, if not necessarily, exclusive genius of this
system of learning, which turned our beautiful religion into a
scandal and curse ; our noble liberty into slavery : I shall not
attempt to trace the waste of time and of means generated by
this adherence to foreign media ; nor, lastly, to urge the very
legitimate presumption that, after all, " the strong man " was
awakened in Europe from the lethargy of ages not by, but in
despite of, exotic lore.

All these general topics I reserve till Mr. T. appear in his
justification.

Meanwhile, and with express reference to his present notion
that the best way of exciting the Indian intellect, and of creating a genuine literary spirit, is to scatter the small Educational
fund at Government's disposal amongst the seventy millions of our
subjects, by picking up at random pauper pupils, teaching them
to prate English for five or six years, and then dismissing them,
to *regenerate their country !* living themselves, I suppose, upon
air, and increasing their store of this *facile* knowledge by certain inspirations of which it were mere impiety to doubt the
probability !!!

Such a plan appears to me radically and hopelessly futile ;
and, certainly, no anticipation of success in *this* method of
naturalising European knowledge in India can be drawn from
the fact of the success which attended the incorporation of Greek
and Roman knowledge with our familiar words and thoughts.

True, the difficult and inapt science of Greece and Rome *was,*
in modern Europe, first mastered in itself, and eventually
worked into our own speech and minds. But how ? by the
employment of means adequate to the end, and by the existence
of circumstances most powerfully efficient to forward that end.
A thousand predisposing causes led a mighty nobility to seek

in this lore the appropriate ornament of their rank and station.
A church, which monopolised a third of the wealth of the continent, called Rome its mother and Greece its foster mother:
and throughout the great part of that continent, the Law,
ecclesiastic and civil, was even lingually Roman. *Hence* the
magnificent endowments and establishments and permanent
inducements of all kinds by which a difficult and exotic learning was at length effectually naturalised amongst us. *Hence*
the scholar, if he pleased, might pursue in retirement letters as
a profession, assured of a comfortable provision *for life;* or, if
he pleased, he might devote himself to the task of instructing
the scions of a most influential and wealthy nobility, all of them,
from peculiar associations, necessitated to become his pupils
whether they profited by his lessons or not, and thereby affording *him* the certainty of an enduring means of livelihood; or, if
he pleased, he might pass from the cloister or the college into the
world, and there find the greater part of its most important con-
cerns subservient (by virtue of special causes that had operated
upon the social system since its very genesis) to the uses and
abuses of his peculiar gifts.

If these things be so, we see at least that, in modern Europe,
due provision and *inducement* existed for the *steady pursuit*
throughout a *long succession* of *laborious lives,* of Greek and
Roman knowledge: in other words, means were forthcoming
adequate to achieve (in the lapse of ages!!) the difficult end
proposed to be accomplished. Now, unless Mr. Trevelyan can
demonstrate that it is much less difficult for the people of India
to master our speech and to transmute its treasures into their
own, I think he will find in the *total absence* of those vast appliances, or of those most potent favouring predispositions, by
virtue of which *alone* Europe was Romanised, a decisive objection to his scheme of direct Anglicisation, being no less than a
demonstration of the utter present and prospective futility of
that scheme. Mr. Trevelyan has insisted, throughout and always,
on the parallel case of European progression by virtue of dead
tongues. The above is my answer, quoad his present specific
plan of operations: the parallel is utterly naught; and the plan,
palpably baseless. Let me add, that I take this plan in its *last*
and *freshest* form, or that indicated in and by the memorable

paragraphs of the Education Committee's Report* already
adverted to. And, if I make no allusions to ground-shifting
between the dates of the Essay and of the Report, I may yet
remind Mr. Trevelyan that the recent vernacularisation of our
Courts has, by sundering the last possible link between sheer
English learning and any material local usefulness, doubled the
cogency of all arguments like that just used against the feasibility of the presently alleged plan. Neither in the associations
nor in the wants of the native society, nor yet in the public or
private institutions of the country, is there sufficient *basis*
whereon to rest Mr. Trevelyan's argument and scheme.†

With respect to my own suggestion of an establishment
devoted to the regular supply of good vernacular books and
good vernacular teachers, I have to observe that, if I have not
very much overstated the overruling and absorbing importance
of the vulgar tongues as media for the communication of all
and any knowledge, it will follow, pretty obviously, from the
admission of that importance, that to *inchoate* and *organise* a
system of *vernacularisation* must be the best employment of the
small *Educational fund in the hands of Government.*

It is obvious that any such measure as the one just suggested
surpasses all individual efforts: but I am very certain that did
Government, by the organisation of the college proposed, provide an enduring and wholesome stock of the appliances of
popular education, there are hundreds of individuals who
would hasten to use and employ that stock (a function quite
within their power), in district schools of their own founding.
Already and everywhere there is a call for vernacular books
and teachers, in very defiance of the Anglicists! Nor need
the seemingly Herculean labour of translating our knowledge
into the vulgar tongues of India, alarm a rational and unpre-
judiced person; for, it is just as certain that not one English
work in 50,000 would require or even justify translation, as
that Hindustani, Hindi and Bengali (and it were folly to

---

* Viz., the paragraphs in which it is asserted that however exclusive the Committee's patronage of English in the meanwhile, it is all with ultimate views to the
formation of a vernacular literature!

† I need hardly remark that Mr. T.'s scheme is the Committee's scheme, and that
those who would know what the Committee have done and purpose to do, must consult Mr. T.'s writings.

perpetuate more media) are competent, each and all, to sustain the weight proposed to be laid on them.*

There is another consideration which, whilst it is well worthy of attention in itself, is calculated to show that the extent of necessary translation is by no means such as the enemies of vernacular media have tried to make it. In educating the people of India it should be our object, not so much to imprint in detail all our express thoughts or facts on their minds, as to instil, generally, our *methods of reasoning,* our mathematical and inductive processes, together with that yet small essence of indisputable truths in science, philosophy, and history, which has been eliminated by those processes, and which forms with us, and should do with them, but the starting-point of fresh and vigorous research.

By the one course we should be apt to trammel the Indian intellect for several generations, if not for ever, assuming that we succeeded in conveying to it, *totidem verbis,* our exotic lore: by the other course, we should at once and at small cost of books set it free to take a vigorous but discriminating range over those topical idiosyncrasies of nature and experience which, in every large section of the globe, exist by God's appointment, subject only to man's modification, but not obliteration.

In the most enlightened parts of Europe the general opinion now is that schools for *teachers* have, in the present century, created a new era in the practical science of education. Why then is Government inattentive to so noble and successful an experiment? Especially since there is about this method of normal instruction, or teaching of teachers, just that sort of definiteness which may be compassed by limited public funds, with yet a concomitant prospect of great and diffusive benefits to the country from the adoption of the measure. But work-

---

* In recently translating Prinsep's Transactions into Hindi, I found no difficulty arising out of the alleged poverty of this vernacular ; and I suspect that those who have clamoured most about the feebleness of the Indian vulgar tongues, know as little about the express *facts* as they do about the *inferred* capabilities or rather incapabilities.

Dante found the Italian language cruder than any Indian vernacular now is ; and yet this *single man,* by a *single work,* made the vulgar tongue of his country capable of supporting the most sublime, novel, and abstract ideas. Ex uno disce omnes.

men must have tools; and good workmen, good tools: wherefore, to a nursery for the regular supply of competent vernacular *schoolmasters*, should be added one for the equally regular supply of sound *books* in the three prime vulgar tongues of our * Presidency, books embodying the *substance only* of our *really useful* knowledge, with stimuli and directions for the various sorts of mental exertion; so that, in the result, there might exist, for the *people at large*, the easy and obvious *bridge* of the vulgar tongues, leading from exotic principles to local practices, from European theory to Indian experience!

The incalculable importance to the public weal of the bridge just adverted to, even when principles and theories have been chiefly deduced from local experience and practice, is the last and greatest discovery of Western meditation upon the many methods of intellectual culture which have been used by nations in the past 3000 years; and as whatever is *exotic* in theory becomes on that account less easily marriageable with home practices and observations, it is doubly incumbent upon us so to indoctrinate the people of this country, that those who learn may pass from our schools to life with alert, instead of with encumbered, minds.

Again, in laying the foundation of the educational regeneration of this land, it is well worthy of the attention of a forecasting Government to avoid coincidence with existing and most injurious prepossessions.

Now, this land is absolutely saturated with *dead* learning; absolutely bloated with the *false pride of that learning;* so much so, that there is *no* prepossession stronger than that which consigns to contempt all knowledge, however valuable in itself, of which the medium is the vernacular, or, as it is significantly said, the *vulgar* tongues. If, then, in taking our first measures, we actually, though unintentionally, countenance this prejudice, what hope that the people will spontaneously, as is alleged, lay it aside; and will, no sooner than they have imbibed, *vernacularise*, our lore? I see no rational prospect of the kind, and conceive that the old *style* of learning (through exotic media) will perpetuate the old *pride* of learning, be the substance of

* Viz., Urdu, Hindi, and Bengali.

that learning Orient or Occident. I am, too, quite certain that the true mystery of vernacularisation (challenge to *all* minds to think, and to think purpose-like on what comes home to the business and bosoms of the community) must, in that event, continue for ages as much out of the range of Indian contemplation as it now is.

I say that the solution of this mystery, in relation to the *happiness and vigour of nations*, is the last and noblest result of European cogitation upon the general effects of all the various systems of education that have anywhere and at any time prevailed in the world: and by so much as both the *materials* and the *habit of such* cogitations are peculiarly beyond the reach of Asiatics, by so much is it folly in us to assert any such readiness at spontaneous vernacularisation !

Though no admirer of the prima philosophia of the Anglicists, I am yet ready to admit that they are far ahead of the people they would proselyte : and since the former have not yet discovered the sublime mystery (it may well be called so) to which I allude, I cannot subscribe to the doctrine that it is level to the *understanding* or *will* of the latter.

Népál, *July*, 1837.

––––––––––––

LETTER IV.

You ask me to give, in a condensed form, my ideas on the general subject of education in India, together with their express application to the proposed Normal College. With regard to the general subject, from much experience of the sentiments and habits of natives, I conclude that the *real uses* of book learning are unknown to them; that they dream not of the great objects of arousing the *many* to think purpose-like on *the actual business of life,* and of making an *easy bridge from theory to practice,* so that the millions shall have a chance of producing a Bacon or a Newton from among their vast number, whilst every practical farmer, trader, and craftsman, is placed within reach of the principles lying at the bottom of his daily toil, and men following

letters as a craft are made to come under the wholesome influence of common sense. *These*, the real objects of national education, are, I think, undreamt of in India, as they were till lately
in Europe; and thus I account for the deplorable (as indubitable)
fact that natives are habitually neglectful of their mother
tongue, and are eager to acquire English, Sanskrit, or Persian,
solely for the power or pelf, thence directly derivable by the individual acquirer of one or the other. Now, I consider that if
we would benefit India by book learning, it must be as we benefit her by our government and laws—that is, by reaching the
many, by discasting book lore or enfranchising it, in fact; and
that, with the objects above spoken of, as the only real and sound
ones, we should make knowledge the handmaid of everyday
utility, and give its acquisition the utmost possible facilities.
Such are my wishes, and therefore I give an unlimited preference to a vernacular medium both for its facility and for its
aptitude, to make the knowledge conveyed through it practically
effective in a beneficial way, and *also* for its diffusible quality,
book-knowledge being so apt to pass away from utility, or to be
abused as a mere engine of selfish aggrandisement. But though
I give the mother tongues of the people the first and second
place, I give English the third; and in my Normal College,
which is not so much an educational establishment as an indirect means of making all such establishments efficient, I would
have the alumni *equally* versed in both tongues—their own
and ours. Again, I think that to indigenate a sound literature
in India, to kindle a wholesome spirit of knowledge and to fit
the spoken tongues of the land for being its organs, are mighty
projects that call for express systematic measures, subsidiary
to education ordinarily so called, but which alone can make suc'
education valuable and effective; and in my college I want to
establish and realise such measures: I want to locate therein a
set of able men of the West, who shall be competent to give to
India the *essence* of our INDISPUTABLE knowledge; and to associate with them other men of this land, English and native,
who, together with them, shall transfer this essence into the
vulgar tongues of India in the most attractive and efficient manner, whilst both classes, as professors and originators of the
great change, shall have under them a set of pupils, chosen

from the best alumni of all our seminaries, for the express and perpetual purpose of diffusing the labours of the professors, in the capacities of teachers and of translators, and of replacing those professors *gradually* as heads of the college: these alumni to have scholarships and to be devoted for their lives as the pioneers of a new literature; bound to translating within the college, and to teaching abroad; giving their undivided time and talents to indigenate European lore; and being to the usual educational establishments a *perpetual fount for the supply of good books and good teachers.* Well begun is half done, emphatically: let us once set the people of India in the right path, and they will follow it successfully. But to accomplish this we must produce the essence of our indisputable knowledge in the most attractive form, and spread it with systematic skill; the books and the teachers should be excellent: and yet we have in India now not only not either of the desiderata, but no adequate means of reaching them, except through a wasteful series of failures. No man among us is competent to select the very best books and parts of books: no man among us nor institution is competent to furnish the best translation that might be had soon on system: no man among us can set afoot in India, without system, the splendid methods of teaching now in use in Europe. As for the alumni we now raise, it is passing absurd to suppose that they either can or will put their shoulders to the wheel of a radical change in knowledge and education. *We* must *devote* a set of select instruments to that work, making them the pioneers of the new literature, *providing for them for life*, and *binding them to teaching and translating for life.* We must also give them exemplars of what is wanted and how to remedy the defect, in the professors of the central or Normal College, and we must choose those professors from among the really able of England and of India, so that their books and their teaching shall be first-rate, and fitted to set going the vast and noble project of the Europeanisation of the Indian mind. It is idle for any of us in India to fancy we are *masters* of any one branch of science, or that, *not* being so, we can transfuse its essence into Indian tongues in the *most effective mode:* and it is still idler to suppose that our random pupils of ordinary schools will ever, voluntarily and unpaid, devote themselves to the *profitless and painful* walks of instruction and literature, either as book makers or book expounders.* Yet we must have the best books best translated; we must have a steady supply of able teachers; we *must* have a corps of native pioneers of the new knowledge; and the professors and alumni of my Normal College are to furnish and to be these; the alumni being provided for well for life and bound for life to letters as their vocation and glory; and the professors, picked men of England and of India, European and native, masters of the most essential branches of knowledge, and capable of attractively transfusing its vital spirit into the spoken tongues of India, through their books and through their alumni, fully trained by them in the art and science of teaching, one of the most noble and most difficult of the arts and sciences and the handmaid of them all, yet supposed " to come naturally " like the Frenchman's discovery of prose ! ! *Ecce totum !* behold my college in its professors and its alumni —the latter the normal teachers of any and every school that wants them, and the heirs of the original professors in their own institution whenever fit to direct it. Abroad, these alumni are to teach in English or in the vernaculars (Hindi, Urdu, or Bengali,† and no more), as the institution which sends for them, and for the time pays them, shall please. At home they are to study the genius of both tongues, Western and Eastern, and to labour subordinately as translators or transfusers (in original works as they are able), whilst they resume their scholarship allowance, suspended so long as they were abroad; their constant, suggestive, and useful labours as translators or as teachers preventing idleness or dreamy habits, and their perpetual scholarship being liable to forfeiture for proven indolence, incapacity, or bad conduct.

Let us thus systematically and adequately set to work, and

* These avocations are never remuneratory till the public has become their patrons, and the public will never become so till a close reference to life and its active aims govern letters and education, a result we are just reaching in Europe, slowly and painfully. But yesterday, there, men of letters and teachers were poor and despised! Can you read my riddle now? I want to make literature and education such in India that the native public will become their munificent patrons, and thus anticipate the work of time—of ages lost in India, as in Europe, for want of rational and adequate foundation-laying.

† *N.B.* Our proposed college was suggested for what used to be called the Bengal Presidency. We would, of course, now include any other generally used vernacular.

we shall lay a solid foundation. Let us fiddle-faddle, as at present, and fifty years hence that foundation will have to be laid with a nearly sheer loss of all *ad interim* labours.—Believe me, &c., B. H. HODGSON.

NÉPÁL, *April,* 1843.

P. S. You perceive that the plan above suggested has nothing exclusive about it; that it aims at establishing a really national system of education for the benefit of the mass of the people; that it has an expansive energy about it not inadequate to realise its great end, for it proposes to train only those who as teachers or translators will each of them be a certain nucleus of knowledge whence it may reach hundreds; that it proposes to supply the two great wants of good books and good teachers, and that in laying an adequate foundation for the efficient working of education all over the land, it reconciles the policy of upholding deep lore with the necessity of adequate facilities, in regard to the general diffusion of such lore by giving the learned tongues of East and West to the lifelong student, and the best fruits of their study to the many in the shape of improved vernacular instruction. Such an institution seems to deserve the attention of the conductors of education: for though Lord Hardinge's measures may result in supplying the country with an able body of native functionaries, they seem little calculated to meet the wants of the mass of the people, their design indeed being to meet those of the Government only.

LETTER V.

SIR,—As you have recently noticed the new edition of my Letters on Education, I take leave through your journal to call public attention to two striking historical confirmations of the great principle I have contended for; viz., that if European knowledge is to be indigenated in India, and brought home effectively through the medium of the vernaculars to the business and bosoms of the many in this vast country, itself so anciently lettered and cultivated, the object can only be attained by systematic preliminary measures, which must precede all educational labours in the ordinary sense, and which alone can make such labours fructify in India. The historical facts I allude to are as follows :—

First. When it was proposed to transfer the Buddhist religion and literature from India to Tibet, that is, to indigenate Indian ideas in a soil entirely alien to them, how was this most difficult design set about, so as to ensure that perfect success which has given an entirely new character to the fierce Nomades of High Asia? Why, a college of translators was created, and a set of ripe scholars (Lotsava), men of India and Tibet, were devoted to the work, and directed, first, to bring together all the leading terms, or terminology, of the subject in the original Sanskrit, and next to ascertain and fix adequate equivalents for each of those Sanskrit terms in the language of Tibet ; which was or-dained to be the medium of conveying the new light.

And those glossaries of equivalents exist to this hour, per-petual monuments of the good sense and sincerity, the adequacy and sound direction of exertion, whereby the greatest moral change that Asia has ever known was accomplished on the soil where it was first attempted, and whence it has been since similarly propagated (such is the expansive vigour of wholesome projects) throughout the vast extent of Central Asia, everywhere transforming the immemorial devastators of the earth into settled, peaceful agriculturists and shepherds! Now, if we consider, on the one hand, the great difficulties opposed to the success of this project by the totally different character and genius of the Cis and Trans-Himalayan tongues and ideas, and, on the other hand, the enduring completeness of that success, in a field, too, where Christianity itself with an excellent start yet failed * to achieve anything beyond an ephemeral triumph, we must, if impressible at all, be strongly impressed by this first historical instance of the value of adequate preliminaries in the case of every great project of change and reform. I proceed now to the other instance.

Second. When the Chinese towards the close of the last cen-tury had established their political dominion as far west as the Belúr Tágh, they were forced by the sad experience of repeated failures upon the reflection how much easier it is to overrun and

---

* The last relics of the Christian missions of High Asia have just been recovered and transmitted to his Holiness the Pope.

subdue, than to retain peacefully, and administer successfully, territories inhabited by numerous races differing widely from each other and from their conquerors in language as in other points. In order to master the difficulties that beset the Chinese, how did this sagacious nation proceed? They assembled able men of the several vanquished tribes, Tungus, Mongol, Turk, Tangutian and Tibetan; and these persons they caused to construct a pentaglot (answering to the five grand distinctions of nations) glossary of all the chief geographic, topographic, and administrative terms, in the shape of a table of equivalents which was completed by a Chinese column, leaving no one material topical feature or administrative function, though cited by whatever people, thereafter liable to possible misconstruction on the part of the Government or of its servants or subjects; the language of administration being at the same time ordained to be the vernacular of each grand ethnical division of the country. The Chinese dominion, theretofore, precarious in High Asia, has since the completion of this wise measure been stably fixed; nor does any one conversant with those countries doubt that this stability has been and is greatly owing to the wisdom of my second instance of the value of deliberate adequate preliminaries to every great change. These polyglot official glossaries of the Chinese have lately fallen into the hands of European scholars: a Guizot has paused over the political sagacity which suggested their compilation; a Klaproth, a Rémusat, a Julien and a Humboldt * have thence learned to deal effectively, as philosophers, with that same confused mass of human kind which had priorly so frustrated the efforts of the Chinese as statesmen. I will not weaken the force of these historical examples by a single word of commentary, but go on to point the moral of my tales, by remarking that the prevalent mere lip tribute to the value of the vernaculars, I for one repudiate as a mischievous delusion. We are told that the vernaculars now at least are allowed fair play, and are on their trial.† I deny it utterly, and maintain that the experiment of educating

* Vide Asia Polyglotta, Mémoires rèlatifs à l'Asie, Mélanges Asiatiques et Asie Centrale.

† A distinguished and valued member of the Education Committee lately told me so, himself convinced that the fact was as stated. Happily he now has some pregnant doubts.

the people of India in their own tongues *never* can have fair play, never can have a chance, until those preliminary measures are carried out upon which alone vernacular education must rest as its foundation. What those measures are, and how they should be effected, are points explained in the fourth letter with the utmost care and precision; and for my part, from much recent correspondence with the most experienced men in the interior, I am convinced that thus, or thus wise, only, can vernacular education be furnished with the "indispensable prerequisites of an adequate steady supply of good books and good teachers." Let vernacularisation be but accepted in good faith and truth, and those who shall be nominated to effect the object will, I trust, not be slow to adopt the sage measure of the Tibetans and Chinese as above described; for that is obviously the first right move on the right road; and that vernacularisation *is* the right road, and the only right road, what better proofs can be asked for, or given, than the two signal ones just cited? None! None! But honest acceptance and adequate inchoation are indispensable to the success of any and every project; and what these mean, in the project before us, let my historical examples tell!

The same correspondence has likewise deepened my prior conviction as to the prevalent notion that Lord Hardinge's measures will result in furnishing at least a "superior class of subordinate native functionaries." That notion is founded upon want of intimate information of the interior economy of this country. In India the rights and duties of all classes have long been minutely systematised and reduced to written forms of the most complex kind.* And this complicity of its relations and records, added to the circumstance of its having been for ages under the dominion of foreigners very little really versed in those relations and records, has given rise to a vast class of subordinate functionaries, whose astonishing practical readiness alone it is that, in the absence of such helps as mechanical science (printing) and other European devices (shorthand, &c.), lend in Europe to the daily transaction of business, keeps the Indian administrative machine in motion.

* I beg to refer the stranger to the Ayin-i Akbari and Gladwin's Revenue accounts, both forthcoming in English.

Now our new aspirants to office know nothing of the wheel within wheel of this machine, and still less are they able to work the machine with that prompt facility which results from a life devoted to that sole task. Whilst the old class are toiling in their vocation from youth upwards, and thus slowly attaining that exquisite skill in details which needs only the general knowledge of Europeans for purposes of superintendence, the new class are learning Shakespeare and Milton, Bacon and Newton; and with that sort of training only they are despatched into the interior to become officials, possessed of but a poor and mimicked semblance of *our* own peculiar knowledge, *though purchased at the expense of* all their *own!* Yet it is expected that grave men, responsible for the weal of the country, should prefer the claims to office of one of these young parrots to the claims of persons growing grey in the constant discharge of the complex peculiar duties of this all-important body of functionaries, the professional scribes of the East, upon whose shoulders from time immemorial has ever rested the real burden of administration.* If justice did not forbid such supercession, expedience would: the Europeans cannot possibly dispense with the old class of functionaries; cannot possibly get through the work with the help of the new class: and thus the scheme which looks so well at Calcutta, finds no serious approver or adopter in the interior. Inquire, Mr. Editor, and I think you will find the matter so; reflect, and you will have the rational of the fact. But then if the fact be so,—I pray you tell me whether the metropolitan expectation of *thus* creating a new and superior class of native functionaries (not to speak of *thus* indigenating a new knowledge †) be not a mere delusion? Young Bengal is notoriously malcontent; and for my part I cannot help thinking that the dilettante as well as exotic character of the steps we have taken in the educational department

---

* In all ages in the East, wise China excepted, the *noblesse de l' épé*, the nobles and gentry or dominant classes, have been haughty and ignorant contemners of letters; and this explains at once the low rank and high qualifications of the subordinate functionaries, whose qualifications *we* are certainly in no condition to dispense with, and are unwise to suffer dilettante educationists to tamper with, even for a moment. What is to become of the country if the subordinate functionaries be allowed to become as vaguely conversant with its intimate affairs as are now the superior functionaries?

† Risum teneatis, amici!

could not have had any other result than that of sending forth
a host of grandiloquent grumblers, as able to clamour as unable
to work. What has been taught them has as little reference to
the real work before the scholars when they set foot in the
world of business, to the living wants and affairs, public or
private, of the land they live in, as has the language in which
that teaching has been conveyed ; and we have in these
doings a fresh and glaring proof of the " inevitable tendency
of unvernacular media to divorce learning from utility." I
know nothing so like it as those contemporaneous Encyclopedic
labours which have reproduced for the benefit of India the
childish fables just exploded by the scholars of Europe ! ! Let
me add, I have no desire or purpose to speak harshly, but only
to impress the necessity for deliberately building on right
foundations. I honour all the labourers in the vineyard of
philanthropy. But the grand projects of Europeanising the
Indian mind, and of meeting the practical wants of this land
and day, by educational means, are, and will be, retarded, not
advanced, by misdirected unsystematised efforts. Considering
how little difference of opinion exists upon these points among
men of the highest experience in the interior, it has been
remarked to me with surprise how singular it is that Calcutta
has not yet begun to suspect the unsoundness of her favourite
educational maxims. But there is no room, alas ! for surprise,
nor much for blame ; and so long as *amour propre* holds its usual
sway in human affairs, so long will Calcutta be biassed against
every vernacular view of the education question, and in favour
of every English one : for at Calcutta the great body of influential men, influential from their stations, their talents, and their
knowledge, are, have been, and must continue to be, strangers
to India, and of course (like all human kind) inclined favour-
ably towards all such projects relating to the commonwealth
as may consist with their predominant weight of opinion and
judgment thereon, and by the same rule averse from all such
projects touching the commonwealth as may *not* consist
with that same predominant weight.—This is plain speaking :
but in a matter of such vast moment, I trust that it will be
pardoned and even profited by. Since this letter was commenced I have seen the last report of the Education Committee.

The President in Council is made to deplore the wretched state of vernacular education and to censure tartly its nominal controllers. But I would ask, Can a carriage go without wheels? Can a workman labour without tools? Can a work advance without workmen or tools? And if not, how can vernacular education advance without books, without teachers, and without any arrangement to furnish either, even prospectively? Yet it is now said that "the vernaculars are allowed a fair trial;" and I foresee it will ere long be said that "the trial has proved a failure." What is now doing is doing nearly in sheer waste, at the rate of 15,000 per annum. That sum, multiplied by the number of years since I backed a proposition of an institution that was to furnish a steady adequate supply of good books and good teachers with the tender of 35,000 Rs. raised by private subscription, would by this time have sufficed to place vernacular education, the one grand stay of a nation's intellectual life, upon an indestructible basis!

The English department of education has obtained a Normal School, that is the means of procuring abundance of good teachers, whilst abundance of good books were, from the circumstances of the case, priorly forthcoming in this department. On the other hand, the vernacular department is kept devoid of organised means of procuring either of these appliances of education. And yet it is clear to demonstration that in the former department there was *not* any indispensable necessity for creative machinery, since books and teachers were forthcoming without it, whilst in the latter department it is as clear that there *was* and *is* that indispensable necessity, since neither books nor teachers were, are, or can be, forthcoming without it. That is, where little or no need existed, much has been done; and where the utmost need, nothing! And, to cap the contrast, the former state of things respects the case of the comparatively able and greedy few, the latter, that of the wholly helpless many, among the objects of these partial proceedings!

Let me add, in conclusion, that in the above two historical examples it has been my more immediate object to show how *sincere* approvers of vernacularisation *proceed to effectuate it.* But the examples equally demonstrate the intrinsic value and power of vernacular media: and, if more historic illustration of the latter point be sought, it may be found in the diffusion of Buddhism in India, and in the character of Chinese, as compared with every other Asiatic, mental culture. Why are the Chinese so remarkable as a people for their good sense, and their Government for its stability, in the fantastic and mutable East? Because *their* knowledge, and *their* knowledge *only,* is vernacular! How did the Buddhists, despite the drawbacks of their mischievous monachism and their sceptical speculative principles, yet contrive to assail and carry the strongholds of Brahmanism, and for fifteen centuries to maintain the ground they had won—*the sole successful assailants of Hinduism to this hour !* Why, expressly by vernacularisation! by teaching and preaching in the vulgar tongues, and by opposing this method of indoctrination to the anti-vernacular instructions of their rivals! These are two remarkable instances of the power and value of living learning as opposed to dead, and, with the other two before cited, embrace the citation of the efficient cause of every great moral change and lasting benefit the East has known.—Yet this is the infant Hercules to which the Education Committee plays the part of the cruel stepmother.

B. H. HODGSON.

DARJEELING, " Friend of India," *March* 16, 1848.

LETTER VI.

VERNACULAR EDUCATION.

SIR,—I have read with attention your remarks upon the subject of education, as called forth by my letter to you which you published in your paper of the 16th instant. No one is better aware than yourself that all practical reforms of moment proceed on the *gutta cavat lapidem* principle. Wherefore I shall make no apology for recurring to this most important topic.

I am very anxious not to be misunderstood upon the point of education in the English language, to which you and others seem to fancy me entirely opposed. And yet so far is this from being the case, that I can as little sympathise as you can with any wish to abandon the support of English education "for those who are able to profit by it;" and I am surprised that you should have inferred anything to the contrary from my writings. Credit me, the only questions on which you and I are at issue, are, *Who* are those likely to profit by such studies? and *How* shall we enable them *really* to reap the benefit with due regard to the educational claims of the masses? For the rest, and speaking as an individual about what an individual may and can do in his own humble sphere in reference to the weal of millions, I beg leave to say distinctly that I have throughout my Indian career uniformly given all the support in my power to the study of English by all those who were *at all likely* to profit by it; that at Kathmandu I took ceaseless pains, for many years, to make two persons, selected by the Minister Bhim Sen for the purpose, competent English scholars, and to induce them to establish a school for the instruction of the sons of the Bharadars or chiefs; that Karbir Khatri, one of the two selected teachers, is yet forthcoming to bear witness by his attainments to the unwearied pains bestowed on him, though the political convulsions of Népál since my departure have had the necessary effect of closing his school; and, lastly, that though my employment as a diplomatic functionary in foreign realms necessarily restricted my exertions to promote the study of our language in the British territories, yet have I done whatever I could there also. Only so lately as last month I sent a present of books to the eldest son of the Rajah of Bettiah in testimony of my approbation of his continued application to English, according to my suggestion to him and his father in 1843. And I have always, where opportunity permitted, given similar advice and encouragement to our substantial Zamindars along the whole extended frontier of Népál. So much for acts. Then for writings; is not the practical result deduced from my reasonings the suggestion of an institution, all the professors and alumni of which are to be thorough English scholars, perpetually engaged, as teachers, translators, and transfusers, in works the whole conception and execution of which imply and exact a complete mastery of our language, and also an assiduous diffusion of its stores, directly and indirectly, according to the wants and demands of the country? This, sir, is very careful provision for profitable English studies — more careful and effective, too, than I can perceive in the present system! And such having been the tenor of my doings and sayings (I must crave pardon for such egotistic allusion to them), I think I may claim as clear an exemption as yourself from the absurd character of an exclusionist; and if any detached part of my writings, which extend over a period of fifteen years, seems to countenance such an imputation, you must remember, sir, that this vast topic has many parts and aspects; that I commenced this discussion in opposition to real and violent exclusives; * and that when a very undue bias has been laid on one side, the equilibrium cannot well be restored without some apparently undue weighting of the other scale. What I *first* complained of—and with reason, as you have often affirmed—was the proscription alike of the learning and of the living languages of the country. What I have *since* complained of, and still do— and again with reason, as you have often admitted and yet do —is a practical adherence to this same proscription, only veiled from scrutiny at present by various unfair devices, such as merely ostensible concessions, barren lip service, antagonistic projects pushed the length of virtual nullification of all things else, and, lastly, damning with faint praise. Is this exaggeration? Let us see. The system of education adverted to, is that dictated by authority and supported by the public funds. It is the only thing like national education which we possess, and it is uniformly styled *the* system of education of the country. Well! the country has some seventy millions of inhabitants; and, whilst nine-tenths of the whole educational funds derived from the seventy millions and designed for the seventy millions' benefit, are appropriated to the training of " 2000 actual, and 5000 prospective scholars " in the English department, the remaining fraction of those funds is all that is allotted to the countless host who are concerned solely with the efficiency of the vernacular department. The one hundred schools nominally

* Remember the denunciation of native literature in the "waste paper" edict, and of the living tongues, on all sorts of occasions, as being impracticably numerous and irredeemably inefficient—a style of talk which, by the way, still lingers in some places, and, it may be, in high ones, though no longer enunciated ex cathedra.

assigned to the vernacular department have necessarily, under such circumstances, been "starved to death;" and whilst additional funds were and are being constantly assigned to the English department, in order to give the highest perfection to its books and its teachers, the official controllers of the vernacular schools have been in vain reporting the utter and complete want of those indispensable appliances of education (teachers and books) in all our seminaries for the many. But this is not all; for, whilst the actual and necessary expenses of teaching in the English department are from ten to twenty times as great as in the other department, the injudicious selection and disposal of the recipients of this very costly training necessitate a total waste of the money in reference to "four-fifths" of those taught, because that large proportion of them does not, and cannot, acquire more than a "useless smattering which they can turn to no account." And all this, sir, has had and has place under the auspices of those who profess to have solely in view the fostering and founding of home-bred learning, "the formation of a vernacular literature," according to the memorable Report of 1837 ! ! ! I quote the very words of that Report, leaving the task of comment thereon to you. The above statistics, sir, are derived from yourself : they are also conformable to my own knowledge ; and with regard to the last important point, or the class of pupils in the English department, I say, let all such gentlemen as are now subject to the delusion that these pupils belong to the highest or to the central grade of native society, call for the muster rolls and interrogate the boys, when they will find that these boys, with hardly an exception, belong most distinctly to neither of those grades, and consequently are *not* amongst those whom the *decus et decorum* of English literature can for one moment be rationally supposed to befit. This is the reason why "four-fifths" (you should have said nine-tenths) of those who are instructed in English, are taught to no earthly purpose, are taught in sheer waste, though at such an extreme cost as to entail necessary helplessness in the vernacular department. And it is because there is nothing in the existing institutions or wants of native society at all in harmony with *such* attainments on the part of *such* persons, that the Education Committee have been driven, by the clamour of their *élèves*, to seek to thrust them all upon the Government, *lest they should starve!* In my last letter I have given my reasons for the opinion I entertain that this expedient—the last plank of Anglomania—will fail. I may now add that with its failure will come a material augmentation of that significant "discontent" which is certainly at present a far more palpable characteristic of Young Bengal, of the Chukerbutties, or Cameronians, as I hear the youths are now dubbed, than is any real tincture of the mind and heart of Europe on their part.

Else, what means the pitiful insincerity of the demonstrations they were lately led (unwisely led) to make in behalf of their most amiable and able, though on this point deluded, patrons? I note the hollowness of those demonstrations as one of the signs of the times! What, sir, say you to this sign? or to that other associated sign, to wit, the proven indifference of the native community, generally, for what they were asserted so authoritatively to take deep and real interest in, namely, the fashionable educational follies of the day?

I most earnestly desire to see the upper, wealthy, and influential classes of native society instructed in English: but those classes have not sent, nor are likely to send, *as you well know*, one single child to our schools; nor, if they did, could much be looked for from those "children of ease" in the way of such severe and abiding labours as can alone originate "the regenerating and elevating of the nation," though English may well serve to grace their rank, refine their taste, and facilitate their social intercourse with their masters.

Look to those whose names are now associated with the revival of letters in Europe, and you will find that the pioneers of knowledge in our quarter of the globe were all men of life-long devotion to incredible toils! Now, the more carefully I advert to the constitution and spirit of native society in India —and I have studied them for a quarter of a century—the deeper becomes my conviction, that this indispensable corps of pioneers will never pick up any effective recruits among the impatient class of paupers craving only for office, which singly and solely fills our English schools. From the same premises I deduce the further conclusions that men of a higher independent stamp will neither seek our schools, nor, if they did so, would they perform the required work. And thence, sir, I derive my general conception as to what English teaching is likely to prove profitable to the recipient or the public, as well as my special impression of the value of the corps above adverted to. But that corps must, according to the same premises, be raised, trained, recruited, equipped, and employed as a standing body, by ourselves, with enduring adherence to the lofty end in view, and in some such manner as I have indicated in my fourth letter, my object, as therein explained, being to reconcile the interests of deep lore (the implanting of a novel and healthful stock of learning) with the current claims of ordinary education, and to ensure satisfactory results by providing that both purposes shall be adequately and harmoniously worked out without waste. That you should have found anything savouring of the rejection of *profitable* English studies in that letter, I confess, surprises me not a little ; for my only rejection is of studies almost wholly profitless, yet eating up all our educational funds ! Nor less is my wonder that with such just ideas as you entertain of the greatness and difficulty of the objects aimed at, and of the consequent necessity there exists for a " Normal vernacular school, well-trained vernacular teachers, a vernacular library, —and a travelling inspector of vernacular seminaries "—you should have anything to object to my proposition : for, sir, in very truth, the desiderata you have enumerated (in the above quotation) comprise the substance of whatever I have contended for for years, or do now still contend for ! My proposition is only so far peculiar that it also involves the exposition of definite adequate means to the ends you insist upon, but insist with hardly admissible oblivion of that excessively wasteful antagonism inseparable from the dominant system, which, so long as that system stands on its present footing, must render all the professions of its partizans in favour of vernacularisation a delusion and a snare. All I say of instruction in English is, that its extreme costliness and no less extreme inappropriateness to ordinary uses, prescribe its employment at the public cost * in a special, instead of a general or pro-

---

* Observe the limitation, at the public cost. For the rest, if there be any real spontaneous demands for an education in "Shakespeare and Milton, Bacon and Newton," private schools of that stamp will flourish, and I heartily wish them

miscuous manner, as at present; and this, as well to ensure efficient or profitable study as to prevent such excessive waste of funds as has heretofore totally crippled, and must still do so, that sort of education which alone is suitable to ordinary wants and therefore primarily entitled to public support.

If, sir, you can persuade the Government to double or quadruple the funds appropriated to education, then I am content to see the present system in the English department "go hand in hand" with such a system in the vernacular department as you have sketched. But if you cannot so persuade the Government, then, sir, it behoves you to consider whether the existing *inevitable as total* sacrifice of the latter to the former, be defensible; for the two are demonstrably incompatible, without a vast addition to the funds now assigned to the promotion of education by the State. I, sir, expect no such addition; and as I know that under the existing constitution of native society men of rank and wealth will never send their children to our schools but abide by domestic education, whilst I feel convinced that in regard to the only sort of children frequenting our schools, so costly, difficult, and peculiar an education as that now in vogue, can neither yield its appropriate fruits in ripe maturity, nor yet find any adequate market for those fruits even if matured,* I would grant no such an education at the public cost to the promiscuous herd of comers, but only to such persons as would consent to thorough training and to the dedication of their rare attainments to the permanent service of the public as normal teachers and translators. Such, sir, is my proposition, and such the grounds of it.

B. H. HODGSON.

DARJEELING, *28th March* 1848.

<hr>

success. But their success is too problematical, their sphere of possible utility too restricted, and their necessary cost too enormous, to warrant the primary or general application of that system, at the public cost, to the necessary annihilation of all effective teaching in the only style suited to the ordinary wants of the people.

* On this point see above, p. 317, f., showing by comparison what means an effective demand for exotic learning.

LETTER VII.

SIR,—In your issue of the 28th ult., you have some observations on Mr. Hodgson's letters on education, in the general tenor of whose views you concur, but say that some of his doctrines are repugnant to your judgment. If, however, you will look more closely into the treatise, you will find that there is really no difference between you and it, for Mr. Hodgson not only does not eschew English, but purposes special and costly means for its cultivation. Mr. Hodgson distinguishes between education for the many—education in any ordinary sense, and all those subsidiary measures which, however connected with the general question as it occurs for consideration and decision in India, yet really belong rather to the literary than educational phase of the question. Mr. Hodgson desires to make ordinary education for the many efficient, and extraordinary education for the few no less efficient. He considers the English language and its higher literature to be fit only for the few, and that studies so difficult cannot possibly yield their appropriate fruit without adequate and special provision for their enduring and effective prosecution. But he holds that neither in the wants of native society nor in the resources at the disposal of our Government, is there anything like a foundation for such costly and enduring studies as the ordinary system of education; that therefore any *general* system for their prosecution must prove a failure, at the same time that it *absorbs all the funds that are available;* and he would therefore limit such studies, so far as they depend on public support, in such a way as to conform with existing wants and means; whilst whatever is learnt is learnt adequately, and these special studies of the few are made perpetually to minister to the universally allowed requirements of instruction for the many.

I think Mr. Hodgson is right in insisting that to create a fresh literary spirit in India requires a special body of pioneers of the new learning; and also that the improvement of the vernaculars is indispensable to the efficient working of the most ordinary system of vernacular education: inquire and you will find that vernacular education is languishing to death for want of books and teachers : inquire again and you will find that the Chakerbutty class of promiscuous smatterers in European languages and lore, neither do nor can make any efficient use of their acquirements. Now, Mr. Hodgson's plan ensures the steady prosecution of English studies to a point that will enable them to yield their appropriate fruit; and that fruit is to assume systematically a shape and flavour suited to the popular stomach. The lifelong teachers and translators—the pioneers of the new literature—are to be equally accomplished in our and their learning—are to study English throughout their learned lives—are to teach in English whenever required so to do—are to translate and transfuse from English whenever not employed in teaching; and thus, while their own adequate studies and teachings must tend effectively to the propagation of a knowledge so difficult as that of our language and literature, the people—the many—will be perpetually reaping all the advantage from such knowledge that they are now capable of; and in this way our noble language and literature will be gradually and surely worked more and more into the frame of the Indian mind. Mr. Hodgson contends only for *adequacy* of study and due regard to the *general* wants and means of *existing society.*—Yours, &c.,

VERNACULARIS.

February 10, 1848.

LETTER VIII.

VERNACULAR EDUCATION.

SIR,—I have attentively followed the course of your recent lucubrations on the education question, as afresh stirred by Mr. Hodgson's letters; and I should probably ere this have attempted a rejoinder had not your rather eccentric movements rendered the task difficult. To avoid labour in waste it seems indispensable to revert to the state of the question.

Now, sir, the subject of debate is at present, and has been for twelve years past, this—Is the existing exclusive patronage of English by the Education Committee, " with a view to the formation of a vernacular literature" (Report of 1836), wisely conceived and honestly worked out.? Or, does it sin against wisdom in origin and fair dealing in progress ? Such, I say, has been, and is, the state of the question ; and therefore you, who ridicule the very idea of the formation of a vernacular literature, are not precisely in a position to judge reasonably of the aptness or otherwise of those historical illustrations of Mr. Hodgson, which necessarily assume the question as it really is, and not as *you conceive* it is, or ought to be. This, sir, is a long-standing debate upon a most extensive topic ; and if, as would seem, the controversy be new to you, I would recommend your consulting Mr. Trevelyan's treatise or Mr. Macaulay's minute, in connection with the statistics and reports of the department, when I conjecture you may discover that Mr. Hodgson's array of facts and reasonings against the ruling system of education has a pertinency you are now little aware of. I say, sir, I so conjecture, and I will tell you why : because you have never approved Mr. Cameron's parting address to his alumni, nor yet, that Chakerbuttyism with which your city is plagued—said addresses being nothing but a *rifacimento* of the doctrines I have just referred you to, and said Chakerbuttyism nothing but the characteristic and inevitable result of those doctrines—doctrines to which, I need but add, Mr. Cameron has remorselessly sacrificed* any and every system of vernacular instruction, as well the system which you contend for, as that Mr. Hodgson has advocated !

You will observe, sir, that the Education Committee's end, and Mr. Hodgson's end, are one and the same ; viz., the formation of a vernacular literature, or the literary application of the spoken tongues of India to the substance of European knowledge. Now, this end may be wise or it may be foolish : you and I cannot discuss that point at present. But I think you must allow that, if the wisdom of the end be granted, the Committee's practical means of realising it are as unfit as Mr. Hodgson's are fit ! What can we reason but from what we know ? Well, we know by the uniform tenor of the Committee's doings for fifteen years past, that the vernaculars are utterly and hopelessly neglected, sacrificed to a vehement determination to push English

---

* Take a recent item as a sample of all ; establishment for normal teaching, English department 900 rupees ; vernacular department 50 rupees—that is, 18 to 1 against the latter.

all lengths and primarily. Thence Mr. Hodgson infers want of judgment and want of sincerity on the Committee's part; and his suggestion for the promotion of vernacularisation amounts to this, primary, direct, systematic, and adequate but *not exclusive* attention to the object professedly aimed at. And now, sir, if you revert to Mr. Hodgson's recent historical illustrations, you will find them, I think, sufficiently pertinent; for what are they? Four signal instances, drawn from Asiatic story, of the vigour and efficacy of living tongues, no more cultivated than those of modern India, as instruments for the successful diffusion of knowledge, two of the instances being, further, successful exemplifications on the largest scale of that very method of procedure in the effectuation of the object for which Mr. Hodgson contends! Now, sir, *quot homines tot sententiæ:* you and I and others may differ till doomsday as to the efficacy of transfused knowledge, as to the best method of transfusion, or as to the adequacy of the express channel or medium of transfusion in the given case. But, sir, it is because such differences of individual opinion on points so weighty are as inevitable as they are obstructive, that adequate precedents—prerogative instances, as Bacon would have called them, of the soundness of what an individual may urge, become so valuable: and where shall we find those over-ruling precedents save in history? And with all due submission I take leave to say that the diffusion of Buddhism throughout High Asia, and the stabilitation of Chinese dominion there, are, as stated by Mr. Hodgson, in all the recorded circumstances and results of either event, signal demonstrations both of the feasibility and of the desirableness of Mr. Hodgson's proposed means and end, in reference to the diffusion of European lore through the medium of the vulgar tongues of India. The historical illustrations, sir, are instances of direct, systematic, combined, and authoritative measures of vernacularisation, conducted by a body of men skilled thoroughly in the transfusing and transfused media, commenced by that most admirable step, the fixation of the true equivalency of the leading and essential terms,* and completed and applied over vast realms with perfect success. Now, Mr.

---

* If you will refer to the reports of the Delhi and Benares Colleges, you will fin t specific lament over the perpetual obstructions caused by the want of these glossaries of primary equivalents.

Hodgson had priorly contended for directness, system, combination, and authoritative support and sanction in this very way, as essential to the success of vernacularisation ; had denounced the total absence of every one of these characteristics in the Committee's plan of vernacularisation, as inevitably nullificatory of the alleged end : and depend upon it, sir, you must resort to some one of your own hypotheses, damnatory of *that end*, ere you can blemish the pertinency of Mr. Hodgson's historical proofs ; for proofs they are, and not merely illustrations ; and when I add that they likewise furnish the strongest presumptions against one and all of your hypotheses, I but state without exaggeration the full force and effect of the two historical facts more specially rested on. Those hypotheses of yours are, that translated knowledge is valueless, and that the spoken tongues of India from their feebleness and plurality are impracticable media for the communication of the knowledge of Europe. I will not irk you by further insisting upon the demonstration involved in the historical instances, all the four, of the fallacy of both your assumptions. I will, instead thereof, refer you to the opinions and the practices of the most eminent men in the educational department—the workmen, I mean, not the talkers—beyond the ditch ; and I answer you, without fear of refutation that the Reports and the works of the Principals of the Benares, Delhi, and (I think also) Dacca Colleges gainsay your assertions— one and the other of them—with all the irresistible authority of ample direct experience supported by correspondent realising labours. These most able men, equally familiar with Western and Eastern learning, whilst they contend for systematic improvement of the vernaculars considered as organs of European knowledge, uphold by word and deed their improvability to any needful extent ; Dr. Ballantyne expressly arguing that " he who cannot convey a European idea through the vernaculars, in conjunction with their founts, may very well suspect that he himself possesses only the shadow, not the substance, of such idea," and all three agreeing that for every practical purpose there are throughout the vast Bengal Presidency but three* vulgar tongues. What say you, sir, to such opinions of such men as

---

* Each of these languages is spoken by a population far more numerous than that using English in Britain ! What is your answer to this fact ?

Drs. Ballantyne and Sprenger? And with regard to the innumer able tongues you are fain to talk of—fifty to wit—how comes it that you are insensible to the broad fact that whilst the adminis- trations of justice, revenue, and police are avowedly vernacular, only three tongues are used in our courts? Wherefore, then, more in our schools? In a word, sir, if you can spare time to look into the whole matter a little more calmly and clearly, I feel convinced you will not again consent to re-echo the old exploded cry of the Anglomaniacs against *all sorts* of vernacular instruction—yours alike and Mr. Hodgson's—to wit, that the living tongues of the people are so numerous and so feeble as to be presently and prospectively unavailable.

I proceed now briefly to notice one or two heresies more peculiarly your own. You insist that learning for the masses ought to be confined to the merest elements of knowledge, con- veyed in the unaltered spoken tongues of those masses; and you instance the example of England—of Europe—in support of this notable maxim. But, sir, you are therein citing an exemplar really and deplorably irrelevant, as, without more recon- dite research, you may satisfy yourself by turning to the " Edin- burgh Review," No. 174, Article 10, and to the " Westminster," No. 95, Article 8, or to the " Calcutta Review," No. 16, p. 303 *et seq.* Your notion that the unimproved language of the masses can be employed at all for educational purposes is a fallacy of which you will be aware if you reflect that the most imperfect colloquial medium (even that of brutes) may very well serve for its customary colloquial ends, and yet prove totally unequal to a new end, such as education, according to any sane concep- tion of it, is and must be. And, accordingly, whilst the opinion and the practice of all the enlightened parts of Europe are daily becoming more decided and consentaneous as to the indispensable necessity of education for the masses of a sort very superior to what you insist is enough, the novel extended measures of popular education now rapidly bringing into operation in Switzerland, England, Holland, Prussia, and Scot- land, are expressly based upon the *proven worthlessness* of sheer elements, attempted to be communicated, as of old, through so utterly inadequate a medium as the unfashioned speech of the many.

Of all this you will find abundant and various confirmation in the recent educational doings of Europe, as cited and referred to in the periodicals above-named ; and I think, sir, you will be a little startled to find, upon perusal of the articles specified, that you have recklessly put forth an educational dogma upon alleged European warranty than which none is more utterly and expressly repudiated by all the best and latest words and deeds of Europe ! "A total reform" of that old apparatus of popular teaching to which you cling is there "imperatively called for;" and in the recent "Peoples' Colleges" at Sheffield and at Birmingham we have ("Westminster," No. 95, p. 437, 8) express samples of that sort of education for the *working classes* which is now deemed to be alone efficacious for them ; and so deemed all over enlightened Europe, as you may learn from Cousin's Reports.

Your notion, however, of elemental education for the masses seems rather vague; for you now insist that it should be limited to "sheer reading, writing, and accounts," and anon you require that the masses aforesaid should be instructed "how best to turn their time and talents to account in industrial pursuits and mechanical arts," and that they should also "be made acquainted with the history of their own country." I agree with you in these latter conceptions, so far as they go. But I ask you, sir, whether such ends can by possibility be achieved or attempted in the unfashioned colloquials of the vulgar ? And, again, whether the attainment of the former end does not most expressly imply and exact, not only cultivation of the Indian vernaculars, but the conveyance into them by translation and transfusion of European knowledge ?

You cannot, I should say, avoid answering these questions so as to make you well nigh a convert to Mr. Hodgson's plan of vernacularisation ; for where, save in the stores of European knowledge, will you find any portion of that lore which turns the peasant into a Briareus, the craftsman into a magician, the trader into an instrument of Providence for the practical diffusion of "peace and good-will upon earth," and the farmer into a servant and interpreter of Nature, performing miracles of production merely by right interpretation of her occult signs ? I love to dwell upon this special phase of a vast topic, and with reference to it I pray you to observe, that in order to render this fine country capable of supporting full and adequate European administration (it is now not half administered) we *must* call forth the industrial energies of the people; that beyond doubt we can do so only by communicating largely and freely the substance of our special and recent knowledge; * that that communication can be effected solely through the ready and familiar channel of the native languages, duly improved and systematically applied to that object; and that the substance of all our really useful and indisputable knowledge *can* be most efficiently conveyed to the masses through that channel! You speak, sir, as if *all* translation must prove "useless, impossible, mischievous:" and yet you are a Protestant Christian, knowing what the translation of the Bible has done!—and yet you are a scholar who cannot have failed to learn that "in the consentaneous judgment of the highest minds of Europe the vernacularisation of learning did more there in disabusing the general intellect of the prejudices of existing institutions and opinions, than all the rest of the glorious events and discoveries of that age which witnessed it, including among those events the invention of printing!"—and yet you are a gentleman of the press, and by the special power of the instrument you daily wield should be prepared to recognise the *perfectly analogous* diffusive vigour of vernacularisation! Why, then, write and speak in the style and spirit of 150 years back, as if all these things were beyond your ken? and as if that sound knowledge, which is the common product and inheritance of all the race of man,† were inseparably connected with this or that particular language? Why, sir, I have but to raise my head from the paper I am now driving my quill over to see opposite me on the shelves of a moderate library fifty books of History, Political Economy, Literature, Philosophy and Science, so translated that their whole treasures of original knowledge are completely secured in the traduction, one-half of them, moreover, preserving unimpaired all the manner as well as matter of the originals! E grege, Sabine's Cosmos, of which the second part has just reached me. There

---

* To wit, the economic applications of chemistry and of mechanics to agriculture, and to the useful arts of primary importance.

† See the splendid concluding paragraphs of Cosmos, vol. 1.

are even some in which the redacteur has been a vast improver, as Dumont's Bentham.   Your objections to translations, sir, have no semblance of validity save in the departments of poetry and oratory; and in those departments you overlook the unquestionable fact that the very same causes which make translations inefficient, debar the foreigner equally almost from adequate appreciation of the original!   Your Chakerbutties and their proners may hold forth, as they will, touching the beauties of Shakespeare and Milton, Burke and Fox and Sheridan.   But unless the greatest critics of poetry and of oratory be dolts, said Chakerbutties are, after all, mere "learned pigs" in such matters; because the soul of eloquence in verse or prose is autocthonous, is so much bound up with the peculiar domestic, social, and political institutions and habits of each land, with its traditional glories and its infantine associations and myths, that a Hindu can scarcely more really appreciate the English masters of song and of oratory in our tongue than he could in his own!   Thus, you perceive, sir, that your objection to translations in general, deduced from the worthlessness of translations in the Homeric and Demosthenian departments of human knowledge, is every way inadmissible, not being really sound even in the special view, and having little or no relevancy in a general view.

But sound knowledge, sir, *generally speaking*, is so far from being "cribbed, cabined, and confined" to the lingual organ which first happened to enshrine it, that nearly every month's mail brings us translations, little, if at all, inferior to the originals, whether those originals be German, Italian, or French. Now, sir, the mere fact that such works are constantly coming to us under the sanction of the highest names, and are in daily profitable use amongst us, is a sufficient answer to your general doctrine of the uselessness of "second-hand works;"*

* In reference to this superficial dogma of pedagogues and pedants, let me beg your attention to the justly world-renowned apophthegm of Hobbes, "Words are the counters of wise men and the money of fools." It may be safely said that he who has a correct notion of the real nature and function of all language will not allow his efforts for the national diffusion of the benefits of knowledge to be impeded by such pedantic hypercriticisms.   Leave them, sir, I pray, to the Anglomaniacs, and when they next dun their nonsense in your ears, ask them if those historical works which are now commanding the best attention of themselves and their countrymen be not simply "second-hand" Niebuhrs, and Rankes, and Michelets, and Thiers, and Lamartines, and Guizots, and Thierries?   And civilly entreat them for a response!

whilst in reply to your incautious reiteration of the Anglomaniac cry against the communication of the same benefits to our sable brethren through their tongues, I can only state that it has been proved, over and over again, by sound induction from philosophy and history, by recent facts, by cogent arguments and by express experiments, that the substance of all really useful English lore *can* be conveyed into the spoken tongues of India with perfect success, provided only that the known and demonstrated conditions of such success be not neglected. —Yours, &c., VERNACULARIS.

March 30, 1848.

APPENDIX.

PROPOSAL OF A NORMAL VERNACULAR COLLEGE FOR SCHOOL-MASTERS AND TRANSLATORS.

IT is believed that very many of the best friends of the cause of education in India, who ardently seek India's regeneration through European knowledge, are yet satisfied that all sound effective national instruction must be conveyed by and through the living languages of the people; that those languages in India—a country so anciently and eminently literary—cannot be and are not inadequate to the communication of European knowledge; and, lastly, that however ardent our zeal in this cause, we must be convinced we cannot *directly* provide for the mental wants of a population so vastly numerous as that of India. From the above simple premises, when viewed in connection with the wonders achieved lately in Europe by the regular *teaching of teachers*, results very obviously the course we should adopt for the educational regeneration of India. Let us not meddle directly with the education of the people in their own tongues; but let us establish an institution having for its object systematically and adequately to furnish the *means* of such education, to provide a *succession of good vernacular books and good vernacular teachers.*

Give to incipient education in European lore in India these

appliances, and that lore cannot fail to take root and flourish, naturally and wholesomely in this soil: withhold these appliances from such education, and it can never so take root and flourish, but will prove a sickly and unwholesome exotic.

Let us then have a school of indigenation—a school to *make all other schools succeed*—a school to furnish good books and good teachers in the living tongues of the people—a school to rear translators, who by staying within its walls, and schoolmasters, who by going abroad, shall together give a solid and safe *beginning* to the Europeanisation of India.

Good books and good teachers! are you not assured that these are what we want; well, then, let us bend our efforts, firstly and chiefly, to their attainment by founding the Normal Institution I have spoken of, and the plan of which may be easily settled by and by in Committee. Meanwhile let us manifest our sincerity and earnestness by coming forward with the requisite funds, and be assured, my friends, that we have but to show the way in order soon to behold it crowded with followers, wondering that these things had never before occurred to them.

PRINTED BY BALLANTYNE, HANSON AND CO
EDINBURGH AND LONDON

LINGUISTIC PUBLICATIONS

OF

TRÜBNER & CO.,

57 AND 59, LUDGATE HILL, LONDON, E.C.

Adi Granth (The); OR, THE HOLY SCRIPTURES OF THE SIKHS, translated from the original Gurmukhī, with Introductory Essays, by Dr. ERNEST TRUMPP, Professor Regius of Oriental Languages at the University of Munich, etc. Roy. 8vo. cloth, pp. 866. £2 12s. 6d.

Ahlwardt.—THE DÍVÁNS OF THE SIX ANCIENT ARABIC POETS, Ennábiga, 'Antara, Tarafa, Zuhair, 'Algama, and Imruolgais; chiefly according to the MSS. of Paris, Gotha, and Leyden, and the collection of their Fragments: with a complete list of the various readings of the Text. Edited by W. AHLWARDT, 8vo. pp. xxx. 340, sewed. 1870. 12s.

Aitareya Brahmanam of the Rig Veda. 2 vols. See under HAUG.

Alabaster.—THE WHEEL OF THE LAW: Buddhism illustrated from Siamese Sources by the Modern Buddhist, a Life of Buddha, and an account of H.M. Consulate-General in Siam; M.R.A.S. Demy 8vo. pp. lviii. and 324. 1871. 14s.

Alif Lailat wa Lailat.—THE ARABIAN NIGHTS. 4 vols. 4to. pp. 495, 493, 442, 434. Cairo, A.H. 1279 (1862). £3 3s.
This celebrated Edition of the Arabian Nights is now, for the first time, offered at a price which makes it accessible to Scholars of limited means.

Amberley.—AN ANALYSIS OF RELIGIOUS BELIEF. By VISCOUNT AMBERLEY. 2 vols. 8vo. cl., pp. xvi. 496 and 512. 1876. 30s.

American Oriental Society, Transactions of. Subscription, £1 5s. per volume.

Andrews.—A DICTIONARY OF THE HAWAIIAN LANGUAGE, to which is appended an English-Hawaiian Vocabulary, and a Chronological Table of Remarkable Events. By LORRIN ANDREWS. 8vo. pp. 560, cloth. £1 11s. 6d.

Anthropological Institute of Great Britain and Ireland (The Journal of the). Published Quarterly.
Vol I., No. 1. January–July, 1871. 8vo. pp. 120–clix, sewed. Illustrated with 11 full page Plates, and numerous Woodcuts; and accompanied by several folding plates of Tables, etc. 7s.
Vol. I., No. 2. October, 1871. 8vo. pp. 121–264, sewed. 4s.
Vol. I., No. 3. January, 1872. 8vo. pp. 265–427, sewed. 16 full-page Plates. 4s.
Vol. II., No. 1. April, 1872. 8vo. pp. 136, sewed. Eight two-page plates and two four-page plates. 4s.
Vol. II., No. 2. July and Oct , 1872. 8vo. pp. 137–312. 9 plates and a map. 6s.
Vol. II., No. 3. January, 1873. 8vo pp. 143. With 4 plates. 4s.
Vol. III., No. 1. April, 1873. 8vo. pp. 136. With 8 plates and two maps. 4s.
Vol. III., No. 2. July and October, 1873. 8vo. pp. 168, sewed. With 9 plates. 4s.
Vol. III., No. 3. January, 1874. 8vo. pp. 238, sewed. With 8 plates, etc. 6s.
Vol. IV., No. 1. April and July, 1874. 8vo. pp. 308, sewed. With 22 plates. 8s.
Vol. IV., No. 2. April, 1875. 8vo. pp. 200, sewed. With 11 plates. 6s.
Vol. V., No. 1. July, 1875. 8vo. pp. 120, sewed. With 3 plates. 4s.
Vol. V., No. 2. October, 1875. 8vo. pp. 132, sewed. With 8 plates. 4s.
Vol. V., No. 3. January, 1876. 8vo. pp. 156, sewed. With 8 plates. 5s.
Vol. V., No, 4. April, 1876. 8vo. pp. 128, sewed. With 2 plates. 5s.

Anthropological Institute—*continued.*
Vol. VI., No. 1.   July, 1876.   8vo. pp. 100, sewed.   With 5 plates.   5s.
Vol. VI., No. 2.   October, 1876.   8vo. pp. 98, sewed.   With 4 plates and a map.
   5s.
Vol. VI., No. 3.   January, 1877.   8vo. pp. 146, sewed.   With 11 plates.   5s.
Vol. VI., No. 4.   May, 1877.   8vo. pp. iv. and 184, sewed.   With 7 plates.   5s.
Vol. VII., No. 1.   August 1877.   8vo. pp. 116, sewed.   With three plates.   5s.
Vol. VII., No. 2.   November, 1877.   8vo. pp. 84, sewed.   With one plate.   5s.
Vol., VII., No. 3.   February, 1878.   8vo. pp. 193, sewed.   With three plates.   5s.
Vol. VII., No. 4.   May, 1878.   8vo. pp. iv. and 158, sewed.   With nine plates.   5s.
Vol. VIII, No. 1.   August, 1878.   8vo. pp. 103, sewed.   With one plate.   5s.
Vol. VIII., No. 2.   November, 1878.   8vo. pp. 126, sewed.   With three plates.   5s.

Apastambíya Dharma Sutram.—Aphorisms of the Sacred Laws of
   the Hindus, by Apastamba. Edited, with a Translation and Notes, by G. Bühler.
   By order of the Government of Bombay.   2 parts.   8vo. cloth, 1868–71.
   £1 4s. 6d.

Arabic and Persian Books (A Catalogue of).   Printed in the East.
   Constantly for sale by Trübner and Co., 57 and 59, Ludgate Hill, London.
   16mo. pp. 46, sewed.   1s.

Archæological Survey of India.—See under Burgess and Cunningham.

Arden.—A Progressive Grammar of the Telugu Language, with
   Copious Examples and Exercises. In Three Parts. Part I. Introduction.—
   On the Alphabet and Orthography.—Outline Grammar, and Model Sentences.
   Part II. A Complete Grammar of the Colloquial Dialect.   Part III. On the
   Grammatical Dialect used in Books.   By A. H. Arden, M.A., Missionary of
   the C. M. S. Masulipatam.   8vo. sewed, pp. xiv. and 380.   14s.

Arnold.—The Iliad and Odyssey of India.   By Edwin Arnold,
   M.A., C.S.I., F.R.G.S., etc.   Fcap. 8vo. sd., pp. 24.   1s.

Arnold.—The Indian Song of Songs.   From the Sanskrit of the Gita
   Govinda of Jayadeva.   By Edwin Arnold, M.A., C.S.I., F.R.G.S. (of
   University College, Oxford), formerly Principal of Poona College, and Fellow
   of the University of Bombay.   Cr. 8vo. cl., pp. xvi. and 144.   1875.   5s.

Arnold.—A Simple Transliteral Grammar of the Turkish Language.
   Compiled from various sources.   With Dialogues and Vocabulary.   By Edwin
   Arnold, M.A., C.S.I., F.R.G.S.   Pott 8vo. cloth, pp. 80.   2s. 6d.

Asher.—On the Study of Modern Languages in General, and of the
   English Language in particular.   An Essay.   By David Asher, Ph.D.   12mo.
   pp. viii. and 80, cloth.   2s.

Asiatic Society.—Journal of the Royal Asiatic Society of Great
   Britain and Ireland, from the Commencement to 1863.   First Series, complete in 20 Vols. 8vo., with many Plates.   Price £10; or, in Single Numbers,
   as follows:—Nos. 1 to 14, 6s. each; No. 15, 2 Parts, 4s. each; No. 16, 2 Parts,
   4s. each; No. 17, 2 Parts, 4s. each , No. 18, 6s.   These 18 Numbers form
   Vols. 1. to IX.—Vol. X., Part 1, op.; Part 2, 5s.; Part 3, 5s.—Vol. XI.,
   Part 1, 6s.; Part 2 not published.—Vol. XII., 2 Parts, 6s. each —Vol. XIII.,
   2 Parts, 6s. each.—Vol. XIV., Part 1, 5s.; Part 2 not published.—Vol. XV.,
   Part 1, 6s.; Part 2, with 3 Maps, £2 2s.—Vol. XVI., 2 Parts, 6s. each.—Vol.
   XVII., 2 Parts, 6s. each.—Vol. XVIII., 2 Parts, 6s. each.—Vol. XIX., Parts 1
   to 4, 16s.—Vol. XX., Parts 1 and 2, 4s. each.   Part 3, 7s. 6d.

Asiatic Society.—Journal of the Royal Asiatic Society of Great
   Britain and Ireland.   *New Series.*   Vol. I.   In Two Parts.   pp. iv. and
   490, sewed.   1861–5.   16s.
   Contents—1. Vajra-chhediká, the "Kin Kong King," or Diamond Sútra. Translated from
   the Chinese by the Rev. S. Beal, Chaplain, R.N.—II. The Páramitá-hridaya Sútra, or, in Chinese,
   " Mo ho-pó-ye-po-lo-mih-to-sin-king," *i.e.* "The Great Páramitá Heart Sútra." Translated

from the Chinese by the Rev. S. Beal, Chaplain, R.N.—III. On the Preservation of National Literature in the East. By Colonel F. J. Goldsmid.—IV. On the Agricultural, Commercial, Financial, and Military Statistics of Ceylon. By E. R. Power, Esq.—V. Contributions to a Knowledge of the Vedic Theogony and Mythology. By J. Muir, D.C.L., LL.D.—VI. A Tabular List of Original Works and Translations, published by the late Dutch Government of Ceylon at their Printing Press at Colombo. Compiled by Mr. Mat. P. J. Ondaatje, of Colombo.—VII Assyrian and Hebrew Chronology compared, with a view of showing the extent to which the Hebrew Chronology of Ussher must be modified, in conformity with the Assyrian Canon. By J. W. Bosanquet, Esq.—VIII. On the existing Dictionaries of the Malay Language. By Dr. H. N. van der Tuuk.—IX. Bilingual Readings: Cuneiform and Phœnician. Notes on some Tablets in the British Museum, containing Bilingual Legends (Assyrian and Phœnician). By Major-General Sir H. Rawlinson, K.C.B., Director R.A.S.—X. Translations of Three Copper-plate Inscriptions of the Fourth Century A.D., and Notices of the Chálukya and Gurjjara Dynasties By Professor J. Dowson, Staff College, Sandhurst.—XI. Yama and the Doctrine of a Future Life, according to the Rig-Yajur-, and Atharva-Vedas. By J. Muir, Esq., D.C.L., LL.D.—XII. On the Jyotisha Observation of the Place of the Colures, and the Date derivable from it. By William D. Whitney, Esq., Professor of Sanskrit in Yale College, New Haven, U.S.—Note on the preceding Article. By Sir Edward Colebrooke, Bart., M.P., President R.A.S.—XIII. Progress of the Vedic Religion towards Abstract Conceptions of the Deity. By J. Muir, Esq., D.C.L., LL.D.—XIV. Brief Notes on the Age and Authenticity of the Work of Aryabhata, Varáhamihira, Brahmagupta, Bhattotpala, and Bháskaráchárya. By Dr. Bháu Dájí, Honorary Member R.A.S.—XV. Outlines of a Grammar of the Malagasy Language. By H. N. Van der Tuuk.—XVI. On the Identity of Xandrames and Krananda. By Edward Thomas, Esq.

Vol. II. In Two Parts. pp. 522, sewed. 1866-7. 16s.

CONTENTS.—I. Contributions to a Knowledge of Vedic Theogony and Mythology. No. 2. By J. Muir, Esq. —II. Miscellaneous Hymns from the Rig- and Atharva-Vedas. By J. Muir, Esq.—III. Five hundred questions on the Social Condition of the Natives of Bengal. By the Rev. J. Long.—IV. Short account of the Malay Manuscripts belonging to the Royal Asiatic Society. By Dr. H. N. van der Tuuk.—V. Translation of the Amitábha Sûtra from the Chinese. By the Rev. S. Beal, Chaplain Royal Navy.—VI. The initial coinage of Bengal. By Edward Thomas, Esq.—VII. Specimens of an Assyrian Dictionary. By Edwin Norris, Esq.—VIII. On the Relations of the Priests to the other classes of Indian Society in the Vedic age By J. Muir, Esq.—IX. On the Interpretation of the Veda. By the same.—X. An attempt to Translate from the Chinese a work known as the Confessional Services of the great compassionate Kwan Yin, possessing 1000 hands and 1000 eyes. By the Rev. S. Beal, Chaplain Royal Navy. —XI. The Hymns of the Gaupáyanas and the Legend of King Asamâti. By Professor Max Müller, M.A., Honorary Member Royal Asiatic Society.—XII. Specimen Chapters of an Assyrian Grammar. By the Rev. E. Hincks, D.D., Honorary Member Royal Asiatic Society.

Vol. III. In Two Parts. pp. 516, sewed. With Photograph. 1868. 22s.

CONTENTS.—I. Contributions towards a Glossary of the Assyrian Language. By H. F. Talbot. —II. Remarks on the Indo-Chinese Alphabets. By Dr. A. Bastian.—III. The poetry of Mohamed Rabadan, Arragonese. By the Hon. H. E. J. Stanley.—IV. Catalogue of the Oriental Manuscripts in the Library of King's College, Cambridge. By Edward Henry Palmer, B.A , Scholar of St. John's College, Cambridge ; Member of the Royal Asiatic Society , Membre de la Société Asiatique de Paris.—V. Description of the Amravati Tope in Guntur. By J. Fergusson, Esq., F.R.S.—VI. Remarks on Prof. Brockhaus' edition of the Kathásarit-ságara, Lambaka IX. XVIII. By Dr. H. Kern, Professor of Sanskrit in the University of Leyden.—VII. The source of Colebrooke's Essay "On the Duties of a Faithful Hindu Widow." By Fitzedward Hall, Esq., M.A., D.C.L. Oxon. Supplement : Further detail of proofs that Colebrooke's Essay, "On the Duties of a Faithful Hindu Widow," was not indebted to the Vivádabhangárnava. By Fitzedward Hall, Esq.—VIII. The Sixth Hymn of the First Book of the Rig Veda. By Professor Max Müller, M.A. Hon. M.R.A.S.—IX. Sassanian Inscriptions. By E. Thomas, Esq.—X. Account of an Embassy from Morocco to Spain in 1690 and 1691. By the Hon. H. E. J. Stanley.— XI. The Poetry of Mohamed Rabadan, of Arragon. By the Hon. H. E. J. Stanley.—XII. Materials for the History of India for the Six Hundred Years of Mohammadan rule, previous to the Foundation of the British Indian Empire. By Major W. Nassau Lees, LL.D., Ph.D.—XIII. A Few Words concerning the Hill people inhabiting the Forests of the Cochin State. By Captain G. E. Fryer, Madras Staff Corps, M.R.A.S.- XIV. Notes on the Bhojpurí Dialect of Hindí, spoken in Western Behar. By John Beames, Esq., B.C.S., Magistrate of Chumparun.

Vol. IV. In Two Parts. pp. 521, sewed. 1869-70. 16s.

CONTENTS.—I. Contribution towards a Glossary of the Assyrian Language. By H. F. Talbot. Part II.—II. On Indian Chronology. By J. Fergusson, Esq., F.R.S.—III. The Poetry of Mohamed Rabadan of Arragon. By the Hon. H. E. J. Stanley.—IV. On the Magar Language of Nepal. By John Beames, Esq., B.C.S.—V. Contributions to the Knowledge of Parsee Literature. By Edward Sachau, Ph.D.—VI. Illustrations of the Lamaïst System in Tibet, drawn from Chinese Sources. By Wm. Frederick Mayers, Esq., of H.B.M. Consular Service, China.— VII. Khuddaka Pátha, a Páli Text, with a Translation and Notes. By R. C. Childers, late of the Ceylon Civil Service.— VIII. An Endeavour to elucidate Rashíduddín's Geographical Notices of India. By Col. H. Yule, C.B.— IX. Sassanian Inscriptions explained by the Pahlaví of the Pársis. By E. W. West, Esq.—X. Some Account of the Senbyú Pagoda at Mengún, near the Burmese Capital, in a Memorandum by Capt. E. H Sladan, Political Agent at Mandalé ; with Remarks on the Subject by Col Henry Yule, C.B.— XI. The Brhat-Sanhitá ; or, Complete System of Natural Astrology of Varáha-Mihira. Translated from Sanskrit into English by Dr. H. Kern.—XII. The Mohammedan Law of Evidence, and its influence on the Administration of

Justice in India. By N. B. E. Baillie, Esq.—XIII. The Mohammedan Law of Evidence in connection with the Administration of Justice to Foreigners. By N. B. E. Baillie, Esq.—XIV. A Translation of a Bactrian Páli Inscription. By Prof. J. Dowson.—XV. Indo-Parthian Coins By E. Thomas, Esq.

Vol. V. In Two Parts. pp. 463, sewed. With 10 full-page and folding Plates. 1871-2. 18s. 6d.

CONTENTS.—I. Two Játakas. The original Páli Text, with an English Translation. By V. Fausböll.—II. On an Ancient Buddhist Inscription at Keu-yung kwan, in North China. By A. Wylie.—III. The Brhat Sanhitâ; or, Complete System of Natural Astrology of Varâha-Mihira Translated from Sanskrit into English by Dr. H. Kern.—IV. The Pongol Festival in Southern India. By Charles E. Gover.—V. The Poetry of Mohamed Rabadan, of Arragon. By the Right Hon. Lord Stanley of Alderley.—VI. Essay on the Creed and Customs of the Jangams. By Charles P. Brown.—VII. On Malabar, Coromandel, Quilon, etc. By C. P. Brown.—VIII. On the Treatment of the Nexus in the Neo-Aryan Languages of India. By John Beames, B.C.S.—IX. Some Remarks on the Great Tope at Sânchi. By the Rev. S. Beal.—X. Ancient Inscriptions from Mathura. Translated by Professor J. Dowson.—Note to the Mathura Inscriptions. By Major-General A. Cunningham.—XI. Specimen of a Translation of the Adi Granth. By Dr. Ernest Trumpp.—XII. Notes on Dhammapada, with Special Reference to the Question of Nirvâna. By R. C. Childers, late of the Ceylon Civil Service.—XIII. The Brhat-Sanhitâ; or, Complete System of Natural Astrology of Varâha-mihira. Translated from Sanskrit into English by Dr. H. Kern.—XIV. On the Origin of the Buddhist Arthakathâs. By the Mudliar L. Comrilla Vijasinha, Government Interpreter to the Ratnapura Court, Ceylon. With an Introduction by R. C. Childers, late of the Ceylon Civil Service.—XV. The Poetry of Mohamed Rabadan, of Arragon. By the Right Hon. Lord Stanley of Alderley. -XVI. Proverbia Communia Syriaca. By Captain R. F. Burton. XVII. Notes on an Ancient Indian Vase, with an Account of the Engraving thereupon. By Charles Horne, M.R.A.S., late of the Bengal Civil Service.—XVIII. The Bhar Tribe. By the Rev. M. A. Sherring, LL.D , Benares. Communicated by C. Horne, M.R.A.S., late B.C.S.—XIX. Of *Jihad* in Mohammedan Law, and its application to British India. By N. B. E. Baillie.—XX. Comments on Recent Pehlvi Decipherments. With an Incidental Sketch of the Derivation of Aryan Alphabets. And Contributions to the Early History and Geography of Tabaristán. Illustrated by Coins. By E. Thomas, F.R.S.

Vol. VI., Part I, pp. 212, sewed, with two plates and a map. 1872. 8s.

CONTENTS.—The Ishmaelites, and the Arabic Tribes who Conquered their Country. By A. Sprenger.—A Brief Account of Four Arabic Works on the History and Geography of Arabia. By Captain S. B. Miles.—On the Methods of Disposing of the Dead at Llassa, Thibet, etc. By Charles Horne, late B.C.S. The Brhat-Sanhitâ; or, Complete System of Natural Astrology of Varâha-mihira, Translated from Sanskrit into English by Dr. H. Kern.—Notes on Hwen Thsang's Account of the Principalities of Tokháristán, in which some Previous Geographical Identifications are Reconsidered. By Colonel Yule, C.B.—The Campaign of Ælius Gallus in Arabia. By A. Sprenger.—An Account of Jerusalem, Translated from the late Sir H. M. Elliott from the Persian Text of Násir ibn Khusrú's Safanámah by the late Major A. R. Fuller.—The Poetry of Mohamed Rabadan, of Arragon. By the Right Hon. Lord Stanley of Alderley.

Vol. VI., Part II., pp. 213 to 400 and lxxxiv., sewed. Illustrated with a Map, Plates, and Woodcuts. 1873. 8s.

CONTENTS.- On Hiouen-Thsang's Journey from Patna to Ballabhi. By James Fergusson, D.C.L., F.R.S.- Northern Buddhism. [Note from Colonel H. Yule, addressed to the Secretary.] —Hwen Thsang's Account of the Principalities of Tokháristán, etc. By Colonel H. Yule, C.B.— The Brhat-Sanhitâ; or, Complete System of Natural Astrology of Varâha-mihira. Translated from Sanskrit into English by Dr. H. Kern.—The Initial Coinage of Bengal, under the Early Muhammadan Conquerors. Part II. Embracing the preliminary period between A.H. 614-634 (A.D. 1217-1236-7). By Edward Thomas, F.R.S.—The Legend of Dipaṅkara Buddha. Translated from the Chinese (and intended to illustrate Plates xxix. and L., 'Tree and Serpent Worship'). By S. Beal.—Note on Art. IX., antè pp. 213-274 on Hiouen-Thsang's Journey from Patna to Ballabhi. By James Fergusson D.C.L., F.R.S.—Contributions towards a Glossary of the Assyrian Language. By H. F. Talbot.

Vol. VII., Part I., pp. 170 and 24, sewed. With a plate. 1874. 8s.

CONTENTS.—The *Upasampadâ-Kammavâcâ*, being the Buddhist Manual of the Form and Manner of Ordering of Priests and Deacons. The Páli Text, with a Translation and Notes. By J. F. Dickson, B.A., sometime Student of Christ Church, Oxford, now of the Ceylon Civil Service.—Notes on the Megalithic Monuments of the Coimbatore District, Madras. By M. J. Walhouse, late Madras C.S.—Notes on the Sinhalese Language. No. 1. On the Formation of the Plural of Neuter Nouns. By R. C. Childers, late of the Ceylon Civil Service.—The Páli Text of the *Mahâparinibbâna Sutta* and Commentary, with a Translation. By R. C. Childers, late of the Ceylon Civil Service —The Brihat-Sanhitâ; or, Complete System of Natural Astrology of Varâha-mihira. Translated from Sanskrit into English by Dr. H. Kern.—Note on the Valley of Choombi. By Dr. A. Campbell, late Superintendent of Darjeeling.—The Name of the Twelfth Imám on the Coinage of Egypt. By H. Sauvaire and Stanley Lane Poole.—Three Inscriptions of Parákrama Bâhu the Great from Pula-tipura, Ceylon (date circa 1180 A.D.). By T. W. Rhys Davids.—Of the Kharáj or Muhammadan Land Tax; its Application to British India, and Effect on the Tenure of Land. By N. B. E. Baillie.—Appendix: A Specimen of a Syriac Version of the Kalîlah wa-Dimnah, with an English Translation. By W. Wright.

Vol. VII., Part II., pp. 191 to 394, sewed. With seven plates and a map. 1875. 8s.

CONTENTS.—Sigiri, the Lion Rock, near Pulastipura, Ceylon; and the Thirty-ninth Chapter of the Mahâvamsa. By T. W. Rhys Davids.—The Northern Frontagers of China. Part I. The Origines of the Mongols. By H. H. Howorth.—Inedited Arabic Coins. By Stanley Lane Poole.—Notice on the Dinârs of the Abbasside Dynasty. By Edward Thomas Rogers.—The Northern Frontagers of China. Part II. The Origines of the Manchus. By H. H. Howorth.—Notes on the Old Mongolian Capital of Shangtu. By S. W. Bushell, B.Sc., M.D.—Oriental Proverbs in their Relations to Folklore, History, Sociology; with Suggestions for their Collection, Interpretation, Publication. By the Rev. J. Long.—Two Old Simhalese Inscriptions. The Sahasa Malla Inscription, date 1200 A D., and the Ruwanwæli Dagaba Inscription, date 1191 A.D. Text, Translation, and Notes. By T. W. Rhys Davids.—Notes on a Bactrian Pali Inscription and the Samvat Era. By Prof. J. Dowson.—Note on a Jade Drinking Vessel of the Emperor Jahângîr. By Edward Thomas, F.R.S.

Vol. VIII., Part I., pp. 156, sewed, with three plates and a plan. 1876. 8s.

CONTENTS.— Catalogue of Buddhist Sanskrit Manuscripts in the Possession of the Royal Asiatic Society (Hodgson Collection). By Professors E. B. Cowell and J. Eggeling.—On the Ruins of Sigiri in Ceylon. By T. H. Blakesley, Esq., Public Works Department, Ceylon.—The Pâtimokkha, being the Buddhist Office of the Confession of Priests. The Pali Text, with a Translation, and Notes. By J. F. Dickson, M.A., sometime Student of Christ Church, Oxford, now of the Ceylon Civil Service.—Notes on the Sinhalese Language. No. 2. Proofs of the Sanskritic Origin of Sinhalese. By R. C. Childers, late of the Ceylon Civil Service.

Vol. VIII., Part II., pp. 157-308, sewed. 1876. 8s.

CONTENTS.—An Account of the Island of Bali. By R. Friederich.—The Pali Text of the Mahâparinibbâna Sutta and Commentary, with a Translation. By R C. Childers, late of the Ceylon Civil Service.—The Northern Frontagers of China. Part III. The Kara Khitai. By H. H. Howorth.—Inedited Arabic Coins. II. By Stanley Lane Poole.—On the Form of Government under the Native Sovereigns of Ceylon. By A. de Silva Ekanáyaka, Mudaliyar of the Department of Public Instruction, Ceylon.

Vol. IX., Part I., pp. 156, sewed, with a plate. 1877. 8s.

CONTENTS.—Bactrian Coins and Indian Dates. By E. Thomas, F.R.S.—The Tenses of the Assyrian Verb. By the Rev. A. H Sayce, M.A.—An Account of the Island of Bali. By R. Friederich (continued from Vol. VIII. N.S. p. 218).—On Ruins in Makran. By Major Mockler. —Inedited Arabic Coins. III. By Stanley Lane Poole.—Further Note on a Bactrian Pali Inscription and the Samvat Era. By Prof. J. Dowson.—Notes on Persian Belûchistan. From the Persian of Mirza Mehdy Khân. By A. H. Schindler.

Vol IX., Part II., pp. 292, sewed, with three plates. 1877. 10s. 6d.

CONTENTS.—The Early Faith of Asoka. By E. Thomas, F.R.S.—The Northern Frontagers of China. Part II. The Manchus (Supplementary Notice). By H. H. Howorth.—The Northern Frontagers of China. Part IV. The Kin or Golden Tatars. By H. H. Howorth.—On a Treatise on Weights and Measures by Eliyá, Archbishop of Nisîbîn. By M. H. Sauvaire.—On Imperial and other Titles. By Sir T. E. Colebrooke, Bart., M.P.—Affinities of the Dialects of the Chepang and Kusundah Tribes of Nipál with those of the Hill Tribes of Arracan. By Captain C. J. F. Forbes F.R.G.S., M.A.S. Bengal, etc.—Notes on Some Antiquities found in a Mound near Damghan. By A. H. Schindler.

Vol. X., Part I., pp. 156, sewed, with two plates and a map. 1878. 8s.

CONTENTS.—On the Non-Aryan Languages of India. By E. L. Brandreth, Esq.—A Dialogue on the Vedantic Conception of Brahma. By Pramadá Dása Mittra, late Officiating Professor of Anglo-Sanskrit, Government College, Benares.—An Account of the Island of Bali. By R. Friederich (continued from Vol. IX. N. S. p. 120).—Unpublished Glass Weights and Measures. By Edward Thomas Rogers.—China viâ Tibet. By S. C. Boulger.—Notes and Recollections on Tea Cultivation in Kumaon and Garhwâl. By J. H. Batten, F.R.G.S., Bengal Civil Service Retired, formerly Commissioner of Kumaon.

Vol. X., Part II., pp. 146, sewed. 1878. 6s.

CONTENTS.—Note on Pliny's Geography of the East Coast of Arabia. By Major-General S. B. Miles, Bombay Staff Corps. The Maldive Islands; with a Vocabulary taken from François Pyrard de Laval, 1602—1607. By A. Gray, late of the Ceylon Civil Service.—On Tibeto-Burman Languages. By Captain C, J. F. S. Forbes, of the Burmese Civil Service Commission.—Burmese Transliteration. By H. L. St. Barbe, Esq., Resident at Mandelay.—On the Connexion of the Môns of Pegu with the Koles of Central India. By Captain C. J, F. S. Forbes, of the Burmese Civil Commission.—Studies on the Comparative Grammar of the Semitic Languages, with Special Reference to Assyrian. By Paul Haupt. The Oldest Semitic Verb-Form.—Arab Metrology. II. El Djabarty. By M. H. Sauvaire.—The Migrations and Early History of the White Huns; principally from Chinese Sources. By Thomas W. Kingsmill.

Vol. X., Part III., pp. 204, sewed. 1878. 8s.

CONTENTS.—On the Hill Canton of Sálár.—the most Easterly Settlement of the Turk Race. By Robert B. Shaw. Geological Notes on the River Indus By Griffin W. Vyse, B.A., M.R.A.S., etc., Executive Engineer P.W.D. Panjab.—Educational Literature for Japanese Women. By Basil Hall Chamberlain, Esq., M.R.A.S.—On the Natural Phenomenon Known in the East by the Names Sub-hi-Kâzib, etc., etc. By J. W. Redhouse, M.R.A.S., Hon. Memb. R.S.L.—On a Chinese Version of the Sânkhya Kârikâ, etc., found among the Buddhist Books comprising the Tripitaka and two other works. By the Rev. Samuel Beal, M.A.—The Rock-cut Phrygian Inscriptions at Doganlu. By Edward Thomas, F.R.S.—Index.

Vol. XI., Part. I., pp. 128, sewed. 5s.

CONTENTS.—On the Position of Women in the East in the Olden Time. By Edward Thomas, F.R.S.—Notice of the Scholars who have Contributed to the Extension of our Knowledge of the Languages of British India during the last Thirty Years. By Robert N. Cust, Hon. Librarian R.A.S.—Ancient Arabic Poetry: its Genuineness and Authenticity. By Sir William Muir, K.C.S.I., LL.D.—Note on Manrique's Mission and the Catholics in the time of Shâh Jahân. By H. G. Keene, Esq.—On Sandhi in Pali. By the late R. C. Childers.—On Arabic Amulets and Mottoes. By E. T. Rogers, M.R.A.S.

Asiatic Society.—TRANSACTIONS OF THE ROYAL ASIATIC SOCIETY OF GREAT BRITAIN AND IRELAND. Complete in 3 vols. 4to., 80 Plates of Fac-similes, etc., cloth. London, 1827 to 1835. Published at £9 5s.; reduced to £5 5s.

The above contains contributions by Professor Wilson, G. C. Haughton, Davis, Morrison, Colebrooke, Humboldt, Dorn, Grotefend, and other eminent Oriental scholars.

Asiatic Society of Bengal.—JOURNAL OF THE ASIATIC SOCIETY OF BENGAL. Edited by the Honorary Secretaries. 8vo. 8 numbers per annum, 4s. each number.

Asiatic Society of Bengal.—PROCEEDINGS OF THE ASIATIC SOCIETY OF BENGAL. Published Monthly. 1s. each number.

Asiatic Society.—THE JOURNAL OF THE BOMBAY BRANCH OF THE ROYAL ASIATIC SOCIETY. Edited by the Secretary. Nos. 1 to 35. 7s. 6d. to 10s. 6d. each number.

Asiatic Society.—JOURNAL OF THE CEYLON BRANCH OF THE ROYAL ASIATIC SOCIETY. 8vo. Published irregularly. 7s. 6d. each part.

Asiatic Society of Japan.—TRANSACTIONS OF THE ASIATIC SOCIETY OF JAPAN. Vol. I. From 30th October, 1872, to 9th October, 1873. 8vo. pp. 110, with plates. 1874. Vol. II. From 22nd October, 1873, to 15th July, 1874. 8vo. pp. 249. 1874. Vol. III. Part I. From 16th July, 1874, to December, 1874, 1875. Vol. III. Part II. From 13th January, 1875, to 30th June, 1875. Vol. IV. From 20th October, 1875, to 12th July, 1876. Each Part 7s. 6d.

Asiatic Society.—JOURNAL OF THE NORTH CHINA BRANCH OF THE ROYAL ASIATIC SOCIETY. New Series. Parts 1 to 11.

Aston.—A GRAMMAR OF THE JAPANESE WRITTEN LANGUAGE. By W. G. ASTON, M.A., Assistant Japanese Secretary, H B.M.'s Legation, Yedo, Japan. Second edition, Enlarged and Improved. Royal 8vo. pp. 306. 28s.

Aston.—A SHORT GRAMMAR OF THE JAPANESE SPOKEN LANGUAGE. By W. G. ASTON, M.A., H. B. M.'s Legation, Yedo, Japan. Third edition. 12mo. cloth, pp. 96. 12s.

Athar-ul-Adhâr—TRACES OF CENTURIES; or, Geographical and Historical Arabic Dictionary, by SELIM KHURI and SELIM SH-HADE. Geographical Parts I. to IV., Historical Parts I. and II. 4to. pp. 788 and 384. Price 7s. 6d. each part.   [*In course of publication.*

Atharva Veda Prátiçákhya.—See under WHITNEY.

Auctores Sanscriti. Edited for the Sanskrit Text Society, under the supervision of THEODOR GOLDSTÜCKER. Vol. I., containing the Jaiminiya-Nyâya-Mâlâ-Vistara. Parts I. to VII., pp. 582, large 4to. sewed. 10s. each part. Complete in one vol , cloth, £3 13s. 6d. Vol. II. The Institutes of Gautama. Edited with an Index of Words, by A. F. STENZLER, Ph.D., Professor of Oriental Languages in the University of Breslau. 8vo. cloth, pp. iv. 78. 4s. 6d. Vol. III. Vaitâna Sûtra. The Ritual of the Atharva Veda. Edited with Critical Notes and Indices, by DR. RICHARD GARBE. 8vo. sewed, pp. 119. 5s.

Axon.—THE LITERATURE OF THE LANCASHIRE DIALECT. A Bibliographical Essay. By WILLIAM E. A. AXON, F.R.S.L. Fcap. 8vo. sewed.
1870. 1s.

Baba.—AN ELEMENTARY GRAMMAR OF THE JAPANESE LANGUAGE, with
Easy Progressive Exercises. By TATUI BABA. Crown 8vo. cloth, pp. xii. and
92. 5s.

Bachmaier.—PASIGRAPHICAL DICTIONARY AND GRAMMAR. By ANTON
BACHMAIER, President of the Central Pasigraphical Society at Munich. 18mo.
cloth, pp. viii.; 26; 160. 1870. 3s.

Bachmaier.—PASIGRAPHISCHES WÖRTERBUCH ZUM GEBRAUCHE FÜR DIE
DEUTSCHE SPRACHE. Verfasst von ANTON BACHMAIER, Vorsitzendem des
Central-Vereins für Pasigraphie in München. 18mo. cloth, pp. viii.; 32; 128;
120. 1870. 2s. 6d

Bachmaier.—DICTIONNAIRE PASIGRAPHIQUE, PRÉCÉDÉ DE LA GRAMMAIRE.
Redigé par ANTOINE BACHMAIER, Président de la Société Centrale de Pasigraphie à Munich. 18mo. cloth, pp. vi. 26; 168; 150. 1870. 2s. 6d.

Baldwin.—A MANUAL OF THE FOOCHOW DIALECT. By Rev. C. C.
BALDWIN, of the American Board Mission. 8vo. pp. viii.–256. 18s.

Balfour.—WAIFS AND STRAYS FROM THE FAR EAST; being a Series of
Disconnected Essays on Matters relating to China. By FREDERIC HENRY
BALFOUR. 1 vol. demy 8vo. cloth, pp. 224. 10s. 6d.

Ballad Society (The).—Subscription—Small paper, one guinea, and
large paper, three guineas, per annum. List of publications
on application.

Ballantyne.—A GRAMMAR OF THE MAHRATTA LANGUAGE. For the
use of the East India College at Haileybury. By JAMES R. BALLANTYNE, of
the Scottish Naval and Military Academy. 4to. cloth, pp. 56. 5s.

Ballantyne.—ELEMENTS OF HINDÍ AND BRAJ BHÁKÁ GRAMMAR. By the
late JAMES R. BALLANTYNE, LL.D. Second edition, revised and corrected
Crown 8vo., pp. 44, cloth. 5s.

Ballantyne.—FIRST LESSONS IN SANSKRIT GRAMMAR; together with an
Introduction to the Hitopadésa. Second edition. Second Impression. By
JAMES R. BALLANTYNE, LL.D., Librarian of the India Office. 8vo. pp. viii.
and 110, cloth. 1873. 3s. 6d.

Ballantyne.—HINDUSTANI SELECTIONS IN THE NASKHI AND DEVANAGARI
Character. With a Vocabulary of the Words. Prepared for the use of the
Scottish Naval and Military Academy, by JAMES R. BALLANTYNE. Royal 8vo.
cloth, pp. 74. 3s. 6d.

Ballantyne.—PRINCIPLES OF PERSIAN CALIGRAPHY, illustrated by
Lithographic Plates of the TA"LIK characters, the one usually employed in
writing the Persian and the Hindūstānī. Second edition. Prepared for the
use of the Scottish Naval and Military Academy, by JAMES R. BALLANTYNE.
4to. cloth, pp. 14, 6 plates. 2s. 6d.

Banerjea.—THE ARIAN WITNESS, or the Testimony of Arian Scriptures
in corroboration of Biblical History and the Rudiments of Christian Doctrine.
Including Dissertations on the Original Home and Early Adventures of Indo-
Arians. By the Rev. K. M. BANERJEA. 8vo. sewed, pp. xviii. and 236. 8s. 6d.

Bate.—A DICTIONARY OF THE HINDEE LANGUAGE. Compiled by J.
D. BATE. 8vo. cloth, pp. 806. £2 12s. 6d.

Beal.—TRAVELS OF FAH HIAN AND SUNG-YUN, Buddhist Pilgrims
from China to India (400 A.D. and 518 A.D.) Translated from the Chinese,
by S. BEAL (B.A. Trinity College, Cambridge), a Chaplain in Her Majesty's
Fleet, a Member of the Royal Asiatic Society, and Author of a Translation of
the Pratimóksha and the Amithába Sútra from the Chinese. Crown 8vo. pp.
lxxiii. and 210, cloth, ornamental, with a coloured map. 10s. 6d.

Beal.—A CATENA OF BUDDHIST SCRIPTURES FROM THE CHINESE. By S. BEAL, B.A., Trinity College, Cambridge; a Chaplain in Her Majesty's Fleet, etc. 8vo. cloth, pp. xiv. and 436. 1871. 15s.

Beal.—THE ROMANTIC LEGEND OF SÁKHYA BUDDHA. From the Chinese-Sanscrit by the Rev. SAMUEL BEAL, Author of "Buddhist Pilgrims," etc. Crown 8vo. cloth, pp. 400. 1875. 12s.

Beal.—THE BUDDHIST TRIPITAKA, as it is known in China and Japan. A Catalogue and Compendious Report. By SAMUEL BEAL, B.A. Folio, sewed, pp. 117. 7s. 6d.

Beal.—TEXTS FROM THE BUDDHIST CANON, commonly known as DHAMMAPADA. Translated from the Chinese by S. BEAL, B.A., Professor of Chinese, University of London. With accompanying Narrative. Post 8vo. pp. viii. and 176, cloth. 7s. 6d.

Beames.—OUTLINES OF INDIAN PHILOLOGY. With a Map, showing the Distribution of the Indian Languages. By JOHN BEAMES. Second enlarged and revised edition. Crown 8vo. cloth, pp. viii. and 96. 5s.

Beames.—NOTES ON THE BHOJPURI DIALECT OF HINDÍ, spoken in Western Behar. By JOHN BEAMES, Esq., B.C.S., Magistrate of Chumparun. 8vo. pp. 26, sewed. 1868. 1s. 6d.

Beames.—A COMPARATIVE GRAMMAR OF THE MODERN ARYAN LANGUAGES OF INDIA (to wit), Hindi, Panjabi, Sindhi, Gujarati, Marathi, Uriya, and Bengali. By JOHN BEAMES, Bengal C.S., M.R.A.S., &c.
Vol. I. On Sounds. 8vo. cloth, pp. xvi and 360. 16s.
Vol. II. The Noun and the Pronoun. 8vo. cloth, pp. xii. and 348. 16s.
Vol III. The Verb. 8vo. cloth, pp. xii. and 316.   [*Just ready.*

Bede.—VENERABILIS BEDÆ HISTORIA ECCLESIASTICA GENTIS ANGLORUM. Ad Fidem Codd. MSS. recensuit JOSEPHUS STEVENSON. With plan of the English Historical Society, by the late John Miller. 8v. pp. xxxv., xxi. and 424, and 2 facsimiles. 7s. 6d.
The same, in royal 8vo., uniform with the publications of the Master of the Rolls. 10s. 6d.

Bellairs.—A GRAMMAR OF THE MARATHI LANGUAGE. By H. S. K. BELLAIRS, M.A., and LAXMAN Y. ASHKEDKAR, B.A. 12mo. cloth, pp. 90. 5s.

Bellew.—A DICTIONARY OF THE PUKKHTO, OR PUKSHTO LANGUAGE, on a New and Improved System. With a reversed Part, or English and Pukkhto, By H. W. BELLEW, Assistant Surgeon, Bengal Army. Super Royal 8vo. pp. xii. and 356, cloth. 42s.

Bellew.—A GRAMMAR OF THE PUKKHTO OR PUKSHTO LANGUAGE, on a New and Improved System. Combining Brevity with Utility, and Illustrated by Exercises and Dialogues. By H. W. BELLEW, Assistant Surgeon, Bengal Army. Super-royal 8vo., pp. xii. and 156, cloth. 21s.

Bellew.—FROM THE INDUS TO THE TIGRIS: a Narrative of a Journey through the Countries of Balochistan, Afghanistan, Khorassan, and Iran, in 1872; together with a Synoptical Grammar and Vocabulary of the Brahoe Language, and a Record of the Meteorological Observations and Altitudes on the March from the Indus to the Tigris. By H. W. BELLEW, C.S.I., Surgeon Bengal Staff Corps, Author of "A Journal of a Mission to Afghanistan in 1857-58," and "A Grammar and Dictionary of the Pukkhto Language." Demy 8vo. cloth. 14s.

Bellew.—KASHMIR AND KASHGHAR. A Narrative of the Journey of the Embassy to Kashghar in 1873-74. By H. W. BELLEW, C.S.I. Demy 8vo. cl., pp. xxxii. and 420. 16s.

Bellows.—ENGLISH OUTLINE VOCABULARY, for the use of Students of the Chinese, Japanese, and other Languages. Arranged by JOHN BELLOWS. With Notes on the writing of Chinese with Roman Letters. By Professor SUMMERS, King's College, London. Crown 8vo., pp. 6 and 368, cloth. 6s.

Bellows.—OUTLINE DICTIONARY, FOR THE USE OF MISSIONARIES, Explorers, and Students of Language. By MAX MÜLLER, M.A., Taylorian Professor in the University of Oxford. With an Introduction on the proper use of the ordinary English Alphabet in transcribing Foreign Languages. The Vocabulary compiled by JOHN BELLOWS. Crown 8vo. Limp morocco, pp. xxxi. and 368. 7s. 6d.

Bellows.—DICTIONARY FOR THE POCKET, French and English, English and French. Both Divisions on same page. By JOHN BELLOWS. Masculine and Feminine Words shown by Distinguishing Types. Conjugations of all the Verbs; Liaison marked in French Part, and Hints to aid Pronunciation. Together with Tables and Maps. Revised by ALEXANDRE BELJAME, M.A., and Fellow of the University, Paris. Second Edition. 32mo. roan, with tuck, gilt edges. 10s. 6d. Persian, 10s. 6d. Morocco, 12s. 6d.

Benfey.—A GRAMMAR OF THE LANGUAGE OF THE VEDAS. By Dr. THEODOR BENFEY. In 1 vol. 8vo., of about 650 pages.   [*In preparation.*

Benfey.—A PRACTICAL GRAMMAR OF THE SANSKRIT LANGUAGE, for the use of Early Students. By THEODOR BENFEY, Professor of Sanskrit in the University of Göttingen. Second, revised and enlarged, edition. Royal 8vo. pp. viii. and 296, cloth. 10s. 6d.

Benfey.—VEDICA UND VERWANDTES. Von THEODOR BENFEY. Cr. 8vo. 7s. 6d.

Beschi.—CLAVIS HUMANIORUM LITTERARUM SUBLIMIORIS TAMULICI IDIO-MATIS. Auctore R. P. CONSTANTIO JOSEPHO BESCHIO, Soc. Jesu, in Madurensi Regno Missionario. Edited by the Rev. K. IHLEFELD, and printed for A. Burnell, Esq., Tranquebar. 8vo. sewed, pp. 171. 10s. 6d.

Beveridge.—THE DISTRICT OF BAKARGANJ; its History and Statistics. By H. BEVERIDGE, B.C.S. 8vo. cloth, pp. xx. and 460. 21s.

Bhagavat-Geeta.—See under WILKINS.

Bibliotheca Indica. A Collection of Oriental Works published by the Asiatic Society of Bengal. Old Series. Fasc. 1 to 235. New Series. Fasc. 1 to 408. (Special List of Contents to be had on application.) Each Fsc in 8vo., 2s.; in 4to., 4s.

Bibliotheca Orientalis: or, a Complete List of Books, Pamphlets, Essays, and Journals, published in France, Germany, England, and the Colonies, on the History and the Geography, the Religions, the Antiquities, Literature, and Languages of the East. Edited by CHARLES FRIEDERICI. Part I., 1876, sewed, pp. 86, 2s. 6d. Part II., 1877, sewed, pp. 100, 2s. 6d.

Bibliotheca Sanskrita.—See TRÜBNER.

Bickell.—OUTLINES OF HEBREW GRAMMAR. By GUSTAVUS BICKELL, D.D. Revised by the Author; Annotated by the Translator, SAMUEL IVES CURTISS, junior, Ph.D. With a Lithographic Table of Semitic Characters by Dr. J. EUTING. Cr. 8vo. sd., pp. xiv. and 140. 1877. 3s. 6d.

Bigandet.—THE LIFE OR LEGEND OF GAUDAMA, the Buddha of the Burmese, with Annotations. The ways to Neibban, and Notice on the Phongyies, or Burmese Monks. By the Right Reverend P. BIGANDET, Bishop of Ramatha, Vicar Apostolic of Ava and Pegu. 8vo. pp. xi., 538, and v. £1 11s. 6d.

Bleek.—A COMPARATIVE GRAMMAR OF SOUTH AFRICAN LANGUAGES. By W. H. I. BLEEK, Ph.D. Volume I. I. Phonology. II. The Concord. Section 1. The Noun. 8vo. pp. xxxvi. and 322, cloth. £1 16s.

Bleek.—A BRIEF ACCOUNT OF BUSHMAN FOLK LORE AND OTHER TEXTS. By W. H. I. BLEEK, Ph.D., etc., etc. Folio sd., pp. 21. 1875. 2s. 6d.

Bleek.—REYNARD IN SOUTH AFRICA; or, Hottentot Fables. Translated from the Original Manuscript in Sir George Grey's Library. By Dr. W. H. I. BLEEK, Librarian to the Grey Library, Cape Town, Cape of Good Hope. In one volume, small 8vo., pp. xxxi. and 94, cloth. 3s. 6d.

Blochmann.—THE PROSODY OF THE PERSIANS, according to Saifi, Jami, and other Writers. By H. BLOCHMANN, M.A. Assistant Professor, Calcutta Madrasah. 8vo. sewed, pp. 166. 10s. 6d.

Blochmann.—SCHOOL GEOGRAPHY OF INDIA AND BRITISH BURMAH. By H. BLOCHMANN, M.A. 12mo. pp. vi. and 100. 2s. 6d.

Blochmann.—A TREATISE ON THE RUBA'I entitled Risalah i Taranah. By AGHA AHMAD 'ALI. With an Introduction and Explanatory Notes, by H. BLOCHMANN, M.A. 8vo. sewed, pp. 11 and 17. 2s. 6d.

Blochmann.—THE PERSIAN METRES BY SAIFI, and a Treatise on Persian Rhyme by Jami. Edited in Persian, by H. BLOCHMANN, M.A. 8vo. sewed pp. 62. 3s. 6d.

Bombay Sanskrit Series. Edited under the superintendence of G. BÜHLER, Ph. D., Professor of Oriental Languages, Elphinstone College, and F. KIELHORN, Ph. D., Superintendent of Sanskrit Studies, Deccan College. 1868-70.

1. PANCHATANTRA IV. AND V. Edited, with Notes, by G. BÜHLER, Ph. D. Pp. 84, 16. 6s.

2. NÁGOJÍBHAṬṬA'S PARIBHÁSHENDUŚEKHARA. Edited and explained by F. KIELHORN, Ph. D. Part I., the Sanskrit Text and Various Readings. pp. 116. 10s. 6d.

3. PANCHATANTRA II. AND III. Edited, with Notes, by G. BÜHLER, Ph. D. Pp. 86, 14, 2. 7s. 6d.

4. PANCHATANTRA I. Edited, with Notes, by F. KIELHORN, Ph.D. Pp. 114, 53. 7s. 6d.

5. KÁLIDÁSA'S RAGHUVAṀSA. With the Commentary of Mallinátha. Edited, with Notes, by SHANKAR P. PAṆḌIT, M.A. Part I. Cantos I.-VI. 10s.6d.

6. KÁLIDÁSA'S MÁLAVIKÁGNIMITRA. Edited, with Notes, by SHANKAR P. PAṆḌIT, M.A. 10s. 6d.

7. NÁGOJÍBHAṬṬA'S PARIBHÁSHENDUŚEKHARA Edited and explained by F. KIELHORN, Ph.D. Part II. Translation and Notes. (Paribhâshâs, i.-xxxvii.) pp. 184. 10s. 6d.

8. KÁLIDÁSA'S RAGHUVAṀSA. With the Commentary of Mallinátha. Edited, with Notes, by SHANKAR P. PAṆḌIT, M.A. Part II. Cantos VII.-XIII. 10s. 6d.

9. NÁGOJÍBHAṬṬA'S PARIBHÁSHENDUṢEKHARA. Edited and explained by F. KIELHORN. Part II Translation and Notes. (Paribhâshâs xxxviii.-lxix.) 7s. 6d.

10. DANDIN'S DASAKUMARACHARITA. Edited with critical and explanatory Notes by G. Bühler. Part I. 7s. 6d.

11. BHARTRIHARI'S NITISATAKA AND VAIRAGYASATAKA, with Extracts from Two Sanskrit Commentaries. Edited, with Notes, by KASINATH T. TELANG. 9s.

12. NAGOJIBHATTA'S PARIBHÁSHENDUSEKHARA. Edited and explained by F. KIELHORN. Part II. Translation and Notes. (Paribhâshâs lxx.-cxxii.) 7s. 6d.

13. KALIDASA'S RAGHUVAṀSA, with the Commentary of Mallinátha. Edited, with Notes, by SHANKAR P. PAṆḌIT. Part III. Cantos XIV.-XIX. 10s. 6d.

14. VIKRAMÂNKADEVACHARITA. Edited, with an Introduction, by G. BÜHLER. 7s. 6d.

15. BHAVABHÚTI'S MÁLATÎ-MÁDHAVA. With the Commentary of Jagaddhara, edited by RAMKRISHNA GOPAL BHANDARKAR. 14s.

Borooah.—A Practical English-Sanskrit Dictionary. By Anundoram Borooah, B.A., B.C.S., of the Middle Temple, Barrister-at-Law. Vol. I. A to Falseness. pp. xx.–580–10. £1 11s. 6d.

Borooah.—A Companion to the Sanskrit-Reading Undergraduates of the Calcutta University, being a few notes on the Sanskrit Texts selected for examination, and their Commentaries. By Anundoram Borooah. 8vo. pp. 64. 3s. 6d.

Borooah.—Bhavabhuti and his Place in Sanskrit Literature. By Anundoram Borooah. 8vo. sewed, pp. 70. 5s.

Bottrell.—Traditions and Hearthside Stories of West Cornwall. By W. Bottrell (an old Celt). Demy 12mo. pp. vi. 292, cloth. 1870. Scarce.

Bottrell.—Traditions and Hearthside Stories of West Cornwall. By William Bottrell. With Illustrations by Mr. Joseph Blight. Second Series. Crown 8vo. cloth, pp. iv. and 300. 6s.

Bowditch.—Suffolk Surnames. By N. I. Bowditch. Third Edition, 8vo. pp. xxvi. and 758, cloth. 7s. 6d.

Bretschneider. — On the Knowledge Possessed by the Ancient Chinese of the Arabs and Arabian Colonies, and other Western Countries mentioned in Chinese Books. By E. Bretschneider, M.D., Physician of the Russian Legation at Peking. 8vo. pp. 28, sewed. 1871. 1s.

Bretschneider.—Notes on Chinese Mediæval Travellers to the West. By E. Bretschneider, M.D. Demy 8vo. sd., pp. 130. 5s.

Bretschneider. — Archæological and Historical Researches on Peking and its Environs. By E. Bretschneider, M.D., Physician to the Russian Legation at Peking. Imp. 8vo. sewed, pp. 64, with 4 Maps. 5s.

Bretschneider.—Notices of the Mediæval Geography and History of Central and Western Asia. Drawn from Chinese and Mongol Writings, and Compared with the Observations of Western Authors in the Middle Ages. By E. Bretschneider, M.D. 8vo. sewed, pp. 233, with two Maps. 12s. 6d.

Brhat-Sanhita (The).—See under Kern.

Brinton. — The Myths of the New World. A Treatise on the Symbolism and Mythology of the Red Race of America. By Daniel G. Brinton, A.M., M.D. Second Edition, revised. Cr. 8vo. cloth, pp. viii. and 331. 12s. 6d.

British Museum.—Catalogue of Sanskrit and Pali Books in the British Museum. By Dr Ernst Haas. Printed by permission of the Trustees of the British Museum. 4to pp. viii. and 188, boards. £1 1s.

British Museum Publications (List of) on Sale by Trübner & Co. [On application.

British Archæological Association (Journal of The). Volumes 1 to 31, 1844 to 1876, £1 11s. 6d. each. General Index to vols. 1 to 30. 8vo. cloth. 15s. Parts Quarterly, 8s. each.

Brockie.—Indian Philosophy. Introductory Paper. By William Brockie, Author of "A Day in the Land of Scott," etc., etc. 8vo. pp. 26, sewed. 1872. 6d.

Bronson.—A Dictionary in Assamese and English. Compiled by M. Bronson, American Baptist Missionary. 8vo. calf, pp. viii. and 609. £2 2s.

Brown.—The Dervishes; or, Oriental Spiritualism. By John P. Brown, Secretary and Dragoman of the Legation of the United States of America at Constantinople. With twenty-four Illustrations. 8vo. cloth, pp. viii. and 415. 14s.

Brown.—Sanskrit Prosody and Numerical Symbols Explained. By Charles Philip Brown, Author of the Telugu Dictionary, Grammar, etc., Professor of Telugu in the University of London. Demy 8vo. pp. 64, cloth. 3s. 6d.

Bühler.—Eleven Land-Grants of the Chaulukyas of Aṇhilvâḍ.
A Contribution to the History of Gujarât. By G. Bühler. 16mo. sewed,
pp. 126, with Facsimile. 3s. 6d.

Bühler.—Three New Edicts of Aśoka. By G. Bühler. 16mo.
sewed, with Two Facsimiles. 2s. 6d.

Burgess.—Archæological Survey of Western India. Vol. 1. Report
of the First Season's Operations in the Belgâm and Kaladgi Districts. Jan. to
May, 1874. By James Burgess. With 56 photographs and lith. plates.
Royal 4to. pp. viii. and 45. £2 2s.
Vol. 2. Report of the Second Season's Operations. Report on the Antiquities of
Kâthiâwâd and Kachh. 1874–5. By James Burgess, F.R.G.S., M.R.A.S., etc.
With Map, Inscriptions, Photographs, etc. Roy. 4to. half bound, pp. x. and
242. £3 3s.
Vol. 3. Report of the Third Season's Operations. 1875–76. Report on the
Antiquities in the Bidar and Aurangabad District. Royal 4to. half bound
pp. viii. and 138, with 66 photographic and lithographic plates. £2 2s.

Burnell.—Catalogue of a Collection of Sanskrit Manuscripts. By
A. C. Burnell, M.R.A.S., Madras Civil Service. Part 1. Vedic Manuscripts.
Fcap. 8vo. pp. 64, sewed. 1870. 2s.

Burnell.—Dayadaçaçloki. Ten Slokas in Sanskrit, with English
Translation. By A. C. Burnell. 8vo. pp. 11. 2s.

Burnell.—Elements of South Indian Palæography. From the
Fourth to the Seventeenth Century a.d. By A. C. Burnell. Second Corrected
and Enlarged Edition, 34 Plates and Map, in One Vol. 4to. pp. xiv.-148.
£2 12s. 6d.

Burnell.—On the Aindra School of Sanskrit Grammarians. Their
Place in the Sanskrit and Subordinate Literatures. By A. C. Burnell. 8vo.
pp. 120. 10s. 6d.

Burnell.—The Sâmavidhânabrâhmaṇa (being the Third Brâhmaṇa)
of the Sâma Veda. Edited, together with the Commentary of Sâyaṇa, an
English Translation, Introduction, and Index of Words, by A. C. Burnell.
Volume I.—Text and Commentary, with Introduction. 8vo. pp. xxxviii. and
104. 12s. 6d.

Burnell.—The Arsheyabrahmana (being the fourth Brâhmaṇa) of
the Sama Veda. The Sanskrit Text. Edited, together with Extracts from the
Commentary of Sayana, etc. An Introduction and Index of Words. By A. C.
Burnell, Ph.D. 8vo, pp. 51 and 109. 10s. 6d.

Burnell.—The Devatâdhyâyabrâhmaṇa (being the Fifth Brâhmaṇa)
of the Sama Veda. The Sanskrit Text edited, with the Commentary of Sâyaṇa,
an Index of Words, etc., by A. C. Burnell, M.R.A.S. 8vo. and Trans.,
pp. 34. 5s.

Burnell.—The Jaiminīya Text of the Arsheyabrāhmaṇa of the
Sâma Veda. Edited in Sanskrit by A. C. Burnell, Ph. D. 8vo. sewed, pp.
56. 7s. 6d.

Burnell. — The Samhitopanishadbrāhmaṇa (Being the Seventh
Brâhmaṇa) of the Sâma Veda. The Sanskrit Text. With a Commentary, an
Index of Words, etc. Edited by A. C. Burnell, Ph.D. 8vo. stiff boards,
pp. 86. 7s. 6d.

Burnell.—The Vaṃçabrâhmaṇa (being the Eighth Brâhmaṇa) of the
Sâma Veda. Edited, together with the Commentary of Sâyaṇa, a Preface and
Index of Words, by A. C. Burnell, M.R.A.S., etc. 8vo. sewed, pp. xliii.,
12, and xii., with 2 coloured plates. 10s. 6d.

Butler.—Hungarian Poems and Fables for English Readers. Selected and translated by E. D. Butler, of the British Museum. With Illustrations by A. G. Butler. Fcap. limp cloth, pp. vi.–88. 1877. 2s.

Buttmann.—A Grammar of the New Testament Greek. By A. Buttmann. Authorized translation by Prof J. H. Thayer, with numerous additions and corrections by the author. Demy 8vo. cloth, pp. xx. and 474. 1873. 14s.

Butrus-al-Bustány.—كتاب وَائِرَة المَعَارِف An Arabic Encylopædia of Universal Knowledge, by Butrus-al-Bustány, the celebrated compiler of Mohit ul Mohît (المُحِيط), and Katr el Mohît (قطر المُحِيط).

This work will be completed in from 12 to 15 Vols., of which Vols. I. to III. are ready, Vol. I. contains letter ا to اب; Vol. II. اب to ار; Vol. III. ار to غ. Small folio, cloth, pp. 800 each. £1 11s. 6d. per Vol.

Byington.—Grammar of the Choctaw Language. By the Rev. Cyrus Byington. Edited from the Original MSS. in Library of the American Philosophical Society, by D. G. Brinton, M.D. Cr. 8vo. sewed, pp. 56. 7s. 6d.

Calcutta Review (The).—Published Quarterly. Price 8s. 6d. per number.

Caldwell.—A Comparative Grammar of the Dravidian, or South-Indian Family of Languages. By the Rev. R. Caldwell, LL.D. A Second, corrected, and enlarged Edition. Demy 8vo. pp. 805. 1875. 28s.

Callaway.—Izinganekwane, Nensumansumane, Nezindaba, Zabantu (Nursery Tales, Traditions, and Histories of the Zulus). In their own words, with a Translation into English, and Notes. By the Rev. Henry Callaway, M.D. Volume I., 8vo. pp. xiv. and 378, cloth. Natal, 1866 and 1867. 16s.

Callaway. — The Religious System of the Amazulu.

Part I.—Unkulunkulu; or, the Tradition of Creation as existing among the Amazulu and other Tribes of South Africa, in their own words, with a translation into English, and Notes. By the Rev. Canon Callaway, M.D. 8vo. pp. 128, sewed. 1868. 4s.

Part II.—Amatongo; or, Ancestor Worship, as existing among the Amazulu, in their own words, with a translation into English, and Notes. By the Rev. Canon Callaway, M.D. 1869. 8vo. pp. 127, sewed. 1869. 4s.

Part III.—Izinyanga Zokubula; or, Divination, as existing among the Amazulu, in their own words. With a Translation into English, and Notes. By the Rev. Canon Callaway, M.D. 8vo. pp. 150, sewed. 1870. 4s.

Part IV.—Abatakati, or Medical Magic and Witchcraft. 8vo. pp. 40, sewed. 1s. 6d.

Calligaris.—Le Compagnon de Tous, ou Dictionnaire Polyglotte. Par le Colonel Louis Calligaris, Grand Officier, etc. (French—Latin—Italian—Spanish—Portuguese—German—English—Modern Greek—Arabic—Turkish.) 2 vols. 4to., pp. 1157 and 746. Turin. £4 4s.

Campbell.—Specimens of the Languages of India, including Tribes of Bengal, the Central Provinces, and the Eastern Frontier. By Sir G. Campbell, M.P. Folio, paper, pp. 308. 1874. £1 11s. 6d.

Carletti.—Idh-har-ul-haqq, Ou Manifestation de la Vérité de El-hage Rahmat-ullah Effendi de Delhi (un des Descendants du Califfe Osman-ben-'Affan). Traduit de l'Arabe, par un éminent, quoique très-jeune, Orientaliste de Tunis. Revu sur le texte, retouché en plusieurs endroits et augmenté d'une preface et d'un appendixe. Par P. V. Carletti. In Two Vols. 8vo. [*In the press.*

Carpenter.—The Last Days in England of the Rajah Rammohun Roy. By Mary Carpenter, of Bristol. With Five Illustrations. 8vo. pp. 272, cloth. 7s. 6d.

Carr.—ఆంధ్రలోకోక్తి చంద్రిక. A COLLECTION OF TELUGU PROVERBS, Translated, Illustrated, and Explained; together with some Sanscrit Proverbs printed in the Devnâgarî and Telugu Characters. By Captain M. W. CARR, Madras Staff Corps. One Vol. and Supplemnt, royal 8vo. pp. 488 and 148. 31s. 6d

Catlin.—O-KEE-PA. A Religious Ceremony of the Mandans. By GEORGE CATLIN. With 13 Coloured Illustrations. 4to. pp. 60, bound in cloth, gilt edges. 14s.

Chalmers.—A CONCISE KHANG-HSI CHINESE DICTIONARY. By the Rev. J. CHALMERS, LL.D., Canton. Three Vols. Royal 8vo. bound in Chinese style, pp. 1000. 21s.

Chalmers.—THE ORIGIN OF THE CHINESE; an Attempt to Trace the connection of the Chinese with Western Nations in their Religion, Superstitions, Arts, Language, and Traditions. By JOHN CHALMERS, A.M. Foolscap 8vo. cloth, pp. 78. 5s.

Chalmers.—THE SPECULATIONS ON METAPHYSICS, POLITY, AND MORALITY OF "THE OLD PHILOSOPHER" LAU TSZE. Translated from the Chinese, with an Introduction by John Chalmers, M.A. Fcap. 8vo. cloth, xx. and 62. 4s. 6d.

Charnock.—LUDUS PATRONYMICUS; or, the Etymology of Curious Surnames. By RICHARD STEPHEN CHARNOCK, Ph.D., F.S.A., F.R.G.S. Crown 8vo., pp. 182, cloth. 7s. 6d.

Charnock.—VERBA NOMINALIA; or Words derived from Proper Names. By RICHARD STEPHEN CHARNOCK, Ph. Dr. F.S.A., etc. 8vo. pp. 326, cloth. 14s.

Charnock.—THE PEOPLES OF TRANSYLVANIA. Founded on a Paper read before THE ANTHROPOLOGICAL SOCIETY OF LONDON, on the 4th of May, 1869. By RICHARD STEPHEN CHARNOCK, Ph.D., F.S.A., F.R.G.S. Demy 8vo. pp. 36, sewed. 1870. 2s. 6d.

Chaucer Society's (The).—Subscription, two guineas per annum. List of Publications on application.

Childers.—A PALI-ENGLISH DICTIONARY, with Sanskrit Equivalents, and with numerous Quotations, Extracts, and References. Compiled by the late Prof. R. C. CHILDERS, late of the Ceylon Civil Service. Imperial 8vo. Double Columns. Complete in 1 Vol., pp. xxii. and 622, cloth. 1875. £3 3s.
The first Pali Dictionary ever published.

Childers.—NOTES ON THE SINHALESE LANGUAGE. No. 1. On the Formation of the Plural of Neuter Nouns. By the late Prof. R. C. CHILDERS. Demy 8vo. sd., pp. 16. 1873. 1s.

Childers.—ON SANDHI IN PALI. By the late Prof. R. C. CHILDERS. 8vo. sewed, pp. 22. 1s.

Childers.—THE MAHÂPARINIBBÂNASUTTA OF THE SUTTA-PITAKA. The Pali Text. Edited by the late Professor R. C. CHILDERS. 8vo. cloth, pp. 72. 5s.

China Review; OR, NOTES AND QUERIES ON THE FAR EAST. Published bi-monthly. Edited by E. J. EITEL. 4to. Subscription, £1 10s. per volume.

Chintamon.—A COMMENTARY ON THE TEXT OF THE BHAGAVAD-GÎTÂ; or, the Discourse between Krishna and Arjuna of Divine Matters. A Sanscrit Philosophical Poem. With a few Introductory Papers. By HURRYCHUND CHINTAMON, Political Agent to H. H. the Guicowar Mulhar Rao Maharajah of Baroda. Post 8vo. cloth, pp. 118. 6s.

Christaller.—A DICTIONARY, ENGLISH, TSHI, (ASANTE), AKRA; Tshi (Chwee), comprising as dialects Akán (Asànté, Akém, Akuapém, etc.) and Fànté; Akra (Accra), connected with Adangme; Gold Coast, West Africa.

| Enyiresi, Twi né Ǹkraṅ | Eṅliši, Otšûi ke Gã̱ |
| nsɛm - asɛkyerɛ - ṅhõma. | wiemɔi - ašišitšomɔ- wolo. |

By the Rev. J. G. CHRISTALLER, Rev. C. W. LOCHER, Rev. J. ZIMMERMANN. 16mo. 7s. 6d.

Christaller.—A GRAMMAR OF THE ASANTE AND FANTE LANGUAGE, called Tshi (Chwee, Twi) : based on the Akuapem Dialect, with reference to the other (Akan and Fante) Dialects. By Rev. J. G. CHRISTALLER. 8vo. pp. xxiv. and 203. 1875. 10s. 6d.

Clarke.—TEN GREAT RELIGIONS : an Essay in Comparative Theology. By JAMES FREEMAN CLARKE. 8vo. cloth, pp. x. and 528. 1871. 15s.

Clarke.—MEMOIR ON THE COMPARATIVE GRAMMAR OF EGYPTIAN, COPTIC, AND UDE. By HYDE CLARKE, Cor. Member American Oriental Society ; Mem. German Oriental Society, etc., etc. Demy 8vo. sd., pp. 32. 2s.

Clarke.—RESEARCHES IN PRE-HISTORIC AND PROTO-HISTORIC COMPARATIVE PHILOLOGY, MYTHOLOGY, AND ARCHÆOLOGY, in connexion with the Origin of Culture in America and the Accad or Sumerian Families. By HYDE CLARKE. Demy 8vo. sewed, pp. xi. and 74. 1875. 2s. 6d.

Clarke.—SERPENT AND SIVA WORSHIP, and Mythology in Central America, Africa and Asia. By HYDE CLARKE, Esq. 8vo. sewed. 1s.

Cleasby.—AN ICELANDIC-ENGLISH DICTIONARY. Based on the MS. Collections of the late Richard Cleasby. Enlarged and completed by G. VIGFÚSSON. With an Introduction, and Life of Richard Cleasby, by G. WEBBE DASENT, D.C.L. 4to. £3 7s.

Cleasby.—APPENDIX TO AN ICELANDIC-ENGLISH DICTIONARY. *See* Skeat.

Colebrooke.—THE LIFE AND MISCELLANEOUS ESSAYS OF HENRY THOMAS COLEBROOKE. The Biography by his Son, Sir T. E. COLEBROOKE, Bart., M.P., The Essays edited by Professor Cowell. In 3 vols.
Vol. I. The Life. With Portrait and Map. Demy 8vo. cloth, pp. xii. and 492. 14s.
Vols. II. and III. The Essays. A New Edition, with Notes by E. B. COWELL, Professor of Sanskrit in the University of Cambridge. Demy 8vo. cloth, pp. xvi.-544, and x.-520. 1873. 28s.

Colleccao de Vocabulos e Frases usados na Provincia de S. Pedro, do Rio Grande do Sul, no Brasil. 12mo. pp. 32, sewed. 1s.

Contopoulos.—A LEXICON OF MODERN GREEK-ENGLISH AND ENGLISH MODERN GREEK. By N. CONTOPOULOS. In 2 vols. 8vo. cloth. Part I. Modern Greek-English, pp. 460. Part II. English-Modern Greek, pp. 582. £1 7s.

Conway.—THE SACRED ANTHOLOGY. A Book of Ethnical Scriptures. Collected and edited by M. D. CONWAY. 4th edition. Demy 8vo. cloth, pp. xvi. and 480. 12s.

Coomára Swamy.—THE DATHÁVANSA ; or, the History of the Tooth-Relic of Gotama Buddha. The Pali Text and its Translation into English, with Notes. By Sir M. COOMÁRA SWÁMY, Mudeliár. Demy 8vo. cloth, pp. 174. 1874. 10s. 6d.

Coomára Swamy.—THE DATHÁVANSA ; or, the History of the Tooth-Relic of Gotama Buddha. English Translation only. With Notes. Demy 8vo. cloth, pp. 100. 1874. 6s.

Coomára Swamy.—SUTTA NIPÁTA ; or, the Dialogues and Discourses of Gotama Buddha. Translated from the Pali, with Introduction and Notes. By Sir M. COOMÁRA SWAMY. Cr. 8vo. cloth, pp. xxxvi. and 160. 1874. 6s.

Cotton.—ARABIC PRIMER. Consisting of 180 Short Sentences containing 30 Primary Words prepared according to the Vocal System of Studying Language. By General SIR ARTHUR COTTON, K.C.S.I. Cr. 8vo. cloth, pp. 38. 2s.

Cowell and Eggeling.—Catalogue of Buddhist Sanskrit Manuscripts in the Possession of the Royal Asiatic Society (Hodgson Collection). By Professors E. B. Cowell and J. Eggeling. 8vo. sd., pp. 56. 2s. 6d.

Cowell.—A short Introduction to the Ordinary Prakrit of the Sanskrit Dramas. With a List of Common Irregular Prakrit Words. By Prof. E. B. Cowell. Cr. 8vo. limp cloth, pp. 40. 1875. 3s. 6d.

Cunningham.—The Ancient Geography of India. I. The Buddhist Period, including the Campaigns of Alexander, and the Travels of Hwen-Thsang. By Alexander Cunningham, Major-General, Royal Engineers (Bengal Retired). With thirteen Maps. 8vo. pp. xx. 590, cloth. 1870. 28s.

Cunningham.—The Bhilsa Topes; or, Buddhist Monuments of Central India: comprising a brief Historical Sketch of the Rise, Progress, and Decline of Buddhism; with an Account of the Opening and Examination of the various Groups of Topes around Bhilsa. By Brev.-Major Alexander Cunningham, Bengal Engineers. Illustrated with thirty-three Plates. 8vo. pp. xxxvi. 370, cloth. 1854. £2 2s.

Cunningham.—Archæological Survey of India. Four Reports, made during the years 1862-63-64-65. By Alexander Cunningham, C.S.I., Major-General, etc. With Maps and Plates. Vols. 1 to 5. 8vo. cloth. £6.

Cust.—A Sketch of the Modern Languages of the East Indies. Accompanied by Two Language Maps. By R. Cust. Post 8vo. pp. xii. and 198, cloth. 12s.

Da Cunha.—Memoir on the History of the Tooth-Relic of Ceylon; with an Essay on the Life and System of Gautama Buddha. By J. Gerson da Cunha. 8vo. cloth, pp. xiv. and 70. With 4 photographs and cuts. 7s. 6d.

Da Cunha.—The Sahyadri Khanda of the Skanda Purana; a Mythological, Historical and Geographical Account of Western India. First edition of the Sanskrit Text, with various readings. By J. Gerson da Cunha, M.R.C.S. and L.M. Eng., L.R.C.P. Edinb., etc. 8vo. bds. pp. 580. £1 1s.

Da Cunha.—Notes on the History and Antiquities of Chaul and Bassein. By J. Gerson da Cunha, M.R.C.S. and L.M. Eng., etc. 8vo. cloth, pp. xvi. and 262. With 17 photographs, 9 plates and a map. £1 5s.

Dalton.—Descriptive Ethnology of Bengal. By Edward Tuite Dalton, C.S.I., Colonel, Bengal Staff Corps, etc. Illustrated by Lithograph Portraits copied from Photographs. 33 Lithograph Plates. 4to. half-calf, pp. 340. £6 6s.

D'Alwis.—A Descriptive Catalogue of Sanskrit, Pali, and Sinhalese Literary Works of Ceylon. By James D'Alwis, M.R.A.S., Advocate of the Supreme Court, &c., &c. In Three Volumes. Vol. I., pp. xxxii. and 244, sewed. 1870. 8s. 6d.

Davids.—Three Inscriptions of Parâkrama Bâhu the Great, from Pulastipura, Ceylon. By T. W. Rhys Davids. 8vo. pp. 20. 1s. 6d.

Davids.—Sìgiri, the Lion Rock, near Pulastipura, and the 39th Chapter of the Mahávamsa. By T. W. Rhys Davids. 8vo. pp. 30. 1s. 6d.

Delepierre.—Supercheries Littéraires, Pastiches Suppositions d'Auteur, dans les Lettres et dans les Arts. Par Octave Delepierre. Fcap. 4to. paper cover, pp. 328. 14s.

Delepierre.—Tableau de la Littérature du Centon, chez les Anciens et chez les Modernes. Par Octave Delepierre. 2 vols. small 4to. paper cover, pp. 324 and 318. 21s.

Delepierre.—Essai Historique et Bibliographique sur les Rébus. Par Octave Delepierre. 8vo. pp. 24, sewed. With 15 pages of Woodcuts. 1870. 3s. 6d.

Dennys.—CHINA AND JAPAN. A complete Guide to the Open Ports of those countries, together with Pekin, Yeddo, Hong Kong, and Macao; forming a Guide Book and Vade Mecum for Travellers, Merchants, and Residents in general; with 56 Maps and Plans. By WM. FREDERICK MAYERS, F.R.G.S. H.M.'s Consular Service; N. B. DENNYS, late H.M.'s Consular Service; and CHARLES KING, Lieut. Royal Marine Artillery. Edited by N. B. DENNYS. In one volume. 8vo. pp. 600, cloth. £2 2s.

Dennys.—A HANDBOOK OF THE CANTON VERNACULAR OF THE CHINESE LANGUAGE. Being a Series of Introductory Lessons, for Domestic and Business Purposes. By N. B. DENNYS, M.R.A.S., Ph.D. 8vo. cloth, pp. 4, 195, and 31. £1 10s.

Dennys.—A HANDBOOK OF MALAY COLLOQUIAL, as spoken in Singapore, Being a Series of Introductory Lessons for Domestic and Business Purposes. By N. B. DENNYS, Ph.D., F.R.G.S., M.R.A.S., etc., Author of "The Folklore of China," "Handbook of Cantonese," etc., etc. 8vo. cloth, pp. 204. £1 1s.

Dennys.—THE FOLK-LORE OF CHINA, and its Affinities with that of the Aryan and Semitic Races. By N. B. DENNYS, Ph.D., F.R.G.S., M.R.A.S., author of "A Handbook of the Canton Vernacular," etc. 8vo. cloth, pp. 168. 10s. 6d.

De Vere.—STUDIES IN ENGLISH; or, Glimpses of the Inner Life of our Language. By M. SCHELE DE VERE, LL.D., Professor of Modern Languages in the University of Virginia. 8vo. cloth, pp. vi. and 365. 12s. 6d.

De Vere.—AMERICANISMS: THE ENGLISH OF THE NEW WORLD. By M. SCHELE DE VERE, LL.D., Professor of Modern Languages in the University of Virginia. 8vo. pp. 685, cloth. 12s.

Dickson.—THE PÂTIMOKKHA, being the Buddhist Office of the Confession of Priests. The Pali Text, with a Translation, and Notes, by J. F. DICKSON, M.A. 8vo. sd., pp. 69. 2s.

Dinkard (The).—The Original Pehlwi Text, the same transliterated in Zend Characters. Translations of the Text in the Gujrati and English Languages; a Commentary and Glossary of Select Terms. By PESHOTUN DUSTOOR BEHRAMJEE SUNJANA. Vols. I. and II. 8vo. cloth. £2 2s.

Döhne.—A ZULU-KAFIR DICTIONARY, etymologically explained, with copious Illustrations and examples, preceded by an introduction on the Zulu-Kafir Language. By the Rev. J. L. DÖHNE. Royal 8vo. pp. xlii. and 418, sewed. Cape Town, 1857. 21s.

Döhne.—THE FOUR GOSPELS IN ZULU. By the Rev. J. L. DÖHNE, Missionary to the American Board, C.F.M. 8vo. pp. 208, cloth. Pietermaritzburg, 1866. 5s.

Doolittle.—A VOCABULARY AND HANDBOOK OF THE CHINESE LANGUAGE. Romanized in the Mandarin Dialect. In Two Volumes comprised in Three Parts. By Rev. JUSTUS DOOLITTLE, Author of "Social Life of the Chinese." Vol. I. 4to. pp. viii. and 548. Vol. II. Parts II. and III., pp. vii. and 695. £1 11s. 6d. each vol.

Douglas.—CHINESE-ENGLISH DICTIONARY OF THE VERNACULAR OR SPOKEN LANGUAGE OF AMOY, with the principal variations of the Chang-Chew and Chin-Chew Dialects. By the Rev. CARSTAIRS DOUGLAS, M.A., LL.D., Glasg., Missionary of the Presbyterian Church in England. 1 vol. High quarto, cloth, double columns, pp. 632. 1873. £3 3s.

Douglas.—CHINESE LANGUAGE AND LITERATURE. Two Lectures delivered at the Royal Institution, by R. K. DOUGLAS, of the British Museum, and Professor of Chinese at King's College. Cr. 8vo. cl., pp. 118. 1875. 5s.

Douglas.—THE LIFE OF JENGHIZ KHAN. Translated from the Chinese, with an Introduction, by ROBERT KENNAWAY DOUGLAS, of the British Museum, and Professor of Chinese, King's College, London. Cr. 8vo. cloth, pp. xxxvi.-106. 1877. 5s.

2

Douse.—GRIMM'S LAW; A STUDY: or, Hints towards an Explanation of the so-called "Lautverschiebung." To which are added some Remarks on the Primitive Indo-European *K*, and several Appendices. By T. LE MARCHANT DOUSE. 8vo. cloth, pp. xvi. and 230. 10*s.* 6*d.*

Dowson.—A GRAMMAR OF THE URDU OR HINDUSTANI LANGUAGE. By JOHN DOWSON, M.R.A.S. 12mo. cloth, pp. xvi. and 264. 10*s.* 6*d.*

Dowson.—A HINDUSTANI EXERCISE BOOK. Containing a Series of Passages and Extracts adapted for Translation into Hindustani. By JOHN DOWSON, M.R.A.S., Professor of Hindustani, Staff College. Crown 8vo. pp. 100. Limp cloth, 2*s.* 6*d.*

Dwight.—MODERN PHILOLOGY: Its Discovery, History, and Influence. New edition, with Maps, Tabular Views, and an Index. By BENJAMIN W. DWIGHT. In two vols. cr. 8vo. cloth. First series, pp. 360 ; second series, pp. xi. and 554. £1.

Early English Text Society's Publications. Subscription, one guinea per annum.

1. EARLY ENGLISH ALLITERATIVE POEMS. In the West-Midland Dialect of the Fourteenth Century. Edited by R. MORRIS, Esq., from an unique Cottonian MS. 16*s.*

2. ARTHUR (about 1440 A.D.). Edited by F. J. FURNIVALL, Esq., from the Marquis of Bath's unique MS. 4*s.*

3. ANE COMPENDIOUS AND BREUE TRACTATE CONCERNYNG YE OFFICE AND DEWTIE OF KYNGIS, etc. By WILLIAM LAUDER. (1556 A.D.) Edited by F. HALL, Esq., D.C.L. 4*s.*

4. SIR GAWAYNE AND THE GREEN KNIGHT (about 1320-30 A.D.). Edited by R. MORRIS, Esq., from an unique Cottonian MS. 10*s.*

5. OF THE ORTHOGRAPHIE AND CONGRUITIE OF THE BRITAN TONGUE ; a treates, noe shorter than necessarie, for the Schooles, be ALEXANDER HUME. Edited for the first time from the unique MS. in the British Museum (about 1617 A.D.), by HENRY B. WHEATLEY, Esq. 4*s.*

6. LANCELOT OF THE LAIK. Edited from the unique MS. in the Cambridge University Library (ab. 1500), by the Rev. WALTER W. SKEAT, M.A. 8*s.*

7. THE STORY OF GENESIS AND EXODUS, an Early English Song, of about 1250 A.D. Edited for the first time from the unique MS. in the Library of Corpus Christi College, Cambridge, by R. MORRIS, Esq. 8*s.*

8 MORTE ARTHURE; the Alliterative Version. Edited from ROBERT THORNTON'S unique MS. (about 1440 A.D.) at Lincoln, by the Rev. GEORGE PERRY, M.A , Prebendary of Lincoln. 7*s.*

9. ANIMADVERSIONS UPPON THE ANNOTACIONS AND CORRECTIONS OF SOME IMPERFECTIONS OF IMPRESSIONES OF CHAUCER'S WORKES, reprinted in 1598; by FRANCIS THYNNE. Edited from the unique MS. in the Bridgewater Library. By G. H. KINGSLEY, Esq., M.D., and F. J. FURNIVALL, Esq., M.A. 10*s.*

10. MERLIN, OR THE EARLY HISTORY OF KING ARTHUR. Edited for the first time from the unique MS. in the Cambridge University Library (about 1450 A.D.), by HENRY B. WHEATLEY, Esq. Part I. 2*s.* 6*d.*

11. THE MONARCHE, and other Poems of Sir David Lyndesay. Edited from the first edition by JOHNE SKOTT, in 1552, by FITZEDWARD HALL, Esq., D.C.L. Part I. 3*s.*

12. THE WRIGHT'S CHASTE WIFE, a Merry Tale, by Adam of Cobsam (about 1462 A.D.), from the unique Lambeth MS. 306. Edited for the first time by F. J. FURNIVALL, Esq., M.A. 1*s.*

Early English Text Society's Publications—*continued.*

13. SEINTE MARHERETE, þE MEIDEN ANT MARTYR. Three Texts of ab. 1200, 1310, 1330 A.D. First edited in 1862, by the Rev. OSWALD COCKAYNE, M.A., and now re-issued. 2s.

14. KYNG HORN, with fragments of Floriz and Blauncheflur, and the Assumption of the Blessed Virgin. Edited from the MSS. in the Library of the University of Cambridge and the British Museum, by the Rev. J. RAWSON LUMBY. 3s. 6d

15. POLITICAL, RELIGIOUS, AND LOVE POEMS, from the Lambeth MS. No. 306, and other sources. Edited by F. J. FURNIVALL, Esq., M.A. 7s. 6d.

16. A TRETICE IN ENGLISH breuely drawe out of þ book of Quintis essencijs in Latyn, þ Hermys þ prophete and king of Egipt after þ flood of Noe, fader of Philosophris, hadde by reuelacioun of an aungil of God to him sente. Edited from the Sloane MS. 73, by F. J. FURNIVALL, Esq., M.A. 1s.

17. PARALLEL EXTRACTS from 29 Manuscripts of PIERS PLOWMAN, with Comments, and a Proposal for the Society's Three-text edition of this Poem. By the Rev. W. SKEAT, M.A. 1s.

18. HALI MEIDENHEAD, about 1200 A.D. Edited for the first time from the MS. (with a translation) by the Rev. OSWALD COCKAYNE, M.A. 1s.

19. THE MONARCHE, and other Poems of Sir David Lyndesay. Part II., the Complaynt of the King's Papingo, and other minor Poems. Edited from the First Edition by F. HALL, Esq., D.C L. 3s. 6d.

20. SOME TREATISES BY RICHARD ROLLE DE HAMPOLE. Edited from Robert of Thornton's MS. (ab. 1440 A.D.), by Rev. GEORGE G. PERRY, M.A. 1s.

21. MERLIN, OR THE EARLY HISTORY OF KING ARTHUR. Part II. Edited by HENRY B. WHEATLEY, Esq. 4s.

22. THE ROMANS OF PARTENAY, OR LUSIGNEN. Edited for the first time from the unique MS. in the Library of Trinity College, Cambridge, by the Rev. W. W. SKEAT. M.A. 6s.

23. DAN MICHEL'S AYENBITE OF INWYT, or Remorse of Conscience, in the Kentish dialect, 1340 A.D. Edited from the unique MS. in the British Museum, by RICHARD MORRIS, Esq. 10s. 6d.

24. HYMNS OF THE VIRGIN AND CHRIST; THE PARLIAMENT OF DEVILS, and Other Religious Poems. Edited from the Lambeth MS. 853, by F. J. FURNIVALL, M.A. 3s.

25. THE STACIONS OF ROME, and the Pilgrim's Sea-Voyage and Sea-Sickness, with Clene Maydenhod. Edited from the Vernon and Porkington MSS., etc., by F. J. FURNIVALL, Esq., M.A. 1s.

26. RELIGIOUS PIECES IN PROSE AND VERSE. Containing Dan Jon Gaytrigg's Sermon; The Abbaye of S. Spirit; Sayne Jon, and other pieces in the Northern Dialect. Edited from Robert of Thorntone's MS. (ab. 1460 A.D.), by the Rev. G. PERRY, M.A. 2s.

27. MANIPULUS VOCABULORUM : a Rhyming Dictionary of the English Language, by PETER LEVINS (1570). Edited, with an Alphabetical Index, by HENRY B. WHEATLEY. 12s.

28. THE VISION OF WILLIAM CONCERNING PIERS PLOWMAN, together with Vita de Dowel, Dobet et Dobest. 1362 A.D., by WILLIAM LANGLAND. The earliest or Vernon Text; Text A. Edited from the Vernon MS., with full Collations. by Rev. W. W. SKEAT, M.A. 7s.

Early English Text Society's Publications—*continued.*

29. OLD ENGLISH HOMILIES AND HOMILETIC TREATISES. (Sawles Warde
and the Wohunge of Ure Lauerd : Ureisuns of Ure Louerd and of Ure Lefdi,
etc.) of the Twelfth and Thirteenth Centuries. Edited from MSS. in the British Museum, Lambeth, and Bodleian Libraries ; with Introduction, Translation, and Notes. By RICHARD MORRIS. *First Series.* Part I. *7s.*

30. PIERS, THE PLOUGHMAN's CREDE (about 1394). Edited from the
MSS. by the Rev. W. W. SKEAT, M.A. *2s.*

31. INSTRUCTIONS FOR PARISH PRIESTS. By JOHN MYRC. Edited from
Cotton MS. Claudius A. II., by EDWARD PEACOCK, Esq., F.S.A., etc., etc. *4s.*

32. THE BABEES BOOK, Aristotle's A B C, Urbanitatis, Stans Puer ad
Mensam, The Lytille Childreues Lytil Boke. THE BOKES OF NURTURE of
Hugh Rhodes and John Russell, Wynkyn de Worde's Boke of Kervynge, The
Booke of Demeanor, The Boke of Curtasye, Seager's Schoole of Vertue, etc.,
etc. With some French and Latin Poems on like subjects, and some Fore-
words on Education in Early England. Edited by F. J. FURNIVALL, M.A.,
Trin. Hall, Cambridge. *15s.*

33. THE BOOK OF THE KNIGHT DE LA TOUR LANDRY, 1372. A Father's
Book for his Daughters, Edited from the Harleian MS. 1764, by THOMAS
WRIGHT Esq., M.A., and Mr. WILLIAM ROSSITER. *8s.*

34. OLD ENGLISH HOMILIES AND HOMILETIC TREATISES. (Sawles Warde,
and the Wohunge of Ure Lauerd: Ureisuns of Ure Louerd and of Ure Lefdi,
etc.) of the Twelfth and Thirteenth Centuries. Edited from MSS. in the
British Museum, Lambeth, and Bodleian Libraries; with Introduction, Translation, and Notes, by RICHARD MORRIS. *First Series.* Part 2. *8s.*

35. SIR DAVID LYNDESAY's WORKS. PART 3. The Historie of ane
Nobil and Wailzeand Sqvyer, WILLIAM MELDRUM, umqvhyle Laird of
Cleische and Bynnis, compylit be Sir DAVID LYNDESAY of the Mont *alias*
Lyoun King of Armes. With the Testament of the said Williame Mel-
drum, Squyer, compylit alswa be Sir Dauid Lyndesay, etc. Edited by F.
HALL, D.C.L. *2s.*

36. MERLIN, OR THE EARLY HISTORY OF KING ARTHUR. A Prose
Romance (about 1450–1460 A.D.), edited from the unique MS. in the
University Library, Cambridge, by HENRY B. WHEATLEY. With an Essay
on Arthurian Localities, by J. S. STUART GLENNIE, Esq. Part III. 1869. *12s.*

37. SIR DAVID LYNDESAY's WORKS. Part IV. Ane Satyre of the
thrie estaits, in commendation of vertew and vitvperation of vyce. Maid
be Sir DAVID LINDESAY, of the Mont, *alias* Lyon King of Armes. At
Edinbvrgh. Printed be Robert Charteris, 1602. Cvm privilegio regis.
Edited by F. HALL, Esq., D.C.L. *4s.*

38. THE VISION OF WILLIAM CONCERNING PIERS THE PLOWMAN,
together with Vita de Dowel, Dobet, et Dobest, Secundum Wit et Resoun,
by WILLIAM LANGLAND (1377 A.D.). The "Crowley" Text; or Text B.
Edited from MS. Laud Misc. 581, collated with MS. Rawl. Poet. 38, MS.
B. 15. 17. in the Library of Trinity College, Cambridge, MS. Dd. 1. 17. in
the Cambridge University Library, the MS. in Oriel College, Oxford, MS.
Bodley 814, etc. By the Rev. WALTER W. SKEAT, M.A., late Fellow of
Christ's College, Cambridge. *10s. 6d.*

39. THE "GEST HYSTORIALE" OF THE DESTRUCTION OF TROY. An
Alliterative Romance, translated from Guido De Colonna's "Hystoria
Troiana." Now first edited from the unique MS. in the Hunterian Museum,
University of Glasgow, by the Rev. GEO. A. PANTON and DAVID DONALDSON.
Part I. *10s. 6d.*

Early English Text Society's Publications—*continued.*

40. ENGLISH GILDS. The Original Ordinances of more than One
Hundred Early English Gilds : Together with the olde usages of the cite of
Wynchestre; The Ordinances of Worcester; The Office of the Mayor of
Bristol; and the Customary of the Manor of Tettenhall-Regis. From
Original MSS. of the Fourteenth and Fifteenth Centuries. Edited with
Notes by the late TOULMIN SMITH, Esq., F.R.S. of Northern Antiquaries
(Copenhagen). With an Introduction and Glossary, etc., by his daughter,
LUCY TOULMIN SMITH. And a Preliminary Essay, in Five Parts, ON THE
HISTORY AND DEVELOPMENT OF GILDS, by LUJO BRENTANO, Doctor Juris
Utriusque et Philosophiæ. 21*s.*

41. THE MINOR POEMS OF WILLIAM LAUDER, Playwright, Poet, and
Minister of the Word of God (mainly on the State of Scotland in and about
1568 A.D., that year of Famine and Plague). Edited from the Unique
Originals belonging to S. CHRISTIE-MILLER, Esq., of Britwell, by F. J.
FURNIVALL, M.A., Trin. Hall, Camb. 3*s.*

42. BERNARDUS DE CURA REI FAMULIARIS, with some Early Scotch
Prophecies, etc. From a MS., KK 1. 5, in the Cambridge University
Library. Edited by J. RAWSON LUMBY, M.A., late Fellow of Magdalen
College, Cambridge. 2*s.*

43. RATIS RAVING, and other Moral and Religious Pieces, in Prose and
Verse. Edited from the Cambridge University Library MS. KK 1. 5, by J.
RAWSON LUMBY, M.A., late Fellow of Magdalen College, Cambridge. 3*s.*

44. JOSEPH OF ARIMATHIE: otherwise called the Romance of the
Seint Graal, or Holy Grail: an alliterative poem, written about A.D. 1350,
and now first printed from the unique copy in the Vernon MS. at Oxford.
With an appendix, containing "The Lyfe of Joseph of Armathy," reprinted
from the black-letter copy of Wynkyn de Worde ; " De sancto Joseph ab
Arimathia," first printed by Pynson, A.D. 1516; and "The Lyfe of Joseph of
Arimathia," first printed by Pynson, A.D. 1520. Edited, with Notes and
Glossarial Indices, by the Rev. WALTER W. SKEAT, M.A. 5*s.*

45. KING ALFRED'S WEST-SAXON VERSION OF GREGORY'S PASTORAL CARE.
With an English translation, the Latin Text, Notes, and an Introduction
Edited by HENRY SWEET, Esq., of Balliol College, Oxford. Part I. 10*s.*

46. LEGENDS OF THE HOLY ROOD ; SYMBOLS OF THE PASSION AND CROSS-
POEMS. In Old English of the Eleventh, Fourteenth, and Fifteenth Centuries. Edited from MSS. in the British Museum and Bodleian Libraries;
with Introduction, Translations, and Glossarial Index. By RICHARD
MORRIS, LL.D. 10*s.*

47. SIR DAVID LYNDESAY'S WORKS. PART V. The Minor Poems of
Lyndesay. Edited by J. A. H. MURRAY, Esq. 3*s.*

48. THE TIMES' WHISTLE : or, A Newe Daunce of Seven Satires, and
other Poems : Compiled by R. C., Gent. Now first Edited from MS. Y. 8. 3.
in the Library of Canterbury Cathedral; with Introduction, Notes, and
Glossary, by J. M. COWPER. 6*s.*

49. AN OLD ENGLISH MISCELLANY, containing a Bestiary, Kentish
Sermons, Proverbs of Alfred, Religious Poems of the 13th century. Edited
from the MSS. by the Rev. R. MORRIS, LL.D. 10*s.*

50. KING ALFRED'S WEST-SAXON VERSION OF GREGORY'S PASTORAL CARE.
Edited from 2 MSS., with an English translation. By HENRY SWEET, Esq.,
Balliol College, Oxford. Part II. 10*s.*

51. ÞE LIFLADE OF ST. JULIANA, from two old English Manuscripts of
1230 A.D. With renderings into Modern English, by the Rev. O. COCKAYNE
and EDMUND BROCK. Edited by the Rev. O. COCKAYNE, M.A. Price 2*s.*

Early English Text Society's Publications—*continued.*

52. PALLADIUS ON HUSBONDRIE, from the unique MS., ab. 1420 A.D., ed. Rev. B. LODGE. Part I. 10s.

53. OLD ENGLISH HOMILIES, Series II., from the unique 13th-century MS. in Trinity Coll. Cambridge, with a photolithograph; three Hymns to the Virgin and God, from a unique 13th-century MS. at Oxford, a photo-lithograph of the music to two of them, and transcriptions of it in modern notation by Dr. RIMBAULT, and A. J. ELLIS, Esq., F.R.S.; the whole edited by the Rev. RICHARD MORRIS, LL.D. 8s.

54. THE VISION OF PIERS PLOWMAN, Text C (completing the three versions of this great poem), with an Autotype; and two unique alliterative Poems: Richard the Redeles (by WILLIAM, the author of the *Vision*); and The Crowned King; edited by the Rev. W. W. SKEAT, M.A. 18s.

55. GENERYDES, a Romance, edited from the unique MS., ab. 1440 A.D., in Trin. Coll. Cambridge, by W. ALDIS WRIGHT, Esq., M.A., Trin. Coll. Cambr. Part I. 3s.

56. THE GEST HYSTORIALE OF THE DESTRUCTION OF TROY, translated from Guido de Colonna, in alliterative verse; edited from the unique MS. in the Hunterian Museum, Glasgow, by D. DONALDSON, Esq., and the late Rev. G. A. Panton. Part II. 10s. 6d.

57. THE EARLY ENGLISH VERSION OF THE "CURSOR MUNDI," in four Texts, from MS. Cotton, Vesp. A. iii. in the British Museum; Fairfax MS. 14. in the Bodleian; the Göttingen MS. Theol. 107; MS. R. 3, 8, in Trinity College, Cambridge. Edited by the Rev. R. Morris, LL.D. Part I. with two photo-lithographic facsimiles by Cooke and Fotheringham. 10s. 6d.

58. THE BLICKLING HOMILIES, edited from the Marquis of Lothian's Anglo-Saxon MS. of 971 A.D., by the Rev. R. MORRIS, LL.D. (With a Photolithograph). Part I. 8s.

59. THE EARLY ENGLISH VERSION OF THE "CURSOR MUNDI;" in four Texts, from MS. Cotton Vesp. A. iii. in the British Museum; Fairfax MS. 14. in the Bodleian; the Göttingen MS. Theol. 107; MS. R. 3, 8, in Trinity College, Cambridge. Edited by the Rev. R. MORRIS, LL.D. Part II. 15s.

60. MEDITACYUNS ON THE SOPER OF OUR LORDE (perhaps by ROBERT OF BRUNNE). Edited from the MSS. by J. M. COWPER, Esq. 2s. 6d.

61. THE ROMANCE AND PROPHECIES OF THOMAS OF ERCELDOUNE, printed from Five MSS. Edited by Dr. JAMES A. H. MURRAY. 10s. 6d.

62. THE EARLY ENGLISH VERSION OF THE "CURSOR MUNDI," in Four Texts. Edited by the Rev. R. MORRIS, M.A., LL.D. Part III. 15s.

63. THE BLICKLING HOMILIES. Edited from the Marquis of Lothian's Anglo-Saxon MS. of 971 A.D., by the Rev. R. MORRIS, LL.D. Part II. 4s.

64. FRANCIS THYNNE'S EMBLEMES AND EPIGRAMS, A.D. 1600, from the Earl of Ellesmere's unique MS. Edited by F. J. FURNIVALL, M.A. 4s.

65. BE DOMES DÆGE (Bede's De Die Judicii) and other short Anglo-Saxon Pieces. Edited from the unique MS. by the Rev. J. RAWSON LUMBY, B.D. 2s.

66. THE EARLY ENGLISH VERSION OF THE "CURSOR MUNDI," in Four Texts. Edited by Rev. R. MORRIS, M.A., LL.D. Part IV. 10s.

67. NOTES ON PIERS PLOWMAN. By the Rev. W. W. SKEAT, M.A. Part I. 21s.

68. The Early English Version of the "CURSOR MUNDI," in Four Texts. Edited by Rev. R. MORRIS, M.A., LL.D. Part V. 25s.

Early English Text Society's Publications—*continued.*

69. ADAM DAVY'S FIVE DREAMS ABOUT EDWARD II. THE LIFE OF
SAINT ALEXIUS. Solomon's Book of Wisdom. St. Jerome's 15 Tokens
before Doomsday. The Lamentation of Souls. Edited from the Laud MS.
622, in the Bodleian Library, by F. J. FURNIVALL, M.A. *5s.*

Extra Series. Subscriptions—Small paper, one guinea; large paper
two guineas, per annum.

1. THE ROMANCE OF WILLIAM OF PALERNE (otherwise known as the
Romance of William and the Werwolf). Translated from the French at the
command of Sir Humphrey de Bohun, about A.D. 1350, to which is added a
fragment of the Alliterative Romance of Alisaunder, translated from the
Latin by the same author, about A.D. 1340; the former re-edited from the
unique MS. in the Library of King's College, Cambridge, the latter now
first edited from the unique MS. in the Bodleian Library, Oxford. By the
Rev. WALTER W. SKEAT, M.A. 8vo. sewed, pp. xliv. and 328. *£1 6s.*

2. ON EARLY ENGLISH PRONUNCIATION, with especial reference to
Shakspere and Chaucer; containing an investigation of the Correspondence
of Writing with Speech in England, from the Anglo-Saxon period to the
present day, preceded by a systematic Notation of all Spoken Sounds by
means of the ordinary Printing Types; including a re-arrangement of Prof.
F. J. Child's Memoirs on the Language of Chaucer and Gower, and reprints
of the rare Tracts by Salesbury on English, 1547, and Welsh, 1567, and by
Barcley on French, 1521 By ALEXANDER J. ELLIS, F.R.S. Part 1. On
the Pronunciation of the XIVth, XVIth, XVIIth, and XVIIIth centuries. 8vo.
sewed, pp. viii. and 416. *10s.*

3. CAXTON'S BOOK OF CURTESYE, printed at Westminster about 1477–8,
A.D., and now reprinted, with two MS. copies of the same treatise, from the
Oriel MS. 79, and the Balliol MS. 354. Edited by FREDERICK J. FURNI-
VALL, M.A. 8vo. sewed, pp. xii. and 58. *5s.*

4. THE LAY OF HAVELOK THE DANE; composed in the reign of
Edward I., about A.D. 1280. Formerly edited by Sir F. MADDEN for the
Roxburghe Club, and now re-edited from the unique MS. Laud Misc. 108, in
the Bodleian Library, Oxford, by the Rev. WALTER W. SKEAT, M.A. 8vo.
sewed, pp. lv. and 160. *10s.*

5. CHAUCER'S TRANSLATION OF BOETHIUS'S "DE CONSOLATIONE
PHILOSOPHIE." Edited from the Additional MS. 10,340 in the British
Museum. Collated with the Cambridge Univ. Libr. MS. Ii. 3. 21. By
RICHARD MORRIS. 8vo. 12s.

6 THE ROMANCE OF THE CHEVELERE ASSIGNE. Re-edited from the
unique manuscript in the British Museum, with a Preface, Notes, and
Glossarial Index, by HENRY H. GIBBS, Esq., M.A. 8vo. sewed, pp.
xviii. and 38. *3s.*

7. ON EARLY ENGLISH PRONUNCIATION, with especial reference to
Shakspere and Chaucer. By ALEXANDER J. ELLIS, F.R.S., etc., etc.
Part II. On the Pronunciation of the XIIIth and previous centuries, of
Anglo-Saxon, Icelandic, Old Norse and Gothic, with Chronological Tables of
the Value of Letters and Expression of Sounds in English Writing. 10s.

8. QUEENE ELIZABETHES ACHADEMY, by Sir HUMPHREY GILBERT.
A Booke of Precedence, The Ordering of a Funerall, etc. Varying Versions
of the Good Wife, The Wise Man, etc., Maxims, Lydgate's Order of Fools,
A Poem on Heraldry, Occleve on Lords' Men, etc., Edited by F. J.
FURNIVALL, M.A., Trin. Hall, Camb. With Essays on Early Italian and
German Books of Courtesy, by W. M. ROSSETTI, Esq., and E. OSWALD,
Esq. 8vo. 13s.

Early English Text Society's Publications—*continued.*

9. THE FRATERNITYE OF VACABONDES, by JOHN AWDELEY (licensed in 1560-1, imprinted then, and in 1565), from the edition of 1575 in the Bodleian Library. A Caueat or Warening for Commen Cursetors vulgarely called Vagabones, by THOMAS HARMAN, ESQUIERE. From the 3rd edition of 1567, belonging to Henry Huth, Esq., collated with the 2nd edition of 1567, in the Bodleian Library, Oxford, and with the reprint of the 4th edition of 1573. A Sermon in Praise of Thieves and Thievery, by PARSON HABEN OR HYBERDYNE, from the Lansdowne MS. 98, and Cotton Vesp. A, 25. Those parts of the Groundworke of Conny-catching (ed. 1592), that differ from *Harman's Caueat.* Edited by EDWARD VILES & F. J. FURNIVALL. 8vo. 7s. 6d.

10. THE FYRST BOKE OF THE INTRODUCTION OF KNOWLEDGE, made by Andrew Borde, of Physycke Doctor. A COMPENDYOUS REGYMENT OF A DYETARY OF HELTH made in Mountpyllier, compiled by Andrewe Boorde, of Physycke Doctor. BARNES IN THE DEFENCE OF THE BERDE : a treatyse made, answerynge the treatyse of Doctor Borde upon Berdes. Edited, with a life of Andrew Boorde, and large extracts from his Breuyary, by F. J FURNIVALL, M.A., Trinity Hall, Camb. 8vo. 18s.

11. THE BRUCE ; or, the Book of the most excellent and noble Prince, Robert de Broyss. King of Scots: compiled by Master John Barbour, Arch-deacon of Aberdeen. A.D. 1375. Edited from MS. G 23 in the Library of St. John's College, Cambridge, written A.D. 1487 ; collated with the MS. in the Advocates' Library at Edinburgh, written A.D. 1489, and with Hart's Edition, printed A.D. 1616 ; with a Preface, Notes, and Glossarial Index, by the Rev. WALTER W. SKEAT, M.A. Part I 8vo. 12s.

12. ENGLAND IN THE REIGN OF KING HENRY THE EIGHTH. A Dialogue between Cardinal Pole and Thomas Lupset, Lecturer in Rhetoric at Oxford. By THOM s STARKEY, Chaplain to the King. Edited, with Preface, Notes, and Glossary, by J. M. COWPER. And with an Introduction, containing the Life and Letters of Thomas Starkey, by the Rev. J. S. BREWER, M.A. Part II. 12s. (*Part I., Starkey's Life and Letters, is in preparation.*)

13. A SUPPLICACYON FOR THE BEGGARS. Written about the year 1529, by SIMON FISH. Now re-edited by FREDERICK J. FURNIVALL. With a Supplycacion to our moste Soueraigne Lorde Kynge Henry the Eyght (1544 A.D.), A Supplication of the Poore Commons (1546 A.D.), The Decaye of England by the great multitude of Shepe (1550-3 A.D.). Edited by J. MEADOWS COWPER. 6s.

14. ON EARLY ENGLISH PRONUNCIATION, with especial reference to Shakspere and Chaucer. By A. J. ELLIS, F.R.S., F.S.A. Part III. Illustrations of the Pronunciation of the XIVth and XVIth Centuries. Chaucer, Gower, Wycliffe, Spenser, Shakspere, Salesbury, Barcley, Hart, Bullokar, Gill. Pronouncing Vocabulary. 10s.

15. ROBERT CROWLEY'S THIRTY-ONE EPIGRAMS, Voyce of the Last Trumpet, Way to Wealth, etc., 1550-1 A.D. Edited by J. M. COWPER, Esq. 12s.

16. A TREATISE ON THE ASTROLABE ; addressed to his son Lowys, by Geoffrey Chaucer, A.D. 1391. Edited from the earliest MSS. by the Rev. WALTER W. SKEAT, M.A., late Fellow of Christ's College, Cambridge. 10s.

17. THE COMPLAYNT OF SCOTLANDE, 1549, A.D., with an Appendix of four Contemporary English Tracts. Edited by J. A. H. MURRAY, Esq. Part I. 10s.

18. THE COMPLAYNT OF SCOTLANDE, etc. Part II. 8s.

19. OURE LADYES MYROURE, A.D. 1530, edited by the Rev. J. H. BLUNT, M.A., with four full-page photolithographic facsimiles by Cooke and Fotheringham. 24s.

Early English Text Society's Publications—*continued*.

20. LONELICH'S HISTORY OF THE HOLY GRAIL (ab. 1450 A.D.), translated from the French Prose of SIRES ROBIERS DE BORRON. Re-edited from the Unique MS. in Corpus Christi College. Cambridge, by F. J. Furnivall, Esq. M.A. Part I. 8s.

21. BARBOUR'S BRUCE. Edited from the MSS. and the earliest printed edition by the Rev. W. W. SKEAT, M.A. Part II. 4s.

22. HENRY BRINKLOW'S COMPLAYNT OF RODERYCK MORS, somtyme a gray Fryre, unto the Parliament Howse of Ingland his naturall Country, for the Redresse of certen wicked Lawes, euel Customs, and cruel Decreys (ab. 1542); and THE LAMENTACION OF A CHRISTIAN AGAINST THE CITIE OF LONDON, made by Roderigo Mors, A.D. 1545. Edited by J. M. COWPER, Esq. 9s.

23. ON EARLY ENGLISH PRONUNCIATION, with especial reference to Shakspere and Chaucer. By A. J. ELLIS, Esq., F.R.S. Part IV. 10s.

24. LONELICH'S HISTORY OF THE HOLY GRAIL (ab. 1450 A.D.), translated from the French Prose of SIRES ROBIERS DE BORRON. Re-edited from the Unique MS. in Corpus Christi College, Cambridge, by F. J. FURNIVALL, Esq., M.A. Part II. 10s.

25. THE ROMANCE OF GUY OF WARWICK. Edited from the Cambridge University MS. by Prof. J. ZUPITZA, Ph.D. Part I. 20s.

26. THE ROMANCE OF GUY OF WARWICK. Edited from the Cambridge University MS. by Prof. J. ZUPITZA, Ph.D. (The 2nd or 15th century version.) Part II. 14s.

27. THE ENGLISH WORKS OF JOHN FISHER, Bishop of Rochester (died 1535). Edited by Professor J. E. B. MAYOR, M.A. Part I., the Text. 16s.

28. LONELICH'S HISTORY OF THE HOLY GRAIL. Edited by F. J. FURNIVALL, M.A. Part III. 10s.

29. BARBOUR'S BRUCE. Edited from the MSS. and the earliest Printed Edition, by the Rev. W. W. SKEAT, M.A. Part III. 21s.

30. LONELICH'S HISTORY OF THE HOLY GRAIL. Edited by F. J. FURNIVALL, ESQ., M.A. Part IV. 15s.

31. ALEXANDER AND DINDIMUS. Translated from the Latin about A.D. 1340-50. Re-edited by the Rev. W. W. SKEAT, M.A. 6s.

Edda Saemundar Hinns Froda—The Edda of Saemund the Learned. From the Old Norse or Icelandic. By BENJAMIN THORPE. Part I. with a Mythological Index. 12mo. pp. 152, cloth, 3s. 6d. Part II. with Index of Persons and Places. 12mo. pp. viii. and 172, cloth. 1866. 4s.; or in 1 Vol. complete, 7s. 6d.

Edkins.—INTRODUCTION TO THE STUDY OF THE CHINESE CHARACTERS. By J. EDKINS, D.D., Peking, China. Roy. 8vo. pp. 340, paper boards. 18s.

Edkins.—CHINA'S PLACE IN PHILOLOGY. An attempt to show that the Languages of Europe and Asia have a common origin. By the Rev. JOSEPH EDKINS. Crown 8vo, pp. xxiii.—403, cloth. 10s. 6d.

Edkins.—A VOCABULARY OF THE SHANGHAI DIALECT. By J. EDKINS. 8vo. half-calf, pp. vi. and 151. Shanghai, 1869. 21s.

Edkins.—A GRAMMAR OF COLLOQUIAL CHINESE, as exhibited in the Shanghai Dialect. By J. EDKINS, B.A. Second edition, corrected. 8vo. half-calf, pp. viii. and 225. Shanghai, 1868. 21s.

Edkins.—A GRAMMAR OF THE CHINESE COLLOQUIAL LANGUAGE, commonly called the Mandarin Dialect. By JOSEPH EDKINS. Second edition. 8vo. half-calf, pp. viii. and 279. Shanghai, 1864. £1 10s.

Edkins.—PROGRESSIVE LESSONS IN THE CHINESE SPOKEN LANGUAGE. With Lists of Common Words and Phrases.   By J. EDKINS, B.A.   Third edition, 8vo. pp. 120. 1869. 14s.

Edkins.—RELIGION IN CHINA.   A Brief Account of the Three Religions of the Chinese.   By JOSEPH EDKINS, D.D.   Post 8vo. cloth.   7s. 6d.

Eger and Grime; an Early English Romance.   Edited from Bishop Percy's Folio Manuscript, about 1650 A.D.   By JOHN W. HALES, M.A., Fellow and late Assistant Tutor of Christ's College, Cambridge, and FREDERICK J. FURNIVALL, M.A., of Trinity Hall, Cambridge. 1 vol. 4to., pp. 64, (only 100 copies printed), bound in the Roxburghe style.   10s. 6d.

Egyptian Calendar for the Year 1295 A.H (1878 A.D.), corresponding with the years 1594, 1595, of the Koptic Era. Demy 8vo. sewed, pp. 98. 5s.

Eitel.—A CHINESE DICTIONARY IN THE CANTONESE DIALECT.   By ERNEST JOHN EITEL, Ph.D. Tubing. Will be completed in four parts. Part I. (A—K). 8vo. sewed, pp. 202. 12s. 6d. Part II. (K—M). pp. 202. 12s. 6d.

Eitel.—HANDBOOK FOR THE STUDENT OF CHINESE BUDDHISM.   By the Rev. E. J. EITEL, of the London Missionary Society. Crown 8vo. pp. viii., 224, cl., 18s

Eitel.—FENG-SHUI: or, The Rudiments of Natural Science in China. By Rev. E. J. EITEL, M.A., Ph.D. Demy 8vo. sewed, pp. vi. and 84. 6s.

Eitel.—BUDDHISM: its Historical, Theoretical, and Popular Aspects. In Three Lectures. By Rev. E. J. EITEL, M.A. Ph.D. Second Edition. Demy 8vo. sewed, pp. 130. 5s.

Elliot.—THE HISTORY OF INDIA, as told by its own Historians.   The Muhammadan Period. Complete in Eight Vols. Edited from the Posthumous Papers of the late Sir H. M. ELLIOT, K.C.B., East India Company's Bengal Civil Service, by Prof. JOHN DOWSON, M.R.A.S., Staff College, Sandhurst.

Vols. I. and II.   With a Portrait of Sir H. M. Elliot. 8vo. pp xxxii. and 542, x. and 580, cloth.   18s. each.
Vol. III. 8vo. pp. xii. and 627, cloth.   24s.
Vol. IV. 8vo. pp. x. and 563 cloth   21s
Vol. V. 8vo. pp. xii. and 576, cloth.   21s.
Vol. VI. 8vo. pp. viii. and 574, cloth.   21s.
Vol. VII. 8vo. pp. viii. and 574, cloth.   21s.
Vol. VIII. 8vo. pp. xxxii., 444, and lxviii. cloth.   24s.

Elliot.—MEMOIRS ON THE HISTORY, FOLKLORE, AND DISTRIBUTION OF THE RACES OF THE NORTH WESTERN PROVINCES OF INDIA; being an amplified Edition of the original Supplementary Glossary of Indian Terms. By the late Sir HENRY M. ELLIOT, K.C.B., of the Hon. East India Company's Bengal Civil Service. Edited, revised, and re-arranged, by JOHN BEAMES, M.R.A.S., Bengal Civil Service; Member of the German Oriental Society, of the Asiatic Societies of Paris and Bengal, and of the Philological Society of London. In 2 vols. demy 8vo., pp. xx., 370, and 396, cloth. With two Lithographic Plates, one full-page coloured Map, and three large coloured folding Maps. 36s.

Ellis.—ON NUMERALS, as Signs of Primeval Unity among Mankind. By ROBERT ELLIS, B.D., late Fellow of St. John's College, Cambridge. Demy 8vo. cloth, pp. viii. and 94. 3s. 6d.

Ellis.—THE ASIATIC AFFINITIES OF THE OLD ITALIANS.   By ROBERT ELLIS, B.D., Fellow of St. John's College, Cambridge, and author of "Ancient Routes between Italy and Gaul." Crown 8vo. pp. iv. 156, cloth. 1870. 5s.

Ellis.—PERUVIA SCYTHICA.   The Quichua Language of Peru: its derivation from Central Asia with the American languages in general, and with the Turanian and Iberian languages of the Old World, including the Basque, the Lycian, and the Pre-Aryan language of Etruria. By ROBERT ELLIS, B.D. 8vo. cloth, pp. xii. and 219. 1875. 6s.

Ellis.—ETRUSCAN NUMERALS. By ROBERT ELLIS, B.D. 8vo. sewed, pp. 52. 2s. 6d.

English and Welsh Languages.—THE INFLUENCE OF THE ENGLISH AND Welsh Languages upon each other, exhibited in the Vocabularies of the two Tongues. Intended to suggest the importance to Philologers, Antiquaries, Ethnographers, and others, of giving due attention to the Celtic Branch of the Indo-Germanic Family of Languages. Square, pp. 30, sewed. 1869. 1s.

English Dialect Society's Publications. Subscription, 1873 to 1876, 10s. 6d. per annum; 1877 and following years, 20s. per annum.

1873.

1. Series B. Part 1. Reprinted Glossaries. Containing a Glossary of North of England Words, by J. H.; five Glossaries, by Mr. MARSHALL; and a West-Riding Glossary, by Dr. WILLAN. 7s. 6d.

2. Series A. Bibliographical. A List of Books illustrating English Dialects. Part I. Containing a General List of Dictionaries, etc.; and a List of Books relating to some of the Counties of England. 4s.

3. Series C. Original Glossaries. Part I. Containing a Glossary of Swaledale Words. By Captain HARLAND. 4s.

1874.

4. Series D. The History of English Sounds. By H. SWEET, Esq. 4s. 6d.

5. Series B. Part II. Reprinted Glossaries. Containing seven Provincial English Glossaries, from various sources. 7s.

6. Series B. Part III. Ray's Collection of English Words not generally used, from the edition of 1691; together with Thoresby's Letter to Ray, 1703. Re-arranged and newly edited by Rev. WALTER W. SKEAT. 8s.

6*. Subscribers to the English Dialect Society for 1874 also receive a copy of 'A Dictionary of the Sussex Dialect.' By the Rev. W. D PARISH.

1875.

7. Series D. Part II. The Dialect of West Somerset. By F. T. ELWORTHY, Esq. 3s. 6d.

8. Series A. Part II. Containing a List of Books Relating to some of the Counties of England. 6s.

9. Series C. A Glossary of Words used in the Neighbourhood of Whitby. By F. K. ROBINSON. Part I. 7s. 6d.

10. Series C. A Glossary of the Dialect of Lancashire. By J. H. NODAL and G. MILNER. Part I. 3s. 6d.

1876.

11. On the Survival of Early English Words in our Present Dialects. By Dr. R. MORRIS. 6d.

12. Series C. Original Glossaries. Part III. Containing Five Original Provincial English Glossaries. 7s.

13. Series C. A Glossary of Words used in the Neighbourhood of Whitby. By F. K. Robinson. Part II. 6s 6d.

14. A Glossary of Mid-Yorkshire Words, with a Grammar. By C. CLOUGH ROBINSON. 9s.

1877.

15. A GLOSSARY OF WORDS used in the Wapentakes of Manley and Corringham, Lincolnshire. By EDWARD PEACOCK, F.S.A. 9s. 6d.

16. A Glossary of Holderness Words. By F. Ross, R. STEAD, and T. HOLDERNESS. With a Map of the District. 4s.

17. On the Dialects of Eleven Southern and South-Western Counties, with a new Classification of the English Dialects. By Prince LOUIS LUCIEN BONAPARTE. With Two Maps. 1s.

18. Bibliographical List. Part III. completing the Work, and containing a List of Books on Scottish Dialects, Anglo-Irish Dialect, Cant and Slang, and Americanisms, with additions to the English List and Index. Edited by J. H. NODAL. 4s. 6d.

19. An Outline of the Grammar of West Somerset. By F. T. ELWORTHY, ESQ. 5s.

1878.

20. A Glossary of Cumberland Words and Phrases. By WILLIAM DICKINSON, F.L.S. 6s.

21. Tusser's Five Hundred Pointes of Good Husbandrie. Edited with Introduction, Notes and Glossary, by W. PAINE and SIDNEY J. HERRTAGE, B.A. 12s. 6d.

22. A Dictionary of English Plant Names. By JAMES BRITTEN, F.L.S., and ROBERT HOLLAND. Part I. (A to F). 8s. 6d.

1879.

23. Five Reprinted Glossaries, including Wiltshire, East Anglian, Suffolk, and East Yorkshire Words, and Words from Bishop Kennett's Parochial Antiquities. Edited by the Rev. Professor SKEAT, M.A. 7s.

24. Supplement to the Cumberland Glossary (No. 20). By W. DICKINSON, F.L.S. 1s.

Etherington.—THE STUDENT'S GRAMMAR OF THE HINDÍ LANGUAGE. By the Rev. W. ETHERINGTON, Missionary, Benares. Second edition. Crown 8vo. pp. xiv., 255, and xiii., cloth. 1873. 12s.

Faber.—A SYSTEMATICAL DIGEST OF THE DOCTRINES OF CONFUCIUS, according to the ANALECTS, GREAT LEARNING, and DOCTRINE of the MEAN, with an Introduction on the Authorities upon CONFUCIUS and Confucianism. By ERNST FABER, Rhenish Missionary. Translated from the German by P. G. von Möllendorff. 8vo. sewed, pp. viii. and 131. 1875. 12s. 6d.

Facsimiles of Two Papyri found in a Tomb at Thebes. With a Translation by SAMUEL BIRCH, LL.D., F.S.A., Corresponding Member of the Institute of France, Academies of Berlin, Herculaneum, etc., and an Account of their Discovery. By A. HENRY RHIND, Esq., F.S.A., etc. In large folio, pp. 30 of text, and 16 plates coloured. bound in cloth. 21s.

Fallon.—A NEW HINDUSTANI-ENGLISH DICTIONARY. With Illustrations from Hindustani Literature and Folk-lore. By S. W. FALLON, Ph.D. Halle. Parts I. to XIX. Roy. 8vo. Price 4s. 6d. each Part.
To be completed in about 25 Parts of 48 pages each Part, forming together One Volume.

Farley.—EGYPT, CYPRUS, AND ASIATIC TURKEY. By J. LEWIS FARLEY, Author of "The Resources of Turkey," etc. Demy 8vo. cl., pp. xvi.-270. 10s. 6d.

Fausböll.—THE DASARATHA-JÁTAKA, being the Buddhist Story of King Ráma. The original Páli Text, with a Translation and Notes by V. FAUSBÖLL. 8vo. sewed, pp. iv. and 48. 2s. 6d.

Fausböll.—FIVE JÁTAKAS, containing a Fairy Tale, a Comical Story, and Three Fables. In the original Páli Text, accompanied with a Translation and Notes. By V. FAUSBÖLL. 8vo. sewed, pp. viii. and 72. 6s.

Fausböll.—TEN JÁTAKAS. The Original Páli Text, with a Translation and Notes. By V. FAUSBÖLL. 8vo. sewed, pp. xiii. and 128. 7s. 6d.

Fausböll.—JÁTAKA. See under JÁTAKA.

Fiske.—MYTHS AND MYTH-MAKERS: Old Tales and Superstitions interpreted by Comparative Mythology. By JOHN FISKE, M.A., Assistant Librarian, and late Lecturer on Philosophy at Harvard University. Crown 8vo. cloth, pp. viii. and 252. 10s. 6d.

Fornander.—AN ACCOUNT OF THE POLYNESIAN RACE: Its Origin and Migrations. By A. FORNANDER. Vol. I. Post 8vo., cloth. 7s. 6d.

Forsyth.—REPORT OF A MISSION TO YARKUND IN 1873, under Command of SIR T. D. FORSYTH, K.C.S.I., C.B., Bengal Civil Service, with Historical and Geographical Information regarding the Possessions of the Ameer of Yarkund. With 45 Photographs, 4 Lithographic Plates, and a large Folding Map of Eastern Turkestan. 4to. cloth, pp. iv. and 573. £5 5s.

Foss.—NORWEGIAN GRAMMAR, with Exercises in the Norwegian and and English Languages, and a List of Irregular Verbs. By FRITHJOF FOSS, Graduate of the University of Norway. Crown 8vo., pp. 50, cloth limp. 2s.

Foster.—PRE-HISTORIC RACES OF THE UNITED STATES OF AMERICA. By J. W. FOSTER, LL.D., Author of the "Physical Geography of the Mississippi Valley," etc. With 72 Illustrations. 8vo. cloth, pp. xvi. and 416. 14s.

Fryer.—VUTTODAYA. (Exposition of Metre.) By SANGHARAKKHITA THERA. A Pali Text, Edited, with Translation and Notes, by Major G. E. FRYER. 8vo. pp. 44. 2s. 6d.

Furnivall.—EDUCATION IN EARLY ENGLAND. Some Notes used as Forewords to a Collection of Treatises on "Manners and Meals in the Olden Time," for the Early English Text Society. By FREDERICK J. FURNIVALL, M.A., Trinity Hall, Cambridge, Member of Council of the Philological and Early English Text Societies. 8vo. sewed, pp. 74. 1s.

Garrett.—A CLASSICAL DICTIONARY OF INDIA, illustrative of the Mythology, Philosophy, Literature, Antiquities, Arts, Manners, Customs, etc., of the Hindus. By JOHN GARRETT. 8vo. pp. x. and 793. cloth. 28s.

Garrett.—SUPPLEMENT TO THE ABOVE CLASSICAL DICTIONARY OF INDIA. By JOHN GARRETT, Director of Public Instruction at Mysore. 8vo. cloth, pp. 160. 7s. 6d.

Gautama.—THE INSTITUTES OF GAUTAMA. *See Auctores Sanscriti.*

Gesenius.—HEBREW AND ENGLISH LEXICON OF THE OLD TESTAMENT, including the Biblical Chaldee, from the Latin. By EDWARD ROBINSON. Fifth Edition. 8vo. cloth, pp. xii. and 1160. £1 16s.

Gesenius.—HEBREW GRAMMAR. Translated from the Seventeenth Edition. By Dr. T. J. CONANT. With Grammatical Exercises, and a Chrestomathy by the Translator. 8vo. cloth, pp. xvi.-364. £1.

Giles.—CHINESE SKETCHES. By HERBERT A. GILES, of H.B.M.'s China Consular Service. 8vo. cl., pp. 204. 10s. 6d.

Giles.—A DICTIONARY OF COLLOQUIAL IDIOMS IN THE MANDARIN DIALECT. By HERBERT A. GILES. 4to. pp. 65. £1 8s.

Giles.—SYNOPTICAL STUDIES IN CHINESE CHARACTER. By HERBERT A. GILES. 8vo. pp. 118. 15s.

Giles.—CHINESE WITHOUT A TEACHER. Being a Collection of Easy and Useful Sentences in the Mandarin Dialect. With a Vocabulary. By HERBERT A. GILES. 12mo. pp 60. 5s.

Giles.—RECORD OF THE BUDDHIST KINGDOMS. Translated from the Chinese by H. A. GILES, of H.M. Consular Service. 8vo. sewed, pp. x.-129. 5s.

Giles.—The San Tzu Ching; or, Three Character Classic; and the Ch'Jen Tsu Wen; or, Thousand Character Essay. Metrically Translated by Herbert A. Giles. 12mo. pp. 28. 2s. 6d.

Giles.—A Glossary of Reference on Subjects connected with the Far East. By H. A. Giles, of H.M. China Consular Service. 8vo. sewed, pp. v.–183. 7s. 6d.

Giles —Hebrew and Christian Records. An Historical Enquiry concerning the Age and Authorship of the Old and New Testaments. By the Rev. Dr. Giles, Rector of Sutton, Surrey, and formerly Fellow of Corpus Christi College, Oxford. Now first published complete, 2 Vols. Vol. I., Hebrew Records; Vol. II., Christian Records. 8vo. cloth, pp. 442 and 440. 1877. 24s.

Gliddon.—Ancient Egypt, Her Monuments, Hieroglyphics, History, Archæology, and other subjects connected with Hieroglyphical Literature. By George R. Gliddon, late United States Consul, at Cairo. 15th Edition. Revised and Corrected, with an Appendix. 4to. sewed, pp. 68. 2s. 6d.

God.—Book of God. By ☉. 8vo. cloth. Vol. I.: The Apocalypse. pp. 647. 12s. 6d.—Vol. II. An Introduction to the Apocalypse, pp. 752. 14s.— Vol. III. A Commentary on the Apocalypse, pp. 854. 16s.

Goldstücker.—A Dictionary, Sanskrit and English, extended and improved from the Second Edition of the Dictionary of Professor H. H. Wilson, with his sanction and concurrence. Together with a Supplement, Grammatical Appendices, and an Index, serving as a Sanskrit-English Vocabulary. By Theodor Goldstücker. Parts I. to VI. 4to. pp. 400. 1856-1863. 6s. each.

Goldstücker.—Panini: His Place in Sanskrit Literature. An Investigation of some Literary and Chronological Questions which may be settled by a study of his Work. A separate impression of the Preface to the Facsimile of MS. No. 17 in the Library of Her Majesty's Home Government for India, which contains a portion of the Manava-Kalpa-Sutra, with the Commentary of Kumarila-Swamin. By Theodor Goldstücker. Imperial 8vo. pp. 268, cloth. £2 2s.

Goldstücker.—On the Deficiencies in the Present Administration of Hindu Law; being a paper read at the Meeting of the East India Association on the 8th June, 1870. By Theodor Goldstücker, Professor of Sanskrit in University College, London, &c. Demy 8vo. pp. 56, sewed. 1s. 6d.

Gover.—The Folk-Songs of Southern India. By Charles E. Gover. 8vo. pp. xxiii. and 299, cloth 10s. 6d.

Grammatography.—A Manual of Reference to the Alphabets of Ancient and Modern Languages. Based on the German Compilation of F. Ballhorn. Royal 8vo. pp. 80, cloth. 7s. 6d.

The "Grammatography" is offered to the public as a compendious introduction to the reading of the most important ancient and modern languages. Simple in its design, it will be consulted with advantage by the philological student, the amateur linguist, the bookseller, the corrector of the press, and the diligent compositor.

ALPHABETICAL INDEX.

Afghan (or Pushto).	Czechian(or Bohemian).	Hebrew (current hand).	Polish.
Amharic.	Danish.	Hebrew (Judæo-Ger-	Pushto (or Afghan).
Anglo-Saxon.	Demotic.	Hungarian. [man).	Romaic(Modern Greek
Arabic.	Estrangelo.	Illyrian.	Russian.
Arabic Ligatures.	Ethiopic.	Irish.	Runes.
Aramaic.	Etruscan.	Italian (Old).	Samaritan.
Archaic Characters.	Georgian.	Japanese.	Sanscrit.
Armenian.	German.	Javanese.	Servian.
Assyrian Cuneiform.	Glagolitic.	Lettish.	Slavonic (Old).
Bengali.	Gothic.	Mantshu.	Sorbian (or Wendish).
Bohemian (Czechian).	Greek.	Median Cuneiform.	Swedish.
Búgis.	Greek Ligatures.	Modern Greek (Romaic)	Syriac.
Burmese.	Greek (Archaic).	Mongolian.	Tamil.
Canarese (or Carnátaca).	Gujerati(orGuzzeratte).	Numidian.	Telugu.
Chinese.	Hieratic.	OldSlavonic(orCyrillic).	Tibetan.
Coptic.	Hieroglyphics.	Palmyrenian.	Turkish.
Croato-Glagolitic.	Hebrew.	Persian.	Wallachian.
Cufic.	Hebrew (Archaic).	Persian Cuneiform.	Wendish (or Sorbian).
Crillic (or Old Slavonic).	Hebrew (Rabbinical).	Phœnician.	Zend.

Grassmann.—WÖRTERBUCH ZUM RIG-VEDA. Von HERMANN GRASSMANN, Professor am Marienstifts-Gymnasium zu Stettin. 8vo. pp. 1775. £1 10s.

Green.—SHAKESPEARE AND THE EMBLEM-WRITERS: an Exposition of their Similarities of Thought and Expression. Preceded by a View of the Emblem-Book Literature down to A.D. 1616. By HENRY GREEN, M.A. In one volume, pp. xvi. 572, profusely illustrated with Woodcuts and Photolith. Plates, elegantly bound in cloth gilt, large medium 8vo. £1 11s. 6d ; large imperial 8vo. 1870. £2 12s. 6d.

Grey.—HANDBOOK OF AFRICAN, AUSTRALIAN, AND POLYNESIAN PHILOLOGY, as represented in the Library of His Excellency Sir George Grey, K.C.B., Her Majesty's High Commissioner of the Cape Colony. Classed, Annotated, and Edited by SIR GEORGE GREY and Dr. H. I. BLEEK.

Vol. I.   Part 1.—South Africa. 8vo. pp. 186. 20s.
Vol. I.   Part 2.—Africa (North of the Tropic of Capricorn). 8vo. pp. 70. 4s.
Vol. I.   Part 3.—Madagascar. 8vo. pp. 24. 2s.
Vol. II.   Part 1.—Australia. 8vo. pp. iv. and 44. 3s.
Vol. II.   Part 2.—Papuan Languages of the Loyalty Islands and New Hebrides, comprising those of the Islands of Nengone, Lifu, Aneitum, Tana, and others. 8vo. p. 12. 1s.
Vol. II.   Part 3.—Fiji Islands and Rotuma (with Supplement to Part II., Papuan Languages, and Part I., Australia). 8vo. pp. 34. 2s.
Vol. II.   Part 4.—New Zealand, the Chatham Islands, and Auckland Islands. 8vo. pp. 76. 7s.
Vol. II.   Part 4 (*continuation*).—Polynesia and Borneo. 8vo. pp. 77-154. 7s.
Vol. III.   Part 1.—Manuscripts and Incunables. 8vo. pp. viii. and 24. 2s.
Vol. IV.   Part 1.—Early Printed Books. England. 8vo. pp. vi. and 266. 12s.

Grey.—MAORI MEMENTOS: being a Series of Addresses presented by the Native People to His Excellency Sir George Grey, K.C.B., F.R.S With Introductory Remarks and Explanatory Notes ; to which is added a small Collection of Laments, etc. By CH. OLIVER B. DAVIS. 8vo. pp. iv. and 228, cloth. 12s.

Griffin.—THE RAJAS OF THE PUNJAB. Being the History of the Principal States in the Punjab, and their Political Relations with the British Government. By LEPEL H. GRIFFIN, Bengal Civil Service ; Under Secretary to the Government of the Punjab, Author of " The Punjab Chiefs," etc. Second edition. Royal 8vo., pp. xiv. and 630. 21s.

Griffis.—THE MIKADO'S EMPIRE. Book I. History of Japan from 660 B.C. to 1872 A.D. Book II. Personal Experiences, Observations, and Studies in Japan, 1870-74. By W. E. GRIFFIS. Illustrated. 8vo cl., pp. 626. £1.

Griffith.—SCENES FROM THE RAMAYANA, MEGHADUTA, ETC. Translated by RALPH T H. GRIFFITH, M.A., Principal of the Benares College. Second Edition. Crown 8vo. pp. xviii., 244, cloth. 6s.

CONTENTS.—Preface—Ayodhya—Ravan Doomed—The Birth of Rama—The Heir apparent—Manthara's Guile—Dasaratha's Oath—The Step-mother—Mother and Son—The Triumph of Love—Farewell!—The Hermit's Son—The Trial of Truth—The Forest—The Rape of Sita—Rama's Despair—The Messenger Cloud—Khumbakarna—The Suppliant Dove—True Glory—Feed the Poor—The Wise Scholar.

Griffith.—THE RÁMÁYAN OF VÁLMÍKI. Translated into English verse. By RALPH T. H. GRIFFITH, M.A., Principal of the Benares College. 5 vols.

Vol. I., containing Books I. and II. Demy 8vo. pp. xxxii. 440, cloth. 1870. 18s.
Vol. II., containing Book II., with additional Notes and Index of Names. Demy 8vo. pp. 504, cloth. 18s.
Vol. III. Demy 8vo. pp. v. and 371, cloth. 1872. 15s.
Vol. IV. Demy 8vo. pp. viii. and 432. 1873. 18s.
Vol. V. Demy 8vo. pp. 368, cloth. 1875. 15s.

Griffith.—THE BIRTH OF THE WAR GOD. A Poem by KÁLIDÁSA. Translated from the Sanskrit into English Verse. By RALPH T. H. GRIFFITH, M.A., Principal of Benares College. Second edition, post 8vo. cloth, pp. xii. and 116. 5s.

Grout.—The Isizulu : a Grammar of the Zulu Language ; accompanied with an Historical Introduction, also with an Appendix. By Rev. Lewis Grout. 8vo. pp. lii. and 432, cloth. 21s.

Gubernatis.—Zoological Mythology ; or, the Legends of Animals. By Angelo de Gubernatis, Professor of Sanskrit and Comparative Literature in the Instituto di Studii Superiori e di Perfezionamento at Florence, etc. In 2 vols. 8vo. pp. xxvi. and 432, vii. and 442. 28s.

Gundert.—A Malayalam and English Dictionary. By Rev. H. Gundert, D. Ph. Royal 8vo. pp. viii. and 1116. £2 10s.

Haas.—Catalogue of Sanskrit and Pali Books in the Library of the British Museum. By Dr. Ernst Haas. Printed by Permission of the Trustees of the British Museum. 4to. cloth, pp. 200. £1 1s.

Háfiz of Shíráz.—Selections from his Poems. Translated from the Persian by Herman Bicknell. With Preface by A. S. Bicknell. Demy 4to., pp. xx. and 384, printed on fine stout plate-paper, with appropriate Oriental Bordering in gold and colour, and Illustrations by J. R. Herbert, R.A. £2 2s.

Haldeman. — Pennsylvania Dutch : a Dialect of South Germany with an Infusion of English. By S. S. Haldeman, A.M., Professor of Comparative Philology in the University of Pennsylvania, Philadelphia. 8vo. pp. viii. and 70, cloth. 1872. 3s. 6d.

Hall.—Modern English. By Fitzedward Hall, M.A., Hon. D.C.L., Oxon. Cr. 8vo. cloth, pp. xvi. and 394. 10s. 6d.

Hall.—On English Adjectives in -Able, with Special Reference to Reliable. By Fitzedward Hall, C.E., M.A., Hon.D.C.L. Oxon. ; formerly Professor of Sanskrit Language and Literature, and of Indian Jurisprudence, in King's College, London. Crown 8vo. cloth, pp. viii. and 238. 7s. 6d.

Hans Breitmann.—See under Leland.

Hardy.—Christianity and Buddhism Compared. By the late Rev. R. Spence Hardy, Hon. Member Royal Asiatic Society. 8vo. sd. pp. 138. 6s.

Hassoun.—The Diwan of Hatim Tai. An Old Arabic Poet of the Sixth Century of the Christian Era. Edited by R. Hassoun. With Illustrations. 4to. pp. 43. 3s. 6d.

Haswell.—Grammatical Notes and Vocabulary of the Peguan Language. To which are added a few pages of Phrases, etc. By Rev. J. M. Haswell. 8vo. pp. xvi. and 160. 15s.

Haug.—The Book of Arda Viraf. The Pahlavi text prepared by Destur Hoshangji Jamaspji Asa. Revised and collated with further MSS.. with an English translation and Introduction, and an Appendix containing the Texts and Translations of the Gosht-i Fryano and Hadokht Nask. By Martin Haug, Ph.D., Professor of Sanskrit and Comparative Philology at the University of Munich. Assisted by E. W. West, Ph.D. Published by order of the Bombay Government. 8vo. sewed, pp. lxxx., v., and 316. £1 5s.

Haug.—A Lecture on an Original Speech of Zoroaster (Yasna 45), with remarks on his age. By Martin Haug, Ph.D. 8vo. pp. 28, sewed. Bombay, 1865. 2s.

Haug.—The Aitareya Brahmanam of the Rig Veda : containing the Earliest Speculations of the Brahmans on the meaning of the Sacrificial Prayers, and on the Origin, Performance, and Sense of the Rites of the Vedic Religion. Edited, Translated, and Explained by Martin Haug, Ph.D., Superintendent of Sanskrit Studies in the Poona College, etc., etc. In 2 Vols. Crown 8vo. Vol. I. Contents, Sanskrit Text, with Preface, Introductory Essay, and a Map of the Sacrificial Compound at the Soma Sacrifice, pp. 312. Vol. II. Translation with Notes, pp. 544. £2 2s.

Haug.—An Old Zand-Pahlavi Glossary. Edited in the Original Characters, with a Transliteration in Roman Letters, an English Translation, and an Alphabetical Index. By Destur Hoshengji Jamaspji. High-priest of the Parsis in Malwa, India. Rev. with Notes and Intro. by Martin Haug, Ph.D. Publ. by order of Gov. of Bombay. 8vo. sewed, pp. lvi. and 132. 15s.

Haug.—An Old Pahlavi-Pazand Glossary. Ed., with Alphabetical Index, by Destur Hoshangji Jamaspji Asa, High Priest of the Parsis in Malwa. Rev. and Enl., with Intro. Essay on the Pahlavi Language, by M. Haug, Ph.D. Pub. by order of Gov. of Bombay. 8vo. pp. xvi. 152, 268, sd. 1870. 28s.

Haug.—Essays on the Sacred Language, Writings, and Religion of the Parsis. By Martin Haug, Ph D., late Professor of Sanskrit and Comparative Philology at the University of Munich. Second Edition. Edited by E. W. West, Ph.D. Post 8vo. pp. xvi. and 428, cloth, 16s.

Hawken.—Upa-Sastra : Comments, Linguistic and Doctrinal, on Sacred and Mythic Literature. By J. D. Hawken. 8vo. cloth, pp. viii.–288. 7s. 6d.

Heaviside.—American Antiquities ; or, the New World the Old, and the Old World the New. By John T. C. Heaviside. 8vo. pp. 46, sewed. 1s. 6d

Hebrew Literature Society (Publications of). Subscription £1 1s. per Series.   1872-3. *First Series.*

Vol. I. Miscellany of Hebrew Literature. Demy 8vo. cloth, pp. viii. and 228. 10s.

Vol. II. The Commentary of Ibn Ezra on Isaiah. Edited from MSS., and Translated with Notes, Introductions, and Indexes, by M. Friedländer, Ph.D. Vol. I. Translation of the Commentary. Demy 8vo. cloth, pp. xxviii. and 332. 10s. 6d.

Vol. III. The Commentary of Ibn Ezra. Vol. II. The Anglican Version of the Book of the Prophet Isaiah amended according to the Commentary of Ibn Ezra. Demy 8vo. cloth, pp. 112. 4s. 6d.

1877.   *Second Series.*

Vol. I. Miscellany of Hebrew Literature. Vol. II. Edited by the Rev. A. Löwy. Demy 8vo. cloth. pp. vi. and 276. 10s. 6d.

Vol. II. The Commentary of Ibn Ezra. Vol. III. Demy 8vo. cloth, pp. 172. 7s.

Vol. III. Ibn Ezra Literature. Vol. IV. Essays on the Writings of Abraham Ibn Ezra. By M. Friedlände, Ph D. Demy 8vo. cloth, pp. x.–252 and 78. 12s. 6d.

Hepburn.—A Japanese and English Dictionary. With an English and Japanese Index. By J. C. Hepburn, M.D., LL.D. Second edition. Imperial 8vo. cloth, pp. xxxii., 632 and 201. £8 8s.

Hepburn.—Japanese-English and English-Japanese Dictionary. By J. C. Hepburn, M.D., LL.D. Abridged by the Author from his larger work. Small 4to. cloth, pp. vi. and 206. 1873. 18s.

Hernisz.—A Guide to Conversation in the English and Chinese Languages, for the use of Americans and Chinese in California and elsewhere. By Stanislas Hernisz. Square 8vo. pp. 274, sewed. 10s. 6d.

The Chinese characters contained in this work are from the collections of Chinese groups, engraved on steel, and cast into moveable types, by Mr. Marcellin Legrand, engraver of the Imperial Printing Office at Paris. They are used by most of the missions to China.

Hincks.—Specimen Chapters of an Assyrian Grammar. By the late Rev. E. Hincks, D.D., Hon. M.R.A.S. 8vo., pp. 44, sewed. 1s.

Hodgson.—Essays on the Languages, Literature, and Religion of Nepal and Tibet; together with further Papers on the Geography, Ethnology, and Commerce of those Countries. By B. H. Hodgson, late British Minister at Nepál. Royal 8vo. cloth, pp. 288. 14s.

Hoffmann.—Shopping Dialogues, in Japanese, Dutch, and English. By Professor J. Hoffmann. Oblong 8vo. pp. xiii. and 44, sewed. 5s.

Hoffmann, J. J.—A Japanese Grammar. Second Edition. Large 8vo. cloth, pp. viii. and 368, with two plates. £1 1s.

Holbein Society.—Subscription £1 1s. per annum. A List of Publications to be had on application.

Hopkins.—Elementary Grammar of the Turkish Language. With a few Easy Exercises. By F. L. Hopkins. M.A., Fellow and Tutor of Trinity Hall, Cambridge. Cr. 8vo. cloth, pp. 48. 3s. 6d.

Howse.—A Grammar of the Cree Language. With which is combined an analysis of the Chippeway Dialect. By Joseph Howse, Esq., F.R.G.S. 8vo. pp. xx. and 324, cloth. 7s. 6d.

Hunter.—A Statistical Account of Bengal. By W. W. Hunter, B.A., LL.D. Director-General of Statistics to the Government of India; one of the Council of the Royal Asiatic Society; M.R.G.S.; and Honorary Member of various Learned Societies.

VOL.	VOL.
I. 24 Parganás and Sundarbans.	X. Dárjíling, Jalpáigurí and Kuch Behar
II. Nadiyá and Jessor.	XI. Patná and Sáran. [State.
III. Midnapur, Húglí and Hourah.	XII. Gayá and Sháhábád
IV. Bardwán, Birbhúm and Bánkurá.	XIII. Tirhut and Champáran.
V. Dacca, Bákarganj, Farídpur and Maimansinh.	XIV. Bhágalpur and Santál Parganás.
	XV. Monghyr and Purniah.
VI. Chittagong Hill Tracts, Chittagong, Noákháli, Tipperah, and Hill Tipperah State.	XVI. Hazáribágh and Lohárdagá.
	XVII. Singbhúm, Chutiá, Nágpur Tributary States and Mánbhúm.
VII. Meldah, Rangpur and Dinájpur.	XVIII. Cuttack and Balasor.
VIII. Rájsháhí and Bográ.	XIX. Purí, and Orissa Tributary States.
IX. Murshidábád and Pábná.	XX. Fisheries, Botany, and General Index.

Published by command of the Government of India. In 20 Vols. 8vo. half-morocco. £5.

Hunter (F. M.)—An Account of the British Settlement of Aden in Arabia. Compiled by Captain F. M. Hunter, F.R.G.S., F.R.A.S., Assistant Political Resident, Aden. Demy 8vo. half-morocco, pp. xii.-232. 7s. 6d.

Ikhwánu-s Safá; or, Brothers of Purity. Describing the Contention between Men and Beasts as to the Superiority of the Human Race. Translated from the Hindustání by Professor J. Dowson, Staff College, Sandhurst. Crown 8vo. pp. viii. and 156, cloth. 7s.

Indian Antiquary (The).—A Journal of Oriental Research in Archæology, History, Literature, Languages, Philosophy, Religion, Folklore, etc. Edited by James Burgess, M.R.A.S., F.R.G.S. 4to. Published 12 numbers per annum. Subscription £2.

Ingleby.—Shakespeare: the Man and the Book. By C. M. Ingleby, M.A., LL.D. 8vo. boards, pp. 172. 6s.

Inman.—Ancient Pagan and Modern Christian Symbolism Exposed and Explained. By Thomas Inman, M.D. Second Edition. With Illustrations. Demy 8vo. cloth, pp. xl. and 148. 1874. 7s. 6d.

Jaiminiya-Nyâya-Mâlâ-Vistara —See under Auctores Sanscriti.

Jami, Mulla.—Salámán U Absál. An Allegorical Romance; being one of the Seven Poems entitled the Haft Aurang of Mullá Jámí, now first edited from the Collation of Eight Manuscripts in the Library of the India House, and in private collections, with various readings, by Forbes Falconer, M.A., M.R.A.S. 4to. cloth, pp. 92. 1850. 7s. 6d.

Jataka (The); together with its Commentary. Being Tales of the Anterior Birth of Gotama Buddha. For the first time Edited in the original Pali by V. Fausböll, and Translated by T. W. Rhys Davids. Vol. I. Text. Demy 8vo. cloth, pp. 512. 28s.

The "Jataka" is a collection of legends in Pali, relating the history of Buddha's transmigration before he was born as Gotama. The great antiquity of this work is authenticated by its forming part of the sacred canon of the Southern Buddhists, which was finally settled at the last Council in 246 B.C. The collection has long been known as a storehouse of ancient fables, and as the most original attainable source to which almost the whole of this kind of literature, from the Panchatantra and Pilpay's fables down to the nursery stories of the present day, is traceable; and it has been considered desirable, in the interest of Buddhistic studies as well as for more general literary purposes, that an edition and translation of the complete work should be prepared. The present publication is intended to supply this want.—*Athenæum*.

Jenkins's Vest-Pocket Lexicon.—An English Dictionary of all except Familiar Words; including the principal Scientific and Technical Terms, and Foreign Moneys, Weights and Masures. By Jabez Jenkins. 64mo., pp. 564. cloth. 1s. 6d.

Johnson.—Oriental Religions. *See* Trübner's Oriental Series.

Kalid-i-Afghani.—Translation of the Kalid-i-Afghani, the Text-book for the Pakkhto Examination. with Notes, Historical, Geographical, Grammatical, and Explanatory. By Trevor Chichele Plowden. Imp. 8vo. pp. xx. and 406, with a Map. *Lahore*, 1875. £2 2s.

Kásiká.—A Commentary on Pánini's Grammatical Aphorisms. By Pandit Jayáditya. Edited by Pandit Bála Sástrí, Prof. Sansk. Coll., Benares. First part, 8vo. pp. 490. 16s.

Kellogg.—A Grammar of the Hindi Language, in which are treated the Standard Hindi, Braj, and the Eastern Hindî of the Ramayan of Tulsi Das ; also the Colloquial Dialects of Marwar, Kumaon, Avadh, Baghelkhand, Bhojpur, etc., with Copious Philological Notes. By the Rev. S. H. Kellogg, M.A. Royal 8vo. cloth, pp. 400. 21s.

Kern.—The Âryabhatiya, with the Commentary Bhatadîpikâ of Paramadiçvara, edited by Dr. H. Kern. 4to. pp. xii. and 107. 9s.

Kern.—The Brhat-Sanhitá ; or, Complete System of Natural Astrology of Varâha-Mihira Translated from Sanskrit into English by Dr. H. Kern, Professor of Sanskrit at the University of Leyden. Part I. 8vo. pp. 50, stitched. Parts 2 and 3 pp. 51-154. Part 4 pp. 155-210. Part 5 pp. 211-266. Part 6 pp. 267-330. Price 2s. each part. [*Will be completed in Nine Parts.*

Khirad-Afroz (The Illuminator of the Understanding). By Maulaví Hafízu'd-dín. A new edition of the Hindústání Text, carefully revised, with Notes, Critical and Explanatory. By Edward B. Eastwick, M.P., F.R.S., F.S.A., M.R.A.S., Professor of Hindústání at the late East India Company's College at Haileybury. 8vo. cloth, pp. xiv. and 321. 18s.

Kidd.—Catalogue of the Chinese Library of the Royal Asiatic Society. By the Rev. S. Kidd. 8vo. pp. 58, sewed. 1s.

Kielhorn.—A Grammar of the Sanskrit Language. By F. Kielhorn, Ph.D., Superintendent of Sanskrit Studies in Deccan College. Registered under Act xxv. of 1867. Demy 8vo. pp. xvi. 260. cloth. 1870. 10s. 6d.

Kielhorn.—Kátyáyana and Patanjali. Their Relation to each other and to Panini. By F. Kielhorn, Ph. D., Prof. of Orient. Lang. Poona. 8vo. pp. 64. 1876. 3s. 6d.

Kilgour.—The Hebrew or Iberian Race, including the Pelasgians, the Phenicians, the Jews, the British, and others. By Henry Kilgour. 8vo. sewed, pp. 76. 1872. 2s. 6d.

Kistner.—Buddha and his Doctrines. A Bibliographical Essay. By Otto Kistner. Imperial 8vo., pp. iv. and 32, sewed. 2s. 6d.

Koch.—A HISTORICAL GRAMMAR OF THE ENGLISH LANGUAGE. By C. F. KOCH. Translated into English. Edited, Enlarged, and Annotated by the Rev. R. MORRIS, LL.D., M.A. [*Nearly ready.*

Koran (The). Arabic text, lithographed in Oudh, A.H. 1284 (1867). 16mo. pp. 942. 7s. 6d.

Koran (The).—*See* Sale, and Trübner's Oriental Series.

Kramers' New Pocket Dictionary of the English and Dutch LANGUAGES. Royal 32mo. cloth, pp. xvi. and 714. 4s.

Kroeger.—THE MINNESINGER OF GERMANY. By A. E. KROEGER. 12mo. cloth, pp. vi. and 284. 7s.

CONTENTS.—Chapter I. The Minnesinger and the Minnesong.—II. The Minnelay.—III. The Divine Minnesong.—IV. Walther von der Vogelweide.—V. Ulrich von Lichtenstein.—VI. The Metrical Romances of the Minnesinger and Gottfried von Strassburg's ' Tristan and Isolde."

Lacombe.—DICTIONNAIRE ET GRAMMAIRE DE LA LANGUE DES CRIS, par le Rév. Père ALB. LACOMBE. 8vo. paper, pp. xx. and 713, iv. and 190. 21s.

Laghu Kaumudí. A Sanskrit Grammar. By Varadarája. With an English Version, Commentary, and References. By JAMES R. BALLANTYNE, LL.D., Principal of the Sanskrit College, Benares. 8vo. pp. xxxvi. and 424, cloth. £1 11s. 6d.

Land.—THE PRINCIPLES OF HEBREW GRAMMAR. By J. P. N. LAND, Professor of Logic and Metaphysic in the University of Leyden. Translated from the Dutch by REGINALD LANE POOLE, Balliol College. Oxford. Part I. Sounds. Part II. Words. Crown 8vo. pp. xx. and 220, cloth. 7s. 6d.

Legge.—CONFUCIANISM IN RELATION TO CHRISTIANITY. A Paper Read before the Missionary Conference in Shanghai, on May 11, 1877. By Rev. JAMES LEGGE, D.D., LL.D. 8vo. sewed, pp. 12. 1877. 1s. 6d.

Legge.—THE CHINESE CLASSICS. With a Translation, Critical and Exegetical Notes, Prolegomena, and Copious Indexes. By JAMES LEGGE, D.D., of the London Missionary Society. In seven vols.

　Vol. I. containing Confucian Analects, the Great Learning, and the Doctrine of the Mean. 8vo. pp. 526, cloth. £2 2s.

　Vol. II., containing the Works of Mencius. 8vo. pp. 634, cloth. £2 2s.

　Vol. III. Part I. containing the First Part of the Shoo-King, or the Books of Tang, the Books of Yu, the Books of Hea, the Books of Shang, and the Prolegomena. Royal 8vo. pp. viii. and 280, cloth. £2 2s.

　Vol. III. Part II. containing the Fifth Part of the Shoo-King, or the Books of Chow, and the Indexes. Royal 8vo. pp. 281—736, cloth. £2 2s.

　Vol. IV. Part I. containing the First Part of the She-King, or the Lessons from the States; and the Prolegomena. Royal 8vo. cloth, pp. 182-244. £2 2s.

　Vol. IV. Part II. containing the 2nd, 3rd and 4th Parts of the She-King, or the Minor Odes of the Kingdom, the Greater Odes of the Kingdom, the Sacrificial Odes and Praise-Songs, and the Indexes. Royal 8vo. cloth, pp. 540. £2 2s.

　Vol. V. Part I. containing Dukes Yin, Hwan, Chwang, Min, He, Wan, Seuen, and Ch'ing; and the Prolegomena. Royal 8vo. cloth, pp. xii., 148 and 410. £2 2s.

　Vol. V. Part II. Contents :—Dukes Seang, Ch'aon, Ting, and Gal, with Tso's Appendix, and the Indexes. Royal 8vo. cloth, pp. 526. £2 2s.

Legge.—THE CHINESE CLASSICS. Translated into English. With Preliminary Essays and Explanatory Notes. By JAMES LEGGE, D.D., LL.D.

　Vol. I. The Life and Teachings of Confucius. Crown 8vo. cloth, pp. vi. and 338. 10s. 6d.

　Vol. II. The Life and Works of Mencius. Crown 8vo. cloth, pp. 412. 12s.

　Vol. III. The She King, or The Book of Poetry. Crown 8vo., cloth, pp. viii. and 432. 12s.

Legge.—INAUGURAL LECTURE ON THE CONSTITUTING OF A CHINESE CHAIR in the University of Oxford. Delivered in the Sheldonian Theatre, Oct. 27th, 1876, by Rev. JAMES LEGGE, M.A., LL.D., Professor of the Chinese Language and Literature at Oxford. 8vo pp. 28, sewed. 6d.

Leigh.—THE RELIGION OF THE WORLD. By H. STONE LEIGH. 12mo. pp. xii. 66, cloth. 1869. 2s. 6d.

Leitner.—INTRODUCTION TO A PHILOSOPHICAL GRAMMAR OF ARABIC. Being an Attempt to Discover a Few Simple Principles in Arabic Grammar. By G. W. LEITNER. 8vo. sewed, pp. 52. *Lahore.* 4s.

Leitner.—SININ-I-ISLAM. Being a Sketch of the History and Literature of Muhammadanism and their place in Universal History. *For the use of Maulvis.* By G. W. LEITNER. Part I. The Early History of Arabia to the fall of the Abassides. 8vo. sewed. *Lahore.* 6s.

Leland.—THE ENGLISH GIPSIES AND THEIR LANGUAGE. By CHARLES G. LELAND. Second Edition. Crown 8vo. cloth, pp. 276. 7s. 6d.

Leland.—THE BREITMANN BALLADS. THE ONLY AUTHORIZED EDITION. Complete in 1 vol., including Nineteen Ballads illustrating his Travels in Europe (never before printed), with Comments by Fritz Schwackenhammer. By CHARLES G. LELAND. Crown 8vo. handsomely bound in cloth, pp. xxviii. and 292. 6s.

HANS BREITMANN'S PARTY. With other Ballads. By CHARLES G. LELAND. Tenth Edition. Square, pp. xvi. and 74, cloth. 2s. 6d.

HANS BREITMANN'S CHRISTMAS. With other Ballads. By CHARLES G. LELAND. Second edition. Square, pp. 80, sewed. 1s.

HANS BREITMANN AS A POLITICIAN. By CHARLES G. LELAND. Second edition. Square, pp. 72, sewed. 1s.

HANS BREITMANN IN CHURCH. With other Ballads. By CHARLES G. Leland. With an Introduction and Glossary. Second edition. Square, pp. 80, sewed. 1s.

HANS BREITMANN AS AN UHLAN. Six New Ballads, with a Glossary. Square, pp. 72, sewed. 1s.

Leland.—FUSANG; or, the Discovery of America by Chinese Buddhist Priests in the Fifth Century. By CHARLES G. LELAND. Cr. 8vo. cloth, pp. xix. and 212. 7s. 6d.

Leland.—ENGLISH GIPSY SONGS. In Rommany, with Metrical English Translations. By CHARLES G. LELAND, Author of "The English Gipsies," etc.; Prof. E. H. PALMER; and JANET TUCKEY. Crown 8vo. cloth, pp. xii. and 276. 7s. 6d.

Leland.—PIDGIN-ENGLISH SING-SONG; or Songs and Stories in the China-English Dialect. With a Vocabulary. By CHARLES G. LELAND. Fcap, 8vo. cl., pp. viii. and 140. 1876. 5s.

Leo.—FOUR CHAPTERS OF NORTH'S PLUTARCH. Containing the Lives of Caius Marcius Coriolanus, Julius Cæsar, Marcus Antoninus, and Marcus Brutus, as Sources to Shakespeare's Tragedies, Coriolanus, Julius Cæsar, and Antony and Cleopatra; and partly to Hamlet and Timon of Athens. Photo-lithographed in the size of the Edition of 1595. With Preface, Notes comparing the Text of the Editions of 1579, 1595, 1603, and 1612; and Reference Notes to the Text of the Tragedies of Shakespeare. Edited by Prof. F. A. LEO, Ph.D. In one volume, folio, elegantly bound, pp. 22 of letterpress and 130 pp. of facsimiles. £1 11s. 6d.

The Library Edition is limited to 250 copies, at the price £1 11s. 6d.

Of the Amateur Edition 50 copies have been struck off on a superior large hand-made paper, price £3 3s. per copy.

Leonowens.—The English Governess at the Siamese Court—being Recollections of six years in the Royal Palace at Bangkok. By Anna Harriette Leonowens. With Illustrations from Photographs presented to the Author by the King of Siam. 8vo. cloth, pp. x. and 332. 1870 12s.

Leonowens.—The Romance of Siamese Harem Life. By Mrs. Anna H. Leonowens, Author of "The English Governess at the Siamese Court." With 17 Illustrations, principally from Photographs, by the permission of J. Thomson, Esq. Crown 8vo. cloth, pp. viii. and 278. 14s.

Literature.—Transactions of the Royal Society of Literature of the United Kingdom. First Series, 6 parts in 3 vols. 4to. plates ; 1827–39. Second Series, 10 vols. or 30 parts, and vol. xi. parts 1 and 2, 8vo. plates, 1843–76. A complete set, as far as published, £10 10s. A list of the contents of the volumes and parts on application.

Lobscheid.—English and Chinese Dictionary, with the Punti and Mandarin Pronunciation. By the Rev. W. Lobscheid, Knight of Francis Joseph, C.M.I.R.G.S.A., N.Z.B.S.V., etc. Folio, pp. viii. and 2016. In Four Parts. £8 8s.

Lobscheid.—Chinese and English Dictionary, Arranged according to the Radicals. By the Rev. W. Lobscheid, Knight of Francis Joseph, C.M.I.R.G.S.A., N.Z.B.S.V., &c. 1 vol. imp. 8vo. double columns, pp. 600, bound. £2 8s.

Ludewig.—The Literature of American Aboriginal Languages. By Herman E. Ludewig With Additions and Corrections by Professor Wm. W. Turner. Edited by Nicolas Trübner. 8vo. fly and general Title, 2 leaves ; Dr. Ludewig's Preface, pp. v.—viii. ; Editor's Preface, pp. iv.—xii. ; Biographical Memoir of Dr. Ludewig, pp. xiii.—xiv. ; and Introductory Biographical Notices, pp. xiv.—xxiv., followed by List of Contents. Then follow Dr. Ludewig's Bibliotheca Glottica, alphabetically arranged, with Additions by the Editor, pp. 1—209 ; Professor Turner's Additions, with those of the Editor to the same, also alphabetically arranged, pp. 210—246 ; Index, pp. 247—256 ; and List of Errata, pp. 257, 258. Handsomely bound in cloth. 10s. 6d.

Luzzatto.—Grammar of the Biblical Chaldaic Language and the Talmud Babylonical Idioms. By S. D. Luzzatto. Translated from the Italian by J. S. Goldammer. Cr. 8vo. cl., pp. 122. 7s. 6d.

Macgowan.—A Manual of the Amoy Colloquial. By Rev. J. Macgowan, of the London Missionary Society. 8vo. sewed, pp. xvii. and 200. Amoy, 1871. £1 1s.

Mackay.—The Gaelic Etymology of the Languages of Western Europe, and more especially of the English and Lowland Scotch, and of their Slang, Cant, and Colloquial Dialects. By Charles Mackay, LL.D. Royal 8vo. cloth, pp. xxxii. and 604. 42s.

McClatchie. — A Translation of Section Forty-nine of the "Complete Works" of the Philosopher Choo-Foo-Tze, with Explanatory Notes. By the Rev. Thomas McClatchie, M.A. Small 4to. pp. xviii. and 162. 12s. 6d.

Maclay and Baldwin.—An Alphabetic Dictionary of the Chinese Language in the Foochow Dialect. By Rev. R. S. Maclay, D.D., of the Methodist Episcopal Mission, and Rev. C. C. Baldwin, A.M., of the American Board of Mission. 8vo. half-bound, pp. 1132. Foochow, 1871. £4 4s.

Mahabharata. Translated into Hindi for Madan Mohun Bhatt, by Krishnachandradharmadhikarin of Benares. (Containing all but the Harivansá.) 3 vols. 8vo. cloth, pp. 574, 810, and 1106. £3 3s.

Maha-Vira-Charita; or, the Adventures of the Great Hero Rama.
An Indian Drama in Seven Acts. Translated into English Prose from the
Sanskrit of Bhavabhúti. By JOHN PICKFORD, M.A. Crown 8vo. cloth. 5s.

Maino-i-Khard (The Book of the). — The Pazand and Sanskrit
Texts (in Roman characters) as arranged by Neriosengh Dhaval, in the
fifteenth century. With an English translation, a Glossary of the Pazand
texts, containing the Sanskrit, Rosian, and Pahlavi equivalents, a sketch of
Pazand Grammar, and an Introduction. By E. W. WEST. 8vo. sewed, pp.
484. 1871. 16s.

Maltby. — A PRACTICAL HANDBOOK OF THE URIYA OR ODIYA LANGUAGE.
By THOMAS J. MALTBY, Esq., Madras C.S. 8vo. pp. xiii. and 201. 1874.
10s. 6d.

Manava-Kalpa-Sutra; being a portion of this ancient Work on Vaidik
Rites, together with the Commentary of KUMARILA-SWAMIN. A Facsimile of
the MS. No. 17, in the Library of Her Majesty's Home Government for India.
With a Preface by THEODOR GOLDSTÜCKER. Oblong folio, pp. 268 of letterpress and 121 leaves of facsimiles. Cloth. £4 4s.

Manipulus Vocabulorum; A Rhyming Dictionary of the English
Language. By Peter Levins (1570) Edited, with an Alphabetical Index, by
HENRY B. WHEATLEY. 8vo. pp. xvi. and 370, cloth. 14s.

Manning. — AN INQUIRY INTO THE CHARACTER AND ORIGIN OF THE
POSSESSIVE AUGMENT in English and in Cognate Dialects. By the late
JAMES MANNING, Q.A.S., Recorder of Oxford. 8vo.pp. iv. and 90. 2s.

March. — A COMPARATIVE GRAMMAR OF THE ANGLO-SAXON LANGUAGE;
in which its forms are illustrated by those of the Sanskrit, Greek, Latin,
Gothic, Old Saxon, Old Friesic, Old Norse, and Old High-German. By
FRANCIS A. MARCH, LL.D. Demy 8vo. cloth, pp. xi. and 253. 1877. 10s.

Mariette. — THE MONUMENTS OF UPPER EGYPT. A Translation of the
Itineraire de la Haute Egypte, of Auguste Mariette Bey. By ALPHONSE
MARRIETTE. Fcap. 8vo. cloth, pp. vii.–261. 7s. 6d.

Markham. — QUICHUA GRAMMAR and DICTIONARY. Contributions towards a Grammar and Dictionary of Quichua, the Language of the Yncas of
Peru; collected by CLEMENTS R. MARKHAM, F.S.A., Corr. Mem. of the University of Chile. Author of "Cuzco and Lima," and "Travels in Peru and
India." In one vol. crown 8vo., pp. 223, cloth. £1. 11s. 6d.

Markham. — OLLANTA: A DRAMA IN THE QUICHUA LANGUAGE. Text,
Translation, and Introduction, By CLEMENTS R. MARKHAM, F.R.G.S. Crown
8vo., pp. 128, cloth. 7s. 6d.

Markham. — A MEMOIR OF THE LADY ANA DE OSORIO, Countess of
Chinchon, and Vice-Queen of Peru, A.D. 1629–39. With a Plea for the
Correct Spelling of the Chinchona Genus. By CLEMENTS R. MARKHAM, C.B.,
F.R.S., Commendador da Real Ordem de Christo, Socius Academiæ Cæsareæ
Naturæ Curiosorum Cognomen Chinchon. Small 4to, pp. 112. With a Map,
2 Plates, and numerous Illustrations. Roxburghe binding. 28s.

Markham. — THE NARRATIVES OF THE MISSION OF GEORGE BOGLE,
B.C.S., to the Teshu Lama, and of the Journey of Thomas Manning to Lhasa.
Edited, with Notes and Introduction, and lives of Mr. Bogle and Mr. Manning,
by CLEMENTS R. MARKHAM, C.B., F.R.S. Demy 8vo., with Maps and Illustrations, pp. clxi. 314, cl. 21s.

Marsden's Numismata Orientalia. New International Edition.
See under NUMISMATA ORIENTALIA.

Mason.—THE PALI TEXT OF KACHCHAYANO'S GRAMMAR, WITH ENGLISH
ANNOTATIONS. By FRANCIS MASON, D.D.   I. The Text Aphorisms, 1 to 673.
II. The English Annotations, including the various Readings of six independent
Burmese Manuscripts, the Singalese Text on Verbs, and the Cambodian Text
on Syntax.   To which is added a Concordance of the Aphorisms.   In Two
Parts. 8vo. sewed, pp. 208, 75, and 28. Toongoo, 1871. £1 11s. 6d.

Mathews.—ABRAHAM BEN EZRA'S UNEDITED COMMENTARY ON THE CAN-
TICLES, the Hebrew Text after two MS., with English Translation by H. J.
MATHEWS, B.A., Exeter College, Oxford. 8vo. cl. limp, pp. x., 34, 24. 2s. 6d.

Mathuráprasáda Misra.—A TRILINGUAL DICTIONARY, being a compre-
hensive Lexicon in English, Urdú, and Hindí, exhibiting the Syllabication,
Pronunciation, and Etymology of English Words, with their Explanation in
English, and in Urdú and Hindí in the Roman Character. By MATHURÁ-
PRASÁDA MISRA, Second Master, Queen's College, Benares. 8vo. pp. xv. and
1330, cloth. Benares, 1865. £2 2s.

Matthews.—ETHNOLOGY AND PHILOLOGY OF THE HIDATSA INDIANS.
By WASHINGTON MATTHEWS, Assistant Surgeon, U.S. Army. *Contents :—*
Ethnography, Philology, Grammar, Dictionary, and English-Hidatsa Voca-
bulary. 8vo. cloth. £1 11s. 6d.

Mayers.—ILLUSTRATIONS OF THE LAMAIST SYSTEM IN TIBET, drawn from
Chinese Sources. By WILLIAM FREDERICK MAYERS, Esq., of Her Britannic
Majesty's Consular Service, China. 8vo. pp. 24, sewed. 1869. 1s. 6d.

Mayers.—THE CHINESE READER'S MANUAL. A Handbook of Biographical, Historical, Mythological, and General Literary Reference. By W.
F. MAYERS, Chinese Secretary to H. B. M.'s Legation at Peking, F.R.G.S.,
etc., etc. Demy 8vo. pp. xxiv. and 440. £1 5s.

Mayers.—TREATIES BETWEEN THE EMPIRE OF CHINA AND FOREIGN
Powers, together with Regulations for the Conduct of Foreign Trade. etc.
Edited by W. F. MAYERS, Chinese Secretary to H.B.M.'s Legation at Peking.
8vo. cloth, pp. 246. 1877. 25s.

Mayers.—THE CHINESE GOVERNMENT. A Manual of Chinese Titles,
Categorically arranged, and Explained with an Appendix. By W. F. MAYERS,
Chinese Secretary to H.B.M.'s Legation at Peking. Royal 8vo. cloth,
pp. viii.–160. 1878. £1 8s.

Mayers.—THE ANGLO-CHINESE CALENDAR MANUAL. A Handbook of
Reference for the Determination of Chinese Dates during the period from
1860 to 1879. With Comparative Tables of Annual and Mensual Designations,
etc. Compiled by W. F. MAYERS, Chinese Secretary, H.B.M.'s Legation,
Peking. 2nd Edition. Sewed, pp. 28. 7s. 6d.

Medhurst.—CHINESE DIALOGUES, QUESTIONS, and FAMILIAR SENTENCES,
literally translated into English, with a view to promote commercial intercourse
and assist beginners in the Language. By the late W. H. MEDHURST, D.D.
A new and enlarged Edition. 8vo. pp. 226. 18s.

Megasthenês.—ANCIENT INDIA AS DESCRIBED BY MEGASTHENÊS AND
ARRIAN. Being a Translation of the Fragments of the Indika of Megasthenês
collected by Dr. SCHWANBERK, and of the First Part of the Indika of Arrian.
By J. W. McCRINDLE, M.A., Principal of the Government College, Patna,
etc. With Introduction, Notes, and Map of Ancient India. Post 8vo. cloth,
pp. xii.–224. 1877. 7s. 6d.

Megha-Duta (The). (Cloud-Messenger.) By Kálidása. Translated
from the Sanskrit into English verse, with Notes and Illustrations. By the
late H. H. WILSON, M.A., F.R.S., Boden Professor of Sanskrit in the University of Oxford, etc., etc. The Vocabulary by FRANCIS JOHNSON, sometime
Professor of Oriental Languages at the College of the Honourable the East India
Company, Haileybury. New Edition. 4to. cloth, pp. xi. and 180. 10s. 6d.

Memoirs read before the ANTHROPOLOGICAL SOCIETY OF LONDON, 1863 1864. 8vo., pp. 542, cloth. 21s.

Memoirs read before the ANTHROPOLOGICAL SOCIETY OF LONDON, 1865-6. Vol. II. 8vo., pp. x. 464, cloth. 21s.

Mills —THE INDIAN SAINT; or, Buddha and Buddhism.—A Sketch Historical and Critical. By C. D. B. MILLS. 8vo. cl., pp. 192. 7s. 6d.

Minocheherji.—PAHLAVI, GUJARÁTI, AND ENGLISH DICTIONARY. By JAMASPJI DASTUR MINOCHEHERJI JAMASP ASANA, Fellow of the University of Bombay, and Member of the Bombay Branch of the Royal Asiatic Society. Vol. I. (To be completed in three volumes.) Demy 8vo. pp. clxxix and 168, with Photographic Portrait of the Author. 14s.

Mírkhónd.—THE HISTORY OF THE ATÁBEKS OF SYRIA AND PERSIA. By MUHAMMED BEN KHÁWENDSHÁH BEN MAHMUD, commonly called MÍRKHÓND. Now first Edited from the Collation of Sixteen MSS., by W. H. MORLEY, Barrister-at-law, M.R.A.S. To which is added a Series of Facsimiles of the Coins struck by the Atábeks, arranged and described by W. S. W. Vaux, M.A., M.R.A.S. Roy. 8vo. cloth, 7 plates, pp. 118. 1848. 7s. 6d.

Mitra.—THE ANTIQUITIES OF ORISSA. By RAJENDRALALA MITRA. Vol. I. Published under Orders of the Government of India. Folio, cloth, pp. 180. With a Map and 36 Plates. £4 4s.

Molesworth.—A DICTIONARY, MÁRATHI and ENGLISH. Compiled by J. T. MOLESWORTH, assisted by GEORGE and THOMAS CANDY. Second Edition, revised and enlarged. By J. T. MOLESWORTH. Royal 4to. pp. xxx and 922, boards. Bombay, 1857. £3 3s.

Molesworth.—A COMPENDIUM OF MOLESWORTH'S MARATHI AND ENGLISH DICTIONARY. By BABA PADMANJI. Second Edition. Revised and Enlarged. Demy 8vo. cloth, pp. xx. and 624. 21s.

Möllendorff.—MANUAL OF CHINESE BIBLIOGRAPHY, being a List of Works and Essays relating to China. By P. G. and O. F. VON MÖLLENDORFF, Interpreters to H.I.G.M.'s Consulates at Shanghai and Tientsin. 8vo. pp. viii. and 378. £1 10s.

Morley.—A DESCRIPTIVE CATALOGUE of the HISTORICAL MANUSCRIPTS in the ARABIC and PERSIAN LANGUAGES preserved in the Library of the Royal Asiatic Society of Great Britain and Ireland. By WILLIAM H. MORLEY, M.R.A.S. 8vo. pp. viii. and 160, sewed. London, 1854. 2s. 6d.

Morris.—A DESCRIPTIVE AND HISTORICAL ACCOUNT OF THE GODAVERY DISTRICT in the Presidency of Madras By HENRY MORRIS, formerly of the Madras Civil Service. Author of a "History of India for Use in Schools" and other works. 8vo. cloth (with a map), pp. xii. and 390. 1878. 12s.

Morrison.—A DICTIONARY OF THE CHINESE LANGUAGE. By the Rev. R. MORRISON, D.D. Two vols. Vol. I. pp. x. and 762; Vol. II. pp. 828, cloth. Shanghae, 1865. £6 6s.

Muhammed.—THE LIFE OF MUHAMMED. Based on Muhammed Ibn Ishak By Abd El Malik Ibn Hisham. Edited by Dr. FERDINAND WÜSTEN-FELD. The Arabic Text. 8vo. pp. 1026, sewed. Price 21s. Introduction, Notes, and Index in German. 8vo. pp. lxxii. and 266, sewed. 7s. 6d. Each part sold separately.

The text based on the Manuscripts of the Berlin, Leipsic, Gotha and Leyden Libraries, has been carefully revised by the learned editor, and printed with the utmost exactness.

Muir.—ORIGINAL SANSKRIT TEXTS, on the Origin and History of the People of India, their Religion and Institutions. Collected, Translated, and Illustrated by JOHN MUIR, Esq., D.C.L., LL.D., Ph.D.

Vol. I. Mythical and Legendary Accounts of the Origin of Caste, with an Inquiry into its existence in the Vedic Age. Second Edition, re-written and greatly enlarged. 8vo. pp. xx. 532, cloth. 1868. 21s.

Vol. II. The Trans-Himalayan Origin of the Hindus, and their Affinity with the Western Branches of the Aryan Race. Second Edition, revised, with Additions. 8vo. pp. xxxii. and 512, cloth. 1871. 21s.

Vol. III. The Vedas: Opinions of their Authors, and of later Indian Writers, on their Origin, Inspiration, and Authority. Second Edition, revised and enlarged. 8vo. pp. xxxii. 312, cloth. 1868. 16s.

Vol. IV. Comparison of the Vedic with the later representations of the principal Indian Deities. Second Edition Revised. 8vo. pp. xvi. and 524, cloth. 1873. 21s.

Vol. V. Contributions to a Knowledge of the Cosmogony, Mythology, Religious Ideas, Life and Manners of the Indians in the Vedic Age. 8vo. pp. xvi. 492, cloth, 1870. 21s.

Müller.—THE SACRED HYMNS OF THE BRAHMINS, as preserved to us in the oldest collection of religious poetry, the Rig-Veda-Sanhita, translated and explained. By F. MAX MÜLLER, M.A., Fellow of All Souls' College; Professor of Comparative Philology at Oxford; Foreign Member of the Institute of France, etc., etc. Volume I. Hymns to the Maruts or the Storm Gods. 8vo. pp. clii. and 264. 12s. 6d.

Müller.—THE HYMNS OF THE RIG-VEDA in the Samhita and Pada Texts. Reprinted from the Editio Princeps. By F. MAX MÜLLER, M.A., etc. Second edition. With the Two Texts on Parallel Pages. In 2 vols. 8vo., pp. 1700, sewed. 32s.

Müller.—LECTURE ON BUDDHIST NIHILISM. By F. MAX MÜLLER, M.A., Professor of Comparative Philology in the University of Oxford; Member of the French Institute, etc. Delivered before the General Meeting of the Association of German Philologists, at Kiel, 28th September, 1869. (Translated from the German.) Sewed. 1869. 1s.

Nagananda; OR THE JOY OF THE SNAKE-WORLD. A Buddhist Drama in Five Acts. Translated into English Prose, with Explanatory Notes, from the Sanskrit of Sri-Harsha-Deva. By PALMER BOYD, B.A., Sanskrit Scholar of Trinity College, Cambridge. With an Introduction by Professor COWELL. Crown 8vo., pp. xvi. and 100, cloth. 4s. 6d.

Nalopákhyánam.—STORY OF NALA; an Episode of the Mahá-Bhárata. The Sanskrit Text, with Vocabulary, Analysis, and Introduction. By MONIER WILLIAMS, M.A. The Metrical Translation by the Very Rev. H. H. MILMAN, D.D. 8vo. cl. 15s.

Naradiya Dharma Sastram; OR, THE INSTITUTES OF NARADA. Translated for the First Time from the unpublished Sanskrit original. By Dr. JULIUS JOLLY, University, Wurzburg. With a Preface, Notes chiefly critical, an Index of Quotations from Narada in the principal Indian Digests, and a general Index. Crown 8vo., pp. xxxv. 144, cloth. 10s. 6d.

Newman.— A DICTIONARY OF MODERN ARABIC —1. Anglo-Arabic Dictionary. 2. Anglo-Arabic Vocabulary. 3. Arabo-English Dictionary. By F. W. NEWMAN, Emeritus Professor of University College, London. In 2 vols. crown 8vo., pp. xvi. and 376—464, cloth. £1 1s.

Newman.—A HANDBOOK OF MODERN ARABIC, consisting of a Practical Grammar, with numerous Examples, Dialogues, and Newspaper Extracts, in a European Type. By F. W. NEWMAN, Emeritus Professor of University College, London; formerly Fellow of Balliol College, Oxford. Post 8vo. pp. xx, and 192, cloth. London, 1866. 6s.

Newman.—THE TEXT OF THE IGUVINE INSCRIPTIONS, with interlinear Latin Translation and Notes. By FRANCIS W. NEWMAN, late Professor of Latin at University College, London. 8vo. pp. xvi. and 54, sewed. 2s.

Newman.—ORTHOËPY: or, a simple mode of Accenting English, for the advantage of Foreigners and of all Learners. By FRANCIS W. NEWMAN, Emeritus Professor of University College, London. 8vo. pp. 28, sewed. 1869. 1s.

Nodal.—ELEMENTOS DE GRAMÁTICA QUICHUA Ó IDIOMA DE LOS YNCAS. Bajo los Auspicios de la Redentora, Sociedad de Filántropos para mejorar la suerte de los Aboríjenes Peruanos. Por el Dr. JOSE FERNANDEZ NODAL, Abogado de los Tribunales de Justicia de la República del Perú. Royal 8vo. cloth, pp. xvi. and 441. Appendix, pp. 9. £1 1s.

Nodal.—LOS VINCULOS DE OLLANTA Y CUSI-KCUYLLOR. DRAMA EN QUICHUA. Obra Compilada y Espurgada con la Version Castellana al Frente de su Testo por el Dr. JOSÉ FERNANDEZ NODAL, Abogado de los Tribunales de Justicia de la República del Perú. Bajo los Auspicios de la Redentora Sociedad de Filántropos para Mejorar la Suerte de los Aborijenes Peruanos. Roy. 8vo. bds. pp. 70. 1874. 7s. 6d.

Notley.—A COMPARATIVE GRAMMAR OF THE FRENCH. ITALIAN, SPANISH, AND PORTUGUESE LANGUAGES. By EDWIN A. NOTLEY. Crown oblong 8vo. cloth, pp. xv. and 396. 7s. 6d.

Numismata Orientalia.—THE INTERNATIONAL NUMISMATA ORIENTALIA. Edited by EDWARD THOMAS, F.R.S., etc. Vol. I. Illustrated with 20 Plates and a Map. Royal 4to. cloth. £3 13s. 6d.
Also in 6 Parts sold separately, viz.:—
Part I.—Ancient Indian Weights. By E. THOMAS, F.R.S., etc. Royal 4to. sewed, pp. 84, with a Plate and a Map of the India of Manu. 9s. 6d.
Part II.—Coins of the Urtuki Turkumans. By STANLEY LANE POOLE, Corpus Christi College Oxford. Royal 4to. sewed, pp 44, with 6 Plates. 9s.
Part III. The Coinage of Lydia and Persia, from the Earliest Times to the Fall of the Dynasty of the Achæmenidæ. By BARCLAY V. HEAD, Assistant-Keeper of Coins, British Museum. Royal 4to. sewed, pp. viii. and 56, with three Autotype Plates. 10s. 6d.
Part IV. The Coins of the Tuluni Dynasty. By EDWARD THOMAS ROGERS. Royal 4to. sewed, pp. iv. and 22, and 1 Plate. 5s.
Part V. The Parthian Coinage. By PERCY GARDNER, M.A. Royal 4to. sewed, pp. iv. and 65, with 8 Autotype Plates. 18s.
Part VI. On the Ancient Coins and Measures of Ceylon. With a Discussion of the Ceylon Date of the Buddha's Death. By T. W. RHYS DAVIDS, Barrister-at-Law, late of the Ceylon Civil Service. Royal 4to. sewed, pp. 60, with Plate. 10s.

Nutt.—FRAGMENTS OF A SAMARITAN TARGUM. Edited from a Bodleian MS. With an Introduction, containing a Sketch of Samaritan History, Dogma, and Literature. By J. W. NUTT, M.A. Demy 8vo. cloth, pp. viii., 172, and 84. With Plate. 1874. 15s.

Nutt.—A SKETCH OF SAMARITAN HISTORY, DOGMA, AND LITERATURE. Published as an Introduction to "Fragments of a Samaritan Targum. By J. W. NUTT, M.A. Demy 8vo. cloth, pp. viii. and 172. 1874. 5s.

Nutt.—TWO TREATISES ON VERBS CONTAINING FEEBLE AND DOUBLE LETTERS by R. Jehuda Hayug of Fez, translated into Hebrew from the original Arabic by R. Moses Gikatilla, of Cordova; with the Treatise on Punctuation by the same Author, translated by Aben Ezra. Edited from Bodleian MSS. with an English Translation by J. W. NUTT, M.A. Demy 8vo. sewed, pp. 312. 1870. 7s. 6d.

Oera Linda Book, from a Manuscript of the Thirteenth Century, with the permission of the Proprietor, C. Over de Linden, of the Helder The Original Frisian Text, as verified by Dr. J. O. OTTEMA: accompanied by an English Version of Dr. Ottema's Dutch Translation, by WILLIAM R. SANDBACH. 8vo. cl. pp. xxvii. and 223. 5s.

Ollanta: A DRAMA IN THE QUICHUA LANGUAGE.   See under MARKHAM and under NODAL.

Oriental Congress.—Report of the Proceedings of the Second International Congress of Orientalists held in London, 1874. Roy. 8vo. paper, pp. 76. *5s.*

Oriental Congress—TRANSACTIONS OF THE SECOND SESSION OF THE INTERNATIONAL CONGRESS OF ORIENTALISTS, held in London in September, 1874. Edited by ROBERT K. DOUGLAS, Honorary Secretary. Demy 8vo. cloth, pp. viii. and 456. *21s.*

Osburn.—THE MONUMENTAL HISTORY OF EGYPT, as recorded on the Ruins of her Temples, Palaces, and Tombs. By WILLIAM OSBURN. Illustrated with Maps, Plates, etc. 2 vols. 8vo. pp. xii. and 461; vii. and 643, cloth. *£2 2s.*

> Vol. I.—From the Colonization of the Valley to the Visit of the Patriarch Abram.
> Vol. II.—From the Visit of Abram to the Exodus.

Otté.—HOW TO LEARN DANISH (Dano-Norwegian). A Manual for Students of Danish (Dano-Norwegian). Based on the Ollendorffian System of Teaching Languages, and adapted for Self-Instruction. By E. C. OTTÉ. Crown 8vo cloth, pp. xix.–338. *7s. 6d.*
Key to the Exercises. Cloth, pp. 84. *3s.*

Palmer.— EGYPTIAN CHRONICLES, with a harmony of Sacred and Egyptian Chronology, and an Appendix on Babylonian and Assyrian Antiquities. By WILLIAM PALMER, M.A., and late Fellow of Magdalen College, Oxford. vols.. 8vo. cloth, pp. lxxiv. and 428, and viii. and 636. 1861. *12s.*

Palmer.—A CONCISE DICTIONARY OF THE PERSIAN LANGUAGE. By E. H. PALMER, M.A., Professor of Arabic in the University of Cambridge. Square 16mo. pp. viii. and 364, cloth. *10s 6d.*

Palmer.—LEAVES FROM A WORD HUNTER'S NOTE BOOK. Being some Contributions to English Etymology. By the Rev. A. SMYTHE PALMER, B.A., sometime Scholar in the University of Dublin. Cr. 8vo. cl. pp. xii.–316. *7s. 6d.*

Palmer.—THE SONG OF THE REED; and other Pieces. By E. H. PALMER, M.A., Cambridge. Crown 8vo. pp. 208, handsomely bound in cloth. *5s.*
Among the Contents will be found translations from Hafiz, from Omer el Kheïyam, and from other Persian as well as Arabic poets.

Pand-Námah. — THE PAND-NÁMAH ; or, Books of Counsels. By ÁDARBÁD MÁRÁSPAND. Translated from Pehlevi into Gujerathi, by Harbad Sheriarjee Dadabhoy. And from Gujerathi into English by the Rev. Shapurji Edalji. Fcap. 8vo. sewed. 1870. *6d.*

Pandit's (A) Remarks on Professor Max Müller's Translation of the "RIG-VEDA." Sanskrit and English. Fcap. 8vo. sewed. 1870. *6d.*

Paspati.—ÉTUDES SUR LES TCHINGHIANÉS (GYPSIES) OU BOHÉMIENS DE L'EMPIRE OTTOMAN. Par ALEXANDRE G. PASPATI, M.D. Large 8vo. sewed, pp. xii. and 652. Constantinople, 1871. *28s.*

Patanjali.—THE VYÁKARANA-MAHÁBHÁSHYA OF PATANJALI. Edited by F. KIELHORN, Ph.D., Professor of Oriental Languages, Deccan College. Vol. I., Part I. pp. 200. *8s. 6d.*

Patell.—COWASJEE PATELL'S CHRONOLOGY, containing corresponding Dates of the different Eras used by Christians, Jews, Greeks, Hindús, Mohamedans, Parsees, Chinese, Japanese, etc. By COWASJEE SORABJEE PATELL. 4to. pp. viii. and 184, cloth. *50s.*

Peking Gazette.—Translation of the Peking Gazette for 1872, 1873, 1874, 1875, 1876, and 1877. 8vo. cloth. *10s. 6d.* each.

Percy.—Bishop Percy's Folio Manuscripts—Ballads and Romances. Edited by John W. Hales, M.A., Fellow and late Assistant Tutor of Christ's College, Cambridge; and Frederick J. Furnivall, M.A., of Trinity Hall, Cambridge; assisted by Professor Child, of Harvard University, Cambridge, U.S.A., W. Chappell, Esq., etc. In 3 volumes. Vol. I., pp. 610; Vol. 2, pp. 681.; Vol. 3, pp. 640. Demy 8vo. half-bound, £4 4s. Extra demy 8vo. half-bound, on Whatman's ribbed paper, £6 6s. Extra royal 8vo., paper covers, on Whatman's best ribbed paper, £10 10s. Large 4to., paper covers, on Whatman's best ribbed paper, £12.

Pfoundes.—Fu So Mimi Bukuro.—A Budget of Japanese Notes. By Capt. Pfoundes, of Yokohama. 8vo. sewed, pp. 184. 7s. 6d.

Philological Society (Transactions of The). A Complete Set, including the Proceedings of the Philological Society for the years 1842-1853. 6 vols. The Philological Society's Transactions, 1854 to 1876. 15 vols. The Philological Society's Extra Volumes. 9 vols. In all 30 vols. 8vo. £19 13s. 6d.

Proceedings (The) of the Philological Society 1842-1853. 6 vols. 8vo. £3.

Transactions of the Philological Society, 1854-1876. 15 vols. 8vo. £10 16s.

⁎ The Volumes for 1867, 1868-9, 1870-2, and 1873-4, are only to be had in complete sets, as above.

Separate Volumes.

For 1854 : containing papers by Rev. J. W. Blakesley, Rev. T. O. Cockayne, Rev. J. Davies, Dr. J. W. Donaldson, Dr. Theod. Goldstücker, Prof. T. Hewitt Key, J. M. Kemble, Dr. R. G. Latham, J. M. Ludlow, Hensleigh Wedgwood, etc. 8vo. cl. £1 1s.

For 1855 : with papers by Dr. Carl Abel, Dr. W. Bleek, Rev. Jno. Davies, Miss A. Gurney, Jas. Kennedy, Prof. T. H. Key, Dr. R. G. Latham, Henry Malden, W. Ridley, Thos. Watts, Hensleigh Wedgwood, etc. In 4 parts. 8vo. £1 1s.

⁎ Kamilaroi Language of Australia, by W. Ridley; and False Etymologies, by H. Wedgwood, separately. 1s.

For 1856-7 : with papers by Prof. Aufrecht, Herbert Coleridge, Lewis Kr. Daa, M. de Haan, W. C. Jourdain, James Kennedy, Prof. Key, Dr. G. Latham, J. M. Ludlow, Rev. J. J. S. Perowne, Hensleigh Wedgwood, R. F. Weymouth, Jos. Yates, etc. 7 parts. 8vo. (The Papers relating to the Society's Dictionary are omitted.) £1 1s. each volume.

For 1858 : including the volume of Early English Poems, Lives of the Saints, edited from MSS. by F. J. Furnivall; and papers by Ern. Adams, Prof. Aufrecht, Herbert Coleridge, Rev. Francis Crawford, M. de Haan Hettema, Dr. R. G. Latham, Dr. Lottner, etc. 8vo. cl. 12s.

For 1859 : with papers by Dr. E. Adams, Prof. Aufrecht, Herb. Coleridge, F. J. Furnivall, Prof. T. H. Key, Dr. C. Lottner, Prof. De Morgan, F. Pulszky, Hensleigh Wedgwood, etc. 8vo. cl. 12s.

For 1860-1 : including The Play of the Sacrament; and Pascon agau Arluth, the Passion of our Lord, in Cornish and English, both from MSS., edited by Dr. Whitley Stokes; and papers by Dr. E. Adams, T. F. Barham, Rev. Derwent Coleridge, Herbert Coleridge, Sir John F. Davis, Danby P. Fry, Prof. T. H. Key, Dr. C. Lottner, Bishop Thirlwall, Hensleigh Wedgwood, R. F. Weymouth, etc. 8vo. cl. 12s.

For 1862-3 : with papers by C. B. Cayley, D. P. Fry, Prof. Key, H. Malden, Rich. Morris, F. W. Newman, Robert Peacock, Hensleigh Wedgwood, R. F. Weymouth, etc. 8vo. cl. 12s.

For 1864 : containing 1. Manning's (Jas.) Inquiry into the Character and Origin of the Possessive Augment in English, etc. ; 2. Newman's (Francis W.) Text of the Iguvine Inscriptions, with Interlinear Latin Translation; 3. Barnes's (Dr.

Philological Society (Transactions of The)—*continued.*

W.) Grammar and Glossary of the Dorset Dialect; 4. Gwreans An Bys—The Creation: a Cornish Mystery, Cornish and English, with Notes by Whitley Stokes, etc. 8vo. cl. 12s.

*** Separately: Manning's Inquiry, 3s.—Newman's Iguvine Inscription, 3s.—Stokes's Gwreans An Bys, 8s.

For 1865: including Wheatley's (H. B.) Dictionary of Reduplicated Words in the English Language; and papers by Prof. Aufrecht, Ed. Brock, C. B. Cayley, Rev. A. J. Church, Prof. T. H. Key, Rev. E. H. Knowles, Prof. H. Malden, Hon. G. P. Marsh, John Rhys, Guthbrand Vigfusson, Hensleigh Wedgwood, H. B. Wheatley, etc. 8vo. cl. 12s.

For 1866: including 1. Gregor's (Rev. Walter) Banffshire Dialect, with Glossary of Words omitted by Jamieson; 2. Edmondston's (T.) Glossary of the Shetland Dialect; and papers by Prof. Cassal, C. B. Cayley, Danby P. Fry, Prof. T. H. Key, Guthbrand Vigfusson, Hensleigh Wedgwood, etc. 8vo. cl. 12s.

*** The Volumes for 1867, 1868-9, 1870-2, and 1873-4, are out of print. Besides contributions in the shape of valuable and interesting papers, the volume for 1867 also includes: 1. Peacock's (Rob. B.) Glossary of the Hundred of Lonsdale; and 2. Ellis (A. J.) On Palæotype representing Spoken Sounds; and on the Diphthong "Oy." The volume for 1868-9—1. Ellis's (A. J.) Only English Proclamation of Henry III. in Oct. 1258; to which are added "The Cuckoo's Song and "The Prisoner's Prayer," Lyrics of the XIII. Century, with Glossary; and 2. Stokes's (Whitley) Cornish Glossary. That for 1870-2—1. Murray's (Jas. A. H.) Dialect of the Southern Counties of Scotland, with a linguistical map. That for 1873-4—Sweet's (H.) History of English Sounds.

For 1875-6: containing the Rev. Richard Morris (President), Fourth and Fifth Annual Addresses. 1. Some Sources of Aryan Mythology by E. L. Brandreth; 2. C. B. Cayley on Certain Italian Diminutives; 3. Changes made by four young Children in Pronouncing English Words, by Jas. M. Menzies; 4. The Manx Language, by H. Jenner; 5. The Dialect of West Somerset, by F. T. Elworthy; 6. English Metre, by Prof. J. B. Mayor; 7. Words, Logic and Grammar, by H. Sweet; 8. The Russian Language and its Dialects, by W. R. Morfill; 9. Relics of the Cornish Language in Mount's Bay, by H. Jenner. 10. Dialects and Prehistoric Forms of Old English. By Henry Sweet, Esq.; 11. On the Dialects of Monmouthshire, Herefordshire, Worcestershire, Gloucestershire, Berkshire, Oxfordshire, South Warwickshire, South North-amptonshire, Buckinghamshire, Hertfordshire, Middlesex, and Surrey, with a New Classification of the English Dialects. By Prince Louis Lucien Bonaparte (with Two Maps), Index, etc. Part I., 6s.; Part II., 6s.; Part III., 6s.

For 1877 8-9: containing the President's (Henry Sweet, Esq.) Sixth and Seventh Annual Addresses. 1. Accadian Phonology, by Professor A. H. Sayce; 2. On *Here* and *There* in Chaucer, by Dr. R. Weymouth; 3. The Grammar of the Dialect of West Somerset. by F. T. Elworthy, Esq.; 4. English Metre, by Professor J. B. Mayor; 5. The Malagasy Language, by the Rev. W. E. Cousins; 6. The Anglo-Cymric Score, by A. J. Ellis, Esq., F.R.S. 8vo. Part I., 3s.; Part II., 7s.

The Society's Extra Volumes.

Early English Volume, 1862-64, containing: 1. Liber Cure Cocorum, A.D. *c.* 1440. -2. Hampole's (Richard Rolle) Pricke of Conscience, A.D. *c.* 1340.— 3. The Castell off Love, A.D. *c.* 1320. 8vo. cloth. 1865. £1.

Or separately: Liber Cure Cocorum, Edited by Rich. Morris, 3s.; Hampole's (Rolle) Pricke of Conscience, edited by Rich. Morris, 12s.; and The Castell off Love, edited by Dr. R. F. Weymouth, 6s.

Philological Society (Transactions of the)—*continued.*

Dan Michel's Ayenbite of Inwyt, or Remorse of Conscience, in the Kentish Dialect, A.D. 1340. From the Autograph MS. in Brit. Mus. Edited with Introduction, Marginal Interpretations, and Glossarial Index, by Richard Morris. 8vo. cloth. 1866. 12s.

Levins's (Peter, A.D. 1570) Manipulus Vocabulorum : a Rhyming Dictionary of the English Language. With an Alphabetical Index by H. B. Wheatley. 8vo. cloth. 1867. 16s.

Skeat's (Rev. W. W.) Mœso-Gothic Glossary, with an Introduction, an Outline of Mœso-Gothic Grammar, and a List of Anglo-Saxon and old and modern English Words etymologically connected with Mœso-Gothic. 1868. 8vo. cl. 9s.

Ellis (A. J.) on Early English Pronunciation, with especial Reference to Shakspere and Chaucer : containing an Investigation of the Correspondence of Writing with Speech in England from the Anglo-Saxon Period to the Present Day, etc. 4 parts. 8vo. 1869–75. £2.

Mediæval Greek Texts: A Collection of the Earliest Compositions in Vulgar Greek, prior to A.D. 1500. With Prolegomena and Critical Notes by W. Wagner. Part I. Seven Poems, three of which appear for the first time. 1870. 8vo. 10s. 6d.

Phillips.—THE DOCTRINE OF ADDAI THE APOSTLE. Now first Edited in a Complete Form in the Original Syriac, with an English Translation and Notes. By GEORGE PHILLIPS, D.D., President of Queen's College, Cambridge. 8vo. pp. 122, cloth. 7s. 6d.

Picard.—A NEW POCKET DICTIONARY OF THE ENGLISH AND DUTCH LANGUAGES. By H. PICARD. Revised and augmented by A. B. MAATJES and H. J. VOGIN. Fifth edition. Small 4to. cloth, pp. xvi. and 1186. 1877. 10s.

Pimentel.—CUADRO DESCRIPTIVO Y COMPARATIVO DE LAS LENGUAS INDÍGENAS DE MÉXICO, o Tratado de Filologia Mexicana. Par FRANCISCO PIMENTEL. 2 Edicion unica completa. 3 Volsume 8vo. *Mexico*, 1875. £2 2s.

Pischel.—HEMACANDRA'S GRAMMATIK DER PRÁKRITSPRACHEN (Siddha-hemacandram Adhyâya VIII.) mit Kritischen und Erläuternden Anmerkungen. Herausgegeben von RICHARD PISCHEL. Part I. Text und Wörtverzeichniss. 8vo. pp. xiv. and 236. 8s.

Pope.—A TAMIL HANDBOOK ; or, Full Introduction to the Common Dialect of that Language, on the plan of Ollendorff and Arnold. With copious Vocabularies, Appendices, containing Reading Lessons, Analyses of Letters, Deeds, Complaints, Official Documents, and a Key to the Exercises. By Rev. G. U. POPE. Third edition, 8vo. cloth, pp. iv. and 388. 21s.

Prakrita-Prakasa ; or, The Prakrit Grammar of Vararuchi, with the Commentary (Manorama) of Bhamaha. The first complete edition of the Original Text with Various Readings from a Collation of Six Manuscripts in the Bodleian Library at Oxford, and the Libraries of the Royal Asiatic Society and the East India House; with copious Notes, an English Translation, and Index of Prakrit words, to which is prefixed an easy Introduction to Prakrit Grammar. By E. B. COWELL. Second issue, with new Preface, and corrections. 8vo. pp. xxxii. and 204. 14s.

Priaulx.—QUÆSTIONES MOSAICÆ ; or, the first part of the Book of Genesis compared with the remains of ancient religions. By OSMOND DE BEAUVOIR PRIAULX. 8vo. pp. viii. and 548, cloth. 12s.

Rámáyan of Válmiki.—5 vols. See under GRIFFITH.

Ram Jasan. — A Sanskrit and English Dictionary. Being an Abridgment of Professor Wilson's Dictionary. With an Appendix explaining the use of Affixes in Sanskrit. By Pandit Ram Jasan, Queen's College, Benares. Publ shed under the Patronage of the Government, N.W.P. Royal 8vo. cloth, pp. ii. and 707. 28s.

Ram Raz. — Essay on the Architecture of the Hindus. By Ram Raz, Native Judge and Magistrate of Bangalore. With 48 plates. 4to. pp. xiv. and 64, sewed. London, 1834. £2 2s.

Rask. — A Grammar of the Anglo-Saxon Tongue. From the Danish of Erasmus Rask, Professor of Literary History in, and Librarian to, the University of Copenhagen, etc. By Benjamin Thorpe. Second edition, corrected and improved. 18mo. pp. 200, cloth. 5s. 6d.

Rawlinson. — A Commentary on the Cuneiform Inscriptions of Babylonia and Assyria, including Readings of the Inscription on the Nimrud Obelisk, and Brief Notice of the Ancient Kings of Nineveh and Babylon, by Major H. C. Rawlinson. 8vo. pp. 84, sewed. London, 1850. 2s. 6d.

Rawlinson. — Outlines of Assyrian History, from the Inscriptions of Nineveh. By Lieut. Col. Rawlinson, C.B., followed by some Remarks by A. H. Layard, Esq., D.C.L. 8vo., pp. xliv., sewed. London, 1852. 1s.

Rawlinson. — Inscription of Tiglath Pileser I., King of Assyria, b.c. 1150, as translated by Sir H. Rawlinson, Fox Talbot, Esq., Dr. Hincks, and Dr. Oppert. Published by the Royal Asiatic Society. 8vo. sd., pp. 74. 2s.

Rawlinson. — Notes on the Early History of Babylonia. By Colonel Rawlinson, C.B. 8vo. sd., pp. 48. 1s.

Redhouse. — The Turkish Campaigner's Vade-Mecum of Ottoman Colloquial Language; containing a concise Ottoman Grammar; a carefully selected Voc bulary, alphabetically arranged, in two parts, English and Turkish, and Turkish and English: also a few Familiar Dialogues; the whole in English characters. By J. W. Redhouse, F.R.A.S. Oblong 32mo. limp cloth, pp. iv. and 332. 6s.

Redhouse. — كتاب لعجة المعانى لجيمس رد حاوص الانكليزى. A Lexicon English and Turkish, showing in Turkish the Literal, Incidental, Figurative, Colloquial, and Technical Significations of the English Terms, indicating their pronunciation in a new and systematic manner, and preceded by a Sketch of English Etymology to facilitate to Turkish Students the acquisition of the English Language. By J. W. Redhouse, M.R.A.S. Second edition, pp. xvii. and 827. 15s.

Redhouse. — A Vindication of the Ottoman Sultan's Title to "Caliph," showing its Antiquity, Validity, and Universal Acceptance. By J. W. Redhouse. 8vo. paper, pp. 20. 3d.

Renan. — An Essay on the Age and Antiquity of the Book of Nabathæan Agriculture. To which is added an Inaugural Lecture on the Position of the Shemitic Nations in the History of Civilization. By M. Ernest Renan, Membre de l'Institut. Crown 8vo., pp. xvi. and 148, cloth. 3s. 6d.

Revue Celtique (The). — A Quarterly Magazine for Celtic Philology, Literature, and History. Edited with the assistance of the Chief Celtic Scholars of the British Islands and of the Continent, and Conducted by H. Gaidoz. 8vo. Subscription, £1 per Volume.

Rhys. — Lectures on Welsh Philology. By John Rhys, M.A., Professor of Celtic at Oxford. Second edition, revised and enlarged. Crown 8vo. cloth, pp. viii. and 466. 15s.

Rig-Veda. — *See* Müller.

Rig-Veda-Sanhita: The Sacred Hymns of the Brahmans. Translated and explained by F. Max Müller, M.A., LL.D., Fellow of All Souls' College, Professor of Comparative Philology at Oxford, Foreign Member of the Institute of France, etc., etc. Vol. I. Hymns to the Maruts, or the Storm-Gods. 8vo. pp. clii. and 264. cloth. 1869. 12s. 6d.

Rig-Veda Sanhita.—A Collection of Ancient Hindu Hymns. Constituting the First Ashtaka, or Book of the Rig-veda; the oldest authority for the religious and social institutions of the Hindus. Translated from the Original Sanskrit by the late H. H. Wilson, M.A. 2nd Ed., with a Postscript by Dr. Fitzedward Hall. Vol. I. 8vo. cloth, pp. lii. and 348, price 21s.

Rig-Veda Sanhita.—A Collection of Ancient Hindu Hymns, constituting the Fifth to Eighth Ashtakas, or books of the Rig-Veda, the oldest Authority for the Religious and Social Institutions of the Hindus. Translated from the Original Sanskrit by the late Horace Hayman Wilson, M.A., F.R.S., etc. Edited by E. B. Cowell, M.A., Principal of the Calcutta Sanskrit College. Vol. IV., 8vo., pp. 214, cloth. 14s.

A few copies of Vols. II. and III. still left.   [*Vols. V. and VI. in the Press.*

Riola.—How to Learn Russian. A Manual for Students of Russian, based upon the Ollendorfian system of teaching languages, and adapted for self instruction. By Henry Riola, Teacher of the Russian Language. With a Preface by W. R. S. Ralston, M.A. Crown 8vo. cloth, pp. 576. 1878. 12s.
Key to the above. Crown 8vo. cloth, pp. 126. 1878. 5s.

Roberts.—Aryan Philology, according to the most recent Researches (Glottologia Aria Recentissima), Remarks Historical and Critical. By Domenico Pezzi, Membro della Facolta de Filosofia e lettere della R. Universit. di Torino. Translated by E. S. Roberts, M.A., Fellow and Tutor of Gonville and Caius College. Crown 8vo. cloth, pp. xvi. and 199. 6s.

Roe and Fryer.—Travels in India in the Seventeenth Century. By Sir Thomas Roe and Dr. John Fryer. Reprinted from the "Calcutta Weekly Englishman." 8vo. cloth, pp. 474. 7s. 6d.

Rœhrig.—The Shortest Road to German. Designed for the use of both Teachers and Students. By F. L. O. Rœhrig. Cr. 8vo. cloth, pp. vii. and 225. 1874. 7s. 6d.

Rogers.—Notice on the Dinars of the Abbasside Dynasty. By Edward Thomas Rogers, late H.M. Consul, Cairo. 8vo. pp. 44, with a Map and four Autotype Plates. 5s.

Rosny.—A Grammar of the Chinese Language. By Professor Leon de Rosny. 8vo. pp. 48. 1874. 3s.

Ross.—A Mandarin Primer. Being Easy Lessons for Beginners, Transliterated according to the European mode of using Roman Letters By Rev. John Ross, Newchang. 8vo. wrapper, pp. 122. 6s.

Ross—A Corean Primer. Being Lessons in Corean on all Ordinary Subjects. Transliterated on the principles of the Mandarin Primer by the same author. By the Rev. John Ross, Newchang. Demy 8vo. stitched. pp. 90. 10s.

Routledge.—English Rule and Native Opinion in India. From Notes taken in the years 1870-74. By James Routledge. Post 8vo. cloth, pp. 344. 10s. 6d.

Royal Society of Literature of the United Kingdom (Transactions of The). First Series, 6 Parts in 3 Vols., 4to., Plates; 1827-39. Second Series, 10 Vols. or 30 Parts, and Vol. XI. Parts 1 and 2, 8vo., Plates; 1843-76.

4

A complete set, as far as published, £10 10s. Very scarce. The first series of this important series of contributions of many of the most eminent men of the day has long been out of print and is very scarce. Of the Second Series, Vol. I.-IV., each containing three parts, are quite out of print, and can only be had in the complete series, noticed above. Three Numbers, price 4s. 6d. each, form a volume. The price of the volume complete, bound in cloth, is 13s. 6d.

Separate Publications.

I. FASTI MONASTICI AEVI SAXONICI : or an Alphabetical List of the Heads of Religious Houses in England previous to the Norman Conquest, to which is prefixed a Chronological Catalogue of Contemporary Foundations. By WALTER DE GRAY BIRCH. Royal 8vo. cloth. 1872. 7s. 6d.

II. LI CHANTARI DI LANCELLOTTO ; a Troubadour's Poem of the XIV. Cent. Edited from a MS. in the possession of the Royal Society of Literature, by WALTER DE GRAY BIRCH. Royal 8vo. cloth. 1874. 7s.

III. INQUISITIO COMITATUS CANTABRIGIENSIS, nunc primum, è Manuscripto unico in Bibliothecâ Cottoniensi asservato, typis mandata : subjicitur Inquisitio Eliensis : curâ N. E. S. A. Hamilton. Royal 4to. With map and 3 facsimiles. 1876. £2 2s.

IV. A COMMONPLACE-BOOK OF JOHN MILTON. Reproduced by the autotype process from the original MS. in the possession of Sir Fred. U. Graham, Bart., of Netherby Hall. With an Introduction by A. J. Horwood. Sq. folio. Only one hundred copies printed. 1876. £2 2s.

V. CHRONICON ADÆ DE USK, A.D. 1377-1404. Edited, with a Translation and Notes, by ED. MAUNDE THOMPSON. Royal 8vo. 1876. 10s. 6d.

Rudy.—THE CHINESE MANDARIN LANGUAGE, after Ollendorff's New Method of Learning Languages. By CHARLES RUDY. In 3 Volumes. Vol. I. Grammar. 8vo. pp. 248. £1 1s.

Sabdakalpadruma, the well-known Sanskrit Dictionary of RAJÁH RADHAKANTA DEVA. In Bengali characters. 4to. Parts 1 to 40. (In course of publication.) 3s. 6d. each part.

Sakuntala.—KÁLIDÁSA'S ÇAKUNTALÁ. The Bengalí Recension. With Critical Notes. Edited by RICHARD PISCHEL. 8vo. cloth, pp. xi. and 210. 14s.

Sakuntala.—A SANSKRIT DRAMA IN SEVEN ACTS. Edited by MONIER WILLIAMS, M.A. Second Edition. 8vo. cl. £1 1s.

Sale.—THE KORAN ; commonly called THE ALCORAN OF MOHAMMED. Translated into English immediately from the original Arabic. By GEORGE SALE, Gent. To which is prefixed the Life of Mohammed. Crown 8vo. cloth, pp. 472. 7s.

Sâma-Vidhâna-Brâhmana. With the Commentary of Sâyana. Edited, with Notes, Translation, and Index, by A. C. BURNELL, M.R.A.S. Vol. I. Text and Commentary. With Introduction. 8vo. cloth, pp. xxxviii. and 104. 12s. 6d.

Sanskrit Works.—A CATALOGUE OF SANSKRIT WORKS PRINTED IN INDIA, offered for Sale at the affixed nett prices by TRÜBNER & Co. 16mo. pp. 52. 1s.

Sarva-Sabda-Sambodhini ; OR, THE COMPLETE SANSKRIT DICTIONARY. In Telugu characters. 4to. cloth, pp. 1078. £2 15s.

Satow.—AN ENGLISH JAPANESE DICTIONARY OF THE SPOKEN LANGUAGE. By ERNEST MASON SATOW, Japanese Secretary to H.M. Legation at Yedo, and ISHIBASHI MASAKATA, of the Imperial Japanese Foreign Office. Imp. 32mo., pp. xx. and 366, cloth. 12s.

Sayce.—An Assyrian Grammar for Comparative Purposes. By A. H. Sayce, M.A. 12mo. cloth, pp. xvi. and 188. 7s. 6d.

Sayce.—The Principles of Comparative Philology. By A. H. Sayce, Fellow and Tutor of Queen's College, Oxford. Second Edition. Cr. 8vo. cl., pp. xxxii. and 416. 10s. 6d.

Scarborough.—A Collection of Chinese Proverbs. Translated and Arranged by William Scarborough, Wesleyan Missionary, Hankow. With an Introduction, Notes, and Copious Index. Cr. 8vo. pp. xliv. and 278. 10s.6d.

Schleicher.—Compendium of the Comparative Grammar of the Indo-European, Sanskrit, Greek, and Latin Languages. By August Schleicher. Translated from the Third German Edition by Herbert Bendall, B.A., Chr. Coll. Camb. Part I. Grammar. 8vo. cloth, pp. 184. 7s. 6d.

Part II. Morphology. 8vo. cloth, pp. viii. and 104. 6s.

Schemeil.—El Mubtaker; or, First Born. (In Arabic, printed at Beyrout). Containing Five Comedies, called Comedies of Fiction, on Hopes and Judgments, in Twenty-six Poems of 1092 Verses, showing the Seven Stages of Life, from man's conception unto his death and burial. By Emin Ibrahim Schemeil. In one volume, 4to. pp. 166, sewed. 1870. 5s.

Schlagintweit.—Buddhism in Tibet. Illustrated by Literary Documents and Objects of Religious Worship. With an Account of the Buddhist Systems preceding it in India. By Emil Schlagintweit, LL.D. With a Folio Atlas of 20 Plates, and 20 Tables of Native Prints in the Text. Royal 8vo., pp. xxiv. and 404. £2 2s.

Schlagintweit.—Glossary of Geographical Terms from India and Tibet, with Native Transcription and Transliteration. By Hermann de Schlagintweit. Forming, with a "Route Book of the Western Himalaya, Tibet, and Turkistan,"the Third Volume of H., A., and R. de Schlagintweit's "Results of a Scientific Mission to India and High Asia." With an Atlas in imperial folio, of Maps, Panoramas, and Views. Royal 4to., pp. xxiv. and 293. £4.

Semitic (Songs of The). In English Verse. By G. E. W. Cr. 8vo. cloth, pp. 140. 5s.

Shakspere Society (The New). — Subscription £1 1s. per annum. List of publications on applic tion.

Shápurjí Edaljí.—A Grammar of the Gujaráti Language. By Shápurjí Edaljí. Cloth, pp. 127. 10s. 6d.

Shápurjí Edaljí.—A Dictionary, Gujrati and English. By Shápurjí Edaljí. Second Edition. Crown 8vo. cloth, pp. xxiv. and 874. 21s.

Shaw.—A Sketch of the Turki Language. As Spoken in Eastern Turkistan (Kàshghar and Yarkand). By Robert Barklay Shaw, F.R.G.S., Political Agent. In Two Parts. With Lists of Names of Birds and Plants by J. Scully, Surgeon, H.M. Bengal Army. 8vo. sewed, Part I., pp. 130. 7s. 6d.

Sherring—The Sacred City of the Hindus. An Account of Benares in Ancient and Modern Times. By the Rev. M. A. Sherring, M.A., LL.D.; and Prefaced with an Introduction by Fitzedward Hall, Esq., D.C.L. 8vo. cloth, pp. xxxvi. and 388, with numerous full-page illustrations. 21s.

Sherring.—The Hindoo Pilgrims. By the Rev. M. A. Sherring, Fcap. 8vo. cloth, pp. vi. and 125. 5s.

Singh.—Sakhee Book; or, The Description of Gooroo Gobind Singh's Religion and Doctrines, translated from Gooroo Mukhi into Hindi, and afterwards into English. By Sirdar Attar Singh, Chief of Bhadour. With the author's photograph. 8vo. pp. xviii. and 205. 15s.

Skeat.—A LIST OF ENGLISH WORDS, the Etymology of which is illustrated by Comparison with Icelandic. Prepared in the form of an Appendix to Cleasby and Vigfusson's Icelandic-English Dictionary. By the Rev. WALTER W. SKEAT, M.A., English Lecturer and late Fellow of Christ's College, Cambridge; and M.A. of Exeter College, Oxford; one of the Vice-Presidents of the Cambridge Philological Society; and Member of the Council of the Philological Society of London. 1876. Demy 4to. sewed. 2s.

Smith.—A VOCABULARY OF PROPER NAMES IN CHINESE AND ENGLISH. of Places, Persons, Tribes. and Sects, in China, Japan, Corea, Assam, Siam, Burmah, The Straits, and adjacent Countries. By F. PORTER SMITH, M.B., London, Medical Missionary in Central China. 4to. half-bound, pp. vi., 72, and x. 1870. 10s. 6d.

Smith.—CONTRIBUTIONS TOWARDS THE MATERIA MEDICA AND NATURAL HISTORY OF CHINA. For the use of Medical Missionaries and Native Medical Students. By F. PORTER SMITH, M.B. London, Medical Missionary in Central China. Imp. 4to. cloth, pp. viii. and 240. 1870. £1 1s.

Sophocles.—A GLOSSARY OF LATER AND BYZANTINE GREEK. By E. A. SOPHOCLES. 4to., pp. iv. and 624, cloth. £2 2s.

Sophocles.—ROMAIC OR MODERN GREEK GRAMMAR. By E. A. SOPHOCLES. 8vo. pp. xxviii. and 196.

Sophocles.—GREEK LEXICON OF THE ROMAN AND BYZANTINE PERIODS (from B.C. 146 to A.D. 1100). By E. A. SOPHOCLES. Imp. 8vo. pp. xvi. 1188, cloth. 1870. £2 10s.

Spurrell.—A GRAMMAR OF THE WELSH LANGUAGE. By WILLIAM SPURRELL. 3rd Edition. Fcap. cloth, pp. viii.-206. 1870. 3s.

Spurrell.—A WELSH DICTIONARY. English-Welsh and Welsh-English. With Preliminary Observations on the Elementary Sounds of the English Language, a copious Vocabulary of the Roots of English Words, a list of Scripture Proper Names and English Synonyms and Explanations. By WILLIAM SPURRELL. Third Edition. Fcap. cloth, pp. xxv. and 732. 8s. 6d.

Steele.—AN EASTERN LOVE STORY. KUSA JÁTAKAYA: a Buddhistic Legendary Poem, with other Stories. By THOMAS STEELE, Ceylon Civil Service. Crown 8vo. cloth, pp. xii. and 260. 1871. 6s.

Steere.—SHORT SPECIMENS OF THE VOCABULARIES OF THREE UN-PUBLISHED African Languages (Gindo, Zaramo, and Angazidja). Collected by EDWARD STEERE, LL.D. 12mo. pp. 20. 6d.

Steere.—COLLECTIONS FOR A HANDBOOK OF THE NYAMWEZI LANGUAGE, as spoken at Unyanyembe. By EDWARD STEERE, LL.D. Fcap. cloth, pp. 100. 1s. 6d.

Stent.—THE JADE CHAPLET, in Twenty-four Beads. A Collection of Songs, Ballads, etc. (from the Chinese). By GEORGE CARTER STENT, M.N.C.B.R.A.S., Author of "Chinese and English Vocabulary," "Chinese and English Pocket Dictionary," "Chinese Lyrics," "Chinese Legends," etc. Cr. 8o. cloth, pp. 176. 5s.

Stent.—A CHINESE AND ENGLISH VOCABULARY IN THE PEKINESE DIALECT. By G. E. STENT. 8vo. pp. ix. and 677. 1871. £1 10s.

Stent.—A CHINESE AND ENGLISH POCKET DICTIONARY. By G. E. STENT. 16mo. pp. 250. 1874. 10s. 6d.

Stoddard.—GRAMMAR OF THE MODERN SYRIAC LANGUAGE, as spoken in Oroomiah, Persia, and in Koordistan. By Rev. D. T. STODDARD, Missionary of the American Board in Persia. Demy 8vo. bds., pp. 190. 10s. 6d.

Stokes.—BEUNANS MERIASEK. The Life of Saint Meriasek, Bishop and Confessor. A Cornish Drama. Edited, with a Translation and Notes, by WHITLEY STOKES. Medium 8vo. cloth, pp. xvi., 280, and Facsimile. 1872. 15s.

Stokes.—GOIDELICA—Old and Early-Middle Irish Glosses : Prose and Verse. Edited by WHITLEY STOKES. Second edition. Medium 8vo. cloth, pp. 192. 18s.

Strangford.—ORIGINAL LETTERS AND PAPERS OF THE LATE VISCOUNT STRANGFORD, upon Philological and Kindred Subjects. Edited by VISCOUNTESS STRANGFORD. Post 8vo. cloth, pp. xxii. and 284. 1878. 12s. 6d.

Stratmann.—A DICTIONARY OF THE OLD ENGLISH LANGUAGE. Compiled from the writings of the XIIIth, XIVth, and XVth centuries. By FRANCIS HENRY STRATMANN. Third Edition. 4to. In wrapper. £1 10s.

Stratmann.—AN OLD ENGLISH POEM OF THE OWL AND THE NIGHTINGALE. Edited by FRANCIS HENRY STRATMANN. 8vo. cloth, pp. 60. 3s.

Strong.—SELECTIONS FROM THE BOSTAN OF SADI, translated into English Verse. By DAWSONNE MELANCTHON STRONG, Captain H.M. 10th Bengal Lancers. 12mo. cloth, pp. ii, and 56. 2s. 6d.

Sunjana.—A GRAMMAR OF THE PAHLVI LANGUAGE, with Quotations and Examples from Original Works and a Glossary of Words bearing affinity with the Semitic Languages. By PESHOTUN DUSTOOR BEHRAMJEE SUNJANA, Principal of Sir Jamsetjee Jejeeboy Zurthosi Madressa. 8vo. cl., pp. 18–457. 25s.

Surya-Siddhanta (Translation of the).—*See* Whitney.

Sweet.—A HISTORY OF ENGLISH SOUNDS, from the Earliest Period, including an Investigation of the General Laws of Sound Change, and full Word Lists. By HENRY SWEET. Demy 8vo. cloth, pp. iv. and 164. 4s. 6d.

Syed Ahmad.—A SERIES OF ESSAYS ON THE LIFE OF MOHAMMED, and Subjects subsidiary thereto. By SYED AHMAD KHAN BAHADOR, C.S.I., Author of the "Mohammedan Commentary on the Holy Bible," Honorary Member of the Royal Asiatic Society, and Life Honorary Secretary to the Allygurh Scientific Society. 8vo. pp. 532, with 4 Genealogical Tables, 2 Maps, and a Coloured Plate, handsomely bound in cloth. £1 10s.

Syro-Egyptian Society.—Original Papers read before the Syro-Egyptian Society of London. Volume I. Part 1. 8vo. sewed, 2 plates and a map, pp. 144. 3s. 6d.

Including, among other papers, Remarks on the Obelisks of Ancient Egypt. By W. H. Yates, M.D.—Notes on the Hieroglyphics of Horapollo Nilous. By S. Sharpe.—Remarks on the Wedge Inscription recently discovered on the Upper Euphrates. By G. F. Grotefend, Ph.D. (With a Copy of the Original Inscription).

Táittiríya-Pratiçakhya.—See WHITNEY.

Tarkavachaspati.—VACHASPATYA, a Comprehensive Dictionary, in Ten Parts. Compiled by TARANATHA TARKAVACHASPATI, Professor of Grammar and Philosophy in the Government Sanskrit College of Calcutta. An Alphabetically Arranged Dictionary, with a Grammatical Introduction and Copious Citations from the Grammarians and Scholiasts, from the Vedas, etc. Parts I. to VII. 4to. paper. 1873–6. 18s. each Part.

Technologial Dictionary.—POCKET DICTIONARY OF TECHNICAL TERMS USED IN ARTS AND SCIENCES. English-German-French. Based on the larger Work by KARMARSCH. 3 vols imp. 16mo. cloth. 12s.

Technological Dictionary of the terms employed in the Arts and
Sciences; Architecture, Civil, Military and Naval; Civil Engineering, including
Bridge Building, Road and Railway Making; Mechanics; Machine and Engine
Making; Shipbuilding and Navigation; Metallurgy, Mining and Smelting;
Artillery; Mathematics; Physics; Chemistry; Mineralogy, etc. With a Preface
by Dr. K. KARMARSCH. Second Edition. 3 vols.

Vol. I. English—German—French. 8vo. cloth, pp. 666. 12s.

Vol. II. German—English—French. 8vo. cloth, pp. 646. 12s.

Vol. III. French—German—English. 8vo. cloth, pp. 618. 12s.

The Boke of Nurture. By JOHN RUSSELL, about 1460–1470 Anno
Domini. The Boke of Keruynge. By WYNKYN DE WORDE, Anno Domini
1513. The Boke of Nurture. By HUGH RHODES, Anno Domini 1577. Edited
from the Originals in the British Museum Library, by FREDERICK J. FURNI-
VALL, M.A., Trinity Hall, Cambridge, Member of Council of the Philological
and Early English Text Societies. 4to. half-morocco, gilt top, pp. xix. and 146,
28, xxviii. and 56. 1867. 1l. 11s. 6d.

Thibaut.—THE SÚLVASÚTRAS. English Translation, with an Introduction. By G. THIBAUT, Ph.D., Anglo-Sanskrit Professor Benares College.
8vo. cloth, pp. 47, with 4 Plates. 5s.

Thibaut.—CONTRIBUTIONS TO THE EXPLANATION OF JYOTISHA-VEDÂNGA.
By G. THIBAUT, Ph.D. 8vo. pp. 27. 1s. 6d.

Thomas.—EARLY SASSANIAN INSCRIPTIONS, SEALS AND COINS, illustrating
the Early History of the Sassanian Dynasty, containing Proclamations of Arde-
shir Babek, Sapor I., and his Successors. With a Critical Examination and
Explanation of the Celebrated Inscription in the Hájíábad Cave, demonstrating
that Sapor, the Conqueror of Valerian, was a Professing Christian. By EDWARD
THOMAS, F.R.S. Illustrated. 8vo. cloth, pp. 148. 7s. 6d.

Thomas.—THE CHRONICLES OF THE PATHÁN KINGS OF DEHLI. Illustrated by Coins, Inscriptions, and other Antiquarian Remains. By EDWARD
THOMAS, F.R.S., late of the East India Company's Bengal Civil Service. With
numerous Copperplates and Woodcuts. Demy 8vo. cloth, pp. xxiv. and 467.
1871. £1 8s.

Thomas.—THE REVENUE RESOURCES OF THE MUGHAL EMPIRE IN INDIA,
from A.D. 1593 to A.D. 1707. A Supplement to "The Chronicles of the Pathán
Kings of Delhi." By EDWARD THOMAS, F.R.S. Demy 8vo., pp. 60, cloth.
3s. 6d.

Thomas.—COMMENTS ON RECENT PEHLVI DECIPHERMENTS. With an
Incidental Sketch of the Derivation of Aryan Alphabets, and contributions to
the Early History and Geography of Tabaristán. Illustrated by Coins. By
EDWARD THOMAS, F.R.S. 8vo. pp. 56, and 2 plates, cloth, sewed. 3s. 6d.

Thomas.—SASSANIAN COINS. Communicated to the Numismatic Society
of London. By E. THOMAS, F.R.S. Two parts. With 3 Plates and a Wood-
cut. 12mo. sewed, pp. 43. 5s.

Thomas.—RECORDS OF THE GUPTA DYNASTY. Illustrated by Inscrip-
tions, Written History, Local Tradition and Coins. To which is added a
Chapter on the Arabs in Sind. By EDWARD THOMAS, F.R.S. Folio, with a
Plate, handsomely bound in cloth, pp. iv. and 64. Price 14s.

Thomas.—JAINISM; or, The Early Faith of Asoka. With Illustrations
of the Ancient Religions of the East, from the Pantheon of the Indo-Scythians.
To which is added a Notice on Bactrian Coins and Indian Dates. By EDWARD
THOMAS, F.R.S. 8vo. pp. viii., 24 and 82. With two Autotype Plates and
Woodcuts. 7s. 6d.

Thomas.—THE THEORY AND PRACTICE OF CREOLE GRAMMAR. By J. J.
THOMAS. Port of Spain (Trinidad), 1869. 1 vol. 8vo. bds. pp. viii. and 135. 12s.

Thorburn.—BANNÚ; or, Our Afghán Frontier. By S. S. THORBURN, I.C.S., Settlement Officer of the Bannú District. 8vo. cloth, pp. x. and 480. 18s.

Thorpe.—DIPLOMATARIUM ANGLICUM ÆVI SAXONICI. A Collection of English Charters, from the reign of King Æthelberht of Kent, A.D., DCV., to that of William the Conqueror. Containing: I. Miscellaneous Charters. II. Wills. III. Guilds. IV. Manumissions and Acquittances. With a Translation of the Anglo-Saxon. By the late BENJAMIN THORPE, Member of the Royal Academy of Sciences at Munich, and of the Society of Netherlandish Literature at Leyden. 8vo. pp. xlii. and 682, cloth. 1865. £1 1s.

Tiele.—OUTLINES OF THE HISTORY OF RELIGION to the Spread of the Universal Religions. By C. P. TIELE, Dr. Theol. Professor of the History of Religions in the University of Leiden. Translated from the Dutch by J. ESTLIN CARPENTER, M.A. Post 8vo. cloth, pp. xix. and 249. 7s. 6d.

Tindall.—A GRAMMAR AND VOCABULARY OF THE NAMAQUA-HOTTENTOT LANGUAGE. By HENRY TINDALL, Wesleyan Missionary. 8vo. pp. 124, sewed. 6s.

Trübner's Bibliotheca Sanscrita. A Catalogue of Sanskrit Literature, chiefly printed in Europe. To which is added a Catalogue of Sanskrit Works printed in India; and a Catalogue of Pali Books. Constantly for sale by Trübner & Co. Cr. 8vo. sd., pp. 84. 2s. 6d.

Trübner's Oriental Series.

I. ESSAYS ON THE SACRED LANGUAGE, WRITINGS, AND RELIGION OF THE PARSIS. By MARTIN HAUG, Ph.D. late Professor of Sanskrit and Comparative Philology at the University of Munich. Edited by Dr. E. W. WEST. Second Edition. Post 8vo. cloth, pp. xvi. and 428. 1878. 16s.

II. TEXTS FROM THE BUDDHIST CANON, commonly known as Dhammapada. With accompanying Narratives. Translated from the Chinese by S. BEAL, B.A., Professor of Chinese, University College, London. Post 8vo. cloth, pp. viii. and 176. 1878. 7s. 6d.

III. THE HISTORY OF INDIAN LITERATURE. By ALBRECHT WEBER. Translated from the German by JOHN MANN, M.A., and THEODOR ZACHARIAE, Ph.D., with the sanction of the Author. Post 8vo. cloth, pp. xxiii. and 360. 1878. 18s.

IV. A SKETCH OF THE MODERN LANGUAGES OF THE EAST INDIES. By ROBERT CUST. Accompanied by Two Language Maps. Post 8vo. cloth, pp. xii. and 198. 1878. 12s.

V. THE BIRTH OF THE WAR GOD. A Poem by KÁLIDÁSA. Translated from the Sanskrit into English Verse. By RALPH T. H. GRIFFITH, M.A., Principal of Benares College. Second Edition. Post 8vo. cloth, pp. xii.-116. 1879. 5s.

The following Works are in Preparation.

A CLASSICAL DICTIONARY OF HINDU MYTHOLOGY AND HISTORY, GEOGRAPHY AND LITERATURE. By JOHN DOWSON, M.R.A.S., late Professor in the Staff College. In One Volume, post 8vo., about 500 pages, price not to exceed 21s.

SELECTIONS FROM THE KU-RAN. With a COMMENTARY. Translated by the late EDWARD WILLIAM LANE, Author of an "Arabic-English Lexicon," etc. A New Edition, Revised, with an Introduction on the History and Development of Islam, especially with reference to India. By STANLEY LANE POOLE. Post 8vo. cloth.

PASSAGES RELIGIOUS, MORAL, PRUDENTIAL, AND NARRATIVE, from the Mahabharata and other Sanskrit Works. Freely Translated or Paraphrased in English Verses. With an Appendix containing Prose Versions of the Original Texts. By JOHN MUIR, LL.D. Post 8vo. cloth.

Trübner's Oriental Series—*continued.*

ORIENTAL RELIGIONS in their Relation to Universal Religion. By
SAMUEL JOHNSON. First Section—India. Second Section—China. In Two
Volumes, post 8vo. cloth.

MISCELLANEOUS ESSAYS Relating to Indian Subjects.   By B. H.
HODGSON, late British Minister at Nepal. In Two Volumes, post 8vo. cloth.

THE GULISTAN; or, Rose Garden of Shekh Mushliu'd-din Sadi of
Shiraz. Translated for the first time into Prose and Verse, with an Intro-
ductory Preface, and a Life of the Author, from the Ātish Kadah, by EDWARD
B. EASTWICK, F.R.S., M.R.A.S., etc. Second Edition, post 8vo. cloth.

THE JATAKA STORIES.   With the Commentary and Collection of
Buddhist Fairy Tales, Fables, and Folk Lore. Translated from the original
Pali by T. W. RHYS DAVIDS. (The first part of the Commentary contains the
most complete account we yet have of the Life of Buddha.) Vol. I., post 8vo.
cloth.

CHINESE BUDDHISM. A Volume of Sketches, Historical and Critical.
By J. EDKINS, D.D , Author of " China's Place in Philology," " Religion in
China," etc., etc. Post 8vo. cloth.

BUDDHIST RECORDS OF THE WESTERN WORLD. Being the SI-YU-KI by
HYEN THSANG. Translated from the original Chinese, with Introduction,
Index, etc.   By SAMUEL BEAL, Trinity College, Cambridge; Professor of
Chinese, University College, London. In Two Vols., post 8vo. cloth.

THE POEMS OF HAFIZ OF SHIRAZ. Translated from the Persian into
English Verse by E. H. PALMER, M.A., Professor of Arabic in the University
of Cambridge. Post 8vo. cloth.

HISTORY OF THE PORTUGUESE IN INDIA.   Based upon Documentary
Evidence, now for the first time made available. By J. GERSON DA CUNHA,
M.D. Post 8vo. cloth.

INDIAN TALES FROM THIBETAN SOURCES. Translated from the Thibetan
into German by ANTON SCHIEFNER. Rendered into English, with Notes, by
W. R. S. RALSTON. In One Volume, post 8vo.

ON THE VICISSITUDES OF ARYAN CIVILISATION IN INDIA. One of the
Florence Prize Essays. By Dr. J. GERSON DA CUNHA. In Two Volumes,
post 8vo.

Trumpp.—GRAMMAR OF THE PAṢTO, or Language of the Afghans, compared with the Irānian and North-Indian Idioms. By Dr. ERNEST TRUMPP.
8vo. sewed, pp. xvi. and 412. 21s.

Trumpp.—GRAMMAR OF THE SINDHI LANGUAGE. Compared with the
Sanskrit-Prakrit and the Cognate Indian Vernaculars. By Dr. ERNEST
TRUMPP. Printed by order of Her Majesty's Government for India. Demy
8vo. sewed, pp. xvi. and 590. 15s.

Van der Tuuk.—OUTLINES OF A GRAMMAR OF THE MALAGASY LANGUAGE
By H. N. VAN DER TUUK. 8vo., pp. 28, sewed. 1s.

Van der Tuuk.—SHORT ACCOUNT OF THE MALAY MANUSCRIPTS BELONGING
TO THE ROYAL ASIATIC SOCIETY. By H. N. VAN DER TUUK. 8vo., pp. 52. 2s. 6d.

Vedarthayatna (The); or, an Attempt to Interpret the Vedas. A
Marathi and English Translation of the Rig Veda, with the Original Saṁhitā
and Pada Texts in Sanskrit. Parts I. to XXVIII. 8vo. pp. 1—896. Price
3s. 6d. each.

Vishnu-Purana (The) ; a System of Hindu Mythology and Tradition.
Translated from the original Sanskrit, and Illustrated by Notes derived chiefly
from other Purāṇas. By the late H. H. WILSON, M.A., F.R.S., Boden Professor of Sanskrit in the University of Oxford, etc., etc. Edited by FITZEDWARD

HALL. In 6 vols. 8vo. Vol. I. pp. cxl. and 200: Vol. II. pp. 343; Vol. III., pp. 348; Vol IV. pp. 346, cloth; Vol. V.Part I. pp. 392, cloth. 10s. 6d. each. Vol. V., Part 2, containing the Index, compiled by Fitzedward Hall. 8vo. cloth, pp. 268. 12s.

Vissering, W.—ON CHINESE CURRENCY. Coin and Paper Money. With Facsimile of a Bank Note. Royal 8vo. cloth, pp. xv. and 219. *Leiden*, 1877. 18s.

Wade.—Yü-YEN TZŬ-ERH CHI. A progressive course designed to assist the Student of Colloquial Chinese, as spoken in the Capital and the Metropolitan Department. In eight parts, with Key, Syllabary, and Writing Exercises. By THOMAS FRANCIS WADE, C.B., Secretary to Her Britannic Majesty's Legation, Peking. 3 vols. 4to. Progressive Course, pp. xx. 296 and 16; Syllabary, pp. 126 and 36; Writing Exercises, pp. 48; Key, pp. 174 and 140, sewed. £4.

Wade.—WÉN-CHIEN TZŬ-ERH CHI. A series of papers selected as specimens of documentary Chinese, designed to assist Students of the language, as written by the officials of China. In sixteen parts, with Key. Vol. I. By THOMAS FRANCIS WADE, C.B., Secretary to Her Britannic Majesty's Legation at Peking. 4to., half-cloth, pp. xii. and 455; and iv., 72, and 52. £1 16s.

Wake.—CHAPTERS ON MAN. With the Outlines of a Science of comparative Psychology. By C. STANILAND WAKE, Fellow of the Anthropological Society of London. Crown 8vo. pp. viii. and 344, cloth. 7s. 6d.

Wake.—THE EVOLUTION OF MORALITY. Being a History of the Development of Moral Culture. By C. STANILAND WAKE, author of "Chapters on Man," etc. Two vols. 8vo. cloth, pp. xvi. and 506, xii. and 474. 21s.

Watson.—INDEX TO THE NATIVE AND SCIENTIFIC NAMES OF INDIAN AND OTHER EASTERN ECONOMIC PLANTS AND PRODUCTS, originally prepared under the authority of the Secretary of State for India in Council. By JOHN FORBES WATSON, M.A., M.D., F.L.S., F.R.A.S., etc., Reporter on the Products of India. Imperial 8vo., cloth, pp. 650. £1 11s. 6d.

Weber.—ON THE RÂMÂYANA. By Dr. ALBRECHT WEBER, Berlin. Translated from the German by the Rev. D. C. Boyd, M.A. Reprinted from "The Indian Antiquary." Fcap. 8vo. sewed, pp. 130. 5s.

Weber.—THE HISTORY OF INDIAN LITERATURE. By ALBRECHT WEBER. Translated from the German by JOHN MANN, M.A., and Dr. THEODOR ZACHARIAE, with the Author's sanction. Post 8vo. pp. xxiii. and 360, cloth, 1878. 18s.

Wedgwood.—A DICTIONARY OF ENGLISH ETYMOLOGY. By HENSLEIGH WEDGWOOD. Third Edition, thoroughly revised and enlarged. With an Introduction on the Formation of Language. Imperial 8vo., double column, pp. lxxii. and 746. 21s.

Wedgwood.—ON THE ORIGIN OF LANGUAGE. By HENSLEIGH WEDGWOOD, late Fellow of Christ's College, Cambridge. Fcap. 8vo. pp. 172, cloth. 3s. 6d.

West.—GLOSSARY AND INDEX OF THE PAHLAVI TEXTS OF THE BOOK OF Arda Viraf, The Tale of Gosht-I Fryano, The Hadokht Nask, and to some extracts from the Din-Kard and Nirangistan; prepared from Destur Hoshangji Asa's Glossary to the Arda Viraf Namak, and from the Original Texts, with Notes on Pahlavi Grammar. By E. W. WEST, Ph.D. Revised by MARTIN HAUG, Ph.D. Published by order of the Government of Bombay. 8vo. sewed, pp. viii. and 352. 25s.

West and Buhler.—A DIGEST OF THE HINDU LAW OF INHERITANCE and Partition, from the Replies of the Sâstris in the several Courts of the Bombay Presidency. With Introduction, Notes and Appendix. Edited by RAYMOND WEST and J. G. BUHLER. Second Edition. Demy 8vo. sewed, pp. 674. £1 11s. 6d.

Wheeler.—The History of India from the Earliest Ages. By J. Talboys Wheeler, Assistant Secretary to the Government of India in the Foreign Department, Secretary to the Indian Record Commission, author of "The Geography of Herodotus," etc. etc. Demy 8vo. cl.

Vol. I. The Vedic Period and the Maha Bharata. pp. lxxv. and 576.

Vol. II., The Ramayana and the Brahmanic Period. pp. lxxxviii. and 680, with two Maps. 21s.

Vol. III. Hindu, Buddhist, Brahmanical Revival. pp. 484, with two maps. 18s.

Vol. IV. Part I. Mussulman Rule. pp. xxxii. and 320. 14s.

Vol. IV. Part II. In the press.

Wheeler.—Early Records of British India. A History of the English Settlement in India, as told in the Government Records, the works of old travellers and other contemporary Documents, from the earliest period down to the rise of British Power in India. By J. Talboys Wheeler. Royal 8vo. cloth, pp. xxxii. and 392. 1878. 15s.

Whitmee.—A Grammar and Dictionary of the Samoan Language. By Rev. George Pratt, forty years a Missionary of the London Missionary Society in Samoa. Second Edition. Edited by Rev. S. J. Whitmee, F.R.G.S. Crown 8vo. cloth, pp. 388. 18s.

Whitney.—Oriental and Linguistic Studies. By William Dwight Whitney, Professor of Sanskrit and Comparative Philology in Yale College. First Series. The Veda; the Avesta; the Science of Language. Cr. 8vo. cl., pp. x. and 418. 12s.
Second Series.—The East and West—Religion and Mythology—Orthography and Phonology—Hindú Astronomy. Crown 8vo. cloth. pp. 446. 12s.

Whitney.—Atharva Veda Prátiçákhya; or, Çáunakíyá Caturádhyáyiká (The). Text, Translation, and Notes. By William D. Whitney, Professor of Sanskrit in Yale College. 8vo. pp. 286, boards. £1 11s. 6d.

Whitney.—Language and the Study of Language: Twelve Lectures on the Principles of Linguistic Science. By W. D. Whitney. Third Edition, augmented by an Analysis. Crown 8vo. cloth, pp. xii. and 504. 10s. 6d.

Whitney.—Language and its Study, with especial reference to the Indo-European Family of Languages. Seven Lectures by W. D. Whitney, Professor of Sanskrit, and Instructor in Modern Languages in Yale College. Edited with Introduction, Notes, Tables of Declension and Conjugation, Grimm's Law with Illustration, and an Index, by the Rev. R. Morris, M.A., LL.D. Cr. 8vo. cl., pp. xxii. and 318. 5s.

Whitney.—Surya-Siddhanta (Translation of the): A Text-book of Hindu Astronomy, with Notes and an Appendix, containing additional Notes and Tables, Calculations of Eclipses, a Stellar Map, and Indexes. By W. D. Whitney. 8vo. pp. iv. and 354, boards. £1 11s. 6d.

Whitney.—Táittiríya-Prátiçákhya, with its Commentary, the Tribháshyaratna: Text, Translation, and Notes. By W. D Whitney, Prof. of Sanskrit in Yale College, New Haven. 8vo. pp. 469. 1871. £1 5s.

Williams.—A Dictionary, English and Sanscrit. By Monier Williams, M.A. Published under the Patronage of the Honourable East India Company. 4to. pp. xii. 862, cloth. 1851. £3 3s.

Williams.—A Sanskrit-English Dictionary, Etymologically and Philologically arranged, with special reference to Greek, Latin, German, Anglo-Saxon, English, and other cognate Indo-European Languages. By Monier Williams, M.A., Boden Professor of Sanskrit. 4to. cloth, pp. xxv. and 1186. £4 14s. 6d.

Williams.—A PRACTICAL GRAMMAR OF THE SANSKRIT LANGUAGE, arranged with reference to the Classical Languages of Europe, for the use of English Students, by MONIER WILLIAMS, M.A. 1877. Fourth Edition, Revised. 8vo. cloth. 15s.

Williams.—A SYLLABIC DICTIONARY OF THE CHINESE LANGUAGE, arranged according to the Wu-Fang Yuen Yin, with the pronunciation of the Characters as heard in Peking, Canton, Amoy, and Shanghai. By S. WELLS WILLIAMS. 4to. cloth, pp. lxxxiv. and 1252. 1874. £5 5s.

Williams.—FIRST LESSONS IN THE MAORI LANGUAGE. With a Short Vocabulary. By W. L. WILLIAMS, B.A. Fcap. 8vo. pp. 98, cloth. 5s.

Williams.—MODERN INDIA AND THE INDIANS. Being a Series of Impressions, Notes, and Essays. By MONIER WILLIAMS, D.C.L. Second Edition. Post 8vo. cloth, pp. 244. 1878. 7s. 6d.

Wilson.—Works of the late HORACE HAYMAN WILSON, M.A., F.R.S., Member of the Royal Asiatic Societies of Calcutta and Paris, and of the Oriental Soc. of Germany, etc., and Boden Prof. of Sanskrit in the University of Oxford.

Vols I. and II. ESSAYS AND LECTURES chiefly on the Religion of the Hindus, by the late H. H. WILSON, M.A., F.R.S., etc. Collected and edited by Dr. REINHOLD ROST. 2 vols cloth, pp. xiii. and 399, vi and 416. 21s.

Vols. III, IV. and V. ESSAYS ANALYTICAL, CRITICAL, AND PHILOLOGICAL, ON SUBJECTS CONNECTED WITH SANSKRIT LITERATURE. Collected and Edited by Dr. REINHOLD ROST. 3 vols. 8vo. pp. 408, 406, and 390, cloth. Price 36s.

Vols. VI., VII., VIII, IX. and X., Part I. VISHNU PURÁNA, A SYSTEM OF HINDU MYTHOLOGY AND TRADITION. Vols. I. to V. Translated from the original Sanskrit, and Illustrated by Notes derived chiefly from other Puránás. By the late H. H. WILSON, Edited by FITZEDWARD HALL, M.A., D.C.L., Oxon. 8vo., pp. cxl. and 200; 344; 344; 346, cloth. 2l. 12s. 6d.

Vol. X., Part 2, containing the Index to, and completing the Vishnu Puráná, compiled by Fitzedward Hall. 8vo. cloth. pp. 268. 12s.

Vols. XI. and XII. SELECT SPECIMENS OF THE THEATRE OF THE HINDUS. Translated from the Original Sanskrit. By the late HORACE HAYMAN WILSON, M.A., F.R.S. 3rd corrected Ed. 2 vols. 8vo. pp. lxi. and 384 ; and iv. and 418, cl. 21s.

Wilson.—SELECT SPECIMENS OF THE THEATRE OF THE HINDUS. Translated from the Original Sanskrit. By the late HORACE HAYMAN WILSON, M.A., F.R.S. Third corrected edition. 2 vols. 8vo., pp. lxxi. and 384 ; iv. and 418, cloth. 21s.

CONTENTS.

Vol. I.—Preface—Treatise on the Dramatic System of the Hindus—Dramas translated from the Original Sanskrit—The Mrichchakatí, or the Toy Cart—Vikram aand Urvasi, or the Hero and the Nymph—Uttara Ráma Charitra, or continuation of the History of Ráma.

Vol. II.—Dramas translated from the Original Sanskrit—Maláti and Mádhava, or the Stolen Marriage—Mudrá Rakshasa, or the Signet of the Minister—Ratnávalí, or the Necklace—Appendix, containing short accounts of different Dramas.

Wilson.—THE PRESENT STATE OF THE CULTIVATION OF ORIENTAL LITERATURE. A Lecture delivered at the Meeting of the Royal Asiatic Society. By the Director, Professor H. H. WILSON. 8vo. pp. 26, sewed. London, 1852. 6d.

Wilson.—A DICTIONARY IN SANSKRIT AND ENGLISH. Translated, amended, and enlarged from an original compilation prepared by learned Natives for the College of Fort William by H. H. WILSON. The Third Edition edited by Jagunmohana Tarkalankara and Khettramohana Mookerjee. Published by Gyanendrachandra Rayachoudhuri and Brothers. 4to. pp. 1008. Calcutta, 1874. £3 3s.

Wilson (H. H.).—See also Megha Duta, Rig-Veda, and Vishnu-Puráná.

Wise.—COMMENTARY ON THE HINDU SYSTEM OF MEDICINE. By T. A. WISE, M.D., Bengal Medical Service. 8vo., pp. xx. and 432, cloth. 7s. 6d.

Wise.—REVIEW OF THE HISTORY OF MEDICINE. By THOMAS A. WISE, M.D. 2 vols. 8vo. cloth. Vol. I., pp. xcviii. and 397; Vol. II., pp. 574. 10s.

Withers.—THE ENGLISH LANGUAGE SPELLED AS PRONOUNCED, with enlarged Alphabet of Forty Letters. With Specimen. By GEORGE WITHERS. Royal 8vo. sewed, pp. 84. 1s.

Wordsworth.—THE CHURCH OF THIBET, and the Historical Analogies of Buddhism and Christianity. A Lecture delivered at Bombay by W. WORDS-WORTH, B.A., Principal of Elphinstone College. 1877. 8vo. pp. 51. 2s. 6d.

Wright.—FEUDAL MANUALS OF ENGLISH HISTORY. A Series of Popular Sketches of our National History, compiled at different periods, from the Thirteenth Century to the Fifteenth, for the use of the Feudal Gentry and Nobility. Now first edited from the Original Manuscripts. By THOMAS WRIGHT, Esq., M.A. Small 4to. cloth, pp. xxiv. and 184. 1872. 15s.

Wright.—THE HOMES OF OTHER DAYS. A History of Domestic Manners and Sentiments during the Middle Ages. By THOMAS WRIGHT, Esq., M.A., F.S.A. With Illustrations from the Illuminations in contemporary Manuscripts and other Sources, drawn and engraved by F. W. Fairholt, Esq., F.S.A. 1 Vol. medium 8vo. handsomely bound in cloth, pp. xv. and 512. 350 Woodcuts. £1 1s.

Wright.—THE CELT, THE ROMAN, AND THE SAXON; a History of the Early Inhabitants of Britain down to the Conversion of the Anglo-Saxons to Christianity. Illustrated by the Ancient Remains brought to Light by Recent Research. By THOMAS WRIGHT, Esq., M.A., F.S.A., etc., etc. Third Corrected and Enlarged Edition. Numerous Illustrations. Crown 8vo. cloth, pp. xiv. and 562. 14s.

Wright.—ANGLO-SAXON AND OLD-ENGLISH VOCABULARIES, Illustrating the Condition and Manners of our Forefathers, as well as the History of the Forms of Elementary Education, and of the Languages spoken in this Island from the Tenth Century to the Fifteenth. Edited by THOMAS WRIGHT, Esq., M.A., F.S.A., etc. Second Edition, edited, collated, and corrected by RICHARD WULCKER. [*In the press.*

Wylie.—NOTES ON CHINESE LITERATURE; with introductory Remarks on the Progressive Advancement of the Art; and a list of translations from the Chinese, into various European Languages. By A. WYLIE, Agent of the British and Foreign Bible Society in China. 4to. pp. 296, cloth. Price, £1 16s.

Yajurveda.—THE WHITE YAJURVEDA IN THE MADHYANDINA RECENSION. With the Commentary of Mahidhara. Complete in 36 parts. Large square 8vo. pp. 571. £4 10s.

Yates.—A BENGÁLÍ GRAMMAR. By the late Rev. W. YATES, D.D. Reprinted, with improvements, from his Introduction to the Bengálí Language Edited by I. WENGER. Fcap. 8vo., pp. iv. and 150, bds. Calcutta, 1864. 3s. 6d.

STEPHEN AUSTIN AND SONS, PRINTERS, HERTFORD.

CPSIA information can be obtained
at www.ICGtesting.com
Printed in the USA
LVHW091022221020
669312LV00068B/107